Religions of the World
Second Edition

Religions of the World

Second Edition

A COMPREHENSIVE ENCYCLOPEDIA OF BELIEFS AND PRACTICES

Volume Three: E–H

J. GORDON MELTON
MARTIN BAUMANN
Editors

TODD M. JOHNSON
World Religious Statistics

DONALD WIEBE
Introduction

 ABC-CLIO

Santa Barbara, California • Denver, Colorado • Oxford, England

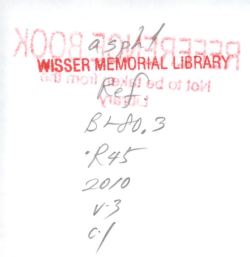
Copyright 2010 by ABC-CLIO, LLC

Library of Congress Cataloging-in-Publication Data

Religions of the world : a comprehensive encyclopedia of beliefs and practices / J. Gordon Melton, Martin Baumann, editors ; Todd M. Johnson, World Religious Statistics ; Donald Wiebe, Introduction. — 2nd ed.
   p.   cm.
  Includes bibliographical references and index.
  ISBN 978-1-59884-203-6 — ISBN 978-1-59884-204-3
  1. Religions—Encyclopedias. I. Melton, J. Gordon. II. Baumann, Martin.
  BL80.3.R45   2010
  200.3—dc22   2010029403

ISBN: 978-1-59884-203-6
EISBN: 978-1-59884-204-3

14 13 12 11 10   1 2 3 4 5

This book is also available on the World Wide Web as an eBook.
Visit www.abc-clio.com for details.

ABC-CLIO, LLC
130 Cremona Drive, P.O. Box 1911
Santa Barbara, California 93116-1911

This book is printed on acid-free paper ∞
Manufactured in the United States of America

Contents

A–Z List of Entries

Note: Core essays are indicated with the symbol ◆; country essays are indicated with the symbol ■.

Volume Five

Volume Six

Religions of the World

Second Edition

A COMPREHENSIVE ENCYCLOPEDIA
OF BELIEFS AND PRACTICES

Volume Three: E–H

E

East Africa Yearly Meeting of Friends

American representatives of the Society of Friends (now the Friends United Meeting) began mission work in Kaunosi, Kenya, in 1902. Work concentrated on the Kakamega and Bungoma districts in the western part of the country and later extended into the Rift Valley, the Nyanza Province, and the two large cities (Nairobi and Mombasa). Over the next four decades, the work grew into the largest Yearly Meeting (association) of Friends in the world. The East Africa Yearly Meeting became self-governing in 1946 and became responsible for all of the properties formerly owned by the mission in 1964. More recently, it became the source of a set of closely related Yearly Meetings.

A group of Kenyan Friends under the leadership of Johnstone Namufweli moved into Uganda in 1948 and founded a Monthly Meeting (congregation) at Kampala. They were joined by others who migrated in the mid-1950s at the invitation of the colonial government. They were set apart as an independent Yearly Meeting in 1969. In 1952 the government of Tanganyika (now Tanzania) invited Kenyans to relocate there, and some Friends were among those who accepted the invitation. The first group settled in Ikoma in the Musoma District, where the first congregation was established. The Tanzania congregations remained a part of the Kenyan work until 1968, when the Tanzania Yearly Meeting was formed.

In 1973, the work in Kenya was reorganized into nine districts, and the first of what became five Yearly Meetings (Elgon Religious Society of Friends) established. In 1979 the East Africa Yearly Meeting (South) held its first meeting and is now the largest of the Friends Yearly Meetings, with some 47,000 members.

Yearly Meetings are congregational associations that are the basic organization unit among Friends. The East Africa Yearly Meeting (North) (with 13,000 members) and the Nairobi Yearly Meeting (with 4,000 members) were established in 1987. Among the five Kenyan associations, the East Africa Yearly Meeting sponsors the Friends Bible Institute (for the training of pastors) and Friends College, both in Aimosi. At the beginning of the new century, the East Africa Year Meeting was a member of the World Council of Churches, but has since withdrawn. It remains a member of the National Council of Churches of Kenya.

East Africa Yearly Meeting (South)
PO Box 35
Tiriki
Kenya

J. Gordon Melton

See also: Friends United Meeting; World Council of Churches.

References

Kimball, Herbert, and Beatrice Kimball, eds. *Go into All the World: A Centennial Celebration of Friends in East Africa*. Richmond, IN: Friends United Press, 2002.

Painter, Levinus King. *The Hill of Vision: The Story of the Quaker Movement in East Africa; 1902–1965*. Kenya: East Africa Yearly Meeting of Friends, 1951.

Quakers around the World. London: Friends World Committee for Consultation, 1994.

Rasmussen, Ane Marie Bak. *A History of the Quaker Movement in Africa*. London: I. B. Tauris, 1995.

East Java Christian Church

The East Java Christian Church (Gereja Kristen Jawi Wetan [GKJW]) dates to the activities of Christian laypeople operating in East Java early in the 19th century. In the 1930s two European laypeople, one a German watchmaker, the other an Indo-Russian farmer, introduced Christianity into the Muslim community around Surabaya. They baptized an initial convert in 1843. During this time, the watchmaker spent several periods in jail for violating the law against proselytizing Muslims. Eventually a small congregation emerged, which in 1850 came under the care of the mission of the Reformed Church of the Netherlands. Over the next generations the mission grew slowly but steadily. In 1931 a synod was organized. At this time there were some 23,000 baptized members, almost all residing in rural areas.

As with other missions in Indonesia, the missionaries remained in control until the Japanese arrived in 1942. The war and period of occupation totally disrupted the church, which took the rest of the decade to recover. Growth began again in the 1950s and resumed its pattern of steady development in what is a predominantly Muslim part of the country. Associated with the church are a set of schools, an orphanage, and a variety of medical facilities.

In 2005 the church reported 130,000 members in 148 congregations. It was a founding member of the World Council of Churches and the World Alliance of Reformed Churches.

East Java Christian Church
Jin Shodanchoo Supriadi 18
Malang 65147 Jawaa Timur
Indonesia

J. Gordon Melton

See also: Reformed Church in the Netherlands (Liberated); World Alliance of Reformed Churches; World Council of Churches.

References

Bauswein, Jean-Jacques, and Lukas Vischner, eds. *The Reformed Family Worldwide: A Survey of Reformed Churches, Theological Schools, and International Organizations*. Grand Rapids, MI: William B. Eerdmans Publishing Company, 1999.

Van Beek, Huibert. *A Handbook of the Churches and Councils: Profiles of Ecumenical Relationships*. Geneva: World Council of Churches, 2006.

Easter

The high feast of the Christian church, Easter celebrates the resurrection of Jesus Christ. Even those churches that typically do not follow the liturgical year calendar will observe Easter. The timing of all of the other moveable feasts in the Christian year revolves around Easter, showing this event's central position in Christian doctrine and worship. Easter Sunday is preceded by the 40 days of Lent and Holy Week. The feast begins a 50-day season of "Eastertide" that includes Ascension Day and leads to Pentecost.

There is biblical and early church evidence that Christians originally celebrated the resurrection of Christ every Sunday. At some point in the first two centuries of the church, however, it became customary to further celebrate the event annually during the Jewish Passover season, the time of year when Jesus was crucified, buried, and raised.

Prior to the fourth century, because of its Passover associations, the holy day was called *Pascha*. The word for Easter in most European languages still derives from this root. However, the English word "Easter," which parallels the German word *Ostern*, has less certain origins. Saint Bede the Venerable (672–735 CE) was the first to suggest that the term comes from *Estre*, the Anglo-Saxon goddess of spring and fertility. A related and more commonly accepted theory is that the word originated from early Christian designation of Easter week as *in albis*, the Latin plural for *alba* ("dawn"). This word evolved into *eostarum* in Old High German, the precursor of the modern German and English term for spring. This parallels the development of the word "Lent," which also has spring connotations.

Easter, like the Jewish Passover, is a moveable feast. Originally, churches in Asia celebrated Easter on the same day as Passover, regardless of the day of the week on which it fell. All other churches in other

Catholics take part in an Easter procession celebrating Jesus Christ's resurrection in Niquinohomo, Nicaragua. (AP Photo/Esteban Felix)

regions celebrated Easter on the first Sunday after Passover.

Based on a formula decided by the Council of Nicaea in 325 CE, Easter is celebrated on the first Sunday following the first full moon after the Spring Equinox. As a result, Easter Sunday can fall between March 22 and April 25, depending on the lunar cycle. To complicate matters further, most Eastern churches use the Julian calendar (as revised early in the 20th century) and a 19-year lunar cycle while Western churches follow an 84-year cycle. Consequently, the Orthodox Easter sometimes falls on the same day as the Western Easter while at other times the two celebrations can occur as much as five weeks apart.

While there are many and varied liturgical customs associated with Easter, the Easter Vigil serves as the core of the event's worship activities. Before sunrise on Easter Sunday, worshippers gather in darkness for the lighting of the Christ, or Paschal, candle. From this new fire, worshippers light other candles to illuminate the entire sanctuary. Readings from the Gospels and songs of praise accompany the celebration of lights.

The sanctuary is newly adorned in the colors of Easter: white and gold. White symbolizes the hope of the resurrection, as well as the purity and newness that comes from victory over sin and death. The gold symbolizes the light of the world brought by the risen Christ who enlightens the world. The cross is no longer draped in black. Instead, it is covered in flowers and the top is draped in white.

The Easter Vigil has evolved into an outdoor sunrise service for many churches. The spreading dawn adds to the celebration of lights and candles. The practice may derive from the Gospel narrative of Jesus' resurrection, which states that Mary Magdalene went to the tomb "while it was still dark" (John 20:1) or as dawn was breaking (Matthew 28:1; Luke 24:1).

926 | Easter Island

From the earliest days of the church, Easter has been the primary time for the baptism of new converts. It is a fitting time to celebrate not only Jesus' resurrection from death to life, but also the symbolism of death and resurrection of the Christian through the waters of baptism. At one time those baptized changed into new white clothes to symbolize their new life in Christ. This has led to the tradition of buying new clothes at Easter.

Easter has accumulated many traditions derived from folk customs, many of which were associated with springtime fertility celebrations. For example, the popular modern Easter symbols of eggs and rabbits are ancient Pagan symbols for fertility. The church prohibited the eating of eggs during the Lenten fast, so by the 13th century the custom arose of collecting and decorating eggs that were laid during Holy Week in anticipation of breaking the fast. The egg itself became a symbol of the resurrection. Just as Jesus rose from the tomb, the egg symbolizes new life emerging from the eggshell.

The custom of associating a rabbit with Easter arose in Protestant areas in Europe in the 17th century but did not become common until the 19th century. The Easter rabbit was said to lay the eggs as well as decorate and hide them.

Kevin Quast

See also: Holy Week; Lent; Liturgical Year; Passover.

References

Aveni, Anthony. "The Easter/Passover Season: Connecting Time's Broken Circle." In *The Book of the Year: A Brief History of Our Seasonal Holidays,* 64–78. Oxford: Oxford University Press, 2004.

Bradshaw, Paul F., and Lawrence A. Hoffman, eds. *Passover and Easter: Origin and History to Modern Times.* Notre Dame, IN: University of Notre Dame Press, 1999.

Cantalamessa, Raneiro. *The Mystery of Easter.* Collegeville, MN: Liturgical Press, 1993.

Chupungco, Anscar. *Shaping the Easter Feast.* Washington, DC: Pastoral Press, 1992.

Holweck, Frederick. "Easter." In *The Catholic Encyclopedia.* Vol. 5. New York: Robert Appleton Company, 1909.

Jones, Cheslyn, Geoffrey Wainwright, Edward Yarnold, and Paul Bradshaw, eds. *The Study of Liturgy, Revised Edition.* New York: Oxford University Press, 1992.

Nocent, Adrian. *The Liturgical Year.* Vol. 3, *The Paschal Triduum, The Easter Season.* Collegeville, MN: Liturgical Press. 1977.

Ramshaw, Gail. *The Three Day Feast: Maundy Thursday, Good Friday, Easter.* Minneapolis, MN: Augsburg Fortress, 2004.

Easter Island

Easter Island, a single isolated volcanic island, is located in the Pacific Ocean some 2,000 miles west of the coast of South America and an equal distance east of the clusters of inhabited islands of the South Pacific. Locally known as Rapa Nui, it received its Western name from Admiral Jacob Roggeveen (1659–1729), whose three ships visited the island on Easter Day in 1722. It would be Roggeveen who informed the world of the giant statues that seemed to peer out to sea from the island. Many interactions would occur between the Easter islanders and the outside world over the next two centuries, but not until the eye-catching work of anthropologist/adventurer Thor Heyerdahl (1914–2002) in the 1940s did the general public become engaged with the questions concerning the origins of the island's residents and its unique statuary.

Following Roggeveen's initial visit, additional ships occasionally stopped. Then early in the 19th century, a visit by a whaling vessel led to the spread of venereal disease. In the 1860s Peruvians raided the islands for slave labor, taking much of its political and religious leadership. The great majority of those taken died within a few years. Disease introduced by others killed most of those who escaped slavery. A mere 111 islanders were alive by the mid-1870s. The sudden loss of the island's religious leadership, who carried the group memories for what was a pre-literate people, led to the significant loss of knowledge concerning the island's history and culture. Through the last decades of the 20th century, anthropologists and other scientists spent many hours attempting to reconstruct the island's past.

The annexation of the island by Chile in 1888 did little to improve the residents' lot, as the island was turned over to commercial interests who ran it much like a slave labor camp. The harsh conditions did not improve when the island was turned over to Chile's navy in 1953.

Thor Heyerdahl came to Easter Island in 1955 bringing his celebrity over the popularization of his idea that the Polynesians originated in the Americas rather than Asia. He focused attention on the mystery surrounding the large stone heads. The team he assembled put together an initial story, which became the subject of several scholarly studies and a popular book. The islands had been inhabited since the fourth century BCE. He also found in the oldest statuary on the island a resemblance to contemporaneous statuary from South America.

Heyerdahl's work had a dramatic effect on the island. The Chilean government saw the possibility of attracting tourists. The islands saw their opportunity to reorder their relationship to their overlords. In 1966, they revolted and forced the writing of a Constitution that included a set of freedoms. Incorporating the island into modern transportation systems opened it to both tourists and scholars. Life steadily improved, and by the end of the century, the population had risen to approximately 2,000.

The archaeological community viewed Heyerdahl's study as merely a first step in understanding Easter Island. He focused his relatively brief study on the statues, locally called *moais*. These male figures stood some 13 feet high and weighed some 14 tons. They had been carved out of the volcanic rock. Their mystery was accentuated by the lack of written records concerning them and the loss of much of the oral tradition. It was also the case that by the 20th century, all of the statues, the existence of which had featured prominently in the early Western accounts of the island, had been toppled. Heyerdahl began the task of replacing the figures in their earlier resting places.

The mystery of the statues opened the door to the more complete study of the island's history and culture. In the late 20th century, UCLA archaeologist Jo Anne Van Tilburg emerged as the chief scholar of Easter Island lore. She deduced that the statues represented stylized images of various chiefs. She dated their initial erection to the years 1400 to 1600, during which time they played a key role in the religious life of the Rapa Nui. They appear to have served as contact points for communication with divine entities. The lack of definitive records, however, has left the door open to variant opinions on the statues and the island's history.

In 1995, Easter Island (Rapa Nui) was added to the list of World Heritage Sites designated by the United Nations.

J. Gordon Melton

References

Fischer, Steven Roger. *Island at the End of the World: The Turbulent History of Easter Island*. London: Reaktion Books, 2006.

Heyerdahl, Thor. *Aku-Aku: The Secret of Easter Island*. London: Allen & Unwin, 1958.

Heyerdahl, Thor. *Easter Island: The Mystery Solved*. New York: Random House, 1989.

Orliac, Catherine, and Michel Orliac. *Easter Island: Mystery of the Stone Giants*. New York: Harry N. Abrams Inc., 1995.

Van Tiburg, Jo Anne, and John Mack. *Easter Island: Archaeology, Ecology, and Culture*. Washington, DC: Smithsonian Institution Press, 1995.

Eastern Orthodoxy

Together, the Eastern Orthodox churches constitute one of the three major traditions of Christianity (Roman Catholicism and Protestantism being the other two). Eastern Orthodoxy emerged as the dominant expression of Christianity in the eastern half of the Mediterranean world in the eastern half of the Roman Empire (which after the fall of Rome in 475 came to be known as the Byzantine Empire), and its organizational focus was on the archbishops at Constantinople (originally Byzantium, later Istanbul), Antioch, Jerusalem, and Alexandria. Greek was the dominant language, as opposed to Latin in the western Mediterranean, where after the fall of Rome the bishop of Rome became more and more important, leading the whole Western church as pope. Through the centuries, the organizational unity of Christendom was gradually weakened

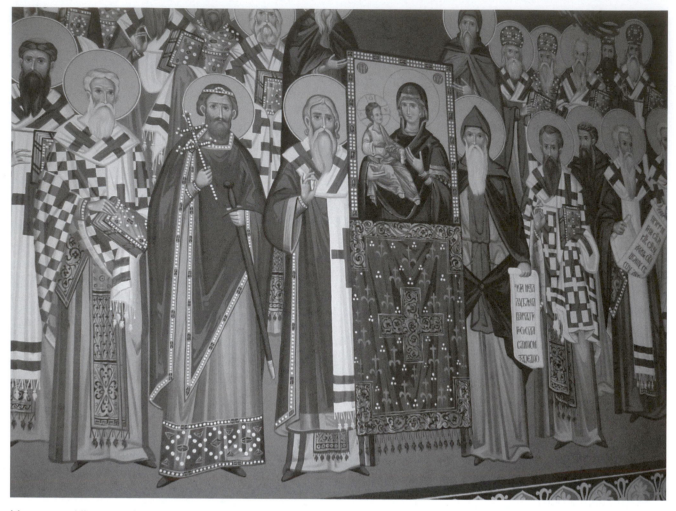

Mosaic in a Ukrainian Orthodox church, Edmonton, Alberta, Canada. (J. Gordon Melton)

by theologically divergent churches in Armenia, Egypt, Persia, and lands to the east. Then in the 11th century, the most significant schism occurred, that between the Roman Catholic Church and the Greek Orthodox churches.

Today, Eastern Orthodoxy consists of a number of churches, which are divided nationally and ethnically, but held together in communion through a shared faith, which finds expression in their version of the Nicene Creed. The Eastern Orthodox have a technical theological disagreement with the Roman Catholic Church concerning the place of the Holy Spirit in the Trinity. In the Nicene Creed as recited in Eastern Orthodox churches, belief is affirmed in "the Holy Spirit, who proceeds from the Father." In the Roman Catholic version of the creed, the phrase "and the Son" is added at this point, so that it reads, "the Holy Spirit, who

proceeds from the Father and the Son." The Eastern church rejected that phrase, believing that it suggested an undue subordination of the Holy Spirit.

The Eastern church also did not develop the ideal of celibacy of the clergy as in the Roman Catholic Church, though it insists that priests marry before receiving Holy Orders and that bishops be drawn from unmarried priests (primarily from its monks, who live in ordered communities).

The archbishop of Istanbul, the ecumenical patriarch, is the symbolic focus of the unity of Eastern Orthodoxy. His jurisdiction, the Ecumenical Patriarchate, includes Turkey (the former base of the Roman Empire in the East, usually referred to as the Byzantine Empire), parts of Greece, all of Europe not specifically assigned to other jurisdictions, and the Greek-speaking Orthodox in North and South America. The remainder of the Mediterranean is divided between the Greek Orthodox Patriarchate of Antioch and All the East, the Greek Orthodox Patriarchate of Jerusalem, and the Greek Orthodox Patriarchate of Alexandria and All Africa.

Through the centuries a variety of autonomous Orthodox jurisdictions have been recognized, most separating from the Ecumenical Patriarchate as they grew in size and their country asserted its independence. Important Orthodox churches include the Russian Orthodox Church (Moscow Patriarchate), the Ukrainian Orthodox Church, the Orthodox Church of Greece, the Bulgarian Orthodox Church, and the Romanian Orthodox Church. There are in addition a number of smaller autonomous jurisdictions.

Also, during the centuries since the schism between the Eastern and Western churches, a variety of Orthodox communities have for various reasons moved back into communion with the Roman Catholic Church and now exist as Eastern-rite Catholic churches. Such Eastern-rite churches now parallel most Orthodox jurisdictions.

There are some Orthodox churches that are not in communion with the Ecumenical Patriarchate. Some of these were formed during the 20th century, as Marxist governments rose in predominantly Orthodox countries. It was the feeling of some members of these churches that they could not remain in communion with bishops who had tacitly offered allegiance to such government authorities. The largest of these anti-Communist Orthodox churches is the Russian Orthodox Church Outside of Russia, formed by Russian bishops who were outside the country at the time of the Russian Revolution and who attempted to reorganize the Russian parishes in the diaspora.

In the late 20th century, as the Orthodox Church began to participate in the ecumenical movement as expressed in the World Council of Churches, the more conservative church leaders saw such relationships as inherently subversive of Orthodox faith and practice. Their protest was focused in the change of most Orthodox churches from the traditional Julian calendar to the more commonly used Gregorian calendar. The conservative dissenting jurisdictions are generally known as "Old Calendar" churches.

J. Gordon Melton

See also: Bulgarian Orthodox Church; Ecumenical Patriarchate/Patriarchate of Constantinople; Greek Orthodox Patriarchate of Alexandria and All Africa; Greek Orthodox Patriarchate of Antioch and All the East; Greek Orthodox Patriarchate of Jerusalem; Orthodox Church of Greece; Roman Catholic Church; Romanian Orthodox Church; Russian Orthodox Church (Moscow Patriarchate); Ukraine, Eastern Orthodoxy in; World Council of Churches.

References

Bartholomew, Patriarch. *Encountering the Mystery: Understanding Orthodox Christianity Today.* Garden City, NY: Doubleday, 2008.

Clendenin, Daniel B. *Eastern Orthodox Christianity: A Western Perspective.* Grand Rapids, MI: Baker Academic, 2003.

Fitzgerald, Thomas E. *The Orthodox Church.* Westport, CT: Greenwood Press, 1995.

Orthodoxia. Regensburg, Germany: Ostkirchliches Institut, issued annually.

Roberson, Ronald G. *The Eastern Christian Churches.* Rome, Italy: Pont. Institutum Studiorum Orientalium, 1988.

Schmemann, Alexander. *The Historic Road of Eastern Orthodoxy.* New York: Holt, Rinehart and Winston, 1963.

ECKANKAR

ECKANKAR, also known as "The Religion of the Light and Sound of God," was founded by Paul Twitchell (ca. 1908–1971) in California in 1965. Although it claims to be the oldest religion in the world, its beliefs and practices bear striking resemblances to the Punjabi Radhasoami tradition, Western Esoteric traditions such as those found in the Theosophical Society and Rosicrucianism (the Ancient and Mystical Order Rosae Crucis), and certain aspects of the Church of Scientology. The essence of ECKANKAR lies in its spiritual practices, which are said to lead the individual into greater union with God and toward becoming a co-worker with God. The practices taught by ECKANKAR include singing the mantra "Hu" (an especially holy name for God) and bilocation (soul travel). Eckists believe that they can be in more than one place simultaneously and that many dreams are actually such experiences. ECKANKAR teaches them how to interpret the spiritual meanings of dreams.

Paul Twitchell wrote several books about and for ECKANKAR, including the first volumes of an open-ended canon of ECKANKAR scriptures known as Shariyat-Ki-Sugmad. Twitchell died in 1971 and was succeeded by Darwin Gross, who was in turn succeeded as "Living ECK Master" (spiritual leader and oracle of God) by Harold Klemp in the early 1980s. Under Klemp and ECKANKAR's president, Peter Skelskey, ECKANKAR relocated its world headquarters from California to Minneapolis, Minnesota, in the late 1980s. The world headquarters includes the Temple of ECK, ECKANKAR's primary worship center, in Chanhassen, Minnesota. The organization does not publish membership statistics but claims to have tens of thousands of adherents worldwide. It is a nonexclusive religious organization, so many members are also members of other religious groups.

The highest authority in ECKANKAR is the Living ECK Master, and Harold Klemp is considered the 973rd such person in world history. ECKANKAR *chelas* (devotees) regard Klemp as their spiritual guide and believe that he appears to them and teaches them in their dreams. Klemp is believed to be in touch with a group of spiritual guides known as the Order of Vairagi Masters. The spiritual teachings and practices of ECKANKAR are determined by Klemp and communicated to the chelas via books, correspondence courses, and magazines published by Illuminated Way Publishing Company. ECKANKAR also produces videos, which often feature talks given by Klemp, and these are shown on cable television. ECKANKAR centers exist in numerous cities in North America, Europe, and Africa.

ECKANKAR has endured several controversies since its founding. Paul Twitchell's autobiography and credibility as a genuine spiritual leader was questioned by at least one scholar. David Christopher Lane's exposé of Twitchell and ECKANKAR, entitled *The Making of a Spiritual Movement: The Untold Story of Paul Twitchell and ECKANKAR,* has plagued ECKANKAR since its first publication in the late 1970s. Controversy surrounded the departure of Darwin Gross and

his succession by Harold Klemp. Many Minnesotans initially objected to the building of ECKANKAR's temple in suburban Minneapolis, claiming that a cult was appearing in their midst. However, under Klemp's capable leadership, ECKANKAR has managed to survive these controversies and has settled into a more stable life among the West's relatively new alternative religions.

ECKANKAR
PO Box 27300
Minneapolis, MN 55427
http://www.eckankar.org

Roger E. Olson

See also: Ancient and Mystical Order Rosae Crucis; Church of Scientology; Theosophical Society (American).

References

Klemp, Harold, *The Spiritual Exercises of ECK.* Minneapolis: ECKANKAR, 1993.

Lane, David Christopher. *The Making of a Spiritual Movement: The Untold Story of Paul Twitchell and ECKANKAR*. Del Mar, CA: Del Mar Press, 1993.

Olson, Roger E. "ECKANKAR: From Ancient Science of Soul Travel to New Age Religion." In *America's Alternative Religions,* edited by Timothy Miller. Albany: State University of New York Press, 1995.

Twitchell, Paul. *ECKANKAR: The Key to Secret Worlds.* Minneapolis: Illuminated Way Publishing, 1969, 1987.

■ Ecuador

Ecuador is located on the Pacific Coast of South America, between Peru to the south and Colombia to the north. This small Andean nation has an area of 109,483 square miles and a population of 14.6 million (July 2009), of which 66 percent is urban and 34 percent is rural. The country also includes the famous Galápagos Islands in the Pacific Ocean, about 600 miles west of the mainland. It is one of only two countries (with Chile) in South America that do not have a border with Brazil.

Ecuador

Religion	Followers in 1970	Followers in 2010	% of Population	Annual % growth 2000–2010	Followers in 2025	Followers in 2050
Christians	5,830,000	13,364,000	97.0	1.14	15,466,000	17,036,000
Roman Catholics	5,844,000	12,532,000	91.0	0.82	14,000,000	15,250,000
Protestants	82,900	532,000	3.9	5.17	850,000	1,000,000
Marginals	13,700	380,000	2.8	3.81	570,000	750,000
Agnostics	19,000	211,000	1.5	5.33	400,000	700,000
Ethnoreligionists	90,000	125,000	0.9	1.24	105,000	100,000
Atheists	6,000	21,000	0.2	1.20	29,000	50,000
Baha'is	16,400	17,200	0.1	1.20	25,000	35,000
Buddhists	2,000	14,600	0.1	1.20	17,500	24,000
Chinese folk	4,000	13,200	0.1	1.20	18,000	21,500
Jews	2,000	4,200	0.0	1.20	4,200	5,000
New religionists	1,000	3,000	0.0	1.20	5,000	7,500
Muslims	0	1,800	0.0	1.19	4,000	9,000
Total population	**5,970,000**	**13,775,000**	**100.0**	**1.20**	**16,074,000**	**17,988,000**

Ecuador's population is very diverse, comprising many races and ethnic groups. In general, Ecuadorans trace their origins to four sources: Amerindians, Europeans, Africans, and Asians. *Mestizos* (mixed Amerindian and Spanish ancestry) are by far the largest of ethnic groups, constituting more than 65 percent of the current population. In second place are Amerindians, who are approximately 25 percent of the population. The whites are mainly *criollos*, who are descendants of Spanish colonists, and are about 7 percent of the population. In addition, there were waves of immigration from the Middle East, Italy, Germany, France, and other European countries. The Afro-Ecuadoran community, descendants of African slaves and freedmen, includes Negros, mulattos, and *zambos*, and it constitutes most of the remaining 3 percent of the population.

Since the early 1900s, Ecuador has experienced increased immigration from the Middle East, Asia (especially China and Japan), North America, and Europe. Today, Ecuador has about 95,000 U.S. expatriates and 30,000 European Union expatriates.

The community of Middle Easterners numbers in the tens of thousands, mostly of Lebanese, Syrian, or Palestinian origin. Many are prominent in commerce and industry, and are concentrated in the coastal cities of Guayaquil, Quevedo, and Machala; most are Eastern Orthodox Christians. The Arab-Ecuadoran community has created many cultural organizations to honor and celebrate their heritage, although most of those born in Ecuador do not speak Arabic. They are well assimilated into the local culture and are referred to commonly as *turcos* since the early Middle Eastern migrants arrived with passports issued by the Ottoman Empire at the beginning of the 20th century.

There are an estimated 225,000 English speakers and 112,000 German speakers in Ecuador of which the majority reside in Quito, mainly descendants of immigrants who arrived in the late 1800s. There are also small communities of Italians, Jews, Armenians, French, and Greeks. The Jewish community, which numbers less than 500, is mostly of German or Italian descent.

Also, there is a small East Asian–Ecuadoran community, estimated at 25,000; it mainly consists of those of Japanese and Chinese descent whose ancestors arrived as miners, farm laborers, or fishermen in the late 1800s.

Until the end of the 19th century, the Ecuadoran population was concentrated in the central highlands (the Andes Mountains run through the center of the country and surround the central highlands, known as the Sierra region), due to the prevalence of malaria and yellow fever in the coastal region, but today's population is distributed about equally between the highlands and the coastal lowlands. Migration toward cities, particularly larger cities, in all regions has increased the urban population to about 55 percent of the national population. The majority of Ecuador's small but vibrant upper- to middle-class population segment is distributed between the capital, Quito, and Guayaquil, each home to 1.5 to 2.0 million inhabitants.

The Oriente region, composed of Amazonian lowlands to the east of the Andes and covering about half the country's total land area, includes some of the headwaters of the Amazon River and remains sparsely populated. It contains only about 3 percent of the population, many of whom are unassimilated Amerindians who maintain a wary distance from the more recent arrivals: mestizo and white settlers. This region is home to nine tribes of indigenous peoples who survive mainly as hunters and gatherers: the Quichua, Shuar, Achuar, Waorani, Siona, Secoya, Shiwiar, Záparo, and Cofan. These groups are all represented politically by the Confederation of Indigenous Nationalities of the Ecuadoran Amazon (CONFENIAE). By contrast, the Colorado Indians (about 2,300 in 2000) inhabit the northwestern jungle area west of Quito, around Santo Domingo de los Colorados, in the Pacific lowlands.

Occasional visits by outsiders to the Oriente region, seeking gold, land, trade, and converts occurred during and after the Spanish colonial period. These early contacts between Europeans and the indigenous people were disastrous because new diseases were introduced that decimated the tribal population. Later, the Amazon rubber boom in the 19th and early 20th centuries brought increased contact with Europeans, causing measles, malaria, and tuberculosis epidemics that further reduced the Native population.

Recent settlers in the Amazonian lowlands are the result of a small wave of immigration (mainly mestizo migrants from the central highlands) that began in the 1960s, when government-sponsored multinational corporations began to exploit petroleum reserves in the region. The boom in the petroleum industry led to mushrooming towns as well as to substantial deforestation, pollution of wetlands and lakes, and the further decline of the indigenous population.

Current Religious Situation The nation's Constitution provides for freedom of religion, and the government has generally respected this right in practice.

The government, at all levels, seeks to protect this right in full and does not tolerate its abuse, by either governmental or private actors. The only limits imposed by the government are "those proscribed by law to protect and respect the diversity, plurality, security and rights of others." The Constitution prohibits discrimination based on religion.

The Catholic Episcopal Conference estimates that 85 percent of the population is Roman Catholic, with 35 percent of Catholics actively practicing. Although no scientific survey has been undertaken, the Episcopal Conference estimates that attendance at Mass increased slightly during the 2000s. Some ethnolinguistic groups, particularly indigenous people who live in the mountains, follow a syncretistic form of Catholicism that combines animistic Amerindian beliefs and practices with orthodox Catholic doctrine. Catholic saints often are venerated in ways similar to those associated with indigenous deities.

Based on research conducted by PROLADES (Programa Latinoamericano de Estudios Socioreligiosos), religious affiliation in Ecuador can be described as follows in 2000: Roman Catholic, 85 percent; Protestant, 12 percent; other religions, 1 percent; and none/no response, 2 percent. The latter category includes atheists and agnostics, but there are no reliable statistics for these specific groups.

While Protestant conversions traditionally have been more numerous among the lower classes, growing numbers of the middle class and professionals are converting to Protestantism or marginal Christian groups. There has been success finding new converts in different regions, particularly among indigenous people in the Andean provinces of Chimborazo, Bolivar, Cotopaxi, Imbabura, and Pichincha, especially among persons who practice syncretistic religions, as well as among the marginalized sectors of society, especially in urban areas.

Historical Overview of Social, Political and Religious Development Evidence of human cultures exists in Ecuador from ca. 3500 BCE. Many ancient civilizations were created and developed throughout Ecuador, such as the Valdivia culture and Machalilla culture on the coast, the Quitus (near present-day Quito), and the Cañari (near present-day Cuenca). Each

ECUADOR

civilization developed its own distinctive architecture, pottery, and religious characteristics. After years of fiery resistance by the Cayambes and other tribes, as demonstrated by the Battle of Yahuarcocha ("Blood Lake"), where thousands of warriors were killed and thrown into the lake, the region succumbed to the expansion of the Incas and was loosely assimilated into the Inca Empire in 1453. The most prominent of the conquered tribes were the Quichua (or Quechua), whose center was located at Quito.

In 1531, the Spanish conquistadors arrived under the leadership of Francisco Pizarro to find an Inca Empire torn by strife and civil war. In subsequent years, the Spanish colonists became the new elite in the Andean region, with their centers of power in the viceroyalties of Lima and New Granada. Warfare and disease decimated the indigenous population during the first decades of Spanish rule, when the Native people were forced into the *encomienda* labor system of the Spanish landlords. In 1563, Quito became the seat of an *audiencia royal* (administrative district) of Spain and part of the Viceroyalty of Lima, and in 1717 it became part of the Viceroyalty of Nueva Granada, which included Colombia and Venezuela.

After nearly 300 years of Spanish colonization, Quito was still a small city of only 10,000 inhabitants. It was there, on August 10, 1809 (now, a national holiday), that the first call for independence from Spain was made in Latin America (Primer Grito de la Independencia), under the leadership of the city's criollos such as Carlos Montúfar, Eugenio Espejo, and Bishop Cuero y Caicedo. Quito's nickname, Luz de América ("Light of America"), comes from the idea that this first attempt produced the inspiration for the rest of Spanish America. Quito is also known as La Cara de Dios ("The Face of God") for its beauty.

On October 9, 1820, Guayaquil became the first city in Ecuador to gain its independence from Spain. On May 24, 1822, the rest of Ecuador gained its independence after Field Marshal Antonio José de Sucre defeated the Spaniard Royalist forces at the Battle of Pichincha, near Quito. Following the battle, Ecuador joined Liberator Simón Bolívar's Republic of Gran Colombia (modern-day Colombia and Venezuela), but withdrew from Gran Colombia and became an independent nation in 1830.

The 19th century was marked by instability in Ecuador, with a rapid succession of rulers. Between 1833 and 1908, the nation had 19 presidents. The opposing political parties were the Conservatives (or Clericals) and the Liberals. The first president was the Venezuelan-born Juan José Flores (r. 1830–1834, 1839–1843, 1843–1845), who was ultimately deposed, followed by many other authoritarian leaders. The Conservative Gabriel Garcia Moreno (r. 1861–1865) unified the country in the 1860s with the support of the Roman Catholic Church. In the late 19th century, world demand for cocoa (chocolate) tied the economy to commodity exports and led to migrations of people from the highlands to the agricultural frontier on the Pacific coast.

The country continued under the leadership of an oligarchy of large landowners. Their stranglehold on the country prevented land reform, and their ineptitude led to the loss of areas of the country to their neighbors. Present-day Ecuador represents approximately 20 percent of the country's original territory at the time of independence from Spain.

The Liberal Revolution of 1895 led by José Eloy Alfaro Delgado (r. 1895–1901, 1906–1911) reduced the power of the Catholic clergy and the Conservative land owners of the highlands, and revoked the Concordat with the Vatican. He is credited with the separation of church and state in Ecuador and for implementing many political and civil rights, such as freedom of speech and the legalization of civil marriage and divorce.

The Ecuadoran Radical Liberal Party (Partido Liberal Radical Ecuatoriano [PLRE]) is the oldest existing political party in Ecuador. The PLRE emerged out of divisions between moderate and radical liberals within the Liberal Party of Ecuador. As in many Latin American countries, Ecuador experienced a great deal of conflict, often violent, between the Liberal and Conservative parties. Alfaro Delgado brought the Liberal Party to power during the revolution of 1895, which adopted a policy of secularization in church matters. The PLRE was officially founded in 1925, and during the next 50 years several of its members served as presidents of Ecuador. The PLRE was in power from 1895 to 1911, from 1921 to 1952, and from 1960 to 1970. Each time it was overthrown by military coups.

The Liberals retained power until the military "Julian Revolution" of 1925, which gave ultimate political freedom to all Ecuadorans, including the Catholic hierarchy. The 1930s and 1940s were marked by instability and the emergence of populist politicians, such as five-time president José María Velasco Ibarra (r. 1934–1935, 1944–1947, 1952–1956, 1960–1961, and 1968–1972 [as dictator]). However, he only served one of those terms (1952–1956) without being ousted by the army.

In 1972, a "revolutionary and nationalist" military junta overthrew the government of dictator Velasco Ibarra (r. 1968–1972). The coup d'état was led by General Guillermo Rodríguez. The new president exiled Velasco Ibarra to Argentina and served as head of the Supreme Government Council until 1976, when he was removed by another military coup. The new military junta was led by Admiral Alfredo Poveda, who was declared chairman of the Supreme Government Council. After the country stabilized socially and economically, this Supreme Government Council proceeded to hold democratic elections and stepped down to hand over the reins of government to the newly elected president. Elections were held in April 1979, under a new Constitution that instituted democratic rule. Jaime Roldós Aguilera (r. 1979–1981) took office as the first constitutionally elected president, but died two years later in a plane crash.

Beginning in the late 1990s, there was a high emigration of Ecuadorans due to the nation's deteriorating economic and political conditions, which culminated in a severe economic and financial crisis in 1999. The emergence of the Amerindian population as an active political constituency has added to the democratic volatility of the country in recent years. The Quichua population, in particular, has been motivated by government failures to deliver on promises of land reform, lower unemployment, and provision of social services, and to stop the exploitation of indigenous territory by the land-holding elite.

At the start of the 2006 presidential campaign, Correa Delgado founded the Alianza PAIS (Patria Altiva y Soberana), a movement that espouses national sovereignty, regional integration, and economic relief for Ecuador's poor and marginalized masses. After 8 ineffective presidents in 10 years, the frustrated population elected the left-leaning Correa Delgado in late 2006 (a friend of Venezuela's current president, Hugo Chavez) who promised major governmental and economic reforms. President Correa Delgado, an economist and self-described "humanist," took office in January 2007. Despite his earlier promises not to do so, in June 2009, Correa Delgado joined the Chavez-backed Bolivarian Alternative for the Americas (ALBA), founded in 2004 between the governments of Venezuela, Cuba, and Bolivia.

The Roman Catholic Church The Spanish introduced Roman Catholicism in the 1530s, and the Bishopric of Quito was established in 1545. Making use of the infrastructure of the Incas, both Spanish authority and the Catholic faith were established throughout the territory. Following the initial diocesan synod in 1595, a program of evangelizing the Amazon lowlands began under the Dominicans.

Missionary work among the different Amerindian tribes on the tributaries of the Amazon was difficult, and the Dominican missions were destroyed in 1599 by the savage Jivaros (Shuar and Achuar). Later, however, the Dominicans re-established themselves and were assisted by the Jesuits who had worked in Quito beginning in 1596. By the close of the 17th century, Ecuador was "well-evangelized," according to Catholic historians.

However, after the expulsion of the Jesuits in 1767, who on the Napo River alone had established 33 missions among an estimated 100,000 inhabitants, the Dominicans were unable to maintain the work and many of the converted Natives left the faith. During the colonial period, the Catholic Church founded institutions of learning such as the University of Quito, and established a printing press at the same place in 1760.

Steady progress in Christianizing the country was pursued through the 18th century; however, the country's independence from Spain in 1822 brought many problems. The church's dependence on Spain for priests, male and female religious workers, and financial support led to a sharp cutback in the services provided. The church's limitations, especially in pastoral leadership and parish work, led to the further development of a popular folk Catholicism, which integrates many elements of traditional Amerindian culture, beliefs, and practices (syncretism).

In 1848, the Diocese of Quito was upgraded to an archdiocese under Archbishop Nicolás Joaquín de Arteta y Calisto, who died in September 1849 and was replaced by Archbishop Francisco Xavier de Garaycoa Llaguno in 1851.

The Catholic Church has always had an important role in Ecuadoran government and society. The Constitution of 1869, approved by the Conservative government of President Gabriel García Moreno (r. 1859–1865 and 1869–1875), declared the Roman

Exterior of a Catholic church in Tena, Ecuador. (iStockPhoto.com)

Part of the animosity García Moreno generated among Liberals was his friendship toward the Society of Jesus (Jesuits). During a period of exile, he helped a group of displaced Jesuits find refuge in Ecuador. He had also advocated legislation that would outlaw secret societies. This action and many similar ones encouraged the anti-Catholic parties of Ecuador, especially the Freemasons, to see in him an inveterate enemy. While the political situation at that time was "extremely convoluted and murky," the fact that García Moreno was elected to a second term of office (r. 1869–1875) clearly indicates his popular appeal, both with the hierarchy of the Catholic Church and with the masses. His vigorous support of universal literacy and education based on the French model was considered both controversial and bold.

Liberal anticlerical forces in control of the government during the administration of President José Eloy Alfaro Delgado (r. 1895–1901) repudiated the Concordat with the Vatican in 1895. In 1899, the Liberal government approved a new Constitution that guaranteed freedom of religion and respected all religions. These actions were a severe blow to the Catholic Church. Religious orders, among them the Capuchins, Salesians, Missionaries of Steyl, and the various sisterhoods, were all banished and Bishop Schumacher was exiled.

In 1910, the state religion was Catholicism but other creeds were tolerated. The state provided for the maintenance of Catholic worship and supported religious educational institutions, such as the three seminaries at Quito and one in each of the six dioceses. At the same time, the state ruled that no new or foreign religious order would be permitted in the country. The Ecuadoran government was controlled by anti-clerical Liberals until 1925, when the so-called Julian Revolution led to the establishment of a new Conservative government that granted political and religious freedom to all Ecuadorans.

Diverse tensions arose within the Ecuadoran Catholic Church during the 1960s and following years, which resulted from challenges posed by the Second Vatican Council (1962–1965), the Conference of Latin American Bishops held in Medellín (Colombia) in 1968, the emergence of Latin American Liberation Theology, and the Catholic Charismatic Renewal move-

Catholic Church the nation's official religion and only Catholics could obtain citizenship. Under the new president, a Concordat was established with the Vatican (1863), new dioceses were established, and schools and missions were given back to the Jesuits, who had been permitted to return.

However, President García Moreno was murdered in August 1875, and his death not only put an end to the Concordat but also led to a wave of persecution against the church under the new political regime. In 1885, when Bishop Pietro Schumacher, C.M., became bishop of Portoviejo (established in 1870), nearly all the Native clergy were suspended and replaced by European priests and a new Conservative hierarchy was established under Archbishop José Ignacio Ordóñez (1882–1893), who participated in the First Vatican Council (December 1869–October 1870) hosted by Pope Pius IX (r. 1846–1878).

ment. These powerful new currents polarized Catholic bishops, priests (diocesan and religious), lay brothers and sisters (members of religious orders), and the laity in general into various factions. *Traditionalists* wanted the church to remain as it was prior to the reforms approved by the Second Vatican Council (mid-1960s), with an emphasis on apostolic authority, orthodox theology, the sacraments, and personal piety. *Reformers* generally supported the church's post–Second Vatican Council stance of modernization and toleration of diversity based on its official social doctrine. *Progressives*, inspired by reforms approved at the Second Vatican and Medellín conferences, sought to implement the new vision for "a preferential option for the poor" through social and political action aimed at transforming Ecuadoran society and establishing social justice through peaceful democratic means. *Radicals* adopted the Marxist-inspired Liberation Theology and advocated violent revolution by the people as a means of overthrowing right-wing military dictatorships and creating a Socialist state that would serve the poor marginalized masses. *Charismatic agents* sought to transform the spiritual and communal life of Catholics by means of the power and gifts of the Holy Spirit (including the "baptism of the Holy Spirit and speaking in tongues"), rather than by political and social activism.

The Catholic Church has traditionally identified with the ruling Spanish elite and was thus unprepared to deal with the radical program introduced by Bishop Leonidas Eduardo Proaño Villalba (r. 1955–1987) of the Diocese of Riobamba in the Province of Chimborazo, who identified his diocese with the rights of the Quichuas and other Amerindian peoples and who introduced a broad range of programs, not only to draw them closer to the church but to bring reforms to secular society in rural areas. By the mid-1970s, Bishop Proaño Villalba was being excluded from meetings of the other bishops, but he was able to retain the support of the Vatican.

In 2004, the Ecuadoran Catholic Church was divided administratively into 4 archdioceses (Quito, Cuenca, Guayaquil, and Portoviejo) and 19 dioceses with 1,151 parishes that were served by 1,779 priests (1,019 diocesan and 760 religious priests), assisted by 69 permanent deacons, 1,360 male religious workers,

and 4,759 female religious workers. Catholic male religious orders include the Franciscans, Mercedarians (Order of Our Lady of Mercy), Dominicans, Augustinians, Carmelites, Capuchins, Jesuits, Salesians, Saint Vincent de Paul (Lazaristas), Oblates, and Congregation of Saint Joseph. The current archbishop of Quito is Monsignor Raúl Eduardo Vela Chiriboga, who was appointed in March 2003.

In addition, there are two Eastern Orthodox denominations in Ecuador that are in communion with the Vatican. The Orthodox Church of the Blessed Virgin Mary (Maronite rite) was founded in 1978 in La Atarazana, Guayaquil, now led by the Reverend Flavio Alexis Alfaro, a former Roman Catholic priest. In 2002, the Holy Orthodox Catholic Church was founded in Quito (Archdiocese of Ecuador and South America) to serve Greek, Slav, and Arab Orthodox Christians; since 2004, this denomination has been led by His Eminence Vladika Chrysóstmos (an Ecuadoran), who supervises the Monastery of Anástasis and the Seminary of St. Basil in Quito.

The Protestant Movement   In the face of almost total Catholic hegemony in Ecuador, James Thompson (1788–1854), a Scottish Presbyterian and agent of the British and Foreign Bible Society (BFBS), initiated a Protestant presence in the country in 1824. This initiative was followed up by BFBS agent Lucas Matthews in 1828. In 1835 the Reverend Isaac Watts Wheelwright, an agent of the American Bible Society (ABS), visited Guayaquil and Quito, where he assisted in the establishment of public education at the request of President Vicente Rocafuerte y Bejarano (r. 1834–1839). It was not until 1892 that another ABS agent visited Ecuador, the Reverend Francisco Penzotti, and distributed the scriptures in Guayaquil.

In 1896, the inter-denominational Gospel Missionary Union (GMU, now Avant Ministries) sent its first three missionaries, who were able to take advantage of the opening provided by the repudiation of the country's Concordat with the Vatican by the Liberal government of Eloy Alfaro (r. 1895–1901, 1906–1911). They initiated work along the Pacific coast and in the Amazonian lowlands among the Shuar and Achuar (Jivaroan) people, known as headhunters, who live in scattered communities along the tributaries of the Rio

Napo and the Rio Paute, but their greatest success was among the Quichua in the Andean highlands. Later, their work was organized as the Gospel Missionary Union Churches (1949), which is now the largest non-Catholic denomination in Ecuador.

The Christian and Missionary Alliance (CMA) opened work in 1897, and today its affiliated churches are called the Ecuadoran Evangelical Church. The Methodist Episcopal Church, now an integral part of the United Methodist Church in the United States, sent its first missionaries in 1900. The Seventh-day Adventist Church initiated work in 1905. Several independent Pentecostal missionaries arrived during the period 1910–1930.

After World War II, Ecuador became a major focus of evangelical Christian missions in South America, in part due to the attention brought by the work of the World Radio Missionary Fellowship. In 1931, Clarence Jones and Reuben E. Larson, both of CMA background, began Ecuador's first radio station with a 250-watt transmitter in Quito. HCJB, or the "Voice of the Andes" as it is best known, also was the first religious radio station established outside the United States.

After World War II, as other groups developed their own radio ministries, they gave support to HCJB and used it to build their various mission activities. The most famous incident associated with the station occurred in 1950s, beginning with the 1956 murder of five evangelical missionaries who, with the assistance of HCJB, had pioneered work among the Auca (Waorani) Indians, a remote tribe of hunters and gatherers located in the Amazonian lowlands. The missionaries' deaths were widely reported and debated in evangelical circles, as well as the relocation of the wife and sister of two of those who were killed to Auca territory, where they bravely engaged in missionary work, which led to the eventual "conversion" of the people who had actually murdered the missionaries.

The only other Protestant groups to begin missionary work in Ecuador prior to 1945 were the Church of the Brethren in 1935 and Child Evangelism Fellowship in 1941. Among the groups that began ministries in Ecuador between 1945 and 1959 were the Missionary Church (Fort Wayne, Indiana, 1945), the Oriental Missionary Society (OMS International, 1946), the Evangelical Covenant Church (1947), Missionary Avia-tion Fellowship (1948), the Southern Baptist Convention (1950), the Lutheran-affiliated World Mission Prayer League (1951), Wycliffe Bible Translators (1953), the General Conference Mennonite Church, now the Mennonite Church U.S.A. (1953), Heifer Project International (1955), the International Church of the Foursquare Gospel (1956), the Evangelical Lutheran Church of Ecuador (Missouri Synod, 1956), the United Pentecostal Church International (1957), the Church of England in Ecuador (1957, later known as the Anglican Catholic Church in 1982 and the Anglican Province of Ecuador in 1982, affiliated with the International Anglican Communion), the Berean Mission (1959), and the Apostolic Church of Faith in Jesus Christ (Pentecostal, 1959).

Several older U.S. mainline denominations—the Evangelical and Reformed Church (now a constituent part of the United Church of Christ), the Presbyterian Church in the U.S., and the United Presbyterian Church in the U.S.A. (both now constituent parts of the Presbyterian Church [U.S.A.]), and the Evangelical United Brethren (now a constituent part of the United Methodist Church) combined their resources in 1945 to create the United Andean Mission in Ecuador. Although they intended to launch work in several countries, their efforts have been limited to Ecuador with only modest success, although its various medical, agricultural, and educational efforts have been well received.

Historically, the establishment of Protestant denominations and service agencies in Ecuador can be described as follows: prior to 1900 (4 groups), 1900–1944 (4), 1945–1959 (15), 1960s (18), 1970s (22), 1980s (18), and the 1990s (10). In summary, the period 1960–1989 witnessed the largest development of new church associations and service organizations in the country.

A number of national Amerindian churches have emerged since the mid-1960s, including the Church of the Holy Spirit (1967), the Universal Independent Church of Christ (1970), and the Voice of Jesus Christ Church, all of which are Pentecostal groups. The Association of Indigenous Evangelical Churches of Chimborazo (GMU-affiliated) was the largest Protestant or Free church association in the country in 1985: 235 congregations with an estimated 30,000 members, an average attendance of 80,000, and 130,000 adherents (*Directorio de la Iglesia Evangélica del Ecuador*). Other GMU-related church bodies at this time were the Association of Gospel Missionary Union Churches (founded in 1896: 8,500 adherents among mestizos), the Association of Indigenous Churches of Cotopaxi (founded in 1972: 2,000 adherents), the Association of Indigenous Churches of Tungurahua (founded in 1978: 2,000 adherents), the Association of (indigenous) Shuar Evangelical Churches (founded in 1980: 2,000 adherents), and the Association of Indigenous Churches of Pinchincha (also founded in 1980: 1,550 adherents).

The largest Protestant denominations in Ecuador in 1995, based on the *World Churches Handbook*, were the following: all GMU-related church associations (560 congregations with 71,800 members and an estimated 123,000 adherents), the United Pentecostal Church (65 congregations with 15,000 members and 30,000 adherents), the Christian and Missionary Alliance (190 congregations with 13,400 members and 32,500 adherents), the Baptist Convention (112 congregations with 12,300 members and 35,000 adherents), the International Church of the Foursquare Gospel (110 congregations with 8,100 members and 26,400 adherents), the Assemblies of God (150 congregations with 5,410 members), and the Evangelical Covenant Church (51 congregations with 3,880 members).

More recently, the Seventh-day Adventist Church reported the following statistics for the period 2001–2007: 84 churches with 42,377 members in 2001 and 150 churches with 74,096 members in 2007 (year-end statistics).

Protestant organizations were usually divided between predominantly indigenous organizations, such as the Council of Evangelical Indigenous People and Organizations (FEINE), and mestizo organizations. In large cities, Protestant mega-churches, some with more than 10,000 members, have continued to grow substantially. There is a high percentage of mestizo Protestants in the Guayaquil area.

Interdenominational work began with the establishment of the Inter-Mission Fellowship, founded in 1950, which included a spectrum of Protestant missionary organizations. It was superseded by the Ecuadoran Evangelical Confraternity (CEE) in 1964, a reflection of the emergence of autonomous Ecuadoran denominations. In 2007, the CEE membership included more than 150 denominations and independent church associations that represented conservative evangelicalism. The CEE is affiliated with the Latin American Confraternity of Evangelicals (CONELA) and the World Evangelical Alliance.

Some of the ecumenical Protestant denominations are affiliated with the Latin American Council of Churches (CLAI), which established its continental headquarters in Quito in 1987. CLAI is associated with the World Council of Churches (WCC) and is active in broader ecumenical scene in the continent. CLAI members in Ecuador are: the Faith, Integrity and Hope Council of Evangelical Indigenous Organizations and Peoples of Ecuador (Consejo de Pueblos y Organizaciones Indígenas Evangélicas del Ecuador/Fe Integridad y Esperanza); the Episcopal Church of Ecuador; the Evangelical Lutheran Church; and the United Evangelical Church of Ecuador.

Other Christian Groups   There are several Western Catholic denominations in Ecuador that are independent of the Vatican. The Priestly Fraternity of Ecuador (affiliated with the International Organization of Married Catholic Priests, based in the United States) is led by the Reverend Alonso Pérez of the parish of Iglesia La Dolorosa in Ambato. The Priestly Fraternity of Saint Pius X, founded in Switzerland by Mons. Marcel Lefèvbre (1905–1991) in 1970, administers a parish in Quito and only celebrates the Mass in Latin; the Old Catholic Church has been led by Bishop José Javier Guanulema in Saquislí since 2005. The Reformed Catholic Church, founded in 2002 in San Camilo, Quevedo, is led by Bishop Vicente Ney Valero, a former Episcopal priest. The Latin Catholic Church, founded in 2003 in Barrio Guamaní in southern Quito, is headed by Luis Bolívar Lara, also a former Episcopal priest; this is a Spiritualist group that performs healing rituals with the "intervention" of a dead Venezuelan medical doctor, Gregorio Hernández, known as a folk healer. Finally, the Ecumenical Catholic Church was founded by Juventino Espinoza in Barrio La Cristianía in northern Quito; its current leader is Bishop José Vicente García, a lawyer.

Many non-Protestant "marginal" Christian groups are also present in Ecuador: the Church of Jesus Christ of Latter-day Saints (LDS—Mormons, founded in 1965; one temple, 294 congregations and 185,663 members in 2007; on August 1, 1999, the Guayaquil Mormon Temple was dedicated by LDS President Gordon B. Hinckley); the Watch Tower Bible and Tract Society (also known as Jehovah's Witnesses: 764 congregations and 64,792 adherents in 2008); the Children of God, also known as The Family International (located in Valle de los Chillos); the Philadelphia Church of God; the Israelites of the New Universal Covenant (also in Peru and Bolivia); Christadelphian Bible Mission; the Unity School of Christianity; the Voice of the Chief Cornerstone (from Puerto Rico); Growing in Grace Ministries International (headquarters in Miami, Florida); Light of the World Church (from Mexico); and the God is Love Pentecostal Church and the Universal Church of the Kingdom of God from Brazil.

Additional Religious Groups Non-Christian religions include Hinduism, Judaism, Buddhism, Baha'i Faith, Islam and Subud. Hindu-derived groups include: the International Society for Krishna Consciousness (ISKON), Vaisnava Mission, the Brahma Kumaris Community, the Singh Rajinder Community, the Divine Light Mission (now Elan Vital), International Sri Sathya Sai Baba Organization, Osho-Bhadra Meditation Center, Srila Sridhar Swami Seva Ashram, Sawan Kirpal Ruhani Mission-Science of Spirituality, the Maharishi Community of Ecuador, and Transcendental Meditation (TM, now organized as the Global Country of World Peace).

There is a small Jewish community in Ecuador, whose approximately 1,000 members are found primarily in Quito and Guayaquil. There are more than 5,000 Chinese in Ecuador, many of whom continue in their Buddhist and Daoist faiths. Buddhist groups include the Buddhist Community of Ecuador (the Pagoda Yuan Heng is located in La Garzota, Guayaquil), the International Zen Association, the Dahrma Buhdi Susila Community, and the Tibetan Buddhist Community. The Baha'i Faith, introduced in the mid-1900s, has experienced growth, especially among some of the Amerindian peoples and those of African descent. Also, the Sunni Muslim (Islamic Center of Ecuador) and the Subud Association have a small following.

The Ancient Wisdom Tradition is represented by Freemasonry (Grand Equinocial Lodge of Ecuador); the Ancient and Mystical Order Rosae Crucis (AMORC); the Grand Universal Fraternity, Order of Aquarius (GFU, founded in Venezuela); the Gnostic Community of Ecuador; and the Universal Gnostic Christian movement.

The Psychic-Spiritualist-New Age traditions are represented by the Center of Esoteric Studies, Providence Spiritual Center, New Age Holistic Center, Ishaya Techniques, the Silvan Method, the Church of Scientology (also known as Dianetics), the Community of Oriental Spirituality, and the Unification Movement (founded in Korea by the Reverend Sun Myung Moon).

Popular Catholic religiosity (syncretistic) is practiced by a majority of the Hispanic white and mestizo population. Among practitioners of Amerindian religions and "popular Catholic religiosity," there are "specialists" who practice witchcraft (*brujería*), shamanism (*chamanismo*), and folk healing (*curanderismo*). The Quichua people make up about 40 percent of the present population of Ecuador. However, it is among the various smaller Amerindian groups in the remotest parts of the country, especially in the headwaters of the Amazon River, that traditional animistic religion has survived relatively untouched by the outside world. Among the Quichua there are still followers of Inti, the traditional Inca sun god.

Clifton L. Holland

See also: Ancient and Mystical Order Rosae Crucis; Agnosticism; Assemblies of God; Atheism; Augustinians; Baha'i Faith; Brahma Kumaris; Capuchins; Christian and Missionary Alliance; Church of Jesus Christ of Latter-day Saints; Church of Scientology; Church of the Brethren; Dominicans; Elan Vital/ Divine Light Mission; Family International, The; Fraternity/Society of Saint Pius X; Freemasonry; Global Country of World Peace; International Church of the Foursquare Gospel; International Society for Krishna Consciousness; International Zen Association; Jehovah's Witnesses; Jesuits; Latin American Council of Churches; Light of the World Church; Lutheran Church–Missouri Synod; Maronite Catholic Church; Moon, Sun Myung; Philadelphia Church of God; Presbyterian Church (U.S.A.); Roman Catholic Church; Salesians; Seventh-day Adventist Church; Southern Baptist Convention; Subud; Unification Movement; United Church of Christ; United Methodist Church; United Pentecostal Church International; Unity School of Christianity; Universal Church of the Kingdom of God; World Evangelical Alliance.

References

Bandelier, Adolph Francis. "Ecuador." In *The Catholic Encyclopedia*. Vol. 5. New York: Robert Appleton Company, 1909. http://www.newadvent.org/cathen/05278a.htm.

Catholic Hierarchy website. http://www.catholichierarchy.org/country/scec1.html.

Crespo, Walter Roberto. *Panorama Religioso en el Ecuador: 2007*. http://www.prolades.com/cra/regions/sam/ecu/crespo_estudio_ecuador.pdf.

Goffin, A. M. *The Rise of Protestant Evangelism in Ecuador, 1895–1990*. Gainesville: University Press of Florida, 1994.

Hamilton, Keith E. *Church Growth in the High Andes*. Lucknow, U.P., India: The Lucknow Publishing House, 1962.

Handelman, Michael. *Culture and Customs of Ecuador*. Westport, CT: Greenwood Press, 2000.

Hatch, Roberto, ed. *Directorio de la Iglesia Evangélica del Ecuador*. Quito, Ecuador: Comité Interdenominacional Pro-Directorio, 1985.

Holland, Clifton L. "A Chronology of Protestant Beginnings in Ecuador." San José, Costa Rica: PROLADES, 2003. http://www.prolades.com/cra/regions/sam/ecu/ecu-chron.pdf.

Lewis, M. Paul, ed. *Ethnologue: Languages of the World,* 16th edition. Dallas, TX: SIL International, 2009. http://www.ethnologue.com/.

Padilla J., Washington. *La iglesia y los dioses modernos: historia del protestantismo en el Ecuador*. Quito, Ecuador: Corporación Editora Nacional, 1989.

Reed, Gerardo. *Los Evangélicos del Ecuador: Un Estudio Analítico*. Quito, Ecuador: Iglesia del Pacto Evangélico, 1975.

Stoll, David. *Is Latin America Turning Protestant? The Politics of Evangelical Growth*. Berkeley: University of California Press, 1990.

U.S. Department of State. *International Freedom of Religion Report 2007: Ecuador*. http://www.state.gov/g/drl/rls/irf/2007/90252.htm.

Weld, Wayne C. *An Ecuadoran Impasse*. Chicago: Department of World Missions, Evangelical Covenant Church of North America, 1968 (originally presented as a master's thesis to the School of World Mission at Fuller Theological Seminary, Pasadena, CA, in 1968).

Ecumenical Patriarchate/Patriarchate of Constantinople

The Patriarchate of Constantinople, also known as the Ecumenical Patriarchate, is one of the autocephalous churches of the Eastern Orthodox communion. It ranks highest in honor among those churches, and serves as a point of unity among them.

After the Emperor Constantine moved the Roman imperial capital to the town of Byzantium in 330 and renamed it New Rome, or Constantinople, the church of that city took on new importance. Thus the First Council of Constantinople in 381 elevated it to a patriarchal rank second only to Rome. The Council of Chalcedon in 451 expanded the boundaries of the Patriarchate and gave it jurisdiction over bishops of dioceses in "barbarian" lands. For the next 1,000 years, the church of Constantinople was the center of the church in the Eastern Roman Empire (usually referred to as the Byzantine Empire). It also presided over expansive missionary activity into the Balkans and the Slavic lands to the northeast. After the schism with the Roman Catholic Church of the West in the 11th century, Constantinople assumed the first rank among the Eastern Orthodox churches. The steady decline of the Byzantine Empire was hastened by the brief Latin conquest by Crusaders in the 13th century and the gradual encroachment of the Ottoman Turkish armies.

The fall of Constantinople to the Turks in 1453 ironically enhanced the authority of the Patriarchate dramatically. Although its territory had been reduced on the eve of the conquest to the small remnants of the

Byzantine Empire, the Ottoman sultans established a new millet (administrative) system, which gave the Patriarchate civil as well as religious authority over all the Orthodox Christians within their vast empire. Then, when the Ottoman Empire went into decline and new Christian states emerged in the Balkans in the 19th century, the Patriarchate began to give up its ecclesiastical authority there and granted autocephalous status to the new churches in those countries. A small Greek kingdom gained independence in 1832, and in the wake of that independence, the expansion of the kingdom in the wake of the Balkan Wars of 1912–1913, and an extensive exchange of populations between Greece and Turkey in the 1920s, the great majority of the Greek-speaking faithful of the Patriarchate have been transferred to the autocephalous Orthodox Church of Greece. Anti-Greek rioting in Istanbul (the modern Turkish name of the city) in the 1950s precipitated another exchange of populations, such that now fewer than 5,000 Greeks remain in Turkey itself.

Nevertheless, the Patriarchate of Constantinople retains jurisdiction over the semi-autonomous Orthodox Church of Crete as well as the Orthodox dioceses in the Dodecanese Islands and the monastic republic of Mount Athos, all of which are in Greece. The Greek Orthodox in the so-called diaspora also come under the Patriarchate's jurisdiction, notably including the faithful in the Americas, Australia, and Western Europe. The total membership has been estimated at 3.5 million. It administers a number of theological institutions in Greece and elsewhere.

Today the Ecumenical Patriarchate of Constantinople continues to serve as a point of unity among the Orthodox churches, with the patriarch's role often defined as "primus inter pares," or first among equals. The Patriarchate does not have the authority to intervene in the internal affairs of the autocephalous churches, but it does coordinate pan-Orthodox activities, such as decisions to participate in ecumenical dialogues with other Christian bodies. Occasionally it calls the Orthodox churches together for common action when problems arise. The Patriarchate is governed by a permanent 12-member Holy Synod, which is presided over by the Ecumenical Patriarch. The Patriarchate's position in Istanbul remains precarious. The Turkish government closed down its only theological school on the island of Halki in 1971, and the tiny Greek community undergoes periodic harassment. But in 1989 the Patriarchate was able to dedicate a new administrative center to replace the one that had been destroyed by fire in 1941. This gave it the capacity to fulfill its role more effectively and to host important church events.

Ecumenical Patriarchate of Constantinople
% His Holiness Bartholomew, Archbishop of
    Constantinople and Ecumenical Patriarch
Rum Patrikhanesi
34220 Fener-Istanbul
Turkey
http://www.ec-patr.org/

                      Ronald Roberson

See also: Constantine the Great; Istanbul; Orthodox Church of Greece; Roman Catholic Church.

References

Geanakoplos, Deno. *A Short History of the Ecumenical Patriarchate of Constantinople (330–1990): "First among Equals" in the Eastern Orthodox Church.* Brookline, MA: Holy Cross Orthodox Press, 1990.

Hussey, J. M. *The Orthodox Church in the Byzantine Empire.* Oxford: Clarendon Press, 1986.

Maximos, Metropolitan of Sardes. *The Oecumenical Patriarchate in the Orthodox Church: A Study in the History and Canons of the Church.* Trans. by Gamon McLellan. Thessaloniki: Patriarchal Institute for Patristic Studies, 1976.

Runciman, Steven. *The Great Church in Captivity: A Study of the Patriarchate of Constantinople from the Eve of the Turkish Conquest to the Greek War of Independence.* Cambridge: Cambridge University Press, 1968.

Eddy, Mary Baker

1821–1908

Mary Baker Eddy, the founder of Christian Science and author of *Science and Health with Key to the Scriptures*, was one of the most influential and controversial religious leaders in 19th century America. Those who dissented from her primary organization, the Church

Mary Baker Eddy, founder of the religion of Christian Science. Eddy established the Church of Christ, Scientist, one of the United States' fastest-growing religious institutions of the late 19th and early 20th centuries. (Library of Congress)

of Christ, Scientist, and its teachings went on to create the modern New Thought movement.

Eddy was born on July 16, 1821, in Bow, New Hampshire, and was raised in the Congregational Church, though she had early doubts about Calvinistic theology. She was married in 1843 to George Washington Glover but he died the following year. She wed Daniel Patterson, a dentist, in 1853 but that union resulted in financial and emotional torment and eventual divorce in 1873. She married again in 1877, this time to her former student Asa Gilbert Eddy.

In 1862 the future Mrs. Eddy traveled to Maine to seek healing at the hands of Phineas Parkhurst Quimby (1802–1866), a self-professed mental healer. Quimby emphasized the role of the mind in healing, and this suited her growing interest in the importance of the spiritual over the material. While she later downplayed his influence on her, Gillian Gill has shown that critics have often overstated the parallels between the two.

Christian Science is usually traced to Eddy's healing from a fall on the ice in Lynn, Massachusetts, on February 1, 1866. Her recovery from the accident followed a realization of the Allness of God. In her 1891 autobiography she called it a miracle wrought by "the divine Spirit." By 1870 she was teaching her views on healing and gathering devoted students to her side. Her most important works are *Science and Health with Key to the Scriptures,* the textbook of the movement, first published in 1875, and the church manual, the movement's organizational guidebook.

The Christian Scientist Association was born in 1876 and the Church of Christ, Scientist was founded in April 1879. By then Eddy was a public figure, both loved by her followers and maligned by ex-students (Josephine Woodbury) and critics, including Mark Twain. Twain was withering in his critique of Eddy but did compliment her for industriousness. As an example of that, in her 87th year she founded *The Christian Science Monitor*. She died at home in New Hampshire on December 3, 1910.

Mary Baker Eddy was a convinced idealist and her statements about the sole reality of Spirit are uncompromising. One of the most famous lines in *Science and Health* reads: "There is no life, truth, intelligence, nor substance in matter. All is infinite Mind and its infinite manifestation, for God is All-in-all" (468). Later, she writes that "Man is not matter, he is not made up of brain, blood, bones, and other material elements." For her "Man is incapable of sin, sickness, and death" (475) and "evil is but an illusion" (480).

Following a fallout, Eddy's student Emma Curtis Hopkins (1849–1925) would move to Chicago and began teaching students who would become the founders of the major New Thought associations, including Charles and Myrtle Fillmore (Unity School of Christianity), Malinda Cramer (Divine Science), and Ernest Holmes (Religious Science).

James A. Beverley

See also: Church of Christ, Scientist; Religious Science; Unity School of Christianity/Association of Unity Churches.

References

Bates, Ernest S., and John V. Dittemore. *Mary Baker Eddy: The Truth and the Tradition*. New York: Knopf, 1932.

Gardner, Gardner. *The Healing Revelations of Mary Baker Eddy*. Buffalo, NY: Prometheus, 1993.

Gill, Gillian. *Mary Baker Eddy*. New York: Perseus, 1998.

Gottschalk, Stephen. *The Emergence of Christian Science in American Religious Life*. Los Angeles: University of California Press, 1973.

Harley, Gail. *Emma Curtis Hopkins: Forgotten Founder of New Thought*. Syracuse, NY: Syracuse University Press, 2002.

Peel, Robert. *Mary Baker Eddy*. 3 vols. New York: Holt, Rinehart and Winston, 1966, 1971, 1977.

Twain, Mark. *Christian Science*. New York: Harper's, 1907.

Églises Baptistes de la RCA

Baptists entered French Equatorial Africa in the 1920s through the efforts of a fundamentalist Baptist missionary, William C. Haas (1873–1924). Haas had been a missionary in the Belgian Congo with the interdenominational Africa Inland Mission, but in 1920 founded an independent Baptist missionary society called Baptist Mid-Missions (now headquartered at 7749 Webster Rd., Cleveland, OH, 44130). Haas joined the first missionary team that established a mission in what is today the Central African Republic in 1921. They established initial stations at Sibut, Crampel, and Bangasou, where Haas was buried after his death in 1924.

The mission had steady growth over the next generation, and by the 1960s it had founded more than 100 churches. It also had established a hospital and six medical dispensaries. In pursuit of its educational ministry, it owns a printing press and has opened several bookstores. Its two Bible schools and seminary have assisted the development of indigenous leadership. It has contributed to the larger effort of translating the Bible into African languages by publishing the Bible for the Sango people. Its workers translated the New Testament and cooperated with the Grace Brethren Mission on the translation of the Old Testament.

In 1963, the mission was organized as the Association of Baptist Churches. The work was hampered by the discovery of some moral problems among the leadership, and the association was dissolved in the 1970s. In 1996, it reorganized under its present name. The work has continued to grow, and by the mid-1990s it reported 6,000 members in 375 churches. It is the largest non-Catholic religious group in the Central African Republic.

The Églises Baptistes has its headquarters at Bangui. As a fundamentalist group, it has no connection with either the Baptist World Alliance or the World Council of Churches. Baptist Mid-Missions remains an independent society, but has the recommendation of the General Association of Regular Baptist Churches, from which it draws much of the resources that it uses to continue its support of the Églises Baptistes. In 1998, it reported 41 associated personnel in the Central African Republic. An account of the work is found at the Baptist Mid-Missions website at http://www.bmm.org/Fields/car.html.

Two schisms of the Églises Baptistes led to the formation of the Union Fraternelle des Églises Baptistes (1977) and the Association des Églises Baptistes Centrafricaines.

J. Gordon Melton

See also: Baptist World Alliance; World Council of Churches.

References

Baptist Mid-Missions. *Field Surveys*. Cleveland, OH: Baptist Mid-Missions, 1977.

Strong, Polly. *Burning Wicks*. Cleveland, OH: Baptist Mid-Missions, 1984.

■ Egypt

Egypt, considered by many Westerners as the cradle of their civilization, was for millennia the home to a flourishing religious tradition (a tradition whose belief and practice lie beyond the reach of this encyclopedia). That religion, which in a revisionist form has

Al-Azhar Mosque and Al-Azhar University in Cairo, founded in 972 CE by the Fatimid caliph. (Paul Cowan/Dreamstime .com)

reappeared outside of Egypt in neo-Paganism, was in stages replaced by Christianity and then Islam, whose entrance into the Nile Valley initiated the modern religious history of the region. Contemporary Egypt sits on the northern boundary of the African continent. The northern border of its 334,000 square miles lies on the Mediterranean Sea with the Red Sea and Gulf of Suez to the east. Sudan is to the south and Libya to the west. Much of Egypt's history has taken place on the Sinai Peninsula, a land mass of 23,000 square miles that lies to the east of the Suez Canal and the Gulf of Suez and forms a bridge between Africa and Asia. Egypt has one of the fastest rates of population growth in the region, which by 2008 reached more than 81 million.

Egypt was incorporated into the kingdom of Alexander the Great (356–323 BCE) and afterward came under the Ptolemaic dynasty, which continued to rule until Egypt became a Roman province (31 BCE). It remained within the Roman Empire through its transformation into the Byzantine Empire until the Arab conquest in 642 CE. The Arabs imposed their language and created the most definitive break with the country's ancient past.

In the 10th century, the Arabs were replaced by the Fatimids, Ismaili Muslims who had emerged at the end of the prior century in Tunisia and spread across North Africa. The Fatimids established their capital in Cairo and established the famed University of Al-Azhar. The Fatimid Empire extended from Palestine to Tunis but in the 12th century was weakened by war with the Christian Crusaders. In 1171, the Arabs were able to drive the Fatimids from power and reestablish themselves as the dominant force in the land. They held sway until 1517, when the rising Ottoman (Turkish) Empire assumed control.

EGYPT

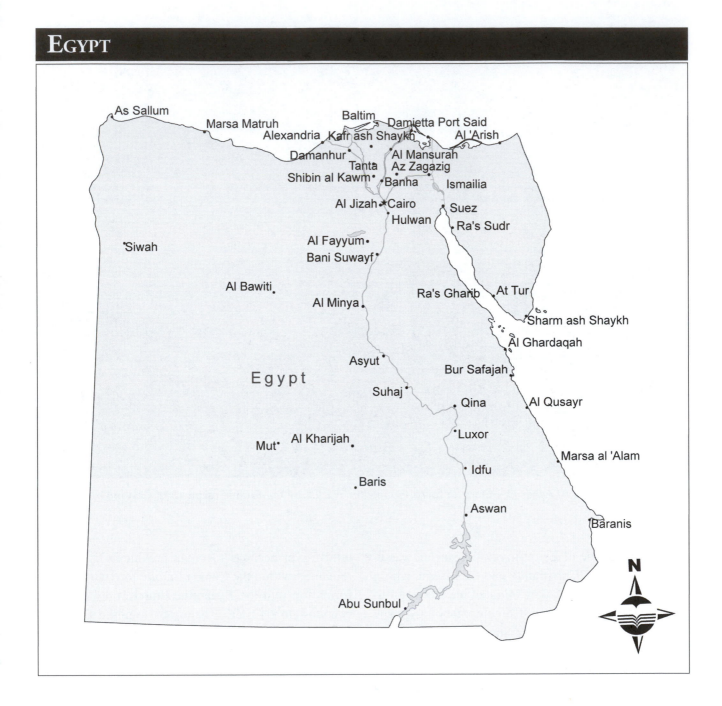

Formally, Egypt remained a part of the Ottoman Empire into the 19th century. In 1805 an Albanian, Muhammad Ali, seized control and began the process of modernization. In the 1860s, Egypt gained a degree of autonomy, but it had already become the object of economic forces operating out of Western Europe. It had joined with the French to create the Suez Canal but in 1874 sold its interest in the canal to pay its debts to the British. In 1882 the British landed an occupation force, and in 1914 Egypt became a British protectorate. Though the protectorate was officially discontinued in 1922, the British presence continued in force through World War II, when Egypt was a staging area for Allied opposition to the Germans in North Africa.

In 1948, the weakened rulers of the country, who claimed royal prerogatives, were overthrown in a coup led by Colonel Gamal Abdel Nasser (1918–1970). Nasser installed a secular government. He created an international crisis by successfully nationalizing the Suez Canal in 1956. Two years later he united Egypt with Syria in the short-lived United Arab Republic (1958–1961). Nasser's last years were overshadowed by the Israeli defeat of Egypt in the 1967 Six-Day War. His successor, Anwar Sadat, reoriented Egypt toward the West and worked out an agreement with Israel, both of which led to his assassination in 1981. He was succeeded by the present president, Hosni Mubarak.

Christianity looks to the account of Mary and Joseph fleeing to Egypt with the infant Jesus (Matthew 2:14–15) as the beginning of Christianity in the country. Then, according to tradition, after the church was established in Jerusalem, Saint Mark was sent to Egypt, where the first Christian church was called together in Alexandria. Over the next centuries, the church spread through the Nile Valley, and the successive bishops of Alexandria became major participants in the evolution of Christian theology through the fifth century. Egypt was also among the first places that Christian monasticism emerged as an important part of church life.

Egyptian Christians faced a major crisis in the middle of the fifth century; as part of the larger theological project of defining the nature of the Trinity, the Christian movement was concerned with defining the nature of Christ. Christ's two natures (human and divine) were defined by the Council of Chalcedon in 451. The Egyptian leadership rejected the formula espoused by Chalcedon and were labeled Monophysites (from the Greek for "one nature") by those who accepted Chalcedon (who in Egypt were called Melkites). The theological battle continued over the next centuries, during which time the majority of the Christians in Egypt were united in their refusal to acknowledge the Chalcedonian position (while claiming that they fully accepted the Nicene Creed and were not Monophysites). Nevertheless, the Egyptian church broke relations with the rest of the Christian world, especially the patriarch in Constantinople (the Ecumenical Patriarchate of Constantinople being the nominal center of Eastern Orthodoxy).

Christian history was then interrupted by the Arab invasion in the seventh century and the entrance of Islam. Christianity was most negatively affected by the subsequent warfare between Egypt, the Muslims headquartered in Baghdad, the Byzantine Empire, and the Crusaders. Many Christians converted to Islam; however, the weakened Coptic Orthodox Church, as it was then called, survived, and eventually the Egyptian Christians becoming a recognizable subgroup in Egyptian society.

Islamic history also followed a somewhat disjunctive course, beginning with the Ismaili Fatimid rulers in 969. The Fatimid caliph established the new city of Cairo as his capital and in 1972 founded Al-Azhar University. The Ismailis represented a form of Shia Islam that looked for leadership of the Muslim world in the descendants of Muhammad through his daughter Fatima and son-in-law Ali. They split with the main body of Shiites in the eighth century when the heir to the throne, Ismail, the son of Imam Ja'far al-Sadiq, died before he could assume authority. Most Shiites threw their support to Ismail's brother, but the Ismailis recognized the descendants of Ismail as the beginning of a new line of imams. The new lineage was named after Fatima.

The Ismailis also proposed the belief that prior to the end of time, a seventh prophet (Muhammad being the sixth) would arise. This prophet, the Mahdi, from the Arabic for "rightly guided," was expected to bring no new revelation, but to bring political unity.

In 1021, a Fatimid prince was declared Ismail resurrected and the one prophesied to overthrow the Arab ruler, a follower of Sunni Islam, then ruling from Baghdad. He failed to accomplish his assigned task, and the resulting splintering of the Ismailis contributed to the weaknesses that led to their overthrow in 1171. Among the groups emerging from the Ismailis was the mystical Tayyibiyya Sufi Brotherhood. Although the reestablishment of Arab leadership in Egypt did not mean the disappearance of the Ismailis, they did move into a minority status, while the Sunni Muslims took the lead. Sunnis are split among the major schools, with the Shafaiite and Malikite schools of Islam dominating in the north and the Hanafite School in the south.

Islam, in its several factions, remains the faith of more than 80 percent of Egypt's 81 million citizens. In the post-Nasser era, Islam in Egypt has developed a set of structures that now offer leadership to the religious community. The Supreme Council for Islamic Affairs has the assigned purpose of spreading Islam in

Egypt

Religion	Followers in 1970	Followers in 2010	% of Population	Annual % growth 2000–2010	Followers in 2025	Followers in 2050
Muslims	28,711,000	68,804,000	86.5	1.92	86,626,000	107,668,000
Christians	6,347,000	10,293,000	12.9	1.29	11,277,000	12,676,000
Orthodox	6,002,000	9,300,000	11.7	1.26	10,000,000	11,000,000
Protestants	136,000	560,000	0.7	0.83	700,000	900,000
Roman Catholics	139,000	340,000	0.4	4.12	450,000	600,000
Agnostics	100,000	355,000	0.4	2.09	500,000	720,000
Atheists	30,000	76,000	0.1	1.83	100,000	140,000
Baha'is	1,100	6,500	0.0	1.83	8,000	12,000
Jews	700	1,500	0.0	−2.17	1,500	1,500
Hindus	0	800	0.0	1.83	1,000	1,600
Total population	**35,190,000**	**79,537,000**	**100.0**	**1.83**	**98,513,000**	**121,219,000**

Egypt and around the world. To that end it prints literature in a number of languages and makes grants for the construction of mosques and the education of youth. Al-Azhar University is one of the leading Muslim centers of higher learning in the world, and its scholars are called upon to make decisions concerning disputed questions in the Muslim community. Reorganized in 1961, it has developed a school for the training of females, a training institute for future Muslim leaders from around the world, and radio and printing facilities to assist in the spread and purifying of Islam. Finally, the Council for Islamic Studies has as its purpose the vivification of Islamic culture. Both the university and the council have been strongly opposed to the more politically radical elements (often lumped together under the term "Islamic Fundamentalism") in Egypt.

Egypt was the originating point of the Muslim Brotherhood, a conservative group allied with the Wahhabi leadership in Saudi Arabia. The brotherhood gained political clout each time the Saudi government put money into the financially ailing Egyptian economy. It has advocated the institution of Islamic law as the law of the land, but has lost considerable support since individuals associated with it were deemed responsible for Anwar Sadat's death. Hosni Mubarak has banned all overt political activity by the brotherhood, while developing friendly relations with the United States. Under Mubarak the country has become more secular, at the same time resisting any attempt to return to the Socialist policies favored by Nasser.

Egyptian Christianity entered the modern world in two main forms, the Coptic Orthodox Church and the much smaller Greek Orthodox Patriarchate of Alexandria and All Africa (in communion with the Ecumenical Patriarchate). Then, in the 17th century, the Roman Catholic Church entered Egypt through missionary activity instituted by the Capuchins and Jesuits. While building up Latin-rite congregations, the spread of Catholicism also led to the formation of the Eastern-rite Coptic Catholic Church. As Egypt's population diversified, congregations of the Maronite Catholic Church and the Melkite Catholic Church also emerged (as have congregations of a variety of Orthodox churches, such as the Russian Orthodox Church [Moscow Patriarchate] and the Armenian Apostolic Church).

Protestants opened work in 1854 through the efforts of the U.S.-based Associate Reformed Presbyterian Church (now a constituent part of the Presbyterian Church [U.S.A.]). Their proselytizing activity, primarily among Coptic Christians, led to the formation of the Coptic Evangelical Church, now known as the Evangelical Church–Synod of the Nile. Other independent evangelical churches and missionary agencies launched missions, among the most substantive being that of the Free Methodist Church in 1899. The work of evangelicals was disrupted by the wars in 1956 and 1967, when foreign missionaries had to leave the country. Several missionary agencies reassigned their missionaries to more friendly locations. Among the churches retaining at least a presence in the country are the Christian Brethren (since 1869) and the Church of God

(Cleveland, Tennessee). Many of the evangelical groups have their base among expatriates (especially Greeks and Lebanese) living and working in Egypt.

Anglicans began work in 1847, and their parishes are now part of the Episcopal Church in Jerusalem and the Middle East, based in Israel.

Egypt, of course, plays a major role in the beliefs of Judaism, and there has been a significant Jewish community in Egypt at least since the fifth century BCE. It was in Egypt that the Hebrew Torah was translated (around 250 BCE) into Greek, a work known as the Septuagint translation. That community survived through the years of Roman and then Muslim rule until 1948. After the establishment of the state of Israel, most of Egypt's Jews migrated, especially spurred by the hostility directed toward them following the wars in 1956 and 1967. At present only some 200 Jews remain in Egypt, supplemented by a small expatriate community that has recently emerged in Cairo. There are four Jewish synagogues in the Cairo metropolitan area.

Few of the newer 20th-century religions have tried to colonize Egypt. Although Buddhists speculate on the possibility that Buddhist missionaries reached Egypt in ancient times, there are no known Buddhist centers in the country at present. There is a small community of the Baha'i Faith, but no Hindus, Sikhs, or representatives of the new religious movements (though it is likely that some of these groups are represented by members in the expatriate community).

J. Gordon Melton

See also: Armenian Apostolic Church (Holy See of Etchmiadzin); Baha'i Faith; Christian Brethren; Church of God (Cleveland, Tennessee); Coptic Catholic Church; Coptic Orthodox Church; Ecumenical Patriarchate/Patriarchate of Constantinople; Episcopal Church in Jerusalem and the Middle East; Evangelical Church–Synod of the Nile; Free Methodist Church of North America; Greek Orthodox Patriarchate of Alexandria and All Africa; Hanafite School of Islam; Jesuits; Malikite School of Islam; Maronite Catholic Church; Melkite Catholic Church; Presbyterian Church (U.S.A.); Roman Catholic Church; Russian Orthodox Church (Moscow Patriarchate); Shafaiite School of Islam; Shia Islam; Wahhabi Islam.

References

Abdo, Geneive, *No God but God: Egypt and the Triumph of Islam*. New York: Oxford University Press, 2002.

Hoffman, Valerie J. *Sufism, Mystics, and Saints in Modern Egypt*. Columbia: University of South Carolina Press, 1995.

Kepel, Gilles. *Muslim Extremism in Egypt*. Berkeley: University of California Press, 1985.

Kramer, Gudrun. *The Jews in Modern Egypt*. London: I. B. Tauris, 1989.

Meinardus, Otto F. A. *Two Thousand Years of Coptic Christianity*. Cairo: American University in Cairo Press, 1999.

Moaddel, Mansoor. *Jordanian Exceptionalism: A Comparative Analysis of State-Religion Relationships in Egypt, Iran, Jordan, and Syria*. London: Palgrave Macmillan, 2002.

Murphy, Carlyle. *Passion for Islam: Shaping the Modern Middle East: The Egyptian Experience*. New York: Scribner, 2002.

Tal, Nachman. *Radical Islam: In Egypt and Jordan*. Eastbourne, East Sussex, UK: Sussex Academic Press, 2005.

Wakin, Edward. *A Lonely Minority: The Modern Story of Egypt's Copts*. Lincoln, NE: iUniverse.com, 2000.

Egypt in Western Religious Imagination

The idea that Egypt is the homeland of profound spiritual wisdom has deep roots in Western culture, and can be found already in Greek sources. Over the centuries, various authors have differed widely in describing the substance of Egyptian wisdom. Statements that were once commonplace, such as the late 18th-century claim that the tarot cards have an Egyptian origin, seem to have become increasingly infrequent. One major reason for such shifts over time is the dissemination among a wider readership of scholarship on the Egyptian system of writing and language. Claims regarding the mystical properties of the hieroglyphs, or of the spiritual import of particular texts translated by paranormal means, have become less common after the decipherment of Ancient Egyptian by Jean-François Champollion (1790–1832) and the popularization of his results and those of subsequent generations of Egyptologists. Another reason is that the nature of these claims adapt to the interests of society at large. In a technological age, claims regarding the profound spirituality of ancient Egyptians are conflated with claims that portray them as masters of an amazingly advanced technology partly built on paranormal foundations.

With the passage of time, the genre of literature and the social forums where the idea of an esoteric or spiritually advanced Egypt is disseminated have also shifted. With the advent of modern archaeological discoveries, conceptions of an esoteric, spiritual Egypt have largely been relegated from mainstream intellectual culture to various new religious movements and alternative (occultist and/or New Age) milieus. Several recent titles presenting alternative claims regarding the paranormal and esoteric insights of the Egyptians have been published by mass-market publishers and have sold millions of copies. Most academic Egyptologists consider such theories pseudoscientific, and the uncharitable label "pyramidiots" has been coined to designate those who accept such alternative claims.

There is no single, coherent image of spiritual Egypt in circulation in these alternative milieus, but rather a number of loosely related claims. Many of these concern the role, nature, and provenance of the pyramids. A first set of narratives suggests that a chamber within the Cheops pyramid functioned as a kind of meditation retreat, where highly initiated members of Egyptian secret societies could receive mystical knowledge. Related narratives suggest more broadly that the core of Egyptian spirituality was secret initiation, and portray a number of key figures in religious history, including Jesus, as the recipient of this hidden knowledge. Much of this alternative history can be traced back to theosophical literature (in particular, Helena P. Blavatsky's *Isis Unveiled*, 1877), or to works historically related to the theosophical current (for example, Rudolf Steiner's interpretations of Egyptian religious history or Edgar Cayce's readings on this topic).

A second set of narratives focuses on the dating of the pyramids themselves. The conventional dating of these monuments to the third millennium BCE is challenged, and alternative accounts push this chronology back several thousand years. These alternative histories do not always agree with each other. Theosophical sources (for example, Helena P. Blavatsky in her work *The Secret Doctrine* [1888], vol. 2, 432) suggest an age of 78,000 years, whereas approximately 10,000 BCE is a common time frame in much of the more recent literature.

The method of construction of the pyramids is also the subject of frequent speculation, with a third group of alternative theories rejecting the standard Egyptological suggestion that the stones were transported on ramps to their final locations on the sides of the pyramid. Rather, paranormal means are invoked, for example, levitation by means of incantations and sound waves. Not infrequently, the ancient Egyptians themselves are given a subsidiary role in the construction of the pyramids, and the main role in the effort is attributed either to extraterrestrials (an idea mentioned by Louis Pauwels and Jacques Bergier in *The Morning of the Magicians* [French original published in 1960, English translation in 1963] and popularized by Erich von Däniken in books such as *Chariots of the Gods* [1968]) or to beings from Atlantis.

A fourth class of narratives insists that the pyramids encode secret or sacred information. In the past, the measurements of the Great Pyramid at Giza have been held to unlock the key to biblical chronologies and the timing of the apocalypse. These suggestions can be traced back to 19th-century speculations by writers such as Charles Taylor (1781–1864) and Piazzi Smyth (1819–1900). Taylor's book *The Great Pyramid: Why was it Built? And Who Built it?* published in 1859 proved particularly significant. Other narratives of this type connect various measurements of the pyramids with astronomical data, for example, the exact duration of the Earth's orbit around the Sun, or the precise distance between the two bodies. The placement of the pyramids at Gizah in relation to each other has also been interpreted as encoding astronomical information. Robert Bauval (b. 1948) has launched the theory that the pyramids correspond to the positions of the stars in the constellation of Orion as they appeared from an Earth-centered perspective approximately 10,000 BCE, that is, the time when the structures were purportedly built by a civilization predating that of the Egyptians.

A fifth, more recent suggestion is that the shape of the pyramids has paranormal properties. A highly publicized book by Sheila Ostrander and Lynn Schroeder, *Discoveries behind the Iron Curtain* (1971), popularized the notion, previously suggested in the 1930s by Antoine Bovis and in the 1950s by Karel Drbal, that objects placed inside pyramids are affected by a paranormal force, pyramid power. It is thus claimed that razor blades remained sharp if placed inside pyramid structures aligned along a north-south axis.

Beside various narratives regarding the pyramids, other archaeological findings are also reinterpreted as evidence of esoteric or paranormal claims. Thus, the Great Sphinx of Giza is frequently mentioned as an object with mysterious properties and a dating that differs radically from that accepted by the vast majority of academic Egyptologists.

Olav Hammer

See also: Blavatsky, Helena P.; Meditation; New Age Movement.

References

Curl, James Stevens. *Egyptomania: The Egyptian Revival*. Manchester, UK: Manchester University Press, 1994.

Hornung, Erik. *The Secret Lore of Egypt: Its Impact on the West*. Ithaca, NY: Cornell University Press, 2001.

Iversen, Erik. *The Myth of Egypt and Its Hieroglyphs in European Tradition*. Princeton, NJ: Princeton University Press, 1993.

Eid al-Adha

Eid al-Adha, or Days of Sacrifice, is a Muslim holiday celebrated for four days during the Islamic month of Dhu al-Hijjah. It celebrates the willingness of the Prophet Abraham (called Ibrahim by Muslims) to sacrifice his son in obedience to God. Like Jews and Christians, Muslims also honor Ibrahim, though their

Muslims slaughter sheep to celebrate Eid al-Adha in Jordan. On this holiday, the meat from slaughtered animals is given to the poor. (Adeeb Atwan/Dreamstime.com)

telling of the story varies somewhat from that found in the biblical book of Genesis, where Abraham as an old man finally becomes the father to a son by his wife Sarah. When Isaac has grown to be a young boy, God orders Abraham to build an altar and kill Isaac. Abraham is about to comply when his hand is stayed and a ram is supplied in Isaac's place.

In the Koran, much more attention is paid to Ibrahim's relation to his first son by the servant Hagar, Ismail. He is believed to have accompanied Ibrahim on a visit to Mecca, where they fixed in place the Kaaba, the cubical structure inside the great mosque in Mecca toward which Muslims prayer daily (Koran 2:125). Muslims also believe that it was Ismail, not Isaac, that was the son who was almost sacrificed by Ibrahim.

Because Allah caused a ram to appear to be sacrificed in Ibrahim's son's place, when commemorating this event, Muslims sacrifice an animal to be eaten. They subsequently share a third of the meat with the poor and a third with friends and family, and keep a third for their own feast. The animals for the sacrifice are sheep, goats, cattle, or camels. The sacrifice must be made during the Days of Sacrifice, and verses in both the Koran and the Hadith indicate the obligatory natures of the sacrifice for all except the poor. The animal must be in good condition—not maimed. Also, the hide must be disposed of properly—one cannot sell it and pocket the money. In the end, the purpose of the holiday is to provide another vehicle for the wealth of the society to be shared with the less fortunate.

Ibrahim's act of obedience is also remembered during the Hajj, the pilgrimage to Mecca required of Muslims at least once in their life. During the Hajj, pilgrims pass a site where Iblis (Satan) attempted to dissuade Ibrahim from making the sacrifice at least three times. Each attempt by Satan is designated with a symbolic pillar. As they pass these pillars, they throw stones at them.

J. Gordon Melton

See also: Abraham/Abram; Islam.

Reference

Algül, Hüseyin. *The Blessed Days and Nights of the Islamic Year*. Somerset, NJ: The Light, 2005.

Eid al-Fitr

See Ramadan.

Eisai

1141–1215

Myoan Eisai, a Japanese Buddhist reformer, is credited with bringing Rinzai Zen (known in China as Linji Chan) to his homeland from China. His work would establish Zen meditation as the primary practice in its own separate community and lead to Zen's emergence as a major Japanese Buddhist tradition. Eisai is also credited with bringing green tea to Japan.

Eisai was born in 1141 into the Kaya family in Bitchu Province (modern Okayama), west of Kyoto. His well-to-do family was associated with both the local Tendai temple and Kibitsu Shinto shrine. Eisai began his appropriation of Buddhism at the Annyoji Temple, where he studied for two years with the priest and tantric practitioner Joshin. He was but 13 when he went to Mount Hiei, the headquarters of the Tendai sect, to further his studies. He was ordained as a Tendai priest in 1154, though still in his early teens. Through his teen years he would travel between his home and Mount Hiei. He would in addition study Shingon (the Japanese form of Vajrayana Buddhism) and emerged as a competent Tantric practitioner. Finally, he also mastered a form of meditation taught within the diverse Tendai tradition.

Early on Eisai had become convinced that Buddhism in Japan had degenerated and was in need of reform. He concluded that he needed to go to China to tap into older purer sources. As he made plans for his journey, he encountered Li Te-chao, a Chinese interpreter in Japan, from whom he learned of Chan centers in southern China. In 1168, he was finally able to make his way to China and while there he visited Mount T'ien-t'ai. During his six-month stay, he delved into the origins of the Tendai tradition and made his first exploration of Chan. He returned to Japan with 60 volumes of Buddhist texts. He now immersed himself in Tendai meditation practices and made plans for a longer visit to China. It would be almost 20 years before he was able to realize his desire in that regard.

Eisai's return visit was delayed by events in Japan, including a civil war, which in the late 1170s forced him to relocate to Kyushu in southwest Japan. He again visited China in 1187. During this visit he concentrated on mastering Zen and received the "seal" (*inkashomei*) of Zen transmission from his instructor, Xuan Huaichang. He also gained a respect for the *vinaya*, the traditional discipline prescribed for Buddhist monks. Upon his return to Kyushu, he established the Hoon-ji, the first Rinzai temple in Japan. At this time he introduced tea drinking to his students, an aid to the strenuous discipline he imposed. He promoted tea based on its health values and in that regard authored a book, *Kissa Yojoki* (*Drinking Tea for Health*), which emphasized tea's general restorative properties. The later popularization of the tea ceremony can be traced to Hoon-ji.

In 1195, authorities at Mount Hiei, who enjoyed official favor with the secular authorities in Kyoto, became aware of what Eisai was attempting on Kyushu and summoned him to defend his practice. This inquiry occasioned the writing of a second book, *Shukke Taiko* (*Essentials for Monks*), in which he defended the vinaya. During his visit, he was able to successfully defend himself, though winning few friends on Mount Hiei in the process. In response to the confrontation, Eisai wrote *Kozen Gokokuron* (*Propagation of Zen and Protection of the Nation*), considered his most important book. He did, however, find important support from members of the powerful Minamoto clan, who sponsored his construction of the Shofukuji Temple on Kyushu. With their help he was able to begin building support at the imperial court in Kyoto, a necessary requirement for Zen to move from its rural beginnings.

In 1204, now in his sixties, he became the abbot of the Kennin-ji Monastery in Kyoto. Among his students was Dogen, who would later in the century also travel to China and transmit Soto Zen (Chodong Chan) to Japan. In 1206 Eisai was asked to rebuild Todaiji Temple in Nara. Work on the temple, damaged in a war, took several years, but was completed in 1213, much to the delight of the emperor. After accepting the honors the emperor bestowed upon him, Eisai retired to Kennin-ji. He died there two years later.

Eisai is considered the first monk to have established Zen teachings in Japan. He not only brought Rinzai practice from China, but through his life lifted it from obscurity and planted it in seats of power in the country. Through his student the second major school of Zen would be introduced and through the 13th century Zen would enjoy a massive expansion throughout the country.

J. Gordon Melton

See also: Meditation; Tian Tai/Tendai Buddhism; Zen Buddhism.

References

Doumoulin, Heinrich. *Zen Buddhism: A History.* Vol. 2, *Japan.* New York: Macmillan Company, 1989.

"Eisai." In *Soka Gakkai Dictionary of Buddhism.* Tokyo: Soka Gakkai, 2002.

Kasahara, Kazuo, ed. *A History of Japanese Religion.* Trans. by Paul McCarthy and Gaynor Sekimori. Tokyo: Kosei Publishing, 2001.

Suzuki, Daisetz T. *Zen and Japanese Culture.* Princeton, NJ: Princeton University Press, 1959.

Ekalesia Niue

The Ekalesia (church) of the tiny island nation of Niue, also known as the Congregational Christian Church of Niue, was initiated by missionaries from Samoa sent by the London Missionary Society in the 1840s. They were joined by Europeans in the 1860s, first William George Lawes (1839–1907) in 1861 and then his successor Frank E. Lawes in 1868. The Lawes brothers organized the mission along Congregationalist lines and trained missionaries who later went to Papua and launched the church there. In successive decades the church developed a close relationship with the Congregational Union of New Zealand. At the same time, the country of Niue developed strong ties to New Zealand. Some 15,000 Niueans now reside in New Zealand, and Niueans have special citizenship rights there.

The mission in Niue became independent in 1966. It has congregations in New Zealand, and a continuing relationship to the Congregational Union of New Zealand and the Presbyterian Church of Aotearoa New Zealand, which also has congregations in Fiji with Niuean members.

The Ekalesia of Niue includes as members 1,300 of the island's 1,896 residents (2005). It is a member of the World Alliance of Reformed Churches, and in 2001 joined the World Council of Churches.

Ekalesia of Niue
PO Box 25
Alofi
Niue (via New Zealand)

J. Gordon Melton

See also: London Missionary Society; World Alliance of Reformed Churches; World Council of Churches.

References

Bauswein, Jean-Jacques, and Lukas Vischner, eds. *The Reformed Family Worldwide: A Survey of Reformed Churches, Theological Schools, and International Organizations*. Grand Rapids, MI: William B. Eerdmans Publishing Company, 1999.

Smith, S. Percy. *Niue: The Island and Its People*. Suva, Fiji: Institute of Pacific Studies, 1983.

Van Beek, Huibert. *A Handbook of the Churches and Councils: Profiles of Ecumenical Relationships*. Geneva: World Council of Churches, 2006.

■ El Salvador

El Salvador is the smallest of the Spanish-speaking countries in Central America, bordered by Guatemala, Honduras, and Nicaragua in the north, east, and south, respectively. El Salvador, known as Cuscatlán ("Land of the Jewel") by the indigenous peoples, is a spectacular land of volcanoes, rolling hills, and lakes, with a long, uninterrupted beach along the Pacific coast. The country has an area of 8,124 square miles and a population of 7.1 million (2007 census). El Salvador has the highest population density in Central America.

An estimated 90 percent of Salvadorans are *mestizo* (mixed Amerindian and Spanish origin) and culturally known as *ladino*; 9 percent are reported to be white: this population is mostly of Spanish descent but it includes others of European and North American descent (mainly French, German, Swiss, and Italian); only about 1 percent is Amerindian. Very few Native Americans have retained their ancient customs, traditions, or languages except for recent Kekchí migrants from Guatemala, an estimated 12,000. There is also a large community of Nicaraguans, 100,000 according to some estimates, many of whom are seasonal migrant workers. Spanish is the nation's official language and is spoken by virtually all inhabitants.

El Salvador has witnessed progress toward greater economic and political stability during the 1990s and into the 21st century, despite the fluctuations of the world economy that have affected traditional exports (mainly coffee and textiles), the revitalized manufacturing sector, the balance of payments (trade deficit and international loans), tourism, and other areas of the economy. One of the most important economic factors in the 1990s and early 2000s was growth in the amount of remittances from relatives living abroad, which helped Salvadoran families to survive the hardships and boosted the nation's staggering economy.

The country's religious landscape has also become divided since the early 1900s, with the arrival of scores of Protestant missionary agencies, mainly from the United States, and the emergence of a strong national evangelical movement, particularly since the 1960s, which have challenged the historically dominant position of the Roman Catholic Church in El Salvador. However, the Constitution explicitly recognizes the Roman Catholic Church and grants it special legal status.

The Constitution provides for freedom of religion, and other laws and policies contribute to the generally free practice of religion. The law at all levels protects this right in full against abuse, by either governmental or private actors. The Constitution states that all persons are equal before the law and prohibits discrimination based on nationality, race, sex, or religion.

A series of public opinion polls between 1988 and 2008 demonstrated that no significant changes had

El Salvador

Religion	Followers in 1970	Followers in 2010	% of Population	Annual % growth 2000–2010	Followers in 2025	Followers in 2050
Christians	3,579,000	6,953,000	97.4	1.46	8,238,000	9,561,000
Roman Catholics	3,313,000	5,800,000	81.2	1.48	6,600,000	7,335,000
Independents	67,900	850,000	11.9	3.74	1,100,000	1,400,000
Protestants	149,000	840,000	11.8	4.08	1,100,000	1,400,000
Agnostics	2,400	105,000	1.5	3.35	180,000	320,000
Ethnoreligionists	9,500	38,100	0.5	1.48	30,000	42,000
Baha'is	5,100	32,000	0.4	1.48	60,000	90,000
Atheists	600	7,000	0.1	3.60	8,500	15,000
New religionists	500	2,400	0.0	1.48	3,500	5,000
Muslims	0	2,000	0.0	1.48	2,500	4,000
Chinese folk	300	850	0.0	1.48	900	1,100
Buddhists	300	650	0.0	1.47	750	1,000
Jews	300	600	0.0	1.46	700	800
Total population	**3,598,000**	**7,142,000**	**100.0**	**1.48**	**8,525,000**	**10,040,000**

taken place in religious affiliation since the mid-1980s. However, between 1995 and 2004, new polls showed a marked increase in the size of the Protestant population, from 16.8 percent to 25.0 percent, with a corresponding decrease in those affiliated with the Catholic Church: from 67.9 percent in 1995 to 56.5 in 2004, a decline of 11.4 percent. All of these studies had a margin of error of plus or minus 2.5 to 3.0 percent. This trend continued between 2004 and 2008, with the Protestant population increasing to 34.4 percent while the Catholic population declined to 50.9 percent. Although an evangelical study published in 1993 claimed that the Protestant population was then more than 30 percent of the total population, in reality this did not happen until the end of 2007 (29.5 percent in November 2007, according to IUDOP-UCA).

It appears that one of the consequences of the end to the nation's civil war (1980–1992), which was followed by a period of relative peace and prosperity after decades of political violence and bloodshed, was a radical shift in religious affiliation from Catholic to Protestant (along with a slight decline in those who previously were religiously indifferent, agnostic, and/or atheist) and a trend toward greater civic and political participation by evangelicals (most were previously apolitical publicly) who have lost their fear of expressing their political views and become involved in so-cial justice and human rights issues in the national context of free and democratic elections and a decline in political violence.

History of El Salvador By 1525, Pedro de Alvarado y Contreras (1495–1541), one of the cruelest Spanish *conquistadores,* had suppressed—with extreme brutality—most of the Amerindian population of Central America. In El Salvador the Pipil, Lenca, and Chortí resisted Spanish colonization but were subdued between 1524 and 1550. The territory of El Salvador became part of the Captaincy-General of Guatemala during the Spanish colonial period, and for some time after independence was part of a federated Republic of Central America (1821–1838) until achieving its full independence in 1838.

The young nation experienced a series of political struggles, assassinations, and revolutions until 1886, when Conservative rule brought about political stability for the next 45 years. During this period communal Amerindian lands were privatized, coffee became the main crop, and the coffee oligarchy consolidated its control of the country's political, economic, and social life.

In 1881–1882, government decrees abolished Pipil communal land holdings, which opened the way for coffee producers to increase their land holdings. The

Pipil were, and still are, concentrated in the western departments of Sonsonate, La Libertad, Ahuachapán, and, to a lesser degree, Santa Ana. As coffee production expanded in the western departments, the Pipil population suffered increasing displacement, which forced them to join the growing labor pool of landless and land-poor peasants who were forced by economic necessity to work on the coffee plantations, especially during harvest season. It was in this context of social dislocation and labor unrest during the period 1900–1930 that the early Protestant churches took root and expanded in the western region.

From 1931—the year of the coup in which General Maximiliano Hernández Martínez (1882–1966) came to power until he was deposed in 1944—there was brutal suppression of any resistance to the military government. Until 1980, all but one Salvadoran temporary president was an army officer. Periodic presidential elections were seldom free or fair, which meant that a virtual military dictatorship controlled El Salvador from 1931 to the 1980s.

From the 1930s to the 1970s, authoritarian right-wing governments employed political repression and limited reform to maintain power, despite the trappings of democracy. The conservative-led National Conciliation Party was in power from the early 1960s until 1979.

During the 1970s, the political situation in El Salvador began to unravel. In the 1972 presidential election, the opponents of military rule united under José Napoleón Duarte, leader of the reformist Christian Democrat Party. Due to widespread electoral fraud, Duarte's broad-based reform movement was defeated. Subsequent protests and an attempted coup were crushed and Duarte was exiled.

These events eroded hope of reform through democratic means and persuaded those opposed to the government that armed insurrection was the only way to achieve needed change. Following decades of continuous social and political turmoil, the Salvadoran civil war generated the large-scale internal displacement (*los desplazados*) of an estimated 265,000 (registered) persons in El Salvador by October 1983, who were forced to leave their homes in embattled areas and wander the countryside in search of a secure town or settlement removed from the violence. The majority

of the internally displaced persons—women and young children and the disabled and elderly—were too poor to leave the country; most of the men had been recruited by the Salvadoran Army or by the leftist guerrilla groups, or they had "disappeared" or had been killed. In addition, another 500,000 or more Salvadorans had fled to neighboring countries or to the United States as economic or political refugees by late 1983, according to international relief and development agencies.

During this tragic period of civil war, the international press reported a series of massacres that shocked the nation and the world and that began to sway U.S. public opinion against its government's support of the repressive Salvadoran government, which needed continued U.S. government assistance to win the war against the Marxist-led revolutionary movement. More than a dozen Roman Catholic priests were killed by right-wing death squads or public security forces during the period 1977–1991, including Archbishop Oscar Arnulfo Romero of San Salvador. Also, in 1980, four U.S. Catholic nuns and lay workers were raped and killed by a military patrol near San Salvador, which led to a temporary suspension of U.S. military aid to the Salvadoran government.

In May 1980, Army Major Roberto D'Aubuisson Arrieta, after heading a failed coup against the ruling military government (1979–1982), organized the Secret Anti-Communist Army to coordinate right-wing death-squad activities. From 1978 to 1992, before and during the civil war, D'Aubuisson commanded secret military and paramilitary death squads. Among his victims was Archbishop Óscar Arnulfo Romero of San Salvador. On May 7, 1980, six weeks after Romero's assassination, D'Aubuisson and a group of civilians and soldiers were arrested on a farm, where investigators found weapons and documents identifying D'Aubuisson and the civilians as death squad organizers and financiers. However, D'Aubuisson and some of his collaborators managed to flee to exile in Guatemala.

In 1981, D'Aubuisson founded the Nationalist Republican Alliance (ARENA), which he led from 1980 to 1985, and his party campaigned in the 1982 election. In March 1982, despite alleged electoral fraud and political violence, the Salvadoran legislative election of a Constituent Assembly was a victory for

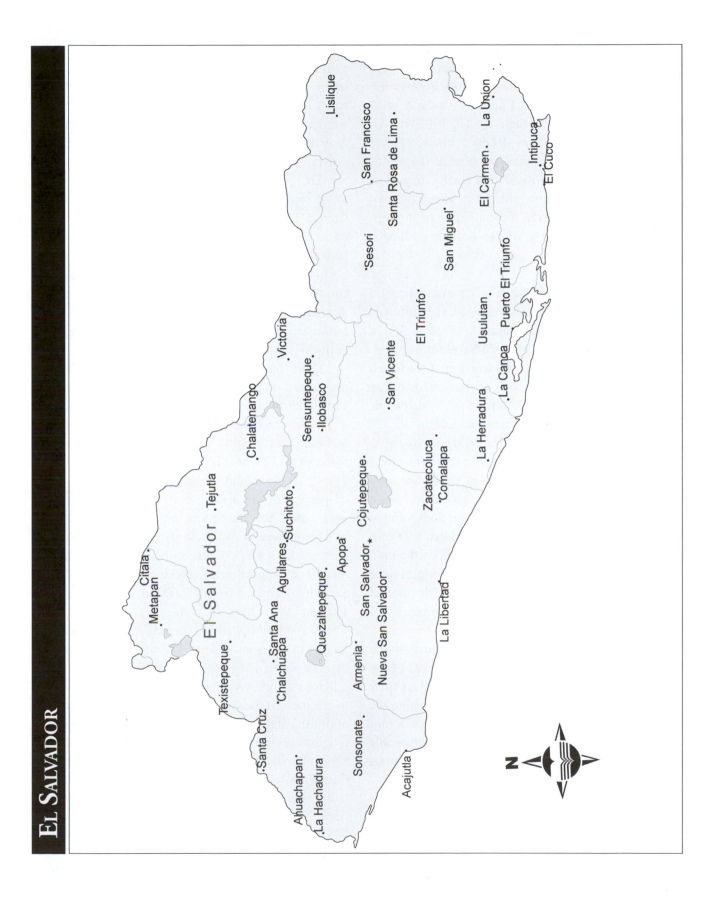

EL SALVADOR

ARENA, which gained 19 of 60 seats, and its allies gained 17 seats. Consequently, D'Aubuisson's supporters were the legislative majority. ARENA dominated Salvadoran presidential politics for the next 17 years under Alfredo Cristiani (r. 1989–1994), Armando Calderón Sol (r. 1994–1999), Francisco Flores Pérez (r. 1999–2004), and Elías Antonio Saca González (r. 2004–2009). The political tide finally turned in the 2009 national election, which was won by Carlos Mauricio Funes Cartagena, the candidate of the left-wing FMLN political party, who took office on June 1, 2009.

The Roman Catholic Church The evangelization of Central America by Catholic missionaries followed the Spanish conquest and occupation of the region in the 1520s. Although the Pipil in El Salvador had a sophisticated religion based on the worship of the forces of nature, there were a number of parallels between their religious practices and Catholicism, which made Spanish missionary efforts somewhat easier.

Following the defeat of the Indian armies by Pedro de Alvarado in 1525, the old gods seemed powerless before the Spanish conquerors and their new religion. The Franciscan friars, after driving out the Native priests and destroying the images of their gods, offered the Amerindians a new religious system that was generally accepted by them and superimposed on their old belief systems. Thousands of indigenous peoples were converted to Catholicism during the Spanish colonial period, when El Salvador was a province and parish of the Captaincy-General of Guatemala.

However, due to the chronic shortage of Catholic priests and other religious workers, the people of the smaller towns and villages learned to conduct their religious life with only occasional assistance from the Catholic clergy. To fill this need, the *cofradía*, a voluntary religious association, developed among the people for planning, organizing, and paying for local religious celebrations during the year.

The status of the Catholic Church in the postcolonial period changed depending on who was ruling the country, the Conservatives or the Liberals. The first anticlerical laws were established by a Liberal government in El Salvador in 1824. In 1871, the Liberal revolution proclaimed freedom of thought and religion, removed cemeteries from clerical control, legalized civil marriage, made education non-clerical, and abolished monastic orders. Priests were not allowed to teach in public schools, but private religious schools were permitted. These policies have remained in force until the present, except for the prohibition of religious orders.

The government does not contribute in any way to the support of religion, but since 1962 the Catholic Church has been allowed to acquire real estate for other than religious purposes. There is no Concordat between the Salvadoran government and the Vatican, but diplomatic representatives are exchanged. The Constitution of 1962 reiterated the separation of church and state and guarantees religious freedom for all faiths, but it precludes the clergy from belonging to political parties and holding public office.

There has always been a shortage of Catholic priests and other religious workers in El Salvador. In 1944, there were 106 parishes with 203 priests and 357 nuns, which increased to 175 parishes, 373 priests, and 803 nuns in 1968. In 1980, among 229 parishes, there were 373 priests (173 diocesan and 200 religious), 70 lay brothers, and 735 nuns. In 1970, about 62 percent of the priests and 19 percent of the nuns were native Salvadorans, which is a high percentage of national priests and a low proportion of native nuns compared to other countries of Latin America at that time. The proportion of priests per inhabitant in El Salvador decreased from 1:7,692 in 1970 to 1:9,090 in 1975 and to 1:12,860 in 1980.

In 1980, 200 Catholic priests in El Salvador belonged to religious orders. The most numerous were the Salesians and the Jesuits. About 50 percent of the religious clergy were dedicated to parishes, 20 percent to teaching, 10 percent to the training and preparation of priests, and the rest to work in the archdiocese. The religious priests assigned to parishes were mainly foreign missionaries, principally from Italy and Spain. The Catholic Church also sponsored 161 private schools with more than 35,000 students. Catholic personnel from the United States included 15 men (6 diocesan, 5 Franciscan, and 4 Maryknoll priests) and 13 women (11 nuns and 2 lay workers).

Since the 1920s, the Catholic Church has also been increasingly divided internally between those who have

Catholics attend a procession with an image of Jesus Christ carried on a donkey on Palm Sunday in Panchimalco, El Salvador. (AP Photo/Edgar Romero)

phasis on apostolic authority, orthodox theology, the sacraments, and personal piety. *Reformers* generally supported the church's post–Second Vatican Council stance of modernization and toleration of diversity based on its official social doctrine. *Progressives*, inspired by reforms approved at the Second Vatican and Medellín conferences, sought to implement the new vision for "a preferential option for the poor" through social and political action aimed at transforming Nicaraguan society and establishing greater social justice through peaceful democratic means. *Radicals* adopted the Marxist-inspired Liberation Theology and advocated violent revolution by the people as a means of overthrowing the Conservative dictatorship and creating a Socialist state that would serve the poor marginalized masses. *Charismatic agents* sought to transform the spiritual and communal life of Catholics by means of the power and gifts of the Holy Spirit (including the "baptism of the Holy Spirit" and "speaking in tongues"), rather than by political and social activism.

Many Catholic families were sundered apart by armed conflict and forced geographical relocation due to the civil war and by internal conflicts between Conservatives, Liberals, and Progressives, in both the political and religious arenas. Monsignor Luis Chávez y González was archbishop of San Salvador from 1939 until 1977. During his tenure, the Salvadoran Catholic Church underwent significant changes. The marginal condition of the peasantry, which had been taken for granted by the church's hierarchy, became a source of growing concern. The traditional approach of charity was seen as ineffective, and the growth of Protestantism loomed as a threat to the Catholic faith in the country. The archbishop addressed this situation by promoting the organization of cooperatives in the countryside, which were followed by the formation of Catholic base communities.

Many *campesinos* were encouraged to find new religious meaning in the message of a socially engaged Jesus and to seek liberation from economic and political oppression, which had significant repercussions. After the armed skirmishes between the army and the Marxist-inspired guerrillas turned into civil war in the 1980s, most Catholic base communities radicalized their activities and became members of peasant associations that provided support for the FMLN.

supported the status quo—the Conservative alliance of church and state—and those who have supported a Liberal and progressive agenda, based on defending the human rights of the marginalized sectors of society.

Diverse tensions arose within the Salvadoran Catholic Church during the 1960s and following years, which resulted from challenges posed by the Second Vatican Council (1962–1965), the Conference of Latin American Bishops held in Medellín (Colombia) in 1968, Latin American Liberation Theology, and the Catholic Charismatic Renewal movement. These powerful new currents polarized Catholic bishops, priests (diocesan and religious), lay brothers and sisters (members of religious orders), and the laity in general into various factions. *Traditionalists* wanted the church to remain as it was prior to the reforms approved by the Second Vatican Council (mid-1960s), with an em-

Relations between the Catholic Church and the state became strained after the rise of General Carlos Humberto Romero to power in January 1977 through a fraudulent election. At about the same time, another Romero, Oscar Arnulfo Romero, was appointed archbishop of San Salvador (1977–1980), apparently the more conservative of the two candidates for that position. However, in a country dominated by terror and injustice, Archbishop Romero soon became a voice for Christian compassion and reason, denouncing the military's systematic repression of the people and pleading for redistribution of land and unification of the country. Tragically, Archbishop Romero was shot through the heart by a sniper in 1980 while celebrating Mass two months after asking U.S. President Jimmy Carter to cease military aid to the Salvadoran government due to its dismal record on human rights.

Archbishop Romero's successor, Archbishop Arturo Rivera y Damas, S.D.B. (1983–1994), expressed his support for the ruling government junta, which he believed was holding its own ground in the political struggle between the forces of the extreme right and left. After Archbishop Rivera y Damas's death in 1994, Bishop Fernando Sáenz Lacalle was appointed as his replacement and served until his retirement in 2008. The current archbishop is Monseñor José Luis Escobar Alas.

In 2002, the Salvadoran Catholic Church reported 8 dioceses with 376 parishes that were served by 429 secular priests and 233 religious priests (a total of 662), in addition to 394 male religious workers (nonordained brothers in religious orders) and 1,542 female religious workers (nuns). The first diocese was established in San Salvador in 1842, while the dioceses of Santa Ana and San Miguel were formed in 1913. San Vicente was added in 1943, Santiago de María in 1958, and Chalatenango and Zacatecoluca in 1987. The Diocese of San Salvador became an archdiocese in 1913 under Archbishop Antonio Adolfo Pérez y Aguilar, who served until his death in 1926.

The Protestant Movement   The history of the Protestant movement in El Salvador is distinct from that of other Central American countries, in that pioneer foreign mission efforts were directed toward the Spanish-speaking population from the very beginning. In other republics, the presence of English-speaking immigrants, largely West Indians, often served as a cultural and linguistic bridge for new missionaries from the United States in their evangelistic and church planting activities prior to engaging in ministry to the Spanish-speaking ladino, or Amerindian, populations.

Since the Amerindian groups in El Salvador are predominantly Spanish-speaking, no Christian churches, either Catholic or Protestant, use an Indian dialect. Consequently, there is little obvious distinction between ladino and Amerindian ethnic groups in terms of general religious practices, and it is difficult to determine the extent of Protestant penetration among the remnants of the Pipil, Lenca, and Chortí. However, in the early 1900s, several Protestant missions began work among the Pipil in the southwestern region and the Chortí in the northwestern region of El Salvador using Spanish; and it is assumed that there are still congregations composed largely of Hispanized Amerindian believers.

The earliest Protestant groups to enter El Salvador were the newly formed Central American Mission (now known as CAM International, with headquarters in Dallas, Texas), whose first missionaries arrived in 1896; the California Friends Mission (Quakers) in 1902; an independent Canadian Pentecostal missionary, Frederick Ernest Mebius, who arrived in 1904; the American Baptists in 1911; the International Pentecostal Holiness Church (Mr. and Mrs. Amos Bradley, 1912–1918); and the Seventh-day Adventists in 1915.

By 1936, most of these Protestant church bodies were well established in El Salvador and had achieved some notable success among the general population of Spanish-speaking mestizos and the remnant of early Amerindians. The Quakers developed an extensive ministry among the Chortí (Mayan) in a region known as the Three-Nation Triangle (El Salvador, Guatemala, and Honduras), which includes northwestern El Salvador. However, the Quakers have not prospered as well as other Protestant groups in El Salvador.

Despite numerous stages of growth and decline, the CAM-supported church association has become one of the largest evangelical non-Pentecostal denominations in the country. From the establishment of its first church in 1898 in Ilapango, near San Salvador, this independent fundamentalist denomination had planted

21 churches and 83 mission stations in 8 of the country's 14 departments by 1936, largely due to the efforts of a team of U.S. missionaries and trained Salvadoran pastors. In 1935, the CAM-related churches were organized under a national council of leaders and became known as the Evangelical Church of El Salvador. In 1978, this association reported 83 churches, 32 missions, and more than 180 preaching points, with about 6,000 members. By 1992, there were about 140 churches with an estimated 13,000 members.

In 1911 the American Baptist Home Mission Society (affiliated with the Northern Baptist Convention, now the American Baptist Churches in the U.S.A.) entered El Salvador, where it soon developed strong educational and church work, especially in the departments of San Salvador and Santa Ana. By 1936, a chain of 19 churches and 50 mission stations had been established with about 1,380 members. Many of the churches were completely under national leadership, and work had begun among the Pipil in the western coastal region, near the city of Santa Ana. The Baptist Association of El Salvador was organized in 1934, but the development of trained national leaders was a slow process. In 1978, the association reported 41 churches with 3,665 members; in 1989 there were 57 churches with 5,700 members; however, by 1992 there were only 51 churches with 4,975 members.

In the 1970s, several other Baptist groups began work in El Salvador, but only two had more than 1,000 members in 1978: the Good Samaritan Baptist Churches with 15 congregations, the Miramonte Baptist Church with 16 congregations, the Baptist Bible Fellowship International, and the International Baptist Mission.

In 1915 the Seventh-day Adventist Church sent a missionary couple to El Salvador, and in 1916 their first church was established in San Salvador. However, the Adventists only reported 5 churches and 325 members in 1936, an effort that was curtailed due to competition with the growing Pentecostal movement. By 1978, there were 61 Adventist churches and 59 mission stations in the whole country, with a total membership of 12,067. Significant church growth occurred thereafter. In 2007, there were 593 congregations with 168,937 members. Three other Adventist-related bodies also exist in El Salvador: the Seventh-day Adventist Reform Movement, founded in 1956; the

Church of God-Seventh Day; and the Israelite Church of God.

In 1904, Frederick Ernest Mebius began one of the first Pentecostal movements in Latin America, known as the Free Apostolic Churches of El Salvador. This occurred about two years prior to the world-renowned Azusa Street Revival that began in Los Angeles, California, in 1906, which is considered to be the modern-day origin of the Pentecostal movement. The Pentecostal doctrine preached by Mebius and his Salvadoran assistants became a source of great upheaval within the emerging Salvadoran evangelical churches, which brought Mebius into conflict with leaders of the CAM-related churches, the American Baptists, and the Adventists. Mebius and his assistants traveled throughout the countryside in an itinerant preaching ministry that eventually produced 25 loosely organized congregations with about 750 baptized members by 1930.

The congregations founded by Mebius became known as the Free Apostolic Churches, but several splinter groups were formed among his early converts, such as the Apostolic Church of the Apostles and Prophets (1935) and the Apostolic Church of the Upper Room (1930s). Two other denominations belong to this same tradition: the Apostolic Church of God in Christ (1950) and the Apostolic Church of the New Jerusalem (1977), as well as many independent congregations. In 1978, there were at least 50 independent churches with about 3,200 members within the Free Apostolic movement, as well as 114 churches and 5,500 members among the organized Apostolic Church associations.

After the arrival of the Assemblies of God in El Salvador in 1930, efforts were made to bring some order to this assortment of independent Free Apostolic Churches, but this attempt was only partially successful. In April 1930, 12 of these churches became founding members of the Assemblies of God, whose missionaries had entered the country at the request of Francisco Ramírez Arbizu, one of the leading Free Apostolic pastors. However, most of the Free Apostolic leaders did not want to submit themselves to the authority of the Assemblies of God in the United States or to its missionaries in El Salvador; consequently, they remained independent with only fraternal ties between them. Nevertheless, under the guidance of British missionary Ralph Williams, the initial groups of Assemblies of God were strengthened, advances were made toward self-support, and new congregations and preaching points were established. By 1936, the Assemblies of God reported 21 churches and 14 mission stations, with 655 members and 965 adherents.

Based on the foundations established by early missionary and national pioneers, the Assemblies of God experienced phenomenal church growth during the next 40 years, especially between 1970 and 1990. These advances made this country a showcase for this denomination's mission work in Latin America. This solid growth is attributed to the employment of "indigenous church principles" during the administration of missionaries Ralph Williams and Melvin Hodges. There was a large spurt of growth between 1935 and 1945, when the total membership increased from 684 to 2,560, and then rapid geographical expansion and membership growth followed.

There was continued growth in the Assemblies of God to the end of the century and into the next. In 2002, 1,395 churches with an estimated 132,525 members were reported. In retrospect, the Assemblies of God have not been immune to schismatic movements, with several splits occurring during the 1960s and early 1970s. At least five church associations were formed by leaders who left the Assemblies of God and began their own organizations: the Pentecostal Evangelical Union (1954), the Evangelical Mission of the Holy Spirit (1960), the Garden of Eden Evangelical Church (1962), the Evangelical Mission of the Voice of God (1969, the largest of these groups), and the Evangelical Pentecostal Church of El Salvador (1974). These 5 associations had a total of 62 churches and 2,830 members in 1978.

The arrival of the Church of God (Cleveland, Tennessee) in El Salvador in 1940 brought the Reverend H. S. Syverson, the general overseer of the Church of God in Central America, in contact with Mebius, who agreed to work together under the auspices of the former, although there were some obvious doctrinal differences between the two church traditions. Nevertheless, Mebius worked with the Church of God for several years, until his death in 1945 at age 76.

The Church of God in the U.S.A. sent a number of short-term missionaries to assist Syverson in El Salvador during the 1940s and early 1950s, but it was not until 1953 that additional full-time missionaries were assigned to the country. Growth over the next 20 years shows a consistent pattern of expansion and development in the Church of God in El Salvador. By 1970 there were 117 churches and 78 preaching points with about 4,300 members; by 1978 the work had grown to 165 churches and 50 preaching points with 6,117 total members. In 1980, there were 191 churches and 56 preaching points with 9,557 members; by 1987 there were an estimated 300 churches and 200 preaching points with 20,122 members; and by 1992 there were 392 churches and 287 preaching points with 19,281 members. Between 1987 and 1992 there was a plateau in church membership due to unexplained causes that need to be investigated.

Additional Pentecostal denominations also began work in El Salvador in the period 1950–1980. The Latin American Council of the Pentecostal Church of God of New York (with 58 churches and 5,665 members in 1992) and the Pentecostal Church of God of Puerto Rico, both with historical ties to the Assemblies of God, arrived in 1966. The Prince of Peace Evangelical Church from Guatemala began work in the early 1960s: PROLADES in 1987 reported 171 churches with 5,050 members; and in 1992 there were 430 churches with 19,111 members. The International Church of the Foursquare Gospel sent its first missionaries to El Salvador in 1973. The Elim Christian Mission from Guatemala established its first congregation in El Salvador in 1977. The Assemblies of God of Brazil arrived in 1978.

The Church of God of Prophecy arrived in 1950, but this denomination, called the Universal Church of God of Prophecy (UCOGP) in El Salvador, has had several divisions: Church of God Holy Zion (1952), Fountain of Life Church of Prophecy (1969, with 74 churches and 6,727 members in 1992), the Fundamental Church of God of Prophecy (1972), the Holy Zion Church of God of Prophecy (1974), and the City of Zion Church of God of Prophecy (also in 1974). The total membership of these splinter groups was 9,871 in 1978 with 175 organized churches, whereas the parent body reported only 38 churches and 4 missions with 1,726 members. In 1982, the UCOGP reported 54 churches and 2,445 members; in 1992 there were 92 churches with 5,151 members.

The Oneness ("Jesus Only") Pentecostal movement is represented in El Salvador by two denominations: the Apostolic Church of Faith in Jesus Christ (1948) and the United Pentecostal Church International (1965). The former had 33 churches, 25 missions, and 600 members in 1978, while the latter had 47 churches and missions, 372 preaching points, and 2,400 members.

Other non-Pentecostal denominations in El Salvador include the Lutheran Church–Missouri Synod (1953), independent Christian Churches and Churches of Christ (1963), Church of the Nazarene (1964, with 32 churches and 2,469 members in 1992), Congregational Holiness Church (1966), Christian Brethren (1970, Cristianos congregados en el nombre del Señor, affiliated with Maurice Johnson's group in California; 45 congregations in 2007), Evangelical Mennonite Church (1968, Beachy Amish), Church of God (1970, Anderson, Indiana), Apostolic Lutheran Church of America (1974), Evangelical Lutheran Synod (1975), Christian Reformed Church (1976), and several smaller groups.

In 1978, the estimated Protestant population of El Salvador was about 295,000, or 6.5 percent of all Salvadorans. The nation's Protestant population had a large proportion of Pentecostals within the total membership (about 68 percent), compared to slightly more than 50 percent for the entire Central American region at that time. The largest Protestant denominations were the Assemblies of God (22,500 members); Seventh-day Adventists (12,000); Church of God (Cleveland, Tennessee) (9,850); the Evangelical Church of El Salvador, related to the Central American Mission (6,000); and the Prince of Peace Evangelical Church (5,000).

Several new Protestant denominations in El Salvador have experienced significant growth during the past 20 or 30 years. Elim Christian Mission of El Salvador is a Pentecostal church founded by Sergio Daniel Solorzano Aldana in 1977, which now claims to have about 115,000 members, led by Pastor General Mario Vega since 1997. "Friends of Israel" Bible Baptist Tabernacle was founded by "Hermano Toby," Edgar

Lopez Bertrand, about 1978; it now claims to have about 10,000 members and is affiliated with Baptist International Missions. "Campground of God" Christian Church–Iglesia Cristiana Campamento de Dios was founded as an independent Charismatic church by Juan Manuel Martinez in 1990; Martinez was the president of the Evangelical Alliance of El Salvador in 2006. International Revival Tabernacle was founded by Carlos H. Rivas in 2001; it now claims to have about 15,000 members.

Ecumenical relations between the various Protestant denominations in El Salvador have been extremely difficult due to strong doctrinal differences and leadership conflicts, mainly between Pentecostal and non-Pentecostal groups. However, the Salvadoran Bible Society has been the major focus of interdenominational cooperation since the 1970s because of its neutral service function of promoting the distribution and reading of the Bible among the general public. More recently, the Latin American Confraternity of Evangelicals (CONELA), affiliated with the World Evangelical Alliance (WEF), has provided a platform for cooperation among conservative evangelicals since the early 1980s. In 1987, the Salvadoran Confraternity of Evangelicals (CONESAL) held its First Interdenominational Congress of Evangelicals in San Salvador. In 2001, CONESAL reported more than 50 member organizations.

The Latin American Council of Churches (CLAI), affiliated with the World Council of Churches (WCC), has the following institutional members in El Salvador: the Baptist Association of El Salvador (affiliated with American Baptist Churches in the U.S.A.), the First Baptist Church of San Salvador, the Emmanuel Baptist Church in San Salvador, the Episcopal Church of El Salvador, the Calvinist Reformed Church of El Salvador (affiliated with the Christian Reformed Church in North America), and the Salvadoran Lutheran Synod (affiliated with the Evangelical Lutheran Church in America).

During the Salvadoran civil war, few Protestants leaders raised their voices to publicly denounce the repression by government security forces and paramilitary death squads. Among the few prophetic voices demanding social justice for the oppressed were the

Reverend Roger Velásquez, senior pastor of the First Baptist Church; the Reverend Edgar Palacios, senior pastor of Emmanuel Baptist Church; and Bishop Medardo E. Gómez of the Salvadoran Lutheran Church (Missouri Synod, established in 1954), all in San Salvador.

In 1985 the Salvadorian Lutheran Synod became an autonomous church. The relationship with the Missouri Synod was disrupted over a spectrum of issues—differing views on Liberation Theology and solidarity with the oppressed, ecumenical commitment, and ordination of women. During the civil war in El Salvador, the Salvadoran Lutheran Synod advocated for justice and assisted displaced persons and the poor. The Lutheran Church paid a high price for its social involvement: one of its pastors was murdered (David Fernández in 1984) and many church workers, including the bishop, received death threats and had to go into hiding or flee the country, as did Baptist pastors Velásquez and Palacios and their families.

Other Christian Groups In addition to the rapid growth of evangelical denominations during past decades, El Salvador has also witnessed the emergence of numerous non-Protestant marginal Christian groups, such as the Jehovah's Witnesses (531 congregations with 30,687 members in 2005), the Church of Jesus Christ of Latter-day Saints (Mormons, established in San Salvador in 1951; in 1965, there were 4,200 members in El Salvador; in 1986, membership was 15,100; in 1990, membership was 38,000; and in 2007, membership was reported to be 102,043 in 161 congregations), and the Reorganized Church of Jesus Christ of Latter-day Saints (now called "Community of Christ") from the United States; the Light of the World Church from Guadalajara, Mexico; Mita Congregation, People of Amos Church and Voice of the Cornerstone from Puerto Rico; the God is Love Church and the Universal Church of the Kingdom of God from Brazil; the Growing in Grace International Ministries (founded by Jose Luis de Jesus Miranda in Miami, Florida), the Unity School of Christianity, and the Christadelphian Bible Mission from the United States, among others.

Additional Religious Groups Also, a few non-Christian religions have appeared, adding to the his-

torical presence of the Jewish community that arrived from Spain (Sephardic) during the colonial period or from other European countries, mainly in the aftermath of World Wars I and II. The first synagogue was founded in 1950, and the first rabbi and spiritual leader of the community was Alex Freund.

Other non-Christian religions in El Salvador include the Baha'i Faith, Islam (mainly among Palestinian Arabs: Comunidad Islámica Shiíta de El Salvador, Centro Cultural Islámico Fátimah Az-Zahra), Buddhism (Buddhist Center of San Salvador [Lhundrup Changchub Ling—Jardín de la iluminación espontánea], Buddhist Group of San Salvador, Budismo Laica Reiyukai, Casa Tibet México–El Salvador, Kusum Ling Study Group, the International Meditation Association of the Supreme Master Ching Hai), and several Hindu-related groups: the Sawan Kirpal Ruhani Mission–Science of Spirituality (Sikhism/Sant Mat), Transcendental Meditation (TM, now organized as the Global Country of World Peace), and the International Society for Krishna Consciousness (ISKON, Hari Krishnas).

The Ancient Wisdom tradition is represented by: the Ancient Mystical Order Rosae Crucis (AMORC) with local chapters in San Salvador, Santa Ana, San Miguel and Sonsonate; Freemasonry (Grand Lodge Cuscatlán of the Republic of El Salvador); the Instituto de Yoga y Escuela de Astrología Gran Fraternidad Universal (GFU, founded in Venezuela by Dr. Serge Raynaud de la Ferrière), and the Salvadoran Christian Gnostic Movement (founded by Samael Aun Weor in Mexico).

The Psychic-Spiritualist-New Age movement is represented by the Theosophical Society in America (with headquarters in Wheaton, Illinois, was established in San Salvador in 1929), the Church of Scientology, and the Unification Movement (founded in Korea by the Reverend Sun Myung Moon).

Some Native American religious traditions (animist) have survived from the pre-Columbian era in some areas of El Salvador. "Popular religiosity" (syncretistic) is practiced by a majority of the Hispanic Catholic population. Among practitioners of Amerindian religions and Hispanic Popular Catholicism, there are "specialists" who practice magic, witchcraft (*brujería*), shamanism (*chamanismo*), and folk healing (*curanderismo*). In addition, there are numerous psychics, mediums, clairvoyants, and astrologers who announce their services in local newspapers.

Clifton L. Holland

See also: American Baptist Churches in the U.S.A; Ancient and Mystical Order Rosae Crucis; Assemblies of God; Baha'i Faith; Baptist Association of El Salvador; Baptist Bible Fellowship International; Christian Brethren; Christian Churches and Churches of Christ; Christian Reformed Church in North America; Church of God (Anderson, Indiana); Church of God (Cleveland, Tennessee); Church of God of Prophecy; Church of Jesus Christ of Latter-day Saints; Church of Scientology; Community of Christ; Evangelical Lutheran Church in America; Franciscans; Freemasonry; Global Country of World Peace; International Church of the Foursquare Gospel; International Pentecostal Holiness Church; International Society for Krishna Consciousness; Jehovah's Witnesses; Jesuits; Latin American Council of Churches; Light of the World Church; Lutheran Church–Missouri Synod; Master Ching Hai Meditation Association; Mita Congregation; Moon, Sun Myung; Roman Catholic Church; Salesians; Salvadoran Lutheran Synod; Seventh-day Adventist Church; Seventh-Day Adventist Reform Movement; Unification Movement; United Pentecostal Church International; Unity School of Christianity; Universal Church of the Kingdom of God; World Council of Churches; World Evangelical Alliance.

References

Barrantes, Enrique. *Cien Años de la Presencia Evangélica en El Salvador: El Movimiento Pentecostal.* http://www.prolades.com/cra/regions/cam/els/IAP_historia_els.pdf.

Barrantes, Enrique. *Así Llegó el Pentecostés: un capítulo en la historia de El Salvador.* San Salvador, El Salvador: self-published by the author, ca. 2002 (revised 2008).

Barrantes, Enrique. *Frederico Ernesto Mebius . . . Su Historia, 1869–1945.* San Salvador, El Salvador: self-published by the author, ca. 2002 (revised 2008).

Barry, Tom. *El Salvador: A Country Guide.* Albuquerque, NM: The Inter-Hemispheric Education Resource Center, 1990.

Berryman, Phillip. *The Religious Roots of Rebellion: Christians in Central American Revolutions.* Maryknoll, NY: Orbis Books, 1984.

Canizález, Carlos Napoleón. *Ensayo de la historia de la Iglesia de Dios en El Salvador, 1941–1996.* San Salvador, El Salvador: Iglesia de Dios, 1997.

Chapin, Mac. "La población indígena de El Salvador." *Mesoamérica*, Año 12, Cuaderno 21, junio de 1991.

CID-Gallup. *Encuestas de Opinión Pública.* San José, Costa Rica: CID-Gallup, May 1995, September 2000, and June 2007.

CONESAL. *Despertar '93: El Desarrollo de la Iglesia Evangélica 1982–1992 y los Desafíos para el Ano 2000.* San Salvador, El Salvador: CONESAL, 1993.

Holland, Clifton L., ed. *World Christianity: Central America and the Caribbean.* Monrovia, CA: MARC-World Vision, 1981.

IUDOP-UCA. *Encuestas de Opinión Pública.* Informes Nos. 17, 111, 112, 114, and 116. San Salvador, El Salvador: Instituto Universitario de Opinión Pública, Universidad Centroamericana (IUDOP-UCA) José Simeón Cañas, 1988–2008.

Jeter de Walker, Luisa. *Siembra y Cosecha.* Tomo 1, *Las Asambleas de Dios de México y Centroamérica.* Deerfield, FL: Editorial Vida, 1990.

Monroy, Daniel, et al. *Breve Historia de la Iglesia Bautista en El Salvador, 1909–1985.* http://www.prolades.com/cra/regions/cam/els/ABEL_historia_els.pdf.

Mullancy, John. *Aiding the Desplazados of El Salvador: The Complexity of Humanitarian Assistance.* Washington, DC: The U.S. Committee for Refugees (USCR), Fall 1984.

PROCADES-IINDEF. *Directorio de Iglesias, Organizaciones y Ministerios del Movimiento Protestante: El Salvador.* San José, Costa Rica: Proyecto Centroamericano de Estudios Sociorreligiosos (PROCADES) del Instituto Internacional de Evangelismo A Fondo (IINDEF), agosto de 1982.

PROLADES. *Public Opinion Polls on Religious Affiliation in El Salvador, 1988–2008.* http://www.prolades.com/cra/regions/cam/els/els_polls_1988-2008.pdf.

Read, William R., et al. *Latin American Church Growth.* Grand Rapids, MI: William B. Eerdmans Publishing Company, 1969.

Secretariado General de la Confederación Latinoamericana de Religiosos (CLAR). *Estudio sociográfico de los religiosos y las religiosas en América Latina.* Bogotá, Colombia: CLAR, 1971.

U.S. Department of State. *International Religious Freedom Report 2008: El Salvador.* http://www.state.gov/g/drl/rls/irf/2008/108525.htm.

Williams, Philip J. "The Sound of Tambourines: The Politics of Pentecostal Growth in El Salvador." Chapter 10 in *Power, Politics and Pentecostals in Latin America*, edited by Edward L. Cleary and Hannah W. Stewart-Gambino. Boulder, CO: Westview Press, 1997.

Wilson, Everett A. "Sanguine Saints: Pentecostalism in El Salvador." *Church History* 52 (June 1983): 186–198.

Elan Vital/Divine Light Mission

Shri Hans Maharaj Ji (1900–1966) founded the Divine Light Mission (DLM, which later became Elan Vital) in India during the 1930s. Hansji Maharaj was a disciple of Sarupanand, a guru in the lineage of Shri Paramhans Advait Mat centered in Guna, a district in the state of Madhya Pradesh. Shri Paramhans Advait Mat (which is based primarily on the teachings of the Sant tradition and *shabd* [sound current] yoga) is a guru-based organization with centers throughout India. The group's teachings are remarkably similar to those of the Radhasoami tradition, which was founded in Agra, India, around the same time period (mid- to late 19th century). Apparently Hansji split with the main center of Shri Paramhans Advait Mat in a succession dispute after his guru's death. This led him to create the Divine Light Mission. Hansji incorporated almost every tenet and practice he had learned in Shri Paramhans Advait Mat into his own teachings, including a nuanced understanding of sound and light meditation, lacto-vegetarianism, mahatmas, initiation, receiving "knowledge," and enjoying divine nectar.

When Maharaj Ji died in 1966, Prem Pal Singh Rawat, the youngest of four sons and only eight years old at the time, declared himself to be his father's spiritual successor and a *satguru,* or Perfect Master. A precocious child, he was said to have meditated from the age of two, and he spoke to crowds at age six. Although ascension to authority usually accrues to the oldest not the youngest son, neither his brothers nor his mother challenged his proclamation. He assumed his father's name Maharaj Ji, but later became known as Maharaji.

In 1971, at the age of 13, Guru Maharaj Ji traveled to England and the United States and was almost immediately a media sensation. He established headquarters in Colorado, but the largest number of devotees (called *Premies,* meaning "lovers of God") was in Britain. Barker estimates there were about 8,500 Premies in the early 1970s. But success was short-lived. In 1973 a mass gathering in Houston's Astrodome, called to proclaim a millennium of peace, drew only a fraction of the crowd anticipated and turned out to be a financial disaster. A year later, at age 16, the young guru married his secretary, who was eight years his senior. This marriage fractured family ties and resulted in a reorganization of DLM. Some of his followers began to drift away.

For the next several years Maharaj Ji struggled with reorganization—how to present the message and how to meet mounting financial obligations. In 1979 headquarters were moved from Denver, Colorado, to Miami, Florida, where the responsibility for meeting payrolls and caring for Premies became an increasing burden. Maharaj Ji came to see the Indian spiritual motif as unnecessary, perhaps even a hindrance to reaching a larger audience. In the early 1980s he began closing down ashrams. He eventually disbanded the Divine Light Mission altogether and formed a new corporate structure through which he would present his teachings: Elan Vital. He also repackaged the message, changed his name to Maharaji and then began to use his given name Prem Rawat, and redefined himself as a teacher by dropping all outward appearances as an Indian guru.

In his new role, Prem Rawat has continued the primary teaching of the Divine Light Mission built around the "receipt of Knowledge." The path to receiving Knowledge is the practice of four meditation techniques. The meditation techniques the Maharaji teaches today are the same he learned from his father, Hansji Maharaj, who, in turn, learned them from his spiritual teacher. "Knowledge," claims Maharaji, "is a way to be able to take all your senses that have been going outside all your life, turn them around and put them inside to feel and to actually experience you . . . What you are looking for is inside you" (http://www.elanvital.org/Knowledge.htm).

The young guru, who willingly accepted the spiritual titles of "Lord of the Universe" and the "Perfect Master," considered these meditation techniques to be fundamental in the quest for spiritual existence. Gradually he came to see the meditation techniques as mere technology, which can be applied to "secular enlightenment." He now claims that "'Knowledge' is not spiritual, nor is it a religion." And, of course, Elan Vital is not a religious organization.

Having set the Radhasoami perspective in a new context, as a secular personal-growth teaching, Maharaji has found a new following. He continues to travel the world lecturing and extending Knowledge to uncounted numbers, while the organization has assumed a low profile in many lands where it was formerly an object of intense controversy. In the process of change, he left behind a number of former members of the Divine Light Mission, who have formed a network to continue to communicate about their experiences. Elan Vital itself supports an Internet site, given below, where organizational contacts in countries around the world are listed.

Elan Vital
PO Box 6130
Malibu, CA 90264–6130
http://www.elanvital.org

Jeffrey K. Hadden and Eugene M. Elliott III

See also: Meditation; Radhasoami; Vegetarianism.

References

Barker, Eileen. *New Religious Movements: A Practical Introduction*. London: Her Majesty's Stationery Office, 1989.
Barrett, David V. *The New Believers*. London: Cassell, 2001.
Cagan, Andrea. *Peace Is Possible: The Life and Message of Prem Rawat*. Dresher, PA: Mighty River Press, 2007.
Downton, James V., Jr. *Sacred Journeys: The Conversion of Young Americans to Divine Light Mission*. New York: Columbia University Press, 1979.
Maharaji. *Listen to the Cry of Your Heart: Something Wonderful Is Being Said*. Malibu, CA: Visions International, 1995.
Maharaj Ji. *The Living Master*. Denver, CO: Divine Light Mission, 1978.
Messner, Jeanne. "Guru Maharaj Ji and the Divine Light Mission." In *The New Religious Consciousness,* edited by Charles Y. Glock and Robert N. Bellah. Berkeley: University of California Press. 1976.

Elim Pentecostal Church

The Elim Pentecostal Movement is the second largest Pentecostal denomination in Great Britain. A 1996 survey reported an overall average Sunday attendance of 63,500 in the 432 churches in the United Kingdom, Channel Isles, and Ireland. The largest British Elim congregation is Kensington Temple, London, operating with 120 satellite churches and more than 7,000 members.

Elim was the large oasis that the children of Israel came upon during their wanderings in the wilderness (Exodus 15:27). In 1915, George Jeffreys (1889–1962), a Welsh evangelist, launched the Elim Evangelistic Band in Monaghan, Ireland. The Band's first church was established in Belfast in 1916. Eventually a formalized constitution was agreed upon in 1922, coinciding with Jeffreys' shift of attention from Ireland to England. In 1929, the group became known as the Elim Foursquare Gospel Alliance, reflecting the group's Pentecostal emphases on Jesus as Savior, Baptizer in the Holy Spirit, Healer, and Coming King (a presentation of the Christian gospel developed by Albert Benjamin Simpson [1843–1919], founder of the Christian and Missionary Alliance). In common with other Pentecostal groups, Elim has a high regard for the Bible, together with an expectation of a personal awareness of salvation and subsequent empowerment by the Holy

Spirit. Distinctive to Elim among British Pentecostals, tongues are not insisted upon as the evidence of the baptism in the Holy Spirit.

In 1934, administrative power passed from Jeffreys to an elected Executive Council. From this time on, there was major conflict between Jeffreys and E. J. Phillips (1893–1973), Elim's chief administrator, concerning both doctrinal and ecclesiological issues. This culminated in Jeffreys' resignation in 1939 to form the Bible Pattern Church Fellowship.

After World War II, there was an emphasis upon organized evangelism, continuing Jeffreys' methodology of gathering large crowds of people and preaching a message of salvation through Christ's death and the possibility of divine healing. However, the results in the postwar period did not match the successes of Jeffreys during 1924–1934. It was the Charismatic movement in the 1960s that provided the spur for a revitalized Pentecostal spirituality and a renewed emphasis upon church growth. From the 1980s on, there has been an increased emphasis upon the social effects of the gospel, with many churches offering such programs as child care, employment schemes, and advice centers.

Elim has international links with churches and workers in 45 countries. These range from large national churches such as the Church of Pentecost, which has approximately one million adherents in Africa, to individual workers working with various local congregations.

The Elim Church is governed by the Conference, made up of ministers and laity, which meets annually. Up to 1998, membership of the Conference was only open to men. The national work is divided into regions, each having its own regional superintendent, who is elected to this position by the ministers and lay representatives from within the region. These officers form the basis of the Executive Council. Each church has a leadership session, consisting of the pastor(s), together with elders and deacons. The church session is responsible for the general oversight of the church, although the minister has the responsibility for the services. The membership of the church is open to any who are "born again."

Elim Pentecostal Church
PO Box 38

Cheltenham, Glos. GL50 3HN
UK
http://www.elim.org.uk

D. N. Hudson

See also: Charismatic Movement; Christian and Missionary Alliance; Church of Pentecost; Pentecostalism.

References

Cartwright, Desmon W. *The Great Evangelists.* Basingstoke, UK: Marshall Pickering, 1986.

Hudson, D. N. "A Schism and Its Aftermath. An Historical Analysis of Denominational Deception in the Elim Pentecostal Church, 1939–1940." Ph.D. diss., King's College, 1999.

Wilson, Brian. *Sects and Society.* London: Heinemann, 1961.

Elizabeth I

1533–1603

Elizabeth I, the daughter of King Henry VIII and Anne Boleyn, led England through a half century of political and religious turmoil. Politically, she had to stave off challenges to her rule from both claimants within her own family (most notably Mary Queen of Scots) and foreign powers (most notably Spain). Coming to the throne at a time when both Protestants and Catholics vied for control of the country, she found a way between the two options that led to the emergence of the modern Church of England, or Anglican Church.

Elizabeth was born September 7, 1533. Previously, Henry had withdrawn his allegiance to the pope and annulled his marriage to Catherine of Aragon, who had produced no male heir. He publicly married Boleyn in January 1533. She was subsequently crowned as his queen. Elizabeth was but three when her mother was beheaded (1536) for, like Catherine, not having borne a male child. Meanwhile, Parliament had passed the Act of Succession that declared Catherine's daughter Mary illegitimate and named Elizabeth the heir to the throne. Elizabeth grew up as Henry, who remained a Catholic in belief and practice, strategized with Protestant leaders in his court for the religious direction of the country.

Portrait of Elizabeth I, queen of England (r. 1558–1603). During her reign, England consolidated its position as a European power and embarked upon becoming a colonial power. (Ann Ronan Pictures/StockphotoPro)

In 1547, Elizabeth's half brother Edward VI (r. 1547–1553) came to the throne. With Edward still a child, the Protestant-controlled Council of Regency took the country in a Protestant direction. Edward's brief reign was followed by that of an angry Mary I (r. 1553–1558), who reintroduced Catholicism with a vengeance. Elizabeth finally came to the throne in 1558 to lead a country that was financially broke, religiously divided, and threatened by both France and Spain. Elizabeth moved to quiet the religious controversy by mandating a position between the two competing religions, though she tended to favor Protestantism, aware that the major political/military challenges to England and her leadership, came from Catholic countries (Spain and France) and her Catholic cousin Mary.

Elizabeth's new format for the Church of England became known as the *via media*. The church would include important elements drawn from both Catholics and Protestants. She retained the church's episco-pal leadership and left room in the liturgy so that the Eucharist could be seen as embodying the real presence of Christ. She had some of the most egregious elements of the Prayer Book introduced under Edward modified to appease the Catholics, though the Catholic bishops were still far from resigned. Aware of the Protestant majority in Parliament, she proposed a doctrinal infused with John Calvin's Reformed theology views and specifically denouncing Roman Catholic doctrine in several points. Finally, she reinstituted several of the supremacy acts by which her father had taken control of the church. Parliament named her supreme governor of the Church of England.

Elizabeth was repeatedly distracted by attempts, led by Roman Catholics, to overthrow and even kill her. Her suppression of a Catholic uprising in 1569 led to her excommunication by Pope Pius V (r. 1566–1572). Through the early 1580s, Jesuits began to call for her assassination and told their audiences that assassination in the cause of the church was not only permitted but a genuine good. Elizabeth finally expelled them from her realm in 1585. Following the clear involvement of Mary Queen of Scots in an attempt to replace her cousin, Elizabeth had her executed in 1587.

The ongoing hostilities between Elizabeth and the Catholics culminated in 1588. Pope Sixtus V (r. 1585–1590) backed Spain's designs on England by helping finance the creation of a fleet of ships. The plan called for the Spanish Armada to attack via the Thames River, while an army originating in Holland (then under Spanish rule) was to create a second front. Unable to match the Spanish fleet, ship for ship, the British built several hundred small but swifter ships. Using privateers, some of whom had gained their experience in pirating adventures, the British defeated the Spanish Armada using hit-and-run tactics assisted by some bad weather. The defeat of the armada changed the basic power balance in Europe, with a Protestantized England emerging as the world's greatest naval power and Catholic Spain beginning is long descent from its former powerful position.

Elizabeth's Catholic problems did not especially improve the status of Protestants (mostly Presbyterians). Some refused to wear the prescribed priestly vestments, and Elizabeth fired them from their jobs as parish priests. Dissatisfaction with the continued Romanish elements in the Church of England led to repeated call for its further purification. Those calling for further change became known collectively as Puritans. Puritan opposition to a church led by bishops resulted both in the emergence of Anglican defenders of episcopal authority and Elizabeth's arrest of Puritan leaders. Some left for Holland, which, having overthrown Spain rule, had become the most religiously tolerant country in Europe.

In spite of opposition from both the most doctrinaire of her Catholic and Puritan subjects, Elizabeth created broad popular support for her political acumen and enjoyed obvious overall success in establishing England as a leading world power. As she outlived many of her critics, she gained more and more support for her mediating position from the next generation.

The problems of Elizabeth's last years were very real, though they pale relative to the momentous decisions and event of the first decades. She was also able to retain her health. She had smallpox in 1562, but survived. The disease had left her face scared and caused partial baldness, but otherwise had few long-term effects. Elizabeth began to develop health problems in 1602, but could still function until March 1603. She went relatively quickly, passing away on March 24, 1603, at Richmond Palace. Plans had already been put in place to proclaim James VI of Scotland as her successor.

Elizabeth had largely created the Church of England as it is known today. Especially in the decades after the defeat of the Spanish Armada, she supported explorers of the likes of Sir Francis Drake who set the stage for the development of England's colonial empire beginning in the next century. Through the 17th century, England would challenge the privileges assigned to Spain and Portugal in 1492 for the development of the world.

J. Gordon Melton

See also: Church of England; Mary I; Roman Catholic Church.

References

Erickson, Carolly. *The First Elizabeth.* New York: St. Martin's Griffin, 1997.

Greaves, Richard L. *Society and Religion in Elizabethan England.* Minneapolis: University of Minnesota Press, 1981.

Marcus, Leah S., Janet Mueller, and Mary Beth Rose, eds. *Elizabeth I: Collected Works.* Chicago: University of Chicago Press, 2000.

Ronald, Susan. *The Pirate Queen: Queen Elizabeth I, Her Pirate Adventurers, and the Dawn of Empire.* New York: HarperCollins, 2006.

Somerset, Anne. *Elizabeth I.* New York: Anchor, 2003.

Watkins, Susan. *In Public and Private: Elizabeth I and Her World.* London: Thames and Hudson, 1998.

Emei Shan

Emei Shan (Mount Emei) is one of the four sacred Buddhist mountains in China. It is located in Sichuan Province south of Chung Du, and is the designated mountain of the west. When visiting Emei, one observes four peaks. The sacred aspect of the mountain is primarily attached to one of the four peaks known as Da'e Mountain. The main peak at Mount Emei rises more than 10,100 feet above sea level, making it higher than any of the five Daoist Holy Mountains.

Buddhism appears to have arrived and the first temple built at Mount Emei during the reign of Emperor Wudi (236–290 CE) of the western Jin dynasty. Additional temples were built during the Sui (581–618) and Tang (618–907) dynasties. Over the centuries the mountain was also identified with the bodhisattva Samantabhadra, the Universal Worthy Great Conduct Bodhisattva, one of the more important bodhisattvas in Pure Land Buddhism, often pictured atop a white elephant. He is a featured character in the Flower Garland Sutra, which happened to spread through China during the western Jin dynasty. Nichiren Buddhists see him as the protector of the Lotus Sutra.

As the association between the bodhisattva and the mountain developed, the understanding grew that Samantabhadra had transformed the mountain into his territory from which he worked to spread Buddhism. Symbolic of the bodhisattva's hegemony, during the Song dynasty (960–1279) a bronze statue of Samantabhadra was installed in Wannian Temple. The emphasis on Samantabhadra peaked at Mount Emei during the Ming and Qing dynasties, when several thousand monks resided at more than 70 temples (of which some 20 have survived).

Of the extant temples, the most notable are the Baoguo Temple, a wood structure with the immense Hall of Seven Buddhas and its many wood and stone carvings; the Wannian Temple, built in the Ming dynasty, known for its architecture and the 20-foot statue of Samantabhadra riding his white elephant; the Fuhu Temple with its Huayan Pagoda inscribed with the text of the Flower Garland Sutra; and Yogming Huazang Temple, atop one peak, whose exterior of copper mixed with gold has given its location the name Jinding (Golden Top) Mountain.

In 1996, Mount Emei was named a United Nations Educational, Scientific and Cultural Organization (UNESCO) World Heritage Site for both its natural beauty and historical sacred significance. Included in its designation as a site was the Giant Buddha of Leshan, a 234-foot-high statue of Maitreya Buddha, until quite recently the largest Buddha statue in the world. The Leshan statue is about 25 miles from Mount Emei.

J. Gordon Melton

See also: Emei Shan; Jiu Hua Shan; Putuo Shan; Samantabhadra's Birthday; Statues—Buddhist; Wu Tai Shan.

References

Hargett, James M. *Stairway to Heaven: A Journey to the Summit of Mount Emei.* Albany: State University of New York Press, 2006.

Nanquin, Susan, and Chün-Fang Yü, eds. *Pilgrims and Sacred Sites in China.* Berkeley: University of California Press, 1992.

Shunxun, Nan, and Beverly Foit-Albert. *China's Sacred Sites.* Honesdale, PA: Himalayan Institute Press, 2007.

The Emissaries

The Emissaries, a new religious group in the Western Esoteric tradition, was founded in Tennessee in 1932 by Lloyd Arthur Meeker (1907–1954), who had come to the realization that "he was completely responsible for the state of his world and the quality of his experience in it"; he published his ideas under the name of Uranda. In 1940 he met Martin Cecil (1909–1988), later the seventh marquess of Exeter, who took Meeker's teachings and developed them into a more systematic and comprehensive system. Their writings and talks are collected in a series of volumes entitled *The Third Sacred School.* Meeker died in a plane crash in 1954, and Cecil took over the leadership.

Most Emissaries live in 8 main communities of from 20 to 150 people, the largest being in the United States, at Sunrise Ranch in Colorado, established in 1945. In 2003 the British community sold the headquarters it had used since 1980 at Mickleton House in Gloucestershire, England, to focus on more localized work.

Until Cecil's death in 1988, leadership was centralized; for example, each community would read a transcript of a talk by Cecil at their Sunday services. After Martin Cecil's death his son Michael Cecil (b. 1935) decentralized the leadership, putting it into the hands of a governing board of trustees and locally selected representatives. After an awkward transition, eventually each community became used to being self-governing. Without the strong charismatic centralized leadership of Martin Cecil, however, membership fell by over two-thirds.

The primary purpose of the Emissaries is "to encourage the experience and expression of divine identity." Individuals working together can "become the critical mass which empowers creative change on a wider scale." They see themselves as part of the wider New Age movement of people "whose passion is to express the spirit of God on Earth." Their main spiritual practice is attunement, "a form of vibrational alignment and healing . . . a process of clarifying and deepening our connection with Being and Source . . . a vital component of the spiritual renaissance emerging in the world today." During attunement, one member will hold his or her hands over areas of another member's body, usually without touching, in order to activate "a free flow of life energy between physical and spiritual dimensions" and to "bring health and well-being on very deep and fundamental levels."

Members, typically ages 40 to 60, tend to come from the professions, the arts, and the media. Emissary communities frequently host conferences, courses, and seminars by a wide range of other New Age groups and teachers. They also practice sustainable organic farming.

The Emissaries are also known as the Emissaries of Divine Light. Earlier names for the movement include the Foundation for Universal Unity, the Ontological Society, and the Integrity Society. The organization is led internationally by eight trustees and spiritual director David Karchere. There is an estimated world membership of 600.

Michael Cecil left the Emissaries in 1996, saying in an interview that he believed they had become too introverted. "I didn't want to be part of an enclave separate from the world," he said. "I felt I needed to move out into the larger sphere myself." In 2000 he co-founded a new group, the Ashland Institute, in Ashland, Oregon; it runs a variety of personal development courses with a focus on spiritual-based transformation. It practices attunement, which it describes as "an approach to healing based on the premise that the body is a dynamic, self-healing expression of a deeper spiritual self."

Emissaries
Sunrise Ranch
5569 North County Road 29
Loveland, CO 80538
http://www.emissaries.org

The Ashland Institute
PO Box 366
Ashland, OR 97520
www.ashlandinstitute.org

David V. Barrett

See also: New Age Movement; Western Esoteric Tradition.

References
Barrett, David V. *The New Believers*. London: Cassell, 2001.
Cecil, Martin. *Being Where You Are*. New Canaan, CT: Keats Publishing, 1974.
Exeter, Martin. *Beyond Belief: Insights to the Way It Is*. Loveland, CO: Foundation House Publications, 1986.
Todd, Douglas. "Leader left Divine Light behind him." *Vancouver Sun*, September 29 2003.

Energy

Concepts of vital or cosmic energy can be found in many cultures and religious traditions, including *pneuma* or spirit in the Greco-Roman world, *prana* in India, and *qi* in China. These concepts are all etymologically derived from native terms for "breath," and imply a connection between the rhythms of breathing and the mystery of life. In the book of Genesis, God breathes the breath of life into clay to make Adam as a living soul; the Hebrew Bible also describes death as the breath's return to God. In the Stoic philosophy of ancient Greece, pneuma is the soul of God (Zeus) and the vehicle through which the divine *logos* organizes inert matter. Pneuma is thus the structuring force of the universe, which, in differentiated expressions, accounts for the variation among beings: the pneuma of state or tension, which gives cohesion to inanimate objects; the vegetative pneuma, which gives growth and life; the animal pneuma, which endows animals with powers of perception and reproduction; and the rational pneuma, which gives humans the power of judgment. In Vedantic philosophy, prana is the life-force and creative power of the universe. It exists primordially as an unmanifest, transcendental energy of pure consciousness, from which emanates a manifest force of creation through which the entire universe comes into being. In Chinese philosophy, qi is typically described as the pervasive life-force that circulates throughout the universe and all beings. Daoist and neo-Confucian thought postulate the emanation of formless qi from the Dao, which then differentiates between pure, ethereal yang qi, which rises to form heaven, and heavy, turbid yin qi, which descends to form the Earth. Qi continues to circulate between yin and yang, heaven and Earth, generating the five phases or elements (wood, fire, earth, metal, and water), and the myriad beings.

While beliefs about energy have become incorporated into a variety of religious and spiritual movements, the world religions typically have focused little attention on the subject. For example, although the

Christian practice of laying on of hands may appear similar to energetic healing techniques, the fundamental belief is that prayer has the power to call God's miracles; positive effects are not based on the concept of energy itself. Likewise, Islam has no teachings specifically dealing with energy although some Muslims believe that by submitting completely to the will of Allah, blocked energetic resources can be released.

Prior to the global dominance of the biomedical model of human anatomy and physiology, many cultures' theoretical models of the human body emphasized a system based on energy. In contemporary society, energy theory is particularly evident within the milieu of complementary and alternative medicine. Many therapies purport to work directly on an energetic level, claiming to cure energetic imbalances that are believed to contribute to pain and illness.

Although therapies with a focus on health and well-being are perhaps not strictly speaking religious, many practitioners do incorporate these beliefs into a worldview that they rely upon to make major life choices. Such a worldview resonates with the beliefs and practices of the New Age movement and would include beliefs in the importance of thinking holistically (for both the individual and the plant), a mind-body connection, and the influence of energy. By learning to work energetically, many in this field describe an increased sense of empowerment and feeling of control over their health and lives. In the contemporary New Age milieu, this kind of energy or life-force is often explored simultaneously from many perspectives; it is often believed that the conceptual systems that developed in distinct historical and cultural contexts are simply different descriptions of what is essentially the same phenomenon.

Indian Concepts of Energy   The Indian traditions have ancient and complex beliefs about what might be translated as "energy." *Shakti* relates to the concept of energy involved with the force and power of creation. Shakti is often personified in the form of the goddess, or Devi, a dynamic feminine manifestation of the divine. Another Indian word for energy, with cognates in most Indo-European languages is *ojas*. In Ayurvedic (traditional Indian) medicine, ojas could be translated as "vital energy" and is conceived as the most essential

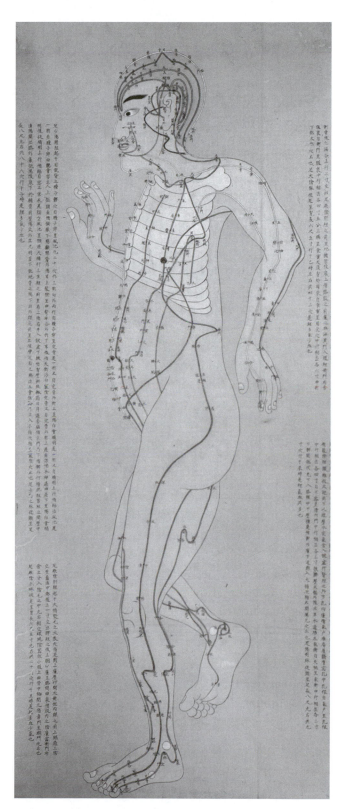

Chinese depiction of energy flow, or *qi*, in the human body. (Bildarchiv Preussischer Kulturbesitz/Art Resource)

element of a body. The strength of an individual's ojas is believed to impact on his or her "potency" or power and influence in the world (Gonda 1952). A related concept is prana, the Sanskrit word for "breath," which is defined as one of the five organs of perception in the *Chandogya Upanishad*, probably composed before 1000 BCE. From at least the time of the *Chandogya Upanishad,* it has been believed that prana is a form of energy that travels in the human body within channels called *nadi*. While the number of nadi vary within different descriptions, there are generally believed to be three main channels: the *Pingala* (associated with the right side of the body, maleness, and the Sun), *Ida* (associated with the left side of the body, femaleness, and the Moon), and the *Sushumna*, a central channel. According to some traditions, energy can be directed into the Sushumna, passing through a series of nodal points (*chakras*) to the crown of the head. When the prana in the central channel (now called *kundalini*) is unblocked, it is believed that an individual can experience the true nature of reality. In the Advaita Vedanta tradition this might be described as *moksha*, or liberation, an experience of the non-dual nature of reality; for a follower of Samkhya it would be described as *kavailya*, the experience of pure consciousness (*purusa*) unfettered by matter (*prakriti*). Esoteric practices aiming to achieve this energetic liberation, known as Tantra, became popular in the Indian subcontinent from around 500 to 700 CE and were incorporated into some Jain, Buddhist, Hindu, as well as later Sufi and Sikh traditions (see White 1996). In the early 20th century, a few Shakti Tantric texts were translated into English by Sir John Woodruff and Bengali collaborators (first published under the pseudonym Arthur Avalon) and these works were incorporated into Karl Jung's theories as well as Western esoteric and ritual magic (Shamdasani 1996; Urban 2006). During the 20th century there have been several published accounts of spiritual awakenings via the raising of kundalini energy and contemporary accounts continue to be published on the Internet.

Energy in China   The concept of qi likewise has ancient origins in Chinese culture. It could be argued that ideas of qi permeate all aspects of Chinese culture, but again, it is not specifically a religious con-

cept. Conceptions of qi have changed over time and practitioners of traditional Chinese medicine, of both Western and Eastern origin, continue to refine the concept in the light of modern understandings (Zhang and Rose 2001). Like prana, qi is believed to be circulated through channels located within the human body. In traditional Chinese medicine these channels are believed to have a role in connecting the surface of the body with the internal organs. Regulating qi is believed to have an important role in maintaining health and increasing an individual's physical and psychological power. The strengthening and manipulation of qi is a key concept in acupuncture, many forms of martial arts, and in the practice of qigong. Consideration of qi in the arrangement of the physical world is known as Feng Shui. Tibetan culture has the concept of rLung, which can be defined as a subtle flow of energy in the body that is intimately related to the healthy functioning of not only the body, but also powers of speech and mind.

Energy in Japan   In Japan, *ki* is often translated as "energy" and has historical and cultural overlaps with the Chinese concept of qi. However, in the Japanese language ki is a common word that has a variety of meanings usually relating to a person's mental state, feelings, or intentions. This link between the mind and body is often emphasized in contemporary presentations of ki as a concept. The Japanese also have a conception of energy traveling in meridians within the body. It is believed that skillful manipulation of this energy can contribute toward improving health, well-being, mental concentration, and spiritual development. Examples include traditional forms of Japanese massage, which form the basis of Shiatsu massage as well as the practice of Reiki, which claims to allow a healer to channel energy from the universe for the healing of a specific human body.

Energy in African Traditions   Many African traditions have a belief in a concept related to energy. For example, the Yorùbá peoples have a belief in *ashé*. Ashé can be understood as mystical, generative force and life-giving energy present in all creation through divine grace. The various *orishas*, or divine beings, are understood as the first anthropomorphic manifestations of this energy. Ashé is considered an ever-present link between creation and the divine; a harmonious interaction with ashé leads to a fulfilling and successful human life. Concepts of ashé are important in Santeria (also known as La Regla Lucumi or Regla de Ocha).

Energy is also an important part of the theology of Haitian Vodou practitioners where the human is seen as a non-discrete being in dialogue with numerous forces external to the human, including spirits and ancestors. The treatments prescribed by Vodou priests could be understood as a kind of healing system that aims to restore an individual's balance with all these energies (Bellegarde-Smith 2005).

Energy in Western Culture In the West, concepts of energy are associated with the vitalistic healing systems of Galenic, Ayurvedic, and Chinese medicine, in which therapies attempt to modify the circulation of vital energies in order to restore the body's energetic harmony. In the Chinese and Indian case, they are also associated with meditation systems (pranayoga and qigong) which aim, through the disciplining of the breath, to control the circulation of qi or prana with one's own consciousness, and to nurture its development and transformations.

Energy-based cosmologies and healing systems have played an important role in the development of alternative spiritualities in late modernity. Although, from the 19th century on, established scientific disciplines such as medicine and chemistry have purged all traces of "vitalism" from their theories and descriptions, energy-based therapies and spiritual techniques have become increasingly widespread in the popular realm. In an increasingly secularized culture in which many people reject the authoritarian monotheism of the established churches, energy therapies and cosmologies can easily be formulated using scientific terminologies such as "rays," "fields," "vibrations," or "biomagnetism," which can be manipulated by anyone through technical operations of the body. This opens a space for spiritualities that can be practiced outside the realm of "religion." The language of energies is shared by a broad array of contemporary therapies and spiritual practices, ranging from kundalini yoga and Anthroposophy to Feng Shui, Chinese martial arts, Reiki, rebirthing-bodywork, Integrative Body Psychotherapy, dowsing, shiatsu, homeopathy, Ayurveda, therapeutic touch, and the like.

Franz Mesmer (1734–1815) believed that health was dependent on the free flow of a kind of energy through channels in the body. He believed he could influence the flow of this energy with "passes" of his hands on and across the body. Although met with a mixed reception during his lifetime, Mesmer's ideas influenced the founding of hypnosis and enjoyed popular interest in Victorian Britain and America (Winter 2000).

In the late 19th and early 20th century, the Theosophical Society was responsible for promoting ideas to do with energy. In particular, the Society popularized the idea of auras or energetic fields visible as colors around individuals and the concept of "astral travel" or moving through space and time in a nonphysical body (Campbell 1980).

In the 20th century, the psychiatrist Wilhelm Reich (1897–1957) generated new ideas about energy. He believed that he discovered ways to access the original primal energy which he termed "orgone." This energy was related to Sigmund Freud's concept of libido and also to sexual orgasm, but Reich emphasized that orgone energy permeated all of the Earth. He built "orgone accumulators," boxes in which healing orgone energy was maximized. He also posited a negative energy, termed "Deadly Orgone," or DOR, which he believed could be harnessed to control the weather. Although his concepts about orgone were not generally accepted, his ideas encouraged the development of somatic psychotherapy (Mann and Hoffmann 1980).

Some Contemporary Religious Views of Energy
There are many ways the various beliefs about energy found throughout the globe have become incorporated in more contemporary religious or spiritual movements. Some New Age worldviews describe the soul as a kind of energy, which actress Shirley MacLaine has described as allowing us to co-create our reality with God (Hanegraaff 1996, 175). This kind of assumption is implicit in many contemporary forms of New Thought, for example, the "power of positive thinking" and more recently "The Secret."

The practice of Esoteric or ritual magick is often associated with the manipulation of energy. The practice of magick could be described as ritual activities that have the aim of changing reality to conform to the practitioner's will. Sometimes the sexual act is used by magicians in an attempt to focus sexual energy into assisting with the magical goals. This practice is associated with Aleister Crowley and some contemporary Gnostic groups.

Contemporary Druids have an interest in energy as evidenced by the concept of "Awen." Awen is a Welsh word usually translated as "lowing spirit" and primarily associated with creative inspiration and intuitive understanding, but which has also been defined by Druids as "the energy of divine inspiration" and "divine energy exchanged." Understandings of Awen tend to be very personal, but accessing and respecting Awen is an important focus for contemporary Druidry.

An interesting approach to prayer energy is taken by the Aetherius Society, a religious movement founded by George King (1917–1997), who believed the "Cosmic Masters" of the Solar System had chosen him as "Primary Terrestrial Mental Channel" for their messages to Earth. King was given instructions by the Cosmic Masters about how to store the energy of prayer in a battery. By storing prayer energy, current members of the Aetherius Society believe they have a uniquely effective way of directing healing prayer energy throughout the world.

The term "energy vampire" or "psychic vampire" has become popular slang for someone who is experienced as a "drain" on energy levels by others. This has also become a self-description for some who consider themselves Human Living Vampires (HLVs). Although not considered a religion by those who self-identify as vampires, beliefs about vampires can become a working worldview with important metaphysical elements. While blood is considered a direct source of energy, most HLV claim to feed on the energy or prana of others, whether emotional, sexual, or ethereal.

Many contemporary practitioners of yoga, tai chi, and martial arts are concerned with energy levels. Most often the concern is not so much with esoteric anatomy, but with regulating levels of physical fitness, tiredness, and an ability to respond to the demands of work, home, and leisure without mental or physical fatigue. Those who practice such techniques often describe their practice as giving them more energy. Additionally, the 1998 Religious and Moral Pluralism Survey indicated that about 15 percent of Europeans understand God as an impersonal spirit or life force.

Suzanne Newcombe and David A. Palmer

See also: Anthroposophical Society; Crowley, Aleister; Daoism; Druidism; New Age Movement; Qigong; Santeria; Tantrism; Vodou; Western Esoteric Tradition; Yoga; Yoruba Religion/Spirituality.

References

Avalon, Arthur (pseud. Sir John George Woodroffe), trans. *The Serpent Power: being the Shat-chakra-nirupana and Paduka-panchaka, two works on Laya yoga / translated from the Sanskrit, with introduction and commentary, by Arthur Avalon.* Madras: Ganesh & Co., 1924.

Bellegarde-Smith, Patrick, ed. *Fragments of Bone: Neo-African Religions in a New World.* Champaign: University of Illinois Press, 2005.

Campbell, Bruce. *Ancient Wisdom Revived—A History of the Theosophical Movement.* Berkeley: University of California Press, 1980.

Gonda, Jan. *Ancient-Indian* Ojas, *Latin* Augos *and the Indo-European nouns in -es/-os.* Utrecht: NVA Oosthoek's Uitgevers Mij, 1952.

Hanegraaff, Wouter. *New Age Religion and Western Culture: Esotericism in the Mirror of Secular Thought.* Leiden: Brill, 1996.

Mann, W. Edward, and Edward Hoffman. *The Man Who Dreamed of Tomorrow: A Conceptual Biography of Wilhelm Reich.* Los Angeles: J. P. Tarcher, 1980.

Shamdasani, Sonu, ed. *The Psychology of Kundalini Yoga.* London: Routledge, 1996.

Urban, Hugh. *Magia Sexualis: Sex, Magic, and Liberation in Modern Western Esotericism.* Berkeley: University of California Press, 2006.

White, David Gordon. *The Alchemical Body: Siddha Traditions in Medieval India.* Chicago: University of Chicago Press, 1996.

Winter, Alison. *Mesmerized: Powers of Mind in Victorian Britain.* Chicago: University of Chicago Press, 2000.

Zhang, Huan Yu, and Ken Rose. *A Brief History of Qi.* Brookline, MA: Paradigm, 2001.

Enlightenment

Enlightenment as a religious goal is mainly associated with Asian traditions, especially Buddhism, Hinduism, and Jainism, though its meaning differs between and within faiths just as the terms "Buddhism" and "Hinduism" are used to categorize a complex and diverse range of religious and philosophical practices. Enlightenment is a pan-Indian concept arising in the sixth century BCE in the early *Upanisads*, in the teachings of Buddha and Mahavira, the founder of Jainism. The enlightenment experiences of seekers are found in their biographies as well as in the religious and philosophical texts they composed. In brief, enlightenment is a profound existential experience that transforms an individual's comprehension of reality. It is said that without the enlightenment experience we are locked into a compelling sense of the reality of the world, while the enlightened being sees the illusion of reality, sees through appearances to the ultimate truth.

Buddhism The biographies of the historical Buddha (ca. 566–486 BCE) reveal the process of achieving enlightenment and his later experience of that achievement. As a 30-year-old prince called Siddartha, he abandoned royal status, family life, and all the comforts of civilization. For six years he wandered through the forests of what is today northern India, living as a celibate ascetic and seeking a solution to the problem of human suffering, which he framed within the endless round of being born, growing old, and dying, only to be reborn once again due to the force of karma, or our own deeds. This cycle is known as *samsara* (transmigration). Prince Siddartha wanted to know if there was a way out (*nirvana*, meaning "extinction" but often glossed as enlightenment or liberation) of samsara. He

Siddhartha Gautama leaves his sleeping wife and baby son, from a Burmese manuscript, 19th century. (The British Library/StockphotoPro)

sought a solution by studying with various ascetic teachers, none of whom could fully satisfy his questions, and by meditating and practicing severe asceticism, such as eating only one sesame seed, one grain of rice, and one juniper berry a day. His determination attracted five male disciples who looked after him.

The world of the forest recluse was predominantly male. A significant part of what Prince Siddartha had rejected in leaving city life was contact with women. The meaning and role of gender are contested issues from the earliest days of Buddhism to the present, with many denying that women can achieve enlightenment, saying they must first reincarnate as men, despite the early record of nuns who achieved enlightenment. Padmanabh Jaini (1991) has a particularly brilliant exposition of the arguments in Jain history and Serinity Young (2004) discusses the Buddhist arguments, all of which raises the troubling question of why enlightenment was believed to be an experience limited to men. Returning to Prince Siddartha, as he sat meditating and wasting away, his dead mother appeared and reminded him of the prediction at the time of his birth that he would achieve enlightenment, which was in jeopardy because of his continued austerities. He reassured her that he would attain his goal and she returned to heaven.

Realizing his body was too weak to achieve enlightenment, he decided to eat solid food. His five male disciples, believing he had abandoned asceticism, deserted him. But several women, human and divine, helped to restore his strength so that he could take his seat under the Bodhi Tree, where he proceeded through a series of ever deepening states of meditation throughout the course of one night. It has long been debated exactly what he experienced on that night, but its outcome, his achievement of enlightenment, is a defining principle of Buddhism that changed the religious face of much of Asia and more recently some of the West. After this experience he was given the title of Buddha, the awakened or enlightened one, from the Sanskrit root *budh* (to wake up) and from which is also derived the term *bodhi*, meaning "awakened or enlightened consciousness." So, from the Buddhist tradition two separate terms, nirvana and bodhi, are translated as enlightenment.

With regard to this experience two points need to be made: first, when the Buddha achieved nirvana he became an enlightened being, and second, when he died he achieved *parinirvana*, meaning he would never be reborn. This understanding postulates that samsara/nirvana are two different kinds of existence, one ruled by desire and the other a realm where desire is extinguished through the enlightenment experience. This is the general view of Theravada Buddhism. A later tradition, Mahayana Buddhism, postulates instead that these are radically different states of mind, consequently putting the emphasis on achieving enlightened consciousness (bodhi).

Both traditions believe that the achievement of enlightenment is accompanied by omniscience and magical powers, and based on the Buddha's experience, that it can be achieved through asceticism, generally understood to mean celibacy, moderation in all things, morality, meditation, and the cultivation of compassion for all living beings. These practices signal a withdrawal from the world, particularly from the entanglements of family life, having few possessions and devoting significant amounts of time to meditation. The idea is to downplay the world of the senses, which are connected to desire. Thus, for much of the Buddhist world, the social reality of seeking enlightenment was and remains structured by a celibate male hierarchy that seeks nirvana or bodhi while being supported by a lay community for whom they perform various religious and educational tasks. Exceptions to this are the later Tantric practices of Buddhists and Hindus that incorporate ritual sexuality into the search for enlightenment and the introduction of married Buddhist clergy in certain sects of Tibetan and East Asian Buddhism.

Hinduism   Although nirvana has meaning in Hinduism as the final emancipation from matter and reunion with the Supreme Spirit (in the *Upanisads* this would be Brahman), the meaning of enlightenment is more often carried by the words *moksa* and *mukti* (both from the Sanskrit root *muc*, meaning "liberation, release"), which are used to contrast with samsara as well as to represent union with Brahman. In other words, the experience of moksa signals release from the endless round of transmigration generated by karma, which may culminate in union with the divine or with a particular deity perceived as the originator of the universe.

Moksa is listed as the highest of the four goals of human life, after duty, enjoyment, and wealth (*Book of Manu*, ca. the beginning of the Common Era), which suggests a different social model than Buddhism in that the Hindu ideal is for a man to wait until he has a grandson, at which time he should abandon his home and family to become a wandering ascetic dependent on the communities he passes through for his food. Of course, throughout history Hindus, like Buddhists, were moved to seek enlightenment at an earlier period in their life. Also like Buddhists, Hindus debated whether or not women were capable of achieving enlightenment or if they had first to reincarnate as men. The issue of gender seems to be tied to the belief that celibacy is a requisite to achieving enlightenment, which problematizes women, often casting them as sexual temptresses. These religions were formulated and developed within patriarchal cultures that put constraints on women that are reflected in their religious beliefs.

The *Bhagavad Gita* (ca. first century CE) introduced three paths to enlightenment: action (good deeds), knowledge (insight into reality), and devotion, in the specific case of the *Gita* devotion to Krishna, but the path of devotion spread to other Hindu traditions, such as those worshipping the god Shiva or the goddess in her many forms. All three paths involve spiritual discipline, such as self-control and meditation. The path of devotion is said to have many forms, such as chanting or singing the praises of god, making offerings as simple as a flower, and performing all acts with one's mind focused on god. Devotion is available to everyone, thus it became and remains very popular with ascetics and non-ascetics alike.

Tantra   Tantra refers to a variety of religious paths that developed mainly in northern India perhaps as early as the third century CE among Buddhists, Hindus, and Jains, although it took several centuries to achieve widespread influence. Its practitioners seek enlightenment through ritual practices that are also believed to give them divine or magical powers; one of its essential features is an abundance of female symbolism. Tantra is considered to be a fast path to enlightenment, claiming that enlightenment can be achieved in one lifetime.

The Tantric ideal type is the *siddha* (from the word *siddhi*, "supernatural power") or *sadhu* (holy man), a wandering yogi who is also a wonder worker, also referred to as a *tantrika*. The behavior of the tantrika is often designed to shock people, to break social taboos that keep people from seeing the enlightened state in which there is no right or wrong.

Tantric rituals often involve the "five m's" (*pañcamakara*): wine, meat, fish, parched grain, and sexual union (respectively, in Sanskrit, *madya, mamsa, matsya, mudra,* and *maithuna*). The first four are described as aphrodisiacs and lead up to the fifth, actual or symbolic sexual union. Theoretically, there are two forms of practice: the right-handed path (*daksinamarga*), which uses substitutes for the first four and visualizes the fifth, sexual union, and the left-handed path (*vamamarga*), which imbibes these substances and involves ritual sexual intercourse. In point of fact though, left-handed practice also frequently uses substitutes and visualization. Generally, Indian left-handed practitioners were wandering yogis while right-handed practitioners were traditional Hindu priests (brahmans). A similar situation arose in Tibet, where free-wheeling Tantric practices were fairly widespread among non-monastics, both householders and wandering yogis, while a more rationalized Tantra flourished in the monasteries. There were, however, exchanges between the two groups.

The five m's are forbidden to orthodox Hindus because they are polluting, but the Tantric practitioner, Buddhist or Hindu, ritually uses these forbidden substances to get beyond the concepts of good and evil, forbidden and allowed, and to achieve an experience of the ultimate union of all opposites, even of female and male. These practices are believed to lead tantrikas to moments of enlightenment that may become a permanent state of awareness. Through visualization practices during rituals or meditation, the adept seeks to merge with the deities, or the buddhas, in union with their consorts, thus sharing in their enlightened consciousness.

Sexual union, whether enacted or visualized involves the belief that women inherently possess something men do not, something that men need to achieve enlightement. In the Buddhist tradition it is *prajña* (wisdom or insight), which advanced male practitioners can access and appropriate through sexual yoga. In the Hindu tradition it is *sakti* (power or energy). For Buddhist female practitioners, men are the source of *upaya*, skillful means, which women can access and appropriate through sexual yoga. During sexual union the adept, who will lose any spiritual benefit if he ejaculates, absorbs his consort's red drops (uterine fluids), mixing them with his white drops (semen), which he then absorbs through his penis up through his body to the top of his head. The female's red drops are not necessarily red, as they are also referred to as the vaginal secretion a woman is believed to ejaculate during intercourse. In other words, they are the female equivalent of semen. This practice imitates the sexual union of the god with the goddess and of the celestial buddhas with their female consorts, which are said to represent enlightened consciousness.

As Asian religious ideas began to penetrate Western thinking beginning in the 18th century and continuing to this day, the concept of enlightenment primarily from Buddhist and Hindu perspectives was incorporated into the service of the individual ideologies of Western translators, scholars, and philosophers, who spread their ideas to the larger culture. In this way, enlightenment has been as fluid a term in the West as it has in the East. Perennial philosophy extended this term to many different religions, a notion that exploded into the general culture of the West beginning in the 1960s and that has been explored recently by Andrew Rawlinson (1998) through the lives of Western teachers of Asian religions. In the end, though, enlightenment is an ineffable experience, one that is beyond the mundane concepts that limit our ability to communicate with one another, as indicated by the truism that those who know don't say while those who don't know do.

Serinity Young

See also: Asceticism; Buddha, Gautama; Devotion/Devotional Traditions; Mahavira; Mahayana Buddhism; Meditation; Monasticism; Perennialism; Reincarnation; Tantrism; Tibetan Buddhism; Women, Status and Role of.

References

Clarke, J. J. 1997. *Oriental Enlightenment: The Encounter Between Asian and Western Thought.* London: Routledge, 1997.

Collins, Steven. *Nirvana and Other Buddhist Felicities: Utopias of the Pali imaginaire.* Cambridge: Cambridge University Press, 1998.

Feuerstein, Georg. *Tantra: The Path of Ecstasy.* Boston: Shambhala, 1998.

Jaini, Padmanabh S. *Gender and Salvation: Jaina Debates on the Spiritual Liberation of Women.* Berkeley: University of California Press, 1991.

Linrothe, Rob, ed. *The Holy Madness: Portraits of Tantric Siddhas.* Chicago: Serinida Publications, 2006.

O'Flaherty, Wendy Doniger, ed. *Karma and Rebirth in Classical Indian Traditions.* Berkeley: University of California Press, 1980.

Rawlison, Andrew. *Book of Enlightened Masters: Western Teachers in Eastern Traditions.* Chicago: Open Court, 1997, 1998.

Welbon, Guy R. *The Buddhist Nirvana and Its Western Interpreters.* Chicago: University of Chicago Press, 1968.

Young, Serinity. *Courtesans and Tantric Consorts: Sexualities in Buddhist Narrative, Iconography, and Ritual.* New York: Routledge. 2004.

Ennôkyô

Ennôkyô is a Japanese new religion founded by Fukata Chiyoko (1887–1925). In 1919 she received a special message from Kami (a Shinto deity) to become the messenger of Kami and a tool for the sake of world. After this revelation from Kami, she began to practice faith healing and to help people avoid misfortune by predicting troubles they would otherwise encounter. Gradually she attracted a number of followers, and in about 1931, six years or so after her death, they organized two groups, Ennô Shûhôkai and Ennô Hôonkai, to carry on her essentially mystical and faith-healing teachings. Both groups dissolved in 1941, but were re-established as Ennôkyô after World War II and registered by the government in 1948. A feature unique to Ennôkyô is Shûhô. Its spiritual training sessions take the form of a dialogue between paired individuals to resolve problems in daily life. Its main scripture is Ennô kyôten, which includes the teachings of *Sei* (sincerity), *Ai* (love), and *Zen* (virtue).

Ennôkyô is currently led by Fukata Mitsuhiro. As the new century began it reported 459,935 members.

Ennôkyô
1-1 Muramori
San Nan-machi, Hikami-gun
Hyogo prefecture
669-3192
Japan

Keishin Inaba

See also: Shinto.

Reference

Hori, Ichiro, et al., eds. *Japanese Religion: A Survey by the Agency for Cultural Affairs.* Tokyo: Kodansha International, 1972.

Epiphany

Falling on January 6, Epiphany is a Christian feast that celebrates the revelation of God in human form in the person of Jesus Christ. In Greek, the word "epiphany" means "manifestation" and in Eastern Christian tradition the event is called "Theophany," which means "manifestation of God." In the Eastern tradition, it falls on January 19. Roman Catholics will often celebrate it on the Sunday closest to January 6.

The Western observance commemorates the visitation of the biblical Magi to the child Jesus, stressing the appearance of Jesus to the Gentiles. In many Hispanic and European churches, it is also known as Three Kings Day. Eastern Christians include the baptism of Jesus in their celebration, highlighting Christ's revelation to the world as the Son of God.

Marking the 12th day of Christmas, Epiphany brings to an end the Advent and Christmas seasons. The day begins an extended period of "Ordinary Time"

in the Christian year that focuses on the mission of the church in the world to reveal Jesus as the Son of God. It is also a time of focusing on Christian unity and fellowship across ethnic and racial lines.

Originating in Eastern Christian churches, the earliest reference to the feast is found in 361 CE in the writings of Ammianus Marcellinus (ca. 330–395 CE). In a sermon delivered on December 25, 380, Gregory of Nazianzus (329–389 CE) referred to the day "the Theophany" and explained how in the coming weeks the church would be celebrating "the holy nativity of Christ." On January 6 and 7, he preached two more sermons, declaring that the celebration of the birth of Christ and the visitation of the Magi had already taken place and now Christ's baptism would be recognized.

Originally, the day was part of the Christmas celebrations of the nativity, but by 534 CE, the Western church had separated it as a commemoration of the coming of the Magi. The Eastern church continued to celebrate January 6 as a composite feast for some time, but eventually reserved January 6 as a commemoration of the baptism of Jesus.

The colors of Epiphany are usually the colors of Christmas, white and gold. Epiphany liturgies stress the universal mission of Jesus Christ and his church to all peoples throughout the whole world.

While Anglicans and Lutherans observe Epiphany, most Protestant churches ignore it and collapse into Christmas their discussion of the visit of the Magi and the related custom of giving gifts. In the last generation, with the spread of the acknowledgment of the liturgical year among some of the large Protestant groups (Methodists, Presbyterians), some notice of Epiphany has emerged.

Epiphany is the reference for the popular Christmas song, "The Twelve Days of Christmas."

Kevin Quast

See also: Christmas; Eastern Orthodoxy; Liturgical Year; Roman Catholic Church.

References

Cullmann, Oscar. "The Origin of Christmas." In *The Early Church*, edited by A. Higgins, 21–36. Philadelphia: Westminster Press, 1956.

Martindale, Cyril Charles. "Epiphany." In *The Catholic Encyclopedia*. Vol. 5. New York: Robert Appleton Company, 1909.

Merras, Merja. *The Origins of the Celebration of the Christian Feast of Epiphany*. Joensuu, Finland: Joensuu University Press, 1995.

Talley, Thomas J. *The Origins of the Liturgical Year*. Collegeville, MN: The Liturgical Press, 1991.

Episcopal Anglican Church of Brazil

The Church of England assumed that South America was not to be considered a missionary field because of the prior presence of the Roman Catholic Church; thus it was left to the Episcopal Church, based in the United States, to initiate the Anglican tradition in Brazil. In 1889, two young seminarians, James W. Morris and Lucien Kinsolving (1862–1929), representatives of the American Church Missionary Society, arrived in Porto Alegre. A decade later Kinsolving became the first Anglican bishop of South Brazil.

In 1905, the Mission Board of the Episcopal Church assumed responsibility for the mission. By 1913 there were 1,304 communicant members. As the mission grew, the Church of England opened chaplaincies in various parts of the country to serve expatriate communities.

By 1962, there were 185 parishes in the Brazilian Church, divided into 3 dioceses. Slowly the church leadership had become indigenous, but few parishes were self-supporting. Following the designation of a fourth diocese, in 1965, the church was set apart as an autonomous province, though it has still continued in a partnership relation with the Episcopal Church, which supplies various resources for it to draw upon.

The church (Igreja Episcopal do Brasil) is led by its primate, currently the Most Reverend Glauco Scares de Lima. There are eight dioceses. The synod of the church, its highest legislative body, meets triennially, and it appoints an executive committee to administer the church's affairs between synod meetings. As the new century began, the church reported a membership of 120,000 (2005) in 84 parishes and 60 missions. It is a member of the World Council of Churches and the worldwide Anglican Communion.

Episcopal Anglican Church of Brazil
Av. Ludolfo Boehl, 256 Teresopolis
CP 11510
Cep 90841-970 Porto Alegre, RS
Brazil

J. Gordon Melton

See also: Anglican Communion/Anglican Consultative Council; Church of England; Episcopal Church; Roman Catholic Church; World Council of Churches.

References

Manross, William W. *A History of the American Episcopal Church*. New York: Morehouse-Gorham, 1950.

Van Beek, Huibert. *A Handbook of the Churches and Councils: Profiles of Ecumenical Relationships*. Geneva: World Council of Churches, 2006.

Van der Bent, Ans J., ed. *Handbook/Member Churches/World Council of Churches*. Geneva: World Council of Churches, 1985.

Episcopal Church

The Episcopal Church is the primary representative of the Anglican tradition in the United States and continues the work of the Church of England established in the British American colonies. The first Anglican worship service appears to have been held in 1587, at the colony originally established at Roanoke, Virginia. The first permanent congregation was assembled in Jamestown, Virginia, in 1607.

Through the 17th century, the church spread through the British colonies, and continued to exist there when Anglicanism was temporarily banned in England during the days of the Commonwealth (1649–1660). In 1692, British authorities finally forced the establishment of a congregation even in Puritan Boston. At the end of the century Dr. Thomas Bray led in the founding of the Society for the Propagation of the Gospel in Foreign Parts (SPG). The American church received the benefits of the society in the form of hundreds of ministers who volunteered to organize and serve American congregations through the next 70 years. Though no bishop was ever appointed for the

As their bishop, William White led the remnants of the Church of England in the United States to form the Protestant Episcopal Church. (Vincent L. Milner, *Religious Denominations of the World*, 1872)

colonies, Bray returned in 1696 as the representative of the church, with some limited episcopal powers.

The American Revolution was a devastating blow to the development of the church. Most members of the church, and especially the ministers, were identified with those settlers who opposed the Revolution. Following the ending of hostilities, all of the SPG missionaries moved to Canada or returned to England. They left only a small group of ministers committed to residing in the new nation and caring for the 400 Church of England congregations.

The immediate problem for the church was the securing of an American bishop. A bishop was needed to perform a variety of functions, not the least being the ordination of new ministers. In 1783 the clergy of Connecticut took the lead and selected Samuel Seabury to go to England for consecration. The British bishops were ready to consecrate him, but he withdrew when he found himself as an American citizen unable to swear allegiance to the British crown. Thwarted, he traveled to Scotland, where he found bishops with the Nonjuring Church of Scotland (now the Scottish Episcopal Church) who in 1784 consecrated him.

Back in the United States, Seabury found the Connecticut clergy ready to follow his leadership, but the churches and ministers in the colonies to the south balking. They still wanted orders directly from England: Some were resentful of the Connecticut brethren acting without consulting them; some did not like Seabury. In the meantime, while Seabury was in Europe, they had met in convocation and found a leader in William White. They developed a constitution for a new church and selected White and Samuel Provost as their prospective bishops. In 1787, the pair sailed for England, where they found that Parliament had passed legislation that allowed for the consecration of men who did not take the oath of loyalty if they were designated for service outside the country. They returned with valid episcopal orders.

In 1789, the Americans organized the Protestant Episcopal Church in the U.S.A. and adopted a constitution. A slightly edited edition of the Prayer Book used as a guide to worship by the Church of England was adopted. It included a basic liturgy reflective of the middle way between Protestantism and Roman Catholicism that had defined Anglicanism since the reign of Elizabeth I. The church also accepted the Church of England's Thirty-nine Articles of Religion.

As the church developed, it served many of America's elite, and a majority of the country's presidents during the early half of the 19th century were drawn from its ranks. It also developed the several recognizable groups that had emerged in British Anglicanism after the Commonwealth. One group, the Anglo-Catholics, followed what was known as a High-Church path and favored rapprochement with the Roman Catholic Church. On the other extreme, those who advocated a Low-Church policy tended to identify with the Protestant community and were noted for their evangelical and missionary zeal. Between the two groups were the Latitudinarians, who followed a middle road between the two extremes.

The Low-Church wing tended to be the strongest in the church through the early half of the 19th century, though the Anglo-Catholic wing was always present. However, during the 19th century Anglo-Catholicism asserted itself in the Church of England, and its influence began to grow in the Episcopal Church. As its support grew, a crisis developed, leading in 1873 to the withdrawal of Kentucky bishop George David Cummins (1822–1876) and many of the Low-Church adherents to found the Reformed Episcopal Church. Although the church weathered the controversy, its worship life was changed. New churches tended to be built in the Gothic Revival style, and the Communion table tended to be replaced with an altar.

In the decades after World War II, the Episcopal Church became deeply involved in the ecumenical movement. A long-time member of the Federal Council of Churches, it was one of the original members of the National Council of Churches in the United States of America. It was also a charter member of the World Council of Churches. As a leader in the liberal Protestant community in America, it was also profoundly affected by the social changes during the last half of the 20th century. Many of the bishops and clergy assumed leadership roles in the civil rights movement, and the church was among the first Anglican bodies to consider the admission of women to the priesthood.

The church faced a new round of significant controversy in the 1970s, controversy created by dissent among members over the church's involvement in various social crusades, the laxity of morals perceived within the clergy, and a set of changes introduced into the Prayer Book. These issues culminated in 1976 when the General Convention of the church approved the ordination of women to the priesthood. As a result of that action, a number of ministers and members left and organized several new denominations that saw themselves as representatives of a Traditional Anglican movement.

The controversy surrounding the ordination of women paled in comparison to the furor unleashed by the election and subsequent consecration of a homosexual living in a long-term committed relationship to the bishopric in 2003. Conservatives who had remained in the church through the 1990s became more vocal and took their case to the other jurisdictions of the worldwide Anglican Communion. A small minority within the American church, the conservatives found

majority support throughout the worldwide Anglican Communion. African and Asian jurisdictions quickly protested the action of the Episcopal Church and threatened the archbishop of Canterbury with withdrawal of their support from the Anglican Communion. Already in 1999, the leaders of the churches in Rwanda and Singapore had consecrated two American bishops to begin to receive dissenting individual Episcopalians and withdrawing congregations.

In 2004, conservative leaders organized the Network of Anglican Communion Dioceses and Parishes as a network of "confessing church clergy and lay member. By 2008, 10 dioceses had indicated their affiliation with the Network, 3 of which took the further step of voting to withdraw from national body. The action of these dioceses are expected to keep the church in litigation for some years into the future.

The Episcopal Church has its headquarters in New York. The church is divided into dioceses, each led by a bishop, and from the bishops, one is selected as the church's presiding bishop. The General Convention is the highest legislative body in the church. In 1967, the General Convention adopted the present name of the church, a shortened form of its original name.

In 2006, Katharine Jefferts Schori became the 26th presiding bishop of the Episcopal Church, the first female to hold the office. In 2006, the church reported 1,796,017 members in 7,095 churches.

The Episcopal Church has primarily seen itself as serving the American Anglican community and concentrated its missionary efforts on growing westward as the United States enlarged itself through the 19th century. It did found congregations and chaplaincies overseas to serve expatriate communities. Through the Convocation of Anglican Churches in Europe, it cooperates with the Diocese of the Church of England and the Lusitanian Catholic Apostolic Evangelical Church (Portugal) to sponsor English-speaking Anglican churches throughout continental Europe.

In 1834 Low-Church forces in the church founded the American Church Missionary Society. The first missionary was an African American, James M. Thompson, appointed for work in Africa. That same year, 1835, Reverend Henry Lockwood was sent as the first missionary to China. Work has expanded to Japan and Haiti. It then became focused on Latin America. The church's Board of Missions took control of the foreign missions in the years after the American Civil War (1860–1865). The work of that board is currently in the hands of the Episcopal Partnership for Global Ministries, the name reflecting the changed relationship between the American church and the now mature Anglican churches worldwide. Some former mission churches have chosen to remain part of the Episcopal Church, and Province II includes the Diocese of Micronesia, Province VIII, the Diocese of Taiwan, and Province IX, the Diocese for Colombia, the Dominican Republic, Ecuador, and Honduras.

In the years immediately after World War II, the Episcopal Church developed a special relationship with the Philippine Independent Church, a church formed by former Roman Catholics in the Philippine Islands. In 1948, Episcopal bishops passed Anglican orders to the Philippine Church, and the two churches have remained in communion since that time.

Episcopal Church
815 Second Ave.
New York, NY 10017
http://ecusa.anglican.org
http://www.episcopalchurch.org

J. Gordon Melton

See also: Anglican Communion/Anglican Consultative Council; Church of England; Lusitanian Church/Lusitanian Catholic Evangelical Church; Philippine Independent Church; Roman Catholic Church; Scottish Episcopal Church; Society for the Propagation of the Gospel in Foreign Parts; Traditional Anglican Communion; World Council of Churches.

References

Elgin, Kathleen. *The Episcopalians: The Protestant Episcopal Church*. New York: D. McKay Co., 1970.

Hein, David, and Gardiner H. Shattuck, Jr., *The Episcopalians*. Westport, CT: Praeger, 2004.

Manross, William W. *A History of the American Episcopal Church*. New York: Morehouse-Gorham, 1950.

Prichard, Robert. *A History of the Episcopal Church*. Harrisburg, PA: Morehouse Publishing, 1991.

Webber, Christopher L. *Welcome to the Episcopal Church*. Harrisburg, PA: Morehouse Publishing, 2000.

Episcopal Church in Jerusalem and the Middle East

The Episcopal Church in Jerusalem and the Middle East brings together the many efforts by members of the Church of England to establish missions from North Africa to the Arabian Peninsula. Though Anglican missionaries had visited the area in the 18th century, it was not until 1818 that permanent work began, in Egypt. Two years later, Joseph Wolff (1795–1862) of the London Church's Ministry among the Jews came to Jerusalem to begin evangelizing the Jewish residents. Wolff's work expanded to neighboring Lebanon and Syria in the next couple of years. The Ministry of the Jews reached Tunisia as early as 1829.

These initial efforts were strongly affected at the beginning of the 1840s by the decision of church leaders in England and Germany to establish a Christian presence in Jerusalem in the form of an Anglican bishop. They chose Michael Solomon Alexander (1799–1845), a German rabbi who had converted to Christianity and subsequently become an Anglican priest. He accepted the position as a means of converting Jews. In 1851, under the leadership of Alexander's successor, Samuel Gobat, the church turned its attention to the Arab population. He built schools and ordained the first Arab priests. Work expanded to Jordan in 1860.

The first Anglican in Iran, Henry Martyn (1781–1812), arrived as a chaplain for the East India Company. A gifted linguist, he translated the Bible into Persian. The fledgling work was given a new infusion of life in 1844 with the arrival of missionaries with the Ministry among the Jews to work with the Jewish community in Tehran. The Church Missionary Society (CMS) arrived in 1869 to begin more general work among the Persian Muslims. The mission grew into a church, and a bishop was named in 1912. The Diocese of Persia remains the most substantial work in the province.

Work on the Arabian Peninsula began in 1839, following the British capture of Aden. Anglican chaplains formed the first church. Over the years, other churches were opened and closed as British presence waxed and waned, but at the beginning of the 21st century those that remain now serve primarily expatriate personnel residing in the area as oil workers.

During the 20th century, Anglican work across North Africa and the Middle East underwent changes as new dioceses were created, and then in the post–World War II world, the move to grant autonomous status to missions took control. In 1920, Egypt and the Sudan were separated from Jerusalem as a new diocese. Sudan became a separate diocese in 1945. With the creation of an independent Israel, in 1948, the majority of the Anglicans left, and many Arab Christians moved to neighboring countries. CMS institutions in Jaffa and Lydda were closed, as was the Bishop Godat school in Jerusalem. Many other properties were abandoned and then destroyed or confiscated by the new government.

In 1957, the bishopric of Jerusalem was elevated into an archdiocese. That same year, the Diocese of Jordan, Lebanon, and Syria was set apart, and the following year, the Diocese of Egypt was suspended and the work attached to Jerusalem. That diocese was revived in 1974 and now included all the work in Egypt, Libya, Tunisia, Algeria, Ethiopia, Somalia, and Djibouti.

Finally, in 1976, the archbishopric was replaced by a new independent Anglican province, the Episcopal Church in Jerusalem and the Middle East. Faik Ibrahim Haddad (r. 1976–1984) was the first bishop of Jerusalem in the new province. At the same time, the Diocese of Jordan, Lebanon, and Syria was absorbed into the Diocese of Jerusalem, and a new Diocese of Cyprus and the Gulf was created by combining the Anglican parishes on Cyprus and the Arabian Peninsula. The Dioceses of Egypt and Iran became a part of the new province.

The province is currently led by the Most Reverend Dr. Mouneer Hanna Anis, the bishop of Egypt. He is president of the Central Synod that represents the four dioceses (Jerusalem, Egypt, Iran, and Cyprus and the Gulf). The president is elected for a five-year term and may be re-elected once. The bishop of Jerusalem, currently the Right Reverend Suheil Dawani, is in a unique position as his church recognizes the primacy of the patriarch of Orthodox Patriarchate of Jerusalem

as the successor of Saint James and hence the rightful bishop of Jerusalem. As a rule, Anglicans would not place a bishop in a city in which an Orthodox bishop had previously established his hegemony.

In 2005, the church reported 37,000 members in 31 parishes. The church oversees St. George's College in Jerusalem. It is a member (since 1976) of the World Council of Churches and the Middle East Council of Churches.

St. George's Close
PO Box 19122
91191 Jerusalem
Israel

J. Gordon Melton

See also: Anglican Communion/Anglican Consultative Council; Church Missionary Society; Church of England; Middle East Council of Churches; World Council of Churches.

References

The Church of England Yearbook. London: Church Publishing House, published annually.

El-Assal, Raih Abu. "Anglicanism in Jerusalem." In *Anglicanism: A Global Communion,* edited by Andrew Wingate et al. London: Mowbray, 1998.

Van Beek, Huibert. *A Handbook of the Churches and Councils: Profiles of Ecumenical Relationships.* Geneva: World Council of Churches, 2006.

Episcopal Church in the Philippines

The Episcopal Church in the Philippines originated in the religious ferment that followed the annexation of the Philippine Islands by the United States in 1898. The Episcopal Church in the United States sent missionaries, who arrived in 1902 with instructions to target those segments of the population not otherwise affiliated with any Christian church. Among groups so identified were the Chinese who lived in Manila, various ethnic groups in northern Luzon, and the Muslims of Mindanao and Sulu.

The work progressed steadily, and a set of primary and secondary schools was established. After World War II, during which the church suffered considerably from the Japanese occupation, a move to build indigenous leadership was vigorously pursued, and the number of Filipino priests increased sharply during the 1950s. The first Filipino bishop was consecrated in 1967.

The church has had a unique relationship with the Philippine Independent Church, which has Anglican orders, and in 1961 the two churches entered into full communion. Until 1990, the work in the Philippines was part of Province VIII of the Episcopal Church in the United States, but in that year it was set apart as an autonomous jurisdiction. The church is at one in faith and practice with the wider Anglican Communion and led by its prime bishop.

The church has six dioceses. In 2005 it reported 125,000 members in 513 parishes. Soon after its independence from the church in the United States, it joined the World Council of Churches (1991).

Episcopal Church in the Philippines
PO Box 10321
Broadway Centrum
1112 Quezon City
Philippines

J. Gordon Melton

See also: Anglican Communion/Anglican Consultative Council; Episcopal Church; Philippine Independent Church.

References

The Church of England Yearbook. London: Church Publishing House, published annually.

Jones, Arun W. *Christian Missions in the American Empire: Episcopalians in Northern Luzon, the Philippines, 1902–1946.* New York: Peter Lang, 2003.

Kane, J. Herbert. *A Global View of Christian Missions.* Grand Rapids, MI: Baker Book House, 1971.

Van Beek, Huibert. *A Handbook of the Churches and Councils: Profiles of Ecumenical Relationships.* Geneva: World Council of Churches, 2006.

Epworth

Epworth is a small town in North Lincolnshire, England. It arose from obscurity in the 18th century as the birthplace of John and Charles Wesley, the founders of Methodism. Their father, Samuel, was the Anglican parish priest in the town from 1695 to 1735. Epworth is located on the Isle of Axholme an island formed by several sounding rivers. The relative isolation of the area was ended when the area was drained, a significant engineering feat of the 1620s.

Samuel Wesley served as rector of the parish church, dedicated to Saint Andrew. It is located on a hill overlooking the town. Architects have dated the oldest part of the church structure to the late 12th century, with later additions primarily from the 14th and 15th centuries. The town itself is much older than the present church.

John and Charles grew up in a large family and Epworth provided a large rectory. However, in 1709, the rectory was burned and during the fire John was trapped and spotted at a second-story window. Because he was eventually rescued, his mother, Susannah, came to believe that he was saved for a purpose, a belief she imposed upon him. It is believed that the fire was set by parishioners angry at Samuel Wesley. Afterward, a new rectory was built. Refurbished and restored, it is maintained as a museum by the World Methodist Council. Samuel Wesley is buried in the church's cemetery.

In 1716 the new rectory became the site of some well-documented psychic disturbances that lasted for several months. They were attributed to a poltergeist whom the family called Old Jeffery. Susannah originally connected the Epworth phenomena to her brother who had disappeared in India, but they came to be connected mostly with John's sister Hetty.

John Wesley later relocated to London, but occasionally returned to Epworth. He is said to have preached in the Market Place from the steps of the Market Cross. British Methodists erected the Wesley Memorial Church on High Street in Epworth in 1889.

Epworth also happened to be the birthplace of Alexander Kilham (1762), one of the founders of the Methodist New Connexion. A forceful writer and speaker, he championed the cause of greater lay representation in the government of the church. The Methodists rejected his views, and in 1796, the Wesleyan Conference tried and expelled him. The next year he became the first secretary of Methodist New Connexion.

J. Gordon Melton

See also: Methodism; Wesley, John; World Methodist Council.

References

Clarke, Ada. *Memoirs of the Wesley Family.* 4th ed. London: W. Tegg, 1860.

Edwards, Maldwyn. *Family Circle: A Study of the Epworth Household in Relation to John and Charles Wesley.* London: Epworth Press, 1961.

Wakeley, J. B. *Anecdotes of the Wesleys: Illustrative of Their Character and Personal History.* New York: Nelson & Phillips, 1869.

Wright, Dudley. *The Epworth Phenomena.* London: William Rider & Son, 1917.

■ Equatorial Guinea

Equatorial Guinea is a small country located on the western coast of Africa. It consists of a small area (28,000 square miles) on the mainland, sandwiched between Cameroon and Gabon, and several islands. The capital, Malabo, is located on one of the islands, Bioko, formerly known as Fernando Po. The territory on the mainland, known as Rio Muni, is largely a rainforest, located less than two degrees from the equator. The major group among the country's 616,000 people (2008) in the country is Bantu, but there are many Ibo and Efik people on Bioko and Fang and Ndowe people on the mainland.

The Ndowe people worked with the European slave traders in the 18th century, while the Fang refused to participate in the slave trade and retreated from the coastal lands. In 1777–1778, Portugal ceded their claims on the area to Spain; before Spain could take control, however, the British moved in and occupied Bioko as a staging area for its conquest of Nigeria. Spain finally took control in the 1850s. Rio Muni had been French territory, but it came into Spanish hands in 1901. Equatorial Guinea remained attached to Spain until independence was proclaimed in 1969. Subsequently, Francisco Macias Nguema (d. 1979) moved quickly to consolidate his power as the new president. He viciously destroyed all visible opposition, and as repression grew, the country went through a decade of bloodshed. In 1978 all churches were ordered closed.

Children play in front of the cathedral in Malabo, Equatorial Guinea. The ornate cathedral, built in 1916 in the Spanish Gothic style, is located near the presidential palace and serves as a place of worship for the country's predominantly Roman Catholic population. (AP/Wide World Photos)

In 1979, Marcus Nguema was arrested and executed following a coup, but the succeeding regime gathered a reputation similar to Nguema's. The leader of the new regime, General Teodoro Obiang Nguema Mba Nzago (b. 1942), continues to lead the country. A slow transition to a more democratic government began in the 1990s.

Each of the peoples of the territory now constituting Equatorial Guinea had a traditional indigenous religion. These religions survive among a small minority

Equatorial Guinea

Religion	Followers in 1970	Followers in 2010	% of Population	Annual % growth 2000–2010	Followers in 2025	Followers in 2050
Christians	257,000	483,000	88.6	2.36	677,000	1,036,000
Roman Catholics	231,000	494,000	90.6	2.66	691,000	1,050,000
Protestants	14,900	26,700	4.9	2.82	43,000	75,000
Independents	5,900	25,500	4.7	2.86	45,000	80,000
Muslims	1,300	22,200	4.1	2.37	32,000	50,000
Agnostics	10,000	18,000	3.3	2.74	33,000	55,000
Atheists	2,800	9,900	1.8	2.37	16,000	25,000
Ethnoreligionists	19,300	9,200	1.7	2.37	10,000	9,000
Baha'is	700	2,800	0.5	2.37	4,200	7,000
Hindus	0	300	0.1	2.39	600	1,000
Total population	**291,000**	**545,000**	**100.0**	**2.37**	**773,000**	**1,183,000**

of the public, mostly among the Fang people, estimated at less than 5 percent of the total population. The Fang acknowledge a supreme deity named Nzame and venerate ancestral spirits called Bekon. The primary religious functionaries are the *uganga* (also called *ngang*), to whom is attributed the ability to contact the spirits and manipulate supernatural powers.

The Roman Catholic Church entered in the 15th century through the successive European powers that operated within the area. Spanish Catholicism provides the major background of the present church. The work was organized under a prefecture in 1855. The prefecture was elevated to a vicariate in 1904. There are presently two dioceses, one for Rio Muni and one for the islands. More than 80 percent of the population are baptized Catholics. The church faced many problems in the 1970s—the expulsion of priests, nuns, and bishops, the arrest of priests and lay leaders, and the closing of churches. However, it rebounded during the 1980s and 1990s.

The first Protestants in Equatorial Guinea were Baptists. They entered in 1841 but were expelled in 1858. Presbyterians began work on the island of Corisco in 1850 and moved into Rio Muni 15 years later. In 1933, the Worldwide Evangelization Crusade (now WEC International), a Protestant sending agency founded by pioneer missionary C. T. Studd (1860–1931), began work in Rio Muni among the Okak (Fang) people. In 1970 the crusade merged its work with the Presbyterians to form the Evangelical Church, an independent Presbyterian body. In 1870, missionaries arrived from the Primitive Methodist Church in England. They established work on Fernando Po, which in 1893 expanded into Nigeria, where it has become a large organization and member of the World Council of Churches. In 1973, the Evangelical Church and the Methodists in Equatorial Guinea united to form the Presbyterian Church of Equatorial Guinea.

Various indigenous movements have appeared in the country. The Bwiti movement, also known as the Church of the Initiates, is a revival of worship of ancestral spirits among the Fang people. Worship includes use of a psychedelic substance found in the *eboga* root. It emerged at the end of the 19th century in neighboring Gabon and has survived in spite of attempts to suppress it.

In 1937 the Presbyterians experienced a schism, when some members adopted a more congregational form of organization and formed as the Assembly of Brethren (Assemblies de los Hermanos). The Jehovah's Witnesses entered the country immediately after World War II.

Among the more interesting groups in the country is the Free Protestant Episcopal Church, a small autonomous Anglican jurisdiction that originated in England and established itself in Nigeria. The work on Bioko, mostly among English-speaking expatriate Africans, is part of the Diocese of West Africa (possibly the most successful arena of the Free church's life).

The Church of Jesus Christ of Latter-day Saints has a small work with less than 100 members that is attached to the Ivory Coast Abidjan Mission. The

EQUATORIAL GUINEA

Seventh-day Adventist Church established its Equatorial Guinea Mission in 1986 and now has several hundred members. The Baha'i Faith entered Equatorial Guinea in the 1960s. There is a minimal Muslim presence, primarily Sunnis of the Malikite School of Islam.

Marcus Nguema was an atheist, and as his regime proceeded, he first supported the spread of atheism and eventually moved against the churches because of their refusal to cooperate with his atheist programs. During this time, atheism became established among one segment of the public.

J. Gordon Melton

See also: Atheism; Baha'i Faith; Bwiti; Church of Jesus Christ of Latter-day Saints; Jehovah's Witnesses; Malikite School of Islam; Roman Catholic Church; Seventh-day Adventist Church; World Council of Churches.

References

Fernàndez, C. *Misiones y misioneros en la Guinea Española.* Madrid: Editorial Co. SA, 1962.

Liniger, Goumaz, Max. *Historical Dictionary of Equatorial Guinea.* Metuchen, NJ: Scarecrow Press, 2000.

Pujadas, P. L. *La Iglesia en la Guinea Ecuatorial.* Madrid: Editorial Iris de Paz, 1968.

■ Eritrea

Eritrea is a relatively new country whose existence was challenged throughout the 20th century. It is a long, narrow country with a long shoreline (more than 650 miles) along the Red Sea between Djibouti and the Sudan. Its long southern border confronts Ethiopia. Its land area of 46,800 square miles is inhabited by some 5.5 million people, split between Islam and Christianity.

What is now Eritrea was originally inhabited by various African peoples believed to have come into the area from the Sudan in ancient times. At some point between 1000 and 400 BCE, the Sabeans, a Semitic group, arrived in Eritrea and integrated with the local population. Because of its long shoreline, the area was a prize seized by different conquering forces over the centuries. Land-bound Ethiopia especially saw Eritrea as its entryway to the ocean. Eritrea was incorporated into the Axum Empire, which reached from its base in northern Ethiopia to include Yemen. Christianity was introduced in the fourth century, and the Ethiopian Orthodox Tewahedo Church, established in 332, became the religion of the nation's ruling elite.

Muslims occupied the islands of the Daklak Archipelago at the beginning of the eighth century, and the religion began to penetrate the coastal area in sub-sequent centuries. Islam enjoyed its greatest success following Ahmad Granj of Harar's establishment of it in the Amhara highlands in 1506. In 1541, a Portuguese fleet called into the area by the Ethiopians destroyed much of the Islamic culture along the coast to the north and east of Ethiopia.

A new era in Eritrean history began in 1885 when Italy occupied the region. Eritrea became the staging area for Italy's subsequent invasion of Ethiopia. Defeated, the Italians received formal control of Eritrea in the subsequent negotiations. They named it a colony in 1900. In the 1930s, Benito Mussolini again tried to invade Ethiopia from Eritrea. Mussolini was defeated in 1941, and the British came into the region to replace the Italians. In 1950 the United Nations named Eritrea a federated state within the Ethiopian Empire. In 1962 it was incorporated fully into Ethiopia, a move rejected by many Eritreans, who had developed a new sense of national identity during the fight against Italy. Efforts to gain Eritrea's independence began in the 1950s, and hostilities aimed at independence began in 1961. After 30 years of warfare, in 1991, while Ethiopia underwent a government change, a provisional government was established in Eritrea by the rebel forces. Following a highly monitored referendum, the new national state was declared in 1993 and most of the world's countries immediately recognized its existence. The capital is in Asmara.

Islam and Orthodox Christianity vie for the hearts of the Eritrean people. The Sunni Muslim community, mostly of the Shafaiite School, is led by Sheikh

Eritrea

Religion	Followers in 1970	Followers in 2010	% of Population	Annual % growth 2000–2010	Followers in 2025	Followers in 2050
Muslims	918,000	2,621,000	49.2	4.19	3,782,000	5,641,000
Christians	857,000	2,512,000	47.2	4.22	3,624,000	5,402,000
Orthodox	760,000	2,260,000	42.5	4.38	3,250,000	4,890,000
Roman Catholics	75,000	170,000	3.2	2.42	225,000	280,000
Protestants	10,000	65,000	1.2	3.46	120,000	190,000
Agnostics	0	155,000	2.9	4.20	250,000	400,000
Ethnoreligionists	71,000	32,000	0.6	4.20	23,000	15,000
Baha'is	500	1,500	0.0	4.21	3,000	4,000
Hindus	500	1,000	0.0	4.19	1,500	2,500
Atheists	0	300	0.0	4.23	500	1,000
Total population	**1,847,000**	**5,323,000**	**100.0**	**4.20**	**7,684,000**	**11,465,000**

ERITREA

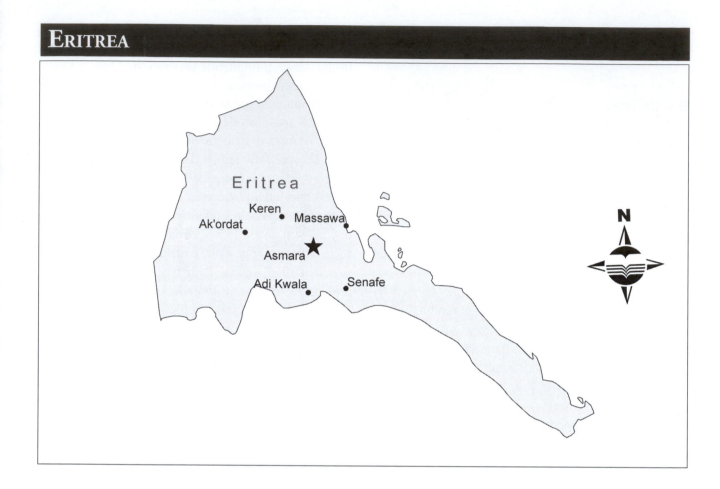

Al-Amin Osman Al-Amin. The Orthodox Church of Eritrea has close relationship with the Coptic Orthodox Church of Egypt, and Pope Shenouda has consecrated most of its bishops. Prior to 1991, the church existed as a Diocese in the Ethiopian Orthodox Tewahedo Church. The Roman Catholic Church has work in both the Latin rite and the Eastern (Ethiopian) rite, with two bishops in Asmara.

In May 2002, Eritrean authorities announced new policies by which it has officially recognized the Eritrean Orthodox Tewahdo Church, Sunni Islam, Catholicism, and the Evangelical Lutheran Church. These groups are exempted from the process of registration required of all other religious bodies. That process requires disclosure of data on their membership, and few groups have been willing to comply. Those few that have submitted information in hopes of registering have received no response.

Protestantism entered Eritrea in 1866 when three representative of the Swedish Evangelical Mission

(representing Lutheranism) arrived in Massawa on their way to the interior of Ethiopia. Blocked from their goal, they stayed and initiated work among the Kunama people. After they had established a center in Massawa, the authorities began to entrust freed slaves to their care. They also began to recruit indigenous leadership. The church became self-governing in 1926, the first autonomous Lutheran body in Africa. In 1911, the church experienced a schism when some of the Swedish missionaries left their affiliation with the Swedish Evangelical Mission to affiliate with the Swedish Mission of Bible True Friends, a conservative movement that had developed to protest liberal trends in the Church of Sweden. The new mission became autonomous in 1957 as the Lutheran Church in Eritrea.

Through the 20th century, various additional Protestant and Free church bodies entered Ethiopia through Eritrea, and the two countries share much religious history in common. Following World War II, the Orthodox Presbyterian Church and the Evangelistic Faith

The minaret of a mosque and the steeple of an Eritrean Orthodox church stand side by side in the religiously mixed market town of Keren. (AP Photo/Boris Grdanoski)

Missions (an American-based sending agency) initiated work in Eritrea. The latter established what has become the Evangelical Church of Eritrea. A year after the declaration of independence in 1993, the Southern Baptist Convention initiated work. These groups all now work outside the official regulations.

J. Gordon Melton

See also: Church of Sweden; Coptic Orthodox Church; Ethiopian Orthodox Tewahedo Church; Free Churches; Lutheranism; Orthodox Presbyterian Church; Roman Catholic Church; Shafiite School of Islam; Southern Baptist Convention;

References

Barrett, David, ed. *The Encyclopedia of World Christianity*. 2nd ed. New York: Oxford University Press, 2001.

Favali, Lyda, and Roy Pateman. *Blood, Land, and Sex: Legal and Political Pluralism in Eritrea.* Bloomington: Indiana University Press, 2003.

Pateman, Roy. *Eritrea: Even the Stones Are Burning.* Trenton, NJ: Red Sea Press, 1998.

Trimingham, J. S. *The Christian Church and Mission in Ethiopia (including Eritrea and the Somalilands).* London: World Dominion Press, 1950.

Eritrean Orthodox Tewahedo Church

The Eritrean Orthodox Tewahedo Church is a Christian body in the tradition of the Coptic Orthodox Church of Egypt. It emerged in the wake of the country gaining independence in 1991.

The Eritrean Orthodox Tewahedo Church traces its history to the founding of the Coptic Orthodox Church and its separation in the fifth century from the larger body of Eastern Orthodox Christianity. By this time Coptic Christianity had been established in Ethiopia, from which it spread to Eritrea. For centuries, the Eritrean orthodoxy was an integral part of the Ethiopian church. Like the Ethiopians, the Eritrean church recognizes Frumentius (fourth century) as its first bishop and it follows the beliefs and practices of Ethiopian Christianity.

The separation of Eritrea from Ethiopia, the result of a freedom movement that began in the 1960s, made the continuation of the Ethiopian church in the new country untenable and ongoing relationships have been strained. When the Eritrean church reorganized as a separate entity in 1994, it turned to the Egyptian church for the consecration and enthronement of its bishops. Four years later, Pope Shenouda III, the patriarch of the Coptic Orthodox Church, traveled to Asmara to elevate one of the bishops, Arbouna Philippos, as the first patriarch of the Eritean Orthodox Tewahedo Church. This ceremony was accompanied by the signing of a formal protocol of mutual recognition by the two churches.

The church is led by its synod, consisting of all the bishops and archbishops and chaired by the patriarch. In 2008, the church claimed 1,700,000 members in its 1,500 churches. The church includes about a third of the population, the remainder of which is primarily

Muslim. The church is currently led by His Holiness Patriarch Antonios, who was enthroned in 2003 by Pope Shenouda.

The church is a member of the World Council of Churches and the All Africa Conference of Churches.

Eritrean Orthodox Tewahedo Church
PO Box 728
Asmara
Eritrea

J. Gordon Melton

See also: All Africa Conference of Churches; Coptic Orthodox Church; Ethiopian Orthodox Tewahedo Church; World Council of Churches.

References

Pateman, Roy. *Eritrea: Even the Stones Are Burning.* Trenton, NJ: Red Sea Press, 1998.

Van Beek, Huibert. *A Handbook of the Churches and Councils: Profiles of Ecumenical Relationships.* Geneva: World Council of Churches, 2006.

Espiritismo

Syncretized ritual systems form the basis of many religions indigenous to the colonial Caribbean. Espiritismo is a less common tradition that takes its place among other syncretized religions in the region such as Vodou, Santeria, and Orisha. Espiritismo is a form of ritual healing indigenous to Puerto Rico and commonly found wherever Puerto Ricans live in substantial numbers. While there is no central authority or institutionalization of Espiritismo practice, it is significant for its common expression throughout Puerto Rican society.

Espiritismo is one of a number of healing traditions that provide participants with an opportunity to relieve stress and to address specific emotional, social, and physical ailments, as well as creating an entertaining drama that satisfies spiritual needs and provides insight into psychic or behavioral crises. As a ritualized healing tradition, it is not practiced as an alternative to mainstream religions such as Catholicism. Ritual specialists (*espiritistas/espiritistos*) are essentially mediums who are able to access, or otherwise influence, spirits and Catholic saints for the benefit of their clients.

Syncretizing elements from a number of spiritual traditions, Espiritismo practitioners continue to adapt their rituals to their contemporary circumstances. Espiritismo has its origins in the writings of Allan Kardec, a Frenchman who attempted to rationalize popular European folk beliefs of the 19th century. In Puerto Rico, Kardec's "science of spiritism" blended with *curanderismo*, which was itself a blend of folk Catholicism, 16th-century European medicine, and earlier Caribbean and Mesoamerican Indian practices. More recently, elements of Santeria, an African-based syncretic faith that developed in Cuba, have also been incorporated into the practice of Espiritismo—especially in New York City, where it has gained wide popularity among Puerto Ricans and African Americans. The syncretism of Santeria and Espiritismo in New York City is still in its incipient form, and it is becoming distinguished as a separate religious/folk medical practice called Santerismo.

When a believing individual or family suffers from persistent pain that has not been relieved by medical doctors, when a husband is cheating on his wife, when someone is facing harassment and unfair treatment at work, or when a child always seems to be in trouble at school, then an espiritista or espiritisto will be consulted. Likewise, newly purchased homes or cars will be "cleansed" and blessed. In the course of her work, an espiritista will have a private consultation with clients at the altar in her home where she will read cards, call upon her spirit guides, and interview the client to assess the nature of the problem. *Guías*, or spirit guides, are the disincarnated spirits with which a medium or medium in development is in direct communication. The guías help the medium and are not understood as "possessing" the espiritista. They talk to the medium, protect her from *causas*, and appear to mount the medium in trance to talk to and help others.

The spirits have personality characteristics that are valued for the strengths they represent or are desired by the medium. Such *protecciónes* are often Catholic saints, the Yoruban powers of Santeria, folk heroes (such as Joan of Arc), idealized ethnic types (such as the Indio, the Hindu, the Negro Africano), a physical

Table set for *Misa Espiritual* (Spiritual Mass) in Houston, Texas. (Mary Ann Clark)

type (a strong black, an old man or woman), a professional type (priest, doctor, missionary), a deceased relative of the individual, or a relative from another existence. They are not understood to be perfect beings, but instead they are called upon as enlightened, elevated spirits. Espiritistas often have many guías.

On the other hand, a causa is a negative and base disincarnated spirit. If such a spirit is identified as the client's problem, then the medium will recommend a *despojo* (a ritual bath) for spiritual cleansing, attending extra Catholic Masses, and participating in a feast night celebration (which she celebrates at the altar in her home or in a *centro*). If the base spirit is particularly resistant, the espiritista will "mount" and interrogate it, sometimes with the assistance of other mediums, in order to remove it from her client. Mounting is a vaguely defined experience of having a spirit ride one person in order to communicate with others. For instance, in Haitian Vodou, people who have the spirit

"on" them are called horses. When an espiritista mounts a spirit, she is metaphorically pinning it down with the weight of her own spiritual power. After the medium has cleansed the client by mounting the causa(s), she will use another ritual to cleanse herself (for example, going to the cemetery where she will ritually pass the causa to a guía, whereupon she returns home to ritually bathe and pray at her altar).

Espiritismo is a particularly Puerto Rican means for negotiating the difficulties of life. It is usually practiced in informal places, such as the home of the spirit medium or in centros, which are basement or storefront sites. Since it is an informal tradition without a central authority, it is extremely difficult to assess the number and distribution of both home and centro sites. Also, Espiritismo is fluid, dynamic, and loosely organized, with mediums having individualized styles and strengths that gain them a following. Still, most people who visit an espiritista consider themselves to be devout Catholics, and they do so only if there is a difficult problem to be solved by spiritual means. Most mediums are found by word of mouth or through their local *botánicas* (neighborhood shops selling spiritual products).

Carolyn V. Prorok

See also: Possession; Santeria; Spiritism; Vodou.

References

Brandon, George. *Santeria from Africa to the New World: The Dead Sell Memories.* Bloomington: Indiana University Press, 1997.

Garrison, Vivian. "The 'Puerto Rican Syndrome' in Psychiatry and Espiritismo." In *Case Studies in Spirit Possession*, edited by Vincent Crapanzano and Vivian Garrison. New York: John Wiley and Sons, 1977.

Koss, Joan D. "Religion and Science Divinely Related: A Case History of Spiritism in Puerto Rico." Paper presented at the 73rd Annual Meeting of the American Anthropological Association, Symposium on Spiritism in Latin America, Mexico City, 1974.

Prorok, Carolyn V. "Boundaries are Made for Crossing: The Feminized Spatiality of Puerto Rican Espiritismo in New York City." *Gender, Place and Culture: A Journal of Feminist Geography* 7, no. 1 (2000): 57–80.

■ Estonia

Estonia is situated at the northeastern part of Europe, at the southern shore of the Finnish Gulf. The capital of Estonia is Tallinn. The population of Estonia is 1.34 million (including 68 percent ethnic Estonians, 25 percent Russians, 2 percent Ukrainians). The official language is Estonian. The majority of the population does not have a religious affiliation.

According to the census data from the year 2000 29 percent of the adult population considered themselves as adherents of some religion. The largest religious group are the Lutherans (13.6 percent of the population), followed by the Orthodox (12.8 percent), Baptists (0.5 percent), Roman Catholics (0.5 percent), Jehovah's Witnesses (0.34 percent), Pentecostals (0.2 percent), Old Believers (0.2 percent), Adventists (0.1 percent), and Methodists (0.1 percent). The largest non-Christian community are Muslims (0.1 percent). Also the indigenous religious traditions have considerable following (0.09 percent) though it is considerably less formally organized compared to other religious traditions. According to the census data, 6 percent of the population considered themselves atheists.

In 1991, after 50 years of Soviet occupation, Estonia reestablished its independence. The early 1990s were characterized by radical socio-political and economical reforms. The governmental regulations were minimized and radical socio-economic as well as political reforms were introduced. The free market ideology was adopted also in the field of religion. The Constitution from 1992 guarantees the freedom of religion and belief. The legislative framework for religious associations has been liberal and the principles of freedom of religion are followed both in legislation as well as in practice. The governmental policy toward religious associations has followed the model of cooperation and equal treatment. The main partner for the government on religion-related issues has been the ecumenical Estonian Council of Churches (1989). Through its member churches the Council represents almost 98 percent of adherents of different Christian churches (Lutherans, Orthodox, Roman Catholics, Baptists, Evangelicals, Methodists, Seventh-day Adventists, Pentecostals, Charismatic Episcopalians, and members of Armenian Apostolic Church).

According to the Constitution, there is no state church in Estonia. As of the end of 2008, Estonia was home to 9 churches (of recognized denominations), 9 congregational associations, and 71 individual congregations. There were also religious communities that have established themselves as nonprofit organizations, as well as some that have maintained themselves as informal associations.

The largest church is the Estonian Evangelical Lutheran Church. The second largest religious community is Orthodox, though divided into two churches: the Estonian Apostolic Orthodox Church and the Estonian Orthodox Church of Moscow Patriarchate. From 1993 to 2002 there was a serious confrontation between these two churches. The main reason for this

Estonia

Religion	Followers in 1970	Followers in 2010	% of Population	Annual % growth 2000–2010	Followers in 2025	Followers in 2050
Christians	618,000	956,000	72.4	0.46	952,000	886,000
Orthodox	280,000	348,000	26.3	0.12	350,000	350,000
Protestants	328,000	238,000	18.0	0.40	242,000	230,000
Independents	350	40,000	3.0	4.76	56,000	60,000
Agnostics	410,000	307,000	23.3	−1.18	240,000	180,000
Atheists	318,000	50,000	3.8	−6.70	50,000	50,000
Muslims	10,000	4,000	0.3	−0.37	5,800	6,000
Jews	8,000	1,500	0.1	−0.37	1,500	1,500
Buddhists	300	800	0.1	4.16	1,000	1,500
Hindus	100	800	0.1	4.16	1,000	1,500
Baha'is	200	500	0.0	−0.40	700	1,000
Total population	**1,365,000**	**1,321,000**	**100.0**	**−0.38**	**1,252,000**	**1,128,000**

was the restitution of the church property nationalized during the Soviet period. The confrontation also had political overtones and had impact on the relations between Estonia and the Russian Federation as well as on the relations between the Ecumenical Patriarchate in Constantinople and the Moscow Patriarchate.

The pre-Christian religion of Estonia was most probably a local form of shamanism like that found among other Finno-Ugric peoples. Nature was considered animated by different spirits or powers, who were called "mothers" and "fathers." The veneration of ancestors was also known. During the 1920s and 1930s, an attempt to restore the pre-Christian religion of Estonians was made under the name Taara-belief. In 1931 the Taara-believers founded their religious organization, Hiis (The Grove).

From the 11th century onward, Christianity was introduced to Estonians by trade and Christian monks. In the beginning of the 13th century the Roman Catholic Church and the Teutonic Order started to Christianize Estonia. By 1227 Estonia was declared Christianized. However, the pre-Christian worldview really started to change as late as the end of the 15th century, and was to a great extent maintained until the first half of the 18th century.

The Lutheran Reformation reached the towns in Estonia in 1524. Soon Lutheranism became the largest denomination. After the Great Northern War (1700–1721) Estonia became part of the Russian Empire. However, this political change did not affect the reli-

gious situation of the country. The Lutheran clergy has played an important role in the processes of forming Estonian cultural and national identity: the first prayer book and catechism in Estonian were Lutheran, printed in 1535, and the Bible was printed by Lutherans in 1739.

In 1727 the first Herrnhut Brethren (Moravians) came to Estonia. The native Estonians had an important role in the development of the Herrnhut movement, especially after 1743, when it was banned and the German Brethren expelled from the country. The movement eventually had a role in the national and cultural development of Estonia by encouraging literacy and various cultural pursuits that were popular in Europe at the time.

The Orthodox Church is one of the oldest churches in Estonia. However, Estonians did not join the Orthodox Church in great numbers until the middle of the 19th century. Then the prime reasons for conversion were economic and social, and the conversions were supported by the czarist Russification policy.

From the 1870s through the end of the first decade of the 20th century, there were several religious revivals in Estonia. During this period Baptists, Seventh-day Adventists, Methodists, Pentecostals, and others were introduced.

Shortly after the collapse of the Russian Empire in 1917, the Estonian Evangelical Lutheran Church was founded on the basis of Lutheran congregations in Estonia. In 1919 the Orthodox congregations in Estonia

ESTONIA

organized themselves as the Estonian Apostolic Orthodox Church (EAOC). In 1920 the patriarch of Moscow gave independence to the EAOC, and since 1923 the EAOC has related to the Ecumenical Patriarchate in Constantinople as an autonomous church.

In 1940, when Estonia was incorporated into the Soviet Union, the religious situation changed dramatically. Already in 1940 some religious organizations were dissolved (for example, the Taara-believers, Salvation Army), religious literature was banned, the property of religious organizations was confiscated, and the Faculty of Theology at the Tartu University was closed. In 1945 the Russian Orthodox Church dissolved the Estonian Apostolic Orthodox Church. The EAOC maintained its legal continuity in exile; the metropolitan of the EAOC had left the country along with approximately 70,000 Estonians who fled from the second invasion of the Soviet troops in 1944. In Esto-

nia, the Russian Orthodox Church established its own diocese. In 1945 the Baptist, Evangelical Christian, Pentecostal, and Free churches were forced by Soviet officials to merge into the Union of Baptists and Evangelical Christians in Soviet Union. The activities of religious organizations were strictly regulated and controlled. The Soviet Marxist ideology of atheism was implemented particularly forcefully in the 1960s. During this period religion and religious institutions were marginalized in the society.

The change began with the national awakening during the end of the 1980s and gained strength with the re-establishment of the independence of Estonia in 1991. During this period religion became significant as the maintainer of ethical and moral norms, and also as a connection to Estonia's past. Because of its links to the past, the Estonian Evangelical Lutheran Church became important. Several religious movements that had previously been banned restarted their activities. In 1993 the EAOC reestablished itself in Estonia. During this period also, many new religious movements emerged. New Age sensibilities, which became noticeable in Estonia in the 1970s, started to gain much popularity among Estonians.

The national awakening also renewed interest in pre-Christian worldviews and religions. This trend is represented by the House of Taara and Native Religions, which together involve roughly 200 active members and approximately 1,000 people who identify themselves with that tradition. The Taara-believers continue the attempts made in the 1930s, whereas the followers of Native religions relate Native Estonian religion to other Finno-Ugric peoples' nature worship. This tradition is essentially person-centered, with the emphasis on a kind of power (*vägi*) that is understood both as a personal quality and as the essence of everything. In addition to Taara- and Earth-believers the local shamanistic tradition of healers (*nõid*) is still alive and popular though it has gained some New Age influences during the last decades.

Islam and Judaism have been traditionally connected to the national minorities in Estonia. In Estonia there are also followers of the Buddhist and Hindu traditions. However, the philosophical ideas of Buddhism and Hinduism are more popular than their religious practices. The most active Hindu group is the local community of the International Society for Krishna Consciousness. The first influences of Buddhism arrived in Estonia during the early 20th century with the Estonian Buddhist monk Vahindra (Karl Tõnisson, also known as Karlis Tennissons). Today the Buddhist tradition is represented by four Tibetan Buddhist congregations, Friends of the Western Buddhist Order Estonia, and a small publishing house.

http://www.eesti.ee/eng/
http://www.estonica.org

Ringo Ringvee

See also: Estonian Apostolic Orthodox Church; Estonian Evangelical Lutheran Church; International Society for Krishna Consciousness; Roman Catholic Church; Russian Orthodox Church (Moscow Patriarchate); Salvation Army; Union of Evangelical Christians—Baptists of Russia.

References

Au, Ilmo, and Ringo Ringvee. *Usulised ühendused Eestis.* Tallinn, Estonia: Allika, 2007.

Raun, Toivo U. *Estonia and the Estonians.* Stanford, CA: Hoover Institution Press, 2001.

Ringvee, Ringo. "State, Religion and the Legal Framework in Estonia." *Religion, State and Society* 36, no. 2 (2008): 181–196.

Vakker, Triin, and Priit Rohtmets. "Estonia: Relations between Christian and Non-Christian Religious Organisations and the State of Religious Freedom." *Religion, State and Society* 36, no. 1 (2008): 45–53.

Vogelaar, Huub. "Ecumenical Relationships in Estonia." *Exchange: Journal of Missiological and Ecumenical Research* 37, no. 2 (2008): 190–219.

Estonian Apostolic Orthodox Church

The Orthodox community is the second largest religious group in Estonia. The Estonian Apostolic Orthodox Church (EAOC; Eesti Apostlik Õigeusu Kirik) is the third largest religious institution in Estonia. It has 3 dioceses with 58 congregations, and according to the EAOC it has approximately 25,000 members. The congregations are served by 27 priests and 10 deacons. The church has also two bishops, and it is led by Metropolitan Stefanus (1999). From 1923 the EAOC has belonged to the canonical jurisdiction of the Ecumenical Patriarchate.

For centuries the Orthodox faith in Estonia was mostly the faith of foreign traders or rulers, or the faith of the cultural minority of Setus in southeastern Estonia. However, during the 19th century, there were two conversion movements pressuring the indigenous peasantry to give up Lutheranism and join the Russian Orthodox Church. The reasons for these conversion movements were both economic and social: the peasantry expected to receive land and hoped to be protected from the Baltic-German landowners if they accepted the official religion of the Russian Empire.

After the declaration of Estonian independence in 1918, the Orthodox congregations in Estonia organized themselves as a church. In 1920, Patriarch Tikhon of Moscow gave autonomous status to the Orthodox Church in Estonia. In 1923 the EAOC came under the canonical jurisdiction of the Ecumenical Patriarchate of Constantinople as an autonomous church.

In 1940, after the incorporation of Estonia into the Soviet Union, the Russian Orthodox Church (Moscow Patriarchate) forced the EAOC to join the canonical jurisdiction of the Moscow Patriarchate, considering the decision from 1923 as schismatic. The situation changed in 1942 when under the German occupation Metropolitan Alexander of the EAOC re-established the church's independence from the Moscow Patriarchate. However, the Russian diocese of the EAOC remained under the jurisdiction of the Moscow Patriarchate.

In 1944, Metropolitan Alexander and 22 priests went into exile just before the Soviet troops invaded Estonia for the second time. In 1945 the representatives of the Russian Orthodox Church (Moscow Patriarchate) dissolved the synod of the EAOC in Estonia and formed a new structure, the Diocese Council of the Russian Orthodox Church. The EAOC was able to maintain its legal continuity in Sweden, serving the Estonian Orthodox community in exile. In 1978 Ecumenical Patriarch Demetrios I declared 1923 tomos to be inoperative in Estonia. In 1993 the EAOC re-established its structures in Estonia. This was followed by a long dispute between the EAOC and the Moscow Patriarchate over issues of church property, which was accompanied by the disputes between the Estonian government and the Moscow Patriarchate as the Estonian administration refused to register the former diocese of the Moscow Patriarchate in Estonia under the name and statute of the EAOC.

In 1996 Ecumenical Patriarch Bartholomew I restored 1923 tomos for the EAOC in Estonia. As the reaction to this, the Moscow Patriarchate cut off communion with the Ecumenical Patriarchate and with the autonomous Finnish Orthodox Church, which had supported the EAOC during the 1990s.

The disagreements concerning property issues ended in 2002 when the disputes on the church property were solved by agreements between the EAOC, EOCMP, and the Estonian government. However, the Moscow Patriarchate refuses to recognize the EAOC as an autonomous church, claiming Estonia as its canonical territory. In 2007 the EAOC became a member of the Conference of European Churches.

Estonian Apostolic Orthodox Church
Wismari 32
10136 Tallinn
Estonia
http://www.eoc.ee

Ringo Ringvee

See also: Ecumenical Patriarchate/Patriarchate of Constantinople; Russian Orthodox Church (Moscow Patriarchate).

References

Papathomas, Grigorios D., and Matthias H. Palli. *The Autonomous Orthodox Church of Estonia/L'Église autonome orthodoxe d'Estonie.* Athens: Épektasis, 2002.

Ringvee, Ringo. "Orthodox Churches in Estonia." *Estonian Culture* 1 (2003): 34–37. http://www.einst.ee/culture/I_MMIII/ringvee.html.

Estonian Evangelical Lutheran Church

The Estonian Evangelical Lutheran Church (EELC; Eesti Evangeelne Luterlik Kirik) is the largest religious organization in Estonia, with 164 congregations in Estonia, 3 congregations in Russia, and 1 congregation in Latvia. In 2007 the EELC reported having approximately 180,000 members. The church's consistory is situated in Tallinn. Since 2004 it has been led by its archbishop, Andres Põder.

Estonia was Christianized during the 13th century by the Roman Catholic Church and the Teutonic Order. The Reformation, in the form of Lutheranism, reached Estonia in 1524. During the period of Swedish rule (1625–1710), the hierarchy of the Lutheran Church was organized along episcopal lines, as was the case with the Church of Sweden. The Lutheran Church with its clergy played an important role in the history of Estonian religion and culture. Then, shortly after the end of the Russian Empire, the Lutheran congregations in Estonia started to develop an indigenous organization. The first Church Congress was held in 1917, and the EELC was officially founded in 1919 at the second Church Congress. The EELC was defined as the "free people's church," as the majority of the population were Lutherans.

After the incorporation of Estonia into the Soviet Union in 1940, major changes concerning the situation of religious organizations took place. By 1939, 53 of the church's 209 pastors had migrated to Germany, due to their German ancestry. In 1940 the Soviet authorities arrested several Lutheran pastors. The theological faculty of the University of Tartu was closed in 1940. Because of this closing, a new Theological Institute of the EELC was founded in 1943 during the years of German occupation. Today this institution still operates as an institution for the preparation of the clergy, as well as Sunday school teachers and the like. In 1944 approximately 70,000 Estonians, among them 72 Lutheran pastors, fled to the West because of the approaching Soviet army. After the war, they took the lead in forming the EELC Abroad.

The Soviet period had serious consequences for the EELC. During this period church life was controlled largely by the Soviet authorities, and the Soviet Marxist atheist campaigns marginalized the role of the EELC in the society. From the late 1980s on, during the period of national awakening that led to the re-establishment of the Estonian independence, the role of the EELC as the most traditional church in Estonia was stressed. In 1995 the Estonian government established a joint committee with the EELC for the discussions on matters concerning both parties. On the legislative level the EELC is treated on the same ground as other religious associations and the EELC does not have any specific privileges.

Internationally the EELC belongs to the World Council of Churches (1961) and to the Lutheran World Federation (1963). In 1996 the EELC signed the Porvoo Declaration, a statement of agreement with the Anglican and Scandinavian Lutheran churches. The ordination of women started in 1967. In 2008, 37 of the 142 EELC clergy were women.

Estonian Evangelical Lutheran Church
Kiriku plats 3
10130 Tallinn
Estonia
http://www.eelk.ee/

Ringo Ringvee and J. Gordon Melton

See also: Estonian Evangelical Lutheran Church Abroad; Lutheran World Federation; Roman Catholic Church; World Council of Churches.

References

Altnurme, Riho. "Foreign Relations of the Estonian Evangelical Lutheran Church as a Means of Maintaining Contact with the Western World." *Kirchliche Zeitgeschichte/Contemporary Church History* 19, no. 1 (2006): 159–165.

Veem, Konrad. *Vaba Eesti Rahvakirik*. Stockholm: EVR, 1988.

We Bless You from the House of the Lord: The Estonian Evangelical Lutheran Church Today. Tallinn, Estonia: Consistory of the EELC, 1997.

Estonian Evangelical Lutheran Church Abroad

The Estonian Evangelical Lutheran Church Abroad (EELCA; Eesti Evangeeliumi Luteri Usu Kirik) was formed in 1944 among Estonian refugees in Sweden. Currently the EELCA has 63 congregations all over the world—in Sweden, Germany, England, France, the United States, Canada, Australia, and Brazil. Its approximate membership is more than 15,000. The church is led by Archbishop Andres Taul (2007) and the consistory of the church, which is located in Toronto.

In 1944, due to the traumatic experiences of the first Soviet occupation (1940–1941), approximately 70,000 Estonians fled from Estonia to the West, mainly Sweden and Germany, before the Soviet troops occupied the country. The majority of the refugees were Lutherans. Among the expatriates were 72 Lutheran pastors, including the head of the Estonian Evangelical Lutheran Church (EELC), Bishop Johan Kõpp. The first new pastors were ordained in 1947 in German refugee camps.

All the statutes of the EELC were reestablished abroad in 1958. The consistory of the EELCA is situated in the country where the archbishop resides. The EELCA has been the maintainer of the Estonian

Dome of the Toomkirik, an Estonian Evangelical Lutheran church in Tallinn, Estonia. (Focus Database/StockphotoPro)

national identity for the diaspora community, which traditionally maintains church services in the Estonian language. Through the last decades of the 20th century the membership declined, as second- and third-generation Estonians assimilated to the population of their country of residence. During the period of Soviet occupation of Estonia, the EELCA provided religious literature for the EELC at home.

On the international level, the EELCA was one of the founding members of the Lutheran World Federation (1947) and of the World Council of Churches (1948). It is also a member of the Conference of European Churches. Since 1978, the EELCA has also sponsored an educational institution for the clergy, the Theological Institute of the EELCA. The negotiations between the Estonian Evangelical Lutheran Church

and the EELCA on the issue of unification of the two churches started in the 1990s.

Estonian Evangelical Lutheran Church Abroad
383 Jarvis St.
Toronto, ON M5B 2C7
Canada
http://eelk.org/index.php
http://www.eelk.ee/eng_EELCabroad.html

Ringo Ringvee

See also: Estonian Evangelical Lutheran Church; Lutheran World Federation; World Council of Churches.

References

Veem, Konrad. *Vaba Eesti Rahvakirik*. Stockholm: EVR, 1988.
We Bless You from the House of the Lord: The Estonian Evangelical Lutheran Church Today. Tallinn, Estonia: Consistory of the EELC, 1997.

Estonian Orthodox Church of Moscow Patriarchate

The Estonian Orthodox Church of Moscow Patriarchate (EOCMP; Moskva Patriarhaadi Eesti Õigeusu Kirik) is the second largest religious institution in Estonia with approximately 170,000 members (2007). The EOCMP has 31 congregations, 44 priests, and 11 deacons. The church is led by Metropolitan Kornily (until 2000 as bishop).

Although the Orthodox Christianity has been in Estonia since 11th century, the official presence of the Moscow Patriarchate in Estonia is dated back to the 18th century, when the Orthodox congregations became part of the Pskov Diocese of the Russian Orthodox Church. In 1920 Patriarch Tikhon of Moscow gave autonomous status to the Orthodox Church in Estonia. In 1923 the Estonian Apostolic Orthodox Church came under the canonical jurisdiction of Ecumenical Patriarchate.

The presence of the Moscow Patriarchate in Estonia was re-established in 1940 after the Soviet occupation of Estonia. In 1945 the diocese of the Russian Orthodox Church was established after the dissolution of the autonomous Estonian Apostolic Orthodox Church. During the Soviet period from 1945 to 1991 many Orthodox churches were closed. Also the ethnic structure of the Orthodox population changed during the Soviet period due to the massive immigration from other parts of the Soviet Union to Estonia; the majority of the Orthodox were now ethnic Russians. The diocese was administrated from 1961 to 1990 by Metropolitan Alexy, who was in 1990 elected patriarch of the Russian Orthodox Church as Alexy II. In 1993 the patriarch of Moscow gave tomos to the diocese, recognizing it as an autonomous church.

In 1993 the Estonian Apostolic Orthodox Church re-established itself in Estonia. Subsequently the Estonian authorities refused to recognize the diocese of the Moscow Patriarchate as legal successor of the pre-Soviet Estonian Apostolic Orthodox Church, which meant that the church property nationalized during the Soviet period was restituted to the Estonian Apostolic Orthodox Church. This decision was followed by serious confrontation between the Moscow Patriarchate and the Estonian government. From 1995 on this conflict became an important factor in the relations between the Russian Federation and Estonia. In 2002 the Estonian authorities registered the former diocese as EOCMP although it was not recognized as the legal successor of the pre-Soviet Estonian Apostolic Orthodox Church. The property issues were regulated by the trilateral agreements between the Estonian Apostolic Orthodox Church, the Estonian government, and the EOCMP.

The Moscow Patriarchate has also two stavropegial institutions in Estonia: Alexander Nevsky Congregation in Tallinn and Pukhtitsa nunnery in Kuremäe.

Estonian Orthodox Church of Moscow Patriarchate
Pikk 64-4
10133 Tallinn
Estonia
http://www.orthodox.ee/

Ringo Ringvee

See also: Estonian Apostolic Orthodox Church; Russian Orthodox Church (Moscow Patriarchate).

References

Alexy, Patriarch. *Pravoslaviye v Estonii.* Moscow: Pravoslavnaja Entsiklopedija, 1999.

Ringvee, Ringo. "Orthodox Churches in Estonia." *Estonian Culture* 1 (2003): 34–37. http://www.einst.ee/culture/I_MMIII/ringvee.html.

■ Ethiopia

Ethiopia, a landlocked northeast African nation, is surrounded by Sudan, Kenya, Somalia, Djibouti, and Eritrea. For a variety of geographical reasons, its 432,000 square miles were able to remain largely free of European colonial ambitions, and its citizens are proud of their ancient civilization.

Ethiopia is home to a variety of Native peoples, the majority being Galla or Amhara. Around 2000 BCE

Bet Giyorgis (St. George's), one of a number of rock-hewn churches built by Lalibela, a Christian king of Ethiopia during the 12th and 13th centuries CE. (iStockPhoto.com)

Ethiopia

Religion	Followers in 1970	Followers in 2010	% of Population	Annual % growth 2000–2010	Followers in 2025	Followers in 2050
Christians	15,921,000	52,477,000	58.6	2.71	75,052,000	112,046,000
Orthodox	11,072,000	35,570,000	39.7	2.70	49,540,000	72,700,000
Protestants	746,000	14,400,000	16.1	3.36	21,800,000	33,050,000
Independents	132,000	1,500,000	1.7	4.14	2,600,000	4,300,000
Muslims	9,000,000	30,457,000	34.0	2.69	42,550,000	62,500,000
Ethnoreligionists	4,875,000	6,400,000	7.1	1.69	7,000,000	8,000,000
Agnostics	0	170,000	0.2	2.62	300,000	700,000
Baha'is	7,000	30,300	0.0	2.62	50,000	75,000
Jews	28,000	13,100	0.0	2.63	14,000	18,000
Atheists	0	12,000	0.0	2.62	20,000	50,000
Hindus	0	6,500	0.0	2.63	10,000	15,000
Total population	**29,831,000**	**89,566,000**	**100.0**	**2.62**	**124,996,000**	**183,404,000**

the Habbashat, an Arab people from Yemen, moved into the region, and it is from them that Ethiopia also became known as Abyssinia. The early center of Ethiopia was Axum, a city along the trade route from the Red Sea to the southern Sudan.

An Ethiopian kingdom arose early in the Christian era and expanded across the Red Sea into present-day Yemen. In the fourth century, the royal family accepted Christianity, and gradually the Christian faith came to dominate the land. The kingdom suffered from the gradual movement of Islam, first through the Arab peninsula and Egypt and then along the East African coast. Feeling somewhat stifled by the Muslim world that now largely surrounded them, the rulers appealed to Christian Europe for assistance in the 15th century. Their appeal finally resulted in the arrival of the Portuguese in the next century and the destruction of Muslim power in Somalia.

The next centuries saw the rivalry between the Amhara (who had ruled Ethiopia) and the Gallas come to the fore. The Gallas gained the throne for a brief period in the middle of the 18th century, but eventually the Amharas re-established control.

At the end of the 19th century, the Italians invaded Ethiopia as part of their dream of an empire in Africa. They were soundly defeated in 1895, but were able to take control of Eritrea and the coast of the southern part of Somalia. The Italians again invaded in 1935, and they held Ethiopia until replaced by the British in 1941. Independence returned in 1948 under Haile Selassie.

Selassie ruled until he was overthrown in 1974. The underlying cause of unrest had been the stranglehold on the country held by Ethiopian royalty and the Ethiopian church, which together owned the great majority of the country. A military government, sympathetic to Marxist socialism, eventually took over in 1977, but faced a number of dissenting groups and constant violence and civil war through the 1980s. The military ruler, Mengistu Haile Mariam (b. 1937), was finally overthrown in 1991 but the new government faced a period of intense social conflict. It worked out a peace with the primary dissident group that controlled Eritrea, which became an independent country, and then turned to deal with the problem of the widespread famine, which had been exacerbated by the war.

Although some traditional African religions still exist in Ethiopia, the majority of the population are Christians and members of the Ethiopian Orthodox Tewahedo Church. Traditional religion is strongest in the southwestern part of the county (in lands bordering Kenya and the Sudan).

Following the acceptance of Christianity by the ruling elite, the Ethiopian church has had a strong relationship with the Coptic Orthodox Church of Egypt and followed it in its break with the larger world of Eastern Orthodoxy during the Monophysite controversy in the fifth century. The Monophysites, whose name comes from the Greek for "one nature," tended to emphasize the divine nature of Christ to the point of sacrificing his fully human nature. The Eastern Ortho-

ETHIOPIA

Map of Ethiopia showing cities including Adi Dairo, Inda Silase, Adigrat, Wik'ro, Abiy Adi, Mek'ele, Maych'ew, Gonder, Azezo, Korem, Lalibela, K'obo, Werota, Weldiya, Bahir Dar, Mot'a, Dese, Bati, Bure, Debre Werk', Debre Mark'os, Mendi, Debra Sina, Erer-Gota, Dire Dawa, Ethiopia, Harar, Jijiga, Addis Ababa, Nek'emte, Debre Zeyit, Dembi Dolo, Giyon, Nazret, Mechara, Metu, Mek'i, Gore, Asela, Agaro, Jima, Awasa, Shashemene, Mizan Teferi, Sodo, Wendo, Goba, Imi, Werder, Dila, Arba Minch', Kibre Mengist, Yabelo, Negele, Kelem, Dolo Odo.

dox in communion with the Ecumenical Patriarchate held that Christ had two natures (human and divine), as defined in the Chalcedonian Creed, adopted at the council held in Chalcedon in 451. In modern perspective, the controversy appears to have been essentially a jockeying for control of the Egyptian church that was fought out in theological terms.

Through the centuries, the relation of the Ethiopian church as a daughter to the Egyptian church was symbolized by the regular appointment of an Egyptian as the *abuna* (archbishop) of the Ethiopian church by the head of the Coptic church. That relationship only ended in 1959, when the head of the church became an Ethiopian, bearing the title of patriarch-catholicos.

Abune Bacilios was named the first patriarch. The church is currently led by Abune Paulos, the fifth patriarch.

The Ethiopian church developed a unique relationship with Islam when some of the early followers of Muhammad visited the country in 662 CE. This visit is often quoted by Muslims as an important event establishing Islam's traditional tolerant stance toward the other religions of the Book (Christianity and Judaism). The Coptic church supported the country's resistance to the expansion of Islam as neighboring lands became predominantly Muslim.

Islam (of the Shafaiite School) gained a permanent stronghold in Ethiopia among several of the peoples in the southeastern part of the country near the border with Somalia. Danan is an important intellectual center, and Goba, a city farther inland and nearer the capital, Adis Ababa, annually hosts thousands of pilgrims on their way to the town of Ginir, where the body of Sheikh Hussein, considered a saint in Ethiopia, is entombed. Other Muslims are concentrated in the far east of the country near the Sudanese border. They currently make up some 30 percent of Ethiopia's residents.

The Roman Catholic Church came into the country in the 16th century, and some attempts were made to absorb the Ethiopian church into Roman Catholicism. Some progress to this end was made in the 17th century, when the head of the church briefly identified as a Catholic. However, some of the missionaries proved tactless and, among other things, attempted to impose the Latin liturgy on the land. In reaction, the missionaries were kicked out of the country and were not allowed to return until the 19th century. However, when they returned, they were identified with the Italians, and they were again ejected. The church survived, however, as Italian lay people were not forced to leave.

The church finally developed an Ethiopic liturgy that retained as much of the Coptic liturgy as was possible. Today a community of several hundred thousand Roman Catholics exists in Ethiopia, the great majority following the Ethiopic liturgy, though Latin- and Ethiopic-rite congregations operate within the same dioceses. The church is led by the archbishop of Addis Ababa.

Protestantism entered the country through the efforts of a spectrum of Lutheran missionaries, beginning in 1866 with some from the Swedish Lutheran Mission. Subsequently, in 1911, Swedish missionaries representing the independent True Friends of the Bible arrived. The two groups united their work in 1938. German missionaries from the Hermannsburg Mission arrived in 1927. Missionaries from Norway, Denmark, Iceland, and the United States arrived through the 1940s and 1950s. Much of the Lutheran work was brought together in the Ethiopian Evangelical Church Mekane Yesus. American Presbyterians arrived in 1920 and began work among the Galla people. When the Italians arrived, the Presbyterian missionaries were expelled, and before leaving they organized their mission as the Bethel Evangelical Church. In the mid-1970s, it merged into the Mekane Jesus Church.

The Sudan Interior Mission (SIM) launched its expansive work in Ethiopia in 1927; Dr. Thomas A. Lambie (1885–1954), who had been working with the Presbyterians, began an independent work that he called the Abyssinian Frontier Mission. He merged his mission into SIM. Working primarily among the Galla people, the mission built a following of some 60 members, but after the expulsion of the missionaries in 1935, expanded rapidly. There were 18,000 by the time the British arrived. By the mid-1970s there were 182,000 members, and as the Word of Life Church/ Kale Heywet, it has become the largest Protestant work in the country, with more than 2 million members as of the 1990s.

In the years since World War II, additional Protestant groups have begun work in Ethiopia, including the Baptist General Conference of America, which entered the country in 1950. Pentecostalism came into the country in the postwar years, and two large indigenous churches have resulted, the Full Gospel Believers Church and Gods All Times Association, which between them have half a million members. Both of these churches have been encouraged by assistance and personnel from Scandinavian Pentecostal bodies.

Among the most interesting of Ethiopian groups has been the Beta Israel, a Jewish group that existed in the Gondar region north of Lake Tana. They were the subject of much persecution at various periods of the 20th century, even as they fought for recognition by the larger Jewish community that had finally taken notice of their existence. In the 1990s, most of the group (which at its height numbered some 28,000) migrated to Israel (which finally recognized them under the Law of Return in 1994). Around 12,000 remain in Ethiopia.

The Baha'i Faith established its first spiritual assembly in 1964. Today there are almost 20,000 adherents. A variety of new religions have arrived, most African Initiated Churches from nearby countries. Though several Buddhist groups responded to Ethiopian needs during the recent famine conditions in the country, no Buddhist or Hindu groups appear to have been formed.

The Ethiopian Constitution guarantees religious freedom. Though the Orthodox church is in the majority, it is not considered the state church and is not officially privileged. Additional regulations forbid the forming of partisan political parties based on religious allegiance and incitement of religious quarrels. All religious groups are required to register themselves and renew such registration tri-annually.

J. Gordon Melton

See also: African Initiated (Independent) Churches; Baha'i Faith; Beta Israel; Coptic Orthodox Church; Ecumenical Patriarchate/Patriarchate of Constantinople; Ethiopian Evangelical Church Mekane Yesus; Ethiopian Orthodox Tewahedo Church; Pentecostalism; Roman Catholic Church; Shafaiite School of Islam; Word of Life Church.

References

Eide, Oyvind M. *Revolution & Religion in Ethiopia: Growth & Persecution Of Mekane Yesus Church.* Athens: Ohio State University Press, 2000.

Engelsviken, T. *Molo Wingel: A Documentary Report on the Life and History of the Independent Pentecostal Movement in Ethiopia, 1960–1975.* Oslo: Free Faculty of Theology, 1975.

Erlich, Haggai. *Saudi Arabia and Ethiopia: Islam, Christianity, and Politics Entwined.* Boulder, CO: Lynne Rienner Publishers, 2006.

Horner, N. A. *Rediscovering Christianity Where It Began: A Survey of Contemporary Churches in the Middle East and Ethiopia.* Beirut: Near East Council of Churches, 1974.

Levine, Donald N. *Greater Ethiopia: The Evolution of a Multiethnic Society.* Chicago: University of Chicago Press, 2000.

Liesel, N. *The Eastern Catholic Liturgy: A Study in Words and Pictures.* Westminster, MD: Newman Press, 1960.

Marcus, Harold G. *A History of Ethiopia.* Berkeley: University of California Press, 2002.

Molnar, Enrico S. *The Ethiopian Orthodox Church.* Pasadena, CA: Bloy House Theological School, 1969.

Trimingham, J. S. *The Christian Church and Mission in Ethiopia (including Eritrea and the Somalilands).* London: World Dominion Press, 1950.

Trimingham, J. S. *Islam in Ethiopia.* London: Routledge, 2007.

Yesehaq, Archbishop. *The Ethiopian Tewahedo Church: An Integrally African Church.* Nashville: Winston-Derek Publishers, 1997.

Ethiopian Catholic Church

The Ethiopian Orthodox Tewahedo Church was a branch of the Coptic Orthodox Church based in Egypt and like it failed to affirm the formulation of doctrine promulgated by the Council of Chalcedon in the fifth century. The Chalcedonian Creed affirmed that Christ existed as one person with both a human and a divine nature. The Monophysites (from the Greek for "one nature"), who predominated in the Egyptian church, held that Christ had only a divine nature. For many centuries after the establishment of Islam across North Africa, Ethiopia was cut off from the rest of the Christian world. It was rediscovered in the 15th century, and missionaries of the Roman Catholic Church launched efforts to bring the Ethiopian church into union with Rome.

In 1622, the king of Ethiopia declared himself Catholic and his nation a Catholic state. The following year, the pope appointed Affonso Mendez, a Portuguese Jesuit, the first patriarch of the new Ethiopian Catholic Church. He was installed in 1626. He lost popular support, however, when he tried to Latinize the liturgy. When the king died, his successor banished Mendez and ended the union of the Ethiopian church with Rome.

Catholic missionaries did not re-enter the country until the end of the 19th century, and the church did not expand significantly until the years of the Italian occupation (1935–1941), and not until 1961 was an episcopal see, headquartered at Addis Ababa, erected. Additional suffragan dioceses were established in Asmara and Adigrat.

In 1993, Eritrea became independent of Ethiopia. Approximately half of the Ethiopian Catholic membership resided in the new country; as a result two additional dioceses (Keren, Barentu), and eventually a third, were created. Most of the 223,000 members of the Ethiopian Catholic Church are in the two countries. The Ethiopian Catholic Church, distinguished by its use of the Ethiopic rite, now has six diocese (eparchies), three in Eritrea and three in Ethiopia. The church is currently headed by Archbishop Berhaneyesus Demerew Souraphiel (b. 1948), who took office in 1999. There is also a large presence of Latin-rite Catholics in Ethiopia whose congregations are organized into five vicariates and two apostolic prefectures. Vicariates and apostolic prefectures may be understood as provisional dioceses that have been established in an area where it is expected that a diocese will be created in the relatively near future.

Ethiopian Catholic Church
Catholic Archbishop's House
PO Box 21903
Addis Ababa
Ethiopia
http://www.ecs.org.et/

J. Gordon Melton

See also: Coptic Orthodox Church; Ethiopian Orthodox Tewahedo Church; Roman Catholic Church.

References
Liesel, N. *The Eastern Catholic Liturgies: A Study in Words and Pictures.* Westminster, MD: Newman Press, 1960.
Roberson, Ronald G. *The Eastern Christian Churches—A Brief Survey.* 5th ed. Rome: Edizioni Orientalia Christiana, Pontificio Istituto Orientale, 1995.

Ethiopian Evangelical Church Mekane Yesus

The Ethiopian Evangelical Church Mekane Yesus was founded in 1959 by the churches that had grown out of the several missions created by different Lutheran missionary agencies that had been operating in Ethiopia through the 20th century. Lutheran work began with missionaries of the Swedish Evangelical Mission in Eritrea in 1866. Through the next decade, they worked with two converts. They eventually opened a mission in Jima, in the Province of Kefa. They purchased slaves who were then invited to become Christians and educated the neighborhood children in their

school. Workers with the mission also helped translate the Bible into one of the Ethiopian languages, Oromo. Through the next decades, the Swedish Evangelical Mission grew primarily among the Oromo-speaking people, though the missionaries encouraged the developing evangelical movement within the Ethiopian Orthodox Tewahedo Church that had resulted from the earlier translation of the Bible into Amharic (or Amarigna).

Through the next decades, other Lutheran groups established work in the country: the Swedish Mission of Bible True Friends (1921), the German Hermannsburg Mission (1927), the Norwegian Lutheran Mission (1948), the Icelandic Mission (1952), and the Danish Ethiopian Mission (1952). The earlier missions suffered during the occupation of the country by the Italians (1936–1941). Not only were the missionaries exiled, but a number of the leaders in the church were arrested and executed. However, the church not only survived, it prospered. In 1941 the congregation in Addis Ababa reorganized apart from the Swedish Evangelical Mission and through the decade emerged as the center of the indigenous Protestant movement in the country. In 1944 it called the first Conference of Ethiopian Evangelical Churches that would meet annually, apart from the missionaries' input and attendance, and work toward the creation of a single Ethiopian evangelical church.

A significant move to unite the Lutheran work in Ethiopia was initiated in 1947 by the Lutheran World Federation, which has called upon Lutherans around the world to seek unity in their own countries. A visit by a Lutheran World Federation representative led to the formation of the Lutheran Missions Committee, which in turn launched several cooperative efforts to assist all the missions, most notably the Ethiopian Evangelical College, opened at Debre Zeyt in 1956. By the mid-1950s, considerable effort was evident in planning for a united Lutheran church, culminating in the formation of the Ethiopian Evangelical Church Mekane Yesus in 1959. The church was received into the Lutheran World Federation in 1963 and the World Council of Churches in 1972.

The church has grown by a series of mergers. In 1965, the Kambata Evangelical Church, formerly a synod of the Word of Life Church/Kale Heywet, merged into the Ethiopian Evangelical Church. Meanwhile in Europe, discussion between Lutheran and Reformed churches led to the Leuenberg Agreement, which offered a statement of understanding and alignment between the two communions. Based upon that agreement, the Evangelical Church Bethel merged into the Ethiopian Evangelical Church. The Bethel church originated in 1919 when a flu epidemic hit Ethiopia and the government requested Thomas Alexander Lambie (1885–1954), a medical missionary working in the Sudan, to come to Ethiopia.

He and other American Presbyterian missionaries who came afterward decided to work toward the renewal of the Orthodox church rather than set up separate Presbyterian church congregations. However, when the missionaries were kicked out in 1936, those who had been affected by their work moved to set up a church in the Reformed tradition in 1940. It was formally constituted as the Evangelical Church Bethel in 1947. In 1970 it was received into the World Alliance of Reformed Churches, though that association was dropped in 1974.

The church has more than four million members (2005). It went through a period of rapid growth between 1977 and 1983 during which the membership doubled. It also has affiliated congregations in Europe formed by members who have moved to Scandinavia. These congregations have organized the Northern Europe Mekane Yesus Fellowship.

The church is organized into synods and the quadrennial synodical convention is the highest legislative body. It is led by a president who is assisted by an executive committee and general secretary. The church supports the Mekane Yesus Seminary in Addis Ababa. In 1998, the church organized a peace, justice, and advocacy commission to work at various levels in the cause of peace-making.

Ethiopian Evangelical Church
Jomo Kenyatta Road
PO Box 2087
Addis Ababa
Ethiopia

J. Gordon Melton

See also: Ethiopian Orthodox Tewahedo Church; Lutheran World Federation; Word of Life Church; World Alliance of Reformed Churches; World Council of Churches.

References

Aren, Gustav. *Evangelical Pioneers in Ethiopia: Origins of the Evangelical Church Mekane Yesus*. Addis Ababa, Ethiopia: Evangelical Church Mekane Yesus, 1978.

Bachmann, E. Theodore, and Mercia Brenne Bachmann. *Lutheran Churches in the World: A Handbook*. Minneapolis, MN: Augsburg Press, 1989.

Bauswein, Jean-Jacques, and Lukas Vischner, eds. *The Reformed Family Worldwide: A Survey of Reformed Churches, Theological Schools, and International Organizations*. Grand Rapids, MI: William B. Eerdmans Publishing Company, 1999.

Edie, Oyvind M. *Revolution and Religion in Ethiopia: The Growth and Persecution of the Mekane Yesus Church, 1974–85*. Abingdon, Oxon, UK: James Currey, 2000.

Van Beek, Huibert. *A Handbook of the Churches and Councils: Profiles of Ecumenical Relationships*. Geneva: World Council of Churches, 2006.

Ethiopian Orthodox Tewahedo Church

Christianity's appearance in Ethiopia is generally attributed to Frumentius (ca. 300–ca. 380), a Greek Christian. According to the story, while on a voyage through the Red Sea, he was captured along with his brother, and both were taken to the ancient capital of Ethiopia at Axum as slaves. Placed in the service of the king, like the biblical Joseph, he won the king's favor and was given a position of trust. As a part of his privileges, he was allowed to preach his Christian faith. He eventually won over the king and court to the new faith, and the door was open to convert the country. Frumentius's brother was ordained as a priest, and in 339 Frumentius was consecrated by the Patriarchate of Alexandria (Egypt) as the first bishop of Ethiopia. He is credited with translating the Bible into the Ethiopian language.

The Ethiopian church developed as a daughter church of the Egyptian church. Several centuries after

Timkat celebration, an important festival in the Ethiopian Orthodox Tewahedo Church, in which people renew their baptismal vows. (Carolyne Pehora/Dreamstime.com)

its founding it became involved in a controversy between the patriarch of Alexandria and the other bishops of the Christian church over the nature of Christ. As part of their attempt to refine Christian understanding of God, the church considered the mystery of Christ's dual nature as both God and human. The patriarch of Alexander argued that Christ's divine nature was primary, an opinion that deemphasized the human nature of Jesus. The rest of the church went on (in the fifth century) to reach a consensus that Christ was both fully human and fully divine. This "orthodox" position was included in the Chalcedonian Creed, adopted by the church's bishops in 451 at the Council of Chalcedon. The patriarch of Alexandria continued to adhere to the Nicene Creed (of 325), which is compatible with both the Monophysite (from the Greek for "one nature") position and that of the "orthodox" churches.

The argument split the church, and most of the Egyptians followed the patriarch into what is now known as the Coptic Orthodox Church.

Except for this question of Christ's nature, the Ethiopian church is at one with Eastern Orthodoxy and traditional Christian faith. The church follows the Coptic Church in its veneration of the Virgin Mary. However, it differs in its acceptance of the Apocrypha (books written between the period of the last books of the Hebrew Bible and the first century CE). It also recognizes some Old Testament figures as saints, holds Saturday as an additional holy day, and observes many Jewish dietary rules.

The Ethiopian church was cut off from the Christian world in the eighth century by the rise of Islam. Isolated, Ethiopia was able to remain autonomous in its mountainous homeland. In the 13th century, the

Christian state reached the height of its power, and King Lalibela gave his name to a city of churches, 10 of which were carved from solid rock. It almost merged into the Roman Catholic Church in the 17th century, but pulled back in reaction to the tactless activities of Catholic missionaries. In the 20th century, responding to attempts to heal the rifts of the ancient church, the Ethiopian Orthodox Tewahedo ("Unity") Church has become a member of the World Council of Churches.

The church does not have an official website. There are several expansive unofficial pages at http://members.nbci.com/redingtn/eth.html and http://www.prairienet.org/dxmages/eotc.htm. The church is headed by its patriarch, currently Abuna Paulos. In 2005, it reports some 38,956,000 members in Ethiopia. There are also dioceses in Sudan, Djibouti (covering East Africa), Jerusalem, London, Trinidad, and the United States. Its membership in neighboring Eritrea was set aside as an autonomous body in 1994.

Ethiopian Orthodox Tewahedo Church
PO Box 728
Asmara
Ethiopia

J. Gordon Melton

See also: Coptic Orthodox Church; World Council of Churches.

References

The Church of Ethiopia: A Panorama of History and Spiritual Life. Addis Ababa: The Ethiopian Orthodox Church, 1970.

Molnar, Enrico S. *The Ethiopian Orthodox Church.* Pasadena, CA: Bloy House Theological School, 1969.

Shenk, C. E. "The Development of the Ethiopian Orthodox Church and Its Relationship with the Ethiopian Government from 1930 to 1970." Ph.D. diss., New York University, 1972.

Van Beek, Huibert. *A Handbook of the Churches and Councils: Profiles of Ecumenical Relationships*. Geneva: World Council of Churches, 2006.

Yesehaq, Archbishop. *The Ethiopian Tewahedo Church: An Integrally African Church*. Nashville: Winston-Derek Publishers, 1997.

Ethiopian Zion Coptic Church

The Ethiopian Zion Coptic Church is a small body that traces its history to Marcus Garvey (1887–1940), the Jamaican reformer and advocate for African Americans, but gained a reputation of a different kind following the arrest of several of its leaders in 1978 for breaking the antidrug laws in the United States. Garvey founded the church in 1914 in Jamaica as a religious affiliate of his Universal Negro Improvement Association, and although it blossomed briefly in the 1920s, it died out in the United States. It survived in Jamaica as a very small body and became associated with the Rastafarians, known for their use of *ganja* (marijuana) as a mood-altering substance for religious purposes.

In 1970, several Americans in Jamaica encountered the church. They joined and established a church center on Star Island off Miami Beach, in Florida. Under the leadership of Thomas Reilly Jr., the American leader, a second center opened in New Jersey. Over the next several years the church had a variety of interactions with government authorities. In 1973, law enforcement authorities seized 105 tons of marijuana from the group. However, that did not prevent the church from finally receiving its tax-exempt status as a religious organization two years later. The church immediately filed a lawsuit against the government, demanding that its members be allowed to use marijuana.

The church had arisen on the heels of the widespread discovery of marijuana and other psychedelic substances by young people in the 1960s and the founding of a spectrum of groups that used various substances (LSD, peyote, and the like), all of which were considered controlled substances by the American government. The Ethiopian Zion Coptic Church believes that smoking marijuana is equivalent to making a burnt offering to God. The members believe that by smoking marijuana and thus consuming the psychoactive ingredient in the plant they will be able to change their body chemistry and thus survive into God's new world after the end of this world. The new world will be a time of peace and brotherhood and of such abundance that people will no longer have to work. They call upon the Bible to support their belief (Genesis 1:29; Exodus 3:2–4; Psalm 104:14; Hebrews 6:7).

In spite of their belief, in 1978 the court ruled against their members being allowed to use marijuana even in a religious context, and immediately afterward law enforcement agents raided the church center on Star Island. Finding illegal substances, the police arrested a number of church leaders, and after a long adjudication process they were convicted in 1981. In jail, they petitioned for the right to have marijuana, but were again denied. Through the 1970s, other drug-oriented churches in the United States (with one exception, the Native American Church) also were handed a series of negative court rulings.

The church survives in the United States, but headquarters remain where members operate a 4,000-acre farm. Unfavorable court rulings decimated the American membership though several thousand member reside in Jamaica. A website is maintained by church member Carl Olsen at http://www.ethiopianzioncoptic church.org/. Olsen has continued the church's legal battle and found hope in the favorable ruling received by members of the Native American Church relative to the use of peyote and the more recent 2006 ruling in favor of the Brazilian-based União do Vegetal that uses ayahuasca. The rulings have been based on provisions of the Religious Freedom Restoration Act. The adjudication process for the Ethiopian Zion Coptic Church continues. On December 8, 2008, Olsen filed a Petition for Writ of Certiorar, a petition to ask the Supreme Court to review the lower court judgments against the church.

Ethiopian Zion Coptic Church
Carl E. Olsen, Director, Incorporator
PO Box 4091
Des Moines, IA 50333
http://www.ethiopianzioncopticchurch.org/

J. Gordon Melton

See also: Native American Church; Rastafarians.

Reference
Marijuana and the Bible. Hialeah, FL: Ethiopian Zion Coptic Church, n.d.

Ethnoreligions

The term "ethnoreligion" designates a group of religions also termed primal religions, Native religions, indigenous religions, and most frequently in this volume traditional religions. The term refers to those thousands of religions practiced by the many, relatively small, surviving ethnic groups around the world. The religions themselves are relatively small in that, compared to Buddhism or Islam, for example, they are confined to a single particular ethnic (or sub-ethnic) group centered in a limited geographical locale. Adherents of the religion are usually tied together by a local language (some 5,000 such local languages still exist) and are related to each other as members of the same kinship group. In general, one is born into the group, and except under unusual circumstances, new members from outside the ethnic group are not admitted. Most of these groups are pre-literary, that is, they exist in cultures in which written languages may have only been introduced in the last two centuries, and what literature exists has not become a factor in the perpetuation of the religion.

In the 19th century, such ethnoreligions were viewed as lower in the evolutionary scale, less advanced forms of the religious life. Those scholars who developed the comparative study of religion often attempted to build a hierarchy of religions, in which invariably Christianity appeared at the apex and these religions formed the base. Over the 19th and 20th centuries, many ethnoreligions disappeared as their adherents were absorbed into one of the larger religious communities.

Various considerations led to a re-evaluation of ethnoreligions in the 20th century. A more sophisticated approach to history has challenged the ease with which presently existing tribal religions are equated with what might have existed in the ancient past. Scholars now understand that religions exist in time and change and develop over time. Scholars are now more hesitant to equate what they find in the present,

Macumba practitioners prepare food for the *orixas* (gods) before a ceremony begins honoring a novice being inducted into the temple, Rio de Janeiro. (Stephanie Maze/Corbis)

even among the most isolated of groups, with what might have existed in the ancient past. They have also discovered that geographically limited communities were frequently tied to large trading networks that operated over large distances and were continuing spurs to transformation.

In the 20th century, scholars also developed a new appreciation of the levels of sophistication and appropriateness of the ideology underlying most ethnoreligions. Such sophistication was often obscured by the Western missionaries who for many years were the main conduits of information concerning the majority of ethnoreligionists. At the same time, rather than seeing a sharp break between "primitive" and "higher" religions, scholars now see a continuum of ethnogroups, which would include literary traditions such as Shinto and Judaism or a relatively new ethnoreligion like

Sikhism. Hinduism can even be seen as a cluster of ethnoreligions.

Shinto, Judaism, and Sikhism aside, most ethnoreligions share characteristics that set them apart as a distinctive set of religions. The great majority of ethnoreligions operate as oral traditions. The chronicles of Christianity, in particular, have been filled in the past centuries with accounts of initial missionaries to a different people who spent their first years reducing a language to writing and producing a grammar, a Bible, and a hymnbook or liturgy. Such work has been integrated into the spread of Christianity since the 17th century among Native Americans and in primal cultures around the world. However, in the face of the global movement of Christianity, Buddhism, and Islam, many people have chosen to remain adherents to their traditional faiths.

While expressing a wide variety of theologies and mythologies, ethnoreligions tend to have a primary concern with power. They developed in situations in which the struggle for basic survival was a constant concern and lacked the contemporary tools that have been supplied by science and technology. They had to deal with disease, natural calamities, and limited resources while seeking means to predict, control, and overcome them. At the same time, they shared the common human experiences of spirit being; heightened states of consciousness; and moments of success, transcendence, and empowerment.

Both their physical environment and inner experience provided the elements from which a worldview would be constructed. That worldview would integrate the totality of existence from the mundane to the transcendent, and it would be developed in such a manner that modern distinctions such as sacred and secular or religious and nonreligious would not exist. Given the holistic nature of many ethnoreligions, some have argued that it is improper to think of the group as having a religion at all, suggesting instead that spirituality pervades their life. One can, however, provide some overview of ethnoreligions based upon a religious analysis.

Most ethnoreligions include reference to a pantheon of deities, usually headed by a being that is seen as a first deity who directly creates or is the source of lesser deities, the created world, and humanity. The account of the world of this deity is told in stories (which together constitute a myth), which account for the origins of the group and the land they inhabit. The primal deity is often remote and inaccessible, and hence any relationships are with the myriad gods and goddesses. The world is also usually seen as alive, as the abode of gods or spirits or itself possessed of spiritual power, or both. Usually introduced into the worldview is a place for ancestors. Many origin stories include accounts of the first humans and make a place for the memory of honored group heroes and the immediate ancestors of living individuals. One of the factors by which ethnoreligions may be distinguished is the relative emphasis placed on deities, various spirits, and the group's ancestors. Each is seen as a source of power, some of good power to be accessed and some of evil power to be avoided or countered.

Most ethnoreligions provide a variety of means to relate to the larger cosmos and the sources of power. The most common means is magic, the utilization of various techniques believed to be the means of manipulating spiritual power. A variety of forms of magic have been distinguished and a variety of names (witchcraft, sorcery, wizardry) applied to them. One generally thinks of magic being invoked when specific mundane goals are being sought, such as the manipulation of weather, the curing of a disease, or the fecundity of a harvest. The life of groups also embodies elements of worship, actions aimed at building positive relationships with the deities, the spirit world, and the ancestors. Some rituals will often combine elements of both magic and worship.

Different primal societies also have a spectrum of religious practitioners, most of whose jobs have elements of secular occupations. The most well known of such practitioners are the shamans, recognized for their abilities to be in direct contact with the spirit world, and the priests, who function as ceremonial leaders in the annual cycle of rituals and otherwise enforce communal rules. The priestly role often overlaps with political leadership. Some groups may have healers, who are repositories of the group's wisdom on alleviating sickness. Oracles and divines are people who have an ability to offer supernatural guidance about a situation or discern the future. Mediums are people especially able to contact spirits. The various functions of magic and worship are merged and divided in numerous ways in different societies, with practitioners combining their "spiritual" roles in very diverse ways with more mundane occupations.

Ethnoreligions rarely have an abstract ethics, there being little time or motivation for the speculative arts, though the groups will have some rules that dictate actions and others that delineate forbidden actions. Researchers in Polynesia encountered the idea of taboo: objects, actions, and even people who were considered dangerous (and hence to be avoided) due to some characteristic—ritual uncleanness, past negative occurrences associated with them, or possession of negative spiritual power. An analogous idea appears to be inherent in many primal cultures. Among the most common taboos are those relating to childbirth, menstruating women, or the bodies of the deceased.

The Jewish Bible (the Christian Old Testament) includes many stories of the conflict of Judaism with neighboring polytheistic ethnoreligions. The rise of Christianity to power in Europe came as it replaced the numerous ethnoreligions that had preceded it across the continent. The Arab-Islamic Empire that spread from the Indus Valley to Morocco, while relatively tolerant of Christian and Jews, saw "polytheists" as major subjects for conversion. Through the succeeding centuries, as Christianity and Islam became global religions, their progress was often at the expense of ethnoreligions, which have been increasingly on the defensive in the modern world.

In spite of the political and scientific power aligned with the major world religions, primal religions have survived, and in places ethnoreligionists have assumed the offensive in preserving their traditional life. In this task, they have been assisted by contemporary ideas of cultural relativity, and they have drawn on those ideas to charge Christian and Muslim missionaries with a form of cultural totalitarianism. Christians, in particular, have been associated with the evils of European colonialism, and ethnoreligionists have reasserted themselves in the now independent former colonies. Ethnoreligions remain a significant factor in the religious life of most African countries south of the Sahara and in Asia, in such countries as South Korea, Laos, Malaysia, and Mongolia, among others.

The interface of ethnoreligions with European colonial authorities and with Islamic and Christian missionaries has in many places led to the emergence of modern movements that draw on traditional religious themes and rituals, but attempt to respond to the pressures applied by the colonial and postcolonial situation. Among the more famous would be the Native American Church, a movement that spread among Native Americans early in the 20th century. It was but one example of a series of such movements that had emerged at various times through the 19th century as the United States expanded across North America. Most of these, such as the Ghost Dance movement, were suppressed by the authorities. Equally well known are the so-called cargo cults that emerged in the South Pacific following World War II.

In Africa, a number of new spirit possession movements, in which contact with the deities is made as participants go into a trancelike state and allow spirit to speak and act through them, appeared throughout the 20th century. Most began as local cults, but some subsequently spread to a variety of different groups across national boundaries. Another type of group was the Mchape (medicine) movement that arose in what is now Malawi in the 1930s, with a concentration on eradicating malevolent magic. It later spread to Uganda, Tanzania, Zambia, and Mozambique. The new traditionalist movements in Africa fit into a spectrum of new religions, which include groups that present a complex mixture of Christian and traditionalist themes such as the African Initiated Churches.

Thousands of ethnoreligions still exist, and only a representative sample could be included in this encyclopedia; these few, however, illustrate both the wide variety and common themes found in primal society worldwide.

As a result of slavery, many Africans were transported to the Americas. In Brazil and the Caribbean Islands especially, new forms of African ethnoreligions emerged in dialogue with Roman Catholicism. Often seen as syntheses of the two faiths, the Afro-Caribbean and Afro-Brazilian faiths have increasingly been seen as surviving African religions with a veneer of Catholicism.

During the 20th century, citizens of developed nations have turned their attention to ancient ethnoreligions and created new religions that attempt to recover religions lost for centuries. Most are known only through archaeological and anthropological reconstructions, or through the writings of representatives of faiths that replaced them. Most noticeable of the revivalist neo-religions are various forms of European Paganism. Attempts to refound Paganism began early in the 20th century, but did not take off until Gerald B. Gardner (1884–1964) founded the neo-religion of Witchcraft, or Wicca. As Gardnerian Wicca spread from England to North America, it inspired further neo-Pagan groups, including a revived Druidism, and provided a legitimation for a modern form of polytheism built around worship of a prime female deity, Goddess Spirituality. In the 1990s, the fall of the Soviet Union became the occasion of a new assertion of national tradition in Northern Europe by those who have revived Pagan traditions in the Baltic nations (Lithuania, Latvia, Estonia) and Poland. (Romuva, Clan of Ausrans, Rodzima Wiara).

J. Gordon Melton

See also: Aboriginal Religions; African Initiated (Independent) Churches; African Traditional Religions; Clan of Ausrans; Dogon Religion; Gardnerian Wicca; Goddess Spirituality; Judaism; Lakota, The; Maori Religion; Native American Church; Navaho, The; Nepal, Indigenous Religions in; Palo Mayombe; Possession; Rodzima Wiara (Poland); Romuva. Santeria; Shinto; Sikhism; Umbanda; Vodou; Wiccan Religion; Yoruban Religion/Spirituality; Zulu Religion.

References

Adegbola, E. A. Ade, ed. *Traditional Religion in West Africa*. Nairobi: Uzima Press, 1983.

Adler, Margot. *Drawing Down the Moon*. Rev. ed. Boston: Beacon Press, 1986.

Alpers, Anthony. *Maori Myths and Tribal Legends*. Auckland, NZ: Longman, 1966.

Bastide, Roger. *The African Religions of Brazil: Toward a Sociology of Interpretation of Civilizations*. Baltimore: Johns Hopkins University Press, 1978.

Beier, Ulli. *The Origin of Life and Death: African Creation Myth*. London: Heinemann, 1966.

Blakely, T. D., E. A. Walter, and L. T. Dennis, eds. *Religion in Africa: Experience and Expression*. London: Heinemann, 1994.

Brandon, George. *Santeria from Africa to the New World: The Dead Sell Memories*. Bloomington: Indiana University Press, 1993.

Collins, John James. *Native American Religions: A Geographical Survey*. Lewiston, NY: Edwin Mellen, 1991.

Eliade, Mircea. *Shamanism: Archaic Technique of Ecstasy*. New York: Pantheon, 1964.

Haynes, Douglas. *Micronesian Religion and Lore*. Westport, CT: Greenwood Publishing Group, 1995.

Hultkrantz, Ake. *Native Religions of North America*. San Francisco: Harper and Row, 1987.

Isizoh, Chidi Denis. "Bibliography on African Traditional Religion." www.afrikaworld.net/afrel/atr_bibliography.htm. Accessed January 15, 2002.

Murphy, Joseph M. *Working the Spirit: Ceremonies of the African Diaspora*. Boston: Beacon Press, 1994.

Olupona, Jacob, ed. *African Spirituality: Forms, Meanings and Expressions*. New York: Crossroad, 2000.

Olupona, Jacob, ed. *African Traditional Religion in Contemporary Society*. New York: Continuum, 1990.

Sullivan, Lawrence E., ed. *Native American Religions: North America*. New York: Macmillan, 1989.

Sullivan, Lawrence E., ed., *Native Religions and Cultures of North America: Anthropology of the Sacred*. New York: Continuum, 2000.

Smart, Ninian. *The Religious Experience of Mankind*. New York: Macmillan, 1984.

Swain, Tony. *Interpreting Aboriginal Religion: An Historical Account*. Special Studies in Religion 5. South Australia: Flinders University, 1985.

Swain, Tony, and Garry Trompf. *The Religions of Oceania*. London: Routledge, 1995.

Turner, Harold W. *Bibliography of New Religious Movements in Primal Societies*. 2 vols. Boston: G. K. Hall, 1977, 1979.

Turner, Harold W. *Religious Innovation in Africa*. Boston: G. K. Hall, 1980.

Walker, Barbara. *The Woman's Encyclopedia of Myths and Secrets*. San Francisco: Harper & Row, 1983.

European Buddhist Union

The European Buddhist Union (EBU) is an international umbrella organization of Buddhist communities, centers, and organizations as well as national unions. The EBU is not affiliated with a particular Buddhist tradition or school. According to its constitution, adopted in 1990 and renewed in 2004, the aims are to promote fellowship and cooperation among Buddhist organizations in Europe and to encourage meetings and friendly relations between their members. The EBU works to support and promote the growth and public recognition of Buddhism in Europe.

The EBU was founded in Paris in 1975. It is headed by a board consisting of a president, two vice presidents, and a treasurer. EBU's first president was French Paul Arnold (r. 1975–1983), followed by British Arthur Burton-Stibbon (r. 1983–1989), and also British Stephen Hodge (r. 1989–1991), Dutch Aad Verboom (r. 1991–1995), and French Lama Denys Teundroup (r. 1995–1998). The current president is Frans Goetghebeur, Belgium. The number of member organizations has grown steadily since the EBU's beginning, with about 30 members from 11 countries in 1991, and 46 members from 14 European countries in 2009.

Apart from national unions from Austria, Belgium, Denmark, Germany, Great Britain, Italy, and Switzerland, members are also Buddhist centers or organizations working on a Europe-wide basis, such as the Friends of the Western Buddhist Order, Dzogchen Community Europe, some Zen and Shin Buddhist groups, the Tibetan Center Hamburg, the Amida Trust (United Kingdom), and the Nalanda Association (Spain). Organizations of Buddhists who have immigrated from Asia (for example, Vietnamese, Cambodian, or Laotian Buddhists) or of Nichiren traditions are not members of the EBU. Thus, the EBU is almost exclusively a representational organization of convert Buddhists, although some migrant Buddhist organizations are affiliated with national unions. The EBU estimates the number of Buddhists in Europe to be between one to four million people. In view of scholarly studies, a much lower figure of around one million Buddhists is, however, more likely.

EBU delegates meet annually at varying Buddhist centers. The main public event of the EBU is the EBU international congress, held every five years (with modifications). Congresses have taken place in Paris (1979, 1988, 2000), Turin (1984), and Berlin (1992). The meetings are aimed at bringing about both a dialogue between Buddhists of the various traditions and a stocktaking of the state of affairs of Buddhism in Europe. During such conferences, visited by up to 1,000 people, notable speakers elaborate on the theme of the congress, be it the public recognition of Buddhism in Europe, educational issues, or the dynamic of the plurality and diversity of Buddhism in Europe. Also, annual meetings take place, synchronizing these every second year with a meeting of Buddhist teachers active in Europe.

The EBU has no permanent headquarters, due to its restricted financial resources and its less strong organizational efforts. Its offices are thus moved in accordance with the current president. For many years it has been acknowledged as a United Nations Educational, Scientific and Cultural Organization (UNESCO) nongovernmental organization (category C) and has been approached by the European Parliament and UNESCO on issues regarding the freedom of religious practice. In 2008, the EBU officially obtained participatory status with the Council of Europe.

Martin Baumann

See also: Tibetan Buddhism; Zen Buddhism.

References

Baumann, Martin. "Buddhism in Europe: Past, Present, Prospects." In *Westwards Dharma: Buddhism beyond Asia*, edited by Charles S. Prebish and Martin Baumann, 85–105. Berkeley: University of California Press, 2002.

Einheit in der Vielfalt-Buddhismus in Europa. Munich: Deutsche Buddhistische Union, 1994.

European Buddhist Union. http://www.e-b-u.org.

Evangelical Baptist Church in Angola

The Evangelical Baptist Church in Angola is the most prominent of several churches of the Baptist tradition working in Angola. The church traces its origins to the launching of work by British missionaries of the Baptist Mission Society. During the last years of colonial rule in Angola, many Baptists moved into exile in the neighboring Democratic Republic of the Congo (1961–1974). Returning after independence was declared, members of the mission organized in 1977 as an autonomous body.

The church continues the faith and practice of the parent Mission Society. All the local churches are represented in the general assembly, the highest legislative body for the church.

In 2006, the church reported 80,000 members, but its influence extends far beyond its formal membership. More than 200,000 children, for example, attend its Sunday school classes. The church oversees a variety of social and self-help programs. Ministers are trained at its seminary in Luanda. Women are accepted into the ordained ministry. The church is a member of the World Council of Churches (2005) and the Baptist World Alliance.

J. Gordon Melton

See also: Baptist World Alliance; World Council of Churches.

Reference

Van Beek, Huibert. *A Handbook of the Churches and Councils: Profiles of Ecumenical Relationships.* Geneva: World Council of Churches, 2006.

Evangelical Baptist Union of Italy

The Evangelical Baptist Union of Italy (UCEBI) is the largest Italian Baptist body.

The first Baptist mission in Italy was established in Bologna in 1863 and was known as the Gospel Mission to the Italians. Its lifespan was short. A more permanent institution, however, was the Spezia Mission for Italy and the Levant, which was founded in 1866 in La Spezia by English pastor Edward Clarke (1820–1912). Later, both an English and an American mission (the latter affiliated with the Southern Baptist Convention) were established in Rome. In 1884, the two missions joined forces together with the Spezia Mission in a federation called Unione Cristiana Apostolica Battista (Christian Apostolic Baptist Union). In 1922, the British Mission left Italy and entrusted its members to the Southern Baptists, while the Spezia Mission maintained an autonomous presence under the leadership of Harry Herbert Pullen (1862–1951). A notable Baptist intellectual of the early 20th century was Giuseppe Gangale (1898–1978). In 1954, the Spezia Mission was reorganized and renamed Associazione Missionaria Evangelica Italiana (Italian Evangelical Mission Association). It merged in 1966 with the Unione Cristiana Evangelica Battista d'Italia (UCEBI; Evangelical Baptist Union of Italy), histori-

cally derived from the Southern Baptist Mission, but independent and in fact more liberal than its U.S. counterpart, thus inducing the more conservative Italian Baptists to establish a separate Assemblea Evangelica Battista Italiana (AEBI; Italian Evangelical Baptist Assembly). In the first decade of the 21st century a strong movement of independent Reformed Baptist churches has also developed independently of UCEBI. The Italian Reformed Baptists regard themselves as heirs of the Calvinistic theology of the particular Baptists in the tradition of John Bunyan (1626–1688), Roger Williams (1603–1683), William Carey (1761–1834), and Charles Spurgeon (1834–1892).

UCEBI now comprises more than 150 churches (not all of them Baptist), with some 50 male and female pastors, 5,000 adult members, and a "population" (including children and irregular attendees) of 25,000. On March 29, 1993, UCEBI entered into a concordat ("Intesa") with the Italian government, which theoretically would have entitled it to share in the national church tax. However, the UCEBI has so far elected not to receive its rightful portion of the tax because of its theological principles about the separation of church and state. The concordat preserves the UCEBI's congregationalist identity, whereby it regards itself as a loose federation of independent churches, despite the fact that in 1990 it adopted a Confession of Faith, which insists on adult baptism and separation of church and state. In 1977, UCEBI joined the World Council of Churches and, in 1990, it signed a protocol for the reciprocal recognition of ministers with the Waldensian and Methodist Union, notwithstanding their differences on infant baptism (clearly spelled out in the protocol).

UCEBI
Piazza San Lorenzo in Lucina 35
00186 Rome
Italy
http://www.ucebi.it

Massimo Introvigne and PierLuigi Zoccatelli

See also: Carey, William; Southern Baptist Convention; World Council of Churches.

References

Maselli, Domenico. *Storia dei battisti italiani (1873–1923).* Turin: Claudiana, 2003.

Sanfilippo, Paolo. *Commento alla confessione di fede dell'U.C.E.B.I.* Rome:UCEBI, 1992.

Scaramuccia, F. *Un'avventura di fede. L'Opera missionaria di Edward Clarke (1820–1912).* Claudiana: Torino, 1999.

Scaramuccia, Franco, and Renato Maiocchi. *L'Intesa battista: un'identità rispettata.* Claudiana: Torino, 1994.

Wardin, Albert W., ed. *Baptists Around the World.* Nashville: Holman Publishers, 1995.

Evangelical Christian Church in Irian Jaya

The Evangelical Christian Church of Irian Jaya (GKI Irja: Gereja Kristen Injili di Irian Jaya) began with the arrival of two independent German carpenters who were supported as missionaries by an independent faith mission in Holland. They settled in northeastern Irian Jaya, a province of Indonesia, in what is known as the Bird's Head in 1855, accompanied by several native Christians from the Moluccan Islands. They had little success, a fact that has been attributed to their extremely low opinion of the culture.

The progress of the mission changed visibly in 1907, when suddenly Christianity spread and many joined the church. Over the next few years the church spread throughout the northern half of the island (the Dutch authorities had given the southern half to the Roman Catholic Church). A teacher training school was opened at Meiji, at which indigenous leadership was trained. However, the Japanese invasion caught the mission unprepared. No indigenous pastors had been ordained, and no pan-congregational structure had been created. The move to formally organize the church was picked up after the war. In 1950 the first Indonesian pastors were ordained, and in 1965 the first synod met. Irian Jaya was incorporated into Indonesia in 1963, at which time the missionaries turned the church over to the local leadership and left the country.

Since it became independent, the church has had to face a variety of problems. The population has changed radically, as different peoples have moved into the area following economic development. The church faces competition with the spread of Roman Catholicism and Islam in its established territory in the north. The church itself has begun to spread into the south of Irian Jaya.

The church is organized on a presbyterian model, with a synod as the highest legislative body. It accepts the ancient Christian creeds as its doctrinal standard. The church has developed an extensive educational system that includes the Sekolah Tinggi Theologia I. S. Kijne (named for the leader of its original training school).

In the 1990s the church reported 650,000 members in 1,869 congregations. It is a member of the World Alliance of Reformed Churches and was until recently a member of the World Council of Churches. It is a partner church with the Presbyterian Church (U.S.A.).

Evangelical Christian Church in Irian Jaya
PO Box 1160
Jalan Argapura No. 21
Jayapura 99222 Irian Jaya
Indonesia

J. Gordon Melton

See also: Presbyterian Church (U.S.A.); Roman Catholic Church; World Alliance of Reformed Churches; World Council of Churches.

Reference

Bauswein, Jean-Jacques, and Lukas Vischner, eds. *The Reformed Family Worldwide: A Survey of Reformed Churches, Theological Schools, and International Organizations.* Grand Rapids, MI: William B. Eerdmans Publishing Company, 1999.

Evangelical Church in Chile

See Evangelical Lutheran Church in Chile.

Evangelical Church in Germany

The Evangelical Church in Germany inherits the history of the Christianity that was introduced into Germany possibly as early as the second century. Three bishoprics were erected in the third century, and over the next centuries Roman Catholicism became the dominant religion. The whole of present-day Germany was included in the Holy Roman Empire, whose emergence is generally dated to the coronation of Charlemagne in 800. By the 16th century, the empire consisted of a number of more or less autonomous countries, principalities, and city-states.

In the 1520s, Martin Luther, a monk and professor at the University of Wittenberg in Saxony, challenged the theological trends of his day and a variety of practices he felt had entered the Roman Catholic Church illegitimately. These trends and practices, he believed, contradicted the teachings of the Bible, which he insisted centered upon the message of the free salvation God offered to believers. The new movement he began championed the ideas of the final authority of the Bible (over and against the authority of tradition and the teaching office of the papacy) and of salvation by faith, apart from any good works performed by humans. These emphases and their implications were embodied in the Augsburg Confession (1530) and a catechism that Luther had authored the year before. These two documents more than any others define the Lutheran tradition.

The religious wars that broke out between Lutherans and Roman Catholics as Luther's ideas spread were brought to a halt in 1555 by the Peace of Augsburg. The treaty signed at that time articulated a principle that was to have far-reaching effects throughout Germany. Both Lutherans and Catholics would exist in the Holy Roman Empire, and the ruler of each principality would decide which church would dominate in his or her land (a principle often expressed, in Latin, as *cuius region, eius religio,* whose region, his religion). In Lutheran lands, the prince assumed the power formerly held by the bishop. The situation was complicated in the ensuing decades as the Reformed tradition (the form of Protestantism developed by John Calvin in Geneva, Switzerland) spread through Germany, and some princes accepted it. Lutherans issued the Formula of Concord (1577) to distinguish the Lutheran faith from the Reformed variation.

Among the more important of the Lutheran principalities was Prussia. In 1613, the ruler adopted the Reformed faith. Although the population remained Lu-

Stiftskirche, an Evangelical Collegiate church in Stuttgart, Germany. (iStockPhoto.com)

theran, a number of Reformed congregations came into being, with the approval of the country's leadership. This development attracted French Huguenots to Prussia to escape the hostile environment in their homeland. In 1817, King Frederick William I (r. 1797–1840) forced a merger of the Lutheran and Reformed churches into what became known as the Evangelical Church of Germany. Though there was one national church organization, local congregations and individual ministers were allowed to choose either the Lutheran or the Reformed faith. Both the Augsburg Confession and the Helvetic Confession (the latter a statement of the Reformed faith) were accepted as official statements of faith, and pastors could choose either Luther's Small Catechism or the Heidelberg Catechism as a tool to instruct the youth. In other lands, similar evangelical churches came into existence. In Baden and the Palatinate, a new catechism that combined Lutheran and Reformed emphases was introduced.

During the course of the 19th century, the many smaller German states were unified into modern Germany, though the border changed frequently as different wars were fought and won or lost. As the country was united, the larger of the former independent German countries became states in the new nation. Each state continued the church that had previously evolved within its boundaries. The various churches existed along a spectrum from those that were predominantly Lutheran to those that were evangelical or United (combining Lutheran and Reformed elements) to those that were predominantly Reformed. Predominantly Lutheran churches were found in Saxony and Bavaria, while the Reformed perspective dominated in Lippe. In Saxony, where the evangelical church had originated, one group of Lutheran separated from the state church as a confessional Lutheran body.

Attempts to bring some unity to this chaotic situation were focused in various gatherings of the territorial churches throughout the 19th century. Then in 1918, church and state was separated, and the Protestant princes handed the episcopal authority they had heretofore held to the church. The church's synods received that authority. They became self-governing churches just in time to experience the era of inflation, economic depression, the rise of National Socialism, and World War II. Each of the territorial churches, one in each of the German states, adopted a new constitution, and continued their relationship with the state to the extent that they still received state money for their maintenance.

In 1922 the German Evangelical Church Federation was formed. It built upon the theological work and relationships of the 19th century. It assumed a basically Lutheran perspective but allowed room for the Reformed minority. Also operating among the churches was the General Evangelical Lutheran Conference, formed in 1868. It worked on building relationships with Lutherans in other lands and led directly to the calling of the Lutheran World Convention in 1923.

The rise of Nazism split the church between those who supported the aims of the state and those opposed to what they saw as an evil government. Pro-government supporters forced the organization of the German Evangelical Church in 1933. The church became the battleground for the two factions, and the battle lasted until suppressed by the war. The war ended with Germany divided into two parts.

The surviving leadership of the anti-Nazi Confessing Church emerged in 1945 to lead in the formation of a new inclusive Protestant church, the Evangelical Church of Germany (Evangelische Kirke in Deutschland [EKD]). The same forces that led to the formation of the Lutheran World Convention led to participation in the formation of the Lutheran World Federation in 1948. The federation had as its immediate task the rebuilding of Europe. That same year, the predominantly Lutheran churches in Germany also founded the United Evangelical Lutheran Church of Germany (VELKD) as a fellowship within the EKD.

Both the EKD and the VELKD included the churches in the two sections into which Germany had been divided, which later became the Federal Republic of (West) Germany and the (East) German Democratic Republic. This attempt to preserve a church that reflected a united Germany proved untenable as the Cold War developed. In 1968 the EKD divided, and the VELKD followed suit the next year. That divided condition remained until the unification of Germany in 1990. The present Evangelical Church in Germany was brought together following the country's reunion.

The Evangelical Church in Germany now consists of 24 autonomous churches, one each in the different states of the German nation. Each church is allowed a considerable variation theologically and administratively and is responsible for the spiritual life of the people in its area. The Evangelical Church in Germany is a cooperative structure through which the churches carry out a variety of functions, including their relationship to various interdenominational ecumenical agencies like the World Council of Churches. Individual churches have also chosen to be members of the Lutheran World Federation or the World Alliance of Reformed Churches.

The highest legislative body in the EKD is its synod, which meets annually. The synod is headed by a seven-person governing board, the Presidium. The synod considers matters of common concern to the churches. It initiates programs through its nine permanent committees: Scripture and Proclamation of the Gospel; Social Services, Mission and Ecumenical Relations; Legal Affairs; Church, Society, and State; Education and Young People; Europe; the Environment; Budget; and Nominations.

The churches that now make up the EKD have experienced various movements concerned with theological revival and personal spirituality over the centuries. In the 19th century, the churches were profoundly affected by the world Protestant mission movement, which had actually begun in Germany among the Moravians. In response a number of missionary societies were formed, drawing their support from the members of one or more of the churches. Prominent among those based in the more Lutheran churches were the Leipzig, the Gossmer, and the North German Missionary societies. Societies drawing primarily from United churches included the Berlin, the Rhenish, and the Basel Missionary societies. The latter, as its name implied, also drew heavily from Swiss Reformed churches. These societies carried German Protestantism around the world and in some places perpetuated the internal differences that existed in the German church.

In 2005 the EKD reported 26 million members.

Evangelical Church in Germany
Herrenhauser Str. 12
Postfach 21 02 20
D-30402, Hanover
Germany
http://www.ekd.de

J. Gordon Melton

See also: Basel Mission; Lutheran World Federation; Lutheranism; Reformed/Presbyterian Tradition; Rhenish Mission; Roman Catholic Church; World Alliance of Reformed Churches; World Council of Churches.

References

Bachmann, E. Theodore, and Mercia Brenne Bachmann. *Lutheran Churches in the World: A Handbook.* Minneapolis, MN: Augsburg Press, 1989.

Van Beek, Huibert. *A Handbook of the Churches and Councils: Profiles of Ecumenical Relationships.* Geneva: World Council of Churches, 2006.

Van der Bent, Ans J., ed. *Handbook/Member Churches/World Council of Churches.* Geneva: World Council of Churches, 1985.

Evangelical Church in Kalimantan

The Evangelical Church in Kalimantan (Kalimantan Evangelical Church, Gereja Kalimantan Evangelis [GKE]) originated in 1935 with the arrival of missionaries from the Rhenish Mission (a German missionary society with roots in both Lutheranism and the Reformed tradition) to begin work among the Dayak people in Kalimantan, a province in the central region of the island of Borneo. In 1838 they formally opened stations among the Dayak, Ngaju, and Maanyan peoples. The people expressed little interest in Christianity, and the local religious leaders were openly hostile to the missionaries. They also resented the attempt of colonial Dutch authorities to establish hegemony in the area. In the 1859 revolt against the Dutch, the mission was seen as part of the Dutch rule and destroyed. The missionaries left the area and relocated on the island of Nias (thus initiating work there).

The mission was re-established once order was restored but continued to make only modest gains for the rest of the century. It was estimated that between 1866 and 1900, only 2,000 Dayak people joined the new religion. In 1920, the Rhenish Mission turned over its work to the Swiss-based Basel Mission. The work began to make progress over the next 15 years, and in 1935 the first Dayak ministers were ordained and the church formally established as an autonomous body. It was given a presbyterial order and adopted the ancient Christian creeds as its doctrinal standards. Among the new ministers was the son of a Dayak chief, F. Dingang, who proved an effective evangelist.

The missionaries continued to serve the church, and until the arrival of the Japanese in 1942, one of the Germans headed the synod board. Church leadership became thoroughly indigenous during the war years. The church saw the peace that followed as a time for expansion and in 1950 adopted its present name a part of a self-conscious attempt to abandon its role as an exclusively Dayak church and become one serving people of all ethnic groups throughout Kalimantan, both the various traditional groups and the many immigrants who have arrived since World War II. It also joined the newly founded Indonesian Council of Churches.

In 1955 the church founded the Centre of Agricultural Training, located at Tumbang Lahang, and in 1967 the Technical High School at Mandomai. In 1987 it capped its vast educational program with the new Christian University, opened at Palangka Raya, the capital of central Kalimantan.

In 2005, the church reported 245,000 members in 1,057 congregations. It is a member of the World Alliance of Reformed Churches and was a founding member of the World Council of Churches

Evangelical Church in Kalimantan
PO Box 86
Jalan Jenderal Sudirman, No. 4, Rt 1
Benjarmasin-Jolly 70114 Kalimantan
Indonesia

J. Gordon Melton

See also: Basel Mission; Lutheranism; Reformed/Presbyterian Tradition; Rhenish Mission; World Alliance of Reformed Churches; World Council of Churches.

References

Bauswein, Jean-Jacques, and Lukas Vischner, eds. *The Reformed Family Worldwide: A Survey of Reformed Churches, Theological Schools, and International Organizations*. Grand Rapids, MI: William B. Eerdmans Publishing Company, 1999.

Van Beek, Huibert. *A Handbook of the Churches and Councils: Profiles of Ecumenical Relationships*. Geneva: World Council of Churches, 2006.

Evangelical Church in New Caledonia and the Loyalty Islands

Christian missionaries began activity on New Caledonia (now the country of Kanaky in the South Pacific) in 1834. In 1841, two Samoan converts from the mission of the London Missionary Society (LMS) arrived in New Caledonia and others began work in the Loyalty Islands. They were joined by European missionaries in 1853, about the same time that the French took over control. The Roman Catholic Church missionaries had arrived two years earlier, and they received the support of the government. Nevertheless, the LMS mission grew steadily through the 19th century.

As French became the dominant language of Kanaky, the mission shifted its primary relationship from the LMS to the Paris Missionary Society (PMS) of the Reformed Church of France, beginning in 1897. Under the PMS, the mission enjoyed a particularly prosperous period, beginning in 1902 during the tenure of Maurice Leenhart (1878–1954).

The church follows the Reformed tradition in theology and is congregational in polity. In the 20th century, it stressed its cultural identification with the Kanak people, the Melanesian group that originally inhabited the island.

The Evangelical Church became independent in 1962. During the century it developed largely indigenous leadership, and few Europeans remain on its staff. The church reports a membership of approximately 40,000 (2005) out of a population of 236,000.

Evangelical Church in New Caledonia and the
   Loyalty Islands
8 rue F. Leriche
BP 277
Noumea
New Caledonia

J. Gordon Melton

See also: London Missionary Society; Paris Mission; Reformed Church of France; Reformed/Presbyterian Tradition; Roman Catholic Church.

References

Bauswein, Jean-Jacques, and Lukas Vischner, eds. *The Reformed Family Worldwide: A Survey of Reformed Churches, Theological Schools, and International Organizations*. Grand Rapids, MI: William B. Eerdmans Publishing Company, 1999.

Van Beek, Huibert. *A Handbook of the Churches and Councils: Profiles of Ecumenical Relationships*. Geneva: World Council of Churches, 2006.

Van der Bent, Ans J., ed. *Handbook/Member Churches/World Council of Churches*. Geneva: World Council of Churches, 1985.

Evangelical Church of Cameroon

The Evangelical Church of Cameroon (Église évangélique du Cameroun) has its roots in the decision of the British Baptist Missionary Association to begin work in West Africa utilizing converts from among the recently freed Africans residing on Jamaica. In 1843, 42 Jamaicans joined 4 European couples in setting up a mission station on Fernando Po (now Bioko), the island that the Spanish had turned into a center of the African slave trade. Two years later, Joseph Merrick, one of the Jamaicans, moved to the coast of Cameroon and began learning the language of the Usubu people. One of the Europeans, Alfred Saker (1814–1880), moved to Cameroon Town (now Duala). He formed the first Baptist church in 1849.

The Baptist work grew until 1884, at which time Germany gained hegemony over Cameroon. The Baptists turned their work over to the Basel Mission, a Swiss missionary society that drew support from Germans and Austrians. The new workers agreed to respect the Baptist faith of the converts; nevertheless, many did not like the manner of the German missionaries or their introduction of practices such as infant baptism. A split occurred. Those who stuck with the Basel Mission experienced a new change as World War I began, when Britain and France replaced the German authorities. The Basel Mission turned its work in French territory (some 15 stations) to the Paris Missionary Society (of the Reformed Church of France). Even though the Basel Mission was allowed to return in 1925, it did not reclaim its stations from the Paris Mission. The resources of the French missionaries, however, had been significantly stretched by many new responsibilities, a fact that hastened indigenous leadership's taking over the church's management and the church gaining its autonomy even before the country became independent. The process toward independency began in 1947, and the church emerged as the fully independent Evangelical Church of Cameroon in 1957.

The Evangelical Church's life had been partly tied to that of the Union des Églises Baptistes du Cameroon, which had also come under the guidance of the Paris Mission and had also become independent, in 1947. The church and the union retain close fraternal ties and both are members of the Council of Baptist and Evangelical Churches.

In 2005 the Evangelical Church reported 2,000,000 members in its 700 churches. It is presbyterially organized and currently has 13 regional synods. A general synod is the highest legislative body. It has a theological college at Ndougué. It is a member of the World Council of Churches.

Evangelical Church of Cameroon
BP 89
Duala
Cameroon

J. Gordon Melton

See also: Basel Mission; Paris Mission; Reformed Church of France; World Council of Churches.

References

Bauswein, Jean-Jacques, and Lukas Vischner, eds. *The Reformed Family Worldwide: A Survey of Reformed Churches, Theological Schools, and International Organizations.* Grand Rapids, MI: William B. Eerdmans Publishing Company, 1999.

Van Beek, Huibert. *A Handbook of the Churches and Councils: Profiles of Ecumenical Relationships.* Geneva: World Council of Churches, 2006.

Evangelical Church of Chad

The Evangelical Church of Chad grew out of the variety of Protestant and Free church missionary efforts launched in various parts of the country during the 20th century, at which time Chad was a part of French Equatorial Africa. The Canadian branch of the Sudan United Mission (SUM), an interdenominational evangelical sending agency, entered in 1925, and while developing its own work in the southwestern Province of Logone, was active in coordinating the efforts of other missionary groups. After World War II the evangelical enterprise entered a growth phase. SUM's effort was focused upon the establishment of a self-supporting church and the development of indigenous leadership among what was and remains a relatively poor land.

In 1958, the Mission franco-romande du Tchad started work in the Ouaddai region, a predominantly Muslim area in eastern Chad, with SUM support. It soon received substantial additional support from the World Evangelization Crusade (now WEC International), a British-based sending agency. In 1962, the leadership of the Sudan United Mission, the WEC, and the French Mennonites, who were also supporting work in the area, began a dialogue in light of the emergence of Chad as an independent country (1960) and the fragmented nature of the Protestant mission scene. Out of these conversations came the SUM Mission, which the government recognized in 1963. The SUM Mission evolved into the Evangelical Church of Chad.

It is a conservative Free church based upon the authority of the Bible and affirming the basic doctrines of evangelical Christianity. In the late 1990s, it reported some 200,000 members, the largest Protestant body in what is a predominantly Muslim country. It oversees several Bible schools and the École supérieure de théologie évangélique. It was an important force in establishing the Comité de Coordination des Activités Missionnaires, which continues to promote amity between the different missionary agencies operating in the country.

In the middle of the first decade of the new century, the Evangelical Church has been one among several religious groups that has suffered as the violence in the Darfur region of Sudan, with whom Chad shares a lengthy border, has spilled over. Church leaders have claimed that the Sudanese government has given support both to militia who have made raids into Chad and to Chadian rebel groups that have been allowed to establish bases in Sudan

Evangelical Church of Chad
BP 821
N'Djamena
Chad

J. Gordon Melton

See also: Free Churches.

Reference

Bauswein, Jean-Jacques, and Lukas Vischner, eds. *The Reformed Family Worldwide: A Survey of Reformed Churches, Theological Schools, and International Organizations.* Grand Rapids, MI: William B. Eerdmans Publishing Company, 1999.

Evangelical Church of French Polynesia

See Maohi Protestant Church.

Evangelical Church of Gabon

The Evangelical Church of Gabon was initiated by missionaries from the American Board of Commissioners for Foreign Missions, the missionary agency founded by American Congregationalists early in the 19th century. Their representatives settled in what is now Gabon in 1842. A generation later, the work was passed to the Presbyterian Church in the U.S.A., now a constituent part of the Presbyterian Church (U.S.A.), which in turn passed its work on to the Paris Mission (the missionary arm of the Reformed Church of France) in 1892. In the late 19th century, France had asserted its hegemony over this part of Africa and in the 1890s demanded that instruction in all schools be in French.

By 1949, the Paris Mission had 8 stations and 20 missionary personnel working in Gabon. That same year the first group of African members returned from having completed their theological studies at the seminary in Cameroon. These five teachers became the first Native pastors. Their arrival also speeded the mission's transformation into an autonomous church, completed in 1961. The church was composed primarily of Fang people and was heavily female in membership.

Many churches have been disrupted because of interference or suppression by the government, but the Evangelical Church of Gabon has been troubled by internal disputes and power struggles. In 1971 the church was split into two factions, which had become visible during the close election of Nang Essono as head of the church. His unsuccessful challenger, Sima Ndong, headed the dissenting faction. The church removed the pastors supporting Ndong from their ministerial roles.

In spite of a number of attempts to settle the dispute, the schism continued for the next 20 years.

It was not until 1989 that what appeared to be a reconciliation was worked out and a single synodal council elected to office. However, in the early 1990s, troubles arose again. On several occasions the disputes led to shooting. By the middle of the 1990s, the church had split into three factions, known informally as the Baraka, the Foyer, and the Gros Bouquet. In 1997, the Baraka and Gros Bouquet factions met in a joint synod, formed a new national council, and elected a new president, Reverend Jean Noël Ogouliguendé. This church is now recognized as the Evangelical Church of Gabon.

In 2005, the church reported 205,000 members. It joined the World Council of Churches in 1961. It supports the Theological School of the African Protestant Church at Yaoundé, Cameroon.

Evangelical Church of Gabon
BP 617
Libreville
Gabon

J. Gordon Melton

See also: American Board of Commissioners for Foreign Missions; Paris Mission; Presbyterian Church (U.S.A.); Reformed Church of France; World Council of Churches.

References

Bauswein, Jean-Jacques, and Lukas Vischner, eds. *The Reformed Family Worldwide: A Survey of Reformed Churches, Theological Schools, and International Organizations.* Grand Rapids, MI: William B. Eerdmans Publishing Company, 1999.

Van Beek, Huibert. *A Handbook of the Churches and Councils: Profiles of Ecumenical Relationships.* Geneva: World Council of Churches, 2006.

Van der Bent, Ans J., ed. *Handbook/Member Churches/World Council of Churches.* Geneva: World Council of Churches, 1985.

Evangelical Church of the Augsburg and Helvetic Confessions in Austria

Martin Luther's first followers in Austria can be traced as early as 1521, and until the beginning of the Thirty Years' War in 1618, Austrian Christians of the Protestant denominations in the upper classes had religious freedom. During the time of its widest spread the Evangelical Church could claim three-quarters of the Austrian population. But when the Austrian emperors Ferdinand II (1578–1637) and Ferdinand III (1608–1657) enforced some burdensome changes, following the victory of the Catholic league in the Battle of the White Mountain (1620), the fate of the Evangelical Church grew far worse. The Roman Catholic Counter-Reformation forced thousands of Protestants to either leave the country or to hide underground for more than 150 years.

Two important historical and legal changes happened in the following centuries. In 1784 Emperor Joseph II (1741–1790) issued the Patent of Tolerance, and Lutherans and Calvinists (and members of the Eastern Orthodox Church) were permitted private religious services, though they were still considered "second-class citizens." Finally, in 1861, Protestants got the same civil rights as members of the Roman Catholic Church in the Austrian monarchy, and in 1867 religious freedom was legally acknowledged as a human right by the Fundamental Law of the State. But religious affairs, including those of the Evangelical Church, remained under the control of the government, which was traditionally dominated by Roman Catholic values. It was not until 1961 that an agreement was signed between the Republic of Austria and the Evangelical Church under which the latter gained full sovereignty and autonomy.

Presently there are about 328,000 members of the 2 bodies that together constitute the Church of the Augsburg and Helvetic Confessions, with sinking numbers during the last decades of the 20th century. The Church of the Augsburg Confession (Lutheran) now comprises 190 parishes and 7 superintendents; the Church of the Helvetic Confession (Reformed) has 9 parishes (with 10,500 persons). Worth mentioning is the existence within both churches of a small number of "mixed" parishes, following both the Augsburg and Helvetic Confessions. The largest number of evangelical Christians in relation to the whole population lives in the Burgenland, an eastern part of Austria bordering Hungary, which was attached to Austria after World War I. Many adherents of the Helvetic Confession live in Vorarlberg, bordering Switzerland.

In both churches people are elected from the community for their offices; the governing body is the synod. Women have been admitted to the ministry; the first female superintendent, Gertraud Knoll, was elected in 1994 for the Burgenland. For theological studies there exists a faculty at the University of Vienna with a full curriculum leading up to the doctorate.

The Evangelical Church was a founding member of the Ecumenical Council of Churches of Austria in 1958; the Augsburg Confession also joined the Lutheran World Federation in 1947, and the Helvetic Confession is a member of the World Alliance of Reformed Churches. Both Confessions are also members of the Conference of European Churches and the World Council of Churches. There are regular and active ecumenical contacts with most of the Protestant Free churches and with the Roman Catholic Church and Old Catholic Church of Austria; with the latter there has been intercommunion since 1986.

Evangelical Church of the Augsburg and Helvetic
  Confessions
Severin-Schreiber-Gasse 3
A-1180 Wien
Austria
http://www.evang.at

Manfred Hutter

See also: Free Churches; Luther, Martin; Lutheran World Federation; Old Catholic Church of Austria; Roman Catholic Church; World Alliance of Reformed Churches; World Council of Churches.

References

Reingrabner, Gustav. *Evangelische in Oesterreich.* Vienna: Evangelischer Presseverband in Österreich, 1996.

Reingrabner, Gustav. *Protestanten in Oesterreich: Geschichte und Dokumentation.* Vienna: Boehlau, 1981.

Evangelical Church of the Augsburg Confession in Poland

The ideas of Martin Luther (1483–1546) came to Poland as soon as Polish merchants and students brought them on their way back home from Wittenberg and Königsberg. The first evangelical (Lutheran) sermons were preached in 1518 in Gdansk and in Slask (Silesia). Already in 1523, the Wroclaw city council had nominated the first evangelical parson. The Lutheran views spread from Lower Silesia and Krakow to the area of Cieszyn and survived the Catholic Counter-Reformation during the reign of the Habsburgs to stay alive until today. In eastern Prussia, in turn, the last Great Master of the Teutonic Order, Prince Albert (1490–1568), under the personal influence of Luther, dissolved his order and then formally paid homage to the Polish king, Zygmunt the Old (aka Sigismund II, 1520–1572). Both the king and his son created favorable conditions for the Augsburg Confession in eastern Prussia. Although the Polish Parliament voted for equality of religions and religious peace in 1573, the act was condemned by the Roman Catholic Church, and the period of the Counter-Reformation started.

Later on, Austrian monarch Joseph I (1678–1711) allowed evangelicals to build six churches in Silesia, and the Edict of Toleration issued by Joseph II (1741–1790) in 1781 allowed evangelical religious life to flourish in the Cieszyn area. The immigration to Polish soil of evangelical craftsmen and farmers from the whole of Europe in the 19th century gave Lutheranism new strength. However, World War II prevented the stabilization of the church. Around 30 percent of the evangelical clergy died in concentration camps and prisons. The politics of the postwar authorities also caused a weakening of the church.

The primary structure of the church is its synod, the church's governing body, consisting of 15 clergy delegates and 390 lay representatives. The synod is elected every five years. The administrative and executive power rests with the eight-member consistory and the superintendent bishop. The consistory is based in Warsaw. Both the president of the synod and the president of the consistory are elected by a special collective electoral body. The inner affairs of the church are regulated by the Fundamental Inner Law, as accepted by the synod. The basic relationship of the church and the Republic of Poland is determined by the law enacted on May 13, 1994.

The church is currently divided into six dioceses in Poland. They are represented by their respective synods, which execute their power through the board and the bishop. There are 132 congregations that serve as worship centers for the 80,000 (as of 2006) members who reside mainly in the area of Cieszyn (Silesia), in Upper Silesia, Mazury (former East Prussia), and Warsaw. They are cared for by approximately 120 priests. The Kosciol Ewangelicko-Augsburski, to give it its Polish name, is a member of the Polish Ecumenical Council and was a founding member of the World Council of Churches.

Evangelical Church of the Augsburg Confession
    (Poland)
ul. Miodowa 21
00–246 Warszawa
Poland

Leslaw Borowsk

See also: Luther, Martin; Lutheranism; Roman Catholic Church; World Council of Churches.

References

Gastpary, Waldemar. *Historia protestantyzmu w Polsce.* Warszawa: ChAT, 1977.

Marceli, Kosman. *Protestanci w Polsce do polowy XX wieku.* Wroclaw: Ossolineum, 1980.

Van Beek, Huibert. *A Handbook of Churches and Councils: Profiles of Ecumenical Relations.* Geneva: World Council of Churches, 2006.

Evangelical Church of the Augsburg Confession in Romania

The Evangelical Church of the Augsburg Confession in Romania derives from the spread of Lutheranism in the German-speaking areas of Transylvania in the 16th century. It shared some of its history with that of the Lutheran Church in Hungary, though existing as a

The "black church" of the Evangelical Church of the Augsburg Confession in Transylvania, Romania. (Christian Draghici/ Dreamstime.com)

separate German-speaking organization. The Lutheran movement arrived in Transylvania just as the Turkish army was establishing its control. German-speaking Transylvanians formed the Church of God of the Saxon Nation, which in 1572 officially accepted the Augsburg Confession as its confessional statement of belief. Hungarian-speaking Lutherans in Transylvania, originally a part of the Lutheran Church in Hungary, were cut off from their counterparts in Hungary with the separation of Transylvania and its incorporation into Romania after World War I. They organized the Synodal Evangelical Presbyterian Lutheran Church of the Augsburg Confession.

Transylvania was incorporated into the Austro-Hungarian Empire in 1691. Although Turkish rule was gone, the new government favored the Roman Catholic Church to the detriment of Protestant churches. In the mid-19th century the church adopted a new constitution (with the approval of ruling authorities in Vienna) that established a presbyterial-synodal governing system but allowed for significant congregational autonomy. The church has always been headed by a bishop. The church also oversaw a large primary and secondary school system.

The church suffered greatly during World War II and the subsequent rise of an aggressive atheist government. At the same time, many Transylvanians accepted the offer of the German government to resettle people of German heritage from Eastern Europe in Germany. With more than 100 pastors accepting this offer, the church has faced a significant leadership problem. The Romanian population also moved into the industrial centers and away from the towns where most Lutheran parishes were located. With the fall of the Ceausescu government in 1989, the church has received greater freedom to develop its life.

The church is headquartered in Sibiu. In 2005 it reported 14,543 members. In the Sibiu headquarters complex there is a school of theology for training pastors. With instruction in German, it serves as an extension school of the United Protestant Theological Institute located in Cluj, where instruction is in Hungarian. The Institute also serves Hungarian-speaking Lutheran, Reformed, and Unitarian educational needs.

The church is very ecumenically minded and is a member of the Lutheran World Federation, the World Council of Churches, and the Conference of European Churches.

Evangelical Church of the Augsburg Confession in Romania
Strada General Magheru 4
R-2400 Sibiu
Romania

J. Gordon Melton

See also: Lutheran Church in Hungary; Lutheran World Federation; Lutheranism; Roman Catholic Church; World Council of Churches.

References

Bachmann, E. Theodore, and Mercia Brenne Bachmann. *Lutheran Churches in the World: A Handbook*. Minneapolis, MN: Augsburg Press, 1989.

Branzea, Nicolae I., and Stefan Lonita. *Religious Life in Romania*. Bucharest: Editura Paideia, 1999.

Cuciuc, Constantin. *Atlasul Religiilor şi al Monumentelor Istorice Religioase din Romania*. Bucharest: Editura Gnosis, 1996.

Van Beek, Huibert. *A Handbook of the Churches and Councils: Profiles of Ecumenical Relationships*. Geneva: World Council of Churches, 2006.

Evangelical Church of the Augsburg Confession in the Slovak Republic

The territory constituting the present Slovak Republic, formerly a part of the Czechoslovak Socialist Republic, emerged as an independent country in 1993, in the wake of the destruction of the Marxist hegemony in Eastern Europe. It had existed under Hungarian rule for most of the second millennium CE. As such, it was eventually incorporated into the Austro-Hungarian Empire. In 1921, in the wake of World War I and the collapse of the empire, the nation of Czechoslovakia was created by the merger of Slovakia with the neighboring provinces of Bohemia and Moravia, which through the centuries had been more identified with German rule.

In 1948, Czechoslovakia became a Socialist country. The government was reorganized as a federal republic in 1968, and Slovakia gained heightened autonomy as a regional government unit. With the fall of Communism, the desire for the formation of a Slovak-speaking state led to the formation of the present Slovak Republic.

Lutheranism had come into Bohemia, Moravia, and Slovakia during the early 16th century. The area had previously been affected by the reforming movement led by John Hus (1372–1415) and the Moravian Brethren. Although the Counter-Reformation led to a resurgent Catholicism in Bohemia and Moravia (and the almost complete suppression of Lutheranism), Lutheranism survived in strength in Slovakia. It was suppressed, but in the two decades after the Edict of Toleration of 1781, the church quickly rebounded. Parishes reappeared and more than 130 church buildings were erected. It received a new level of recognition in 1848, when it was accorded full ecclesial equality.

Until the formation of Czechoslovakia, Slovakian Lutheranism had been a part of the larger Lutheran Church in Hungary, which was controlled by a Hungarian-speaking leadership. The setting up of the new country was the occasion for establishing a separate Slovak-speaking Lutheran body. The present church continues that organization into the now independent nation of the Slovak Republic.

The church accepts the Augsburg Confession as its doctrinal standard. It has a rich liturgical life, which includes the use of the Kralice Bible (a Czech translation of 1577) and the hymnal of Wittenberg-trained pastor-poet Juraj Tranovsky (1592–1637). Ecumenically oriented, the church was a founding member of the World Council of Churches and the Ecumenical Council of Churches of the former Czechoslovakia. It is currently a member of the Ecumenical Council of Churches in the Slovak Republic.

The church is organized into 14 districts and 2 dioceses, the latter each headed by a bishop. The general convention is the primary legislative body, and the administration of the national church is left in the hands of a presidium and the bishop-general. In 2005, the church reported 372,858 members. It oversees some Slovak parishes in the Czech Republic and has strong ties to Slovak-speaking Lutherans in the countries of the former Yugoslavia and Slovak-heritage congregations in the United States.

It sponsors the Slovak Theological Faculty, which trains pastors for Slovak-, Slovene-, and Polish-speaking congregations, both in the Slovak Republic and in neighboring countries. A separate Polish-speaking Lutheran church also exists in the Slovak Republic.

Evangelical Church of the Augsburg Confession in
  the Slovak Republic
Palisady 46
81106 Bratislava
Slovak Republic
http://www.ecav.sk

J. Gordon Melton

See also: Lutheranism; World Council of Churches.

References
Bachmann, E. Theodore, and Mercia Brenne Bachmann. *Lutheran Churches in the World: A Handbook*. Minneapolis, MN: Augsburg Press, 1989.
Van Beek, Huibert. *A Handbook of the Churches and Councils: Profiles of Ecumenical Relationships*. Geneva: World Council of Churches, 2006.

Evangelical Church of the Congo

The Evangelical Church of the Congo began in 1910 when missionaries from the Mission Covenant Church of Sweden arrived in Madzia, then in French Equatorial Africa. They were soon joined by colleagues from Norway and Finland. A thriving mission resulted, and a seminary was created at Ngouedi. In 1947, a period of spiritual awakening broke out at the seminary and soon spread through the church and led to a burst of membership growth. In 1961, a year after the Congo gained its independence, the mission also became independent.

The new church followed the Pietist and evangelical teachings of its parent body. It has no creed and regards the Bible as the only source of its faith and practice. Only adult baptism is practiced. The church has a centralized government headed by a synod. The church is divided into districts, each headed by a su-

Service in an evangelical church, Brazzaville, Congo. (Pascal Deloche /Godong/Corbis)

perintendent. The church manages a number of health facilities and several schools for girls.

The 1990s were a time of social unrest in the country and tensions within the church, many of which were based on ethnic differences. In 1997, during a civil war, much of the church's property was destroyed or looted. The church has worked for democratic government to become a reality in the Congo, one of the primary goals of the Institute for Training and Information, a joint project of the church and the Mission Covenant Church in Sweden.

In 2005 the church reported 150,000 members in 118 congregations. It is a member of the World Alliance of Reformed Churches and the World Council of Churches.

Evangelical Church of the Congo
BP 3205
1 rte de Djoué-Moukounizgouaka
Bacango-Brazzaville
People's Republic of the Congo

J. Gordon Melton

See also: Mission Covenant Church of Sweden; World Alliance of Reformed Churches; World Council of Churches.

References

Bauswein, Jean-Jacques, and Lukas Vischner, eds. *The Reformed Family Worldwide: A Survey of Reformed Churches, Theological Schools, and International Organizations.* Grand Rapids, MI: William B. Eerdmans Publishing Company, 1999.

Van Beek, Huibert. *A Handbook of the Churches and Councils: Profiles of Ecumenical Relationships.* Geneva: World Council of Churches, 2006.

Van der Bent, Ans J., ed. *Handbook/Member Churches/World Council of Churches.* Geneva: World Council of Churches, 1985.

Evangelical Church of the Czech Brethren

The Evangelical Church of the Czech Brethren (Ceskobratrská církev evangelická) emerged in 1918 through the coalescence of the former Calvinist Evangelical Church of the Helvetic Confession and the Evangelical Church of the Augsburg Confession, both of which dated to the movement of the Protestant Reformation into the Czech lands in the 16th century. Its emergence came as a result of long-term efforts of Czech Calvinists and Lutherans to unite. The unification had originally been planned for the year 1915 to honor the 500th anniversary of the martyr's death in flames of Czech religious reformer Jan Hus. However, the outbreak of World War I prevented it. After the war, the fall of the Austro-Hungarian monarchy and the foundation of the new, independent, Czechoslovak Republic created space for the emergence of this new church. All the Czech congregations affiliated with the two churches joined this new church at its beginning.

The church is actively involved in the ecumenical movement: In 1927 it helped to establish the Union of Evangelical Churches in the Republic of Czechoslovakia; in 1955 it was one of the cofounders of the Ecumenical Council of Churches; and later it cooperated in the ecumenical translation of the Bible into Czech. It is also a member of the World Alliance of Reformed Churches, the World Council of Churches, and the Conference of European Churches.

One of the specific features of this church is its embracing of four confessions: the Brethren Confession (1535), the Bohemian Confession (the common confession of Evangelical Christians in the Czech countries, stemming from Hussite times and presented to the emperor Maximilian II in 1575), the Augsburg Confession (1539), and the Second Helvetic Confession (1566). However, the overall common denominator of its doctrine and practice is the Calvinism of the Helvetic Confession. Members acknowledge two sacraments: baptism and the Eucharist.

The organizational structure of this church is presbyterian. The church is divided into 13 seniorates, which are presided over by committees comprised of both ministers and laypeople. The highest body is the synod, which holds annual meetings and is comprised of elected deputies. The Synod Council, headed by a synod senior, controls the work of the church.

In 2005, the church reported 117,000 members meeting in 270 congregations.

Evangelical Church of the Czech Brethren
PO Box 466
Jungmanova 9
CZ-111 21 Praha 1
Czech Republic

Dušan Lužný

See also: World Alliance of Reformed Churches; World Council of Churches.

References

Bauswein, Jean-Jacques, and Lukas Vischner, eds. *The Reformed Family Worldwide: A Survey of Reformed Churches, Theological Schools, and International Organizations.* Grand Rapids, MI: William B. Eerdmans Publishing Company, 1999.

Di Domenzio, Daniel G. *Religion in Secularized Culture: The Czech Experience.* Lewiston, NY: Edwin Mellen Press, 2004.

Van Beek, Huibert. *A Handbook of the Churches and Councils: Profiles of Ecumenical Relationships.* Geneva: World Council of Churches, 2006.

Evangelical Church of the Disciples of Christ in Argentina

The Evangelical Church of the Disciples of Christ in Argentina is the major body representing the Restoration tradition of Free church Christianity that originated with the work of Barton Stone, Alexander Campbell, and their colleagues on the American frontier in the early 19th century. Representatives of one of the three major bodies of the tradition, the Christian Church (Disciples of Christ), arrived in Argentina in 1906. The mission remained small, with a focus in two areas, metropolitan Buenos Aires and the Province of Chaco in the extreme northern part of the country near the border with Paraguay.

The mission became an autonomous body in 1959. In 2006 it reported 7 congregations and 700 members. Two of the Buenos Aires congregations are joint congregations with the Methodist Church. It is one of the smallest member churches of the World Council of Churches, and is also a member of the Disciples Evangelical Consultative Council. Its commitment to ecumenical activity has made it one of the most visible entities in the various Christian cooperative projects operating in Argentina.

Evangelical Church of the Disciples of Christ in
    Argentina
Terrada 2324
1416 Buenos Aires
Argentina

J. Gordon Melton

See also: Disciples Ecumenical Consultative Council; World Council of Churches.

Reference

Van Beek, Huibert. *A Handbook of the Churches and Councils: Profiles of Ecumenical Relationships.* Geneva: World Council of Churches, 2006.

Evangelical Church of the Lutheran Confession in Brazil

The Lutheran presence in Brazil began with the movement of the Portuguese royal family to Brazil during the Napoleonic era. During his stay in Brazil, the king devised a plan to introduce European-style farming into the southern part of the country. He recruited farmers from the Catholic section of Switzerland, but unable to fill his needs, he turned to Germany. Most who accepted the offer of a new life in Brazil came from the poorer areas of the Rhine River Valley in the Palatinate. The first group arrived in 1823 and settled at Nova Friburgo, northeast of Rio de Janeiro. Subsequent settlers were located farther south in Rio Grande do Sul. In all some 5,000 people migrated, and included among them were a few German Lutheran pastors. The first church was organized in 1824.

The church overcame a number of obstacles during its first generation. It always had a shortage of pastors, a problem only remedied when several of the German mission societies became involved in the 1860s. Some settlements became victims of imposters. In mid-century, the Jesuits entered the area, and their vigorous pro-Catholic work soured what had been good relations between Lutherans and Roman Catholics. Nevertheless, immigration continued, and eventually four separate Lutheran synods emerged, serving communities in different parts of the country. The Synod of Rio Grande do Sul was formed in the south in 1886. Then came the Lutheran Synod (1901), the Synod of Santa Catarina and Parana (1911), and the Middle Brazilian Synod (1912).

The new century brought a new set of obstacles, not the least being the arrival of missionaries from the Lutheran Church–Missouri Synod who, rejecting the theological latitude in the evangelical church, which included those of the Reformed tradition, took members away from the church to found a conservative, exclusively Lutheran, rival church. World War I brought pressures for the German-speaking communities to drop their German language, only to be followed in the 1930s by the attractiveness of National Socialism and Adolf Hitler. Then in 1938, the Brazilian government nationalized all the foreign-language school.

On a more positive note, in 1922, steps had been taken to start theological education in Brazil, a must if the churches were ever to free themselves from dependence on the home country. World War II led to the arrest of some pastors and speeded the transition to Portuguese. In 1946 the founding of the Faculdade de Teologia (now the Escola Superior de Teologia) became an important event uniting the four synods. They united in a federation just two years later and under that loose organization joined the World Council of Churches in 1950 and the Lutheran World Federation in 1952. The church is a charter member of the National Council of Churches in Brazil. It adopted its present name in 1954. At the time it was the largest non-Catholic body in Brazil, though that is no longer the case.

The new Evangelical Church moved to improve its ecumenical ties, especially with a long-term program of contacts with the Roman Catholic Church. It has also supported the continued improvement of its educational facilities and encouraged faculty members and pastors to pursue further education in Germany.

Although no longer the largest Protestant body in Brazil, it is by far the largest Lutheran Church body in South America. In the 2005, it reported 715,959 members. It experienced a membership boost as Lutherans from Europe moved to Brazil after World War II. The church is led by a general assembly that meets biennially, and the administration is in the hands of a church council. Its 1,812 congregations are divided among 18 synods.

Evangelical Church of the Lutheran Confession
Rua Señor dos Passos 202, 5 andar
Caixa postal 2876
90001-970 Porto Alegre, RS
Brazil

J. Gordon Melton

See also: Jesuits; Lutheran World Federation; Lutheranism; Reformed/Presbyterian Tradition; Roman Catholic Church; World Council of Churches.

References

Bachmann, E. Theodore, and Mercia Brenne Bachmann. *Lutheran Churches in the World: A Handbook*. Minneapolis, MN: Augsburg Press, 1989.

Van Beek, Huibert. *A Handbook of the Churches and Councils: Profiles of Ecumenical Relationships*. Geneva: World Council of Churches, 2006.

Van der Bent, Ans J., ed. *Handbook/Member Churches/World Council of Churches*. Geneva: World Council of Churches, 1985.

Evangelical Church of the River Plate

Lutheranism in Argentina began among German immigrants in Buenos Aires in the years after the country gained independence (in 1816). German Protestants initially gathered in the Anglican Church, but in 1842 petitioned the Evangelical Mission Society in Bremen, Germany, for a pastor. August Ludwig Siegel arrived the following year. It took the members a decade to raise the funds and construct their own building, which was dedicated in 1853. Meanwhile, immigration increased, especially after the unrest in 1848 encouraged many to leave Europe. Others were lured by a scheme to populate Argentina's interior. Some also settled in nearby Uruguay, and ties developed with similar congregations in Brazil, Paraguay, and Chile. In the 1890s a pastor was sent to travel a preaching circuit among the German Lutheran congregations across the southern half of South America, and in 1900 an association, the German Lutheran La Plata Synod, held its first meeting.

For the next three decades, the pastor of the Buenos Aires congregation also served as the president of the synod, but in 1932 a dean was appointed from Germany to take the burdens of the synod's office from the pastor. The church continued to grow, especially in the years after World War II, when many Germans moved to South America. It became independent of the Evangelical Church in Germany in 1956, and for the next generation church leaders pushed members to become more integrated into South American society. The success of their efforts was manifest in 1980, when the first Argentinean-born pastor, Rodolfo Reinach, was elected the synod's president.

Today the church continues to serve the descendants of German and Swiss immigrants, and as adaptation has occurred, Spanish services have superseded German-language worship. Gradually, the majority of pastors have also come from among men trained at the Instituto Superior Evangélico de Estudios Teologicos, a Protestant seminary supported by several denominations in Buenos Aires.

The church has been a leader in ecumenical efforts. It is a member of the Argentine Federation of Evangelical Churches and the Latin American Council of Churches. It helped to form the Lutheran Council of the River Plate, which includes the three larger Lutheran bodies in Argentina, as well as a number of independent churches and smaller associations. It is one of four Argentinian churches to sign the Leuenberg Agreement, which has led to pulpit and table fellowship with the other signing churches, namely, the Presbyterian Church of Argentina, Reformed Churches in Argentina, and the Evangelical Congregational Church. It is also a member of the World Council of Churches and the Lutheran World Federation.

The church is headquartered in Buenos Aires. It includes congregations in Paraguay and Uruguay in its membership, last reported in 2005 at 25,000.

Although largely Lutheran, the church has adopted a position as a "United Protestant" church, meaning that it follows a program initiated in Germany of uniting Lutheran and Reformed churches into a single organization and reconciling what are considered minor differences. It is estimated that approximately 10 percent of the members are from the Reformed tradition.

Evangelical Church of the River Plate
Sucre 2855, piso 3
C1428 DVY Buenos Aires
Argentina

J. Gordon Melton

See also: Evangelical Church in Germany; Latin American Council of Churches; Lutheran World Federation; Lutheranism; Reformed/Presbyterian Tradition; World Council of Churches

References

Bachmann, E. Theodore, and Mercia Brenne Bachmann. *Lutheran Churches in the World: A Handbook.* Minneapolis, MN: Augsburg Press, 1989.

Van Beek, Huibert. *A Handbook of the Churches and Councils: Profiles of Ecumenical Relationships.* Geneva: World Council of Churches, 2006.

Evangelical Church of the West Indies

The Evangelical Church of the West Indies grew out of the work of a team of independent evangelical Christian missionaries in Cuba in 1928. The work was initiated by Elmer Thompson (b. 1901) and his wife Evelyn McElheran (b. 1905), who were soon joined by Bartholomew Lavastida (1890–1994), a Cuban national, and Isabel Junco, a Spanish woman converted by Lavastida. They opened a Bible school in which the students were quickly engaged in evangelistic endeavor. Prior to Fidel Castro's coming to power, the work had formed more than 100 congregations, and the school had trained some 400 evangelists.

In 1936 the group decided to establish work in the Dominican Republic. Alexander Mersdorf, a missionary who had joined the original team, stopped at Port-au-Prince, Haiti, on the way to his destination, and he was immediately asked by some Haitians to provide some training to a small group of Christians who had great zeal but had never been instructed in the Christian life. They lacked a Bible in their language and were desirous of a minister. He placed the need before the mission in Cuba, and they responded to it and postponed their thrust into the Dominican Republic. The opening of the mission in Haiti occasioned the team's adoption of a name, the West Indies Mission. The work in Haiti eventually became the Evangelical Mission of South Haiti.

The work subsequently spread to the Dominican Republic (1939), Jamaica (1945), and Guadeloupe (1947). Then in 1949, the Mission began a thrust into a number of the small English-speaking islands of the Eastern Caribbean—St. Lucia, St. Vincent, Grenada (the Windward Islands), and Trinidad and Tobago. Over the years, this effort matured and was eventually set apart as an autonomous church, the Evangelical Church of the West Indies (ECWI).

In St. Lucia there are 10 churches, all led by St. Lucian pastors, with a total membership of 1,000. The Mission first entered St. Vincent in 1952 when missionaries began witnessing in small coastal towns. Today there are 10 churches dotting the island with a membership of 650. In Grenada, the 5 churches have a total membership of approximately 250. The ministry on Trinidad was started in 1951 by Lloyd Cross and Dave Whitemore. They focused on the north coast, where they perceived a lack of Christian presence. There are now 18 ECWI churches scattered from Blanchisseuse in the north to Siparia in the south, including all the key towns of the island, with a combined membership of approximately 1,500.

Along the way the West Indies Mission became WorldTeam and continued to expand the number of countries in which it had work. It opened work in South America in 1955 and in Europe in 1970. Then, in 1995, WorldTeam merged with the British-based RBMU (Regions Beyond Missionary Union) International to form World Team (1431 Stuchert Rd., Warrington, PA 18976), and has continued to open new fields of operation.

The Evangelical Church of the West Indies has continued to work in close relationship with World Team. In 1990 it welcomed a new openness toward religion shown by the Castro regime in Cuba and has once again begun to grow, by forming of cell groups in different towns, many towns having been without a church since the rise of the Castro regime.

The church is headed by its president. Each island nation has its own structure, headed by a national moderator and national superintendent. A General Council meets biennially. In 1998 that council authorized the church's own missionary sending agency, which adopted a mission in French Guinea as its first responsibility.

Evangelical Church of the West Indies
Box 143
Old Montrose, Kingstown
St. Vincent

J. Gordon Melton

See also: Evangelical Mission of South Haiti.

Reference

"About World Team: A History of World Team 1928–1995." http://www.worldteam.org/about/wthist.htm. Accessed November 1, 2000.

Evangelical Church of West Africa

The Evangelical Church of West Africa is the result of the missionary initiative of the Sudan Interior Mission, an independent evangelical missionary society founded in 1893 in the United States. In 1935 it sent missionaries into the Borno Province of Nigeria, who established a station at Kukar Gadu near the Bauchi Province border. This area is predominantly Muslim, but the missionaries targeted four communities of non-Muslims for attention, the Kare-Kare, Bade, Ngamo, and Ngizim peoples. They first had significant success from a station in Gashua among the Bade people opened in 1938.

They successively opened stations in Gadaka among the Ngamo (1951) and in Garin Maje as an outpost among the Ngizim (1952). In 1954 the several churches that had been created were united as the Association of Evangelical Churches in West Africa. The church had spectacular success, primarily in the northeast of the country. In the 1990s it reported 2,200,000 members, and it is the largest of the several churches of the Reformed tradition operating in Nigeria.

The Evangelical Church of West Africa has retained a conservative theological stance, which it teaches through its 15 Bible training school, 3 theological colleges, and 2 seminaries. It is organized congregationally. The congregations are grouped into 18 districts. There is a general council to oversee the church's denominational endeavors, which include extensive medical and educational facilities. The church is a member of the World Evangelical Alliance.

Evangelical Church of West Africa
PO Box 63
Jos, Plateau State
Nigeria

J. Gordon Melton

See also: Evangelicalism; Reformed/Presbyterian Tradition; World Evangelical Alliance.

Reference

Bauswein, Jean-Jacques, and Lukas Vischner, eds. *The Reformed Family Worldwide: A Survey of Reformed Churches, Theological Schools, and International Organizations.* Grand Rapids, MI: William B. Eerdmans Publishing Company, 1999.

Evangelical Churches of Vietnam

The Evangelical Churches of Vietnam (Hoi Thánh Tin Lành), one of the few Christian religious communities operating in Vietnam, began in 1911 after missionaries

of the Christian and Missionary Alliance (from the United States) obtained permission from the French colonial government to pursue evangelistic work in Da Nang. Very early, several influential members of the community identified with the church, and it grew rapidly. Local leadership developed, and it was granted autonomy as the Evangelical Churches of Vietnam in 1927. The government recognized it in 1929 and lifted restrictions on its work. It quickly expanded among various ethnic groups, especially the Raday and Kobo peoples. A Bible and Theological Training Institute was opened at Nhatrang and later others at Dalat and Ban Me Thot. The church developed with a congregational polity, and there is no national synod.

The end of French colonialism, the division of Vietnam into two countries, and the years of the Vietnam War created significant changes in the church. Following the withdrawal of the French, many church members moved into the southern half of the country. However, the work in the north, including the Bible school at Nhatrang, continued to operate throughout the years of the Vietnam War. In 1972, church leaders in the north made contact with the National Council of Churches in the United States, at which time they expressed criticism of the American role in the war. The following year they made contact with the World Council of Churches, which initiated aid to rebuild the church following the close of the war.

The final fall of South Vietnam and the withdrawal of American forces were accompanied by the immigration of many church leaders and pastors. In the 1980s, some American Vietnamese converts returned to Vietnam to start new congregations and revive the church. By the end of the 1990s, there were more than 1,000 congregations and some 400 Christian pastors working with the evangelical churches. Some 40 congregations were to be found in Ho Chi Minh City and its immediate environs.

During the first decade of the new century, the evangelical churches were granted official recognition and were allowed to register two congregational associations in the north and south regions of the country as the Southern Evangelical Church of Vietnam (SECV or ECVN-S) and Evangelical Church of Vietnam North (ECVN), two of the four Protestant churches that have been granted such recognition. Problems persist in the registration of local congregations. The official government count on membership of all Protestant churches is 610,000 (2007) though unofficially Protestant spokespersons claim as many as 1.6 million.

The evangelical churches may be contacted through the Evangelical Church in Vietnam-Hoahung, 625 Cach mang thang 8 P.15 Q.10, 155 Tran Hung Dao Q.1, Hochiminh City, SouthEast 84-8, Vietnam. This congregation has an Internet presence at http://www.netministries.org/see/churches.exe/ch26215.

J. Gordon Melton

See also: Christian and Missionary Alliance; World Council of Churches.

Reference

Bauswein, Jean-Jacques, and Lukas Vischner, eds. *The Reformed Family Worldwide: A Survey of Reformed Churches, Theological Schools, and International Organizations.* Grand Rapids, MI: William B. Eerdmans Publishing Company, 1999.

Evangelical Church–Synod of the Nile

The Evangelical Church–Synod of the Nile derives from missionary work begun by American Presbyterians in Egypt in 1854. Unable by law to proselytize among Muslims, they found their converts from people raised as members of the Coptic Orthodox Tewahedo Church. The church built its program around evangelism, charitable activity (hospitals and schools), and Bible study groups using an Arabic Bible. By the turn of the century, four presbyteries had been founded, and work spread into the Sudan.

Through the 20th century, the Evangelical Church has spread to other North African and Middle Eastern countries, primarily from the immigration of its members responding to job offers. In 1967 it became an autonomous body and the following year fully independent, though it retains a working relationship with the Presbyterian Church (U.S.A.). It presently has seven presbyteries united by the Synod of the Nile, the highest legislative body in the church.

In 2005 the church reported 250,000 members, though attendance at its 315 churches indicates a sig-

nificantly larger constituency that for various reasons maintains official religious membership elsewhere. The church sponsors a theological seminary in Cairo. It is a member of the World Alliance of Reformed Churches and since 1963 of the World Council of Churches.

Evangelical Church–Synod of the Nile
PO Box 1248
Cairo
Egypt

J. Gordon Melton

See also: Coptic Orthodox Church; Presbyterian Church (U.S.A.); World Alliance of Reformed Churches; World Council of Churches.

References

Bauswein, Jean-Jacques, and Lukas Vischner, eds. *The Reformed Family Worldwide: A Survey of Reformed Churches, Theological Schools, and International Organizations.* Grand Rapids, MI: William B. Eerdmans Publishing Company, 1999.

Sharkey, Heather J. *American Evangelicals in Egypt: Missionary Encounters in an Age of Empire.* Princeton, NJ: Princeton University Press, 2008.

Van Beek, Huibert. *A Handbook of the Churches and Councils: Profiles of Ecumenical Relationships.* Geneva: World Council of Churches, 2006.

Evangelical Confederation of Latin America

The Evangelical Confederation of Latin America (Confraternidad Evangélica Latinoamericana [CONELA]) was officially organized in Panama City, Panama, in April 1982, led by a group of conservative evangelical leaders who were active in the Lausanne Movement for World Evangelization. The organization of CONELA was supported and financed mainly by the Billy Graham Evangelistic Association (BGEA), the Luis Palau Evangelistic Association (LPEA, founded in 1967), and other organizations. Palau is a well known and popular Argentine evangelist who previously worked with the BGEA in crusade evangelism in many Latin American and Caribbean countries during the 1960s

Evangelist Luis Palau preaches in Bolivia during a three-city campaign, 1995. (AP Photo/Gary S. Chapman)

and 1970s. CONELA is affiliated with the World Evangelical Alliance (WEF).

Participating in the organizational meeting in Panama were delegates from 84 conservative evangelical denominations representing 4.2 million church members, according to official reports. Also participating were representatives of 64 para-church agencies, with media organizations comprising the largest number along with organizations specializing in mass evangelism.

However, absent from this event were representatives of the more fundamentalist denominations and service agencies that were not interested in joining anything interdenominational or ecumenical, which would be considered a betrayal of their basic principles.

In addition, according to David Stoll, the CONELA leadership wanted to keep out of the new organization those defined as "ecumenical Protestants" and those evangelicals who desired to remain in dialogue with the former, including members of the Latin American Theological Fraternity (FTL) who participated in the ecumenical Conference on Mission and Evangelism, held in Melbourne, Australia, in May 1980, sponsored by the World Council of Churches (WCC).

In part, according to Stoll, the creation of CONELA was a reaction against the formation of the Latin American Council of Churches (CLAI, Concilio Latinoamericano de Iglesias), which was initially established in 1978 in Oaxtepec, Mexico, by Latin American "ecumenical Protestants" whose denominations and service agencies were affiliated with the WCC. The defined purpose of CLAI was to promote evangelism as well as social change through its members, which initially included about 100 denominations and service agencies in Latin America. Since its inception CLAI has depended on WCC funding and technical assistance for its operation.

However, according to the Reverend Norberto Saracco, a Pentecostal leader from Buenos Aires and a member of the Lausanne Coordinating Committee, the birth of CONELA took place as a reaction against presentations by "ecumenical Protestants" at CLADE II (Congreso Latino-americano de Evangelización [Latin American Congress on Evangelization]) in Huampaní, Peru, regarding the politicization of the gospel in the Latin American context by supporters of Liberation Theology. CLADE I (Bogotá, Colombia, in 1969), CLADE II (Huampaní, Peru, in 1979), CLADE III (Quito, Ecuador, in 1992), and CLADE IV (at Seminario Sudamericano (SEMISUD), Quinto, Ecuador in 2000) were sponsored by the FTL, which represents the progressive wing of evangelicals in Latin America (Saracco 2009).

In order to increase its membership and representation internationally, CONELA leaders targeted conservative denominational, national and female leaders; representatives of evangelical alliances, councils, pastors' associations, and fellowships; directors of service agencies; representatives of international mission organizations; and pastors of local churches in each Latin American country. The principal motivational factor for organizing national chapters of CONELA in each country or for attracting existing evangelical alliances, councils, and fellowships to become affiliated with CONELA was to build bridges "in the spirit of the Lausanne Congress on World Evangelism," inspired and united by the Lausanne Covenant as a modern, worldwide multinational, and multi-ethnic expression of evangelical faith. The initial Lausanne event in 1974 was convoked by a committee headed by well-known evangelist Billy Graham and drew more than 2,300 evangelical leaders from 150 countries. Lausanne I introduced the term "unreached people groups," hailed as one of the milestone events in contemporary missiology. In contradistinction to those calling for a moratorium on foreign missions, such as many WCC leaders, the idea of unreached people groups pointed toward thousands of groups that remained without a single Christian witness.

In May 1980, approximately 650 worldwide "ecumenical Protestant" church leaders participated in the WCC-sponsored event in Melbourne, called the Tenth World Conference on Mission and Evangelism, which used the theme "Your Kingdom Come" to explore the place of the poor in the church's worldwide mission. Liberation Theology had an especially strong influence on the conference discussions, with a focus on questions of power connecting the work of the church with the need to end political and economic oppression around the world. The conference also highlighted how the life and work of Jesus Christ exemplified Christian solidarity with the poor.

In June 1980, the Lausanne Committee on World Evangelization sponsored a Consultation on World Evangelization (COWE), held in Pattaya, Thailand, which gathered almost 900 evangelicals from around the world to consider strategic issues of reaching the unreached for Jesus Christ. Among the participants was a small group of Latin American evangelical leaders who held a private meeting to discuss the possibility of creating a CONELA-type organization to further the vision and goals of the Lausanne movement throughout Latin America among conservative evangelicals.

Lausanne II was held in Manila, Philippines, in July 1989 on the theme, "Proclaim Christ until He Comes: Calling the Whole Church to Take the Whole Gospel to the Whole World." This event was significant in its *representation*: 4,300 in attendance from 173 countries, including the Soviet Union and Eastern Europe, and with a larger proportion of women, laypersons, and younger leaders than at previous Lausanne-sponsored conferences. A large group of Latin American church leaders participated in this event, which was an important networking opportunity between leaders of different countries. The Manila Congress played a significant role in a movement that stands for completing the task of world evangelization, for cooperation in that cause, and for networking between evangelical leaders in that task.

The congresses and consultations sponsored by the Lausanne Committee on World Evangelization were instrumental in strengthening support among participating Latin American evangelical church leaders for their involvement in CONELA as a vehicle for carrying out the Lausanne mandate. CONELA members helped to establish evangelical fellowships, alliances, and councils in their respective countries in the "spirit of Lausanne."

In the mid-1980s, the leadership of CONELA summoned evangelical leaders to a meeting in Mexico City for the purpose of organizing the first Ibero-American Missionary Congress to discuss issues related to the Lausanne mandate of urgently taking the gospel of Christ to people in every tongue, tribe, people, and nation (that is, ethno-linguistic "people groups") who have not yet heard the "good news" of salvation proclaimed by Jesus of Nazareth. In response, steps were taken to plan, organize, and promote the first Ibero-American Missionary Congress, which was held in November 1987 in Sao Paulo, Brazil. About 3,300 people from 35 countries registered as participants in the Congress. The emphasis at the event was raising awareness as well as training and mobilizing Latin Americans as missionaries to the yet unreached "people groups" around the world, beginning with crosscultural and transcultural evangelization and church planting in every country of Latin America and the Iberian Peninsula (Spain and Portugal) and from there to the rest of the world.

The major outcome of the Ibero-American Missionary Congress was the establishment of Ibero-American Missionary Cooperation (COMIBAM, Cooperación Misionera Iberoamericana). Since its establishment, COMIBAM has produced a substantial amount of literature about transcultural missions and has organized several missionary congresses and conferences at the national, regional, and continental levels, particularly in Latin America. COMIBAM-affiliated organizations have recruited, trained, and sent out hundreds of Latin Americans as missionaries among targeted "unreached people groups" in many nations, with an emphasis on the 10/40 Window, a concept defined by the Reverend Luis Bush of Argentina. The 10/40 Window is an area of the world that contains the largest population of non-Christians. The area extends from 10 degrees to 40 degrees north of the equator, and stretches from North Africa across to China. This 10/40 focus is on finishing the call of scripture to reach every tribe and nation and thus to plant the church of Jesus Christ among *all* people groups. Bush led COMIBAM during its initial phase (1985–1986) and later served as the international director of the AD2000 and Beyond Movement from 1989 to 2001.

The CONELA Constitutional Assembly was held in Panama City, Panama, in April 1982, followed by the I General Assembly in Maracaibo, Venezuela (April 1986); the II General Assembly in Acapulco, Mexico (April 1990); the III General Assembly in 1994; the IV General Assembly in Miami, Florida (June 2001); the V General Assembly in Panama City, Panama (May 2004); and the VI General Assembly in Bogotá, Colombia (April 2007).

The current president of CONELA is the Reverend Ricardo A. Luna Miño (an Ecuadoran), who took office in April 2007 at the VI General Assembly in Bogotá, Colombia, which also marked the 25th anniversary of CONELA. Previously he served as the Latin America director of the ministry Open Doors with Brother Andrew. Later, he founded Oasis Life International and is the current Latin America director for Book of Hope International (OneHope), with headquarters in Miami, Florida.

Mr. Ricardo A. Luna, President of CONELA
Latin America Director of OneHope
600 SW 3rd Street
Pompano, FL 33060
http://www.onehope.net

Clifton L. Holland

See also: AD2000 and Beyond Movement; Latin American Council of Churches; Lausanne Movement; World Council of Churches; World Evangelical Alliance.

References

"COMIBAM." In *Evangelical Dictionary of World Missions,* edited by Moreau, A. Scott, Harold Netland, and Charles Van Engen, 211–212. Grand Rapids, MI: Baker Books, 2000.

CONELA. www.conela.com.

Holland, Clifton L. Personal conversations and correspondence with Virgilio Zapata, Galo Vásquez, Luis Bush, Luis Palau, David Howard and Ricardo Luna regarding CONELA and COMIBAM, 1980–2009.

Lausanne Committee for World Evangelization. http://www.lausanne.org.

Luna, Ricardo. "La Nueva CONELA." http://transform-world.net/newsletters/2008/08/CONELA.pdf.

Saracco, Norberto. "El origin y desarrollo de CONELA" (The origin and development of CONELA). Address in the chapel of the Evangelical University of the Americas (UNELA), San José, Costa Rica, August 10, 2009, sponsored by the Costa Rican Chapter of the Latin American Theological Fraternity.

Stoll, David. "The Evangelical Awakening in Latin America." Chapter 5 in *Is Latin America Turning Protestant? The Politics of Evangelical Growth*. Berkeley: University of California Press, 1990.

Evangelical Congregational Church in Angola

The Evangelical Congregational Church in Angola (Igreja Evangelica Congregacional em Angola) dates to the arrival of representatives of the American Board of Commissioners for Foreign Missions (now the Global Ministries Board of the United Church of Christ) in 1880. The mission, originally opened at Sailundo among the Ovimbundu people, grew very slowly. They were joined by Canadian Congregationalists (now a constituent part of the United Church of Canada) in 1886. As World War I began in 1914, they had gathered only 300 members; however, they experienced a growth phase in the 1920s and 1930s.

The mission has been greatly affected by the changes that came with the ending of colonial rule in Angola. In 1951 Portugal signaled its desire to retain control in Angola by making it an overseas province of Portugal. However, with independence coming to some of its African neighbors, Angola broke into civil war in 1960. In 1961, suspecting the missionaries of supporting the insurgents, the government began systematically denying visa renewals. The number of missionaries dropped significantly. In 1967, the United Church of Christ and the United Church of Canada withdrew the remaining non-Angolan personnel as a protest against the Portuguese policies in Angola.

In the meantime, in 1957, the two Congregationalist missions had united as the Evangelical Church of Central Angola. However, as the missionaries withdrew, the church itself divided, one part of it going into the underground with the rebels. After independence in 1975, the other faction established itself as the Evangelical Congregational Church in the People's Republic of Angola. The two groups remained in contact, and over the two decades after independence worked toward reunion. That was accomplished in 1996.

In 2005 the Evangelical Congregational Church in Angola reported 950,000 members. It was a founding member of the Council of Christian Churches in Angola and since 1985 of the World Council of Churches. The church had developed one of its earliest centers at Dondi, where they founded a seminary and a publication center. Today, ministers are trained at an ecumenical Protestant seminary at Huambo. The church is noted for its extensive medical facilities, the best in the country.

Evangelical Congregational Church in Angola
Avenida Cmdte Gika 3-46
PO 1552
Luanda
Angola

J. Gordon Melton

See also: American Board of Commissioners for Foreign Missions; United Church of Canada; United Church of Christ; World Council of Churches.

References

Bauswein, Jean-Jacques, and Lukas Vischner, eds. *The Reformed Family Worldwide: A Survey of Reformed Churches, Theological Schools, and International Organizations*. Grand Rapids, MI: William B. Eerdmans Publishing Company, 1999.

Van Beek, Huibert. *A Handbook of the Churches and Councils: Profiles of Ecumenical Relationships*. Geneva: World Council of Churches, 2006.

Evangelical Covenant Church

The Evangelical Covenant Church has its roots in the same revival of piety and spirituality in Sweden that led to the formation of the Mission Covenant Church of Sweden. Through the 1850s and 1860s, people who had been affected by the revival migrated to the United States. Most affiliated with Lutheran congregations and attempted to carry on their Pietist quest. However, as in Sweden, they found life in the Lutheran churches too confining, and in the 1870s they began to form their own churches. In 1873 the first synod, the Swedish Lutheran Mission Synod, was organized. A second synod, the Swedish Lutheran Ansgarius Synod, was created in 1884. The next year, the two synods merged to form the Swedish Evangelical Mission Covenant Church of America. The church went through several name changes in the 20th century to emerge as the Evangelical Covenant Church.

Although operating out of the central Western Christian doctrinal tradition, the church is non-creedal and accepts the Bible as the only perfect rule of faith and practice. Its non-creedal position emphasizes the role of the Christian life over that of theological speculation. In 1981, the church backed the publication of an important theological volume, *Covenant Affirmations*, issued as a means of clarifying the church's perspective. It emphasized the centrality of the Bible, the necessity of the new birth, the church as the gathered community of believers, the conscious dependence of the believer on Christ, and the reality of the free life in Christ. Unlike the Baptists, the church practices infant baptism.

The church is organized congregationally, and there is an annual assembly of representatives of the congregations where business affecting the whole covenant is carried out. The church developed an extensive mission program early in the 20th century, and retains a partnership relationship with former mission churches in South America, Asia, continental Europe, and the Democratic Republic of the Congo. In 2006 it reported 114,283 members in the United States and 1,384 members in Canada. It has joined with other churches that came out of the same Free church impulse in Europe in the 19th century and the former mission churches to create the International Federation of Free Evangelical Churches. It has been a member of the World Council of Churches but has in recent years withdrawn.

Evangelical Covenant Church
5101 N. Francisco Ave.
Chicago, IL 60625
http://www.covchurch.org

J. Gordon Melton

See also: International Federation of Free Evangelical Churches; Mission Covenant Church of Sweden; World Council of Churches.

References

Anderson, W. D. B. *The Covenant Church in Canada, 1904–1994: A Time to Remember*. Winnipeg: Evangelical Covenant Church of Canada, 1995.

Matson, P., E. B. Larsson, and W. D. Thornbloom, eds. *Covenant Frontiers*. Chicago: Board of Mission, Evangelical Mission Covenant Church of America, 1941.

Olsson, Karl A. *A Family of Faith*. Chicago: Covenant Press, 1975.

Olsson, Karl A. *Into One Body . . . By the Cross*. Chicago: Covenant Press, 1985.

Van der Bent, Ans J., ed. *Handbook/Member Churches/World Council of Churches*. Geneva: World Council of Churches, 1985.

Evangelical Free Church of America

The Evangelical Free Church of America grew out of the 19th-century Free church revival that swept through Europe and had a special focus in Sweden, where it led to the formation of the Mission Covenant Church of Sweden. Many who had been inspired by the revival immigrated to the United States, where in the 1870s they began to form independent congregations. Some of these congregations joined together in 1873 to form the Swedish Lutheran Mission Synod. However, some congregations, prizing their freedom, rejected any involvement in a synod. They preferred a loose association of congregations. Such an association was formed at Boone, Iowa, in 1884 as the Swedish Evangelical Free Church.

At about the same time, immigrants from Norway and Denmark, where the Swedish revival had spread, also began to organize congregations in America. In 1889, a periodical, *Evangelisten*, appeared to promote their fellowship. An initial organization appeared two years later as the Western Evangelical Free Church Association, followed a few months later by an Eastern association. These two associations merged in 1909 to form the Norwegian-Danish Evangelical Free Church Association.

In 1950, the Swedish and Norwegian-Danish churches united as the Evangelical Free Church of America. By this time, the new church had become identified with the emerging evangelical movement, which had grown out of the Fundamentalist-Modernist controversy of the 1920s. Their position was in contrast to the Evangelical Covenant Church, the other American body that had grown out of the same Swedish revival, which had identified itself with the more liberal Protestant churches and the contemporary ecumenical movement. One sign of the direction of the Evangelical Free Church was its adoption of a confession of faith that emphasized the essential affirmations of the Protestant Reformation, the Bible as the inspired word of God, and the premillennial imminent Second Coming of Christ.

In 2008, the church adopted a new statement of faith that retained its conservative theological perspective and reflected its adherence to the Princeton Theology that emphasized Biblical inerrancy: "As the verbally inspired Word of God, the Bible is without error in the original writings, the complete revelation of His will for salvation, and the ultimate authority by which every realm of human knowledge and endeavor should be judged. Therefore, it is to be believed in all that it teaches, obeyed in all that it requires, and trusted in all that it promises."

In 2006 the Evangelical Free Church reported 130,000 members in the United States and 8,400 in Canada. The church is organized congregationally, and a national annual meeting of congregational representatives oversees the cooperative endeavors of the fellowship. High among these endeavors is a mission program that supports personnel across continental Europe, in Latin America and Asia, and in the Democratic Republic of the Congo. Many of the former missions of the church have in the last generation become autonomous sister churches. The church also supports a college, a university, and a theological seminary in the United States and a spectrum of medical, educational, and social service institutions overseas. The church is a member of the National Association of Evangelicals through which it relates to the World Evangelical Alliance.

Evangelical Free Church of America
901 East 78th Street
Minneapolis, MN 55420
http://www.efca.org

J. Gordon Melton

See also: Evangelical Covenant Church; Evangelicalism; Fundamentalism; Mission Covenant Church of Sweden; World Evangelical Alliance.

References

Forstrom, Jim. *A Living Legacy: Evangelical Free Church of America—A Pictorial History*. St. Louis, MO: G. Bradley Pub., 2002.

Norton, W. Wilbert, et al. *The Diamond Jubilee Story*. Minneapolis, MN: Free Church Publications, 1959.

Olson, Arnold Theodore. *Believers Only*. Minneapolis, MN: Free Church Publications, 1956.

Olson, Arnold Theodore. *This We Believe*. Minneapolis, MN: Free Church Publications, 1961.

Evangelical Church of French Polynesia

See Maohi Protestant Church.

Evangelical Friends International

Evangelical Friends International (EFI) was founded in 1965 as a networking association for four autonomous Quaker groups that represented the most conservative wing of the Friends movement. Each had been deeply affected by the Wesleyan Holiness movement in the 19th century and had come to exist in the space between the two communities. The Evangelical Friends

Alliance, Eastern Division, was founded in 1813 as the Ohio Yearly Meeting of Friends and was one of the original Friends groups influenced by the preaching of Joseph John Gurney (1788–1847), a Quaker preacher deeply influenced by Methodist Holiness teachings.

The Kansas Yearly Meeting was formed in 1872 and in 1900 affiliated with the Five Years Meeting (now the Friends United Meeting). However, through the early 20th century its members were influenced by Holiness teachings, and in 1937 it withdrew from the Five Years Meeting. By this time it had established its first missionary program in the part of the Congo now known as Burundi. In the 1970s it changed its name to the Mid-America Yearly Meeting.

In the late 19th century, Friends began to move into the Willamette Valley in Oregon. In 1893 they dropped their affiliation with the Iowa Friends and formed the independent Oregon Yearly Meeting. In 1902, they too affiliated with the Five Years Meeting and like the Kansas Meeting withdrew after being influenced by Holiness ideas. The Oregon Meeting has been active in education and has established George Fox College in Newberg, Oregon. It later assumed the name Northwest Yearly Meeting.

In 1957 Friends in Colorado withdrew from the Nebraska Yearly Meeting (affiliated with the Five Years Meeting) and formed the Rocky Mountain Yearly Meeting. They did not keep their former affiliation with the Five Years Meeting. Rather, in 1965 they joined with the three other conservative Friends Meetings in the Evangelical Friends Alliance. Over the years that association took on the trappings of a denominational structure. The change of name to Evangelical Friends International in 1990 was a recognition of the change that had taken place.

In 2006, Evangelical Friends International North American Region reported an inclusive membership of 39,569 in 283 churches. It supports two colleges, one university, and a graduate school of theology. It carries out missionary work in Burundi, Mexico, Rwanda, Taiwan, Peru, Bolivia, and India. The Evangelical Friends Alliance, Eastern Division, is a member of the Christian Holiness Partnership, though Evangelical Friends International is not. Evangelical Friends International is a member of the National Association of Evangelicals, through which it is related to the World Evangelical Alliance.

Evangelical Friends International
No central headquarters. For information, contact:
Dr. John P. Williams
Regional Director for North America
5350 Broadmoor Circle, NW
Canton, OH 44709
http://www.evangelical-friends.org

J. Gordon Melton

See also: Christian Holiness Partnership; Friends United Meeting; Friends/Quakers; Holiness Movement; World Evangelical Alliance.

References

The Association of Evangelical Friends: A Story of Quaker Renewal in the Twentieth Century. Newberg, OR: Barclay Press, 1975.

DeVol, Charles E. *Focus on Friends.* Canton, OH: Missionary Board of the Evangelical Friends Church–Eastern Division, 1982.

The Story of Friends in the Northwest. Newberg, OR: Barclay Press, n.d.

Evangelical Lutheran Church in America

The Evangelical Lutheran Church in America is one of the two primary bodies continuing the Lutheran tradition in the United States. Formed in 1988, it stands in direct continuity with the earliest Lutheran organizations in America, formed in the 18th century, but is also the product of a series of mergers that occurred through the 20th century that saw more than 100 separate Lutheran churches merge into a single ecclesiastical unit.

Lutherans came to the United States from the different countries of northern Europe and through the 19th century spread out across the vast frontier then opening to settlement. As groups settled in different areas, churches were formed and synods established. Each synod typically served a single language group in a relatively limited area. A minority of synods rep-

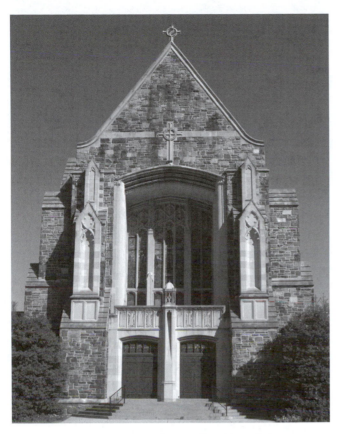

First English Evangelical Lutheran Church in Baltimore, Maryland. (Gaja Snover/StockphotoPro)

resented variant trends in Lutheranism toward a more conservative doctrinal approach or an emphasis upon piety and the religious life. The earliest mergers tended to bring those of the smaller synods together that were of like language or national heritage.

As Americanization proceeded, mergers across the boundaries of national heritage became feasible. Numerous German Lutherans were among the 17th-century immigrants to the American colonies. These settlers formed the backbone of the earliest synods, the Philadelphia Ministerium (1748) and New York Ministerium (1786). The Philadelphia Ministerium, part of the New Ministerium, and the North Carolina Synod had merged in 1820 to form the General Synod of the Lutheran Church. Similar mergers in other parts of the country led to the formation of the General Synod of the South and the General Council. These three groups merged in 1918 to form the United Lutheran Church in America, the largest Lutheran body

in America through the mid-20th century. This body included most of the German American Lutherans.

In 1962, the United Lutheran Church in America created a multiethnic church by its merger with the Finnish Evangelical Lutheran Church (Soumi Synod), the Augustana Evangelical Lutheran Church (of Swedish heritage), and the American Evangelical Lutheran Church (of Danish heritage). Their union created the Lutheran Church in America.

In 1930, a group of German American synods in the middle of the United States—the Ohio, Buffalo, Texas, and Iowa synods—united to form the American Lutheran Church. In 1960 the American Lutheran Church merged with the United Evangelical Lutheran Church, itself the product of a merger of Danish American churches and the Evangelical Lutheran Church, of Norwegian background. The new church retained the name American Lutheran Church.

Through the 1970s the American Lutheran Church and the Lutheran Church in America were the two largest Lutheran bodies in the United States. They also formed the more liberal and ecumenically oriented wing of American Lutheranism, in contrast to the more conservative, confessionally strict, churches such as the Lutheran Church–Missouri Synod and the Wisconsin Evangelical Lutheran Synod. The two churches entered into merger negotiation soon after they were organized. In the meantime, a controversy had developed within the Missouri Synod, in which a number of professors at the synod's main seminary in suburban St. Louis, Missouri, were accused of straying from strict orthodox doctrinal standards. The controversy brought the more liberal pastors and members to the scholars' defense. The controversy resulted in the more liberal group leaving the Missouri Synod and forming the Association of Evangelical Lutheran Churches.

The Association of Evangelical Lutheran Churches was invited into the union meetings of the Lutheran Church in America and the American Lutheran Church. The effort of the three groups culminated in their merger as the Evangelical Lutheran Church in America, a merger that became effective on January 1, 1988. The new church established its headquarters in Chicago. In 2006 it reported an inclusive membership of 4,774,203 members. The church is headed by its presiding bishop, currently the Reverend Mark S. Hanson (b. 1946). Hanson is also the president of the Lutheran World Federation. The church is divided into 65 synods, each of which is in turn headed by a bishop. The work of the church at the national level is channeled through a number of national boards and agencies. The church supports a number of colleges, universities, and seminaries, reflective of a rich intellectual heritage.

The church accepts the Bible and the Augsburg Confession as its standards of doctrine; it has, however, adopted a contemporary theological approach to doctrinal issues that draws from a variety of theological currents that emerged in the 19th and 20th centuries. The church is ecumenically oriented and a member of both the Lutheran World Federation and the World Council of Churches. In 1997, the church voted intercommunion with the Presbyterian Church (U.S.A.), the United Church of Christ, and the Reformed Church in America. In 2001 intercommunion was established with the Episcopal Church. In 2005, the church approved an interim Eucharistic sharing agreement with the United Methodist Church that is expected to evolve into full intercommunion.

Some of the Lutheran churches that are now constituent parts of the Evangelical Lutheran Church were active in missions, often in cooperation with the missionary sending agencies of the various Lutheran churches in continental Europe. Already by the time of the 1988 merger, most of these missionary efforts had evolved into independent churches. The Evangelical Lutheran Church retains a partnership relationship with many of these churches and continues to supply significant financial support to some of them in the poorer countries. The church also supports congregations across Europe that serve English-speaking expatriates. In 1967 and 1986, respectively, the American Lutheran Church and the Lutheran Church in America released their affiliated Canadian parishes. These parishes eventually merged to form the Evangelical Lutheran Church in Canada.

Evangelical Lutheran Church in America
8765 Higgins Rd.
Chicago, IL 60631
http://www.elca.org

J. Gordon Melton

See also: Episcopal Church; Evangelical Lutheran Church in Canada; Lutheran Church–Missouri Synod; Lutheran World Federation; Lutheranism; Presbyterian Church (U.S.A.); Reformed Church in America; United Church of Christ; United Methodist Church; Wisconsin Evangelical Lutheran Synod; World Council of Churches.

References

Almen, Lowell G. *One Great Cloud of Witnesses!: You and Your Congregation in the Evangelical Lutheran Church in America*. Minneapolis, MN: Augsburg Fortress Publishers, 2006.

Chilstrom, Herbert W. *Foundations for the Future*. Minneapolis, MN: Publishing House of the Evangelical Lutheran Church in America, 1988.

Nelson, E. Clifford. *The Lutherans in North America*. Philadelphia: Fortress Press, 1980.

Nichol, Todd W. *All Those Lutherans*. Minneapolis, MN: Augsburg Publishing House, 1986.

Evangelical Lutheran Church in Canada

Lutherans are those who trace their roots to the 16th-century reforms initiated by the German Reformer Martin Luther (1483–1546). Behind many of these reforms was Luther's belief in the necessity of justification by grace through faith alone, as well as his conviction that only holy scripture has authority in matters of belief.

The first Lutheran congregation in Canada was established in Halifax in 1752. The location of churches originally depended on the pattern of German immigration. Support for the churches came primarily from their affiliations with American Lutheran groups. Early churches tended to be in rural Nova Scotia, Ontario, and the prairies. Since World War II, the largest concentrations of Lutherans are found in Kitchener–Waterloo, Winnipeg, and Edmonton.

The Evangelical Lutheran Church in Canada (ELCIC) is one of the two main Lutheran denominations in Canada (the other is the Lutheran Church–Canada). In 1986, the ELCIC was formed from the merger of two Lutheran denominations, the Lutheran

An Evangelical Lutheran church in Canada. (Frederic Sune/ Dreamstime.com)

Church of America and the Evangelical Lutheran Church of Canada. The ELCIC has its head office in Winnipeg, Manitoba, and is comprised of five synods, with each synod presided over by a bishop. Membership is numbered around 200,000. In July 2001 the ELCIC entered into full communion with the Anglican Church of Canada. This allows for the free exchange of members and clergy, although both denominations remain distinct church bodies. The ELCIC is a member of the Canadian Council of Churches, the Lutheran World Federation, and the World Council of Churches. Its denominational periodicals are entitled *Canada Lutheran* and *Esprit*.

The ELCIC uses the term "evangelical" in the way it was used in the 16th century, not necessarily in the way many use it today. Services are primary in English. The ELCIC is a "confessional" church, subscribing to the beliefs of the Reformers expressed in the confessions contained in the *Book of Concord*. Two sacraments are practiced in the church: baptism and

holy Communion. Infant baptism is practiced, with the hope that confirmation will occur at a later date, after the child has been nurtured in the faith. Holy Communion is often celebrated every week, presided over by an ordained minister, and is usually open to all baptized Christians. The ELCIC ordains both men and women and seeks to be active in the promotion of ethical and social issues in Canada and abroad.

Evangelical Lutheran Church in Canada
302-393 Portage Ave.
Winnipeg, Manitoba R3B 3H6
Canada
http://www.elcic.ca

Gordon L. Heath

See also: Anglican Church of Canada; Luther, Martin; Lutheran World Federation; Lutheranism; World Council of Churches.

References

Cronmiller, Carl. R. *A History of the Lutheran Church in Canada*. Toronto: Evangelical Lutheran Synod of Canada, 1961.

Pfrimmer, David. "A Lutheran Witness in Canadian Society." In *Church and Canadian Culture*, edited by Robert E. VanderVennen. Lanham, MD: University Press of America, 1991.

Ward, Kenn. *This Evangelical Lutheran Church of Ours*. Winfield, BC: Wood Lake Books, 1994.

Evangelical Lutheran Church in Chile

The Evangelical Lutheran Church in Chile continues the spread of Lutheranism in Chile that began with the arrival of German-speaking people in the 19th century. An early center was in the southern part of the country near the towns of Valdivia and Osomo, and as early as 1852 two pastors arrived to form and lead congregations. About the same time, a professor of botany at the University of Chile began to organize Lutherans in the Santiago area and recruit pastors from Germany. They were allowed to meet only in private locations, religious freedom not yet being a part of Chilean life. He was assisted by the Gustav-Adolf-Werk, an organization established to assist Lutherans residing in predominantly Roman Catholic lands.

Pastors were obtained from several of the Lutheran bodies in Germany via Argentina, and they were considered part of a mission of the Evangelical Church in Germany. A synod was formed in 1904. It operated in an informal manner until 1937, when the German Evangelical Lutheran Church was formally organized. The church joined the Lutheran World Federation in 1955 and four years later adopted a new constitution and assumed their present name. The program of the church also shifted significantly away from preserving German heritage to Chileanization. The increasing use of Spanish in worship was accelerated by a cooperative program with American Lutherans that aimed at missionary work among the urban poor and the rural indigenous population.

The church ran into major internal problems following the fall of the Allende regime. Pastors tended to be more attuned to the needs of those least supportive of the new government, while many of the laypeople were staunchly conservative. The expulsion from the country of Helmut Frenz, who had headed an ecumenical commission caring for political refugees, became the occasion for a split in the church. Eight of 12 congregations left; some became independent, and some founded the Lutheran Church in Chile. In the 1980s, most Lutherans joined a Council of Lutheran Churches in Chile to work toward reunion, but such a union has not yet occurred.

The Evangelical Lutheran Church in Chile was left with only 2,000 members at the time of the disruption of 1975 and has added only a few hundred more in the ensuing decades. In 2005 it reported 3,000 members. Most of its 13 congregations and work are in the Santiago metropolitan area. It is a member of the World Council of Churches.

The church is led by its president and the synod, the highest legislative body among the rather loosely associated congregations. It continues a program of cooperation with the Evangelical Lutheran Church in America and has attempted to extend it into communities south of Santiago.

Evangelical Lutheran Church in Chile
Av.

Pedro de Valdivia 3420 H depot.33
Casill 167-11
ÑuÑoa–Santiago
Chile

J. Gordon Melton

See also: Evangelical Church in Germany; Evangelical Lutheran Church in America; Lutheran World Federation; Lutheranism; World Council of Churches.

References

Bachmann, E. Theodore, and Mercia Brenne Bachmann. *Lutheran Churches in the World: A Handbook.* Minneapolis, MN: Augsburg Press, 1989.

Van Beek, Huibert. *A Handbook of the Churches and Councils: Profiles of Ecumenical Relationships.* Geneva: World Council of Churches, 2006.

Evangelical Lutheran Church in Congo

The Evangelical Lutheran Church in Congo (Église évangélique luthérienne au Congo) originated among a group of Christian believers in the eastern part of the Democratic Republic of the Congo (then Zaire) who had been inspired by listening to the Radio Voice of the Gospel, a Lutheran radio station that operated out of Addis Ababa in the 1960s. They expressed a desire to affiliate with the Lutheran Church and were placed in contact with representatives of the Lutheran Church in Tanzania and the Lutheran World Federation. Leaders in the Congo group were invited to receive training in Tanzania. In 1975, the first graduate from the Makumira Theological School was ordained for an initial congregation, Kalémié. The following year, the association of Lutheran churches was received into the Church of Christ in Zaire (now the Church of Christ in the Congo), the state-recognized organization for all Protestant churches. The Lutheran Church received official government recognition in 1981.

Through the 1980s, the group grew as more pastors were graduated and ordained. A general assembly was organized. As the Evangelical Lutheran Community in Zaire East, the new church joined the Lutheran World Federation in 1986 and most recently, under its new name, a name that reflects the changes that brought the Democratic Republic of the Congo into existence, has been received into membership by the World Council of Churches.

The congregations of the Lutheran Church in Congo are in the easternmost section of the country, with its primary center in Lubumbashi, on Lake Tanganyika. The church is currently led by Bishop Ngoy Kasukuti. In 2005, it reported 52,000 members. Its 96 congregations have been organized into 6 dioceses. The church has survived through the violence and war that has continued to haunt the Congo in recent decades, a primary reason for its establishing its headquarters office and contact point in neighboring Zambia.

Evangelical Lutheran Church in Congo
PO Box 23294
Kitwe
Zambia

J. Gordon Melton

See also: Evangelical Lutheran Church in Tanzania; Lutheran World Federation; World Council of Churches.

References

Bachmann, E. Theodore, and Mercia Brenne Bachmann. *Lutheran Churches in the World: A Handbook.* Minneapolis, MN: Augsburg Press, 1989.

Van Beek, Huibert. *A Handbook of the Churches and Councils: Profiles of Ecumenical Relationships.* Geneva: World Council of Churches, 2006.

Evangelical Lutheran Church in Denmark

Beginning with the Lutheran Reformation (1536), the Evangelical Lutheran Church was for centuries the only ecclesiastical body allowed in Denmark. It superseded the Roman Catholic Church, which had been introduced into Denmark around 825 CE by a Benedictine monk named Ansgar. Following the Reformation it adopted the Augsburg Confession and aligned itself in belief and practice with the Lutheran Church in Germany.

An Evangelical Lutheran church in Ebeltoft, Denmark. (Lorna/Dreamstime.com)

Through the centuries revivals were watched carefully and sects suppressed. During this period, by the grace of the king and in the economic self-interest of the state, Jews, Calvinists, Roman Catholics, and Moravians were allowed to settle in connection with embassies or in strictly limited areas. With the abolition of the absolute state, Denmark became a constitutional monarchy (1849) that allowed freedom of expression, association, assembly, printing, and religion. Since then citizens have been entitled to freedom of worship, and their religious organizations, financing, and rites may not be touched as long as they respect the public order and morality. No one is obliged to contribute to a religion that the person concerned does not affiliate with. No one can be deprived of civil and political rights because of his or her religious conscience.

Following the establishment of the constitutional monarchy, it was not expected that the majority church should be of the same standing as other religious communities. The national church, which was then called Folkekirken, or the People's Church, had to be Evangelical Lutheran, and for the last 150 years it has been protected and supported economically by the state.

Even in the early 21st century, the sovereign must be a member of a Lutheran community. In the mid-19th century 98 percent of the population belonged to the People's Church, which still today includes about 86 percent of the population. The situation is complex; church and state resemble a divorced couple continuing to live together, with one party having the upper hand. It is a strange fusion of a religious community and public administration, with Parliament as the ruling subject of the church, the institution that supports it, and the authority that gives and withdraws competence. The state can intervene in the external and internal matters of the church. However, it has seldom meddled with the internal affairs and the People's Church is not cowed by the state.

Since 1912 the influence of laypersons has been strong, thanks to local congregational councils, and for almost a century the church has given a lopsided amount of power to the local level. Today church-state relations represent a peculiar mixture of comparatively tight centralizing state administration and extensive self-government locally. This state of affairs has indisputably strengthened the People's Church locally, but it also explains the impotence of a church that is unable to manifest itself as an independent entity in relation to the state. The church has no synod and no one, neither bishop, priest, nor any layperson, can function as the "voice of the church" in, for example, ecumenical matters.

Denmark is an old maritime nation, and colonial power and church circles have always supported the religious and cultural life of Danes abroad, just as since the 18th century they have played a major role concerning Christian mission activities all over the world. At home Lutherans for the last 30 years have had to deal with the growing influence of other—and especially new—religious movements. In 1998, 4.1 percent of the population belonged to "recognized religious communities" outside the People's Church, and among them about 120,000 from Muslim countries. Only 10.1 percent did not in 1998 belong to any religious community at all.

In 2009, the church reported 4,494,589 members. Affiliated congregations, primarily for expatriates, are found in a number of countries across Europe. The church is a member of the Lutheran World Federation and the World Council of Churches.

Evangelical Lutheran Church in Denmark
c/o Secretary International Church Relations
Nørregade 11
DK-1165 København K
Denmark
http://www.folkekirken.dk/ (in Danish with a link to
    English page)

Frands Ole Overgaard

See also: Lutheran World Federation; Roman Catholic Church; World Council of Churches.

References

Bachmann, E. Theodore, and Mercia Brenne Bachmann. *Lutheran Churches of the World: A Handbook.* Minneapolis, MN: Augsburg, 1989.

Bruhn, Verner. *A People and Its Church: The Lutheran Church in Denmark.* Kobønhavn: Council on Inter-Church Relations, 1994.

Evangelical Lutheran Church in Iceland

The religious landscape of Iceland has been changing rapidly in the recent years mainly due to immigration of people of other faiths. When the Evangelical Lutheran Church in Iceland was established in the first constitution of the country in 1874, it was the only religious organization in the country. Now it is one among many, counting 80 percent of the population as members, or 252,000. Endeavoring to be faithful to the gospel, and its unique history and culture, it is open to the challenges of a multi-cultural and multi-religious society.

In the early years of the 21st century extensive strategic planning was done throughout the church, involving some 1,000 people of different walks of life. Intensified work in Christian education for young and old was called for, renovation of worship life and music, development of youth work and leadership training, and more support for families and homes in Christian formation and prayer. There was also an emphasis on

An Evangelical Lutheran church in Budir, Iceland. (Dalibor Kantor/Dreamstime.com)

reaching out to cooperate with others in contributing to the strengthening of a hospitable society.

Today Iceland is a highly urbanized society with an increasing pluralism of belief. In spite of the cultural and demographic changes, the Evangelical Lutheran Church still holds a key position. Almost all of the children are baptized within their first year, around 90 percent of all 14-year-olds are confirmed, 75 percent of all marriages occur in the church, and 99 percent are buried in the church. Most children are taught evening prayers in their homes. The primary schools teach Bible stories, and children's services are an important part of the worship life of most parishes. The State Broadcasting transmits worship services every Sunday morning, and daily devotions morning and night. Recent polls show 12 percent of adults in Iceland attend church services at least once a month. But different worship services throughout the week seem to be gaining ground in the parishes.

Iceland takes pride in its culture, language, and history. The church is an integral part of that. Iceland is unique among European nations in that from the very beginning of human habitation Christianity has been present. The first people in Iceland were Celtic hermits, seeking refuge to worship Christ. Later Norse settlers drove them out. When Iceland was constituted as a republic in the year 930 it was based on the Norse religion. At the end of the 10th century Christianity had gained ground. Soon the nation was divided into two hostile camps. Thus, in the year 1000, at the Alþing (legislative assembly) held at Thingvellir, the leaders of the two groups, realizing the danger that threatened them, chose a person that everybody respected, a Norse priest and chieftain, Thorgeir of Ljósavatn, to decide which way the people should go. After a day-long contemplation of the problem, Thorgeir announced his decision: "Let it be the foundation of our law that everyone in this land shall be Christian and believe in one God, Father, Son and Holy Spirit." The people bowed to his decision. Soon afterward, missionary priests from Germany, England, and Eastern Europe organized the people within the Roman Catholic Church. The first Icelandic bishop, Isleifur, was consecrated in Bremen in 1056. He established his see at Skálholt, which remained the center of Christian learning and spirituality up through the 18th century. A second diocese centered on Hólar was created in 1106.

In 1262 Iceland came under the rulership of Norway and later Denmark. The Danish church joined the Lutheran camp in 1536, and thus four years later, the Reformation of Martin Luther was established in Iceland, enforced by the Danish Crown. The king ordered the dissolving of the monasteries and confiscated much of the church's property, as he now assumed position as the supreme head of the church. Most of the former Roman priests though continued in their parishes under the new regime and the life of the parishes went on as before. The translation of the Bible and the publication of devotional books and poetry contributed to cementing the Reformation and preserving the Icelandic language and culture.

In 1801 the two old dioceses were merged into a new single diocese with one bishop headquartered in Reykjavík. The 19th century saw the beginning of a national revival in Iceland and a movement toward political independence. The Constitution of 1874 guaranteed religious freedom but also decreed that the "Evangelical Lutheran Church is a national church and as such it is protected and supported by the State." This provision remained in the new Constitution of the Republic of Iceland adopted in 1944. This is the only article in the Constitution that can be changed by law, but which then has to be submitted to a national referendum. Church legislation was revised at the beginning of the 20th century, at which time parish councils were established and the congregations gained the right to elect their pastors.

In the early 1900s, liberal theology was introduced in Iceland, and textual criticism of the Bible became quite influential in the newly founded Department of Theology of the University of Iceland. At the same time Spiritualist and Theosophical ideas found support in intellectual circles. Conservative leaders opposed both trends, and the ongoing conflict marred church life well into the 1960s.

On January 1, 1998, a new law redefined the relationship of the Evangelical Lutheran Church to the government. The church remains established by law, but is otherwise autonomous. The state supports the church and collects membership dues for its parishes as for all registered denominations and religious communities. Church legislation, previously the domain of the Alþing, is now handled by the Kirkjuþing (church assembly), the highest legislative authority of the church. It has 29 elected representatives, 12 clergy, and 17 laypeople, and a layperson as a president. The highest executive authority is the Church Council (Kirkjuráð) elected by the Kirkjuþing and presided over by the bishop of Iceland. The bishop's office in the Church House is at the same time the office of the Kirkjuráð. Besides dealing with financial matters and personnel, the council also has departments of church education, and diakonia (service), church music, liturgy, and ecumenical relations.

Annually the bishop summons all the pastors and theologians of the church to the pastors' meeting, the synod, to discuss the affairs of the church and society. The synod has a say in all matters of theology and liturgy to be decided by the bishop and Kirkjuþing. At the old episcopal sees of Skálholt and Hólar there are assistant or suffragan bishops (vígslubiskup). They assist the bishop of Iceland in pastoral matters and with him form the Bishops' Meeting. There are 280 Lutheran parishes nationwide, with approximately 160 priests and 10 ordained deacons. Ten priests and five deacons work in specialized ministries in hospitals and other institutions, and others serve Icelandic congregations abroad. The Theological Faculty of the University of Iceland, founded in 1911, educates the clergy and deacons of the Church. Many theologians go abroad for further studies in seminaries and universities on both sides of the Atlantic.

The Evangelical Lutheran Church in Iceland is a member of the Lutheran World Federation, the Conference of European Churches, the Nordic Ecumenical Council, and the World Council of Churches. It is also a member of the Porvoo agreement between the Anglican Churches of the British Isles and the Nordic and Baltic Lutheran churches. The Union of Missionary Societies of Iceland, in cooperation with the Norwegian Missionary Federation, has operated missions in China, Ethiopia, and Kenya. The Icelandic Church Aid has worked in cooperation with foreign relief and developmental agencies in development work and emergency aid in various parts of the world.

Evangelical Lutheran Church in Iceland
Bishop's Office
Laugavegur 31
IS-150 Reykjavik
Iceland
http://www.kirkjan.is/index.shtml?english

Karl Sigurbjörnsson

See also: Lutheran World Federation; Roman Catholic Church; World Council of Churches.

References

Fell, Michael. *And Some Fell into Good Soil: A History of Christianity in Iceland*, New York: Peter Lang, 1998

Sigurbjörnsson, Karl. *The Church of Iceland: Past and Present*. Reykjavik: Church of Iceland, 2007.

Hjálmarsson, Jón R. *History of Iceland: From the Settlement to the Present Day*. Reykjavik: Iceland Review, 1993.

Evangelical Lutheran Church in Kenya

The Evangelical Lutheran Church in Kenya is one of two Lutheran denominations in Kenya. It has a unique history and is not to be confused with the Kenya Evangelical Lutheran Church.

Lutheranism came to Kenya as a result of the Italian invasion of Ethiopia. In 1936, the Italians expelled all the Protestant missionaries. Among those who left the country were the representatives of the Swedish Mission of the True Bible Friends, an independent missionary organization founded in 1911 in protest of the liberalism its members felt had arisen in the Church of Sweden. The expelled missionaries began to look for an alternative field where they could both continue their evangelism and stay in some minimal contact with their colleagues in Ethiopia. At this juncture, they made contact with some Ethiopian refugees who had escaped the Italian occupation but were having a difficult time in Kenya.

The first representatives of the True Bible Friends arrived in 1939. In the process of helping the Ethiopians, they discovered a new field for evangelism. They settled in the area east of Lake Victoria and began to evangelize the Kisii and Luo peoples. The church had immediate success, and the missionaries moved quickly to train Native leadership. By 1958, the mission was ready to become independent, and a constitution for the Evangelical Lutheran Church in Kenya was adopted. At the same time the first candidate for the ministry, who had been trained at the Lutheran seminary in Tanzania, was ordained. Following revision of the constitution in 1963, the church was registered as an independent church in 1965.

Even though the church was brought into existence by the True Bible Friends (who continue to support it), since its formation four other Lutheran bodies have added their support. These include the Swedish Lutheran Evangelical Association in Finland; the World Mission Prayer League, based in the United States; the Lutheran Evangelical Association of Finland; and the Norwegian Lutheran Mission.

Work has concentrated among the Kisii and Luo peoples, and editions of Luther's Catechism have been produced for both languages. There is both a hymnal and New Testament in Kisii. More recently, the church has reached out to other groups, including the Pokot, the Boran, and the Samburu. The Boran's land is along Kenya's border with Ethiopia.

In 2008 the church reported 85,000 members in 8 parishes. The general assembly is the highest legislative body and administration has been placed in the hands of an executive committee. In 1978 the church established the Matongo Lutheran Theological College and Bible School. It is a member of the Lutheran World Federation and the National Christian Council of Kenya. It joined the World Council of Churches in 1985, but has recently withdrawn from membership.

Evangelical Lutheran Church in Kenya
Nile Rd.
PO Box 54128
Nairobi
Kenya

J. Gordon Melton

See also: Church of Sweden; Kenya Evangelical Lutheran Church; Lutheran World Federation; World Council of Churches.

References

Bachmann, E. Theodore, and Mercia Brenne Bachmann. *Lutheran Churches in the World: A Handbook.* Minneapolis, MN: Augsburg Press, 1989.

Van Beek, Huibert. *A Handbook of the Churches and Councils: Profiles of Ecumenical Relationships.* Geneva: World Council of Churches, 2006.

Van der Bent, Ans J., ed. *Handbook/Member Churches/World Council of Churches.* Geneva: World Council of Churches, 1985.

An Evangelical Lutheran church in Swakopmund, Namibia. Dating from 1912, it is the second-oldest church in Namibia. (Choups/StockphotoPro)

Evangelical Lutheran Church in Namibia

The Evangelical Lutheran Church in Namibia is the largest of several churches that have grown out of the work of the Rhenish Mission in Namibia. The effort began at the urging of the London Missionary Society, which had initially surveyed the area in 1814. However, it was 1842 before representatives of the mission arrived. Latvian-born Carl Hugo Hahn (1818–1895) established work among the Hereros people. While waiting for his first convert, he reduced the language to writing.

After his initial converts in the 1860s, he founded a Christian colony at Otjimbingwe, where he trained some lay workers who led the mission into a growth phase. The work soon outstripped the resources available from the Rhenish Mission, and Hahn found additional support from the Finnish Missionary Society, the missionary arm of the Church of Finland. The expansion of Hahn's work into the land of the Ovambo people (and later the Kawango people) was the first foreign missionary endeavor undertaken by the church. This new support required some negotiation, as the Rhenish leadership was representative of the Evangelical Church in Germany, a church that had combined Lutheran and Reformed roots. However, Hahn's work was allowed to move toward a more exclusive Lutheran identity, as the Finns required. During World War I, the Finns assumed full responsibility for the growing work, and its success has been attributed to a peculiar affinity between the people and the Finnish missionaries, more than 200 of whom had been commissioned by 1970.

The Finnish work included the creation of a publishing center, a hospital (opened in 1911), and an educational system, which began with a teacher-training school in 1913. The move to indigenous leadership began soon afterward, and the first Ovambo pastor was ordained in 1925. The mission became independent as the Evangelical Lutheran Ovambokawango Church in 1954. It adopted its present name in 1984.

It became a prominent part of the anti-apartheid campaign in the last decades of the 20th century, a further reflection of its widespread social concerns ministries. The church also sponsors a public library, a rehabilitation center, two hospitals, and self-help programs. Its printing press is used for church projects and is made available to the public. Future ministers and church workers are trained at the Paulinum Theological Seminary, co-sponsored with the Evangelical Lutheran Church in the Republic of Namibia.

In 2005, the church reported 609,093 members. It is a member of the Lutheran World Federation and since 2001 of the World Council of Churches.

Evangelical Lutheran Church in Namibia
c/o Bishop Kleopas Dumeni
Private Bag 2018
Ondangwa
Namibia

J. Gordon Melton

See also: Evangelical Church in Germany; Evangelical Lutheran Church in the Republic of Namibia; London Missionary Society; Lutheran World Federation; Rhenish Mission; World Council of Churches.

References

Bachmann, E. Theodore, and Mercia Brenne Bachmann. *Lutheran Churches in the World: A Handbook*. Minneapolis, MN: Augsburg Press, 1989.

The Evangelical Lutheran Church in the Republic of Namibia in the 21st Century. Windhoek, Namibia: Gamsberg Macmillan, 2000.

Hellberg, Carl J. *Mission, Colonialism, and Liberation: The Lutheran Church in Namibia, 1840–1966*. Windhoek, Namibia: New Namibia Books, 1997.

Van Beek, Huibert. *A Handbook of the Churches and Councils: Profiles of Ecumenical Relationships*. Geneva: World Council of Churches, 2006.

Evangelical-Lutheran Church in Romania

The Evangelical-Lutheran Church in Romania (formerly known as the Evangelical Synodal Presbyterial Church of the Augsburg Confession in Romania) dates to the movement of the Lutheran faith into Hungary and Transylvania in the 16th century. There it found a response among both German-speaking and Hungarian-speaking peoples. These churches existed in what was then a part of the Ottoman Empire. In 1691, Transylvania was incorporated into the expanding Hapsburg Empire and existed through a period during which the government supported efforts of the Roman Catholic Church to reclaim Protestant believers. Lutherans in Transylvania were initially incorporated into the Lutheran Church in Hungary, but were separated following the transfer of Transylvania to Romania following World War I.

The Evangelical-Lutheran Church in Romania continues the Hungarian-speaking Lutheran tradition that has been present in Transylvania since the Reformation. It had experienced a revival in the 1780s following the granting of religious tolerance by the government in 1781, during which time many of its prominent buildings were erected. Following the changes after World War II, the Hungarian (and Slovak) Lutherans decided to organize separately from the German-speaking Lutherans, now within the Evangelical Church of the Augsburg Confession in Romania.

The Hungarian church is organized on a presbyterial system with congregations organized into presbyteries. A general synod is the highest legislative body. The church is led by a bishop who is assisted by a lay president. In 2005, the church reported a membership of some 33,000 in its 39 congregations. It is a member of the World Council of Churches and the Lutheran World Federation. With the Unitarians and Reformed churches, it supports the United Protestant Theological Institute in Cluj at which most of its ministers are trained.

Evangelical-Lutheran Church in Romania
Str. General Magheru 4
RO-55018 Sibiu-Hermannstadt
Romania

J. Gordon Melton

See also: Evangelical Church of the Augsburg Confession in Romania; Lutheran Church in Hungary; Lutheran World Federation; Roman Catholic Church; World Council of Churches.

References

Branzea, Nicolae I., and Stefan Lonita. *Religious Life in Romania.* Bucharest: Editura Paideia, 1999.

Cuciuc, Constantin. *Atlasul Religiilor şi al Monumentelor Istorice Religioase din Romania.* Bucharest: Editura Gnosis, 1996.

Van Beek, Huibert. *A Handbook of the Churches and Councils: Profiles of Ecumenical Relationships.* Geneva: World Council of Churches, 2006.

Evangelical Lutheran Church in Southern Africa

The Evangelical Lutheran Church in Southern Africa was constituted in 1975 by the merger of four previously existing Lutheran churches, which have retained some organizational continuity as dioceses in the new ecclesiastical body. The first Lutheran missionaries, representatives of the Berlin Mission, entered the Cape of Good Hope in 1834, and their work eventually spread through the colony and into the Orange Free State. In 1911 the mission was organized as two synods, one in each territory. These two synods came together to form a regional church in 1963 and subsequently joined the Lutheran World Federation.

In 1854 missionaries unable to settle in Ethiopia, as planned, came to the Transvaal. They were joined four years later by missionaries from the Berlin Mission who established work among the Bakoba people. The mission spread among different peoples and into Botswana and Lesotho. In 1962 the work in the Transvaal was constituted as the Lutheran Church–Transvaal Region and affiliated with the Lutheran World Federation.

Lutheran work in Natal began in 1844 when five missionaries from the Norwegian Missionary Society arrived. They were joined by Norse-American missionaries in 1870. The Berlin Missionary Society spread their work to the area in 1847. They opened a school at their center in Emmaus. They later expanded their work into Swaziland and in 1911 constituted the Zulu-Xhosa-Swazi Synod. In 1857 the Hermannsburg Missionary Society added their strength to the growing work and opened a school to train parish workers. Finally, in 1876, missionaries from the Church of Sweden settled in the interior of Natal. In 1912, these several missions formed the Cooperating Lutheran Missions in Natal-Zululand. This structure matured into the Lutheran Church in South Africa–South-Eastern Region. As such it joined the Lutheran World Federation and the World Council of Churches.

In 1857, the Hermannsburg Missionary Society opened work among the Tswana people of the Transvaal. They found a ready acceptance of Christianity due to the prior activity of David Modipane. Some 20 years earlier, Modipane, then a war prisoner, had converted to Christianity. In the 1840s, he returned to his people and began to preach. He did not baptize or form a church, but told those who listened to him that soon others would come with proper authority. The missionaries purchased land from the Tswana and formed several Christian villages that became the church's centers. By 1959, when the independent Lutheran Botswana Church was constituted, there were some 100,000 members. That church became the Evangelical Lutheran Church in Southern Africa in 1963 and soon affiliated with the Lutheran World Federation.

Shortly after the merger of these four regional churches to form the Evangelical Lutheran Church in Southern Africa, two additional dioceses were created, one serving the Johannesburg area and one for the members in Botswana. The church has an episcopal polity and is led by its presiding bishop. The church assembly, the highest legislative body, meets biennially. The church council oversees the administration at the national level.

Given the racial divisions in modern South Africa, the reception in 1984 of five congregations whose members were predominantly of Indian heritage became a step forward of significance far beyond the bounds of the church. These congregations were the result of a mission opened in the 1970s by the Norwegian Missionary Society, the Hermannsburg Mission, and the Church of Sweden. The church struggled through the 1980s to deal with the many races, people, and languages in the church, all of which, given the apartheid system imposed by the government, continually threatened its unity. With the end of apartheid, the church has worked to overcome its divided past.

In 2005, the church reported 589,502 members. The church oversees two seminaries, the Lutheran Theological College Umpumulo at Mapumulo and the Marang Theological Seminary in Tihabane, Bophuthatswana. Several smaller churches, primarily of white South Africans, which share much of the history of the Evangelical Lutheran Church, have remained independent of the larger united body.

Evangelical Lutheran Church in Southern Africa
24 Geldenhuys Rd., Kempton Park
PO Box 7331
Bonaero Park, 1622
South Africa
http://www.geocities.com/Heartland/Meadows/7589/
elcsa.html

J. Gordon Melton

See also: Lutheran World Federation; World Council of Churches.

References

Bachmann, E. Theodore, and Mercia Brenne Bachmann. *Lutheran Churches in the World: A Handbook*. Minneapolis, MN: Augsburg Press, 1989.

Van Beek, Huibert. *A Handbook of the Churches and Councils: Profiles of Ecumenical Relationships*. Geneva: World Council of Churches, 2006.

Van der Bent, Ans J., ed. *Handbook/Member Churches/World Council of Churches*. Geneva: World Council of Churches, 1985.

Evangelical Lutheran Church in Tanzania

The Evangelical Lutheran Church in Tanzania (ELCT) was born in June 1963 with the formal amalgamation of seven churches that had previously worked together as a federation. These seven churches trace their beginnings to the 19th-century missionary activities in East Africa. Both African-initiated groups and German missionary societies became very active in creating congregations and parishes that later developed into self-governing churches. Before World War I there were three German mission societies operating in what was then Tanganyika: the Berlin Mission, which worked in the southern part of the colony and later on the eastern coast; the Leipzig Mission, which worked in the northern and central parts of the territory; and Bethel Mission, which worked in the northeast and later in the northwest. In the northwest, Protestant African groups, largely influenced by the Anglican Church in Uganda, invited Bethel Mission to work with them.

New mission societies arrived after World War I. The Augustana Mission, based in America, took over the work of the Leipzig Mission and Berlin Mission. The Norwegian Mission (Free Church) took charge of the Mbulu area in the northern part of the country. The Methodist Mission from South Africa became responsible for the northwest area, but did not remain there long after it got into conflict with the African Christian group.

During and after World War II, representatives from several Lutheran mission societies from Scandinavia arrived and worked together with the already established churches. It was during this time that these established churches of different background formed a Federation of Lutheran Churches in Tanganyika, which later, on June 19, 1963, merged to become the Evangelical Lutheran Church in Tanzania.

The former 7 churches have established 20 church units known as dioceses. Each diocese has its own constitution and diocesan leadership. These 20 different dioceses together constitute the Evangelical Lutheran Church in Tanzania, which in 2005 reported a membership of approximately 3 million members. It is the second largest Christian body in Tanzania and the largest Lutheran body in Africa. The head of the church is called *mkuu wa kanisa* (a Swahili title meaning "the one taking responsibilities of church leadership") and is elected from among the 20 bishops. The first mkuu wa kanisa was the late Bishop Stefano Moshi (1906–1976) from the Northern Diocese, who was succeeded by the late Bishop Sebastian Kolowa (r. 1976–1992) from the North Eastern Diocese, who was in turn succeeded by Bishop Samson Mushemba (b. 1960) from the North Western Diocese. It is currently led by presiding Bishop Alex Gehaz Malasusa, who succeeded Bishop Mushemba in 2007. The church has a general secretary who works with the executive secretaries of different church departments. There is a General Assembly, which meets every four years, and an Executive Council, which meets four times annually.

The church has pursued its mission both within Tanzania and in neighboring countries. In the 1960s and 1970s it supported work in Kenya and the Congo (formerly Zaire). In the 1980s it worked in Malawi and Zambia, and more recently has opened work in Mozambique and Uganda. Within Tanzania it has established new mission areas where the work of *diakonia* ("service") is very strongly emphasized. Education has become a strong priority, leading the church to establish secondary schools, colleges, and a university as expressions of its missionary task.

In order to continue the longstanding relationships between the church and the former mission societies, the Lutheran Christian Service body, since 1997 known as the Lutheran Mission Cooperation, was established in 1973. Its offices are within the church's headquarters in Arusha. This body works together with the Evangelical Lutheran Church in Tanzania to fulfill its mission objectives.

The Evangelical Lutheran Church in Tanzania is a member of the Christian Council of Tanzania, the All-Africa Conference of Churches, the Lutheran World Federation, and the World Council of Churches. Through these ecumenical bodies the church has shared its leadership talents with the larger Christian community. One of the former presidents of the Lutheran World Federation was the late Bishop Josiah M. Kibira (1977–1984), an ELCT bishop.

Evangelical Lutheran Church in Tanzania
PO Box 3033
Boma Rd.
Arusha
Tanzania

Wilson B. Niwagila

See also: All Africa Conference of Churches; Lutheran World Federation; World Council of Churches.

References
Bachmann, E. Theodore, and Mercia Brenne Bachmann. *Lutheran Churches in the World: A Handbook*. Minneapolis, MN: Augsburg Press, 1989.
Van Beek, Huibert. *A Handbook of the Churches and Councils: Profiles of Ecumenical Relationships*. Geneva: World Council of Churches, 2006.
Van der Bent, Ans J., ed. *Handbook/Member Churches/World Council of Churches*. Geneva: World Council of Churches, 1985.

Evangelical Lutheran Church in the Kingdom of the Netherlands

See Protestant Church in the Netherlands.

Evangelical Lutheran Church in the Republic of Namibia

The Evangelical Lutheran Church in the Republic of Namibia dates to 1842 and the beginning of the Rhenish Missionary Society efforts in southern Africa in what in 1884 became German South West Africa and continued after Germany lost control of the region following World War I. Today the area is the independent country of Namibia. Originally developed in various parts of the territory, the work in the north was soon turned over to the Finnish Lutherans and evolved separately (and is now known as the Evangelical Lutheran Church in Namibia). The Rhenish Mission work evolved into the Evangelical Lutheran Church in South-West Africa (Rhenish Mission) in 1957 and assumed it present name in 1990.

The church follows the belief and practice of the Evangelical Church in Germany, which includes an amalgam of Lutheran and Reformed trends. The church also has become socially active and sponsors leadership education programs for women, an anti-AIDS program, and programs to care for the elderly and ill. Among the educational institutions supported are the Martin Luther High School and the Palinum Theological Seminary, jointly sponsored with the Evangelical Lutheran Church in Namibia.

The church is ecumenically active and has been a member of the World Council of Churches since 1992. It is also a member of the Lutheran World Federation. In 2005 it reported 350,000 members in 54 congregations.

Evangelical Lutheran Church in the Republic of
    Namibia
Private Bag 2018, Onipa
Ondangwa
Namibia

J. Gordon Melton

See also: Evangelical Lutheran Church in Namibia; Lutheran World Federation; World Council of Churches.

Reference

Van Beek, Huibert. *A Handbook of the Churches and Councils: Profiles of Ecumenical Relationships*. Geneva: World Council of Churches, 2006.

Evangelical Lutheran Church in Zimbabwe

Lutheranism entered what is today known as Zimbabwe in 1903 when missionaries from the Church of Sweden, which had previously established a work in Natal, moved into southern Rhodesia. There the London Missionary Society, a British Protestant sending agency, and other churches had already initiated missionary work, and an agreement was reached by which the Church of Sweden would concentrate its activity in the southwestern part of the country. Here the missionaries encountered the Ndebele people (a Zulu-related people). The work spread across the southern part of the country, where its strength remains, though as members have migrated into the cities it now has congregations across the country.

In the 1930s the initial steps toward autonomy were taken that resulted in 1941 in a new Constitution, which outlined the several responsibilities of the Church of Sweden and the resident church members. Then in 1961, the church became autonomous. Three years

later, southern Rhodesia became independent, though rule by the white minority continued until 1979.

The church is centered on the city of Bulawayo. Its parishes are organized into two districts. Legislation for the church is done at its biennial delegated assembly. The church is led by its presiding bishop, currently Naison Shava, who in 2006 succeeded Litsietsi Maqethula Dube (r. 2001–2006), who had in turn succeeded Dr. Ambrose Moyo (r. 1996–2001). Mayo moved on to become the executive director of the Lutheran Communion in Southern Africa. In 2005, the church reported 134,000 members in 396 congregations. Most of the church's pastors are trained at the United Theological College in Harare, a joint project of five Protestant denominations.

The church is characterized by a noticeable female majority among the active membership. They created a volunteer organization, Vashandiri, in the 1930s, which has been a significant part of the church's life and development. They manage a program of adult education, including both Bible and theological training as well as secular topics such as child care. Vashandiri is headquartered at a women's center in Gweru, which is also used for retreats, weddings, and various church meetings.

The church has an education program that includes several secondary schools and a youth center at Njube. An early emphasis on medical missions now manifests as joint support with other churches of four hospitals. The church cooperates with the world Lutheran community on various projects, especially Lutheran World Service, which has developed a spectrum of programs in response to the devastating drought in 1984–1986. The church is a member of the World Council of Churches, the Lutheran World Federation, the Fellowship of Evangelical Lutheran Churches in Southern Africa, and the Council of Churches in Zimbabwe.

Evangelical Lutheran Church in Zimbabwe
PO Box 2175
Bulawayo
Zimbabwe

J. Gordon Melton

See also: Church of Sweden; London Missionary Society; Lutheran World Federation; World Council of Churches.

References

Bachmann, E. Theodore, and Mercia Brenne Bachmann. *Lutheran Churches in the World: A Handbook*. Minneapolis, MN: Augsburg Press, 1989.

Van Beek, Huibert. *A Handbook of the Churches and Councils: Profiles of Ecumenical Relationships.* Geneva: World Council of Churches, 2006.

Van der Bent, Ans J., ed. *Handbook/Member Churches/World Council of Churches*. Geneva: World Council of Churches, 1985.

Evangelical Lutheran Church of Finland

The Evangelical Lutheran Church of Finland came into being as a fruit of the 16th-century Reformation of the Roman Catholic Church. At that time, Finland was a part of Sweden. In the 19th century, the country was a part of Russia, and finally in 1917 it became independent.

Two main factors can be seen in the process of the Reformation in Finland. King Gustavus Vasa of Sweden (1496–1560) had political reasons to be in favor of the Reformation. Wealth and power were transferred from the church to the king when Sweden, and Finland as a part of it, became Protestant. At the same time, however, Swedish and Finnish priests studied in Germany and were significantly inspired by the new perspective of the Reformers. The church thus made the transition from Roman Catholicism to Lutheranism, the latter perspective lasting to the present.

In the 19th century, four revival movements started in the Finnish church, all of which continue to exist. Each has its own theological emphases, songbooks, and summer festivals. The largest of the four revival movements is the Laestadian movement, which especially reflects church life in northern Finland. A so-called fifth revival began after World War II and maintains links to the international evangelical movement. In addition to the several revival movements, there are many other organizations, including missionary societies and student organizations within the church; most recently the international charismatic movement has also gained a foothold in the church.

Oulu Cathedral, of the Evangelical Lutheran Church of Finland. (iStockPhoto.com)

According to the Constitution Act of the state from 1919, the state is neutral in respect of religion, and the citizens are guaranteed religious freedom. Still the Lutheran and the Orthodox churches have some privileges, among the more important being their taxing power. The Lutheran Church is a majority church, but no longer a state church. However, in the 1990s additional reforms occurred that further loosened the connection between church and state.

In 1999, 85.3 percent of the population, or 4.4 million people, belonged to the Evangelical Lutheran Church. The church plays, particularly through its ceremonies, a role in most people's lives: a vast majority are baptized, confirmed, married, and buried by Lutheran pastors.

There are approximately 600 parishes located in 8 dioceses. All the Swedish-language parishes in different parts of the country belong to one diocese (5.8 percent of Finns speak Swedish as their native language). The archbishop, who is often regarded as the head of the church is in Turku, the town where the first bishopric of Finland was established in the 13th century. The church's supreme decision-making body is the Synod (107 members). Other authoritative bodies are the Ecclesiastical Board, the Bishops' Conference, and the Church Council for International Relations. The central offices of the church are located in Helsinki. Altogether, the church employs almost 20,000 people full-time or part-time. Out of these, 1,800 are ordained ministers. One-fourth of the clergy are women. Women have been ordained since 1988, but even before that hundreds of female theologians worked in the parishes.

The financial basis of the church is its taxing power. Most funds are spent on parish work and maintenance of buildings. Parish work includes, for example, children's clubs, family counseling, hospital pastoral care, and work among the disabled, the unemployed, old people, and prisoners.

In 2008, the Evangelical Lutheran Church of Finland reported 4.5 million members in 548 parishes organized in 9 dioceses, plus some members who reside outside the country. The spiritual head of the church is Jukka Paarma, the archbishop of Turku. The Evangelical Lutheran Church of Finland is a member of the World Council of Churches, the Conference of European Churches, the Lutheran World Federation, and the Nordic Ecumenical Council.

Department for International Relations
PO Box 185
Satamakatu 11
161 Helsinki
Finland
http://www.evl.fi/english

Laura Maria Latikka

See also: Lutheran World Federation; World Council of Churches.

References

Evangelical Lutheran Church of Finland. *Church in Finland: The History, Present State and Outlook for the Future of the Evangelical Lutheran Church of Finland*. Documents of the Evangelical Lutheran Church of Finland 1. Helsinki: Evangelical Lutheran Church of Finland, 1989.

Heino, Harri, K. Salonen, and J. Rusama. *Response to Recession: The Evangelical Lutheran Church of Finland in the Years 1992–1995*. Tampere, Finland: Research Institute of the Evangelical Lutheran Church of Finland, no. 47, 1997.

Työrinoja, P., ed. *The Evangelical Lutheran Church in Finnish Society*. Documents of the Evangelical Lutheran Church of Finland 6. Helsinki: Church Council for Foreign Affairs, Church Council, 1994.

Sentzke, G. *Finland: Its Church and Its People*. Helsinki: Publications of the Luther-Agricola Society. Series B 3, 1963.

Evangelical Lutheran Church of France

When the Protestant Reformation spread into France, the Reformed Church based in French-speaking Geneva found significantly more support than did Lutheranism. However, a Lutheran movement did emerge in the Montbéliard region (then a part of the German Duchy of Württemberg) and in Alsace-Lorraine (a French area bordering Germany). Beginning with the ministry of Guillaume Farel (1489–1565) and Martin Bucer (1491–1551), the church has been conscious of its role as a mediating force between German Lutheranism and French Reformed emphases. Over the centuries it has produced a number of significant figures in spiritual renewal, such as Pietist leader Phillip Jacob Spener (1635–1705) and Johann Friedrich Oberlin (1740–1825).

The first Lutheran congregation (expatriate Swiss) was founded in Paris in 1626. A Danish congregation soon followed. However, only with the coming of Napoleon and his establishment of a set of laws that both recognized the existence of Protestant churches and regulated their life, were Lutherans allowed to worship openly in France. The presence of Lutheranism in Paris grew in the 20th century with the development of work within the German expatriate community.

In 1871, as a result of the Franco-Prussian War, many of the French Lutherans suddenly found themselves in Germany with the annexation of Alsace-Lorraine. Those Lutherans who remained in France were found primarily in Montbéliard and Paris. In 1906, following the separation of church and state in France, the Lutherans were finally free to form a national organization. The Evangelical Lutheran Church of France is one of the two bodies that continue the life of the Lutheran Reformation in France. When Alsace-Lorraine was returned to France after World War I, the Lutherans there organized the Church of the Augsburg Confession of Alsace and Lorraine, which has remained a separate body.

The Evangelical Lutheran Church of France is a member of the Protestant Federation of France, the World Council of Churches, and the Lutheran World Federation. In 2005, the church reported 36,000 members in 54 congregations.

Evangelical Lutheran Church of France
24 Avenue Wilson
F-75200 Paris
France

J. Gordon Melton

See also: Church of the Augsburg Confession of Alsace and Lorraine; Lutheran World Federation; Lutheranism; World Council of Churches.

References

Bachmann, E. Theodore, and Mercia Brenne Bachmann. *Lutheran Churches in the World: A Handbook*. Minneapolis, MN: Augsburg Press, 1989.

Van Beek, Huibert. *A Handbook of the Churches and Councils: Profiles of Ecumenical Relationships*. Geneva: World Council of Churches, 2006.

Van der Bent, Ans J., ed. *Handbook/Member Churches/World Council of Churches*. Geneva: World Council of Churches, 1985.

Evangelical Lutheran Church of Ghana

The Evangelical Lutheran Church of Ghana originated in 1958 with the efforts of missionaries of the Lutheran Church–Missouri Synod. The work grew steadily and was formally registered as a new ecclesiastical institution in 1964. The church continues the conservative Lutheran theology and practice of its parent body. The church has also developed a widespread program of social endeavors throughout Ghana, including medical facilities aimed at assisting the blind and deaf, improving agriculture, and providing clean water. Evangelistic efforts are punctuated with a popular Bible correspondence course and a broadcast ministry built around the weekly *This Is the Life* television program.

The church has expanded its mission into neighboring Uganda, Nigeria, Benin, and Cote d'Ivoire. In 1998, it founded a ministerial training facility, the Lutheran Clergy Study Programe, based in Accra. In 2005 it reported 26,000 members in 150 congregations and 300 preaching stations. In spite of its ties to the Lutheran Church–Missouri Synod, the church joined the World Council of Churches in 2000. It is also a member of the All Africa Conference of Churches and the Lutheran World Federation.

Evangelical Lutheran Church of Ghana
PO Box K 197
Kaneshie
Ghana

J. Gordon Melton

See also: All Africa Conference of Churches; Lutheran Church–Missouri Synod; Lutheran World Federation; World Council of Churches.

Reference

Van Beek, Huibert. *A Handbook of the Churches and Councils: Profiles of Ecumenical Relationships*. Geneva: World Council of Churches, 2006.

Evangelical Lutheran Church of Lithuania/Lithuanian Evangelical Lutheran Church in Diaspora

The Lutheran Church in Lithuania dates to the spread of the Protestant Reformation in the 1520s. Neighboring Prussia was the first country to declare Lutheranism its state religion (1525), and Lithuanians studied in Wittenberg, Leipzig, and other Protestant universities. The Reformation spread through all parts of society, and the initial Reformers faced harsh resistance by Catholic authorities. In 1539 Abraomas Kulvietis (Abraham Culva, ca. 1509–1545) established a college in Vilnius without permission of the local Catholic

An Evangelical Lutheran church in Vilnius, Lithuania. (Alma Pater)

bishop, and the college was shut down three years later. The college founders sought asylum in Prussia, where Kulvietis, as well as another prominent figure of the Lithuanian Reformation, Stanislovas Rapolionis (often referred to by his Latin name, Stanislaus Rapagelanus; ca. 1485–1545), contributed to the founding of Königsberg University in 1544.

The Reformation eventually found support among the Lithuanian nobility (especially the influential Radvila family), and the country became predominantly Protestant. In response, the bishop of Vilnius invited the Jesuits, already working in Poland, to spearhead the Counter-Reformation. They founded Vilnius University in 1579, and by the end of the century, the Roman Catholic Church had basically regained its former primacy.

Though now in a minority position, Lutherans contributed significantly to Lithuanian culture. The first book ever printed in the Lithuanian language was Luther's Small Catechism, published in 1547 by Martynas Mažvydas (in Latin, Martinus Mosvidius; 1520–1563) in Königsberg. In 1590 Jonas Bretkūnas (Iohannes Bretke; 1536–1602) completed the translation of the Bible into Lithuanian, although it was never published.

In 1648 the synod of the Evangelical Lutheran Church in Lithuania adopted the model of the Saxonian Church of the Augsburg Confession. In 1780 the church's synod established an independent consistory (which started functioning in 1782), and two years later the synod divided Lithuania into three church districts.

In 1832 both the synod and the consistory were abolished by order of the Russian czar, an action made possible because a major part of Lithuania had fallen under Russian occupation in 1795. Lithuania's Lutheran parishes were joined to the Curonian Consistory, with its administrative center in St. Petersburg. Later, parishes in part of Vilnius County and on the right bank of the Nemunas River were joined to the Warsaw Consistory.

Meanwhile, beginning in 1613, Lithuania Minor had its own consistory, established in Königsberg. When in 1660 Prussia ultimately united with Brandenburg, the Königsberg Consistory was integrated into the Berlin General Consistory. In 1817, by decision of the king of Prussia, Fredrick William III, Lutheran and Reformed churches were formally merged to become the Prussian Evangelical Church. Some Lutheran parishes never accepted the Prussian Union.

Lithuania regained its independence in 1918, and the northern part of Lithuania Minor, the Klaipėda District (Memel gebiet), was joined to the Republic of Lithuania in 1923. Of the Klaipėda District's population, 97 percent (more than 150,000) was Lutheran, and there was a strong desire to unite all Lutheran parishes in Lithuania under one administration. Nevertheless, Lutherans in the Klaipėda Distinct remained under the supervision of the Köenigsberg Synod. Only in 1955, after World War II, were the remaining parishes in the district formally joined to the Evangelical Lutheran Church of Lithuania.

In the rest of Lithuania, Lutherans numbered approximately 70,000, but they were divided by language. Thirty thousand were ethnic Lithuanians, 26,000 were German-speaking, and 14,000 were Latvian-speaking. As a result, between 1920 and 1941, each ethnic group formed its own synod, which in turn elected delegates for the consistory, the supreme body of the Evangelical Lutheran Church of Lithuania (ELCL). At the time, the president of the Republic of Lithuania appointed the president and the vice president for the consistory. As World War II loomed (1938), 9.56 percent of the 2.7 million Lithuanians were evangelical (Lutherans and Reformed being counted together).

Due to Soviet occupation and Lithuania's incorporation in the Soviet Union in 1940, a considerable part of the population fled to the West or was deported to the Soviet Union. The number of Lutherans decreased by almost 90 percent. After 1944 large numbers of Lithuanian Lutherans and nearly all pastors found asylum in the West. In 1946 in Germany the constituting synod formed the Lithuanian Evangelical Lutheran Church in Exile, which (as a Lithuanian Evangelical Lutheran Church in Diaspora since 1993) continues to exist today. The church's bishop, Hans G. Dumpys, may be reached at its headquarters, 6641 S. Troy St., Chicago, IL 60629. It is a member of the Lutheran World Federation. As the new century begins, it counts about 5,000 members.

A few pastors who remained in occupied Lithuania tried hard to keep the church alive under repression. A consistory was constituted in 1941 and 1950. Only in 1955 did the first synod meeting since World War II take place. By 1988 there were only 25 parishes in Lithuania.

National revival and the restoration of Lithuania's independence in 1991 provided the ELCL with an opportunity to re-establish parishes and various activities. In 2001 ELCL consisted of 55 parishes, served by some 25 clergy (including deacons). Since 1990, synods have taken place regularly every five years. Between the synods, the church is administered by the consistory.

Lutherans total about one percent of Lithuania's 3.6 million population. ELCL is a member of the Lutheran World Federation (since 1967) and the Leuenberg Church Fellowship. A relatively conservative body, it was a member of the World Council of Churches, but has recently withdrawn. Since 1993, a Department of Evangelical Theology has functioned at Klaipėda University. Bishop Jonas Kalvanas resides in the church headquarters in Tauragė.

Evangelical Lutheran Church of Lithuania
Vokieciu str. 20
1130 Vilnius
Lithuania
http://www.liuteronai.lt/ (in Lithuanian)

Kęstutis Pulokas

See also: Jesuits; Lutheran World Federation; Lutheranism; Roman Catholic Church.

References

Bachmann, E. Theodore, and Mercia Brenne Bachmann. *Lutheran Churches in the World: A Handbook.* Minneapolis, MN: Augsburg, 1989.

Gudaitis, Kristupas. *Evangelikų bažnyčios Lietuvoje.* Vilnius: Lietuvos enciklopedijų redakcija, 1991.

Lukšaitė, Ingė. *Reformacija Lietuvos Didžiojoje Kunigaikštystėje ir Mažojoje Lietuvoje.* Vilnius: Baltos lankos, 1999.

Van Beek, Huibert. *A Handbook of Churches and Councils: Profiles of Ecumenical Relations.* Geneva: World Council of Churches, 2006.

Evangelical Lutheran Church of Papua New Guinea

Lutheran work in Papua New Guinea originated with two thrusts into the region following the establishment of a German colony on the northeast corner of the island of New Guinea in the 1880s. Johannes Flierl (1858–1947) moved to the German colony from Australia, where he had been working with the Aboriginal people. A missionary with the Neuendettelsau Mission, he established an initial station near Finschhafen. Missionaries from the Rhenish Mission joined him the following year. Work began on reducing the local languages to writing and then translating the Bible. As churches slowly emerged, each congregation was assigned an area for evangelization, and beginning in 1908 native teachers were sent out to evangelize their neighbors.

The missions made significant progress when they adopted a method developed by Christian Keyser (1877–1961) of gaining the consent of a whole people to convert before beginning baptisms. This method helped considerably in the preservation of much of the culture of the region. The mission was severely affected by World War I, when the missionaries had to withdraw, but as elsewhere the effect had a positive value in forcing the further creation of indigenous leadership. Until the Germans were allowed to return (1927), American and Australian Lutherans supplied some guidance to the emerging church.

The mission continued to grow through the 1930s, but was even more severely disrupted by the Japanese occupation of the island. A number of missionaries and church leaders were killed and many church buildings destroyed. The mission was quickly reconstructed after the war (with American and Australian assistance), and in 1956 the organization of the Evangelical Lutheran Church occurred. The present name of the church was adopted in 1976 with the establishment of the independent country of Papua New Guinea and the granting of full independence by the several missionary bodies that had until then overseen its operation. Partnership relationships were maintained with German, American, and Australian Lutherans. One of the major programs of the new church was the translation of the Bible into Pidgin, the language that had emerged as the most commonly spoken language in the country's multi-language environment.

In 1976 the Siassi Lutheran Church, a product of the Neuendettelsau Mission, which had been turned over to the Evangelical Lutheran Church of Australia in 1936, merged into the Evangelical Lutheran Church of Papua New Guinea.

The church is led by its bishop, who resides in Lae, and the church convention that meets biennially. Congregations are divided into geographic districts. Zurewe K. Zurenuo, elected in 1973, was the first New Guinean selected for the episcopacy, though at the time he had yet to be ordained to the ministry.

In 2005 the church reported membership at 900,000 worshipping in 2,000 congregations. It is a member of the Lutheran World Federation and the World Council of Churches. It sponsors three seminaries for the training of ministers and church leaders. It also continues to oversee an extensive system of primary and secondary schools, as well as a teacher's college, also located at Lae.

Evangelical Lutheran Church of Papua New Guinea
PO Box 80
Lae 411, Morobe Province
Papua New Guinea

J. Gordon Melton

See also: Lutheran World Federation; World Council of Churches.

References
Bachmann, E. Theodore, and Mercia Brenne Bachmann. *Lutheran Churches in the World: A Handbook*. Minneapolis, MN: Augsburg Press, 1989.

Van Beek, Huibert. *A Handbook of the Churches and Councils: Profiles of Ecumenical Relationships*. Geneva: World Council of Churches, 2006.

Van der Bent, Ans J., ed. *Handbook/Member Churches/World Council of Churches*. Geneva: World Council of Churches, 19

Evangelical Lutheran Free Church of Norway

Significant dissent from the established Church of Norway emerged toward the end of the 19th century when a group appeared asking for independence of the church from state control. The Reverend Paul Peter Wettergren (1835–1889), a former missionary of the church in South Africa, emerged as the spokesperson of the group, arguing that Jesus Christ, not the king of Norway, must be recognized as head of the church. In Norway, the Parliament acted as the Church of Norway's legislature, and the king retained the power of pastoral appointments and of promulgating church law.

The suggestion that the secular authority should not interfere in church affairs was bolstered by complaints that church discipline had become lax, doctrinal aberrations had appeared, and moral standards had been lowered. Wettergren and his associates suggested that congregations be given the privilege of choosing their own pastors and begin exercising the powers now in the hands of the king. The arguments were not accepted, and Wettergren and his followers withdrew from the state church.

The new church made a firm commitment to the standard Lutheran confession of faith and developed a presbyterial polity to organize its congregations. The synod, the highest legislative authority, meets semiannually and elects the church's officers. Congregations call their pastors in cooperation with a district board. The church has established a Bible and Theological Seminary.

The church has a strong program of evangelism, especially among the more secularized adults in the suburbs of Norway's cities. It also has an extensive evangelism program, with missionaries in Japan, Ethiopia, Taiwan, and Cameroon.

In 2008 the church reported 21,775 members. Though challenging the Church of Norway, the Free church has built increasing good relations with it. It has remained aloof from other Free churches in Norway, but has friendly relationships with the Church of the Lutheran Brethren in the United States and sends observers to the Conference of Lutheran Free Churches in Europe. It remained aloof from the Lutheran World Federation for many years, but finally affiliated in 2005.

Evangelical Lutheran Free Church of Norway
St. Olavsplass
PO Box 6787
N-0130 Oslo 1
Norway

J. Gordon Melton

See also: Church of Norway; Free Churches; Lutheran World Federation.

Reference
Bachmann, E. Theodore, and Mercia Brenne Bachmann. *Lutheran Churches in the World: A Handbook*. Minneapolis, MN: Augsburg Press, 1989.

Evangelical Mennonite Conference

Mennonites trace their roots to the more radical element of the 16th-century Protestant Reformation. During a period of continuing persecution, many turned to the former Roman Catholic priest Menno Simons (1496–1559) for his mature leadership. His teachings shaped the movement, which spread from Europe to Russia in the 18th century.

The Evangelical Mennonite Conference's (EMC) origins can be traced back to a split in the Mennonite community in southern Russia in 1812. The leader of the reform movement, Klaas Reimer (1770–1837), concerned about lax discipline in the church, established a separate church entitled the Kleine Gemeinde (German: Little Community). The reason for the title is debated.

It most likely was due to its size in comparison with the Grosse Gemeinde (Large Community).

In 1874–1875 the group immigrated to North America to escape government pressure. About one-third of the group settled in Nebraska, and the other two-thirds settled in two colonies in Manitoba. The Canadian immigrants at that time numbered around 50 families. From the 1880s to the years immediately following World War II, the Kleine Gemeinde experienced a series of divisions within the community, political and cultural pressures to conform, and a loss of members as many immigrated to Mexico. The Kleine Gemeinde kept its name until 1952, when it was changed to the Evangelical Mennonite Church. In 1959 its name was changed to the present-day Evangelical Mennonite Conference.

The modern-day EMC has more than 7,000 members in 53 churches. Its churches are located in central and western Canada. Although its membership still reflects its Dutch-German background, it is increasingly becoming more ethnically diverse. The EMC is a supporting member of the Mennonite Central Committee and the Evangelical Fellowship of Canada.

The denomination holds that the "the Scripture has final authority in faith and practice, a belief in Christ's finished work, and that assurance of salvation is possible." It also adheres to historic Mennonite convictions regarding the necessity of discipleship, believer's adult baptism, social concern, and pacifism. Women can serve on national boards, and in a wide variety of areas of ministry in the church, but they cannot be ordained as ministers. The EMC practices three ordinances: water baptism, the Lord's Supper, and foot washing. Missions work and educational institutions are also an important part of the ministry of the EMC. Local church autonomy is stressed, with the churches of the conference organized under the conference council (which meets twice a year) and the moderator.

Evangelical Mennonite Conference
440 Main Street
Box 1268
Steinbach, Manitoba R0A 2A0
Canada
http://www.emconf.ca

Gordon L. Heath

See also: Mennonites.

References

Epp, Frank H. *Mennonites in Canada, 1786–1920: The History of a Separate People*. Toronto: Macmillan, 1974.

Epp, Frank H. *Mennonites in Canada, 1920–1940: A People's Struggle for Survival*. Scottdale, PA: Herald Press, 1982;

Regehr, T. D. *Mennonites in Canada, 1939–1970: A People Transformed*. Toronto: University of Toronto Press, 1996.

Evangelical Methodist Church in the Philippine Islands

Following the change of administration in the Philippines as a result of the Spanish-American War, the Methodist Episcopal Church (MEC, now an integral part of the United Methodist Church) launched missionary activity in the predominantly Roman Catholic country. The mission grew rapidly, but did not respond in a timely way to expressed desires for indigenous leadership. The desire for a greater leadership role was initially expressed in the formation of "The Truth," an evangelistic effort created by Filipino evangelists. Church leaders discouraged the independent effort. Thus it was that Nicholas Zamora, the first Filipino ordained to the ministry, assumed leadership of some 3,000 members who broke with the MEC to form the Evangelical Methodist Church in 1909. The church was self-governing, self-supporting, and self-propagating. The church had grown to some 20,000 members by the mid-1920s.

Initially the church followed the parent body in organization and adopted a slightly edited version of the MEC *Discipline* as its organizational manual. In 1948, however, it placed the leadership of the church in the hands of a newly created consistory of elders, consisting of 11 ministers and 2 laypersons. The consistory was elected every four years by the church's general conference. The consistory names one of its ministerial members as the church's general superintendent. He, in turn, names the district superintendents who head the geographic districts into which the church is divided.

The church has developed a strong program of economic assistance and industrial development among the poorer people of the Philippines. It has taken a strong stand against racial discrimination, drug addiction, and divorce.

In 2005, the church reported 34,381 members. It is a member of the World Methodist Council and the World Council of Churches.

Evangelical Methodist Church in the Philippine
    Islands
Beulah Land IEMELIF Center
Marytown Circle, Greenfields 1 Subd.
Novaliches, Quezon City 1123
Metro Manila 1000
Philippines

J. Gordon Melton

See also: United Methodist Church; World Council of Churches; World Methodist Council.

References

Deats, Richard L. *The Story of Methodism in the Philippines*. Manila: National Council of Churches in the Philippines, 1964. http://users.drew.edu/loconer/books/deats/deats.htm.

Van Beek, Huibert. *A Handbook of the Churches and Councils: Profiles of Ecumenical Relationships*. Geneva: World Council of Churches, 2006.

Van der Bent, Ans J., ed. *Handbook/Member Churches/World Council of Churches*. Geneva: World Council of Churches, 1985.

World Methodist Council, Handbook of Information, 2002–2006. Lake Junaluska, NC: World Methodist Council, 2003.

Evangelical Methodist Church of Argentina

As early as 1825, the Missionary Society of the Methodist Episcopal Church (now a constituent part of the United Methodist Church) proposed the opening of a mission in Argentina, but the proposal was not acted upon immediately. Then in 1932, an unnamed Methodist wrote from Argentina saying that he had founded a Methodist class and requested that the church send a

John P. Newman, Methodist Episcopal bishop of Omaha and San Francisco, about 1865. (Library of Congress)

missionary to offer assistance. In 1835 the Reverend Fountain E. Pitts (1808–1874) visited the country and returned to the United States to make his recommendation that missionaries be dispatched to the Plate River (Rio de la Plata) area.

John Dempster (1794–1863) arrived in Buenos Aires in December 1836. Over the next five years he built a school and congregation and then was succeeded by William H. Norris (1801–1878), who had been working in Uruguay. Under Norris's guidance, the work was extended into the interior of Argentina and into Paraguay, though the real expansion did not occur until the 1860s. All preaching was in English until that time. In 1874 the Woman's Foreign Missionary Society added their strength to the work and sent two missionaries to found a school for girls (now Colegio Americano).

In 1892, the General Conference authorized the founding of the South America Annual Conference (similar to a diocese in Methodism), and Bishop John

P. Newman (1826–1899) held the first session in 1893. Work now also included missions in Brazil, Peru, and Chile. There were 886 members in Argentina. The South America Conference gave way to the Latin American Central Conference in 1924, the central conference structure offering some degree of autonomy. In 1932, the conference elected the first Latin American Methodist bishop, Juan E. Gattinoni (1878–1970), pastor of Central Church in Buenos Aires.

Argentina was set apart as a separate conference in 1956, and in 1968, the uniting conference of the United Methodist Church voted positively on a proposal that the Argentina Annual Conference be allowed to become an autonomous church. That transformation occurred the next year when the Evangelical Methodist Church of Argentina was organized. Carlos E. Gattinoni (b. 1907), the son of Juan Gattinoni, was elected as the first bishop of the new church. He, like his father, had been the pastor of Central Church when he was called to the episcopate.

The new church continued the structure and beliefs of the parent denomination, except that it established a committee to oversee pastoral appointments, rather than leaving that task in the hands of the bishop alone.

In 2005, the church reported 8,940 members. It is a member of the World Methodist Council and since 1991 of the World Council of Churches.

Evangelical Methodist Church of Argentina
Av. Rivadavia 4044, 3 Piso
1205 Buenos Aires
Argentina
http://www.cristianet.com/iema/

J. Gordon Melton

See also: United Methodist Church; World Council of Churches; World Methodist Council.

References

Harmon, Nolan B. *Encyclopedia of World Methodism.* 2 vols. Nashville: United Methodist Publishing House, 1974.

Van Beek, Huibert. *A Handbook of the Churches and Councils: Profiles of Ecumenical Relationships.* Geneva: World Council of Churches, 2006.

World Methodist Council. Handbook of Information, 2002–2006. Lake Junaluska, NC: World Methodist Council, 2003.

Evangelical Methodist Church of Bolivia

Methodist work in Bolivia is dated from the arrival of bishop-to-be William Taylor (1821–1902) on an exploratory mission in 1877. In 1879, Jose Mongiardino began distributing Bibles in the country, but his work ended abruptly with his murder. Several other attempts to begin a mission met with mixed results, and it was not until 1906 that a stable work was begun, under Francis M. Harrington (1865–1908). He organized the first Methodist church in La Paz and the following year opened the American Institute, which subsequently grew to become the Colegio Evangelista Metodista. The single church carried Methodism for the next 34 years, even though the nation was designated a Mission Conference.

In 1952, Bolivia passed through a revolution, which brought among other changes a new openness to Protestantism. In 1956 the Methodist Episcopal Church (now an integral part of the United Methodist Church) committed funds for a new "Land of Decision" program in Bolivia, which at the time had eight churches in what had been designated a provisional annual conference. Work was launched in Spanish-speaking areas, as well as among the indigenous Native population. Schools were founded, and medical work increased. The original clinic in La Paz is now the Pfeiffer Memorial Hospital. The United Church of Christ in Japan, into which Japanese Methodists had moved, sent missionaries to work among the increasing Japanese expatriate community.

In 1968, at the time of the merger that created the United Methodist Church, the conferences in Latin America requested autonomy, and the conference that had presided over the merger acted favorably on their request. The 1969 annual conference meeting in Bolivia completed the organization of the Evangelical Methodist Church in Bolivia. Reverend Mortimer Arias (b. 1924) was elected as the first bishop of the new church. The bishop is elected for a four-year term. The church continues to work closely with its parent body.

In 2005, the church reported 9,053 members in 188 churches. The church is a member of the World Council of Churches and the World Methodist Council. Within the church, congregations are active among the Aymará, Quechua, and Castellanos peoples.

Evangelical Methodist Church of Bolivia
Landaeta 423
Casilla 356 y 8347
La Paz
Bolivia

J. Gordon Melton

See also: Methodism; United Church of Christ in Japan; United Methodist Church; World Council of Churches; World Methodist Council.

References

Harmon, Nolan B. *Encyclopedia of World Methodism.* 2 vols. Nashville: United Methodist Publishing House, 1974.

McCleary, Paul. *Bolivia—Land of Opportunity.* New York: Board of Missions, The Methodist Church, 1964.

Van Beek, Huibert. *A Handbook of the Churches and Councils: Profiles of Ecumenical Relationships.* Geneva: World Council of Churches, 2006.

Van der Bent, Ans J., ed. *Handbook/Member Churches/World Council of Churches.* Geneva: World Council of Churches, 1985.

World Methodist Council. Handbook of Information, 2002–2006. Lake Junaluska, NC: World Methodist Council, 2003.

Evangelical Methodist Church of Costa Rica

Methodism entered Costa Rica in the 1880s in the person of Francisco G. Penzotti (1851–1925), who had formerly worked as a pastor and missionary in South America. Born in Italy, he had moved to Uruguay, where as a young man he had had a dramatic conversion experience. He entered Costa Rica as an agent of the American Bible Society. The Methodist Episcopal Church (now a constituent part of the United Methodist Church) was formally established in 1918 by George A. Miller (1868–1961), then superintendent of the church's Panama Mission. The first congregations were organized in towns along the Inter-American Highway between San José and the Panama border. A major project was the development of educational institutions, including a training school for church workers (later the Methodist Theological Seminary) and the Colegio Methodista, which became the first Protestant-sponsored school whose students were admitted to the national university.

The work was included in the Central American Mission Conference organized in 1940. The Costa Rica Provisional Annual Conference was organized in 1961. The work continued in affiliation with its American parent through the several mergers in 1939 and 1968 that produced the United Methodist Church. In 1973 it became autonomous as the Methodist Church of Costa Rica. The church is headed by its bishop, who is elected by the conference of ministers and lay delegates.

The church is a member of the World Methodist Council but has withdrawn from membership in the World Council of Churches. In 2002, it reported 9,500 members serving a wider church family of 12,500.

Evangelical Methodist Church of Costa Rica
Apartado 5481-1000
San José
Costa Rica

J. Gordon Melton

See also: United Methodist Church; World Council of Churches; World Methodist Council.

References

Harmon, Nolan B. *Encyclopedia of World Methodism.* 2 vols. Nashville: United Methodist Publishing House, 1974.

Van Beek, Huibert. *A Handbook of the Churches and Councils: Profiles of Ecumenical Relationships.* Geneva: World Council of Churches, 2006.

World Methodist Council. Handbook of Information, 2002–2006. Lake Junaluska, NC: World Methodist Council, 2003.

Evangelical Methodist Church of Italy

The Evangelical Methodist Church of Italy is the largest Italian Methodist body. Methodist missionaries have been active in Italy since the 19th century, with autonomous missions from both England (from what is now the Methodist Church) and the United States (from what is now the United Methodist Church). The first Wesleyan missionary, William Arthur (1819–1901), arrived in Italy in 1859. He was followed by Richard Green (1829–1907), who established an outpost in Florence and initiated cooperative contacts with independent Italian evangelical churches, including the anti-Catholic Free Christian Church, which had been established by a former Catholic priest, Alessandro Gavazzi (1809–1889). The debate on whether the Methodists should establish an Italian Methodist Church, or join in the efforts of those aiming to establish a national Protestant Church in Italy, continued for several decades. The British Wesleyan mission expanded under the leadership of Henry J. Piggott (1831–1917) and Thomas W. S. Jones (1831–1916), who in 1870 incorporated the Evangelical Methodist Church in Italy. The most distinguished Italian member was the philosopher Pietro Taglialatela (1829–1913), another former Catholic priest.

American missions took a separate path. Following a proposal by Charles Elliott (1782–1869), the Missouri–Arkansas Conference in 1871 decided to dispatch Leroy Monroe Vernon (1838–1896) to Italy. Attempts to join forces with the British Methodists were not successful, and in 1874 Vernon incorporated, in Bologna, the Episcopal Methodist Church of Italy, which in 1875 opened a temple in Rome. Vernon's successor, William Burt (1852–1936), developed a liaison with Italian Freemasonry, at that time a very anti-Catholic institution. A number of Italian Freemasons, however, were not Christians of any persuasion, but Secular Humanists. A former Wesleyan Methodist who had joined the Episcopal Methodists, Saverio Fera (1850–1915), promoted a schism in Italian Freemasonry, by gathering in a splinter organization around himself of anti-Catholic Freemasons who were nonetheless Christian and Protestant, and opposed Secular Humanism. Fera was a controversial figure, and his initiatives were ultimately detrimental to Italian Methodism, while a largely independent pastor, Riccardo Santi (1871–1961), acquired national and international respect with the foundation of Casa Materna, established in 1905 as an orphanage for the destitute street children of Naples.

After World War II (during which Methodists suffered discrimination as members of a "foreign" church), in 1946 the American and British branches merged to become the unified Methodist Church of Italy, which was eventually given official recognition by the Italian government on March 20, 1961. Still pursuing their original aim of unifying Italian mainline Protestantism within a single church, the Methodists signed a "pact of integration" with the Waldensian Church in 1975. This pact became officially effective in 1979. It was not, technically, a merger, because the Waldensians and the Methodists also maintained separate institutions, as well as separate international contacts. They decided, however, to be governed by one synod, responsible for the newly constituted Union of Waldensian and Methodist Churches. The Evangelical Methodist Church of Italy remained also incorporated separately, according to legal proceedings completed in 1979, while the Union of Waldensian and Methodist Churches entered into a concordat with the Italian government in 1984.

Evangelical Methodist Church of Italy
Via Firenze 38
00184 Rome
Italy

Massimo Introvigne and PierLuigi Zoccatelli

See also: Methodist Church; United Methodist Church; Waldensian Church; World Methodist Council.

References

Chiarini, Franco. *Storia delle Chiese Metodiste in Italia 1859–1915*. Torino: Claudiana, 1999.

Chiarini, Franco, ed. *Il metodismo italiano (1861–1991)*. Torino: Claudiana, 1997.

Evangelical Methodist Church of Uruguay

The Evangelical Methodist Church of Uruguay (Iglesia Evangelica Metodista) dates to the 1835 tour of Fountain E. Pitts (1808–1874), a minister in the Methodist Episcopal Church (now an integral part of the United Methodist Church). He not only assessed the possibility of initiating a Methodist ministry in Argentina, Brazil, and Uruguay, but founded a Methodist class in Montevideo. During a six-month stay, he called for the church to send a full-time missionary to the area. As a result Reverend John Dempster (1794–1863) arrived in Buenos Aires in 1836. During his tenure he visited Montevideo and requested a full-time missionary worker for the country. That worker was William H. Norris (1801–1878), who arrived in 1839; however, even though he was able to get permission to build a church, the war between Uruguay and Argentina and internal unrest in the country prevented much success in his missionary activities. He withdrew in 1842.

In 1870, a new attempt to found Methodism in Uruguay was started by John F. Thompson (1843–1933), though he also had little success. Finally in 1876, Thomas B. Wood (1844–1922) arrived and was able to create a stable growing organization. He was aided by Francisco G. Penzotti (1851–1925), converted under Thompson's ministry, and other Native Uruguayans. They had some difficulty from a hostile government and on occasions were arrested because of their evangelistic endeavors. They were able to get some relief after William Tallen became pastor of an American church in Montevideo and used the pulpit as a forum to defend Protestantism in general. He also occasionally spoke at the university and attracted several well-educated Uruguayans to the church. In 1884, the mission joined in the development of a theological school as a joint venture with the Waldensian Church (there being a large Italian expatriate community in Montevideo).

Uruguay operated as a branch of the Argentina work until 1893, when the Methodist Episcopal Church organized its South America Conference. Uruguay (including a small part of Argentina and Brazil) became a separate district. During this time, the Crandon Institute, the most important of the church's educational institutions, was founded. It eventually offered a complete education from elementary school through junior college. A ministerial training school founded in Montevideo was later transferred to Buenos Aires and became Union Theological Seminary. In the 1960s the church entered into merger negotiations with the Waldensians and the Christian Church (Disciples of Christ), but the merger was not consummated.

As the work in South America developed, the Argentina and Uruguay districts were separated into the River Plate Conference. That conference was dissolved in 1952, and Uruguay was set apart as the Uruguay Provisional Conference. Having recruited the necessary number of ministers (25), in 1964 it became the Uruguay Annual Conference. In 1968, at the time of the formation of the United Methodist Church, the general conference gave the Uruguay Conference permission to become an autonomous body. It completed that process in 1969, and Reverend Emilio Castro was elected as president of the new church. As secretary of the World Council of Churches, Castro went on to become one of the most outstanding voices in the world ecumenical community.

The Methodist Church is a relatively small church, with approximately 1,000 members in its 21 congregations (2005), but it has been a member of the World Council of Churches and of the World Methodist Council. It has sponsored a radio show since the 1940s, *La Voz Evangelical* (*The Evangelical Voice*).

Evangelical Methodist Church of Uruguay
San José 1457
11.200 Montevideo
Uruguay

J. Gordon Melton

See also: Christian Church (Disciples of Christ); United Methodist Church; Waldensian Church; World Council of Churches; World Methodist Council.

References

Harmon, Nolan B. *Encyclopedia of World Methodism*. 2 vols. Nashville: United Methodist Publishing House, 1974.

Talolon, Alberto G. *Historia del Metodismo en el Rio de la Plata*. Buenos Aires: Imprensa Metodista, 1936.

Van Beek, Huibert. *A Handbook of the Churches and Councils: Profiles of Ecumenical Relationships.* Geneva: World Council of Churches, 2006.

World Methodist Council. Handbook of Information, 2002–2006. Lake Junaluska, NC: World Methodist Council, 2003.

Evangelical Mission of South Haiti

The Evangelical Mission of South Haiti grew somewhat accidentally out of the work of a team of independent evangelical Christian missionaries in Cuba. In 1928 Elmer Thompson (b. 1901), his wife, Evelyn McElheran (b. 1905), a Cuban national named Bartholomew Lavastida (1890–1994), and Isabel Junco opened a Bible school. As part of their study, they had the students engage in evangelistic efforts. The work of the students and graduates expanded to the point that in 1936 a decision was made to expand the effort to the Dominican Republic. Alexander Mersdorf, a missionary who had joined the original team, was sent to survey the situation, but stopped at Port-au-Prince, Haiti, on the way to Santo Domingo. While there, he encountered some Haitians who had been converted to Christianity while working on a sugarcane plantation in Cuba. They knew little of the Christian life beyond the absolute basics and had no Bible in their Native Creole language. They were looking for a minister who could provide them with some training and guidance.

Upon his return to Cuba Mersdorf placed the needs of the Haitians before the group at the Bible school and they decided to postpone work in the Dominican Republic and concentrate instead on Haiti. The work in Haiti eventually became the Evangelical Baptist Mission in South Haiti. The Haitian mission began in 1937 by founding a Bible school in Les Cayes and growing the mission through its graduates. Over the next years it also founded a seminary, a hospital, and a radio network.

In 2008 the mission reported that its fellowship had grown to include some 487 churches, a significant expansion in the last decade. The West Indies Mission, the name assumed by the work that grew in the islands from Thompson's original effort later changed its name to WorldTeam. In 1995 it merged with RBMU Inter-national to become World Team (1431 Stuchert Rd., Warrington, PA 18976). The Evangelical Mission of South Haiti retains close relations with World Team. It also works with Reciprocal Ministries International (5475 Lee St., Suite 301, Lehigh Acres, FL 33971), an evangelical missionary agency, whose program "Hope for Kids" builds schools for children in Haiti.

Evangelical Mission of South Haiti
MFI-M.E.B.S.H.
Box 15665
West Palm Beach, FL 33416-5665

J. Gordon Melton

See also: Baptists; Evangelicalism.

References

Reciprocal Ministries International. http://www.rminet.org/. Accessed April 24, 2009.

World Team. http://www.worldteam.org. Accessed April 24, 2009.

Evangelical Pentecostal Mission of Angola

The Evangelical Pentecostal Mission of Angola dates to the arrival of American Pentecostal missionaries in the country in 1950. Their initial work was soon supplemented by additional personnel representing the Portuguese Assemblies of God. The work grew relatively rapidly and by 1974, when Angola became independent, the mission was ready to organize as a denomination and was recognized as such by the government under its present name. The church developed an expansive program with worship services daily. It also developed a broad program of social service that included programs in education, health care, and rural development, and soon found itself advocating on issues of peace and justice as well as human rights.

The Evangelical Pentecostal Mission has a distinctive perspective on the Christian sacraments. It celebrates the Eucharist and baptism (by immersion), but also designates its ceremonies of member consecration, marriage, and burial as sacraments.

The Mission is ecumenically oriented. In 1985, it joined the World Council of Churches, has affiliated with the World Pentecostal Fellowship, and maintains an active relationship with Portuguese-speaking Pentecostals, especially those in Brazil. In 2005 it reported a membership of 75,000.

Evangelical Pentecostal Mission of Angola
CP 219
Porto Amboim
Angola

J. Gordon Melton

See also: Pentecostalism; World Council of Churches.

Reference

Van Beek, Huibert. *A Handbook of the Churches and Councils: Profiles of Ecumenical Relationships.* Geneva: World Council of Churches, 2006.

Evangelical Presbyterian Church in Iran

The Evangelical Presbyterian Church in Iran, a church in the Reformed tradition, is the product of 19th-century Protestant missionary efforts in the Middle East. Work began in Iran in 1834. Given the hostility to conversionist initiatives by Muslims, missionaries concentrated on the older Orthodox Christian community, in this case the Apostolic Catholic Assyrian Church of the East. One rationale for the mission was to revitalize the Church of the East as a missionary organization in its own culture. That approach did not work, and those few church members influenced by the missionaries ultimately withdrew and organized separately. The first congregations were formed in the mid-1850s in and around Rezaich. Work spread to other parts of the country. The first presbytery was organized in 1862.

In 1934, all of the Protestant churches, some of which included people of Zoroastrian and Jewish background, came together to form a united Protestant church that in 1963 reorganized as the Evangelical Presbyterian Church in Iran. The church is led by its synod, which is made up of representatives from the three presbyteries.

In 2005, the church reported 1,500 members in 7 congregations. The small body is a member of the World Council of Churches, the World Alliance of Reformed Churches, and the Middle East Council of Churches.

Synod of the Evangelical Church in Iran
PO Box 11365-4454
Teheran
Iran

J. Gordon Melton

See also: Apostolic Catholic Assyrian Church of the East; Middle East Council of Churches; World Alliance of Reformed Churches; World Council of Churches.

Reference

Van Beek, Huibert. *A Handbook of the Churches and Councils: Profiles of Ecumenical Relationships.* Geneva: World Council of Churches, 2006.

Evangelical Presbyterian Church in South Africa

The Evangelical Presbyterian Church in South Africa began in 1875 when Reformed Church missionaries from Switzerland initiated work among the Tsonga people of the northern Transvaal of South Africa. They were later joined by workers from the Paris Mission (associated with the Reformed Church of France). The work spread throughout the Transvaal, especially after the mining industry developed. With the movement of people pursuing jobs, it spread to the Orange Free State and into Zululand. It has remained a largely ethnic church, with worship being conducted in the Tsonga language.

The mission matured as the Tsonga Presbyterian Church. In 1962 it became autonomous. Once organizationally independent, it began the long process of becoming financially self-sufficient. Its doctrine and practice follows that of its parent body. The synod is the highest legislative body. It appoints an executive committee that administers the church on a day-by-day basis.

In 2005 the Evangelical Presbyterian Church reported 48,000 members. It is a member of the World Council of Churches and the World Alliance of Reformed Churches.

Evangelical Presbyterian Church in South Africa
PO Box 31961
Braamfontein 2017, Johannesburg
South Africa

J. Gordon Melton

See also: Paris Mission; Reformed Church of France; World Alliance of Reformed Churches; World Council of Churches.

References

Bauswein, Jean-Jacques, and Lukas Vischner, eds. *The Reformed Family Worldwide: A Survey of Reformed Churches, Theological Schools, and International Organizations.* Grand Rapids, MI: William B. Eerdmans Publishing Company, 1999.

Van Beek, Huibert. *A Handbook of the Churches and Councils: Profiles of Ecumenical Relationships.* Geneva: World Council of Churches, 2006.

Van der Bent, Ans J., ed. *Handbook/Member Churches/World Council of Churches.* Geneva: World Council of Churches, 1985.

Evangelical Presbyterian Church of Portugal

The first congregation in the Reformed tradition in Portugal was founded by a Scottish physician, Robert Reid Kelley, in 1845 on the island of Madeira. However, the church was suppressed and the members scattered. One of the members eventually found his way to Lisbon and was instrumental in founding the first Presbyterian church in that city. The movement spread with the assistance of Brazilian and American missionaries. Paralleling the Presbyterians, Manuel dos Santos Carvalho led in the founding of the first Congregational church in the 1880s. That church cooperated with the Evangelical Church of Rio de Janeiro, with whom it founded the Evangelical Union and Mission of Brazil and Portugal.

After World War II, Presbyterian and Congregational leaders began to look toward the formation of a national Portuguese church, and in 1947 a constitution was promulgated. The first synod of the new church, the Evangelical Presbyterian Church of Portugal (Igreja Evangélica Presbiteriana de Portugal), was held in 1952. In this effort, the United Presbyterian Church in the United States (now a part of the Presbyterian Church [U.S.A.]) provided guidance and support. Those Congregationalist churches that chose not to join the united church formed the Union of Evangelical Congregationalist Churches.

The church has its headquarters in Lisbon, Portugal. It has benefited from the changes that brought religious freedom to Portugal and the new relations between Protestant and Roman Catholics following the Second Vatican Council, but remains a small church with 25 congregations and around 3,000 members (2005). It cooperates with the Spanish Methodists in supporting the Evangelical Seminary of Theology in Lisbon. It is a member of the World Council of Churches.

Evangelical Presbyterian Church of Portugal
Rua Tomás de Anunciação n 56, 1-D
P-1300 Lisbon
Portugal

J. Gordon Melton

See also: Presbyterian Church (U.S.A.); World Council of Churches.

References

Bauswein, Jean-Jacques, and Lukas Vischner, eds. *The Reformed Family Worldwide: A Survey of Reformed Churches, Theological Schools, and International Organizations.* Grand Rapids, MI: William B. Eerdmans Publishing Company, 1999.

De Azevedo, C. *Churches of Portugal.* New York: Scala Books, 1985.

Van Beek, Huibert. *A Handbook of the Churches and Councils: Profiles of Ecumenical Relationships.* Geneva: World Council of Churches, 2006.

Evangelical Presbyterian Church of Togo

The Evangelical Presbyterian Church of Togo originated with the Norddeutsche Mission, founded in Hamburg, Germany, in 1836. It drew support from Pietist Lutherans, Moravians, and Reformed Protestants from across northern Germany, and in 1847 it sent the first missionaries into Togo to work among the Ewe people. Their work soon spread across the border into the Gold Coast.

In 1884, Germany assumed hegemony over what was then Togo, but during World War I the British and French took control, dividing the country into an eastern (British) and a western (French) part. In 1918, both governments expelled the German missionaries operating in their territories, and in 1922 the mission reorganized as the Evangelical Ewe Church, which included congregations in French Togo, British Togo, and the Gold Coast. The church tried to affirm its unity across national boundaries, but increasingly the British and French segments were divided by language and custom.

In the Gold Coast, the United Free Church of Scotland, a Presbyterian church, assumed control of the former work of the Basel Mission and then increasingly became influential over the congregations of the Evangelical Ewe Church. Meanwhile in French Togo, the Ewe church founded its own theological school and began to build a relationship with the Paris Mission (Reformed Church of France), which began to assume more and more control. It also began to spread among the Kabye people in the northern part of the country. In 1955 the United Church of Christ from the United States added its support to the work through its United Church Board of World Ministries.

The church became fully independent in 1959 as the Evangelical Church of Togo. The next year Togo became independent of France. In the next decades the church grew to a considerable extent and emerged as the largest non-Catholic body in the country. More recently it assumed its present name, an indication of its leaving its early congregational organization behind and adopting a presbyterial structure.

In 2005, the church reported a membership of 180,000 in 591 congregations. It is a member of the Christian Council of Togo and the World Council of Churches.

Evangelical Presbyterian Church of Togo
BP 2
rue Tokmake 1
Lomé
Togo

J. Gordon Melton

See also: Basel Mission; Paris Mission; Reformed Church of France; United Church of Christ; World Council of Churches.

References

Bauswein, Jean-Jacques, and Lukas Vischner, eds. *The Reformed Family Worldwide: A Survey of Reformed Churches, Theological Schools, and International Organizations.* Grand Rapids, MI: William B. Eerdmans Publishing Company, 1999.

Van Beek, Huibert. *A Handbook of the Churches and Councils: Profiles of Ecumenical Relationships.* Geneva: World Council of Churches, 2006.

Evangelical Presbyterian Church, Ghana

In 1847, missionaries from the Bremen, the Norddeutsche, and the Basel Missions began work among the Ewe people in what was then called Togoland. These societies drew their support from the Lutheran and Reformed churches of Germany and German-speaking Switzerland. Germany assumed control of this area in 1884, and the mission experienced a period of growth beginning in the 1890s and extending to World War I.

Germany lost its African colonies as a result of World War I, and England and France divided Togoland. That part assigned to Britain was incorporated into the colony of the Gold Coast. The congregations that had been formed among the Ewe people were essentially left without missionary oversight, and in 1922 their leadership met for the first synod of the Ewe church. A congregational church order was developed, and the synod took oversight of the churches in both the French and English territory. Two synods were set up to function in the two new colonies, but a joint synod of the whole church was to meet every four years.

In 1923 missionaries from the Church of Scotland moved into the Gold Coast and began to work with the Ewe church members, while in 1929 missionaries from the Paris Mission (associated with the Reformed Church of France) assumed similar duties in French Togo. The two Ewe synods shared a constitution, but over the years developed in divergent directions. As the Gold Coast became Ghana and Togo became an independent country, the two synods became independent churches, though they continue to have close fraternal relations and to meet in their joint synod quadrennially.

The church in Ghana expanded far beyond its original base among the Ewe to include mission stations among the Twi, Guan, Konkomba, Kabre, and Akposso peoples. It has also had a turbulent history, as various groups have formed separate indigenous churches. As early as 1954, some 20 congregations among the Beum and Krachi peoples divided over issues of language and polygamy, the allowance of polygamy, common in some societies, being a persistent problem for African Christian churches. This split became the occasion for the Ewe Presbyterian Church to change its name to the Evangelical Presbyterian Church (The church in Togo made a similar name change.) Other churches that have their roots in the Evangelical Presbyterian Church include the Apostolic Revelation Society, the White Cross Society, the Evangelical Presbyterian Reformed Church, and the Lord's Pentecostal Church. Most recently, the Charismatic movement spread through the church and along with new life brought schism. Those most supportive of the movement have formed the Evangelical Presbyterian Church of Ghana.

In 2005 the church reported 200,000 members in 787 congregations. It supports Trinity College at Legon jointly with the Anglican, Methodist, and other Presbyterian churches. It is a member of the World Alliance of Reformed Churches and the World Council of Churches.

Evangelical Presbyterian Church, Ghana
PO Box 18
Ho-Kpodzi, HO Volta Region
Ghana

J. Gordon Melton

See also: Basel Mission; Church of Scotland; Paris Mission; Reformed Church of France; World Alliance of Reformed Churches; World Council of Churches.

References

Bauswein, Jean-Jacques, and Lukas Vischner, eds. *The Reformed Family Worldwide: A Survey of Reformed Churches, Theological Schools, and International Organizations.* Grand Rapids, MI: William B. Eerdmans Publishing Company, 1999.

Gifford, Paul. *Ghana's New Christianity: Pentecostalism in a Globalising African Economy.* Bloomington: Indiana University Press, 2004.

Van Beek, Huibert. *A Handbook of the Churches and Councils: Profiles of Ecumenical Relationships.* Geneva: World Council of Churches, 2006.

Van der Bent, Ans J., ed. *Handbook/Member Churches/World Council of Churches.* Geneva: World Council of Churches, 1985.

Evangelical Reformed Church of Angola

The Evangelical Reformed Church of Angola grew out of the work of Anglican missionary Archibald Patterson and Swiss minister Ernest Niklaus, who in 1922 started mission work in the Province of Uige. The work grew through the 1960s as the Igreja Evangélica do Norte de Angola. However, in 1961, when civil war broke out, the church faced severe government repression. Most church leaders were either forced underground or out of the country. Only in 1977, after independent Angola had been established, was the church able to reorganize. The members chose the name Evangelical Reformed Church of Angola.

The new church faced some immediate problems, not the least being the departure of 18 ministers who founded a separate church, which led to the formation of the United Evangelical Church–Anglican Communion of Angola. However, the main body of the church continued. Headquarters were moved to the capital in Luanda, and the church developed evangelical efforts designed to transform it into a national church, rather than simply a regional organization. It now has work in 11 of the 18 provinces of Angola.

In 2005 the church reported 200,000 members in 452 congregations. Its General Assembly is the highest legislative body in the church. Administration is in the hands of its executive committee. It is a member of both the Council of Christian Churches in Angola and the World Council of Churches.

Evangelical Reformed Church of Angola
Caixa Postal 2594-C
Luanda
Angola

J. Gordon Melton

See also: World Council of Churches.

References
Bauswein, Jean-Jacques, and Lukas Vischner, eds. *The Reformed Family Worldwide: A Survey of Reformed Churches, Theological Schools, and International Organizations.* Grand Rapids, MI: William B. Eerdmans Publishing Company, 1999.
Van Beek, Huibert. *A Handbook of the Churches and Councils: Profiles of Ecumenical Relationships.* Geneva: World Council of Churches, 2006.

Evangelical Synodal Presbyterial Church of the Augsburg Confession in Romania

See Evangelical Lutheran Church in Romania.

Evangelicalism

Evangelicalism is a hybrid of theological and social components as complex as it is long-standing. While an unsophisticated and ahistorical answer to the question of its source might be "the New Testament," a historically grounded response observes that evangelicalism's roots run at least as deeply as the Reformation. Evangelicalism's resemblance to 17th-century Puritanism is noteworthy, but the most straightforward connection is with the ideas and practices of 18th-century spiritual revitalization movements on both sides of the Atlantic. It has grown to become the largest single North American mode of collective religious practice and one of the world's prominent religious movements.

The label "evangelical" derives from the Greek for "good news." Elements commonly isolated to describe the core that distinguishes evangelicalism from other forms of Christianity include the preponderant stress on personal conversion (conversionism). The second salient signal, a corollary of the first, is activism, whether in generalized service or in evangelism. Third is the immense respect evangelicals hold for the Bible (biblicism). The final factor is the cross's centrality in the redemption process (crucicentrism), although the rise of Charismatic influence has attenuated this somewhat, refocusing attention on the resurrection. The presence of these four features is sufficient to classify a movement as evangelical, neither wrongly including non-evangelical groups nor excluding those that are clearly evangelical yet eschew the title (a number of African-descended denominations, in both North America and Africa, thus qualify). These four features also hint at evangelicalism's inherent fluidity. Never as monolithic as sometimes portrayed, the movement is in constant flux. Some organizations or denominations that once manifested these impulses no longer do so, while others that stood apart may choose to adopt them.

Evangelicalism is a specifically Christian manifestation of the massive Western paradigm shift known as the Enlightenment. The 17th to 19th centuries saw Christians struggling to clarify their relationship with Enlightenment rationalism. Hans Küng's (b. 1928) adaptation of Thomas Kuhn's (1922–1996) theory of paradigm shifts suggests that evangelicalism was a "meso-change," a course correction involving several specific tenets, while not challenging basic orthodoxy. Evangelicals rarely abandon the first five Ecumenical Councils' christological pronouncements. Thus evangelicalism enjoys extensive continuity with the historic faith, yet evinces its spirituality in ways consonant with the broader culture's orientation, rendering it a profoundly conservative form of modernism.

The 18th Century By the third decade of the 18th century, religious revitalization was underway on both sides of the Atlantic. In England, the varying forms of Methodism preached by Anglicans George Whitefield (1714–1770) and John Wesley (1703–1791) provided spiritual outlets for tens of thousands of working people not vitally linked to the state church. Whitefield became a transatlantic phenomenon, preaching to thousands in the northern colonies. This broad upturn in spirituality, the Great Awakening, also included revivals in response to native-born New Englander Jonathan Edwards's (1703–1758) preaching. The New Lights valued the place of emotions in conversion and re-evaluated humans' role in the process of evangelism and discipleship. By mid-century, the Church of England began internal renewal through clergy like John Newton (1725–1807) and Bishop Thomas Sherlock (1678–1761). Sherlock's apologetics addressed issues using Enlightenment categories. So successful was his adaptation to the new paradigm that his argumentation remained in use until the late 20th century, when postmodernism limited its effectiveness. William Wilberforce (1759–1833) and the Clapham Sect forced justice issues (particularly slavery) onto the public agenda. On the continent, evangelicalism flourished through the influence of Lutheran Pietism on the Moravians' guardian, Nicholas von Zinzendorf (1700–1760), and early foreign missions sponsored by the Danish Crown. After the American Revolution, the New Light Stir served as high-water mark of a process by which New England's Baptists separated from state-sanctioned Congregational churches to form voluntarist churches.

The 19th Century Activism was evangelicalism's dominant 19th-century feature. One form was renewed emphasis on conversionism. The 1801 Great Camp Meeting at Cane Ridge, Kentucky, marked the onset of the Second Great Awakening. The Awakening set in motion a demographic process that transformed American society. Church membership soared from roughly 10 percent in the post-Revolutionary period to approximately a quarter of the population by 1850. By century's end, as many as one in three Americans were church members, the largest segment found among the Methodists, Baptists, and other revivalist-oriented Christians.

Acceptant of society's fervor for progress, mingled with postmillennial eschatology, evangelicals' concern that faith have practical outcomes led to the promulgation of a plethora of service societies. English evangelicals launched what became worldwide movements: the British and Foreign Bible Society (1804), the Young Men's Christian Association (1844), the Young Women's Christian Association (1854), the Evangelical Alliance (1846). Labor and health issues also garnered British evangelicals' attention. Inspired partly by the 18th-century advocacy of Thomas Coke (1747–1814) and William Carey (1761–1834), concern for foreign missions surged on both sides of the Atlantic. Significant resources were mobilized, often by women, to recruit and equip crosscultural missionaries. New American societies added antislavery agitation and strong temperance notions. Revivalism began transforming under the Holiness movement's influence. Indicative of revivalism's increasing success, there were fewer unconverted non-Christians and they became more resistant to evangelistic efforts. Focus shifted to promoting spiritual maturity of those claiming rebirth. If children were indeed moral blank slates, educating them with Christian values held profound potential for social amelioration. Higher education embraced the Baconian inductive method, imparting a new flavor to evangelical systematic reflection through the Princeton Theology.

Evangelicalism encountered several difficulties in the 1800s. While a number of communitarian and utopian collectives quietly promoted their eclectic eschatological views, William Miller (1782–1849) fomented broad anxiety with his dramatic interpretation of biblical prophecy, leaving premillennialism unpopular for decades. Revivalism was tamed after the Civil War, transforming raucous camp meetings into sedate and safe Christian resorts. Evangelicals experienced competition from an alternate conservativism, Anglo-Catholicism. It provided Anglicans with a less boisterous means to express profound and historically rooted piety. Darwinism quickly was perceived as a threat; the potential disruptiveness of rising commercialism and consumerism was not.

The Early 20th Century Much of evangelicalism's history in the early 20th century is bound up in the

Aimee Semple McPherson, early-20th-century itinerant evangelist. (Library of Congress)

Fundamentalist-Modernist Controversy. A reaction to the divisive influence of Higher Criticism, Darwinism, and other modern ideas, the controversy severely disrupted Protestantism, literally dividing some denominations.

A new alternate evangelicalism, a form of Restorationism known as Pentecostalism, appeared in 1901, soaring after the 1906 Azusa Street Revival. Disconcerted Methodist preachers were particularly attracted to Pentecostalism in the 1920s. Flamboyant Pentecostal ministries included that of Aimee (Kennedy) Semple McPherson (1890–1944). Born in rural Canada to Methodist and Salvation Army parents, she converted to Pentecostalism in 1907. She married Robert Semple, an evangelist; the couple became missionaries to China, where he died. Her second marriage ended in divorce, her frequent evangelistic trips being cited as abandonment by her spouse. Adventuresome, she moved beyond her initial territory, the American East-

ern Seaboard, planting her ministry base in Los Angeles. She broadened her constituency, eventuating in the formation of the International Church of the Foursquare Gospel. To traditional evangelical accents it added healing. Her later ministry was plagued by scandals and her untimely death.

McPherson's use of radio, while sensationalized, was not unprecedented. The New England Fellowship (a precursor to the National Association of Evangelicals) and the Midwest's Moody Bible Institute also realized broadcasting's potential. The New England Fellowship became a major regional lobby, attracting hundreds of pastors by the early 1930s. Fundamentalist ideas also began penetrating denominations hitherto quite unrelated. For some ethnic denominations, Fundamentalist ideas offered a means to indigenize. For groups once considered on the fringe, such as the minority conservative wing of the American Christian Convention, Fundamentalism was an avenue to broader community acceptance. The relative absence of Afro-Americans in Fundamentalism's ranks is sadly noteworthy.

The Emergence of Neo-Evangelicalism By the late 1930s leaders such as Donald Barnhouse (1895–1960) broke ranks to criticize fellow Fundamentalists' shrill sectarianism. As the World Christian Fundamentals Association lost momentum, two rival entities supplanted it. The uncompromising Fundamentalists' American Council of Christian Churches (1941) was countered by a group committed to exploring a more cooperative approach. They opted for constructive cross-denominational cooperation, not merely opposition to the liberal-oriented Federal Council of Churches. The 1942 National Conference for United Action Among Evangelicals marked the genesis of the National Association of Evangelicals (NAE). Within 5 years, 30 denominations, representing 1.3 million members, were full-members with an influence base of a further 3 million. Non-Fundamentalists, including increasingly respectable Pentecostals, accepted membership. The NAE's analog, the Evangelical Fellowship of Canada did not form until 1964.

Carl Henry's (1913–2003) *Uneasy Conscience of Modern Fundamentalism* (1947) served as a neo-evangelical manifesto. The goal was the movement's reinvigoration, ending its inward (some insiders called it "cultic") focus, shedding its cultural hostility to the purpose of renewed social impact, both through conversionism and broader activism. The term "new-evangelical" (later "neo-evangelical") was bruited in 1948 by Harold Ockenga (1905–1985), a student of J. Gresham Machen (1881–1937), who had in 1936 become the prominent pastor of Park Street Church (Boston) and the NAE's first president. The timing of Henry's and Ockenga's initiatives may reflect renewed optimism about mission in light of America's postwar secular leadership (as did a resurgence of foreign mission activity under evangelical auspices). Ockenga was also emerging as an educational leader; his guiding hand helped shape two quintessentially evangelical seminaries. In 1947, with funds provided by radio evangelist Charles Fuller, Ockenga was a key figure in the launch of Fuller Theological Seminary in California. Back in New England, in 1969, Ockenga fa-

The evangelical reverend Billy Graham in 1966. (Library of Congress)

cilitated the merger of two existing seminaries into Gordon-Conwell Theological Seminary (the school's distance education center is named in Ockenga's honor). These new schools attest that neo-evangelicals felt less threatened by biblical scholarship and the gospel's social application than Fundamentalists.

The growing rift between on-going Fundamentalists and neo-evangelicals is well illustrated by the theory and practice of ecclesiastical separation. Drawing upon verses such as 2 Corinthians 6:17, separation placed a premium on putative purity over ostensible unity. As it evolved, the concept recognized three modes of denominational interaction between Fundamentalists and liberals. A denomination could be mixed, both parties coexisting in the same structure. The next step, in which a denomination maintained oversight such that only Fundamentalists were members but members were free to associate with Fundamentalists in mixed settings, was known as "first degree separation." The third option, known as "second degree separation," applies to those whose denominations also consist solely of known Fundamentalists, but whose members associate only with Fundamentalists in other denominations practising first or second degree separation. Carl McIntire (1906–2002), instigator of the American Council of Christian Churches, insisted members adhere to second degree separation; failure to do so implied one's tacit approbation of liberalism. Dispensationalism emphasized the need for separation, true believers associating only in pure churches until Christ's return to relieve a beleaguered church. Fundamentalists who subscribed to a non-dispensational premillennialism possessed less motivation to adhere to the practice. Neo-evangelicals, notably evangelist Billy Graham (b. 1918), were willing to collaborate not only with denominations following first degree separation, but with persons in mixed denominations. The openness removed impediments to cooperation between predominantly Calvinist evangelicals, generally Arminian Holiness proponents and Pentecostals, whose numbers included both Calvinists and Arminians. Although some groups, such as the Full Gospel Business Men's Fellowship International (1951), had been founded under Pentecostal influence and stressed the contemporary availability of healing, they nonetheless attracted support from some non-Pentecostal evangelicals.

Publications figured centrally in neo-evangelicalism's expansion. *Christianity Today*, founded in 1956 with Carl Henry as editor and Ockenga chairing the board, sought to propagate conservative theology yet with a parallel commitment to engagement in social action. Within a quarter of a century, twice as many North American ministers read *Christianity Today* than its liberal foil, *The Christian Century*. The left-wing of evangelicalism was represented by *Sojourners* magazine. The translation and publication of the Bible became controversial in this era. While the 1901 publication of the entire American Standard Bible (ASB) had been generally uncontroversial, the release of the Revised Standard Version (RSV; New Testament 1948; Old Testament 1952) created a firestorm. Conservatives felt its rendering of certain Old Testament passages undermined prophecies of Jesus' Virgin Birth. At least one denomination made reading of RSV in public wor-

ship an error sufficient to discipline pastors. A more conservatively undertaken New American Standard version emerged (NAS; New Testament 1963; Old Testament 1971); the New International Version (NIV; New Testament 1973; Old Testament 1978) was more broadly accepted, either because or in spite of its "dynamic equivalence" translation philosophy.

Para-church organizations increasingly marshalled evangelicals' energy. The InterVarsity Christian Fellowship, imported from Great Britain to Canada in 1928, whose members exported it to the United States in 1938, provided an alternative to what had become the liberal-dominated Student Christian movement. Typical of the minimalism of transdenominational organizations' statements of faith, InterVarsity's 1933 symbol required assent only to scripture's "inspiration, integrity and authority"; Jesus' deity and saving death; the Holy Spirit's role in regeneration; and Christ's triumphal return. The Navigators (1933), Youth for Christ (1946), and Campus Crusade (1951) not only mobilized myriad volunteers, but reinforced evangelicalism's transdenominational character. The 1966 World Congress on Evangelism, held in Berlin and chaired by Carl Henry, elicited insight from a broadly representative, worldwide group of evangelical leaders and thinkers. Eight years later, John Stott helped orchestrate the First International Congress on World Evangelism in Lausanne, Switzerland. At a time when older Protestant denominations advocated a moratorium on missions, evangelicals became more reflective and sophisticated in mission efforts.

The relaxed atmosphere for dealing with diversity simplified evangelicalism's reaction to the emergence in the early 1960s in the Western world of the Charismatic movement. Arising in both Protestantism and Catholicism, this renewal movement's relationship with older Pentecostalism was often strained, despite their similarities. Both emphasize experience more than theology, valuing spiritual intuition concerning the Holy Spirit's presence, yet they were sometimes at odds with each other. The Charismatic movement's acceptance, in turn, has helped lower barriers between evangelicals and Roman Catholics, allowing cooperative work on ethical issues (although to the consternation of separatist Fundamentalists).

Current Situation Evangelicalism's regaining of some broader cultural credibility was marked by *Newsweek*'s declaration of 1976 as the "Year of the Evangelical." Some, concerned that the improved evangelical image might have been secured at the expense of a weakened stance on the inspiration of scripture, issued the 1978 *Chicago Statement on Inerrancy*, defending the Princetonian doctrine. Growth has continued for three decades. On any given Sunday in North America, a majority of those who attend church and report other forms of regular Christian practice during the week (such as routine Bible reading or praying) assent to the core evangelical tenets. Collectively, in the United States, the largely white, evangelical Protestant denominations enjoy rough parity with Roman Catholicism. Until the 1970s, evangelicals appeared less likely to be involved in politics than the general population, though during the Reagan administration political activism grew significantly, and evangelicals currently constitute a significant element of the Republican Party. Meanwhile, a number of evangelical authors have decried the relative absence of evangelical participation in academic roles or as public intellectuals.

Similar trends are evident in Canada, where participation in public religious activities during the second half of the 20th century was much lower than in the United States. This not only reflected broad abandonment of Catholicism among the large Francophone minority during the "Quiet Revolution," but a dramatic downturn in evangelicalism's popularity among the Anglophone majority. In the past 20 years, however, sociologists like Reginald Bibby discovered a strong resurgence, with self-identified evangelicals' numbers possibly doubling, from roughly one-tenth of the population to one-fifth. Charismatic renewal in Anglican and Roman Catholic churches accounts for some of this growth.

Transatlantic connections are stronger in evangelicalism than Fundamentalism; there are more commonalities on both sides of the Atlantic due to evangelicalism's broader base in both cultures. Fundamentalism has stronger appeal to North Americans, where there is no state church and voluntarist churches are the majority. British evangelicalism has its own emphases, however, such as generally being more open to the ecumenical movement and sharing in the general culture's sense of deference to upper social classes. Legal restrictions limit British evangelicals' use of television. British evangelical biblical scholarship, under the postwar influence of the Tyndale Fellowship, repudiated Fundamentalism; Dispensationalism is viewed as a Plymouth Brethren eccentricity. Pentecostalism has made far deeper inroads in the United States than in the United Kingdom, where the Keswick movement claimed many of its potential converts.

In continental Europe, evangelicalism has long been represented by small Pietist movements, whether existing within state-sanctioned Protestant churches or voluntarist in nature. In German, *Evangelische* means "Protestant" and should not be confused with the movement examined in this article. The fall of Communism has resulted in renewed legal evangelistic activity in Central and Eastern Europe. Efforts are impeded by growing alignment of general nationalist sympathy with long-standing national Orthodox churches.

Barriers to non–Roman Catholicism's presence in Latin America, including both social sanctions and execution, were gradually removed in the early 20th century, but profound penetration by evangelicals occurred only in the final third of the 1900s. In some countries, particularly in Central America, evangelicals grew to be a sizeable and vocal minority. As the century closed, Charismatic variants of evangelicalism predominated.

Sub-Saharan Africa is another area sustaining notable evangelical growth. Much of this growth is among Pentecostal or Charismatic groups; one-fifth of the population of Ghana is said to belong to one of two indigenous Pentecostal denominations. Some North American evangelicals find such expressions of faith in non-Western paradigms disturbing, perhaps without realizing that evangelicalism itself is highly culturally adapted. Recent years have witnessed increased violence in transitional areas, where predominantly Muslim cultures abut preponderantly Christian ones. Some evangelical Anglicans, especially from East Africa, have reversed a two-century-long trend, adopting North America as a mission field. Recently several Americans have been consecrated as missionary bishops.

Christianity of any description continues as a distinct minority in most of Asia, despite a long history of evangelical missions. The major exception is South Korea, where evangelicals constitute a sizeable minority who now undertake foreign missions, often to countries where Western missionaries are barred. China's sheer size translates the small percentage of its population that are evangelicals into millions of members. Violence against evangelicals has occurred in a number of Asian regions, from Muslim, Hindu, and Eastern Orthodox Christian sources.

Postmodernism's impact on evangelicalism is increasing. Disaffection with tradition undermines fixed denominational loyalty; lifelong adherence to a single group is increasingly rare. Individuals' successive membership in denominations once considered profoundly different is not uncommon. Some abandon organized faith communities altogether. The house church movement, dissatisfied with what it perceives as medieval and modern cultural accretions to ecclesiology, seeks non-hierarchical and non-clerical community. Affective bonding concerns adherents more than fine points of doctrine, although the movement still displays evangelicalism's core features. Largely successful in China, during radical Communist oppression, the movement is progressively popular in North America and Britain.

C. Mark Steinacher

See also: Baptists; Carey, William; Charismatic Movement; Clapham Sect; Congregationalism; Fundamentalism; Holiness Movement; International Church of the Foursquare Gospel; Pentecostalism; Roman Catholic Church; Salvation Army; Wesley, John.

References

Bebbington, David. "Evangelicalism in Its Settings: The British and American Movements since 1940." In *Evangelicalism: Comparative Studies of Popular Protestantism in North America, the British Isles, and Beyond 1700–1990,* edited by Mark A. Noll, David Bebbington, and George A. Rawlyk. Oxford: Oxford University Press, 1994.

Brackney, William Henry. *Christian Voluntarism: Theology and Praxis.* Manlius, NY: REV/Rose Publishing, 1997.

Carpenter, Joel A., ed. *The Fundamentalist-Modernist Conflict: Opposing Views on Three Major Issues.* New York and London: Garland Publishing, 1988.

Gauvreau, Michael. *The Evangelical Century: College and Creed in English Canada from the Great Revival to the Great Depression.* Montreal and Kingston: McGill-Queen's University Press, 1991.

Hans Küng, "Paradigm Change in Theology: A Proposal for Discussion." In *Paradigm Change in Theology: A Symposium for the Future,* edited by Hans Küng and David Tracy, translated by Margaret Köhl. New York: Crossroad Publishing, 1991.

Marsden, George. *Reforming Fundamentalism: Fuller Seminary and the New Evangelicalism.* Grand Rapids, MI: William B. Eerdmans Publishing Company, 1995.

Noll, Mark A. *A History of Christianity in the United States and Canada.* Grand Rapids, MI: William B. Eerdmans Publishing Company, 1992.

Stackhouse, John G., Jr. *Canadian Evangelicalism in the Twentieth Century: An Introduction to Its Character.* Toronto: University of Toronto Press, 1993.

Wells, David. "On Being Evangelical: Some Theological Differences and Similarities." In *Evangelicalism: Comparative Studies of Popular Protestantism in North America, the British Isles, and Beyond 1700–1990,* edited by Mark A. Noll, David Bebbington, and George A. Rawlyk. Oxford: Oxford University Press, 1994.

Evola, Julius

1898–1974

Julius Evola was a Traditionalist philosopher, critic of modernity, and synthesizer of Eastern and Western Esoteric currents. Giulio Cesare Evola was born in Rome on May 19, 1898, to a Catholic family of Sicilian origin. He was sometimes called "Baron," and preferred the Latin version of his first name. Little is known of his youth until World War I, when he served as an artillery officer.

After engineering studies, Evola joined the Dadaist movement and produced poetry and paintings, some of these now in museums. In 1922 he abandoned the arts and turned to philosophy. It was probably experiences with ether that first convinced him of the autonomy and absolute quality of the self, and of a "transcendent" state that would remain his guiding star throughout his life. The resulting two-volume study of "magical idealism" and the "absolute individual" won some recognition from the philosophical establishment. For recreation, he made several daring mountaineering ascents.

During the 1920s, Evola moved among Theosophists, Anthroposophists, Esoteric Freemasons, and proponents of neo-Pagan spirituality. He studied the literature of Esoteric traditions, both East and West, especially Daoism, Tantrism, and alchemy, and published the first Italian edition of the *Tao Te Ching* (1923). With Arturo Reghini he formed the Gruppo di UR for the practical application of these traditions, raising the concept of "magic" to a high intellectual level. After the UR group dissolved in 1929, Evola wrote a work on spiritual alchemy (*The Hermetic Tradition,* 1931) that impressed both Carl. G. Jung (1875–1961) and Mircea Eliade (1907–1986).

Evola's longest work is *Rivolta contra il mondo moderno* (*Revolt against the Modern World,* 1934), which traces the decline of human culture and aspirations from prehistoric times to the present. It was influenced by the classical and Hindu system of four Ages or Yugas, by René Guénon's notion of a "primordial tradition," and by Herman Wirth's vision of a prehistoric Arctic culture. Unlike Wirth, Evola regarded matriarchy and goddess religions as a symptom of decadence, preferring a hyper-masculine, warrior ethos. The same attitude marks his later work *The Metaphysics of Sex* (1958).

Although Evola never joined the Fascist Party, he hoped that it might restore a "Pagan imperialism" echoing that of ancient Rome, and wrote much journalism promoting his esoterically inspired politics. After Italy's alliance with the Third Reich, he devised a "spiritual" theory of race in preference to the Nazis' "biological" theory. Fluent in German, he lectured to SS and other groups, but documents have revealed that the Nazi leaders regarded him as a crank.

During World War II, Evola turned to Buddhism and wrote his most serene work, *The Doctrine of Awakening* (1943). In 1945 he was in Vienna, reputedly studying the confiscated archives of secret societies, when he was injured during a bombardment. This left his legs permanently paralyzed. In 1951 he was arrested under suspicion of inspiring neo-Fascist activity, but acquitted after six months in custody. In *Men among the Ruins* (1953) he was still hoping for an "order" that might restore a decadent world, but in *Ride the Tiger* (1961) he preached "apoliteia"—the renunciation of any political solution.

In his last years Evola seemed more sympathetic to Catholicism, but the religious attitude was always alien to him. In this he differs from other "Traditionalists" such as Guénon, Marco Pallis, or Frithjof Schuon. The essence of Evola's work is its call to the "superior individual" to realize the identity of self with the Absolute, and the contention that this is the core of all authentic traditions.

Evola lived with his parents during their lifetimes and never married. He died in Rome on June 11, 1974. Since then, his 20 full-length books and innumerable shorter works have been widely republished and translated.

Joscelyn Godwin

See also: Anthroposophical Society; Theosophical Society (America); Western Esotericism.

References

Evola, Julius. *The Doctrine of Awakening: The Attainment of Self-Mastery According to the Earliest Buddhist Text.* Trans. by H. E. Musson. Rochester, VT: Inner Traditions, 1943, 1995.

Evola, Julius. *Revolt against the Modern World.* Trans. by Guido Stucco. Rochester, VT: Inner Traditions, 1934, 1995.

Evola, Julius, and the UR Group. *Introduction to Magic: Rituals and Practical Techniques for the Magus.* Trans. by Guido Stucco. Rochester, VT: Inner Traditions, 1929, 2001.

Opere di Julius Evola. Series editor: Gianfranco de Turris. Rome: Edizioni Mediterranee, 1990–.

Sedgwick, Mark. *Against the Modern World: Traditionalism and the Secret Intellectual History of the Twentieth Century.* Oxford: Oxford University Press, 2004.

Evolution

See Creationism.

Evolutionary Enlightenment

Evolutionary Enlightenment was founded in the late 1980s as the Moksha Foundation by Advaita Vedanta teacher Andrew Cohen (b. 1955). Cohen had been raised in a Jewish home, but at the age of 16 he had a spontaneous spiritual awakening that eventually led him to India and Hinduism. His search for an explanation of what had occurred to him led him initially to Swami Hariharananda Giri (a master of kriya yoga) and then to the practice of martial arts and Zen meditation.

His search reached a first plateau in 1986 when he met Harivansh Lal Poonja, who followed the teachings of Sri Ramana Maharshi's Advaita Vedanta. The teachings emphasized that human beings as pure consciousness in the Absolute are already in a state of spiritual freedom. They do not need to seek or attain it, but rather simply realize what they already are. Cohen felt an immediate agreement with the message of Poonjaji (as he is respectfully called) and after studying with him for a brief period, began to teach himself, initially in Lucknow, India. He taught in England, Holland, and Israel prior to his return to the United States and the founding of the Moksha Foundation in Cambridge, Massachusetts. In 1989 he moved to Marin County, California (north of San Francisco), and published the first of many books, *My Master Is My Self*, which described his spiritual search.

In Marin County, a small community of close disciples began an experiment in living as if the teachings were true and trying to discover the implications of them for daily life. This group continues as the Sangha. The Sangha became an issue with Poonjaji, whose own perspective was that the realization of Oneness had nothing to do with the visible world. Cohen came to believe that there were stages of realization of one's own unity with the absolute and that there were implications for individuals living in the world. This issue led to his separation from Poonjaji.

The Moksha Foundation renamed itself in the late 1990s, calling itself the International Fellowship for Impersonal Enlightenment, and has more recently adopted its present name. It publishes a popular newsstand magazine, *What Is Enlightenment?* IEF centers are found in the United Kingdom, Holland, France, Germany, Denmark, Israel, and India.

Evolutionary Enlightenment
PO Box 2360
Lenox, MA 01240
http://www.andrewcohen.org/

J. Gordon Melton

See also: Hinduism; Meditation; Zen Buddhism.

References

Cohen, Andrew. *Autobiography of an Awakening.* Corde Madera, CA: Moksha Foundation, 1992.

Cohen, Andrew. *In Defense of the Guru Principle.* Lenox, MA: Moksha Press, 1999.

Cohen, Andrew. *My Master Is My Self.* N.p.: Moksha Foundation, 1989.

"A History of Evolutionary Spirituality." http://www.andrewcohen.org/teachings/history-evolutionary-spirituality.asp. Accessed June 15, 2009.

Exorcism

In the most literal sense, "exorcism" refers to the ritual process of expelling a spirit that is controlling or possessing a person, animal, object, or a geographic domain. The Greek term (*exorkízō*), from which the English is derived, refers to ordering someone who is under an oath (for example, in Matthew 26:63, Jesus is *adjured* to tell the truth about his messianic status). This is the underlying process of exorcism across a variety of religious traditions, which typically involves one or more specialists binding the possessing being(s) in some way and then forcing it (or them) to leave the host. This can range from a crisis exorcism of one

Catholic priest Pamphile Fanou (right) of the Cotonou archdiocese holds an exorcism session in Cotonou, Benin. (Fiacre Vidjingninou/AFP/Getty Images)

spirit from an individual (Shoko 2006, 354) to a public exorcism of an individual (Singleton 1975, 305–307) to an annual ritual exorcising the spirits from a village (Kalsang 1999, 194ff.).

Exorcism is found in every major religion on every continent (Betty 2005; DeWoskin 1981; Nasir 1987). In mainstream Christianity, Judaism, and Islam spirit beings that possess hosts are considered evil and the normal recourse is exorcism. In other religious traditions, some spirits are evil and need to be exorcised while others are good or helpful to the individual or community and therefore welcome to possess human hosts (Vodou and other Afro-Caribbean popular religions). In some religions exorcists are specially trained to bind and cast out spirits. In some cases the specialists may limit their duties exclusively to exorcism, though more frequently they perform exorcisms as one of the tasks within their full scope of responsibilities.

While the specifics of exorcism vary from tradition to tradition, it is possible to identify several common elements. First is the need to identify when exorcism is appropriate. In some cases this means that the person goes through several stages of illness and attempted remedies prior to the decision to attempt an exorcism (Nasir 1987, 160; Nguyên 2008, 306). In others the symptoms are recognized immediately as possession and exorcism is the only recourse (Singleton 1975, 305). The symptoms may indicate the nature of the possession and, if so, the type of specialist needed for exorcism.

Once the need for an exorcism is confirmed, in most cases the exorcist, the possessed, and sometimes the community of the possessed will prepare for the ritual. Frequently the exorcist is a trained individual with perhaps an assistant or two (Nguyên 2008). In some cases, however, it is part or all of the community of the possessed that participates in the exorcism (for example, a local parish community in Tanzania, Singleton 1975; an entire village in the *Baithak* ritual in Pakistan, Nasir 1987).

The exorcist may partake of special foods or substances, fast, meditate, or recite prescribed prayers to prepare. The victim may follow similar procedures, including being required to sacrifice something of value to demonstrate commitment to the process. The victim's community (nuclear or extended family, clan, or village) may also need to prepare in some way, perhaps through a community ritual to cleanse them as a whole from ritual defilement or atone for taboo violations.

An appropriate location (for example, the special compounds in Madagascar of the Lutheran Church called *tob*, Roschke 2006) and time (for example, the evening for the *woto* ceremony among the Tourag of Niger, Rasmussen 1994, 75) for the ritual may be indicated by the nature of the possession, or may need to be discerned by the exorcist or the victim's community. Prior to the ritual itself there may be additional preparations for the location where the exorcism will take place. Additionally, the exorcist may rehearse the ritual or engage in additional preparation, depending on the type of exorcism needed.

Once all participants are deemed ready, the ritual itself is performed. The exorcism itself requires a means to either entice or force the spirit to leave the host. Enticing may involve providing a suitable alternate host (whether human, animal, or object) and some enticement or persuasive element to convince the spirit to leave the current host for the new one.

When the spirit can only be removed by force, a variety of means may be used. They may be mediums whose controlling spirits are more powerful than those controlling the victim, and when possessed themselves they are able to force the lesser spirit(s) to leave (Nguyên 2008; Singleton 1977). They may use magical rituals

to force more powerful spirits to obey them, and then command them to banish the weaker spirits from the possessed (Heissig 1986). Alternately, they may also utilize consecrated paraphernalia such as oil or holy water, special incense, animal parts (feathers, horns, teeth), or religious symbols (crucifixes, statues, bells) that are believed to have power to force the possessing spirits to leave the victim. Or they may cast powerful magical spells through ritual actions, offerings, or sacrifices. These spells, when properly done, force the possessing spirit(s) to leave.

One of the most disturbing exorcism practices is physically torturing the victim to effect the exorcism. In some cases the participants believe that only the possessing spirit feels the effects of the torture (Betty 2005, 16). In other cases they believe that the spirit will react to the physical misery of the victim and depart to find a more acquiescent host. It is disturbing that the beatings, burning with boiling water or oil, and other gruesome acts can result in permanent injury or even death of the possessed when not properly handled.

After the exorcism, those close to the victim observe the efficacy of cure, since exorcisms are not always effective (Rasmussen 1994, 74). When the cure is incomplete, the initial exorcism might be repeated, or more powerful exorcisms are applied until the community is satisfied either that the possessed is delivered or that delivery is simply not possible. The latter may be due to a variety of reasons, such as the spirits claiming the host for some purpose (for example, to become a medium) or the host being a scapegoat for the entire community.

Christians have long noted that Jesus did not perform rituals to exorcise demons; he simply commanded them to leave and they did (Berends 1975, 361; Singleton 1975, 304–305). The apostles followed his lead, commanding spirits to leave in Jesus' name without engaging in the ritual activities of their forbearers (Acts 8:6–7; 16:16–18). The ability of Pentecostal Christians in Africa, Asia, and Latin America to expel demons has powerfully impacted the growth of the churches on those continents over the past century (Anderson 2006; Asamoah-Gyadu 2004; Bergunder et al. 2001; Hollenwager 1980, 71–72).

Until the 1600s, many branches of Christianity included exorcistic formulas in baptismal rituals. Exorcism continues today among Christians who believe in spirit beings and possession, though not without internal examination and debate (Theron 1996; Warrington 2004). In the United States there is contention among practicing Christian medical professionals on when or whether exorcism is appropriate for the treatment of dissociative disorders (Rosik 2003). In Africa there are questions on the extent to which Catholic Christians should accommodate themselves to traditional beliefs in exorcistic practice (Shorter 1980) and the extent to which they should performed exorcisms in traditional idiom but interpret them in anthropological or psychological terms (Singleton 1977).

Finally, despite the assumption that medical, psychological, and social advances of modernity would eventually displace religious practices such as exorcism, this has simply not been the case in many countries of the world (for example, England, Malia 2001; Ghana, Onyinah 2004; India, Bergunder et al. 2001; Japan, Young 1990; Panama, Moore 1983; the United States, Whitehead 1995; Vietnam, Nguyên 2008; more generally see Goodman 1988 and Wilkinson 2007). Given this reality, perhaps a more appropriate question is the extent to which contemporary scientific perspectives can be integrated within the various beliefs and traditions related to exorcism.

A. Scott Moreau

See also: Pentecostalism; Possession; Roman Catholic Church.

References

Anderson, Allan H. "Exorcism and Conversion to African Pentecostalism." *Exchange* 35, no. 1 (2006): 116–133.

Asamoah-Gyadu, J. "Mission to 'Set the Captives Free': Healing, Deliverance, and Generational Curses in Ghanaian Pentecostalism." *International Review of Mission* 93, nos. 370–371 (2004): 389–406.

Austnaberg, Hans. *Shepherds and Demons: A Study of Exorcism as Practised and Understood by Shepherds in the Malagasy Lutheran Church.* New York: Peter Lang, 2008.

Berends, Willem. "Biblical Criteria for Demon-Possession." *Westminster Theological Journal* 37, no. 3 (1975): 342–365.

Bergunder, Michael, Ralph Woodhall, and Allan H. Anderson. "Miracle Healing and Exorcism: The South Indian Pentecostal Movement in the Context of Popular Hinduism." *International Review of Mission* 90, nos. 356–357 (2001): 103–112.

Betty, L. S. "The Growing Evidence for 'Demonic Possession': What Should Psychiatry's Response Be?" *Journal of Religion and Health* 44, no. 1 (2005): 13–30.

Boyd, Katie. *Devils and Demonology in the 21st Century.* Atglen, PA: Schiffer, 2009.

Bull, Dennis. "A Phenomenological Model of Therapeutic Exorcism for Dissociative Identity Disorder." *Journal of Psychology & Theology* 29, no. 2 (2001): 131–139.

Chajes, Jeffrey H. *Between Worlds: Dybbuks, Exorcists, and Early Modern Judaism.* Philadelphia: University of Pennsylvania Press, 2003.

DeWoskin, Kenneth J. "A Source Guide to the Lives and Techniques of Han and Six Dynasties Fang-Shih." *Society for the Study of Chinese Religions Bulletin,* no. 9 (1981): 79–105.

Dwyer, Graham. *The Divine and the Demonic: Supernatural Affliction and Its Treatment in North India.* London and New York: Routledge-Curzon, 2003.

Goodman, Felicitas. *How About Demons? Possession and Exorcism in the Modern World.* Bloomington: Indiana University Press, 1988.

Heissig, Walther. "Banishing of Illnesses into Effigies in Mongolia." *Asian Folklore Studies* 45, no. 1 (1986): 33–43.

Hollenweger, Walter J. "Charismatic Renewal in the Third World: Implications for Mission." *Occasional Bulletin of Missionary Research* 4, no. 2 (1980): 68–75.

Kalsang, Norbu, Yongzhong Zhu, and Kevin Stuart. "A Ritual Winter Exorcism in Gnyan Thog Village, Qinghai." *Asian Folklore Studies* 58, no. 1 (1999): 189–203.

Kiely, David M., and Christina McKenna. *The Dark Sacrament: True Stories of Modern-Day Demon Possession and Exorcism.* New York: HarperOne, 2007.

Maarouf, Mohamm. *Jinn Eviction as a Discourse of Power: A Multidisciplinary Approach to Moroccan Magical Beliefs and Practices.* Leiden and Boston: Brill, 2007.

Malia, Linda. "A Fresh Look at a Remarkable Document: Exorcism: The Report of a Commission Convened by the Bishop of Exeter." *Anglican Theological Review* 83, no. 1 (2001): 65–88.

Moore, Alexander. "Lore and Life: Cuna Indian Pageants, Exorcism, and Diplomacy in the 20th Century." *Ethnohistory* 30, no. 2 (1983): 93–106.

Nasir, Mumtaz. "Baithak: Exorcism in Peshawar (Pakistan)." *Asian Folklore Studies* 46, no. 2 (1987): 159–178.

Nguyên, Thi H. "Yin Illness: Its Diagnosis and Healing within Lên Đông (Spirit Possession) Rituals of the Viêt." *Asian Ethnology* 67, no. 2 (2008): 305–321.

Peck, M. Scott. *Glimpses of the Devil: A Psychiatrist's Personal Accounts of Possession, Exorcism, and Redemption.* New York: Free Press, 2005.

Pratnicka, Wanda, and Jacek Laskowski. *Possessed by Ghosts: Exorcisms in the 21st Century.* Gdynia, Poland: Centrum Publishers, 2002.

Rasmussen, Susan J. "The 'Head Dance,' Contested Self, and Art as a Balancing Act in Tuareg Spirit Possession." *Africa (London, England: 1928)* 64, no. 1 (1994): 74–98.

Roschke, Ronald W. "Healing in Luke, Madagascar, and Elsewhere." *Currents in Theology and Mission* 33, no. 6 (2006): 459–471.

Rosik, Christopher. "Critical Issues in the Dissociative Disorders Field: Six Perspectives from Religiously Sensitive Practitioners." *Journal of Psychology & Theology* 31, no. 2 (2003): 113–128.

Shoko, Tabona. "Super Roma: Towards a New Theology of Healing in the Roman Catholic Church in Zimbabwe." *Svensk missionstidskrift* 94, no. 3 (2006): 349–370.

Shorter, Aylward. "Mediumship, Exorcism and Christian Healing." *AFER* 22, no. 1 (1980): 29–33.

Singleton, Michael. "The Public Confession of an Extempore Exorcist." *AFER* 17, no. 5 (1975): 303–309.

Singleton, Michael. "Spirits and Spiritual Direction: The Pastoral Counselling of the Possessed." *Missiology* 5, no. 2 (1977): 185–194.

Sorensen, Eric. *Possession and Exorcism in the New Testament and Early Christianity.* Tübingen: Mohr Siebeck, 2002.

Theron, Jacques. "A Critical Overview of the Church's Ministry of Deliverance from Evil Spirits." *Pneuma* 18, no. 1 (1996): 79–92.

Twelftree, Graham H. *In the Name of Jesus: Exorcism among Early Christians.* Grand Rapids, MI: Baker Academic, 2007.

Wilkinson, Tracy. *The Vatican's Exorcists: Driving Out the Devil in the 21st Century.* New York: Warner Books, 2007.

Young, Richard F. "Magic and Morality in Modern Japanese Exorcistic Technologies: A Study of Mahikari." *Japanese Journal of Religious Studies* 17, no. 1 (1990): 29-49.

F

■ Faeroe Islands

The Faeroe Islands is a group of 18 islands in the Atlantic Ocean north of Scotland with some 540 square miles of land and approximately 480,000 residents (2004). The islands were originally settled by Scandinavians, who over the centuries developed their own Faeroese language. For centuries they worshipped as Roman Catholics. Following the Reformation of the 16th century, the Roman Catholic Church was replaced with the Lutheran Church, which continues to dominate the religious community.

Today, the Faeroe Islands are a dependency of Denmark. The Lutheran community is a part of the Evangelical Lutheran Church in Denmark and officially under the authority of the bishop of Copenhagen. An assistant bishop resides in Tórshavn, the capital. A small Roman Catholic Church community reappeared in the 1930s and today is attached to the bishop in Copenhagen.

Interestingly, the Christian Brethren, the open branch of the Plymouth Brethren, initiated work in the Faeroes in 1865 and have had success on several of the northernmost islands. They are by far the largest of several Free church groups, including the Salvation Army and the Seventh-day Adventist Church, which now have work. The first Jehovah's Witnesses came around 1950, and there is one kingdom hall. There is also a small group of the Baha'i Faith.

J. Gordon Melton

See also: Baha'i Faith; Christian Brethren; Evangelical Lutheran Church in Denmark; Jehovah's Witnesses; Roman Catholic Church; Salvation Army; Seventh-day Adventist Church.

References

Gaffin, Dennis. *In Place: Spatial and Social Order in a Faeroe Islands Community*. Long Grove, IL: Waveland Press, 1995.

Leckey, Colin. *Dots on the Map*. London: Grosvenor House Publishing, 2006.

West, J. F. *Faroe: The Emergence of a Nation*. London: C. Hurst, 1972.

Wylie, J. *The Faroe Islands: Interpretations of History*. Lexington: University of Kentucky Press, 1987.

Faeroe Islands

Religion	Followers in 1970	Followers in 2010	% of Population	Annual % growth 2000–2010	Followers in 2025	Followers in 2050
Christians	38,700	48,900	98.0	0.74	52,400	55,600
Protestants	38,400	47,800	95.8	0.71	51,200	54,200
Independents	60	250	0.5	3.71	320	400
Roman Catholics	50	160	0.3	2.90	200	300
Agnostics	0	860	1.7	1.98	1,500	2,000
Baha'is	40	160	0.3	0.73	250	300
Total population	**38,700**	**49,900**	**100.0**	**0.76**	**54,100**	**57,900**

FAEROE ISLANDS

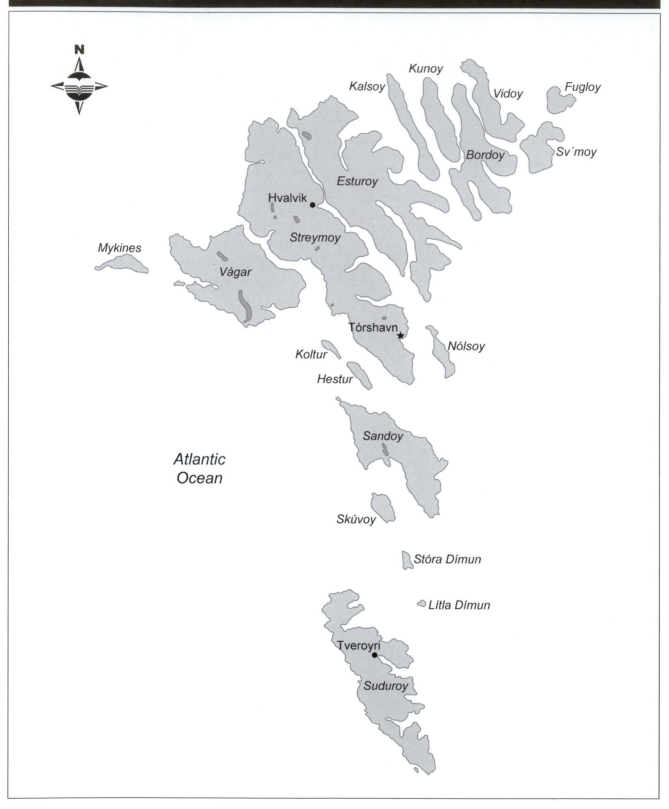

Falashas

See Beta Israel.

■ Falkland Islands/Malvinas Islands

The Falkland Islands, also known as the Malvinas Islands, are a disputed territory in the Atlantic Ocean off the coast of Argentina. Their 4,700 square miles of land are home to 3,140 residents (2008), overwhelmingly of a British background.

In 1982, after Argentina asserted its hegemony of the islands through an occupying force, it fought a war with the United Kingdom and was forced to withdraw. The Falklands include more than 100 islands first discovered in 1520 by Spanish explorers. They were initially inhabited by the British, who founded the community of Port Egmont in the 1690s. They later returned the islands to Spain, which renamed the community Port Soledad. Then in the 18th century French fishers and seal hunters settled on the islands and named them for Saint Malo.

Following Argentina's independence, the islands were considered part of the new nation. In 1833, Great Britain, as part of a larger issue involving trade along the south Atlantic coast, occupied the islands. They also brought settlers with them. These settlers eventually became the overwhelming majority of the islands' inhabitants.

British control of the islands was not disputed until the UN review after World War II. In the end, the UN recognized Argentinean sovereignty, a decision from which the United Kingdom dissented. Since the 1982 war, the United Kingdom has remained in control of the islands, and their status, like their name, is a continuing issue.

The settlers who arrived with the British in 1833 were primarily Anglican, but a chaplain from the Church of England did not arrive until 1845. Missionaries of the South American Missionary Society arrived a decade later. L. S. Brandon, who stayed in the islands for 30 years (1877–1907), is remembered as the person who largely built the Anglican establishment.

The Diocese of the Falkland Islands was created in 1869 and included British expatriates through most of South America. In 1910, work in Argentina and eastern South America was separated, but reunited in 1946. In 1974, jurisdiction over the work in the Falklands passed to the Consejo Anglicano Sud-Americano (CASA), a transition structure leading to the formation of the Anglican Province of the Southern Cone of America. However, the English-speaking residents of the Falklands formally protested their inclusion in what had become a predominantly Spanish-speaking Anglican body, and in 1977 the archbishop of Canterbury assumed authority over the Falklands. The work there remains an integral part of the Archdiocese of Canterbury. The Anglican Church remains the largest religious group on the island though it is no longer supported by the majority of residents.

The Roman Catholic Church began work among the British expatriates in 1857, and their small work remains attached to the bishop of London. A Presbyterian minister arrived in 1872 as the beginning of what

Falkland Islands/Malvinas Islands

Religion	Followers in 1970	Followers in 2010	% of Population	Annual % growth 2000–2010	Followers in 2025	Followers in 2050
Christians	1,900	2,600	82.3	0.31	2,600	2,500
Anglicans	1,000	820	26.5	−0.24	750	700
Protestants	500	620	20.0	−0.33	600	600
Roman Catholics	210	660	21.3	1.34	720	750
Agnostics	60	360	11.6	2.27	450	550
Baha'is	40	90	2.9	0.46	130	150
New religionists	30	60	1.9	0.37	90	120
Atheists	10	30	1.0	0.70	40	60
Buddhists	0	10	0.3	0.00	20	30
Total population	**2,000**	**3,100**	**100.0**	**0.53**	**3,300**	**3,400**

FALKLAND ISLANDS/MALVINAS ISLANDS

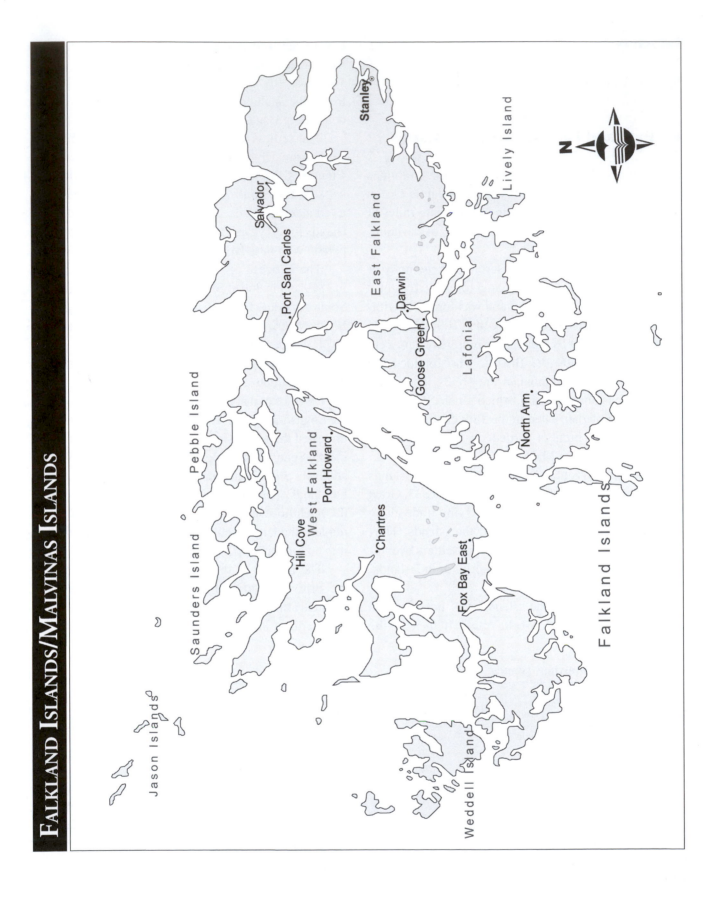

became the United Free Church of the Falkland Islands, in which Lutherans and Baptists have also found a home. The church has fraternal relations with the Church of Scotland.

The Jehovah's Witnesses arrived in the 1960s and have established a small work, as have members of the Baha'i Faith.

J. Gordon Melton

See also: Anglican Province of the Southern Cone of America; Baha'i Faith; Church of England; Church of Scotland; Jehovah's Witnesses; Roman Catholic Church.

References

Barrett, David, ed. *The Encyclopedia of World Christianity*. 2nd ed. New York: Oxford University Press, 2001.

Bissio, Roberto Remo, et al. *Third World Guide 93/94*. Montevideo, Uruguay: Instituto del Tercer Mundo, 1992.

Cannan, Edward. *Churches of the South Atlantic Islands, 1502–1991*. Oswestry, UK: Anthony Nelson, 1992.

Gerry-Hoppé, J. F. "The History of the Non-Conformist Church in the Falkland Islands." *Falkland Islands Journal* 6, no. 1 (1992): 17–25.

Murphy, G. *Christ Church Cathedral: The Falkland Islands—Its Life and Times, 1892–1992*. Stanley: Lance Bidwell, 1991.

Fall Equinox

The Fall Equinox was one of four points in the year (the others being the Winter and Summer Solstices and the Spring Equinox) discovered and marked by ancient peoples who observed the heavens. At the Summer Solstice, from an observer in the Northern Hemisphere, the Sun rises at a point farthest to the north and is in the sky the greatest amount of time. As the days pass, the Sun rises at a point slightly farther south each day and finally reaches a point, 3 months later, around September 21, when it is in the sky for 12 hours and below the horizon for 12 hours. That point is the Equinox. Viewed from above Earth, the Equinox is that point where the center of the Sun is passing through the plane created by the Earth's equator. Following the Winter Solstice, the Sun will appear to be moving north and again reach a point where the day and night are equal—the Spring Equinox. In the Southern Hemisphere, the Fall Equinox is around March 21.

The Fall Equinox was celebrated in temperate climates as the end of the harvest season. Greek mythology had a popular story for this time, related to Persephone (or Kore), the young maiden who was the symbol of fertility. At the Fall Equinox, she goes (or is abducted by Hades) into the underworld, where she reigns for six months, and her mother, Demeter, mourns for her. Without Persephone, the world grows infertile for half the year and awaits rebirth in the spring. Thus the fall festival would be a time of joyfulness, celebrating a full harvest, but with a note of sadness over the coming winter.

Around the world, most cultures celebrated a mid-autumn harvest festival, but it would become an Equinox festival for cultures that operated on a solar calendar. Thus much of Asia did not have their harvest festival on the Equinox, as they operated primarily on a lunar calendar.

The Fall Equinox was not recognized as a significant event in either the Christian or Jewish calendar, and Muslims operated on a strictly lunar calendar. As these three religions rose to prominence, any celebration of the Fall Equinox was almost totally abandoned.

The celebration of the Fall Equinox has been revived by the modern Wiccan/neo-Pagan movement and its eight equally placed annual holidays (usually called Sabbats). The Fall Equinox is acknowledged as the harvest festival, but as few modern Pagans are farmers, the Sabbat (sometimes called Mabon) has become a time for inner reflection. All of the myths related to journeys to the underworld have been collected and related to the inner exploration of the subconscious and unconscious, to contemplate death and understand the cycles of life, death, and new birth. In the Common Era calendar, September 21 is the beginning of fall, thus Mabon becomes the moment for a last summer outing to a Pagan gathering, functioning in the United States, for example, in a manner similar to the purely secular celebration of Labor Day (the first Monday in September).

J. Gordon Melton

See also: Calendars, Religious; Spring Equinox; Wiccan Religion.

References

Crowley, Vivianne. *The Principles of Paganism.* London: Thorsons, 1996.

Dugan, Ellen. *Autumn Equinox: The Enchantment of Mabon.* Woodbury, MN: Llewellyn Publications, 2005.

Farrar, Janet, and Stewart Farrar. *A Witches Bible Complete.* New York: Magickal Child, 1984.

Falun Gong

Starting in 1979, China's leadership introduced radical social and economic reforms. The four modernizations —economic, scientific, military, and agricultural— were presented in an optimistic mode and showed a real willingness on the government's part to experiment with social structure and management. In fact, no one was quite sure what the outcome would be of many of these experiments. One unexpected result has been the flourishing of spiritual and religious movements within the bounds of the new liberalism. Falun Gong is the most significant of the many groups to arise in the 1980s and 1990s.

Falun Gong is an indigenous Chinese spiritual movement that has grown swiftly using modern communication and organizational tools. It formed in 1992 in Chang Chun, an industrial city in northeastern China. At that time it was but one of many qigong practice groups. By the late 1990s it had spread into most Chinese cities and to overseas centers such as Hong Kong, Taiwan, Japan, and the United States. It rose to prominence on April 25, 1999, when more than 10,000 Falun Gong followers surrounded the leadership compound of Zhongnanhai in central Beijing to stage a peaceful but dramatic protest of perceived mistreatment by police. The mistreatment had followed a mass protest in Tianjin that resulted from sharp criticism of qigong and Falun Gong in particular by two writers. At that point Falun Gong ceased being simply an unknown meditation group and became, partly through ongoing intense international media focus, a political opponent of the Chinese government.

Falun is the Wheel of the Law or Dharma, in this case referring to the absolute truth taught by the Buddha, which inexorably rolls forward. Gong refers to a technique or practice, with a particular sense of a spiritual or meditation practice. Thus Falun Gong is the practice or implementation of the spiritual truth, and, by extension, the totality of practitioners who follow these teachings. (The group also refers to itself as Falun Dafa, the Great Law of the Wheel of Dharma.) In practice the label Falun Gong refers to followers of Li Hongzhi, who is said to be enlightened and the sole possessor of the Buddha's truth.

Li Hongzhi (b. 1952; some sources claim 1951) served in the army and worked for a government grain corporation before starting Falun Gong around 1992. Falun Gong literature states that he studied with Daoist and Buddhist masters.

It is not known how large the movement is overall at this stage. At one point Falun Gong literature estimated there were more than 40 million followers in China. Since the group was banned in China, most of these have ceased to participate in group activities; some who believe strongly have been driven underground. Although there are Falun Gong groups around the world that continue to protest and practice in public, the total number of active followers worldwide currently probably numbers in the thousands.

The key Falun Gong texts are *Zhuan Falun* (*The Turning of the Wheel of Dharma*) and *Falun Fofa* (*Buddha Law of the Wheel of Dharma*), which like most Falun texts are collections of Li Hongzhi's speeches. Li has also issued a collection of his poetry, *Hong Yin* (*Torrential Sighs*). One key aspect of Falun Gong's growth has been the adept use of the Internet. Key texts, speeches, and messages from Li Hongzhi are found on the group's websites, in several language options.

Falun Gong espouses a life oriented around both practice and cultivation, in order to cleanse oneself and cease being "ordinary." Practice means performing the set sequences of five physical and meditation exercises. These are often done in groups in the mornings, sometimes in neighborhood parks. Cultivation involves "removing your demon-nature and fulfilling yourself with Buddha-nature."

Zhuan Falun emphasizes that the basic nature of the universe is *zhen-shan-ren*, truthfulness, benevolence,

Banner advertising Falun Gong, Taipei, Taiwan. (J. Gordon Melton)

and forbearance. This compact statement of the fundamental character of the universe is the Great Law (*dafa*). These original universal properties are shared by humans upon birth. We are, however, trapped in the state of ordinary consciousness and cannot see the truth of the universe. The way out of this situation of ignorance is cultivation.

The individual in Falun Gong is described as a container filled with some good elements and some bad elements, the Buddha-nature and the demon-nature. These dual natures are visible to those of higher perceptions as white or black substances. The white is *de*, translated as a physical field surrounding the body, which is accumulated through hardships, and the black is called karmic force (*yeli*), accumulated through bad actions over innumerable lifetimes. The goal of Falun cultivation is to transform de to *gong*, cultivation energy, through the assistance of the master. This de/gong energy level is apparent because it grows in a

vertical spiral, the *gongzhu*, from the top of the head, which again is visible to some.

In addition to gong energy, an individual is characterized by his or her *xinxing* (mind nature) level. Xinxing is an aspect of the person that includes de, plus other characteristics such as tolerance, "enlightenment quality," the abandonment of attachments, and the ability to suffer difficulties. Xinxing thus develops in tandem with de/gong.

A key aspect of cultivation is facing the travails encountered in life. Ordeals are necessary, for they function as tests of xinxing. Conflict in everyday life is similarly part of cultivation. Suffering overall is explained as the repayment of one's karmic debts, and these debts must be repaid in some form.

Falun Gong teaches that the current cycle of the universe is bound to expire and end in catastrophe, "the Final Period of the Last Havoc." The resulting new age will be a period of advancement and ease based on material progress.

Falun Gong's organization is a dispersed yet informed linkage of leaders versed in training and functioning in a cell-like network with maximum flexibility and focus. In its early stages in China, Falun Gong established assistance centers (*fudao zhongxin*) with assistants and branch heads, in addition to general assistance centers (*zong fudao zhongxin*) at the provincial and municipal levels and a Research Society (*yanjiuhui*). The General Society (*zonghui*) arranged national or international meetings. Finally, there were Law Assemblies, *fahui*, at which cultivation experiences could be discussed. Many of these organizational structures fell apart with the crackdown in China. In contrast, Falun Gong in Hong Kong in 2000 was and is a loose collection of practitioner groups, each of which gets together daily to practice the exercises, with a minimum of leadership. However, there is some degree of coordination beyond this, as is evident in the dissemination of information, the training of new members, and the frequent public demonstrations on public holidays. A Hong Kong Association of Falun Gong officially promotes lectures.

Not all Falun Gong groups follow Li Hongzhi, however. Claims by Hong Kong followers of Belinda Peng Shanshan that she is the rightful master of Falun Gong may be a first case of intergroup fissuring.

Zhuan Falun repeatedly states that Falun Gong does not follow the rituals of the past. This does not, however, mean Falun Gong practitioners lack ritual. The carefully choreographed daily exercises so emblematic of Falun Gong practice are a form of group ritualization. In addition such actions as installation of the *falun* (wheel) in the practitioner's abdomen and the opening of the *tianmu* (celestial eye) are clearly initiatory rites.

The movement was officially banned in China on July 20, 1999, and since then has been actively suppressed by public security throughout China. Members caught engaging in the practice, demonstrating in public, or attending meetings have been arrested. Some have been sent to re-education camps or prison. Central government media coverage has also focused on painting the movement in a negative light. Newscasts have interviewed former members who have repudiated the group's principles. Graphic examples of suicide and murder have been attributed to the excesses of Falun Gong beliefs.

In January 2000 seven followers (some reports claim five) attempted suicide by self-immolation in Tiananmen Square, the heart of Beijing. Two subsequently died. Falun Gong spokespersons overseas doubted that the protesters were authentic Falun Gong members, since, they said, Falun Gong principles uphold the sanctity of life. These statements implied that the incident was staged, a contention denied by the Chinese government. Regardless, the constant media reporting of this incident has clearly served to discredit the group in the minds of many Chinese citizens.

Despite Falun Gong's strategic positioning of itself as in opposition to the surrounding society and its "ordinary" mentalities, the interaction has been mutual, with many of the forms found within Falun taken from the Socialist context in which the movement surfaced. These include organization into cells, concern with control over mass media releases, and the centrality of unified doctrinal and organizational practice, all characteristics of Chinese Marxism and the Chinese Communist Party, as well as many sectarian religious groups. The advent of Falun thus shows the resiliency of the tradition of popularly based religious movements within Chinese culture as a whole, as well as the undeniable influence of Chinese socialism.

Falun Gong in some ways fits well in this traditional model of an uneasy relationship between the central government and newly arisen religious groups. It is grassroots based; members are often farmers newly arrived in urban centers, or former state workers thrown out of work due to economic restructuring. And like similar rebellious groups, Falun Gong is consistently critical of the dominant ideologies, including both the established Communist ethos and the new it-is-glorious-to-be-rich game plan.

But in terms of modern (post-1911) Chinese history, there have been very few overtly political religious movements. The myriad groups, such as Tian Dao, which rose in the 1930s, generally had no avowed political agendas. And since the Communist victory in 1949, all but the largest religious organizations, such as Catholicism and Buddhism, have been repressed in mainland China. In this socio-political sense of being a political player, Falun Gong is unique among modern Chinese religious movements.

Falun Gong's success is most likely tied to a combination of the appeal of a clear, simple exercise and ritual practice with the vision expressed in Li Hongzhi's teachings. Clearly, it is not enough to say that Falun Gong grew simply because it filled a gap in a rapidly transforming Chinese socio-spiritual landscape, a gap associated with recent liberalization and modernization of China's economy; the many chapters overseas indicate it appeals to people untouched by China's rapid economic transformation as well.

The treatment of Falun Gong is often portrayed as an example of human rights violations in China, and consequently the group continues to surface as an international news subject. Falun Gong's prospects solely as a religious movement, however, are unclear. Falun Gong may continue to survive outside China simply as one of many spiritual-religious groups based on traditional Chinese cultural practices. Falun Gong has established numerous national organizations throughout the Chinese communities in the diaspora world. They are best contacted through the many Internet sites. In addition a Falun Gong–backed newspaper, *Epoch Times*, is widely distributed.

The issues between Falun Gong and the People's Republic remain unresolved. The movement has become invisible within China, though many people who were members have continued quietly to practice. Outside of China, Falun Gong continues daily protests at embassies and consulates where it passes out literature accusing Chinese authorities of torturing, killing, and experimenting medically on Falun Gong practitioners in confinement. At the same time, China has published numerous reports and pamphlets detailing the harmfulness of practicing Falun Gong and arguing for the legitimacy of its repression of the movement.

A major source of information on Falun Gong is the Internet. There one may easily find numerous sites in a variety of languages from a variety of perspectives. Especially good starting points are some of the official Falun Gong sites, such as http://www.faluninfo.net and http://falundafa.org/eng/books.htm. From the latter site, the complete text of Master Li's main book, *Zhuan Falun*, may be downloaded; additional books have been posted at other sites. For a learned appraisal and periodically updated bibliography, see the site maintained at the Sinological Institute at the University of Leiden, http://www.let.leidenuniv.nl/bth/falun.htm.

Edward A. Irons

See also: Buddhism; Chinese Buddhist Association; Chinese Catholic Patriotic Association; Energy; Qigong; Tian Dao.

References

Haar, Berend J. "Falun Gong: Evaluation and Further References." http://website.leidenuniv .nl/~haarbjter/falun.htm. Accessed June 15, 2009.

Li Hongzhi. *China Falun Gong*. Rev. ed. Hong Kong: Falun Fo Fa Publishing Company, 1998.

Li Hongzhi. *Falun Buddha Law* (Lectures in the United States). Hong Kong: Falun Fo Fa Publishing Company, 1999.

Ownby, David. *Falun Gong and the Future of China*. New York: Oxford University Press, 2008.

Porter, Noah. *Falun Gong in the United States: An Ethnographic Study*. Dissertation.com, 2003.

Wong, John, and William Ti Liu. *The Mystery of China's Falun Gong: Its Rise and Sociological Implications*. Singapore: World Scientific Publishing/Singapore University Press, 1999.

Family International, The

The Family International, originally known as the Children of God (COG), emerged out of the Jesus People movement of the late 1960s. David Brandt Berg (1919–1994), an itinerant evangelist loosely associated with the Christian and Missionary Alliance, established the movement in 1968 in Southern California. COG soon developed into a highly structured communal organization noted for an aggressive style of evangelism, high levels of tension with the outside world, strong internal discipline, and sustained antiestablishment rhetoric aimed at American society and the conventional churches of the day. The Family has spread around the world and is the most globally successful religious community to come out of the Jesus People movement. The Family has generated considerable controversy and occasional governmental repression, primarily due to the highly unconventional sexual ethos.

In 1969, Berg (known until his death as Father David or simply Dad) took his young disciples on the road, eventually establishing a permanent community on a ranch near Thurber, Texas. Here the organization grew to more than 200 young people, and the basic pattern of community life was established. In 1972, Berg ordered his disciples out of North America to begin the missionary task of reaching the entire world with the message of Jesus. Throughout the 1970s the movement grew and flourished. Berg withdrew from personal contact with members, but maintained control through the leadership structure and his written correspondence, known as MO Letters.

In 1978, due to serious internal conflicts and a leadership crisis, Berg fired almost all of the administrative personnel and essentially disbanded the organization. Continuing individual communities maintained ties through written correspondence. Other disciples formed smaller units and traveled nomadically. In 1980, Berg called the communities together again as the Family of Love, then simply the Family. By this time he had selected a young woman, Maria, from among the members as his spouse and successor.

In 1976, Berg introduced a revolutionary new sexual ethic. "Flirty Fishing," the use of sexual allure up to and including sexual intercourse, was advocated as

Youthful members of the Children of God sing at their headquarters in Los Angeles in 1971. (AP Photo)

a means of witnessing and establishing supportive friends. Family women began frequenting bars and nightclubs, and some joined escort services in order to meet potential converts and establish relationships with potential supporters. Flirty Fishing was never intended as a recruitment tool for new disciples, and few joined as a result of being "fished." However, a substantial number of disciples left the movement in response to this sharp change in sexual ethic.

The new sexual ethos also included open sexual relationships between disciples, termed "sharing." Disciples were allowed and encouraged to establish sexual fellowship with other members. Consent of all parties was required, but many homes experienced substantial social pressure to participate in this new aspect of Family life. Nudity and open sexuality became common features of most Family homes during the early 1980s.

A number of disciples interpreted some of Berg's writings and his example as authorizing sexual contact between children and between minors and adults. Family children were considered adults when they turned 12 years of age, and sexual contact between adults and young teens was common during the early 1980s. In 1986, Maria became aware of a number of problems regarding teen/adult sex. Rigid age categories were defined, and sexual contact between adults and minors was prohibited. Flirty Fishing was discontinued the next year, and sexual contact with outsiders is now strictly forbidden. Sexual sharing among consenting adults continues, but sex between adults and minors is an excommunication offense. In the late 1990s, Maria introduced a new form of autoerotic religious sexual practice called "Loving Jesus."

From the beginning, the Children of God focused primarily on a spiritual mission. In 1991, Berg issued a message entitled "Consider the Poor," directing members to begin assisting the poor and helpless "just like Jesus did." Disciples now conduct ministries to prisoners, street gangs, illegal aliens, refugees, unwed mothers, drug addicts, and abused children all over the world.

In October 1994, Berg died. Shortly after his death, Maria and Peter Amsterdam were married and now lead the Family together. In 1994, they issued the "Love Charter," which spelled out the rights and responsibilities of Family members. Although final authority remained at the top, local leadership became far more democratic, and disciple life became less regimented.

The Family does not reveal the address of its leadership, and contact is best made through one of its homes or through the Internet. There is an official Family site at the address given below, and a number of sites sponsored by various continental and national units. By 1986, the greater percentage of disciples and the bulk of the missionary enterprise were located in Latin America and Asia. They had a particularly strong presence in India, Thailand, Japan, the Philippines, Argentina, and Brazil. With the collapse of the Soviet Union in 1989, a new missionary field opened, and in the early 1990s hundreds of disciples left for Eastern Europe. The vast majority were second-generation members under age 25. In the late 1990s, Family leadership identified Africa as the next area of focus, and over the past five years numerous Family homes have been established there.

In 1989, the Family drew a distinction between members who were willing and able to carry the full burden of disciple life, and those unwilling or unable to bear the yoke of full-time membership. Fully committed disciples are known as Charter Members, and the less committed are Fellow Members. In 2004 membership was subdivided into five categories: Family Disciples, Missionary Members, Fellow Members, Activated Members, and General Members. The last two constitute "Outside Members." These are persons who have been led to faith in Jesus by Family disciples and look to the Family for religious guidance and instruction, but have never joined as full-time disciples. In the year 2000 the Family moved to place greater emphasis on the growth, care, and spiritual development of Outside Members. This is now the major thrust of Family ministry.

The Family is a highly diverse movement, counting disciples from a wide range of national, ethnic, racial, and socio-economic backgrounds. Family theology has generally reflected its evangelical Protestant roots. Members are bound together by a set of core theological beliefs. These core beliefs center on Jesus and salvation, Berg as God's Prophet, the end times, and the spirit world.

From the very beginning, the disciples have understood themselves as Jesus people. They pray to Jesus, sing to Jesus, and spend their lives telling others about Jesus. And the disciples are convinced that they are the true and most dedicated followers of Jesus. Personal salvation through faith in Jesus Christ is the linchpin of Family theology. Witnessing for Jesus and persuading others to pray to receive Jesus as their savior is the defining task of disciple life.

David Berg is the defining personality of the Family. By the early 1970s, he had defined his role as God's Prophet for the end times as an essential aspect of Family life. Berg claimed absolute spiritual and political authority over his young charges. The disciples have a high view of the Bible, and use Father David's writings as authoritative interpretations of the scripture. Today, Maria is acknowledged as Berg's successor and God's Prophetess.

It is believed that Berg still leads the Family from the spirit world. He speaks regularly though dreams and prophetic experiences of Maria, Peter, and other Family members. Direct encounter with Jesus, Berg, departed saints, and other residents of the spirit world is a regular feature of Family life.

Family disciples hold end-time beliefs similar to those held widely in the Evangelical Protestant world. The Antichrist will arise and take over the world, persecuting Jesus' followers. During this time of tribulation, the disciples will suffer greatly, but also lead the other Christians in resistance to the Antichrist. Jesus will return and defeat the Antichrist at the Battle of Armageddon, establishing a 1,000-year reign of peace on the Earth. At the end of the 1,000 years, Satan will be released for one final confrontation. After Jesus defeats Satan, God will judge the world and establish the kingdom of heaven, in which Family disciples will serve as rulers and priests. Family theology is distinguished by the special role assigned Family disciples and the intensity of their conviction that the end is near. There has been no formal change in end-time theology, but the intensity level seems to be waning, particularly among second- and now third-generation disciples.

Total commitment is another significant aspect of the Family belief system. Disciples must forsake all and commit their lives to witnessing and Family duties. At one time disciples generally relinquished most contacts with the outside world. With the Love Charter and the growing number of Fellow Members, Family literature now acknowledges "concentric circles" of commitment, though total commitment is still the ideal.

Recruitment of new disciples was a high priority until the late 1980s, when the Family began looking to the second generation as the key to growth and survival. The Family continues to recruit new disciples, but at a much more modest pace. As of the beginning of 2008 the Family reported 4,442 Family Discipleship Members, 2,904 Missionary Members, and 2,090 Fellow Members. They report 1,027 Active Members in 53 countries and 3,456 General Members in 62 countries. In addition, there are 38,773 persons studying in the Activated program and in the pipeline to become General then Activated Members. For 2007, the Family reported 995,818 "souls won" as a result of their missionary effort. In July 2008 The Family initiated "The Offensive," the marshaling of the maximum amount of energy, time, and resources toward enlarging existing Activated congregations and developing new ones.

The normal Family term for the broader society is "the System." Since the earliest days of the Children of God, the disciples have lived in high tension with the System. Disciples generally limited interaction with outsiders to witnessing and raising funds. However, as an increasing number of teens and young adults left the movement, parents have attempted to maintain contact with their children, thus softening the hard line between insider and outsider.

The Family's peculiar lifestyle generated considerable hostility and even persecution from the social environment. Through the years, the Family response had been to go underground. However, beginning in 1989, Family adults were accused of physically and sexually abusing their children. Homes worldwide were subject to raids by law enforcement and social service agencies. To date (2001), all children taken into "protective custody" have been returned to their parents, and no disciple has been convicted of any offense.

However, the ongoing ordeal forced the Family into greater interaction with the legal system, social service agencies, and the academy.

http://www.thefamily.org

James D. Chancellor

See also: Christian and Missionary Alliance; Communalism.

References

Chancellor, James D. *Life in the Family: An Oral History of the Children of God*. Syracuse, NY: Syracuse University Press, 2000.

Fontaine, David, and John Weaver. *Thrilling Pictures of the Future!* Zurich, Switzerland: World Services, 1989.

Lewis, James R., and J. Gordon Melton, eds. *Sex, Slander and Salvation: Investigation of the Family/Children of God*. Stanford, CA: Center for Academic Publication, 1994.

Melton, J. Gordon. *The Children of God: "The Family."* Salt Lake City, UT: Signature Books.

Shepherd, Gary, and Gordon Shepherd. "Accommodation and Reformation in The Family/Children of God." *Nova Religio* 9, no. 1 (August 2005): 67–92.

The Love Charter. Zurich, Switzerland: The Family, 1998.

Van Zandt, David. *Living in the Children of God*. Princeton, NJ: Princeton University Press, 1991.

Fatima

Fatima is a small town in central Portugal some 90 miles north of Lisbon that in 1917 was the site of what became the most famous modern apparitions of the Virgin Mary (Our Lady of Fatima). It was here that three children—Lucia Dos Santos (age nine), Francisco Marto (age eight), and Jacinta Marto (age six)—initially experienced visitations from an angelic being in the spring of 1916. The angelic visitation heralded the first vision of the "beautiful young Lady," dressed all in white and bathed in light, who appeared to them on May 13, 1917. The three children were told to come to the place where this first visit had occurred on the

Portuguese Army officers carry the statue of Our Lady of Fatima through a crowd of worshippers waving white handkerchiefs, May 13, 1997 in Fatima, Portugal. Hundreds of thousands of Catholic pilgrims from all over the world participated in the celebrations of the 80th anniversary of the first apparition of the Virgin in Fatima. (AP Photo/ Armando Franca)

13th of every month for the next five months. She then challenged the children with a seemingly mature query for their youthful age, "Do you wish to offer yourselves to God in order to accept all the sufferings He wishes to send you, in reparation for sin and for the conversion of sinners?"

As announced, subsequent apparitions occurred on the 13th day of each month. Meanwhile, the children faced ridicule from many of the townspeople and the press and hostility from authorities. Then on October 13, the apparitions culminated with a miraculous promised occurrence. As some 70,000 people trekked to the site of the previous apparitions, where nothing had been seen by any but the 3 children, all were treated to a spectacular meteorological occurrence. The rain stopped, the clouds parted, and a bright round disk shone in the sky. The disk began to spin, throwing

off sparks of light. The phenomenon of the dancing "sun" continued for almost half an hour. All, believer and nonbeliever alike, saw it. At the close of the event, the Sun seemed to plunge downward toward the crowd and all felt the heat as their rain-soaked clothing dried.

Over the months of the apparitions, the Blessed Virgin had little by little communicated a significant body of material to the children. Most of the content concerned the people's need to pray for Russia, then in the throes of revolution. The Lady asked the pope to consecrate Russia to Mary's Immaculate Heart. The most intriguing part of the message given to the children remained confidential for the time being. This secret message, in three parts, was partially revealed in 1927. The first part concerned a vision of hell and the second spoke of the consequences of sin and the need to spread the message of the Immaculate Heart. The third part was until the year 2000 known to only a small circle of church leaders in the Vatican. It was a prophecy of an assassination attempt against the "bishop in white." Since 1981, this prophecy was seen by many who knew of it to speak of the assassination attempt on Pope John Paul II (r. 1978–2005) that occurred on May 13, 1981 (coincidentally the anniversary of the first apparition at Fatima). As it happened, the would-be assassin pulled the trigger of his gun just as the pope reached down to bless someone carrying a picture of the Virgin. He later attributed his surviving the incident to Mary's intervention. He subsequently visited Fatima and oversaw (and nurtured) the process of canonization of two of the children, Francisco (d. 1919) and Jacinta (d. 1920).

Lucia died in 2005, the same year as Pope John Paul, on the 13th of February, keeping alive the importance of the 13th of the month for events relative to the apparitions. Most recently, on the third anniversary of Lucia's death, Pope Benedict XVI, who succeeded Pope John Paul II, announced that he had waived the normal five-year waiting period before formally opening the process leading toward canonization as a saint. This waiver had also been exercised in the case of Mother Teresa and Pope Benedict's predecessor, thus putting all three on the fast track to future canonization.

Fatima has been officially recognized as a place of pilgrimage since 1930, still drawing about five million visitors a year. Especially after World War II, devotion to Our Lady of Fatima has spread worldwide, and is expressed, among other ways, through active support from the Vatican and in dozens of church-acknowledged branch shrines elsewhere in the world. Pope John Paul's actions elevated Fatima beside Lourdes as one of the two most important of the many sites that have experienced apparitions of the Virgin Mary. The recent attention given Fatima also culminated the efforts begun in 1947 by Father Harold Colgan who founded the Blue Army, an organization that has had the single purpose of spreading the Fatima message. It is one of the major Catholic devotions in the world.

In addition to being a "mainstream" Marian devotion, Fatima has a particular function as a standard-bearer for a conservative, even fundamentalist Marian movement, made up of a large number of conservative Catholic groups and institutions, some acknowledged by the church, some not and even actively contested, which take their inspiration from the messages (including the secret messages) that were given at Fatima. Generally these groups function autonomously, are often well organized, can command ample resources, and sometimes have large numbers of adherents (for example, Marian Movement of Priests, www.msm-mmp.org/, approximately 100,000; Blue Army of Our Lady of Fatima, c/o World Apostolate of Fatima, PO Box 976, Mountain View Road, Washington NJ 07882, www.wafusa.org/, more than 10 million).

According to the organizations and devotees involved, the messages of Fatima should form the basis for a worldwide re-evangelization and missionary program, in order to save the degenerate world and church from the ever-present Satan. Among the typical themes in the messages are penitence, prayer, conversion of all sinners, the rosary, war, and anti-Communism. Only after the world gives itself over to the Immaculate Heart of Mary (and acknowledges her salvific work) and the conversion of Russia takes place, a kingdom of peace will be realized on Earth, in which all those who believe in Jesus Christ, ask for remission of sins, and subject themselves to the pope will be protected against the devil. The formal dedication of Russia occurred in 1952. Also after this dedication, the Third Secret of Fatima, which the visionary Lucia shared only with the pope, continued to inspire end-time prophecies and speculations of an eschatological and apocalyptic nature about the further course of the world and the concrete beginning of the end times. During the Cold War, Our Lady of Fatima was *the* model for the church in the struggle against Communism, atheism, and apostasy. Communism did not remain quiet; an Italian parliamentary commission concluded that the assault by Ali Agca on John Paul II in 1981 was plotted by the Soviets. The pope ascribed, on his turn, his survival to Our Lady of Fatima.

Since the 1970s the interpretation of the messages has begun to take on a life of its own, and Fatima has increasingly begun to function as the paradigm for new fringe devotions, often in connection with new Marian apparitions.

The fall of the Communist regimes, growing interest in the end of the world caused by the millennium, his own personal devotion to Fatima, and her protection during the assault led Pope John Paul II to reveal the Third Secret during the Jubilee of 2000. The content appeared less dramatic and apocalyptic than many had expected. Fundamentalist circles continue to suggest that the message has not yet been fully revealed, and that the end of time was not to begin in 2000 but in the cataclysmic year 2012, with a comet impact, nuclear war, and total darkness. In this way Fatima remains an important source of nourishment for groups and individuals within the global network of divergent Marian devotion.

Santuário de Nossa Senhora de Fátima
Apartado 31
2496-908 Fátima
Portugal
http://www.santuario-fatima.pt
Service account for pilgrims:
sepe@santuario-fatima.pt

World Apostolate of Fatima Blue Army
   Shrine
674 Mountain View Road East
Washington, NJ 07882
http://www.wafusa.org/

Peter Jan Margry

See also: Devotion/Devotional Traditions; Lourdes; Marian Devotion, World Network of; Mary, Blessed

Virgin; Medjugorje; Pilgrimage; Roman Catholic Church; Saints.

References

Blackbourn, David. *Marpingen.* New York: Alfred A. Knopf, Inc., 1994.

De Marchi, John. *Fatima: From the Beginning.* Trans. by I. M. Kingsbury. Fatima, Portugal: Edições Missões Consolata, 2004.

The Fatima Network. www.fatima.org/. Accessed July 1, 2009.

Kohle, Hubert. "Fundamentalistische Marienbewegungen." In *Handbuch der Marienkunde,* edited by Wolfgang Beinert and Heinrich Petri, vol. 2. Regensburg, Germany: F. Pustet, 1997.

Kondor, Louis. *Fatima in Lucia's Own Words.* Fatima, Portugal: Postulation Centre, 1989.

Kselman, Thomas, and S. Avella. "Marian Piety and the Cold War in the United States." *Catholic Historical Review* 72 (1986): 403–424.

The Message of Fatima. Vatican City: Libreria Editrice Vaticana, 2000.

Morgan, David. "Aura and the Inversion of Marian Pilgrimage: Fatima and Her Statues." In *Moved by Mary: Pilgrimage in the Modern World*, edited by Anna-Karina Hermkens, Willy Jansen, and Catrien Notermans. Oxford: Ashgate, 2009.

Pelikan, Jaroslav. *Mary through the Centuries.* New Haven, CT: Yale University Press, 1996.

Pelletier, Joseph, A. *The Sun Danced: Revised and Expanded.* New York: Image Books, 1983.

Rossi, Serero, and Aventino de Oliveira. *Fatima.* Fatima, Portugal: Consolata Missions' Publications, 1984.

Zimdars-Swartz, Sandra L. *Encountering Mary: Visions of Mary from La Salette to Medjugorje.* New York: Avon Books 1992.

Zimdars-Swartz, Sandra L. *Encountering Mary.* Princeton, NJ: Princeton University Press, 1991.

Federation of Swiss Protestant Churches

The Reformation in Switzerland began in 1521 in Zurich, where Ulrich Zwingli (1484–1531), one of the

Ulrich Zwingli, 16th-century Swiss religious leader. Zwingli was the founder of Zwinglianism, a Reformation movement that challenged the Catholic Church's literal interpretation of the Bible. (Library of Congress)

more radical voices of the period, was pastoring. Reformed ideas spread through the German-speaking cantons during the remainder of the decade and were evident in the French-speaking territories by the beginning of the 1530s. Zwingli had read Martin Luther's writings as they appeared, and he came to believe that only that which the Bible taught should be binding upon Christians or allowable in the church. This principle took the Lutheran Reformation belief that those things that the Bible prohibited should be abandoned one step further. Thus Zwingli moved to get rid of church vestments, statues of saints, and the Mass (to be replaced with a simplified memorial meal, the Lord's Supper). In 1524, he married.

Zwingli was killed in a battle with the Catholic cantons. The battle proved decisive, in that the spread of the Reformation in Switzerland was essentially halted at that point. By the end of the decade, the Swiss phase of the Reformation had a new champion in the person of Jean Calvin (1509–1564). A Frenchman, Calvin moved to Geneva somewhat by accident in 1536, the year his magnum opus, *The Institutes of the Christian Religion*, was published. He initially attempted to build a model community, but ran into opposition that forced him from the city. However, he returned in 1541 and remained the head of the church until his death.

The Institutes of the Christian Religion essentially defined the Reformed faith. Calvin affirmed the basic Lutheran positions of biblical authority and salvation by faith as the free gift of God, as opposed to what the Reformers saw as the Roman Catholic position, advocating a system of salvation by human works. Calvin differed from Luther on the sacraments, teaching that Christ's presence in the Eucharist was spiritual rather than real. This position also differed from Zwingli's understanding of the Lord's Supper as in essence a memorial meal (a position later championed by the Baptists and most Free church groups).

Calvin's Geneva became the disseminating point of the Reformed Church, which spread eastward to Hungary and westward to Holland and the British Isles. Swiss Protestants were able to join in a united front when Calvin worked out an agreement with Heinrich Bullinger, Zwingli's successor in Zurich. The agreement was written up in the *Consensus Tiguinus* in 1549.

The Reformed position could also be seen as broadly opposed to the Free church position. Christianity was viewed as intimately integrated with the state, and Calvin spent his time keeping the state from interfering with the church, while asking the church to move against those who taught other than Reformed theology. Like Zwingli, he opposed the Anabaptists, who argued for a church separated from the state and open only to those who accepted Christ as adults and were subsequently baptized. Reformed churches aimed to be coterminous with the state and to baptize all its citizens as infants. The Reformed Protestant position was published in a series of confessional documents, the Second Helvetic Confession, authored by Bullinger in 1566, being especially important. Over the centuries these have tended to become less authoritative among Swiss Protestants.

For several centuries, the Protestant churches existed as separate state churches, one in each of the cantons. In 1884 the Swiss Confederation was instituted. A decade later a Swiss Church Conference began meeting annually. Then in 1920, the Federation of Swiss Protestant Churches was founded, as a result of probes by the Federal Council of Churches in the United States, which was seeking a European partner to coordinate its efforts to rebuild Europe after the destruction of World War I. The Methodists aligned with the Federation in 1922.

The Federation now includes 22 cantonal churches, the Evangelical-Methodist Church of Switzerland, and the Free Church of Geneva. It exists as an association of the Reformed churches in Switzerland, but performs many denominational functions, such as holding the membership of those churches in the World Council of Churches and the World Alliance of Reformed Churches. The member churches vary in membership from the large church in the Canton of Bern, with more than 700,000 members, to those in predominantly Roman Catholic cantons such as Ticino and Glarus, with only about 20,000 members in each. In 2005, the Federation reported 2,400,000 members in 982 congregations.

The several larger member churches support a set of theological schools in Switzerland. The churches have a structure that models that of the Swiss cantons; they are supported by state funds.

The Swiss Protestant community was significantly affected by the Pietist movement, a movement emphasizing personal religious faith. That movement led to the establishment of a variety of Free churches, opposed to state interference in church life, and to the establishment of a variety of organizations that helped revive the faith life of the churches. Among the more important was the Basel Mission, founded in 1815, which became one of the important structures carrying Protestantism around the world in the 19th century. The Basel Mission drew support from both Lutheran and Reformed churches in Switzerland, Germany, and Austria.

Federation of Swiss Protestant Churches
Postfach 36

Sulgenauweg 26
CH-3000 Bern 23
Switzerland
http://www.ref.ch (in German)

J. Gordon Melton

See also: Baptists; Basel Mission, Calvin, John; Free Churches; World Alliance of Reformed Churches; World Council of Churches.

References

Bauswein, Jean-Jacques, and Lukas Vischner, eds. *The Reformed Family Worldwide: A Survey of Reformed Churches, Theological Schools, and International Organizations.* Grand Rapids, MI: William B. Eerdmans Publishing Company, 1999.

Van Beek, Huibert. *A Handbook of the Churches and Councils: Profiles of Ecumenical Relationships.* Geneva: World Council of Churches, 2006.

Westin, Gunnar. *The Free Church through the Ages.* Nashville: Broadman Press, 1958.

Fellowship of Irian Java Baptist Churches

The Fellowship of Irian Jaya Baptist Churches (Persekutuan Gereja-Gereja Baptis Irian Jaya) began in the 1950s with the work of Mennonites from Holland who launched a mission in Irian Jaya, the eastern half of the island of New Guinea, now a part of Indonesia. They established churches in the Bird's Head region in northwest Irian Jaya near the border with Papua New Guinea. The Mennonite missionaries withdrew in 1963, when Irian Jaya was incorporated into Indonesia, but the work they had founded continued.

In 1955 missionaries connected with the Baptist Union of Australia expanded their work in Papua New Guinea to Irian Jaya. It was their desire to reach those peoples who were still following their traditional religion. Evangelism began among the Dani people in the Balien Valley the following year. The first converts were received in 1962; however, the sight of the burning of their traditional religious artifacts angered many, and four months after the baptismal ceremony, some of the traditionalists attacked and killed some of the converts.

This action was broadly condemned, and the dead, considered to be martyrs for the church, became a catalyst that led to heightened growth. The Fellowship of Irian Jaya Baptist Churches was founded in 1966 among the Dani believers.

In 1977, some of the leaders of the Fellowship were in Jayapura, the regional capital in northwest Irian Jaya, and there encountered some university students who had grown up in the churches founded by the Mennonites. This chance encounter led to communication between the two groups, and the Mennonite work was later merged into the Fellowship.

In the 1990s the Fellowship reported 49,000 members in 170 congregations. It is a member of the Baptist World Alliance.

Fellowship of Irian Java Baptist Churches
Kotari, Jayapura
Irian Jaya, Kotak Pos 1212
Jayapura 99012
Indonesia

J. Gordon Melton

See also: Baptist World Alliance.

References

Nance, John Irvin. "A History of the Indonesian Baptist Mission, 1950–1960." M.A. thesis, Baylor University, 1969.

Wardin, Albert W., ed. *Baptists around the World.* Nashville: Broadman and Holman, 1995.

Fellowship of Isis

The Fellowship of Isis was founded in 1976 at Clonegal Castle, Enniscorthy, Ireland, by Olivia Robertson with Lawrence and Pamela Durdin-Robertson, her brother and sister-in-law. Since Lawrence Durdin-Robertson's death, the Fellowship has been led by Olivia Robertson. Succession planning in January 1999 created a decentralized organization with an Archpriesthood Union of 32 archpriestesses and archpriests acting as custodians of the Fellowship of Isis.

The Fellowship of Isis is multi-religious, multi-racial, and multi-cultural. Members are free to maintain other religious allegiances. The Fellowship of Isis is active in interfaith dialogue and has taken part in the Parliament of the World's Religions. Olivia Robertson was one of 2 women and 16 men who gave a platform address at the opening plenary at the Parliament's Centennial Session in 1993.

Around 26,000 people from 93 countries have taken up membership, but not all are active. Outside Western countries, the Fellowship of Isis is particularly active in Nigeria. The Fellowship has three principles that all members acknowledge—Love, Beauty, and Truth, which are considered to be the divine attributes of the goddess. Membership is seen as a way to promote closer communion between members and the goddess. While it was founded to promote goddess worship, the Fellowship of Isis is not exclusively a goddess organization. Male deities are also venerated.

The Fellowship of Isis has around 700 Iseums, or centers of worship, mainly in members' own homes. These are considered "Hearths of the Goddess." They offer initiation, celebratory rites, and fellowship. Seasonal celebrations are also held at Clonegal Castle and at public venues. A standard liturgy of rites is available for group worship, but Iseums are free to adapt these to their own needs. Members can conduct their own rites, but if they wish, women and men may train for the priesthood. The priesthood is believed to be linked to ancient Egypt through Olivia and Lawrence Durdin-Robertson's descent from a hereditary priesthood. Training in the priesthood is provided through around 110 College of Isis Lyceums. Each Lyceum provides an original course of study culminating in a rite from the Lyceum Liturgy. There are around 950 priestesses and priests. For those not seeking a vocation to the priesthood, there is a system of personal initiation involving 32 initiation rites and a 33rd level of "spontaneous mystical awakening."

The Fellowship of Isis publishes a magazine, *Isian News*, available by subscription. Membership itself is free. The Fellowship of Isis also has its own Druid Order and a body called the Noble Order of Tara that focuses on nature conservation. The Fellowship of Isis has a strong environmental ethos and venerates all life—animal, plant, and mineral. Every human, animal, bird, and tree is considered to be "an eternal offspring of the Mother Goddess's Divine Family of Life."

Fellowship of Isis
Clonegal Castle
Enniscorthy, Ireland
www.fellowshipofisis.com/

Vivianne Crowley

See also: Council for a Parliament of the World's Religions; Druidism; Goddess Spirituality; Wiccan Religion.

References

Adler, Margot. *Drawing Down the Moon: The Resurgence of Paganism in America.* New York: Penguin, 1997.

Robertson, Olivia. *Isis of Fellowship: How the FOI Was Founded.* Enniscorthy, Ireland: Fellowship of Isis, n.d.

Robertson, Olivia, and Connia Silver. *Fellowship of Isis Handbook.* Enniscorthy, Ireland: Cesara Publications, 1992.

Witt, R. E. *Isis in the Graeco-Roman World.* London: Thames and Hudson, 1971.

■ Fiji Islands

The Fiji Islands are an archipelago in the South Pacific that appears to have been populated as early as 2000 BCE. Of the approximately 500 islands, Viti Levu and Vannnua Levu are the largest and include most of the country's 7,000 square miles of land. The majority of the 932,000 residents also reside there. Also included in the islands' political hegemony, Rotuma, an island some 400 miles north, is a dependency of Fiji.

Melanesians settled there in the sixth century BCE. They were first contacted by Europeans in 1643, by Abel Tasman (1603–1659) (for whom Tasmania would later be named). Subsequently, James Cook (1728–1779) visited in 1774, and in 1789 William Bligh (1754–1817), the famous captain of the HMS *Bounty,* stopped there and wrote the first lengthy account of island life.

Toward the beginning of the 19th century, a Fijian leader, Na Ulivau, was able to unite the islands into one community. Then in 1830, the first Christian missionaries arrived, representatives of the London Missionary Society (LMS). However, by agreement

Fiji Islands

Religion	Followers in 1970	Followers in 2010	% of Population	Annual % growth 2000–2010	Followers in 2025	Followers in 2050
Christians	262,000	529,000	61.9	1.01	566,000	579,000
Protestants	188,000	403,000	47.2	0.61	430,000	426,000
Roman Catholics	43,500	96,700	11.3	2.05	105,000	110,000
Independents	3,600	68,000	8.0	3.50	60,000	65,000
Hindus	209,000	253,000	29.6	0.03	261,000	246,000
Muslims	40,500	52,500	6.1	0.11	52,000	53,000
Agnostics	2,600	9,100	1.1	1.63	12,000	15,000
Sikhs	3,200	5,000	0.6	0.18	7,000	7,000
Baha'is	1,000	2,300	0.3	1.05	3,000	4,000
Jains	1,000	1,600	0.2	−0.38	2,000	2,500
Chinese folk	200	900	0.1	0.63	1,600	2,200
Ethnoreligionists	100	340	0.0	0.66	400	500
Atheists	0	200	0.0	0.67	300	500
Jews	0	120	0.0	0.55	130	150
Total population	**520,000**	**854,000**	**100.0**	**0.65**	**905,000**	**910,000**

among the Protestant missionaries working in the South Seas, the Methodists received hegemony over Fiji, and in 1835 the LMS missionaries withdrew and two British Methodists assumed their post. They made little progress until 1854, when Na Ulivau's son, Ratu Seru Cakobau, converted and was baptized. The new king went on to become a great admirer of the Western world, and in 1858 actually offered his kingdom for annexation to the United States. Caught up in the approaching Civil War, the government ignored his offer.

Eventually, England annexed Fiji in 1874 and began the development of large sugar plantations. The local inhabitants would not leave their land to work the plantations, and in 1879 the British began importing laborers from India. Eventually, the Indians brought their wives from their homeland and settled in Fiji. They soon constituted the majority of the population, a fact that has been a continual source of conflict.

The islands became independent in 1970, but political turmoil and ethnic tensions have led to government coups in 1978, 2000, and 2006. The most recent government change saw the ousting of Prime Minister Laisenia Qarase by military leader Commodore Voreqe Bainimarama, who was named interim prime minister.

The ancient religion of the Melanesians predominated on the Fiji Islands until the 19th century. It has virtually disappeared as a distinct religion, though remnants are kept alive in periodic revivals of traditional culture. In 1885, the prophet Ndungumoi arose as a spokesperson of traditional religion and led a movement opposed to the further spread of Christianity. His movement was notable for its espousal of ritual cannibalism.

The British Methodist Church had a 25-year head start on other Protestant churches in building its work and remains the largest religious group in the islands. After the Indians began arriving in numbers, in 1892 the church opened an Indian Mission. The church had over the years been closely identified with the Fijian government and was severely affected by the coup that occurred in 1987 and by the political unrest during the 1990s. The Methodist Church in Fiji and Rotuma is the only Fijian-based church in the World Council of Churches.

The Church of England established its initial work in the islands in 1860. The present-day Anglican parishes are part of the Anglican Church in Aotearoa, New Zealand, and Polynesia. It was followed by missionaries from the Presbyterian Church (1876) and the Seventh-day Adventist Church (1989). Through the 20th century, a variety of Protestant groups, from the Assemblies of God to the Christian Brethren, also arrived.

FIJI ISLANDS

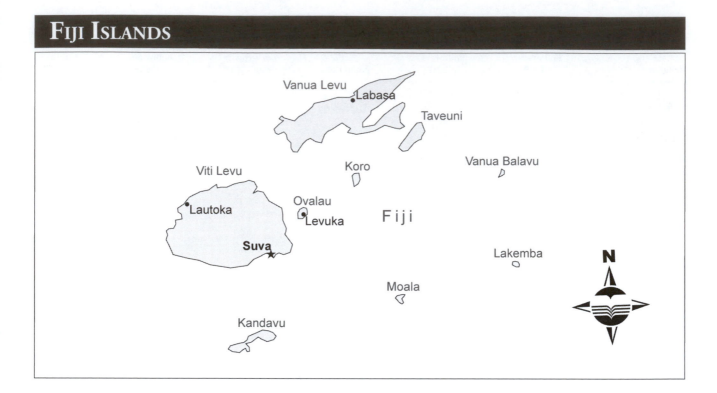

The older missionary churches operating in Fiji formed the Fiji Council of Churches in 1924. It is affiliated with the World Council of Churches (WCC). Also, the regional Pacific Conference of Churches, itself affiliated with the WCC, is headquartered in Suva, Fiji. One result of this cooperative activity was the creation of the Pacific Theological School in 1966 with the sponsorship of the Anglicans, Methodists, Congregationalists, and Presbyterians.

Among the more interesting groups on the islands are several indigenous movements, such as the Church of Time (1945) and the Messiah Club (1965), both schisms of the Methodist Church. The Jehovah's Witnesses, the Church of Jesus Christ of Latter-day Saints (who have a special role for South Sea islanders in their understanding of salvation), and the Reorganized Church of Jesus Christ of Latter Day Saints (now known as the Community of Christ) are active in Fiji. The Church of Christ, Scientist, visible in the 1970s, has disappeared.

The Indian laborers brought Hinduism, in several varieties, with them. Of the 60,000 who arrived prior to World War I, one-fourth were from South India and the rest from North India. The Arya Samaj, a 19th-century reform movement opposed to temple worship,

was brought to Fiji by the North Indians. In opposition, representatives of the Sanatan Dharm, based in the more traditional temple worship, established what is now the largest group in the Hindu community of the Fiji Islands. Competing with it are the TISI Sangam and the Gujarati Samaj, both more traditional groups serving Telugu-speaking and Gujarati-speaking segments of the population. All three have emphasized the construction of temples and the preservation of traditional worship. It is the largest group in the Hindu community of the Fiji Islands. Fiji has also participated in the popular spread of Hinduism worldwide. The International Society for Krishna Consciousness, formed in New York in 1965, has established a Krishna temple in Lautoka, and Adidam, an Advaita Vedanta group, purchased one of the Fijian islands as a home for its guru.

Islam also came to Fiji through the immigration of Indians (and Pakistanis). Their community includes both Sunnis and Shias. Most Muslims are related to the Fuji Muslim League, which in 2000 reported some 56,000 Muslims in Fiji. It cooperates with the Islamic Council for the South Pacific, founded in 1984, which promotes cooperation among Muslims in Australia, New Zealand, Papua New Guinea, Fiji, Venuatu, and Tonga, and the Regional Islamic Da'wa Council for

South East Asia and the Pacific, based in Kuala Lumpur, Malaysia. There is also an active group of Ahmadiyyas, which may have the allegiance of as many as a third of the islands' Muslims.

Several thousand Sikhs from the Punjab joined in the migration of workers from India. More recently, spiritual assemblies of the Baha'i Faith have appeared.

The division of the country into two groupings, one of native Fijians and one of Indian origin, has become an increasing problem in Fiji since World War II. In 1987, Fiji was the subject of a military coup led by people who believed that the native Fijians were being deprived of their rights. The coup led to a new Constitution being promulgated in 1990. Then in 2000, during the term in office of Mahendra Chaudhry, the country's first prime minister of Indian descent, a second coup attempt occurred, which led to the country being taken over by the military. The coup attempts placed the Methodists, the largest religious body in Fiji, whose membership is almost totally native Fijians, in the middle. Many identified the church with the failed Fijian coup attempts.

J. Gordon Melton

See also: Adidam; Anglican Church in Aotearoa, New Zealand, and Polynesia; Arya Samaj; Assemblies of God; Baha'i Faith; Christian Brethren; Church of Christ, Scientist; Church of England; Church of Jesus Christ of Latter-day Saints; Community of Christ; International Society for Krishna Consciousness; Jehovah's Witnesses; London Missionary Society; Methodist Church; Methodist Church in Fiji and Rotuma; Seventh-day Adventist Church; World Council of Churches.

References

Bayliss-Smith, Tim, Richard Bedford, Harold Brookfield, and Marc Latham. *Islands, Islanders and the World: The Colonial and Post-colonial Experience of Eastern Fiji.* Cambridge: Cambridge University Press, 2006.

Foreman, J. C. W., ed. *Island Churches: Challenge and Change.* Suva, Fiji: University of the South Pacific/Institute of Pacific Studies, 1992.

Forman, Charles H. *The Island Churches of the South Pacific: Emergence in the Twentieth Century.* Maryknoll, NY: Orbis, 1982.

Garrett, J. *To Live among the Stars: Christian Origins in Oceania.* Geneva: World Council of Churches in cooperation with the University of the South Pacific/Institute of Pacific Studies, 1982.

Ross, C. S. *Churches and Church Workers in Fiji.* Geelong, Australia: H. Thacker, 1909.

Tippett, Alan Richard. *The Growth of an Indigenous Church: A Collection of Essays on the Emergence of the Methodist Church in Fiji.* Pasadena, CA: Fuller Theological Seminary, 1967.

Fiji Islands, Hindu Community of the

Hinduism came to Fiji with the indentured laborers who were brought from India to Fiji by the British colonialists to work on plantations. Indentured migration to Fiji took place between 1879 and 1916 and involved some 60,000 Indians (45,000 from North India, 15,000 from the south), 80 percent of whom were Hindus. The majority of them decided to stay in Fiji after the end of their indenture, and they were later joined by free migrants from Gujarat and Punjab. According to the 1996 national census, there were 261,097 Hindus in Fiji (259,775 were of Indian origin, the others being converts from other ethnic groups) and 3,076 Sikhs. The overall number of Indo-Fijians was 338,818, or 44 percent of Fiji's total population.

Whereas in India, Hinduism and the caste system are closely related, the latter determining social status, marriage, occupation, and commensality, the caste system did not even survive the journey of Hindus from India to Fiji, let alone plantation life in Fiji. Only the Brahmin status was re-created, while Hindus of all castes lived and ate together, did the same work, and even shared the scarce women. The fading away of the caste system meant that Hindu society in Fiji became more egalitarian and that religion lost its central position in life.

Since Hinduism is closely bound to the Indian soil with its holy rivers, shrines, and gods, a feeling of loss, rootlessness, and guilt is widespread among Hindus in the diaspora. This is one of a number of reasons why most Indo-Fijians cut all ties with India once they embarked on the ships. Free migrants on the other hand

Sri Siva Subramaniya Swami Temple, a Hindu temple in Fiji. (PacificStock/StockphotoPro)

kept close ties to India and were therefore important in keeping Hindu traditions alive.

In the early decades, the absence of proper caste and family life meant that many traditional ceremonies were either not observed at all or persisted in a simplified form. A popularized ritualistic version of Hinduism with a focus on devotion and little intellectual content was practiced, rituals and ceremonies became the essence of the religion, and Brahmins derived their authority from a command of these rituals rather than from religious learning and an ideal lifestyle. From the plurality of Hindu practices in India, Indo-Fijians have chosen those that made most sense to them and their social and economic situation. The Ramayana became the most popular text, not only because it is simple and casteless, but more important because its central theme is exile, suffering, struggle, and eventual return. In the barracks of the indentured workers, the Ramayana was recited, and Ram Lila performances were staged.

Especially after the 1920s, a number of formal religious societies were established that were active in the religious, educational, and cultural fields. For North Indians the most important were the Arya Samaj and the Sanatan Dharm; for South Indians, the Then India Sanmarga Ikya Sangam (PO Box 9, Nadi, Fiji) or TISI Sangam. The Arya Samaj, officially known as Arya Pratinidhi Sabha of Fiji (1 Ono Street, Samabula, Suva, Fiji), started in 1904 but did not register officially until 1917. The major aim in these early years was the provision of educational facilities for Indian children at a time when Christians ran most schools and there was fear of conversion. On the religious side, Arya Samaj stands for simplified ceremonies, a rejection of the caste system and of idol worship, social reform, and conversion of non-Hindus. All these appealed to many Hindus in Fiji who were dissatisfied with the lack of intellectual content in traditional Hinduism, the time-consuming rituals, and idol worship. Today, there are about 20,000 Arya Samajis in Fiji, and their ceremonies, most important the fire ceremony, *hawan*, are held in schools throughout the country as well as in three community centers. The headquarters is in the capital, Suva.

Sanatan Dharm missionaries were called from India in the 1920s to support Hinduism in Fiji and combat the Arya Samaj. The first convention was held in 1934, and an official organization, Shree Sanatan Dharm Pratinidhi Sabha (PO Box 1082, Lautoka, Fiji), formed in 1958. Over the years, the majority of Hindus in Fiji accepted it as their organization. It maintains a number of schools and the majority of temples in Fiji.

The TISI Sangam, a regional organization for South Indians, was formed in 1926. In addition to religious, social, and educational work, it is devoted to the preservation of the Tamil and Malayalam languages. It maintains about 30 temples in the country. In 1941, South Indians of Telugu-speaking origin broke away and formed the Dakshina India Andhra Sangam of Fiji, which runs a few schools and one temple. Apart from these major organizations, there are a number of religious movements and religious-cum-cultural societies. The Gujarati Samaj is the major organization for the 6,000 Gujaratis. The Satya Sai Baba Organization (PO Box 271, Lautoka, Fiji) has about 2,500 followers and 37 centers countrywide, with the headquarters in Fiji's second city, Lautoka. The International Society for Krishna Consciousness maintains a temple in Lautoka (Sri Krishna Kaliya Temple, 5 Tavewa Avenue, PO Box 125, Lautoka, Fiji) and three centers around the country. There are about 300 initiated followers in Fiji.

It is important to note that Hindus in Fiji have not come up with new religious movements or a distinct form of Hinduism that would reflect their unique experiences and needs in the diaspora, but have instead imported a variety of movements from India. There are no holy rivers or great places of pilgrimage in Fiji, though some places have acquired some importance, such as the Cobra Rock Temple outside Labasa, built around a snake-shaped rock that is believed to grow in size. In the course of the relatively short history of Hinduism in Fiji, there has already been a major shift in ritual practices: During the first decades, Holi was the major Hindu festival in the annual calendar. At present Diwali is the principal festival and even a national holiday. This can be interpreted as a shift from play- and transcendence-oriented devotionalism, with Lord Krishna in the center, to a duty- and perfection-oriented devotionalism, focused on Lord Ram. Since no distinct form of Hinduism exists in Fiji, the estimated 100,000 Indo-Fijians who live outside Fiji (most of whom left after the military coups in 1987 and the subsequent state-sanctioned discrimination against them) are sharing temples with Hindus of other origins. In Australia and New Zealand, which are the major countries of resettlement, Indo-Fijians split along lines based on India's, not Fiji's, geography (South versus North Indians) in their choice of temple. However, Indo-Fijians have established branches of their major organizations, especially the Arya Samaj, Sanatan Dharm, and TISI Sangam.

Carmen Voigt-Graf

See also: Arya Samaj; Devotion/Devotional Traditions; Hinduism; International Society for Krishna Consciousness; Sathya Sai Baba Movement.

References
Gillion, K. L. *Fiji's Indian Migrants.* Melbourne: Oxford University Press, 1962.

Kelly, John D. "From Holi to Diwali in Fiji: An Essay on Ritual and History." *Man* (n.s.) 23, no. 1 (1988): 40–55.

Kelly, John D. *A Politics of Virtue: Hinduism, Sexuality, and Countercolonial Discourse in Fiji.* Chicago: University of Chicago Press, 1991.

■ Finland

Finland, the easternmost of the Scandinavian countries, is sandwiched between Sweden and Russia. It has a long coastline on the Baltic Sea and Gulf of Bothnia as well as the Gulf of Finland. There are 5.2 million people who reside on its 131,000 square miles of territory.

The largest religious community in Finland is the Evangelical Lutheran Church of Finland. In 1999, 85.3 percent of the population (approximately 5 million) were members of this church, and 1.1 percent belonged to the Finnish Orthodox Church. The third

Finland

Religion	Followers in 1970	Followers in 2010	% of Population	Annual % growth 2000–2010	Followers in 2025	Followers in 2050
Christians	4,439,000	4,778,000	89.8	0.02	4,780,000	4,551,000
Protestants	4,476,000	4,506,000	84.7	−0.03	4,445,000	4,208,000
Independents	14,900	100,000	1.9	3.25	150,000	180,000
Orthodox	56,800	61,500	1.2	0.75	70,000	75,000
Agnostics	113,000	397,000	7.5	2.79	500,000	600,000
Atheists	49,000	107,000	2.0	1.03	125,000	140,000
Muslims	920	27,000	0.5	7.47	40,000	50,000
Buddhists	0	3,800	0.1	7.78	4,500	6,000
New religionists	1,000	2,700	0.1	1.42	4,800	6,500
Baha'is	1,500	1,700	0.0	0.80	2,000	2,400
Chinese folk	0	4,400	0.1	25.53	6,800	2,500
Jews	1,500	1,300	0.0	0.27	1,300	1,300
Total population	**4,606,000**	**5,323,000**	**100.0**	**0.27**	**5,464,000**	**5,360,000**

largest group was the Pentecostals, and the fourth was Jehovah's Witnesses. More than 10 percent did not belong to any religious communities, and those who dismiss religious beliefs as irrational have formed organizations in order to promote thinking and culture that is free from religious bonds, and have produced nonreligious ceremonies that can replace Christian baptism, wedding ceremonies, and so on. They think that freedom of thought, conscience, conviction, and religion are not yet achieved in society. The adherence to these organizations has so far been modest.

Finland was one of the last European countries to be reached by Christianity. The ancient religion of the Finns consisted of myths; worship of the dead; and worship of nature beings, sprites, and personal gods. There were also shamans and wise men. Worship of the dead was mainly based on the fear of ghosts. In the same way, worship of different beings like fairies, elves, and gnomes often aimed at propitiating these beings. Among the Sami people who populate northernmost Finland, the pre-Christian religion was preserved longer than among the Finns, although they, too, later became Lutheran or Orthodox Christians. Finnish mythology is found in the 19th-century poem collection, the *Kalevala*. It is a work of one man, Elias Lönnrot (1802–1884), who collected the stories in different provinces of Finland but probably also wrote some parts himself. In the 16th century, the church Reformer Mikael Agricola had published a list of ancient Finn-

ish gods. Otherwise the sources of information about the old Finnish mythology are few. Today, there are some small groups of people, neo-Pagans, who wish to revive the religion that Finns had before Christianity.

The first Christian influences have been traced to the ninth century. Items with Christian symbols and Christian vocabulary came from both east and west. Finnish culture and language are not related to the cultures and languages in neighboring countries (except Estonia): Finns are neither a Slavic nor a Scandinavian people. Christianity was established during the first three centuries of the second millennium, and in 1216 the Finland of that time became a part of the diocese of Uppsala (Sweden). Some years later, the first bishop of Finland was appointed. By the end of the 13th century, the Roman Catholic Church had established its position in the country.

The Lutheran phase of the Protestant Reformation of the 16th century reached Finland rather early, the first influences felt already in the 1520s. The Christian New Testament was published in Finnish in 1548. It was translated by Mikael Agricola, later a Lutheran bishop. His literary work had an impact far beyond the church, as it became significant for the literacy of the Finns, for the written Finnish language, and for the national literature.

In theological respects, the Reformation was carried out moderately in Finland, and the historic episcopal succession, or apostolic succession of bishops, was

FINLAND

St. Elias Church, a Finnish Orthodox church in rural Finland. (Sandra Kemppainen/Dreamstime.com)

not broken. The most visible changes were abandoning Latin as the church language and regarding only baptism and holy Communion as sacraments. Economically, the Reformation proved disastrous for the church in the Kingdom of Sweden, of which Finland was still a part. The church's wealth and much of its power were transferred to the king. This did not mean a disaster for Christianity, though, as the Reformation brought about a deepening of knowledge about the Christian faith to the people. Later, especially in the 19th century, several nationwide revivals were experienced among the people. Some of these took place in and still have influence in the Lutheran Church. Others resulted in the establishment and growth of other denominations.

Besides the Lutheran Church and the Pentecostal congregations, the strongest Protestant denomination is the Finnish Orthodox Church (14,000 members). It started at the end of the 19th century as a renewal movement inside the Lutheran Church, but separated as an independent church after the declaration of religious freedom in 1923. The Roman Catholic Church, which had to close down its activities in the 1520s, returned to Finland at the end of the 18th century. Now there are 7,000 Catholics in the 7 parishes of the Diocese of Helsinki. The number of Catholics, of whom many are foreigners, is increasing, and several Catholic religious orders have made their appearance.

The relations between churches became increasingly cordial through the 20th century. The Ecumenical Council of Finland, which is the oldest ecumenical body in the country and which also has the most member churches and organizations, was founded in 1917. The Council includes 12 member churches and communities and 18 observers. A change in the relationship between the majority church and the minority churches occurred recently when the annual official church services (for example, on Independence Day), which members of the government and the Parliament attend, became ecumenical.

The first Jews came to Finland from Sweden at the end of the 18th century, but the community has remained small. The majority of Jews have their roots in Russia. Today, there are 2 synagogues and 1,150 Jews in Finland. In Helsinki the Jewish community also maintains a kindergarten, a school, and a hospital.

The first Muslim community was founded in 1925 by Tatars who immigrated from Russia. This community retains much of its ethnic distinctiveness, as do most of the newer communities. There are not yet any Muslim schools, nor are there recognizable mosques. The registered Muslim communities are still small and few in number. Estimates on the actual size of Islam in Finland vary between 15,000 and 20,000; however, the number of Muslims in Finland is increasing, mainly due to immigration.

Several internationally known new religious movements are present in Finland, but they have remained small. Only Jehovah's Witnesses and the Church of Jesus Christ of Latter-day Saints have gained a notable numbers of members. There are no remarkable indigenous new religious movements.

Religious freedom is guaranteed for everyone, as far as the activities involved are not otherwise in opposition to the law. The legislation came into force in 1923. A new Religious Freedom Act, introduced in 2000, was passed in 2004 and has modernized the 1923 law in several areas. While religion continues to be regulated, the autonomy of the many groups other than the Church of Finland was increased. A minimum of 20 members is needed to formally organize a new religious group. Individuals may be a member of several religious communities at once. The registration procedure for new groups has been greatly simplified.

Laura Maria Latikka

See also: Church of Jesus Christ of Latter-day Saints; Evangelical Lutheran Church of Finland; Finnish Orthodox Church; Jehovah's Witnesses; Pentecostalism; Roman Catholic Church.

References

Heino, Harri. *Changes in Religiosity from the Finnish Viewpoint.* Publication No. 37 of the Research Institute of the Lutheran Church in Finland. Tampere: Research Institute of the Lutheran Church in Finland, 1988.

Kaplan, Jeffrey. *Beyond the Mainstream: The Emergence of Religious Pluralism in Finland, Estonia and Russia (Kotimaisten Kielten Tutkimuskeskuksen Julkaisuja).* Helsinki: Suomalaisen kirjallisuuden seura, 2000.

Pentikäinen, Juha. *Cultural Minorities in Finland. An Overview towards Cultural Policy.* Ed. by J. Hiltunen. Helsinki: Publications of the Finnish National Commission for UNESCO, 1995.

Pentikäinen, Juha. *Kalevala Mythology.* Trans. and ed. by Ritva Poom. Bloomington: Indiana University Press, 1989.

Pentikäinen, Juha. *Shamanism and Culture.* Tampere, Finland: Etnika, 1998.

Sakaranaho, Tuula. *Religious Freedom, Multiculturalism, Islam: Cross-reading Finland and Ireland.* Leiden: Brill, 2006.

Finnish Orthodox Church

The roots of the Finnish Orthodox Church reach back to the missionary work done at the beginning of the second millennium in the easternmost area settled by Finnish tribes, that is, the Province of Karelia. This work primarily originated from the monasteries and was carried out by Orthodox monks. The monastery at Valamo, founded according to tradition by the Greek-born monk Sergius and his younger assistant Herman, was the most important base. As time went by, several other monasteries were founded to back up the church's work. None of the Orthodox parts of Karelia formed part of Sweden–Finland politically until the latter half of the 16th century, and more came to do so in the 17th century. In 1809–1917, when Finland was a Grand Duchy of the Russian Empire, a separate diocese was established for the Orthodox parishes (1892), centered on Vyborg (Karelia). When Finland became independent in 1917, the church's administrative links with the Russian church were broken. After various intermediate stages, the Orthodox Church's standing in Finland was formalized through government action: In 1923 it canonically became an autonomous Orthodox church under the ecumenical patriarch of Constantinople, gaining extensive self-government in internal matters. As early as 1918 the Finnish government had endorsed, through a special decree, its status as the second national church, the other being the Evangelical Lutheran Church of Finland. The Current Act on the Orthodox Church of Finland dates from 1969, with a supplementary decree the following year.

Administratively, the Finnish Orthodox Church, which has some 61,000 members (2006), is divided into three dioceses: Karelia, Helsinki, and Oulu. The bishop of the diocese of Karelia is also archbishop (Archbishop John, archbishop of Karelia and All Finland), the other bishops being metropolitans (Metropolitan Leo of Helsinki and Metropolitan Ambrosius of Oulu). There is also an assistant bishop, called the bishop of Joensuu (Bishop Panteleimon), in the Diocese of Karelia. The church's supreme decision-making body is the General Assembly, made up of representatives of the clergy and laymen, to which the bishops belong by right. Decisions on doctrines and canons must be ratified by the Bishops' Synod. The ordinary decision-making body is the Board of Administration, which consist of bishops, a priest, and laymen. General Assembly decisions can only become acts and decrees following approval by the Finnish state. The church's publications committee takes growing responsibility for all Orthodox literature published. The Orthodox periodicals with the largest circulation are *Aamun Koitto*, *Ortodoksiviesti*, and *Paimen-Sanomat*. The committee also publishes a theological yearbook and a periodical on Orthodox culture. The dioceses are divided into 25 parishes, many of which cover an extensive geographical area. There are some 160 churches and chapels, and about 110 clergy, more than 20 of them currently in retirement. There is one monastery (called in Finnish Uusi-Valamo, or simply Valamo) and one convent (Lintula Convent). Most parishes use only Finnish for services, though Church Slavonic is also used regularly in Helsinki and occasionally in other places Swedish and Greek.

The Finnish Orthodox Church is primarily financed out of the church tax collected with the other national

taxes and paid to the church by the state on a monthly basis. The salaries of the Orthodox clergy, for instance, come out of this money. The central and diocesan administrations are financed by the state. For 70 years (1918–1988), the Orthodox clergy were trained at a seminary maintained by the state. In 1988, however, the seminary was placed under the University of Joensuu, which has a Department of Orthodox and Western Theology for the purpose. There is also an Orthodox seminary subordinate to the church, which is responsible for service rituals and liturgical practices. The university trains teachers of religion and cantors as well as Orthodox priests. Religious instruction in public schools is confessional, and if there are enough of them, Orthodox pupils are entitled to separate instruction. The church usually arranges Orthodox teaching for groups too small to warrant this. The foreign and ecumenical contacts of the Orthodox Church of Finland have been growing steadily ever since the 1960s, and the church is now a member of the World Council of Churches. The church has associated parishes among Finnish Americans in the United States and in 1977 began cooperative work with the Greek Orthodox Patriarchate of Alexandria and All Africa in Kenya and Uganda. Since World War II, there has also been a growing interest in reviving the tradition of icon painting and there are several active groups at the moment in various parts of the country. This art form has awakened interest outside the Orthodox Church, too, like many other manifestations of Orthodox tradition and culture.

Finnish Orthodox Church
Karjalankatu 1
FIN-70110 Kuopio
Finland
http://www.ort.fi

Kari M. Räntilä

See also: Evangelical Lutheran Church of Finland; Greek Orthodox Patriarchate of Alexandria and All Africa; World Council of Churches

References
Piironen, E. "The Orthodox Church in Finland." *International Review of Mission* 62, no. 245 (1973): 51–56.

Purmonen, V., ed. *Orthodoxy in Finland: Past and Present*. 2nd ed. Kuopio, Finland: Orthodox Clergy Association, 1984.

Venkula-Vauraste, L. "800 Years of Orthodox Faith in Finland." *Look at Finland* 5 (1977): 42–47.

Flagellation

Flagellation is the act of whipping the human body by using flexible instruments such as the whip, the scourge, or cat-o'-nine-tails. Flagellation can be located in the context of law, religion, medicine, or sexual excitation. In many cases the juridical and religious aspects are indivisible, whereas sexual arousal by (self-) flagellation is a distinguished phenomenon of Western modernity. In two monotheistic traditions—Roman Catholicism and Shia Islam—self-flagellation plays a role until today.

Flagellation in Antiquity The use of flogging instruments has been a long legal tradition of corporal punishment. The Latin word *flagellum* designates a multi-thong type scourge (whip, lash) with interlaced pieces of metal or bones that inflicts severe wounds on the body of the convict. The Roman law prescribed punishment by the flagellum either to extract a confession or as an overture to execution or as a distinct penalty. In the ancient Latin world flagellation was considered an extreme, gruesome penalty that caused not only tremendous pain but oftentimes grave mutilation and even death. Roman citizens were exempt from being sentenced to scourging whereas noncitizens were subject to it. Furthermore, the whipping of slaves was a common practice throughout the antique world.

The ritualistic usage of the whip was practiced in various Greco-Roman and Egyptian cults, namely, the cult of Isis, the Dionysian cult, the Thargelia festival, or the Roman festival of Lupercalia. Especially the old Spartan cult of Artemis Orthia was famous for its ritual flagellation (*diamastigosis*) of adolescent men (*ephebos*), as related by Plutarch, Xenophon, Pausanius, and Plato. Self-flagellation was practiced by the priests of Attis. Well documented is the ritual scourging in the course of diverse initiation ceremonies of mystery religions (especially Isis mysteries).

The motifs and motivations behind such ritualistic practices differed widely. Consequently there is no scholarly agreement on the general meaning of ancient cultic flagellation. Whipping is seen as a technique of inducing altered states of consciousness or as a ritual of manhood. Blood-letting caused by ritual scourging is interpreted as a substitute for human sacrifice or self-castration or as a means to increase fertility.

Flagellation and Self-Flagellation in Roman Catholic Christianity The first Christian emperors adopted the Roman legal system in varying degrees and by it flogging as a punishment procedure. The whip as an instrument of castigation made its way to early monastic rules. Vigorous corporal punishment was part and parcel of early Christian cloister life from Egypt to Ireland. The authoritative and most influential Rule of Benedict of Nursia (480–547), for example, prescribes flagellation of the stubborn and the hardheaded as well as the novices. Medieval Christian monasteries served as educational laboratories aimed at the fundamental transformation of the souls of monks and nuns. The Christian virtue of willing obedience was the object of the transformation. For the construction of humility and an obedient will, punishment was indispensable. In this context, the Latin word *disciplina* (discipline) was the common term for legally prescribed flogging. Monastic penance that was performed in front of the assembled monks served a dual purpose: it promoted subjection to the law and it paved the way to Christian virtue. Such rites of penance, however, were not directed toward the breaking of the will, but to the forming of religious desires and obedience by choice.

Self-flagellation as a monastic exercise emerged from the penitential *disciplina* and refers to the episode of the flagellation of Christ tied to the pillar, reported in the four canonical Gospels. The scourging of Christ by Roman soldiers preceded the death penalty by crucifixion. Aside from a few exceptions, the ideal of self-mortification and the practice of self-flagellation emerged relatively late in Christianity. Saint Pardulf (657–ca. 737), an abbot in Aquitaine, is reckoned as an early practitioner if not "inventor" of voluntary flogging. The incorporation of self-flagellation in the monastic routine was successfully implemented by Peter

Flagellants, from a 15th-century woodcut. (Ann Ronan Pictures/StockphotoPro)

Damian (1007–1072), a hermit, church reformer, and cardinal in Italy. In various writings, especially in his *De laude Flagellorum* (*In Praise of the Whip*), he propagates ritual self-flagellation as a useful form of purification and repentance. Submitting to the whip was not understood as a denial of the body but as a spiritual *imitatio Christi,* a way to engage the body and the imagination in the task of communicating with God.

By the 11th century, a Passion-centered piety mushroomed in Western Christianity. Self-inflicted suffering became increasingly appreciated by the religious virtuoso. The willing acceptance and evocation of suffering was not only a means of expressing devotion to Christ, but also of expiating guilt in this life and of pre-empting punishment in the afterlife. German Do-

minican mystics, such as Heinrich Seuse (1295/97–1366), Elsbeth von Oye (1290–1340), and Margareta Ebner (1291–1351), practiced drastic forms of self-mortification, among which self-flagellation constituted the rather harmless component.

Besides the individual self-mortification of mystics hidden behind cloister walls, flagellant processions appeared in public spaces in the mid-13th century. A famous flagellant processional happened in 1260, starting in Perugia (Italy) and spreading across the Alps to Germany, Bohemia, and Poland. Earthquakes and the Black Death stirred up another flagellant movement in 1349–1350, which appeared in different waves all over Europe. Huge crowds of clergy and laypeople traveled from town to town and performed new rituals combining collective self-scourging with sermons and hymn chanting. The flagellant movement of 1349–1350 was accompanied by millennial enthusiasm and massacres of Jews. Due to heretical tendencies Pope Clement VI (r. 1342–1352) forbade the processions in 1349. Notwithstanding, flagellant movements, smaller or bigger, are known until the late 15th century in Germany, northern Italy, France, and northern Spain.

During the Catholic reform in the 16th and 17th centuries the Jesuits enthusiastically promoted all kinds of sensual piety such as the veneration of saints and Jesus' mother Mary, paintings and architecture, musical drama and theater. Under their dramaturgical guidance processions, especially flagellant processions during Lent, were encouraged with great ambition as well as theatrical re-enactments of the Passion of Christ.

Since the late 17th century church criticism emerged denouncing the Jesuits as perverts. In the new literary genre of pornography lascivious clerics whipping or watching whippings became standard motifs. At the same time flagellation as a technique of sexual arousal was associated with medicine. Evoking sexual fantasies by flogging was explained with reference to Galen's humoral pathology.

The non-European history of self-flagellation started in the 16th and 17th centuries. The colonial ambitions and missionary fervor of the Spaniards brought Passion plays and the practice of self-flagellation to Mexico and the Philippines. In both countries Iberian "Calvary Catholicism" was introduced with great success. Flagellation in public became popular either as a theatrical element of Passion plays or as separate performance by confraternities or by individuals. The adoption of such rites of self-mortification was accompanied by local reinterpretation. In the Philippines, for instance, self-flagellation is associated with a private vow, the well-being of the family, corporeal purification, and healing, far less with guilt and atonement. Self-flagellation as Lenten ritual is part of popular piety all over the Catholic world, be it the U.S. Southwest, Mexico, the Philippines, or Mediterranean countries such as Italy, Spain, or Portugal. Penitential self-flagellation as an individual act is tolerated and encouraged at least to some degree in lay brotherhoods or congregations (such as Opus Dei) and in penitential orders by the Catholic Church until today.

Self-Flagellation in Shia Islam Self-flagellation in Shia Islam is part of ritualized commemoration of the martyrdom of Imam Husayn (626–680), son of Imam Ali (d. 661) and grandson of Muhammad, which happened in 680 CE. In the power struggle over the legitimate succession of the prophet, one faction encouraged Husayn to fight for leadership. His alleged supporters of Kufa (Iraq), however, betrayed him and his attempted coup failed. In company of only 72 devoted followers and relatives, Imam Husayn was surrounded and besieged by the troops of Omayya ruler Yazid in the Iraqi desert near Kerbela. On the 10th of Muharram, day of Ashura, Yazid's army stormed the camp and massacred Husayn and nearly all of his followers. The corpses were buried in situ and there the shrine of Karbala was erected afterward.

All over the Shiite world the tragedy of Karbala is remembered as a traumatic event and has become a key element of Shiite identity. The glorification of the martyrdom of Husayn and the sorrow over the betrayal is the core of mourning rituals, which are performed annually during the first 10 days of the month of Muharram. Ritual components are the wearing of black clothes, intense weeping, reciting the death narrative of Imam Husayn, somber musical performances, and fasting. The most spectacular and violent parts are processions of men who beat their bare chests with their fists, flagellate their backs with chains (*zanjir*), or cut their foreheads with swords, razorblades, or knives (*tatbir*). Theatrical re-enactments of the Battle of Karbala and Husayn's sacrifice are called *ta'ziya* (Persian: *'aza dari*).

Originally, some individuals who called themselves *tawabun* (repenters) collected at the gravesite of Husayn praising his sacrifice, regretting not fighting and dying alongside him and cursing the killers. Further commemoration gatherings (*majlis*) were held in private rooms, while in Karbala the ritualized visitation of the grave of Husayn (*ziyarah*) flourished, in spite of all efforts of Abbasid caliphs to ban the pilgrimage and to prevent the construction of the shrines. In the year 963, the Buyids, a Shiite Persian dynasty, declared the 10th of Muharram as an official feast and public processions on the day of Ashura occurred with regularity shortly afterward.

In early historical sources the blood-shedding rituals are never mentioned. In the shrine cities of Najaf and Karbala self-flagellation with swords and chains became customary as recently as in the early 19th century. According to the documents, non-Arab participants, Persians and Qizilbash-Turks, introduced these practices.

In the 20th century, the theatrical performances of self-mortification caused legal controversies. The practice of flagellation as a means of identification with Imam Husayn was seriously questioned. Even Ayatollah Khamenei released a fatwa against self-mutilation in 1994 but the attempts to outlaw blood-shedding in Husayn's name have remained ineffective as a whole.

During the Islamic revolution in Iran (1978–1979) the Muharram processions and the mourning slogans were successfully utilized to mobilize emotions and the mass upheavals. "Every day is Ashura; every place is Karbala; every month is Muharram"—this slogan was chanted by the crowds, intoned on radio and television, and written on the walls. Since then this most important Shiite ritual has been constantly politicized by reinterpretation. In countries such as Lebanon, Iraq, and Iran the Ashura commemorations are occasionally transformed from a mourning ritual to emphasizing Islamic activism.

At present, the Muharram observances are carried out in all countries with a noteworthy Shiite population, including Afghanistan, Iran, Iraq, Pakistan, Lebanon, India, Bahrain, and even in Jamaica and Trinidad and Tobago. Laborers from India brought the commemoration rituals to the Caribbean. The main feature of the "Hosay" festival there are colorful parades of cenotaphs for Husayn attended by all ethnic and religious communities. Flagellation, ceremonial chest beating, and other forms of self-mutilation are absent.

Peter J. Bräunlein

See also: Ali ibn Abi Talib; Ashura; Dominicans; Al-Husayn ibn Ali ibn Abi Talib; Jesuits; Karbala; Lent; Mary, Blessed Virgin; Monasticism; Muhammad; Roman Catholic Church; Shia Islam.

References

Asad, Talal. *Genealogies of Religion: Discipline and Reasons of Power in Christianity and Islam*. Baltimore: Johns Hopkins University Press, 1993.

Constable, Giles. *Attitudes Toward Self-Inflicted Suffering in the Middle Ages*. Brookline, MA: Hellenic College Press, 1982.

Dawkins, Richard M., ed. *The Sanctuary of Artemis Orthia at Sparta*. London: Macmillan, 1929.

Ende, Werner. "The Flagellations of Muharram and the Shi'ite Ulama." *Der Islam* 55, no. 1 (1978): 20–36.

Gougaud, Louis. *Dévotions et pratiques ascétiques du Moyen Age*. Paris: Desclée de Brouwer, 1925.

Halm, Heinz. *Shi'a: From Religion to Revolution*. Princeton, NJ: Markus Wiener, 1997.

Hussain, Ali J. "The History of Mourning and the Mourning of History: The Evolution of Ritual Commemoration of the Battle of Karbala." *Comparative Studies of South Asia, Africa and Middle East* 25, no. 1 (2005): 78–88.

Korom, Frank J. *Hosay Trinidad: Muharram Performances in an Indo-Caribbean Diaspora*. Philadelphia: University of Pennsylvania Press, 2003.

Largier, Niklaus. *In Praise of the Whip: A Cultural History of Arousal*. New York: Zone Books, 2007.

Weigle, Marta. *Brothers of Light, Brothers of Blood: The Penitentes of the Southwest*. Santa Fe, NM: Ancient City Press, 1989.

Fludd, Robert

1574–1637

Robert Fludd was a Christian Hermeticist, defender of the Rosicrucians, and author of encyclopedic works on the macrocosm and the microcosm.

Fludd was born in 1574 at Milgate House, Kent, England, the son of Sir Thomas Fludd. In 1592 he entered St. John's College, Oxford, where he moved in High-Church (anti-Puritan) circles, and became a close friend of the future royal physician, William Paddy. He graduated with a master's degree in the arts in 1598.

Fludd then traveled for six years throughout the European continent. In France he acted as tutor to Catholic aristocratic families, notably that of the duc de Guise. In Rome he met "Grutherus" (possibly Matthäus

Greuther), who taught him engineering and introduced him to "magnetic medicines," including the weapon-salve. In Avignon he contested with the Jesuits over geomancy, a system of divination from randomly thrown pebbles. In Padua he met William Harvey, discoverer of the circulation of the blood. Fludd also visited Spain and Germany, where he became a convert to the Paracelsian system of medicine.

On his return to England in 1605, Fludd entered Christ Church, Oxford, and in the same year passed his doctorate in medicine. But his unorthodox views hindered his acceptance by the College of Physicians, and he was not admitted as a Fellow until 1609. He lived thereafter in London as a successful practitioner, treating many distinguished patients. He never married, and prided himself on his lifelong continence.

Fludd's worldview was a synthesis of Hermeticism, Christian Kabbalah, neo-Platonism, alchemy, and "occult philosophy" in the tradition of Cornelius Agrippa (1486–1535). He also aspired to universal knowledge of the arts and sciences. During his European travels he had written treatises on arithmetic, geometry, perspective, military science, music, the art of memory, cosmography, geomancy, astrology, and engineering. He now incorporated these into a vast *History of the Macrocosm and the Microcosm* (*Utriusque Cosmi Maioris scilicet et Minoris Metaphysica, Physica atque Technica Historia*, 1617–1621). The first volume treated the external world (macrocosm) in two divisions: first the works of God, then those of man, including the arts and sciences. The second volume explained man himself (the microcosm), both in his God-given faculties (such as the physical body and paranormal powers) and in his own inventions that lead to self-knowledge (including palmistry and geomancy). The first part was printed in Germany and dedicated to King James I (1566–1625). Four other parts followed, but the ambitious scheme was never completed. The work is noted for its fine symbolic illustrations of the process of creation, the structure of the macrocosm, the harmony of the spheres, and the nature of the human being. Fludd's second encyclopedic project was *Catholic* [in the sense of "universal"] *Medicine* (*Medicina Catholica*, 1629–1631). Also unfinished, it expounds a system of medicine that combines astrology, analysis of urine and the pulse, meteorology, and a firm belief in demonic influences.

Fludd's proud and contentious nature involved him in several controversies. One concerned his use of the weapon-salve, an ointment applied not to a wound but to the weapon that caused it. Another was with the astronomer Johannes Kepler (1571–1630), who criticized Fludd's unscientific interpretation of the harmony of the spheres. Further critics were Marin Mersenne (1588–1638) and Pierre Gassendi (1596–1655), who objected to Fludd's Hermeticism and his leanings toward magic.

Fludd was among the earliest defenders of the Rosicrucians, a fictitious order of world reform proclaimed in 1614–1615. Certainly his philosophy accorded with that of the Rosicrucian manifestos, and believers in the Order, up to the present day, have counted him among its chief members.

Fludd died in London on September 8, 1637. His works were largely forgotten until the 20th century, when they became of interest to the modern Rosicrucian orders and to historians of ideas and of science.

Joscelyn Godwin

See also: Agrippa, Cornelius; Astrology.

References

Fludd, Robert. *Essential Readings*. Ed. by William H. Huffman. London: Aquarian Press, 1992.

Fludd, Robert. *A Philosophical Key*. Ed. by Allen G. Debus. New York: Science History Publications, 1979.

Godwin, Joscelyn. *Robert Fludd, Hermetic Philosopher and Surveyor of Two Worlds*. London: Thames & Hudson, 1979.

Huffman, William H. *Robert Fludd and the End of the Renaissance*. London: Routledge & Kegan Paul, 1988.

Yates, Frances A. *Theatre of the World*. Chicago: University of Chicago Press, 1969.

Foguangshan

Founded in Kaohsiung, Taiwan, in 1967, Foguangshan (Buddha's Light Mountain) had by the opening of the

21st century developed into one of the most influential Buddhist organizations in the Republic of China and had opened nearly 100 temples elsewhere around the world. Its founder, Master Xingyun, is regarded as a leading exponent of Humanistic Buddhism (Renjian Fojiao), by which is meant a refocusing of Chan (Zen) and Pure Land practice to more directly deal with the challenges of contemporary life.

Master Xingyun (b. 1927) took vows of renunciation at age 12 in 1939 at Qixia Temple in Nanjing, China. Ten years later, he followed the Nationalist army as it retreated to Taiwan. As his following among both mainland transplants and native Taiwanese grew, he established Foguangshan in the southern part of the island. The monastery's eight-story-high statue of Amitabha Buddha and its Pure Land Cave (which was modeled on Disney World's "It's a Small, Small World") have over the years attracted millions of pilgrims and tourists. Since the 1990s, Foguangshan has undertaken an ambitious campaign to spread the teachings of Humanistic Buddhism around the world.

Rather than exerting their efforts toward being reborn in a pure land elsewhere in the universe, as is usually advocated by the Pure Land School, Humanistic Buddhism exhorts practitioners to transform our own world into a pure land and thereby attain universal enlightenment. Master Xingyun believes that radical, confrontational reforms are not effective means for achieving that goal, since such tactics create too much suffering and remain within dualistic thinking. Instead, he espouses gradual amelioration through each person, whether monastic or lay, engaging in a daily regimen of recitation, meditation, and self-reflection, while simultaneously devoting the rest of his or her time to improving others' material and spiritual conditions. Hence, Foguangshan sponsors a variety of social, educational, and missionary enterprises, including two orphanages, a medical clinic, several preschools, a high school, and a liberal arts university.

Foguangshan projects are typically undertaken in cooperation with political and corporate leaders. Because of this, Master Xingyun's detractors have saddled him with the pejorative labels of "political monk" and "commercial monk." He counters that creating close working relationships with the powerful is an expedient means (in Chinese, *fangbian*; in Sanskrit, *upaya*) for achieving Buddhist goals.

Although improving people's material well-being is seen as essential to establishing a pure land on Earth, the key to realizing such a utopia nonetheless remains cultivating people's wisdom and compassion through exposure to Buddhism. Foguangshan is therefore especially well known in Taiwan for its publishing empire, which includes a punctuated edition of the Buddhist canon; a six-volume encyclopedia of Buddhism; and scores of books, cassettes, and videos by Master Xingyun on Humanistic Buddhism. The emphasis on promoting Buddhist teachings is also seen in Foguangshan's missionary efforts. Although the vast majority of devotees in Foguangshan branch temples outside of Taiwan are overseas Chinese Buddhists, the organization has also devoted considerable energy to bringing others into its fold. Hsi Lai Temple (Hacienda Heights, California), Nan Tien Temple (Wollengong, Australia), and Nan Hua Temple (Bronkhorstspruit, South Africa) have been at the forefront of Foguangshan missionary activity.

Approximately 1,300 monks and nuns were within the Foguang ranks in the year 2008, and the order's lay society, known as the Buddha's Light International Association, had a membership of at least 400,000 and perhaps more than one million.

Foguangshan
Tashu Township
Kaohsiung County, Taiwan
Republic of China
http://www.ibps.org

Stuart Chandler

See also: Pure Land Buddhism; Zen Buddhism.

References

Chandler, Christopher Stuart. *Establishing a Pure Land on Earth: The Foguang Buddhist Perspective on Modernization and Globalization.* Honolulu: University of Hawaii Press, 2004.

Chandler, Christopher Stuart. "Spreading Buddha's Light: The Internationalization of Foguang Shan." In *Buddhist Missionaries in the Era of*

Globalization, edited by Linda Learman. Honolulu: University of Hawaii Press, 2005.

Jiang Canteng. *Taiwan Dangdai Fojiao*. Taipei: Nantian Press, 1997.

Jones, Charles Brewer. *Buddhism in Taiwan: Religion and State, 1660–1990*. Honolulu: University of Hawaii Press, 1999.

Foundation for the Preservation of the Mahayana Tradition

The Foundation for the Preservation of the Mahayana Tradition (FPMT) is the most widespread Tibetan Buddhist group of the Gelugpa School outside Tibet. The Gelugpa School is the reformed Tibetan school generally identified with the Dalai Lama and the FPMT may be seen as the Dalai Lama's main support group within the Buddhist world though he has no official position within the organization.

The founder of the Foundation for the Preservation of the Mahayana Tradition, Lama Thubten Yeshe (1935–1984), was born in Tibet. He was identified as the reincarnation of the abbess of Chi-me lung Gompa and joined Sera Je College near Lhasa, where he remained until he was 25. In 1959 he fled into northeast India along with many other Tibetans and there continued his studies. Here he met Lama Thubten Zopa Rinpoche (b. 1945), who became his first disciple. In 1965 the lamas first came into contact with a number of Westerners, many of whom were on the hippie trail to India, most important, Zina Rechevsky, an American heiress. Her request to be taught by the lamas resulted in her ordination as a nun by the Dalai Lama in 1967. The trio moved to Nepal in 1969, where they founded Kopan Monastery.

Over the following years Kopan attracted a large influx of Westerners, and the seeds of a new Buddhist movement were sown. Lama Yeshe developed a distinctive teaching style tailored to Western understanding and began to visit many groups, which had arisen throughout the West. By 1975 the extent of the movement was such that Lama Yeshe formed a group in order to oversee the diverse activities that were then taking place. This group was named the Council for the Preservation of the Mahayana Tradition (CPMT) and comprised directors of Dharma centers, rural retreat centers, and training institutes, which were all part of the expanding organization that came to be known as the FPMT. It has now spread into over 26 countries across 4 continents. In 2008, the FPMT reported 147 centers, study groups, and projects in 31 countries worldwide under its spiritual direction.

Lama Yeshe died of a heart attack in a California hospital in 1984, and Lama Zopa succeeded him as spiritual director. In 1984 Osel Hita Torres was born to Spanish parents and was soon identified by His Holiness the Dalai Lama as the reincarnation of Lama Yeshe. He is now training at Sera Je monastery in southern India. In the future he will replace Lama Zopa as the spiritual director of the FPMT.

Conishead Priory in the United Kingdom was purchased in 1976 and was named the Manjushri Center. It became a thriving training and retreat center under the spiritual directorship of Geshe Kelsang Gyatso. However, tensions grew between the FPMT, then situated far away in Nepal, and the Manjushri Center. After much antagonism the Manjushri Center eventually split away from the FPMT and a new movement, the New Kadampa Tradition, was founded under the spiritual guidance of Geshe Kelsang (b. 1931). The two groups have no affiliation today.

At present Lama Zopa Rinpoche remains the spiritual director, and his authority is shared with the FPMT via the board of directors. The CPMT is responsible for representing all members of the various centers around the world. The FPMT Inc. Office (international office) is responsible for administration, legal and financial matters, education, and other coordinating functions, as well as the implementation of ideas stemming from the FPMT board of directors and from the CPMT. Many centers have Tibetan *geshes* as their resident teachers; the geshe is often assisted by a Western monk or nun.

Central to the FPMT teaching is the *Lam Rim Chen Mo*, which is a synopsis of the Perfection of Wisdom literature, though many other Buddhist texts are referred to as and when necessary. Although various meditation and Tantric practices are taught, the FPMT describe their main practice as "following the spiritual advice of Lama Zopa Rinpoche," which is based on the Mahayana Gelug sect of Tibetan Buddhism and follows the lineage of Lama Tsong Khapa.

Lama Yeshe and Lama Zopa also began the Maitreya Project, an effort to build a 500-foot bronze statue of Maitreya Buddha (one of the main deities in the Mahayan Buddhist pantheon) at Kushinagar, Uttar Pradesh, in northern India. The statue will be seated on a throne, and the throne will be a building that will house several temples, a museum and library, and welcoming centers for tourists and pilgrims. When completed, the statue will become the largest religious statue in the world.

Foundation for the Preservation of the Mahayana
    Tradition
125B La Posta Rd.
Taos, NM 87571
http://www.fpmt.org

Jamie Cresswell

See also: Dalai Lama III, Sonam Gyatso; Gelugpa; New Kadampa Tradition–International Kadampa Buddhist Union; Statues—Buddhist; Tibetan Buddhism; Tsong Khapa.

References

Batchelor, Stephen. *The Awakening of the West: The Encounter of Buddhism and Western Culture.* Berkeley, CA: Parallax 1994.

Mackenzie, Vicki. *Reincarnation: The Boy Lama.* London: Bloomsbury, 1988.

Yeshe, Lama, Lama Zopa Rinpoche, et al. *Wisdom Energy: Basic Buddhist Teachings.* Boston: Wisdom Publications, 2000.

Zopa Rinpoche, Lama. *Dear Lama Zopa: Radical Solutions for Transforming Problems into Happiness.* Boston: Wisdom Publications, 2007.

Fox, George

1624–1691

George Fox, a critic of the Church of England in 17th-century England, withdrew his membership and, after experiencing what he interpreted as communications from God, founded the Society of Friends, popularly

George Fox was the founder of the Society of Friends, better known as the Quakers. (Vincent L. Milner, *Religious Denominations of the World,* 1872)

known as the Quakers. The Quakers subsequently grew into an international movement best known for its work on peace concerns.

Fox was born in July 1624 in Fenny Drayton, Leicestershire, England. While a teenager apprenticed to a shoemaker, he began to focus his thoughts on religious issues. He found himself dissatisfied with the religious trappings of the Church of England and he withdrew. Though still in his teens, as early as 1643, he began speaking against the church's ornate buildings and the presence of ordained ministers as being unhelpful and even a hindrance to the basic element of the religious life, establishing a personal relationship with God. He moved from his critique of religion toward a more positive message following an intense experience of the divine in 1646. He now spoke of God dwelling within every individual and emphasized that communication with God was a possibility. God had given each person the Inner Light through which it was possible to speak to Christ.

The original core of people who gathered around Fox was termed the Friends of Truth. One by one, they also withdrew from the Church of England and, most important, refused to pay any church tithes. Fox exhorted the group to tremble before the word of God, an admonition they took somewhat literally. That characteristic led to their being derisively called Quakers, a term traced to Justice Bennet of Derby.

The movement, now termed the Society of Friends, emerged more or less informally during the period of the Commonwealth in England (1649–1660) and came to include some 20,000 adherents. With the restoration of the monarchy, however, Fox and the Friends suffer severe setbacks. During the reign of Charles II (r. 1660–1685), who leaned toward Catholicism, more than 13,000 Friends were imprisoned, some being sent into slavery. They developed a reputation for refusing to recognize differences of social rank, to take oaths (including the oath of loyalty to the Crown), and to pay church tithes. Margaret Fell (1614–1702), the wife of the vice chancellor of the Duchy of Lancaster and an early convert, provided a haven for some of her fellow believers at her estate, Swarthmore Hall. Following the death of her husband, in 1669 she married Fox.

As the movement grew throughout England, Fox extended his travels. He visited Germany and Holland in Europe and crossed the Atlantic to visit the British American colonies, Barbados, and Jamaica. He found a valued colleague in William Penn, who used his inheritance to found two havens for Quakers in the American colonies. When possible, Penn also traveled with Fox. Fox continued to travel until shortly before his death.

Fox organized the movement around a hierarchy of Monthly (congregational), Quarterly (district), and Annual (national) Meetings. Leadership was provided by elders appointed to care for ministry and overseers who took charge of the needs of the poor and the children. Members lived in simplicity. Meetings centered upon waiting for communications from the Inner Light. Women played a prominent role in the developing movement from the beginning.

Fox died January 13, 1691, in London. Active to the end, he had preached earlier that day at the meeting house on Gracechurch Street. Over the next several years, Penn led a group that assembled and published Fox's *Journal*, which appeared in 1694.

J. Gordon Melton

See also: Church of England; Friends/Quakers.

References
Canby, Jones T. *George Fox's Attitude toward War.* Richmond, IN: Friends United Press, 1984.
Fox, George. *The Journal of George Fox.* Ed. by John L. Nickalls. Philadelphia: Philadelphia Yearly Meeting of the Religious Society of Friends, 1995.
Gura, Philip F. *A Glimpse of Sion's Glory: Puritan Radicalism in New England 1620–1660.* Middletown, CT: Wesleyan University Press, 1984.
Ingle, H. Larry. *First Among Friends: George Fox and the Creation of Quakerism.* New York: Oxford University Press, 1994.

■ France

France is located in the very heart of Western Europe, and its capital is Paris. Around 64 million inhabitants dwell in the country, according to the latest census. French is the dominant language, and the country embraces a wide spectrum of linguistic and cultural variations. France ranges among the most developed countries (with a GNP up to $34,000 per person); it is primarily urban (76 percent of the total population), politically secure (as a republic system devoid of major trouble since World War II), and economically stable (despite the fact that 3 percent of the national wealth goes to the poorest 10 percent of the citizens, compared to 25 percent that goes to the richest 10 percent).

Since 1905 and the official separation between state and church, France is supposed to be a model secularized country. However, and despite the political system of *laïcité* (that prohibited, for instance, the teaching of religion in school and the survey of denominations), Roman Catholicism retains a major cultural influence, and new forms of religious activities (the "sects" and the religious heritage of migrants) have spread out in the public spheres, challenging the ideal of a lay national citizenship.

Notre Dame Cathedral in Paris exemplifies the Gothic architectural style. (J. Gordon Melton)

The religious history of France is thoroughly related to Roman Catholicism, which shaped the social and political basis for the foundation of the nation-state, as well as the framework of French culture. France has traditionally been considered "the eldest daughter of the (Roman) Church."

Originally, the ancient territory now called Gaul (from the Latin *Gallia*), forerunner of France, was home to a pre-Celtic and Celtic pastoral and tribal civilization, whose religion was Druidism. After Greek (sixth century BCE) and Roman (second century BCE on) rule, Gaul was absorbed by the Roman Empire. The Gallic provinces began to be converted to Christianity in the first century of the new era.

The Franks, a Pagan Germanic tribe, invaded Gaul, along with other Germanic tribes, in the fifth century, but the baptism of the Frankish leader, Clovis (ca. 466–511), and his people inaugurated a lineage of Christian emperors and kings whose power was legitimated by the blessing of the church. This lineage stretched from the early Merovingian, Carolingian, and Capetian kings, to the late Napoleonic Empire (1804–1814) and the Second Empire (1852–1870).

Recurring barbarian invasions and endless territorial wars between feudal kingdoms in the Middle Ages and the early Renaissance did not allow the lasting foundation of a centralized and powerful state. Despite the success of Charlemagne (742–814) in having himself crowned emperor of the Romans by the pope (800), his unification of many territories into an empire (from the eighth to the 10th centuries) proved fragile, and the Holy Roman Empire that was based on his achievement turned out to be a rival of France rather than an extension of its power. For a time, nevertheless, France grew into the most powerful of feudal monarchies. Simultaneously, Roman Catholic institutions settled in France by way of the building of abbeys (Cluny, 927–942), monasteries, and cathedrals all over the country. The propagation and the reinforcement of the faith were achieved by means of evangelism and Crusades (1096–1291). The Catholic organization of the country was founded upon the model of Roman administrations and reflected the traditional structures of the pre-Christian civilization. This "parish civilization" (a territorial structuring in dioceses) persisted as the main religious and social form of organization in France until the 20th century.

After France recovered from the struggle with England later called the Hundred Years' War, the French monarchy became stable and strong enough to survive the Wars of Religion of the 16th century, brought on by the Protestant Reformation, and to keep France Catholic. At the same time, the French monarchy avoided domination by the pope, and it was among the French clergy that Gallicanism originated as a movement that favored the restriction of papal control and the achievement by the clergy of each nation of administrative autonomy. Moreover, the Edict of Nantes (1598) granted the French Protestants (of the Reformed tradition; called Huguenots) a high degree of religious freedom and even power in some areas.

The absolutist French monarchy of the second half of the 17th century was shaped by a cardinal, the famous Richelieu (1585–1642), and came to its greatest power under Louis XIV (1638–1715), who saw himself as the greatest champion of the Roman Catholic Church and answerable only to God. He encouraged unity of religion, gradually undermining the freedoms and privileges of the Protestants and finally revoking the Edict of Nantes (1685), thus driving many Huguenots out of France and greatly weakening the French economy. The oppressiveness of the political system seemed inextricably linked with the power of the church, and the *philosophes* of the Age of Enlightenment, such as Voltaire (1694–1778), risked their lives when they questioned either.

It is thus not surprising that the French Revolution of 1798 brought about a quick laicization of institutions (public records, health, and social services) and originated a first major rupture with Rome. During the Reign of Terror there was even an effort to completely de-Christianize France—in 1793 the Cathedral of Notre Dame de Paris was proclaimed a Temple of Reason, and widespread persecutions occurred, especially in 1793–1794. On the other hand, ultimately the Revolution contributed to the recognition by state institutions of denominational pluralism (1795). Despite the dispossession of Roman Catholic Church properties during the First Empire, Napoleon I (1769–1821), knowing that most of his subjects were still Roman Catholics and wishing a return to stability, reestablished relationships with Rome; the Concordat of 1801 made the Roman Catholic Church once again the established church of France, supported by the state, yet kept the church firmly Gallican, that is, under the control of the French government. After the first defeat of Napoleon I, the monarchy was restored, but it was a constitutional monarchy and remained one (after a brief hiatus in 1815, ended by Napoleon I's final defeat at Waterloo) until the Revolution of 1848. The Roman Catholic Church remained the established church, and Catholicism continued the revival it had experienced under Napoleon I, but the principle of religious toleration remained in force. It was only with the fall of the Second Empire (1870) and the establishment of the Third Republic (1871) that a republican political and social system came into being that completed the laicization of France.

French aesthetics, literature, and science have slowly separated from religious influences, starting in the 18th century. Further, the progress of industrialization and urbanization, together with the rise of new social strata (proletariat, bourgeoisie), contributed to the process of secularization in France. Emerging ideologies of the 18th and 19th centuries, such as Humanism, Positivism, and Rationalism, also played a key role in this process, in addition to politicized anticlerical movements (even stronger since the mid-19th century) and to the rise of Freethought in the upper classes of society (which had begun in the 17th century). At the same time, Catholicism got more involved in social action (especially in the mid-19th century) and political life (especially between 1860 and 1875). Even so, the educational system was laicized in 1882, and the separation of state and church was decreed in 1905.

From that time, although Catholic Christianity in France has seen various religious renewals (through evangelism, especially in Christian youth movements [1935–1965]), it has on the whole weakened, and there has been a rapid growth of atheism. At the same time, since the mid-1970s the decay of the Catholic Church has favored the rise of new forms of Christian religiosity through traditional community forms (Mennonites, Baptists, or Friends [Quakers]) or evangelical movements (Adventists, Pentecostalism, Jehovah's Witnesses), introduced in France in the years 1900–1930.

Nevertheless, despite the weakening of Catholic institutions and organizations, statistical estimates place the native Catholic population of France at about 56 percent (according to social scientific sources) to 74 percent (according to religious sources). In comparison, Protestants (including Reformed, Lutherans, and Baptists) represent currently between 1 and 2 percent of the French population, while Eastern Orthodox adherents only account for 0.5 percent. Protestantism is represented in France most notably by such bodies as the Reformed Church of France, the Reformed Church of Alsace and Lorraine, the Evangelical Lutheran Church of France, and the Church of the Augsburg Confession of Alsace and Lorraine. The Protestant Federation of France includes these churches and additional groups such as the Salvation Army and the Federation of Evangelical Baptist Churches of France. The Paris Mission, supported by the Reformed Church, has been an important force in the worldwide spread of Protestantism since the 19th century.

France

Religion	Followers in 1970	Followers in 2010	% of Population	Annual % growth 2000–2010	Followers in 2025	Followers in 2050
Christians	42,558,000	42,990,000	68.8	0.47	41,351,000	38,820,000
Roman Catholics	44,579,000	45,240,000	72.4	0.24	43,220,000	40,775,000
Independents	279,000	1,550,000	2.5	1.17	1,950,000	2,000,000
Protestants	860,000	1,350,000	2.2	0.25	1,600,000	1,800,000
Agnostics	4,575,000	10,078,000	16.1	1.10	12,600,000	15,900,000
Muslims	1,353,000	5,250,000	8.4	0.60	6,700,000	7,500,000
Atheists	1,524,000	2,500,000	4.0	0.69	3,200,000	3,800,000
Jews	550,000	610,000	1.0	0.60	600,000	600,000
Buddhists	27,000	480,000	0.8	0.60	600,000	800,000
Chinese folk	30,000	245,000	0.4	3.19	300,000	350,000
New religionists	70,000	160,000	0.3	0.59	200,000	250,000
Ethnoreligionists	50,000	113,000	0.2	0.60	110,000	120,000
Hindus	20,000	50,000	0.1	0.60	70,000	85,000
Spiritists	12,000	26,000	0.0	0.60	30,000	36,000
Baha'is	3,100	4,500	0.0	0.60	7,000	8,500
Zoroastrians	400	650	0.0	0.60	800	1,000
Total population	**50,772,000**	**62,507,000**	**100.0**	**0.60**	**65,769,000**	**68,270,000**

Existing along with Christianity are "foreign" religions, imported through migration: Judaism, Islam, and various Asian religious groups. The presence of Jews dates to the late Middle Ages. They encountered a challenging integration in France, due to a long-lasting tradition of anti-Semitism. Jews acquired French citizenship in 1790–1791 and soon benefited from the official recognition of their religious life owing to integrative laws (1808) and later antidiscrimination laws (1846). Anti-Semitism then gained renewed life as a popular and influential movement in the late 19th century, culminating in the Dreyfus Affair, which began with the unjust sentencing of a Jewish officer, Alfred Dreyfus (1859–1935), to life in prison for treason (1895). A national movement led by some of France's greatest intellectuals fought to exonerate him, and anticlericalism was strengthened by the role the Catholic Church was perceived as having played in his ordeal. Nevertheless, the 1930s crisis reinforced anti-Semitism, and the collaborationist government of Vichy during World War II joined the Nazis in deporting many French Jews to concentration camps. In the second half of the 20th century, the massive settling of migrants from North Africa led to a revitalization of Jewish faith in France, especially propelled by the Jews of Algeria. Following independence in 1962, the Algerian government moved to suppress the Jewish community by, among other actions, depriving Jews of their economic rights. As a result, almost 130,000 Algerian Jews immigrated to France. At the end of the 20th century, Jews made up approximately one percent of the total population of France (some 600,000).

The 1989's "veil" affair (two young Muslim schoolgirls refused to remove their traditional veil, or *hijab*, in school) propelled Islam (mainly Sunnis of the Malikite School) to the forefront of public debates. Islam came to France with the migration influxes of the 1960s from Morocco (one million), Tunisia, and Algeria (more than one million), as well as Turkey (200,000) and sub-Saharan African countries. The Muslim community now includes some 4 to 5 million adherents. It is the largest Muslim presence in Western Europe, and the most substantial since medieval Spain. There are only less than a dozen formal mosques, but between 1,600 and 2,000 less formal prayer and worship centers. The Grand Mosque in Paris serves as a symbolic center of the rather diverse community, but has faced internal tensions regarding the issue of the diversity of denominational and ethnic trends in French Islam. Since the mid-1970s, socially and sometimes politically active Muslim movements have emerged among the migrants and their naturalized offspring, who are

FRANCE

torn between marginalization and integration, and who suffer an enduring xenophobic stigmatization because of their native religion. The multiplication of places of worship, the increasing number of French converts, and the argument against the principles of laïcité by some Muslim groups in France have motivated political considerations concerning religious pluralism. Since the early 2000s, the French model of assimilation, by which citizenship is predominantly based upon denomination and ethnicity, is slowly and difficultly shifting toward a model of multiculturalism, inspired by the Anglo-Saxon experiences.

Asian religions entered the French soil through migration influxes, mainly from the French ex-colonies of

Laos, Vietnam, and Cambodia (Indochina), carrying Buddhism (from 350,000 to 500,000 adherents) and other forms of beliefs and practices (Daoism, Confucianism, and more recent indigenous groups such as Caodism). The United Buddhist Church transferred its headquarters from Vietnam to rural France. The International Zen Association is a large international Japanese Zen movement headquartered in Paris. Hindu immigrants from India and Tamil refugees from Sri Lanka number around 50,000 adherents.

Another and last face of the French religious landscape is the development of new religious movements beginning in the 1950s, including various Asian movements that have spread through the West in the last generation (the Unification Movement, Transcendental Meditation, the International Society for Krishna Consciousness) as well as Western Esoteric groups (Rosicrucians, Fratenité Blanche Universelle, the Acropole) and several uniquely French groups and organizations (Invitation à la Vie [IVI], the Aumist Religion [Mandarom], Ares). The increase in numbers of New Age, or "alternative," movements (more than 300 groups with from several dozens to thousands of members) and the controversy that began in the mid-1990s (following the murder and suicide deaths of members of the Solar Temple) about "sects" has focused public debates on issues of religious freedom, denominational pluralism, and secularization in France. The result has been the passing of a series of laws aimed as suppressing the "sects" in France, with the Jehovah's Witnesses, the Church of Scientology, the Aumists, and the Buddhist movement Soka Gakkai International being primary targets. The UNADFI (Union Nationale des Associations de Défense de la Famille et de l'Individu) is struggling against the sectarian groups supposed to disregard the laws and norms of French society. In 1998, the government launched a Mission Interministérielle de Lutte contre les Sectes (MILS), replaced in 2002 by a Mission Interministérielle de Vigilance et de Lutte contre les Dérives Sectaires (MIVILUDES), whose mission is to watch over the developments of these "alternative" spiritualities.

As a final point, mention must be made of the subtle but ongoing persistence of indigenous beliefs in overseas French territories (French Polynesia and Guyana, as well as islands such as Réunion, Martinique, and Guadeloupe), despite their formal conversion to Roman Catholicism.

Lionel Obadia

See also: Adventism; Atheism; Aumist Religion; Baptists; Church of Scientology; Church of the Augsburg Confession of Alsace and Lorraine; Evangelical Lutheran Church of France; Fratenité Blanche Universelle; Freethought; Friends/Quakers; Humanism; International Society for Krishna Consciousness; International Zen Association; Jehovah's Witnesses; Malikite School of Islam; Mennonites; New Age Movement; Pentecostalism; Reformed Church of Alsace and Lorraine; Reformed Church of France; Reformed/Presbyterian Tradition; Roman Catholic Church; Soka Gakkai International; Solar Temple, Order of the; Unification Movement; Unified Buddhist Church.

References

Annuaire de la France Protestante. Paris: Fédération Protestante de France, issued annually.

Boyer, Alain. *L'Islam en France*. Paris: Presses Universitaires de France, 1998.

Cholvy, Gérard. *La religion en France, de la fin du XVIIIe à nos jours*. Paris: Hachette, 1991.

Introvigne, Massimo, and J. Gordon Melton, eds. *Pour en finir avec les sectes: Le débat sur le rapport de la commission parlementaire*. Paris: Dervy, 1996.

"Les religions dans la société." *Cahiers français*. Paris: La Documentation française Editions, no. 340, September–October 2007.

Messner, Francis, Pierre-Henri Prélot, and Jean-Marie Woehrling, eds. *Traité de droit français des religions*. Paris: Editions du Juris-Classeur, 2003.

Vernette, Jean, and Claire Moncelon. *Dictionnaire des groupes religieux aujourd'hui*. Paris: Presses Universitaires de France, 1995.

Willaime, Jean-Paul, *Europe et religions: les enjeux du XXIe siècle*. Paris: Fayard, 2004.

Francis of Assisi

ca. 1182–1226

One of the most beloved figures in Western Christian history, Francis of Assisi is revered by Protestants as a

Saint Francis of Assisi talks to the birds, engraving from a 13th-century psalter. (iStockPhoto.com)

gentle soul and venerated by Roman Catholics as a saint. Best known as the founder of the Franciscan Order, now existing in multiple branches, he is acknowledged for his championing of the virtue of poverty in the religious life and for his concern for animals and nature. His best recognized literary work is also the first known Italian poem/hymn, the "Canticle to the Sun."

Francis was born in Assisi, in the Province of Perugia, in central Italy, around 1181 or 1182, the son of Pietro and Pica di Bernadone. His father was relatively wealthy with income derived from trade in cloth, banking, and land ownership. Francis traveled widely from his home in Assisi in his early years, enjoyed parties, and had a fighting streak. He wanted to become a knight. He also seems to have had a right inner life

from an early age and people knew him as a person who experienced vivid dreams and even visions.

At one point, he became a soldier and was captured in battle. Following his repatriation, he began to spend times in prayer. He developed a piety built around fasting and alms giving. This new turn, however, did not stop his return to the battlefield. On his way, he stopped by a long-neglected church building, the chapel of San Damiano. While at prayer, he heard what he understood to be the voice of Christ speaking to him. He took the words he heard, "Rebuild my church," quite literally. Reversing his course, he returned to Assisi, where he sold some expensive bolts of cloth and gave the proceeds to the priest in charge of the chapel.

His angry father took Francis to court. The trial was held before the local bishop. Francis reacted to the whole proceeding by stripping naked and renouncing his inheritance. He subsequently donned a simple robe with a hood (later to become the common habit of the Franciscan Order). Now on his own, he began to engage in the physical rebuilding of some chapels in Perugia. During a worship service at the chapel of Santa Maria degli Angeli, known as the Portiuncula ("Little Portion"), he again heard Jesus speak: "Preach as you go, saying, 'The kingdom of heaven is at hand'" (Matthew 10:17). Though an untutored layman, he began to preach. He attracted a group of young men, most of noble birth, around him. As their numbers grew, they spread out in pairs and preached through central Italy and into France and Spain.

The emergence of this group around Francis occurred contemporaneously with the appearance of a variety of medieval movements that had received negative attention from the church due to their heretical notions and extraordinary piety. Aware of the church's reaction to these other movements, Francis and some of his associates traveled to Rome in 1209 to ask papal approval for what would be a new religious order. In initial conversations with officials at the Vatican, he was told to adopt the rules of the more established orders. Francis rejected the suggestions, as he had a very different order in mind. He not only wanted members of the order to take personal vows of poverty, chastity, and obedience; he wanted the order collectively to renounce ownership of property. Rather than reside in one place (as a monastic order), he wanted the brother to itinerate around the countryside, without a home. The ideal of poverty would be thorough. It would allow them to concentrate on their work, identify with common people, and preach the gospel simply.

Francis offered a simple rule designed to copy the life of the Apostles as portrayed in the New Testament and emphasizing love of God and one's neighbor. The brothers were supposed to preach to the poor and oppressed while attempting to alleviate the suffering of the sick and homeless. Finally, Pope Innocent III (r. 1198–1216) granted his tentative approval. The order now experienced a spurt of growth, attracting many young men and even a few women. Most notably, Clare di Favarone, a young noble woman of Assisi, adopted Francis's life and became the founder of the second Franciscan order called the Poor Clares. Laypeople attracted to Francis, but not ready to accept the full life of a wandering mendicant, formed a spiritual association called the Brothers and Sisters of Penance.

The Franciscan movement was taking shape. The Benedictines, who owned the Chapel of Santa Maria degli Angeli, would give it to the brothers as a mother church. The Poor Clares would adopt a life similar to cloistered Benedictines and would receive San Damiano as a home base. The Brothers and Sisters of Penance would evolve into the Franciscan Third Order and would early on become known for using their wealth to assist victims of war and purchasing medicine for the poor. In 1219, some 3,000 friars arrived in Assisi for the annual meeting of the order held each Pentecost.

In 1213 Francis made the first of several international journeys to preach to the Muslims in Spain. In 1219 he made his way to Egypt where Crusaders were fighting the forces of the sultan al-Malik al-Kamil (1180–1238). Francis found a way to slip through the battle lines and engage the sultan in conversations. The following year found him in Acre, Palestine, one of the cities most in contention during the Crusades.

While in Acre, Francis learned of a controversy that was splitting his order in Italy. Church leaders were never happy with the challenge Francis presented to their often opulent life in spite of their personal renouncing of ownership of property and wealth. Bowing to pressure, the brothers had, in Francis's absence, amended the rules to allow corporate ownership of property. Unable to reimpose the rule on absolute poverty, Francis resigned his leadership in favor of Peter of Catanio (d. 1221). Francis continued attempts to amend the rule, but failed to reinstitute the older strictures relative to poverty. The rule was finally approved by Pope Honorius III (r. 1216–1227) in 1223.

Francis's association with animals comes from the later phase of his life. At one point, while on retreat, he staged a re-enactment of the birth of Christ in a cave using live animals. That event was followed by his distributing food to the poor and to the local stable animals. This became an annual tradition. Today, because of Francis, many Catholic and other churches hold annual blessings for animals.

Francis's visionary life also persisted into his later years. Most notably, in 1224 while in retreat with Francis, Brother Leo observed the appearance of an angel who imposed upon Francis the stigmata (the five wounds Christ received on his body during the crucifixion). Francis became the first person in Christian history known to experience this phenomenon, though a number would experience it in successive centuries.

Francis died October 3, 1226, at Assisi. At the moment of death, he lay on the ground naked, as he had requested. The cause of his death was the multiple diseases he had acquired in his travels, including tuberculosis and probably leprosy.

Francis's influence remains strong. The three orders created in his lifetime grew into large international organizations and were particularly important in the spread of Catholicism around the world. A number of additional orders have emerged over the centuries following the Franciscan rule, both within the Roman Catholic Church and among Anglicans and Lutherans.

His love of animals and nature led to his "Canticle to the Sun," a hymn on God and his creation:

Be praised, my Lord, with all your creatures,
Especially my master Brother Sun,
Through whom he gives us the day and through
    whom light shines.
He is beautiful and radiant with great splendor;
Of you, most High, he is the symbol.

Interestingly enough, the literary piece most associated with Francis, a prayer to peace, is a much later anonymous literary production ascribed to Francis in the 20th century.

> Lord, make me an instrument of Thy peace;
> where there is hatred, let me sow love;
> where there is injury, pardon;
> where there is doubt, faith;
> where there is despair, hope;
> where there is darkness, light;
> and where there is sadness, joy.

This prayer became well known during and immediately after World War II as a result of its wide distribution by Archbishop Francis Cardinal Spellman of New York.

Pope Gregory IX (r. 1227–1241) canonized Francis in 1229. Roman Catholics celebrate his feast day on October 4.

J. Gordon Melton

See also: Franciscans; Roman Catholic Church.

References

Cunningham, Lawrence L. *Francis of Assisi: Performing the Gospel Life*. Grand Rapids, MI: William B. Eerdmans Publishing Company, 2004.

House, Adrian, and Karen Armstrong. *Francis of Assisi: A Revolutionary Life*. Mahwah, NJ: Paulist Press, 2003.

Moorman, J. R. H. *Sources for the Life of St. Francis of Assisi*. Manchester: Manchester University, 1940.

Short, William, Regis J. Armstrong, and Wayne J. Hellman. *Francis of Assisi: Early Documents*. 3 vols. Hyde Park, NY: New City Press, 2002.

Francis Xavier

1506–1552

Francis Xavier, a first-generation Jesuit priest, was a pioneer Roman Catholic missionary to Asia. He established the church in India and Japan and prepared the way for the re-entrance of Christianity into China.

Francis was born April 7, 1506, in Navarre. During the war that added Navarre to the new united Spain, the castle of the Francis's family was destroyed (1512). Sent to Paris for his college education, he met Ignatius Loyola while at the Sorbonne. Xavier became one of Loyola's close associates and was one of the original members of the Jesuit Order (the Society of Jesus) who took their vows with him on August 15, 1534.

Meanwhile Xavier earned his doctorate and became a college professor. He settled at Venice and was ordained while there in 1537. In 1540, King John of Portugal called for priests to serve in India, where the Portuguese had been establishing colonies for several decades. Xavier volunteered to go and was named apostolic nuncio (papal ambassador with the authority of an archbishop) to Asia. He sailed for India in 1541 and reached Goa in 1542. He initially settled at Cape Comorin to work among the pearl-fishers. He assumed leadership of the Jesuit college, and in 1544 Loyola named him the first provincial of the Society of Jesus in Goa. In 1545, he further expanded his mission by moving to Malaysia (Malacca) and Indonesia (the Moluccas).

The most famous segment of his life began in 1547, when he encountered a Japanese man named Yajio. Yajio convinced Xavier to establish work in Japan and subsequently became his translator. He arrived in Japan in 1549 and was given some limited freedom to preach by the local ruler (daimyo) at Kagoshima. With Yajiro's help, he produced a catechism in Japanese.

While in Japan, Xavier developed a vision of evangelizing China. To that end, in 1552, he moved to Shangchuan, an island near Canton. He would die there December 3, 1552, while waiting to gain entrance into the Chinese kingdom. He was buried in the Good Jesus Church at Goa, India.

Xavier's work was all the more notable as it brought good news to Rome about the expansion of the church at the very time it was suffering setbacks due to the Muslim invasion of Europe along the Danube and the loss of much of Northern Europe to the Protestant Reformation. The church would expand rapidly throughout Asia through the century following Francis's death. Pope Paul V (r. 1605–1621) beatified Xavier in 1619, and just three years later, Pope Gregory XV (r. 1621–1623) canonized him (at the same time Francis's mentor Ignatius Loyola was canonized). Today Francis is hailed as the patron saint of missionaries. The Roman Catholic Church celebrates his feast day on December 3.

The work initiated by Xavier continues in India, Malaysia, Japan, and China. In the half century after Xavier's death, a Christian community of some 300,000 emerged in Japan. Then, in 1614, the shogun banned the faith. Christianity went underground and survived until the opening of Japan in the 19th century. A new generation of missionaries discovered communities of "hidden Christians" at various locations across the country.

J. Gordon Melton

See also: Ignatius of Loyola; Jesuits; Roman Catholic Church.

References

Brodrick, James. *A Biography of St. Francis Xavier.* New York: Wicklow, 1952.

Schurhammer, Georg. *Francis Xavier: His Life, His Times.* Rome: Jesuit Historical Institute, 1973.

Venn, Henry. *The Missionary Life and Labours of Francis Xavier Taken from His Own Correspondence: with a sketch of the general results of Roman Catholic missions among the heathen.* Ithaca, NY: Cornell University Library, 1862; rpt. Whitefish, MT: Kessinger Publishing, 2007.

Xavier, Francis. *The Letters and Instructions of Francis Xavier.* St. Louis: Institute of Jesuit Sources, 1992.

Franciscans

The Order of Friars Minor is the primary group referred to by the designation Franciscan. There are also two other groups: the order of contemplative nuns popularly known as the Poor Clares (or Second Order) and a lay order, the Third Order of St. Francis. The Order of Friars Minor traces its beginning to Saint Francis of Assisi (ca. 1181–1226). As a young man from a well-to-do family, he felt a call to "rebuild Christ's church" and to live the renounced life: poverty, preaching the gospel, and penance. Others were attracted to him, and he authored a rule that was, according to the order's tradition, verbally approved by Pope Innocent III (r. 1198–1216) in 1209, the founding date of the order.

The rule underwent a number of revisions over the next century, some caused by the need to adapt the rule to the quickly growing membership, the need to interpret ambiguous parts of the text, and the question of how property was to be handled in light of Francis's rather austere understanding of poverty. The legal and practical problems of handling possessions caused tensions in the order for decades, though some moderation was found during the leadership of Saint Bonaventura (1217–1274), considered the order's second founder. The tendency to adopt a more absolutist position on poverty, however, continued to attract many Franciscans. The next generation of the more radical Franciscans was called the Spirituals, and they were vigorously suppressed by the church.

In the 14th century, laxity in the main body of the order led to the emergence of a new subgroup, the Observants, who tended to retire to remote locations where they could practice the rule of Saint Francis in all its austerity. By the end of the century the movement had spread from Italy to France and Spain. Gradually a split developed between the main body of the order, the Conventuals, and the Observants, officially recognized in 1517. The Observants, which constituted the majority of the Franciscans at the time of the split, became the base of other reforming efforts that further split the order. Most of these additional reformed groups were reunited into the Observant branch of the order in 1897. The union of 1897 left three major branches of Franciscans—the Conventuals, the Observants, and the Capuchins (officially recognized in 1619).

In the meantime, the Franciscan movement had spread throughout the known world. Franciscans spread across Europe, were given special responsibility for the Holy Land, and founded the first Catholic churches in China. In the 18th century, the Jesuits had taken the lead in the Catholic Church's missionary work outside Europe, especially in the Americas. Thousands of Franciscans moved to the Americas in the 17th century, and after the Jesuits were suppressed in 1773, Franciscans were in most cases called to take their place. The international role of the Franciscans continued through the 19th century (in spite of ups and downs in various

Ruins of the Franciscan monastery of San Francisco, built between 1512 and 1544, in Santo Domingo, Dominican Republic. (Corel)

particular locations), and by the middle of the 20th century their centers could be found in more than 135 countries. Since the 1960s, they have reasserted an emphasis on ministering to the poor.

The Order of Friars Minor (continuing the Observant tradition) has its international center at Mediatrice 25, I-00165 Rome, Italy. It has a website at http://www.ofm.org/.

The Order of Friars Minor Capuchins has its international center at Curia Generalis Ord. Min. Cap. Via Piemonte 70, I-00187 Rome, Italy. It has several websites sponsored by the different Provinces, including http://capuchin.org and http://www.capuchinfriars.org .au. The order is currently active in 76 countries. The most famous Capuchin in the 20th century was undoubtedly Padre Pio, an Italian monk noted for his having the stigmata, the five wounds of Christ, in his hands, feet, and side. Although a number of cases of the stigmata have been reported over the centuries, he

was the first priest in the history of the church in which they were manifest. He was beatified (a step toward sainthood) by Pope John Paul II on May 2, 1999.

The Order of Friars Minor Conventuals has its international center at Piazza SS. Apostoli 51, I-000187, Rome, Italy.

Contemporaneous with the founding of the Franciscans, a counterpart for females, the Poor Clares, was founded by Saint Francis and Saint Clare (1194–1243) in 1214. Cardinal Ugolino (later Pope Gregory IX) gave the order its first rule in 1219. Over the centuries, like their male counterpart, the Clares split into several branches. The Urbanists follow the rule of Pope Urban IV (1263), which allows some exemption from corporate poverty as well as personal poverty; the Collettines are named after Saint Collette, who restored the principle of corporate poverty in her houses in the 15th century. A Capuchin branch originated in the 16th century, paralleling developments in the male branches of the order. Most of the convents of the Poor Clares are purely contemplative and are strictly enclosed.

J. Gordon Melton

See also: Capuchins; Francis of Assisi; Jesuits; Monasticism; Roman Catholic Church.

References

Carmody, Maurice. *The Franciscan Story*. Twicjenham, UK: Athena Press, 2008.

Hanley, Boniface, and Salvator Fink. *The Franciscans: Love at Work*. Patterson, NJ: St. Anthony Guild Press, 1962.

Jackson, Robert H., and Edward Castillo. *Indians, Franciscans, and Spanish Colonization: The Impact of the Mission System on California Indians*. Albuquerque: University of New Mexico Press, 1996.

Pitchford, Susan. *Following Francis: The Franciscan Way for Everyone*. New York: Morehouse Publishing, 2006.

Robson, Michael. *St Francis of Assisi: The Legend and the Life*. London: Geoffrey Chapman, 2000.

Frankel, Zachariah

1801–1875

Zachariah Frankel was a German Jewish theologian who sought a means to introduce reforms in Jewish life and worship without giving in to the more radical program of Reform Judaism. He developed what was termed the Positive Historical School of Jewish thought that would lead to Conservative Judaism.

Frankel was born September 30, 1801, in Prague (now the Czech Republic) and inherited rabbinical lineages on both sides of his family. After studying at the local yeshiva, in 1925 he entered the university at Budapest. He was ordained a rabbi and in 1836 became the chief rabbi at Dresden. He was early on attracted to the Reform cause, but soon became unenamored with the extremes he saw it taking. In 1845 he walked out of a Reform conference that was discussing the elimination of Hebrew from the Sabbath service. He would later become the rabbi in Leipzig, Germany, and director of the rabbinical seminary in Breslau.

Frankel arrived at what would be his mature position by 1859 when he published *Darkhei HaMishnah* (*The Ways of the Mishnah*). Based upon his broad survey of traditional texts, he concluded that Jewish law developed as a response to changing historical conditions. By the term "Positive Historical Judaism," he was asserting that Jews had developed an ability to be committed to Jewish law (halakhah) as well as a rational faith, and, most important, the idea that the authority of Jewish law rested on its use by Jews over the generations. To bolster his opinion, he demonstrated in great detail how Judaism had changed and evolved over the centuries. The clear implication was that while the Torah may be of divine origin and hence true, the Jewish community has taken charge of the emergent Jewish legal system.

Frankel's basic position would become the philosophical foundation later taken to America upon which Conservative Judaism would emerge a generation later. The Conservative position views the community as the active agent in determining the shape of Jewish belief and practice generation by generation.

Frankel died in Breslau on February 13, 1875.

J. Gordon Melton

See also: Conservative Judaism; Reform Judaism.

References

Gillamn, Neil. *Conservative Judaism: The New Century*. Springfield, NJ: Behrman House, Inc., 1993.

Meyer, Michael A. *Response to Modernity: A History of the Reform Movement in Judaism*. Oxford: Oxford University Press, 1988.

Fraternité Blanche Universelle

The Fraternité Blanche Universelle (Universal White Brotherhood) grew out of the White Brotherhood that had been founded in Bulgaria at the beginning of the 20th century by Peter Deunov (1864–1944). In 1937, as the movement peaked, the aging Deunov sent Omraam Michael Aivanhov (1900–1986), one of his accomplished students, to Paris to open a center. His settlement in Paris was quickly followed by World War II, Deunov's death, and the rise of Soviet power in

Bulgaria. With the suppression of the movement in its land of origin, Aivanhov emerged as the leader of the movement in the West and a spiritual teacher in his own right.

The ultimate authority for the White Brotherhood is believed to be a fraternity of highly evolved beings who reside on a higher plane of existence. The earthly organization is seen as a visible reflection of this invisible Brotherhood, and the leadership is believed to be in contact with its members. The purpose of the Brotherhood is to pass on the eternal religion of Christ; it continues the tradition of the Church of St. John, considered by many as the genuine embodiment of Christian spirituality. The Church of St. John is seen as following the spirit rather than the letter of Christ's teaching (which the visible Church of St. Peter is seen as following). This tradition embodies a Christian version of Western Esotericism.

Aivanhov teaches that the goal of one's life is to know oneself, to unite one's human self with the divine self. Having made that connection, one is attuned to the White Brotherhood and ready to participate in the great work. The masters of the Brotherhood are attempting to bring the kingdom of God into reality on Earth. Aivanhov expounded on this basic idea at length in his writings and public discourses. These are published in two collections, *The Complete Works* (35 volumes) and the *Izvor Collection* (36 volumes).

Aivanhov's works are published in several languages by Editions Prosveta. In the decades following the war, the Brotherhood expanded in France, where it now has some 5,000 members and began to establish centers in other French-speaking countries. In the early 1980s the first center was opened in the United States. In 2008, it reported work in 23 countries, including countries in Western Europe, North and South America, and Africa. The largest concentration of members remains in French-speaking countries such as France (5,000) and Quebec (4,000). Since Aivanhov's death, the Brotherhood has developed a decentralized leadership. Anyone may join the Brotherhood and participate in its activities of spreading the teachings and attend the congresses held several time annually.

Universal White Brotherhood
2, rue du Belvedere de la Ronce

92310 Sèvres
France
http://www.fbu.org/

J. Gordon Melton

See also: Western Esoteric Tradition; White Brotherhood.

References

Feuerstein, Georg. *The Mystery of Light: The Life and Teachings of Omraam Michael Aivanhov.* Salt Lake City, UT: Passage Press, 1992.

Lejbowicz, Agnes. *Omraam Michael Aivanhov, Master of the Great White Brotherhood.* Fréjus, France: Editions Prosveta, 1982.

Renard, Opierre. *The Solar Revolution and the Prophet.* Fréjus, France: Editions Prosveta, 1980.

Who Is Omraam Michael Aivanhov? Fréjus, France: Editions Prosveta, 1982.

Fraternity/Society of Saint Pius X

The Fraternity, or Society, of Saint Pius X is a large body of traditionalist Roman Catholics, regarded by the Vatican as schismatic although an ongoing dialogue aimed at a reconciliation is in process. Monsignor Marcel Lefebvre (1905–1991), a French Roman Catholic missionary priest working in Africa, became first a bishop there, then the apostolic delegate for the whole of French-speaking Africa, and finally archbishop of Dakar in 1955. In 1962, he returned to France to become bishop of Tulle, while at the same time remaining superior general of his missionary religious order, the Fathers of the Holy Spirit. He resigned in 1968, however, finding himself unwilling to cooperate with the *aggiornamento* program requested for religious orders by the Second Vatican Council. In 1970, he opened near Fribourg, Switzerland, a seminary for young Catholic men seeking a "traditional" preparation for the priesthood. After a few months, the seminary moved to Ecône, in the Swiss Diocese of Sion, where the bishop had already granted his approval and incorporation of Lefebvre's organization as the Fraternity of Saint Pius X. In 1974, however, the Vatican started to investigate complaints that the seminary was offering a formation program incompatible

Catholic Archbishop Marcel Lefebvre in 1977. Lefebvre founded the Society of Saint Pius X in 1970. (AP Photo)

with the Second Vatican Council, and in 1975 an ad hoc commission of cardinals requested Lefebvre to refrain from performing further priestly ordinations. He rejected the injunction, however, and on June 29, 1976, defied the Vatican by ordaining 13 new priests.

On July 22, 1976, the Vatican suspended Lefebvre from his functions as bishop and as priest (a lesser sanction than excommunication; Lefebvre was not excommunicated and was still recognized as a Catholic in good standing, but no longer authorized to operate as a bishop, or even as a priest).

A dialogue, in fact, continued between Lefebvre and Rome, and on May 15, 1988, it seemed to have achieved its goal, when the French bishop signed the preliminary version of an agreement making the Fraternity of Saint Pius X an independent organization within the Roman Catholic Church, headed by a bishop selected by the Vatican from the Fraternity's own

ranks (although other than Lefebvre) and authorized to celebrate the pre–Second Vatican Council Catholic Mass. Several of Lefebvre's key aides regarded the agreement as unacceptable, however, and on June 19, 1988, negotiations were interrupted. On June 20, Lefebvre initiated what Rome regarded as a schism, by consecrating, without Vatican authorization, four new bishops (Bernard Fellay [b. 1958], Bernard Tissier de Mallerais [b. 1945], Richard N. Williamson [b. 1940], and Alfonso de Galarreta [b. 1957]). This time, he was promptly excommunicated, together with the conservative Brazilian bishop Antonio de Castro Mayer (1904–1991), who had assisted Lefebvre in the consecration ceremony. On July 2, 1988, Pope John Paul II (r. 1978–2005) published the apostolic letter *Ecclesia Dei*, in which he denounced the new schism, but left a door open to dialogue and allowed Lefebvre's ex-followers who wished to remain in communion with

Rome to obtain a special status and be authorized to celebrate the old Catholic liturgy.

Although separated from Rome, the Fraternity (incorporated in the United States as the Society of Saint Pius X) grew, creating several new male and female religious orders along its path (again, not recognized by the Vatican). It currently has 6 seminaries (in Switzerland, Germany, France, the United States, Argentina, and Australia), 162 homes in 31 countries, 2 universities, 20 high schools, and 50 elementary schools, as well as 486 priests, 192 seminarians, and some 100 male and 240 female members of the religious orders it has created. The Catholic Jubilee year 2000 saw the opening of a new dialogue between the Fraternity and the Vatican, and in March 2001 the Holy See officially confirmed that negotiations were in progress. An obstacle to the dialogue in the 2000s was the affair of the Brotherhood of Saint Josaphat, a traditionalist Ukrainian group of Roman Catholics of the Greek rite, founded in 2000 by Father Vasyl Kovpak. Its 40 priests and seminarians, and 25,000 lay members, are critics of the Second Vatican Council and are now part of the Fraternity of Saint Pius X. Kovpak and his followers were excommunicated by the Vatican in 2007.

In fact, although the media often report that the main disagreement between the Fraternity and Rome is liturgy, and the Fraternity's wish to celebrate the old Mass, there are in fact several other problems that have not yet been resolved. During his last years (he died in 1991), Lefebvre insisted that he regarded Second Vatican Council teachings on religious liberty as the most critical issue. Religious liberty was a notion he rejected for both theological and political reasons. He was also a staunch opponent of ecumenism and interreligious dialogue, which he regarded as conducive to relativism. In the course of its ongoing dialogue with the Fraternity, the Vatican has been quite open on liturgical questions, while the other issues have understandably proved more problematical.

On July 7, 2007, Pope Benedict XVI (b. 1927) published a *motu proprio* (a personal communication issued by the pope) called *Summorum Pontificum*, which significantly liberalized the rules for Catholic priests to celebrate the old Tridentine Mass in Latin. This was seen as a first step toward a reconciliation with the Fraternity, which issued a statement of appreciation for the pope's move. Then in March 2009, Benedict rescinded the excommunication issued against the four bishops that Lefebvre had consecrated in 1988. This action unleashed a storm of controversy as he apparently was unaware that one of the bishops, Richard N. Williamson, had on several occasions publicly denied that six million Jews had been killed in the Nazi Holocaust. Williamson apologized for his remarks, but the issue remains unresolved (2009) as Benedict turned his attention to repairing his relationship with the Jewish community.

Fraternity/Society of Saint Pius X
Priorat Mariæ Verkündigung
Schwandegg, CH-6313 Menzingen
Switzerland
http://www.sspx.org
Massimo Introvigne and PierLuigi Zoccatelli

See also: Roman Catholic Church.

References
Lefebvre, Marcel. *A Bishop Speaks: Writings and Addresses, 1963–1975.* Kansas City, MO: Angelus Press, 2000.
Lefebvre, Marcel. *I Accuse the Council.* Kansas City, MO: Angelus Press, 1998.
Lefebvre, Marcel. *Open Letter to Confused Catholics.* Kansas City, MO: Angelus Press, 1999.

Free Churches

As developed in the 18th century, the term "Free church" referred to those Protestant Christian churches that operated free of entanglements with the state governments of Europe. Free churches had emerged at the time of the Protestant Reformation, when leaders of the Swiss Brethren called for a more radical reformation of the church than that being asked for by Martin Luther (1483–1546), Ulrich Zwingli (1484–1531), and later John Calvin (1509–1564). They wanted a pure church consisting of adults who had been converted to Christianity and who had made a conscious decision to affiliate with the church. By definition, such a church could not be coterminous with the state

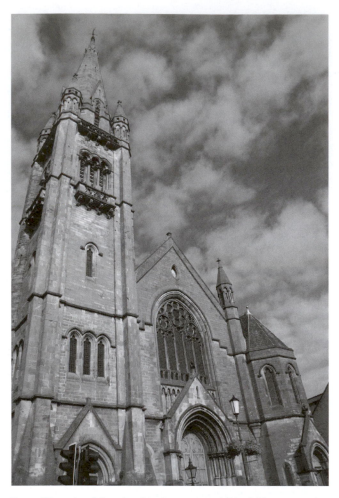

Free Church of Scotland in Inverness. (iStockPhoto.com)

and include all of the citizens whether they had or wanted any relationship with God or not. In such a church, ecclesiastical discipline operated only among church members and was limited to expulsion of a misbehaving member from the church's fellowship.

A primary symbol of the Free church came to be adult baptism. State churches (including the Lutheran, Reformed, and Anglican) generally baptized the children of members soon after their birth. The Free churches generally baptized those who had reached an age at which they were deemed accountable for their Christian profession and had made such a profession. Members who had been previously baptized as infants were typically re-baptized.

The emphasis on baptism within the Free churches led to further concern about, for example, the proper mode of baptism, with many following the lead of the Baptists in opting for immersions. A few, including the Church of the Brethren, advocated triune immersion. Baptists divided over the necessity of the act of baptism for individual salvation.

The Free church impulse led first to the spread of the Mennonites and Baptists and then took form across Europe with the formation of such groups as the Friends (Quakers), the Mission Covenant Church of Sweden, the Evangelical Lutheran Free Church of Norway, and the Free Church of Scotland. In North America there were also the churches of the Restoration movement, the Churches of Christ, the Christian Churches and Churches of Christ, and the Christian Church (Disciples of Christ). In the 20th century, most Pentecostal churches have adopted the Free church approach to Christian community.

In the 19th century, the term "Free" was added to the name of various churches claiming additional freedoms. The Free Methodist Church of North America was an advocate both of immediately freeing African Americans held in slavery and of free pews (as opposed to other Methodist churches, which accepted a fee from members who wished to have a family pew in the local church building). "Free church" also came to mean without a creed (other than the Bible) or free of various forms of ecclesiastical hierarchy. Most Free churches have adopted a congregational polity, though originally the Congregational Church movement was not a Free church and remained tied to the state of Massachusetts into the 19th century. Groups such as the Churches of Christ and the Primitive Baptists have adopted an ultra-congregational polity, which limits any governance functions by structures above the local congregations. Other Free churches, such as the Southern Baptist Convention and the Christian Church (Disciples of Christ), grant denominational structures considerable power to build and control programs operated for the denomination as a whole.

In the last half of the 20th century, a new wave of Free churches adopted an anti-denominational stance that equated denominationalism with traditional hierarchical church governance (episcopal and presbyterian) and the multiplication of denominational boards and agencies. Most such anti-denominational denominations have organized as congregational associations.

J. Gordon Melton

See also: Baptists; Calvin, John; Christian Church (Disciples of Christ); Christian Churches and Churches of Christ; Church of the Brethren; Churches of Christ (Non-Instrumental) ; Evangelical Lutheran Free Church of Norway; Free Methodist Church of North America; Friends/Quakers; Luther, Martin; Mission Covenant Church of Sweden; Southern Baptist Convention.

References

Davies, Horton. *The English Free Churches.* 2nd ed. Oxford: Oxford University Press, 1963.

Harrison, Paul M. *Authority and Power in the Free Church Tradition.* Princeton, NJ: Princeton University Press, 1959.

Littell, Franklin H. *The Free Church.* Boston: Starr King Press, 1957.

Payne, Earnest A. *The Free Church Tradition in the Life of England.* London: SCM Press, 1951.

Westin, Gunnar. *The Free Church through the Ages.* Nashville: Broadman Press, 1958.

Wright, Nigel. *Free Church, Free State: The Positive Baptist Vision.* Colorado Springs, CO: Authentic, 2006.

Free Methodist Church of North America

The Free Methodist Church, one of the leading churches of the 19th-century Holiness movement, emerged as a conservative movement within the Methodist Episcopal Church (now a constituent part of the United Methodist Church) in the 1850s. Leaders of the movement felt that the main body of the church had slipped from Wesleyan standards, especially as related to an emphasis on the call to lead the sanctified life. Methodist founder John Wesley (1703–1791) had taught that it was possible to be sanctified in this life and had proposed that Christians should strive to be sanctified, to become perfect in love, in this life. Two signs of the Methodists' falling from this standard were the membership of many in secret societies and their toleration of slavery. Most of those who eventually made up the Free Methodist Church were abolitionist. The Methodist Episcopal Church, although against slavery generally, held that abolitionism was an extremist position.

The issues raised by the conservatives culminated when Reverend Benjamin Titus Roberts (1823–1893) and others were expelled from the church. They appealed to the General Conference that met in 1860. When their appeal was denied, they formed the Free Methodist Church. Their name related to another complaint of theirs, the selling of pews to particular church members. The Free Methodists declared that all the pews in their churches were freely open to all.

Formally, the Free Methodists had no doctrinal quarrel with its parent body. Increasingly, however, the Methodist Episcopal Church distanced itself from the particular version of the Holiness perspective that had been popularized in the church in the 19th century; the Free Methodists later added a statement on sanctification to the Twenty-five Articles of Religion, to which most Methodists adhere. A new set of articles of religion was adopted in 1974 that spelled out the Holiness perspective and gave the biblical references that underpin them. The church teaches that all Christians may be inwardly cleansed from sinful rebellion against God. This sanctification of the affections occurs instantaneously when believers, already having experienced justification from sin, in a moment of faith are open to the work of the Holy Spirit in their lives.

Outwardly the life of holiness includes conformity to a set of guidelines that the church feels should be normative for the Christian life. Church members refrain from alcohol, tobacco, and recreational drugs. They tithe their income. They refrain from membership in secret societies. They are antiracist. They hold marriage and sexual purity in high regard.

The church is organized with a modified episcopacy. The highest legislative body is the General Conference, consisting of an equal number of ministers and laity. The Conference elects the bishops (or general superintendents). The congregations are divided among annual conferences, which appoint ministers to their pastoral charges. In 1996, the church reported 74,059 members in the United States and 7,603 in Canada (2006). During the 19th century, the church joined in the world missions movement, and today 90 percent of its members are found in its conferences overseas, which reported 731,791 members (including the United States) in 34 countries (2008). The church is a member of the Christian Holiness Partnership and the National Association of Evangelicals, through which it is related to the World Evangelical Alliance.

Free Methodist Church of North America
World Ministries Center
770 North High School
Indianapolis, IN 46214
PO Box 535002
Indianapolis, IN 46253
http://www.fincna.org

J. Gordon Melton

See also: Christian Holiness Partnership; Holiness Movement; Wesley, John; World Evangelical Alliance.

References

Hogue, William T. *History of the Free Methodist Church.* 2 vols. Chicago: Free Methodist Publishing House, 1918.
McKenna, David L. *A Future with a History: The Wesleyan Witness of the Free Methodist Church, 1960–1995.* Winona Lake, IN: Light & Life Communications, 1997.
Marston, Leslie R. *From Age to Age a Living Witness.* Winona Lake, IN: Life and Light Press, 1960.
Roberts, Benjamin T. *Holiness Teachings.* Salem, OH: H. E. Schmul, 1964.
Snyder, Howard A. *Populist Saints.* Grand Rapids, MI: William B. Eerdmans Publishing Company, 2006.

Free Pentecostal Missions Church of Chile

Free Pentecostal Missions Church of Chile, one of three Pentecostal bodies in Chile that have joined the World Council of Churches, was founded in 1974 by Pentecostal Bishop Victor Labbe Dias, who felt led to begin independent evangelistic/missionary work. The constitution of the new fellowship was approved in 1977 and subsequently officially registered in the country. The beliefs and practices follow those of other Chilean Pentecostal churches, the differences being purely administrative. The church has identified with the poor in the country, and in the 30 years of its exis-

tence spread to all sections of the country, though membership is concentrated in the Biobio, Araucanía, and Los Rios districts (south-central Chile) among the Mapucho and Chilote peoples.

The church carries on an active program of evangelism and membership nurture with a social program primarily aimed as health issues. By 2005, the church reported 13,600 members in 45 congregations.

Casilla 349 Correa 3
Santiago
Chile

J. Gordon Melton

See also: Pentecostalism; World Council of Churches.

Reference

Van Beek, Huibert. *A Handbook of the Churches and Councils: Profiles of Ecumenical Relationships.* Geneva: World Council of Churches, 2006.

Free Wesleyan Church of Tonga

Methodism, now divided into four bodies, forms the largest religious community in the multi-island nation of Tonga, and the Free Wesleyan Church of Tonga is the largest of the four Methodist denominations. Methodist work on Tonga began in 1822, but the original missionary, Walter Lawry (1793–1859), had to withdraw after 14 months. On June 28, 1826, John Thomas (1769–1881) and John Hutchinson landed on Ha'atafu and settled in Kolovai. They had been preceded by two converts from Tahiti named Hope and Tafeta, who had started work on Nuku'alofa. As other missionaries (from Australia) arrived, the work spread to Ha'apai and Vava'u.

Success was scant until 1934, when the efforts of an early Tongan convert led to a mass conversion on Vava'u, and the success was soon repeated on Ha'apai. As it turned out, the ruler of Ha'apai, Taufa'ahau Tupouin, in the 1850s became the person who unified Tonga into a nation and became its first ruler. An admirer of the British, he chose the name George I, by which he was commonly known. He also encouraged his new subjects to become Christian, and by the end of the 1850s almost all Tongans were at least nominally Christians. Most Tongans were Methodists, though the Roman Catholic Church had established a small mission.

In 1890, the aging king and his prime minister, Shirley Baker (1836–1903), a former Methodist missionary, expressed their concern about the continuing control of the church from Australia. Their desire to break the administrative relationship led to a schism, and the king and his supporters formed the Wesleyan Free Church. Further, he ordered his subjects (as far as he could, given the religious freedom that had been proclaimed in 1855) to join it, and the Methodist Mission and the new church were bitter rivals for the next four decades. Finally in 1924 the new ruler, Queen Salote, worked out a reconciliation, and the two bodies merged to become the Tonga Conference of the Methodist Church of Australia. Some 6,000 people stayed out of the merger and formed the Free Church of Tonga.

The Tonga Conference continued its relationship with the Australian Methodists until 1977. The merger of the Australian Methodists into the Uniting Church in Australia became the occasion of the Tongan Conference becoming autonomous as the Free Wesleyan Church of Tonga. It sponsors an extensive education program that includes some 60 percent of the secondary education in the country.

During the 19th century, the Tongan church became crucial to the spread of Methodism through the South Pacific, as Tongan converts accompanied many Methodist missionaries, assisting in the foundation of the church in many island systems. In the 20th century, many Tongans migrated to New Zealand, Australia, and the United States, and congregations that retain their relationship directly with the Free Wesleyan Church can now be found in each of these countries.

The Free Wesleyan Church of Tonga is a member of the World Council of Churches. It has a baptized membership of approximately 38,692, but claims a constituency that would double that number.

Free Wesleyan Church of Tonga
PO Box 57
Nuku'alofa
Tonga

J. Gordon Melton

See also: Roman Catholic Church; Uniting Church in Australia; World Council of Churches.

References
Forman, Charles H. *The Island Churches of the South Pacific: Emergence in the Twentieth Century.* Maryknoll, NY: Orbis, 1982.
Loatoukefu, S. *Church and State in Tonga: The Influence of the Wesleyan Methodist Missionaries on the Political Development of Tonga, 1826–1875.* Canberra, Australia: Australian National University, 1967.
Rutherford, Noel. *Shirley Baker and the King of Tonga.* Honolulu: University of Hawaii Press, 1996.
Swain, Tony, and Garry Trompf. *The Religions of Oceania.* London: Routledge, 1995.
Van Beek, Huibert. *A Handbook of the Churches and Councils: Profiles of Ecumenical Relationships.* Geneva: World Council of Churches, 2006.
Wood, A. H. *Overseas Missions of the Australian Methodist Church.* 3 vols. Melbourne: Aldersgate Press, 1975–1978.

Freemasonry

Although there is much debate over the ties of modern Freemasonry to medieval guilds of stone masons, there is little doubt that what is today called Freemasonry emerged at the end of the 17th century with the formation of the lodges of speculative Freemasons in Great Britain culminating in the formation of the first Grand Lodge in 1717 by the merger of four previously existing lodges in England. These initial lodges had emerged as older Masonic organizations accepted non-Masons into their community. Devoid of any interest in erecting buildings, these non-Masons used their gatherings to speculate about metaphysical issues quite apart from the theological perspectives of either the Church of England or the other dissenting churches operating in the country at the time, choosing instead to follow the Western Esoteric teachings previously spread under the label of Rosicrucianism. Among the first prominent exponents of Western Esotericism

Freemasons membership certificate, 1861. (Library of Congress)

in England were Robert Fludd (1574–1637) and Elias Ashmole (1617–1692). The Reverend John Theophilus Desguliers, who became the grand master of the British lodge, was also chaplain to the prince of Wales, and his political connections facilitated the spread of the movement throughout the British Isles and into the European continent and beyond.

Grand Lodges were formed in Ireland in 1723 and in Scotland in 1736. The first speculative lodge was founded in Germany in 1733, and similar lodges were soon established in Italy and France. The first papal statements against Freemasonry were issued in 1738 and 1751. The Grand Lodge of Massachusetts was founded in 1733, and others followed beginning with South Carolina in 1737. The Masonic lodges would become hotbeds not only of metaphysical speculation but of new democratic political ideals. These Masonic ideals would flow through the salons of Paris in the decades prior to the French Revolution and would

become part of the consensus shared by many of the American revolutionaries. The Marquis de Lafayette was a Mason as was Benjamin Franklin (who largely financed the American Revolution) and future American presidents George Washington, James Madison, and James Monroe.

English Masons led in the founding of speculative lodges in France early in the 18th century. The first national French Masonic body, the English Grand Lodge of France, was formed in 1728. It operated under British leadership until 1738, when the duke of Antin became the first French grand master. During the 1730s, the French work became fully independent and took its present name, the Grand Lodge of France. The French work became important in the 19th century as Freethought became important to French intellectual and political culture. In 1849, the Grand Lodge declared that the existence of God and the immortality of the soul were foundational principles of Freemasonry. However, in 1877, the French declared that absolute liberty of conscience and the solidarity of humanity were the basic principles. At the same time, all references to God were removed from the rituals. These actions led to the British or American lodges severing relations with the French. The French action appeared to have been made in reaction to Catholic criticism that Freemasonry had become a rival religion.

Freemasonry operates through an initiatory system in which members are brought step by step into the basic ideas and practices, a basic worldview being presented in the initial three degrees. There are various elaborate degree systems, the most famous being the 33 degrees of the ancient and accepted rite, the system used in most British and American lodges. The cosmos is viewed as a series of levels that the soul travels through as it rises to the realm of the Divine.

The endpoint of metaphysical speculation is an omnipresent, eternal immutable principle beyond the conceptualization of language (which many call God). That principle finds expression in natural law. There also exists space and motion, concepts basic to all human perception. Underlying the cosmos is Spirit/consciousness, which manifests as both energy and matter. The cosmos is in eternal flux and creation proceeds as universal energy and proto-matter interact and produce the seven basic levels of existence. These seven levels—physical, life principle, astral, karma, manas, buddha, atmi—are also reflected in the individual. Masonic rituals provide the material to reflect upon the universe and humanity's rightful place within it.

There are a variety of rites (ritual schemes) used in the different Masonic lodges. A Grand Lodge unites lodges that use the same rite. A Grand Orient unites lodges that may use a variety of rites. The eastern star was founded in 1876 as a Masonic auxiliary for women, Masonry being basically a male endeavor. Through the 20th century several forms of Masonry termed Co-Masonry, which accepted female members, have been founded.

Today, the Masonic movement is organized in a set of national Grand Lodges and Grand Orients, the most prominent of which is the United Grand Lodge of England, the governing body of Freemasonry in England, Wales, and the Channel islands. The Supreme Council 33 Degrees of Ancient and Accepted Scottish Rite of Freemasonry of the Southern Jurisdiction of the United States of America is the leading American organization. Speculative Freemasonry has been an important transmitter of the Western Esoteric tradition, having been constructed from Rosicrucian teachings and serving as a basis for a spectrum of 19th-century Esoteric groups from Theosophy to ceremonial magic groups such as the Ordo Templi Orientis (OTO). To the present it raises questions about the religious nature of its teachings and the essential nature of the several grand lodges as religious bodies.

United Grand Lodge of England
Freemasons Hall
Great Queen St.
London WC2B 5AZ
UK
http://www.ugle.org.uk/

The Supreme Council, 33°
1733 16th St. NW
Washington, DC 20009-3105
http://www.srmason-sj.org/

J. Gordon Melton

See also: Ancient and Mystical Order Rosae Crucis; Ordo Templi Orientis; Theosophical Society (Adyar); Western Esoteric Tradition.

References

Dumenil, Lynn. *Freemasonry and American Culture, 1880–1930*. Princeton, NJ: Princeton University Press, 1984.

Gould, R. F. *History of Freemasonry throughout the World.* New York: Charles Scribner's Sons, 1936.

Mackey, A. G. *Encyclopedia of Freemasonry.* Philadelphia: Louis H. Everts, 1946.

Hamilton, John D. *Material Culture of the American Freemasons.* Lebanon, NH: University Press of New England. 1994.

Jacob, Margaret C. *Living the Enlightenment: Freemasonry and Politics in Eighteenth-Century Europe.* Oxford: Oxford University Press. 1991.

Knoop, Douglas, and Gwilym Peredur Jones. *The Genesis of Freemasonry: An Account of the Rise and Development of Freemasonry in Its Operative, Accepted, and Early Speculative Phases.* Manchester, UK: Manchester University Press. 1947.

Mackey, A. G. *Encyclopedia of Freemasonry.* Philadelphia: Louis H. Everts, 1946.

Roberts, Allen E. *Freemasonry in American History.* Richmond, VA: Macoy Publishing and Masonic Supply Co., 1985.

Voorhis, Harold V. B. *Masonic Organizations and Allied Orders and Degrees.* N.p.: Press of Henry Emmerson, 1952.

Voorhis, Harold V. B. *Masonic Rosicrucian Societies.* New York: Henry Emerson, 1958.

Waite, A. E. *A New Encyclopedia of Freemasonry.* 2 vols. London: William Rider; New York: David McKay, 1921; rpt., New Hyde Park, NY: University Books, 1970.

Freethought

Freethought, or Freethinking, as a term to describe unbelief or dissent from specific religious propositions, appears to have arisen at the end of the 17th century in England. The term emerged during the struggle of science to free itself from ongoing theological debates, as it followed a "free way" in inquiry. Eventually, the term became applied to the conscious reaction to conscious rejection of some parts of traditional religion. The use of the term implies that the freethinker has a

Robert Green Ingersoll, popular orator and leading proponent of Freethought during the 19th century. (Library of Congress)

thought that encompassed not only individuals but groups that included a reference to Freethought in their names. The leading exponent of freethinking unbelief in America was Robert Green Ingersoll (1833–1899), a popular lecturer, who identified himself as a freethinker. He noted in his 1890 lecture, "Has Freethought a Constructive Side?":

A denial of all orthodox falsehoods—an exposure of all superstitions. This is simply clearing the ground, to the end that seeds of value may be planted. It is necessary, first, to fell the trees, to destroy the poisonous vines, to drive out the wild beasts. Then comes another phase—another kind of work. The Freethinker knows that the universe is natural—that there is no room, even in infinite space, for the miraculous, for the impossible. The Freethinker knows, or feels that he knows, that there is no sovereign of the universe, who, like some petty king or tyrant, delights in showing his authority. He feels that all in the universe are conditioned beings, and that only those are happy who live in accordance with the conditions of happiness, and this fact or truth or philosophy embraces all men and all gods—if there be gods.

By this time, Freethought had became a synonym for atheism, with the added polemic point that religious thinkers were somehow bound by outdated religious doctrines and institutions that hindered their logic and prevented their following the logic of their affirmations.

Among the oldest of Freethought organizations was the Free Inquirers, founded by utopian thinker Robert Dale Owens (1801–1877) in 1828. Several other Free Inquiry associations appeared in the next few years, the most notable being Abner Kneeland's (1774–1844) First Society of Free Enquirers in Boston, Massachusetts. Among the largest was Die Freien Gemeinden, founded by German-speaking Americans in 1859. It developed chapters in a number of urban centers and remained active through the 1920s.

By the end of the 19th century, there were a number of Freethought institutions across the North American continent and Europe and around the world, including the Hindu Freethought Union (founded in India in 1875), General Freethought Association (Canada,

special loyalty to the process of thinking and to the freedom that would allow such thinking to go wherever logic takes it. As it developed, Freethought came to apply to any revision or rejection of contemporary religious doctrines, or the application of critical and rational thinking to specifically religious subjects.

In the 1690s, there appeared a pamphlet that included reference to the "New Religious Fraternity of Freethinkers," and in 1708 Jonathan Swift, in his *Sentiments of a Church of England Man*, used the term to refer collectively to those espousing unbelief. Then, in 1713, Anthony Collins accepted the term in his *Discourse of Free-Thinking*, and from that point, the identification of the term and religious unbelief began to appear in popular discourse, though those opposed to Freethinking often included references to any kind of religious heterodoxy, a more common phenomenon than unbelief.

In the 18th century, individuals began to identify themselves as freethinkers, and in the last half of the 19th century, one could identify a movement of Free-

1880s), the Brisbaine Freethought Association (Australia, 1888), the Freethought Association (South Africa, 1888), the Deutscher Freidenker Bund (Germany, 1881), and the Union des Libres Penseurs (France, 1904). The International Federation of Freethinkers was founded in Brussels in 1880 and has been known since 1936 as the World Union of Freethinkers (c/o Jean Kaech, PO Box CH-3001, Berne, Switzerland). *The Freethinker*, a British journal founded by George W. Foote (1850–1915) and espousing unbelief, began publication in 1881 and continues to be issued as a "Voice of Atheism."

In the 20th century, atheists, Humanists, Rationalists, and freethinkers came to see themselves as forming one international community of unbelief, and numerous Freethought organizations have arisen, which are hardly distinguishable from other groups espousing unbelief. Many are members of the International Humanist and Ethical Union. Among the oldest and most influential are the Freidenker-Vereinigung der Schweiz (Switzerland), Vapaa-ajattelijain liitto (Finish Freethought Union), Libre Pensée (France, founded in 1848), and De Vrije Gedachte (The Dutch Freethinking Association).

A Freethought Trail connecting sites associated with prominent American Freethinkers has been designated in upstate New York to honor Freethought pioneers and social activists.

J. Gordon Melton

See also: Atheism; International Humanist and Ethical Union.

References

Jacoby, Susan. *Freethinkers: A History of American Secularism.* New York: Metropolitan Books, 2004.

Robertson, J. M. *A Short History of Freethought.* New York: Russell and Russell, 1957.

Stein, Gordon. *The Encyclopedia of Unbelief.* 2 vols. Buffalo, NY: Prometheus Books, 1985.

Tribe, David. *100 Years of Freethought.* London: Elek, 1967.

■ French Guiana

French Guiana is an overseas department of France located on the Atlantic coast of South America immediately north of Brazil and east of Suriname. It is a tropical land, whose capital, Cayenne, is only five degrees from the equator. Its 34,400 square miles of land is home to 191,000 people (2008), most of African descent.

The primary people found by the Spanish when they first visited the area were the Caribs, who had displaced earlier residents, the Arawaks. Farther inland were other peoples, including the Oyampi, Cussaris, and Emerillon. They practiced a variety of related indigenous religions, some of which have survived.

The Spanish and then the French, who occupied the coast in 1604, brought Catholicism with them. The land was disputed territory through the rest of the century and at different times was controlled by the Dutch, the British, and the Portuguese. French control was finally re-established in 1676. Various efforts to build the colony with French citizens met with mixed results, due to the climate, and even now most of the population resides along the coast and on the nearby islands (one of which was the famous penal colony, Devil's Island).

Catholicism was established in 1636 and became the leading religion soon afterward. Efforts were made to convert the indigenous population, and most immigrants were of a Catholic background. The Diocese of Cayenne was erected in 1956. The church was very slow in creating indigenous leadership, and no native Guianan was ordained as a priest until 1971.

Challenges to Catholic hegemony did not really begin until the 20th century. At the beginning of the century, a member of the Christian Brethren (the Open Plymouth Brethren) came to Guiana from Barbados to begin work. He was followed by representatives of the Seventh-day Adventist Church (1940), the Jehovah's Witnesses (1945), the Southern Baptist Convention (1982), the Evangelical Church of the West Indies (ECWI) (1986), the Church of the Nazarene (1988), and the Church of God of Prophecy (1991). The ECWI is an association of churches initiated by an American-based evangelical sending agency, World Team, in the Caribbean.

Also, through the 20th century, numerous people moved into French Guiana from other lands, especially Brazil, Surinam, and Haiti. There is also a measurable community of Asians, mostly of Chinese and Indian

FRENCH GUIANA

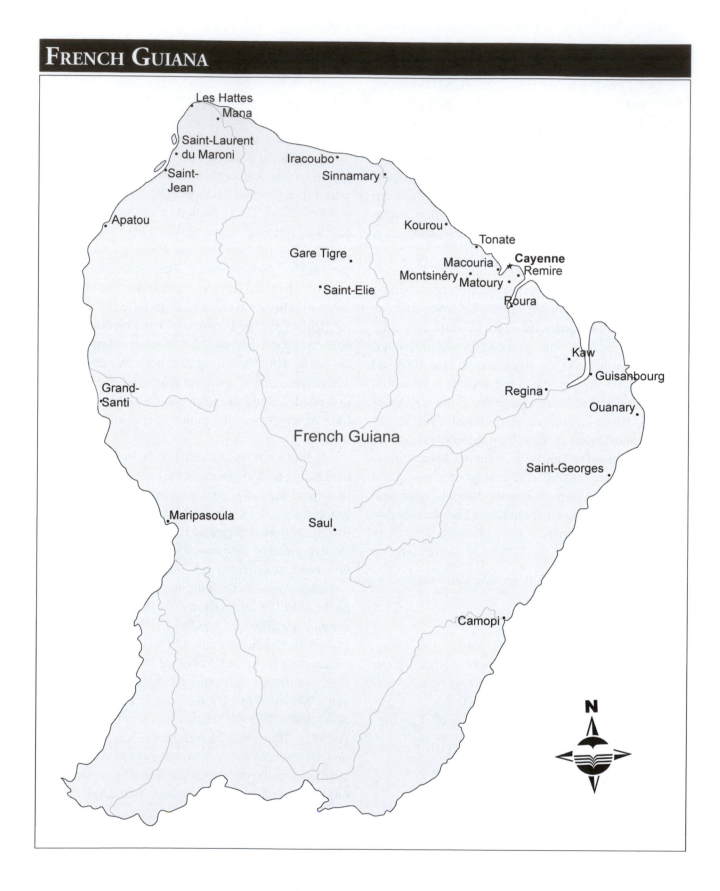

French Guiana

Religion	Followers in 1970	Followers in 2010	% of Population	Annual % growth 2000–2010	Followers in 2025	Followers in 2050
Christians	43,800	183,000	84.3	3.08	242,000	331,000
Roman Catholics	42,500	168,000	77.4	1.39	218,000	291,000
Protestants	2,800	11,000	5.1	4.11	15,500	25,000
Marginals	300	4,000	1.8	3.13	6,000	10,000
Chinese folk	670	7,800	3.6	3.07	10,500	15,000
Spiritists	960	7,200	3.3	3.07	11,000	15,000
Agnostics	480	6,800	3.1	3.07	12,400	21,200
Ethnoreligionists	1,200	4,600	2.1	2.70	4,500	5,000
Hindus	0	3,500	1.6	3.07	6,000	10,000
Muslims	480	2,000	0.9	3.06	3,000	4,000
Atheists	0	1,000	0.5	3.04	1,600	2,100
Baha'is	300	910	0.4	3.05	1,500	2,300
New religionists	50	240	0.1	3.08	350	500
Jews	20	130	0.1	3.16	220	300
Total population	**48,000**	**217,000**	**100.0**	**3.07**	**293,000**	**406,000**

heritage. The massive movement of immigrants into French Guiana has led to the establishment of a variety of different religions, including Afro-Brazilian spirit-possession groups, Spiritism, Vodou, Hinduism, and Buddhism. There are a few Muslims, most of Javanese or Lebanese extraction. French immigrants have brought Rosicrucianism, most noticeably members of the Ancient and Mystical Order Rosae Crucis (an American-based group that has been quite successful in France).

J. Gordon Melton

See also: Ancient and Mystical Order Rosae Crucis; Christian Brethren; Church of God of Prophecy; Church of the Nazarene; Evangelical Church of the West Indies; Jehovah's Witnesses; Seventh-day Adventist Church; Southern Baptist Convention.

References

Barrett, David, ed. *The Encyclopedia of World Christianity*. 2nd ed. New York: Oxford University Press, 2001.

Bissio, Roberto Remo, et al. *Third World Guide 93/94*. Montevideo, Uruguay: Instituto del Tercer Mundo, 1992.

Rodway, James. *Guiana: British, Dutch, and French*. Charleston, SC: BookSurge Publishing, 2002.

■ French Polynesia

The islands presently grouped together as French Polynesia include some 120 islands of the Society, Gambier, Austral, Marquesas, and Tuamotu archipelagoes. The 1,413 square miles of land include the most famous island, Tahiti. More than three-fourths of the islands' 283,000 residents are Polynesians, with the Chinese forming the primary minority group (12 percent).

The islands were inhabited in prehistoric times by the Polynesians. Spanish explorers visited the Marquesas in 1595, but little attention was paid to them until the discovery of Tahiti in 1767 by the English explorer Samuel Wallis. The islands were then visited by Captain James Cook, and in 1789, Tahiti, the largest island, was the destination from which the HMS *Bounty* had just sailed when the famous mutiny occurred in 1789.

In 1840, the French occupied the island. In 1843 they named it a protectorate and in 1880 designated it a colony, calling it the French Establishments of Oceania. Beginning in 1966, French Polynesia was for a period the site of some very controversial French nuclear tests. Finally in 1984, the islands were granted local autonomy, the provisions of which were strengthened

French Polynesia

Religion	Followers in 1970	Followers in 2010	% of Population	Annual % growth 2000–2010	Followers in 2025	Followers in 2050
Christians	107,000	256,000	93.9	1.57	294,000	321,000
Protestants	47,000	104,000	38.1	0.60	120,000	128,000
Roman Catholics	36,100	108,000	39.6	1.95	130,000	137,000
Marginals	7,900	37,200	13.6	1.53	45,000	55,000
Agnostics	2,400	12,400	4.5	2.08	19,000	27,000
Atheists	200	1,500	0.5	1.60	2,000	2,800
Chinese folk	1,000	1,200	0.4	1.60	1,300	1,400
Baha'is	200	550	0.2	4.03	1,500	3,000
New religionists	100	340	0.1	1.58	500	700
Buddhists	300	400	0.1	1.57	500	800
Ethnoreligionists	100	250	0.1	1.57	300	400
Jews	20	150	0.1	0.13	150	150
Total population	**111,000**	**273,000**	**100.0**	**1.60**	**319,000**	**357,000**

Église de la Sainte Famille, a Catholic church in Haapiti on the southwest coast of Moorea, French Polynesia. (iStockPhoto.com)

FRENCH POLYNESIA

in 1996 and 1998. France remains in control of the country's military affairs and the currency.

Prior to the coming of Christianity, the residents of the islands worshipped a pantheon of deities headed by a supreme god called Ta'aroa. The other deities were ascribed hegemony over vital areas of island life, such as the sea or the weather. The traditional religion has been all but obliterated by the modern import of Christianity.

An initial effort at evangelization by Roman Catholics in the islands began as early as 1659. A second attempt began in 1772 by some Franciscans from Peru. More permanent efforts were begun in the Gambier Islands in 1831 by French priests. They subsequently found their way to the Marquesas in 1838, Tahiti in 1842, and Tuamotu in 1849. In the decades following World War II, the church experienced significant growth, which some attributed to the spread of a devotional movement centered upon the recitation of the rosary. The Living Rosary movement had begun in France under the leadership of Pauline Jaricot (1799–1862). Today, the church is centered on the Archdiocese of Papeete (Tahiti). There is also a diocese

headquartered in the Marquesas and serving the northern islands.

In 1797, missionaries of the London Missionary Society (LMS) arrived in Tahiti, one of their very first missionary targets. A party of 18 settled on the island (and another 11 went on to Tonga). The group encountered a variety of unexpected problems, and by the turn of the century, only seven (five men and two women) remained, the rest having left for Australia and two having been dismissed for marrying local women. Crucial to the success of the mission, in 1815 King Pomare converted and requested to be baptized. He then saw to the building of a large church. At the king's urging, most of the people abandoned their old religion in favor of Christianity. The establishment of French rule and the introduction of Roman Catholic missionaries made the British-based LMS missionary work increasingly difficult, and in 1886 the missionaries turned their work over to representatives of the French Reformed Church's Paris Evangelical Missionary Society, which had already begun separate work on Tahiti. In 1963, the mission became autonomous as the Église Evangélique de Polynésie Française. The church is a member of the Pacific Conference of Churches and the World Council of Churches.

Both the Church of Jesus Christ of Latter-day Saints (the Mormons) and the Reorganized Church of Jesus Christ of Latter-day Saints (now known as the Christian Community) established missions in the islands. The former arrived first in 1844, and the Mormons have built extensive work, given the special role they have given Polynesians in their scheme of salvation. The work begun by Elder Addison Pratt (1802–1872) is considered the first Mormon mission to a non-English-speaking area of the world. The French closed the mission in 1852. It was reopened in 1892 and churches built for the remnant of loyal members. A temple was opened in Papeete in 1983. Most recently, the church reported 14,000 members. The Reorganized Church began with a schism in the LDS in the Tuamotu Islands in 1884.

The Seventh-day Adventist Church began work in 1892, and the Jehovah's Witnesses in 1932. The Evangelical Church has also been the scene of a number of schisms, among the most interesting being the Mamaia group, founded in the mid-1920s by a man with messianic pretensions and a calling to evict all white people from the islands. There have been several schisms since World War II, most on administrative issues. In 1968, the Chinese members left to found the Polynesian Pentecostal Churches. In 1977, Baptists made their first appearance in the area, with the entrance of the very conservative Baptist Bible Fellowship International.

Chinese had first arrived in the islands in 1865 and now constitute approximately 12 percent of the population. Although many are Christian, they have also established Buddhist centers. As in other French territories, the Ancient and Mystical Order Rosae Crucis is present, and the Baha'i Faith has been growing since it arrived in 1955.

J. Gordon Melton

See also: Ancient and Mystical Order Rosae Crucis; Baha'i Faith; Baptist Bible Fellowship International; Christian Community (Movement for Religious Renewal); Church of Jesus Christ of Latter-day Saints; Jehovah's Witnesses; London Missionary Society; Paris Mission; Reformed Church of France; Roman Catholic Church; Seventh-day Adventist Church; World Council of Churches.

References

Bolyanatz, Alexander H. *Pacific Romanticism: Tahiti and the European Imagination*. Westport, CT: Praeger Publishers, 2004.

Ellsworth, S. G., and K. C. Perrin. *Seasons of Faith and Courage: The Church of Jesus Christ of Latter-day Saints in French Polynesia, a Sesquicentennial History, 1843–1993*. Sandy, UT: Yves R. Perrin, 1994.

Forman, Charles H. *The Island Churches of the South Pacific: Emergence in the Twentieth Century*. Maryknoll, NY: Orbis, 1982.

Mauer, D. *Protestant Church at Tahiti*. Paris: Nouvelles Editions Latines, 1970.

O'Reilly, P. *Tahitian Catholic Church*. Paris: Société des Océanistes, 1969.

Trompf, Gary. *The Religions of Oceania*. New York: Routledge, 2004.

Friends General Conference

The Friends General Conference is the more liberal wing of the Friends movement, the wing that grew out of the ministry of Elias Hicks (1748–1830), an eloquent speaker who moved among American Quakers in the 1820s. He emphasized the more subjective side of the Quaker tradition, the reliance on the Inner Light for guidance, and tended to denigrate any outward forms. Among the implications of his approach was the gathering of Quakers for meetings without any prior planning (or programming). Thus those meetings attracted to Hicks's messages came to be known as "unprogrammed." Within the Hicksite faction, a new level of theological diversity became manifest.

Hicks's approach created open controversy in 1823 in the Philadelphia Yearly Meeting (the center of the Quaker community at the time), and over the next four years the controversy became harsher. Then in 1827 the Hicksite faction withdrew from the Philadelphia Meeting, and subsequently similar separations occurred in Friends' communities across the East and Midwest. Within a few years seven Hicksite Yearly Meetings were formed.

Further organization began after the American Civil War with the formation of a Sunday School Conference in 1868. It facilitated communication among the far-flung unprogrammed congregations, led to several other organizations focused on additional concerns, and culminated in the formation of the Friends General Conference in 1900.

With some 32,000 members (2002), the Friends General Conference is the smallest of the three main Friends denominations, with members confined to North America.

Friends General Conference
1216 Arch St., 2B
Philadelphia, PA 19107
http://www.fgcquaker.org

J. Gordon Melton

See also: Friends/Quakers.

References

Dandelion, Pink. *The Quakers: A Very Short Introduction.* New York: Oxford University Press, 2008.

Doherty, Robert W. *The Hicksite Separation.* New Brunswick, NJ: Rutgers University Press, 1967.

Friends World Committee for Consultation. *Quakers around the World.* London: Friends World Committee for Consultation, 1994.

Jones, Rufus M. *The Latter Periods of Quakerism.* 2 vols. Westport, CT: Greenwood Press, 1970.

Friends United Meeting

Formed in 1902, the Friends United Meeting brings together the primary elements of the Friends, or Quaker, movement in the United States, which dates to the colonial era. The Friends movement developed around relatively small autonomous associations of congregations in a particular area, and by this means the movements spread across the United States during the 19th century and funded missionaries in Africa and

Engraving of Elias Hicks, about 1830. Hicks was a spiritual leader of Friends United Meeting who emphasized the Inner Light over the authority of scripture. (Library of Congress)

Latin America. The Friends United Meeting has brought together one set of these yearly meetings (as the congregational associations are called).

The United Meeting traces its origins to the earlier arrival of Quakers in the American colonies in the 1650s. As in England, most colonists did not welcome them. The Congregationalists in New England saw them as disturbers of the peace, whose presence distracted from the religious uniformity they hoped to build. Quakers found a haven in the religiously free Rhode Island, and there they organized the first congregation (Quarterly Meeting). The real strength of the movement, however, was in Pennsylvania, where William Penn (1644–1718), a wealthy Quaker, created a colony, in large part to provide a refuge for Quakers and others who were suffering from religious persecution both in England and on the European continent.

The first organization of Quakers above the congregational level, the General Meeting of Friends, gathered in 1681 in Burlington, New Jersey. It became the seed from which the Philadelphia Yearly Meeting eventually grew.

The Friends movement developed on the radical fringe of the Puritan movement. While accepting a basic Protestant belief structure, including belief in the fatherhood of God, the lordship of Jesus Christ, salvation by faith, and the priesthood of all believers, Friends have tended to withdraw from participation in the state and are confirmed pacifists. At various times, their refusal to participate in wars has earned them the contempt of neighbors, which they have countered with a strong emphasis on social service. The Friends have also dropped the practice of water baptism, interpreting the one baptism referred to in Ephesians 4:4–5 as a baptism of the Spirit.

Friends have been known for their unique worship services based upon their understanding of the guidance of the Inner Light. They were known to sit in silence, waiting for the Holy Spirit to move in the hearts of those who had gathered. This emphasis made them the subject of two very different trends in the early 19th century. In the 1820s, many Friends were attracted to the teachings of Elias Hicks (1748–1830), who placed total reliance on the Inner Light and advocated an approach to worship that included no preplanning. Those Meetings that accepted his idea became known as "unprogrammed" Meetings. The Hicksite Friends now form the Friends General Conference. Another group of Friends were attracted to the Holiness teachings of Methodist John Wesley (1703–1791), as delivered by Joseph John Gurney (1788–1847). Most of those Yearly Meetings affected by the Holiness teachings are now gathered in the Evangelical Friends International.

Those Meetings that rejected both the approach of Hicks and that of Gurney continued as the largest faction of the movement. In the 1880s, efforts to bring the Yearly Meetings into a closer relationship were initiated. Conferences were held every five years through the last decades of the century, and in 1902 a loose association, called appropriately the Five Years Meeting, came into existence. The Five Years Meeting evolved into the Friends United Meeting in 1965. At the end of the 1990s, it included 27 Yearly Meetings. The Yearly Meetings cover the United States, but three-fourths of the 170,000 members are now found outside the United States, in the Yearly Meetings in Kenya (with some 120,000 members), Cuba, Jamaica, Mexico, and Israel.

Administratively, the work of the Friends United Meeting is carried out through the General Board. The Department of World Ministries relates American Friends to the associated Meeting overseas. The Meeting is a member of both the National Council of Churches of Christ in the U.S.A. and the World Council of Churches and cooperates fully with the Friends World Committee for Consultation.

Friends United Meeting
101 Quaker Hill Dr.
Richmond Hill, IN 47374
http://www.fum.org

J. Gordon Melton

See also: Evangelical Friends International; Friends General Conference; Friends World Committee for Consultation; Friends/Quakers; World Council of Churches.

References

"Friends United Meeting." In *Friends in the Americas,* edited by Francis B. Hall. Philadelphia: Friends World Committee, Section of the Americas, 1976.

Friends World Committee for Consultation. *Quakers around the World*. London: Friends World Committee for Consultation, 1994.

Friends World Committee for Consultation

The Friends World Committee for Consultation (FWCC) was the major product of the Second World Conference of Friends (Quakers) that was held at Swarthmore, Pennsylvania, in 1937. It expressed the desire for greater unity among Quakers, who had been split by doctrinal difference in the 19th century but had found a new sense of unity in their peace witness as a result of World War I. Also, by the 1930s, after several centuries as primarily a movement in England and North America, the Friends had become a worldwide movement. The initial work of the Committee was somewhat inhibited by the outbreak of World War II soon after its founding.

FWCC rebounded after the war and in 1952 organized the next World Conference, which was held in Oxford, England, in 1952. Since that time it has worked on its multifaceted program of assisting Friends to transcend their doctrinal differences, coordinating various social programs, representing Friends in different ecumenical settings, and providing a united voice for Quaker witness on social issues, especially those related to peace and social justice. Most of the Yearly (district and national) Meetings around the world are affiliated to the Committee.

The Committee is divided into four sections—Africa, the Americas, Asia and the West Pacific, and Europe and the Middle East. The Committee holds a large international Meeting ever three years. An Interim Committee and a staff headed by the executive secretary carry on the work of the Committee between the triennial gatherings. The Committee sees as one of its essential functions the maintenance of communication between Friends worldwide, many of whom live as small minorities within their own countries, and providing a sense of the global nature of their work and witness.

There are some 70 related Yearly Meetings, and several hundred thousand Friends worldwide.

Friends World Committee for Consultation
4 Byng Pl.
London WC1E 7JH
UK
http://www.quaker.org/fwcc/FWCC.html

J. Gordon Melton

See also: East Africa Yearly Meeting of Friends; Evangelical Friends International; Friends General Conference; Friends United Meeting.

References

Dandelion, Pink. *The Quakers: A Very Short Introduction*. New York: Oxford University Press, 2008.

Friends World Committee for Consultation. *Quakers around the World*. London: Friends World Committee for Consultation, 1994.

Peck, George. *What Is Quakerism? A Primer*. Wallingford, PA: Pendle Hill Publications, 1988.

Friends/Quakers

The Friends movement, commonly known as the Quakers, emerged in 17th-century England as the most radical expression of the Puritan movement, which attempted to complete the work of the Reformation in the Church of England by purifying it of non-biblical elements that had accumulated over the centuries. George Fox (1624–1691), the movement's founder, was a mystic and social activist who began to preach in 1647, during the English Civil War, following his experience of inner illumination. His comments on the social scene drew fire during the years of the Commonwealth (1649–1660), when he was first arrested for his pacifist views.

The beginnings of a movement became visible in 1667 when Fox's followers organized a set of Monthly (congregations), Quarterly (district), and Yearly (national) Meetings. The Society of Friends was built around Fox's idea that the Bible was not the end of revelation, but that each believer had access to the Inner Light that provided immediate contact with the living Spirit. Gatherings were centered upon quietly waiting for the Spirit to speak. Bodily movements that appeared in these meeting gave members the popular appellation, Quakers. The messages received and the guidance they offered would then be tested by the teachings and example of Jesus.

Fox taught that Friends should lead simple lives, avoiding the vanities of the world. Members did not wear colorful clothing, wigs, or jewelry. Their language was characterized by their refusal to use "you" when addressing social superiors, as was customary; they addressed everyone with the familiar "thee" and "thou," which further set them apart. They became known for their participation in various social causes, including abolition, prison reform, and, most notably, pacifism. Heightened tension over their pacifism regularly arose in times of war.

Persecuted in England, Quakers found a haven in the American colonies when William Penn (1644–1718) founded Pennsylvania and invited his fellow

Apponegansett Quaker Meeting House, Dartmouth, Massachusetts, built in 1791. (Phillip Caper)

believers to settle there. They first arrived in 1655. Pennsylvania subsequently became a major source of American ideals of freedom of religion.

The Friends remained a small minority group in both England and the United States, and their support for the antislavery cause further limited their growth in the American South. However, through the 19th and early 20th centuries, they spread across North America. As early as 1681 the first General Meeting of Friends was held in New Jersey. It evolved into the General Yearly Meeting of Friends in Philadelphia, East Jersey, and Adjacent Provinces, and as the Philadelphia Yearly Meeting continues as the oldest Quaker association in North America.

During the 19th century, several issues split the Friends, and various Yearly Meetings arose that advocated several distinct perspectives. As the number of Yearly Meetings proliferated across the United States, various associations of Yearly Meetings appeared, the most important being the Friends United Meeting, the Friends General Conference, and the Evangelical Friends International. Friends have also organized for joint efforts on various social issues through the Friends World Committee for Consultation (FWCC). The movement began to spread in the late 19th century as Friends participated in the global Protestant missionary movement, and Yearly Meetings are now found on every continent. Their greatest success was in Kenya, where the East Africa Yearly Meeting of Friends became the largest Quaker association in the world.

The organizational center of the Society of Friends remains in England, where the FWCC and the London Yearly Meeting are headquartered.

J. Gordon Melton

See also: East Africa Yearly Meeting of Friends; Evangelical Friends International; Fox, George; Friends General Conference; Friends United Meeting; Friends World Committee for Consultation.

References

Comfort, William Wistar. *The Quaker Way of Life*. Philadelphia: Blakiston, 1945.

Cooper, Wilmer A. *Living Faith: A Historical and Comparative Study of Quaker Beliefs*. Richmond, IN: Friends United Press, 2001.

Dandelion, Pink. *The Quakers: A Very Short Introduction*. New York: Oxford University Press, 2008.

Friends World Committee for Consultation. *Quakers around the World*. London: Friends World Committee for Consultation, 1994.

Peck, George. *What Is Quakerism? A Primer*. Wallingford, PA: Pendle Hill Publications, 1988.

Whitmire, Catherine. *Plain Living: The Quaker Path to Simplicity*. Notre Dame, IN: Sorin Books, 2001.

Yount, David. *How the Quakers Invented America*. Latham, MD: Rowman & Littlefield Publishers, 2007.

Fuji, Mount

Mount Fuji is Japan's highest peak at 12,389 feet, and its conical shape is a major reminder of the island's ongoing tectonic dynamics. The mountain became a sacred site in the prehistoric era, and its wide appeal found a home in both Shinto and Buddhism. It has erupted periodically, averaging twice a century since records have been kept; the last major activity in 1707 covered Tokyo in ash.

The mountain appears to be named for the fire goddess Fuchi, a deity of the Ainu people, the early inhabitants of Hakkaido. It came to be seen as the home of Sengen, the wife of Ninigi, the grandson of Amaterasu, the Shinto Sun-goddess. Sengen gave birth to three sons—Po-deri-no-mikoto ("Fire-shine"), Po-suseri-no-mikoto ("Fire-full"), and Po-wori-no-mikoto ("Fire-fade"). Po-wori-no-mikoto is seen as the grandfather of Japan's first emperor. Sengen is believed to reside within a luminous cloud in the mountain's crater. She is usually pictured dressed in white.

Among the earliest recorded reactions to the mountain were dances performed by young women dressed in white robes, identified with two mythic females known for their beauty and heroism. Their dance mimicked the puffs of smoke seen coming from the

Mount Fuji, the highest peak in Japan and a national symbol, is considered sacred by many Japanese. (Corel)

mountain's crater. Also, early on, the mountain became home to female shamans/mediums, who could be found inhabiting the caves near its base.

As Buddhism was introduced to Japan in the sixth century CE and became a major religious force in the next century, Shugendo, a mountain-based religion, reacted to what its practitioners saw as the attempt to impose Buddhism on the country. Mount Fuji became a natural site for the new religion's development. Shugendo drew teachings and practices from a wide variety of religions then becoming available in Japan (including the magical practices of Shingon Buddhism). Its practitioners, the Yamabushi (literally, "those who sleep in the mountains"), constituted a male fraternity, which withdrew from ordinary society, adopted a special diet, and underwent a variety of physical trials, all of which contributed to their developing psychic/spiritual powers. In the mountains the Yamabushi could be in direct contact with the divine entities they believed resided there. Shugendo remained an active religious tradition until the Meiji reforms in the late 19th century and still exists today.

Quite apart from Shugendo, many Japanese climbed Mount Fuji over the years, though the oldest path to the top had been created by and dominated by Shugendo practitioners. Later three additional paths were developed. Then in the 13th century, stories began to circulate about Hitoana, a large cave located near Fujinomiya, a town in the mountain's foothills. It was also seen as the home of Sengen, a female being who was discovered by Nitta Shiro Tadsune (d. 1203), a representative of the shogun and later a favorite subject of Japanese fiction writers.

Religious reverence focused on Mount Fuji was significantly elevated in the 17th century following the founding of a new religion, Fuji Ko, by Hasegawa Kakugyo (1541–1646). He settled in Hitoana, where he lived an ascetic life and claimed numerous revelations. These revelations, including a set of undecipherable symbols, provided the content for Fuji Ko, which exists to the present day. Kakugyo's successors merged the veneration of the bodhisattva Maitreya, the future Buddha, into Fuji Ko. Japanese authorities were upset over the spread of Fuji Ko across Japan, especially the offshoots it spawned such as the Millennial Fuji Ko. These marginalized groups have enjoyed a revival in the midst of the post–World War II secularization of Japanese culture and the international promotion of pictures and replicas of the mountain for tourists.

J. Gordon Melton

See also: Mountains; Shingon Buddhism; Shinto; Shugendo.

References

Kasahara, Kazuo. *A History of Japanese Religion.* Tokyo: Kosei Publishing, 2001.

Uhlenbeck, Chris, and Merel Molenaar. *Mount Fuji: Sacred Mountain of Japan.* Leiden: Hotei Publishing, 2000.

Fundamentalism

Fundamentalism has polyvalent meanings. Taken broadly, it serves academic purposes, as in Martin Marty's 11-point delineation of "fundamentalisms" (Kaplan 1992). Also broadly, it is a media and pop culture debased shorthand for fanatical extremists. However, the term enters religious discourse in reference to a conservative Christian movement deriving its name from a series of pamphlets published between 1910 and 1915, *The Fundamentals: A Testimony to the Truth*, upon which this entry will focus.

"Christian Fundamentalism" remains an elusive term. For followers, it is a modern restoration of "the faith once delivered to the saints." For opponents, it is a religion distinct from mainstream Christianity, even a North American analog to European Fascism. The academic consensus is that Christian Fundamentalism's struggle with theological Liberalism was rooted in 19th-century developments, which particularly polarized Protestantism in the 20th century's second and third decades. The suggestion that Fundamentalism was merely millenarianism renamed has fallen from favor, although the profound dissonance of religious optimism in the late 1800s and early 1900s against the troubled culture in which evangelicals found themselves was one factor leading many to divest themselves of the postmillennial eschatology (common to the Protestant Reformers of the 16th century) and embrace Dispensationalism. Yet not all Fundamentalists were Dispensationalists, nor were they all Calvinists. Fundamentalism's additional facets include Scottish Common Sense Realist philosophy and anti-evolutionism. A subset of evangelicalism, Fundamentalism coexisted uneasily with other evangelical traditions, including such diverse groups as the Wesleyan tradition, Pentecostalism, and the Missouri Synod Lutherans. Southern Baptists, annoyed by Northern Baptist Fundamentalists' insistence on premillennialism, stood aloof, even though both sets of Baptists defended conservative Calvinism against theological liberalism and secularization.

Nineteenth-century precursors of the Fundamentalist movement include the Christian Conference (from 1878) and the Niagara Prophecy Conferences (1878, 1883–1897). Appealing to broad constituencies, these meetings introduced Christian Brethren–derived dispensational eschatological theology to leading denominations, including Anglicans/Episcopalians, Baptists, Methodists, and Presbyterians. Growing disillusionment with Progressive ideals' failure to produce profound social improvement rendered pessimistic apocalyptic scenarios more credible than the hitherto prevailing postmillennial vision. American audiences were particularly prepared by the Civil War's horrors; European disenchantment grew only as World War I's atrocities unfolded. The Civil War also divided American denominations into northern and southern regional branches. Some conservatives considered Darwinian thought and biblical Higher Criticism as adopted by liberals end-time threats.

Fundamentalism's precise belief structure is not easily discerned. Despite some authors' assertion that the 1895 Niagara Prophecy Conference adopted five famous foundational points, their only creedal statement was a 14-point document issued by the 1878 conference. The General Assembly of the Presbyterian Church in the United States of America adopted a statement in 1910 (reaffirmed in 1916 and 1923) including scriptural inerrancy in the original documents, the deity of Jesus (including the virgin birth), the substitutionary atonement, the physical resurrection, and Jesus' miracle-working power. The weakness of this description is that Roman Catholics, who generally found Fundamentalism puzzling, share these beliefs. Fundamentalists also affirm human depravity (distinguishing them from the Methodists and Holiness churches), justification by faith alone (distinguishing them from Roman Catholics), the personal, bodily return of Christ, and a literal heaven and a literal hell.

Central to understanding Fundamentalism is the question of the movement's grasp of new scientific understandings of the world that were propounded in the 19th century. Often Fundamentalists are characterized as militant anti-modernists, fixated on supernaturalist perceptions that are counter-rational. Indeed, Fundamentalists went to great lengths to defend the Bible's miracles, Jesus' deity and resurrection, as well as a non-evolutionary cosmogony. Yet the Fundamentalists' forerunners insisted that theirs was a truly scientific view, taking into account observable facts in nature as well as biblical information. By the early 1880s, Presbyterian conservatives and moderates tussled over intellectual high ground, the scientific credibility each side believed they possessed. Systematization was the order of the day. Each applied a version of Baconian inductive method to study of the Bible, with predictably varying results. Theirs was an Enlightenment confidence in the potential for a thoroughly unbiased, neutral, objective and systematic grasp of the Bible's content. Future Fundamentalist leader Reuben Torrey (1856–1928) touted a rigidly inductive, modern scientific method in his 1898 *What the Bible Teaches*. On a more sophisticated level, the Princeton Theology framed by Presbyterian scholars such as Charles Hodge (1797–1878), his son, Alexander Archibald Hodge (1823–1886), and Benjamin Breckinridge Warfield (1851–1921) adumbrated an extremely high and intricate doctrine of biblical inspiration. The individual words in the original autographs (that is, the first handwritten copy of a text) were divinely inspired, specifically chosen by God. These scholars were quite rationalistic, building with elements of Scottish Common Sense Realist philosophy and attempting to adapt to the modern scientific project.

As the 19th century neared its close, secular scientists increasingly realized the logical fallacy their method entailed, but theologians lagged in adapting. Instead of creating leading edge thinking, evangelicals naively treated the Bible as if it were a child's building toy, the pieces of which needed to be assembled correctly in order to create something useful. Their ahistorical readings displayed an underlying tendency to essentialism, or the conviction that the essence of biblical truth on any given biblical issue existed in a timeless state, so that a single specific formula could express that truth in any and every cultural setting. This reflects the massive abandonment of precedent woven into the fabric of the North American worldview that systematically devalued previous generations' (or other nations') wisdom. Anti-traditionalism encouraged self-confidence that bordered on arrogance, yet which was also tinged with innocence. Whether Princeton-bred or autodidact, late-19th-century evangelicals simply failed to grasp the problem that their hermeneutic shrouded the reality that all interpretation is in fact interpretation, conditioned by the interpreter's setting. Their Bible reading tended to atomize the text, handling individual verses as if they were self-standing. They were insouciant that they did not take into account the situation in which the biblical writer committed those words to paper.

At the same time, a new pragmatic brand of ministry training emerged. From 1882, Bible or missionary colleges began providing task-oriented preparation for evangelists, lay workers, and missionaries. Avoiding more speculative theological disciplines sidestepped the growing influence in universities of German Higher Criticism. Suspicious of academic freedom, founders aimed to reinforce faith's fundamentals. Denominationally based colleges naturally viewed the upstarts as a threat to their stability.

As the 20th century dawned, evangelicalism began to fragment. The largest group probably consisted of those unwilling or unable to align themselves with the two emerging, theologically opposed poles. This is understandable, as both extremes agreed on practical points of ethical interest and action, such as urbanization, immigration, and secularism, differing on abstractions. One wing, valuing primarily the gospel's social implications, moved toward theological liberalism. Another, which valued particularly the gospel's provision for personal piety, emerged as Fundamentalism. Polarity would soon provide clarity.

The Fundamentals Writing articles for *The Fundamentals* was an international project, but one dominated by Americans contributors (33 authors prepared 51 articles). The next largest identifiable group is English; 9 authors contributed 10 articles. Six Canadians wrote 8 articles. Two Scots furnished a total of 7 articles; one Irish and one German contributor round out the list of those whose nationality may be readily established. The American-Canadian border was especially porous for Fundamentalists, people, and ideas following lines of theological, rather than nationalist, interests. Publication costs were met by oil entrepreneurs Milton and Lyman Stewart (1840–1923), whose beneficence extended also to the creation of BIOLA (the Bible Institute of Los Angeles).

Given Fundamentalism's predominantly Calvinistic nature, it is no surprise that Presbyterians wrote numerous articles. Warfield's essay "The Deity of Christ" graced the first volume. The most prolific pamphleteers, each penning four articles, were the Scottish historian and theologian James Orr (1844–1913; vols. 1, 4, 6, 9) and American missionary statesman and evangelist Arthur Pierson (1837–1911; vols. 1, 6, 9, 10).

Their work appears consistently throughout the series' progress, from the early stages, sometimes characterized as more reasoned and philosophical, to the later stages, when some detect a more distressed and strident tone that presaged a future sense of alienation.

Baptists also figured prominently, with Amzi Dixon (1854–1925) as series co-editor and author of volume 5's "The Scriptures." Also on the editorial committee sat Elmore Harris (1854–1911). Son of a wealthy industrialist, he used family wealth to initiate both Walmer Road Baptist Church and the Toronto Bible Training School (1894; precursor of Tyndale University College and Seminary). An adjunct faculty member at his alma mater, McMaster University, he involved himself in academic politics, objecting to the 1905 appointment of I. G. Matthews as professor of Hebrew and Old Testament. Unable to block Matthews, Harris charged him with heresy in 1909. Again, Harris failed. Using fellow contributor William J. Erdman (1833–1923; vol. 10) as his son's namesake indicates how deeply friendship developed among some contributors. In 1911, Harris died in India on a round-the-world trip. Matthews earned his doctorate the next year from the liberal-leaning University of Chicago. When he left McMaster in 1919, his replacement was a strong conservative, a temporary victory for Fundamentalists.

Despite turn-of-the-century Congregationalism's well-earned reputation for liberalism, some key *Fundamentals*' contributors were Congregationalist pastors. Reuben Torrey (vols. 1, 5, 12) was one of the chief organizers and editors, a fulcrum of the American Fundamentalist community. The Englishman G. Campbell Morgan (1863–1945; vol. 1) was well known on both sides of the Atlantic as a prodigious preacher and author. The most controversial Congregationalist was Cyrus Scofield (1843–1921; vol. 11). His *Scofield Reference Bible* powerfully inculcated Dispensational doctrine. Less sophisticated readers occasionally mistook Scofield's notes as part of the infallible text. Harris and Pierson were two of seven consulting editors for the 1909 edition; revisions emerged in 1919 and 1966.

Methodists were under-represented among Fundamentalists. Methodists' postmillennialism remained largely intact, buffering the denomination from Christian (Plymouth) Brethren influence and keeping many

Fundamentalist British theologian and preacher G. Campbell Morgan, 1914. (Library of Congress)

aloof from Fundamentalism. The Southern Methodist evangelist Leander Munhall (1843–1934; vol. 7) and Arno Gaebelein (1861–1945; vol. 11), who assisted Scofield's editing of his Bible notes, were notable exceptions. Gaebelein's later departure from Methodism underscores its tenuous relationship with Fundamentalism. Despite coolness toward Fundamentalism, Canadian Methodist conservatives successfully ejected radical professors. George Workman's (1848–1936) challenge of Old Testament prophecy not only led to his forced departure from Victoria College, but provided direct motivation for William Caven's (1830–1904) rejoinder, a tract reprinted posthumously in volume 4. Principal of Toronto's Presbyterian Knox College and president of the Toronto Branch of the Evangelical Alliance, Caven provided a spirited defense of biblical authority. Methodism would prove fertile ground for another alternative Protestantism, Pentecostalism, in which it was over-represented.

Anglicans' (Episcopalians') contribution to Fundamentalism is complex. The Evangelical Party never formed a majority, although some dioceses contained concentrations of conservatives. Long experience as England's mandated state church created a pattern different from most Protestant denominations for dealing with strife; withdrawal was unconscionable. Osborn Troop's (1854–1932; vol. 10) biographer, while immensely proud of her father's evangelical credentials, omitted mention of his article. Two Canadian Anglicans were unusually influential in Fundamentalism. Toronto-born Dyson Hague (1857–1935; vols. 1, 8, 11) was professor of pastoral theology and homiletics at Toronto's conservative Wycliffe College from 1897. One of only seven to contribute three or more articles to *The Fundamentals*, Hague became the hub of the Canadian Fundamentalist network after Harris's death, until Thomas Todhunter Shields's (1873–1955) rise. American academics generally ignored *The Fundamentals*, except to portray Fundamentalists as ignorant country bumpkins or to predict prematurely their demise. British Anglican theologians, however, offered thoughtful rebuttal in *Foundations* (1912). Edited by Burnett Hillman Streeter (1874–1937), originator of the Synoptic Gospel Two Source Hypothesis, the tome went through several editions and earned the editor's symbolic excommunication from the conservative bishop of Zanzibar. The legacy of English-born and -educated William Henry Griffith Thomas (1861–1924; vol. 8) was his co-founding (along with Lewis Sperry Chafer, 1871–1952) of a premier Fundamentalist institution, Dallas Theological Seminary. He died shortly before the seminary opened; his library was donated to the seminary. Winifred Griffith Thomas Gillespie, his daughter, edited and published some of his work. Gillespie also served on the oversight committee of the New King James Version, a Fundamentalist-inspired update of the 1611 original.

Developments after the Great War Apocalyptic hopes ran high among Dispensationalists as reports of Great War (World War I) conquests in Palestine reached the West. Prophetic disillusionment was only one of several disappointments. More than one conservative editor of a denominational journal was ousted. Social Gospel topics displaced evangelistic discussion in many university student fellowships. Theological liberals increasingly secured leading denominational positions. Although not a contributor to the pamphlets, the Baptist William Bell Riley (1861–1947) continued his earlier leadership by guiding the 1919 inauguration of the World's Christian Fundamentals Association (WCFA). Delegates approved a nine-point Confession of Faith drafted by Riley and edited by a Torrey-led committee that included affirmation of the Bible's verbal inerrancy, Christ's personal, premillennial, and imminent return, the Trinity, Jesus' deity, human sinfulness, the substitutionary atonement, the bodily resurrection, justification by faith, and the bodily resurrection of the just and the unjust. July 1920 saw the adoption of the now infamous moniker, Fundamentalism, attributed to the journalist Curtis Lee Laws.

Going on the offensive, Fundamentalists managed the 1924 election of Clarence Macartney (1879–1957) as moderator of the Presbyterian Church in the United States of America. Working in tandem with J. Gresham Machen (1881–1937), the last of the Princeton theologians, Macartney sought to rally flagging Fundamentalist Presbyterians. Momentum was soon lost, conservatives opting to withdraw from Princeton in 1929 to form Westminster Seminary. Becoming a Westminster board director, Macartney later parted company with Machen over the 1933 creation of the Independent Board for Presbyterian Foreign Missions. Thirteen of 28 Westminster trustees resigned over the issue. Despite Machen's insistence on the centrality of the substitutionary atonement, his distaste for both Dispensationalism and the Fundamentalist label resulted in his exclusion from the 1930 WCFA meeting.

One of the most publicly recognized non-clerical Fundamentalists, William Jennings Bryan (1860–1925) thrice obtained the Democratic nomination for the presidency and served as Woodrow Wilson's secretary of state. A supporter of peace initiatives, a single standard of sexual morality for both sexes, and women's suffrage, he confounded Fundamentalist stereotypes. Nor was Bryan a Dispensationalist. Not given to invective against his enemies, Bryan nevertheless suffered a loss of reputation from his role as prosecutor in the so-called Scopes Monkey Trial of 1925. Technically, he won the case, but Fundamentalism lost in the court of cultural influence. This may explain the persistent

citation of H. Richard Niebuhr's error; he posited Fundamentalism's strength lay in poor, underdeveloped, rural southern states. Older historiography also leaned heavily on deprivation theory, suggesting Fundamentalists' fervor was compensation for a dearth of tangible affluence. Subsequent research highlights the opposite: Fundamentalism's principal strongholds actually were predominantly urban, middle-class, and northern.

Fundamentalism's relationship to theological education was ambivalent. The existing network of Bible colleges and Bible institutes expanded as suspicion grew concerning the theological probity of older Christian universities' teaching. Sensitive to charges of obscurantist anti-intellectualism, in 1927 the Baptist Bible Union acquired the bankrupt Des Moines University, appointing T. T. Shields chairman of the board. Success eluded the Union, however, with students staging spectacular on-campus riots that led to the university's entering receivership and permanent damage to the Union. More successful was the 1927 foundation of Bob Jones College (from 1947, University), honoring Methodist evangelist Bob Jones Sr. (1883–1968). Still in operation, the school was accredited only in 2005. The 1929 creation of Westminster Seminary under Machen's leadership marked the final abandonment of Princeton Seminary, Fundamentalism's original intellectual core.

In the short term, liberalism appeared ascendant to the point of nearly wiping out its erstwhile opponents. The creation of the United Church of Canada (1925) may be seen as an institutional triumph for theological liberalism. Lingering embers of cultural optimism were snuffed out by the Depression and World War II. Yet Fundamentalism lived on, despite liberal academics' pre-emptively dismissive declaration of its death. Newly invented radio broadcasting provided wound-licking Fundamentalists a medium by which to appeal to new audiences. Vitriolic exchanges in the late 1920s between two Canadian Fundamentalist broadcasters led to revocation of all faith-based radio licenses in Canada. In the 1930s, Fundamentalism began to recover, as non-Fundamentalist Northern European Protestants (such as Swedish Baptists and the Christian Reformed Church) were increasingly attracted, Fundamentalism's opening a route to their acceptance into mainstream culture. Another trend maturing over ensuing decades was Fundamentalists' tendency to migrate from denominational churches to independent ones.

Many Fundamentalists perceived a new, possibly more insidious threat in the 1940s and 1950s. The WCFA was not flourishing by 1940. Presbyterian Carl Macintire (1906–2002), perceiving alterations of the Fundamentalist consensus by neo-evangelicals as insider defection, or even betrayal, inaugurated the American Council of Christian Churches (ACCC) in 1941 (the related global organization, the International Council of Christian Churches in 1948). The next year, neo-evangelicals launched the National Association of Evangelicals (NAE). The key difference between the ACCC and the NAE, otherwise almost theologically identical groups, was the question of separatism.

Trends since 1970 Fundamentalism continues as a viable and significant branch of the broader evangelical movement. The Baptist Jerry Falwell (1933–2007) turned his back on earlier anti-intellectualism by establishing Liberty University in 1971. Currently attracting approximately 38,000 students, the university offers a broad range of majors, in addition to traditional biblical and theological courses. Socially conservative, as well as theologically, Falwell intoned controversially against homosexuality and pornography. The Moral Majority lobby group he launched in 1979 was one of the first and leading movements in the broader Religious Right campaign. The Religious Right's voter mobilization may have aided Ronald Reagan's (1911–2004) 1980 presidential victory. Harold Lindsell (1913–1998), a strongly Calvinistic apologist, fomented a "Battle for the Bible" with his 1976 eponymous volume that accused some evangelicals of abandoning a sufficiently rigorous doctrine of inspiration. Repercussions continue to be felt in the Evangelical Theological Society. The American Council of Christian Churches continues to function, but as a vestigial group of 7 denominations representing approximately 200 congregations. One of the more highly visible current Fundamentalists is Texas megachurch pastor John Hagee (b. 1940). In keeping with Dispensational tenets, he is a Christian Zionist and vocal supporter of modern Israel.

C. Mark Steinacher

See also: Christian Brethren; Congregationalism; Creationism; Evangelicalism; Homosexuality; International Council of Christian Churches; United Church of Canada.

References

Gauvreau, Michael. *The Evangelical Century: College and Creed in English Canada from the Great Revival to the Great Depression*. Montreal and Kingston: McGill-Queen's University Press, 1991.

Kaplan, Lawrence. *Fundamentalism in Comparative Perspective*. Amherst: University of Massachusetts Press, 1992.

Marsden, George M. *Fundamentalism and American Culture: The Shaping of Twentieth Century Evangelicalism, 1870–1925*. New York: Oxford University Press, 1980.

Noll, Mark A. *The Scandal of the Evangelical Mind*. Grand Rapids, MI: William B. Eerdmans Publishing Company, 1994.

Russell, C. Allyn. *Voices of American Fundamentalism: Seven Biographical Studies*. Philadelphia: Westminster Press, 1976.

Sandeen, Ernest R. *The Roots of Fundamentalism: British and American Millenarianism, 1800–1930*. Chicago: University of Chicago Press, 1970.

Sweet, Leonard I., ed. *The Evangelical Tradition in America*. Macon, GA: Mercer University Press, 1984.

Szasz, Ferenc Morton. *The Divided Mind of Protestant America, 1880–1930*. Tuscaloosa: University of Alabama Press, 1982.

G

G12 Vision

This Charismatic movement was initiated in the nation of Colombia in 1972 by two North American leaders, Father Francis McNutt (b. 1925) and Ruth Carter Stapleton (1929–1983), who visited Bogotá and held a series of meetings there that included both Catholics and evangelicals. A decade later (1983), the movement they initiated would influence the founding of the International Charismatic Mission (MCI) by César Castellanos Domínguez and his wife, Claudia. By 2000, the MCI had developed a large central church in Bogotá (with a weekly attendance of more than 40,000) and had established large daughter churches in other Colombian cities, as well as in other countries—such as Costa Rica, where the MCI had one central church with more than 3,000 in attendance weekly in July 2000.

A few years after the founding of the Bogotá church, Castellanos visited the Reverend David Yongi Cho in South Korea. Cho had implemented a cell structure at his Yoido Full Gospel Church in Seoul, which was subsequently grown to become the largest Christian congregation in the world (with some 830,000 members in 2007). While in South Korea, Castellanos claimed to have received a revelation in which God promised to increase the size of Castellanos's church in great measure and assist him in caring for the growing numbers of people.

Castellanos subsequently reorganized his 600-member church into cell groups of 12 adults (called the G12 Vision), while his brother-in-law, César Fajardo, did the same with the youth. Between 1991 and 1994, Castellanos's church grew from 70 to 1,200 members; and between 1994 and 1999, the church reportedly established 20,000 cell groups with a regular weekly church attendance of 45,000 people. In 2009, the MCI claimed 25,000 weekly cell groups with more than 150,000 people in attendance in Bogotá alone. Between 1990 and 2009, the MCI expanded its ministry throughout the country and established more than 200 local churches and hundreds more in North American, Central and South America, and Europe.

In 2000, evangelical church leaders from around the world traveled to the MCI in Bogotá, Colombia, to learn about the G12 Vision. In 2001, Castellanos formed an international G12 board of directors, with leaders from various countries. However, by 2005 some of these leaders decided to cut their affiliation with Castellanos and his G12 Vision, which they denounced as being too authoritarian. Defectors include César Farjardo, Castellanos's former youth pastor, who established Sin Muros Internacional (Without Borders International), and Ricardo Rodríguez, who founded Centro Mundial de Avivamiento (World Revival Center), both centered in Bogotá. Rodríguez went on to establish his own TV station in Bogotá, called the Avivamiento Broadcasting Network (TV-ABN), which began broadcasting in June 2001. The station is owned by the Centro Mundial de Avivamiento, which is pastored by Ricardo Rodríguez and his wife, María Patricia. In December 2008, Rodríguez held a giant rally at Parque Simón Bolívar in Bogotá, with an estimated 300,000 people in attendance. During that same week, about 15,000 pastors from 50 countries attended his annual "Avivamiento Leadership Conference."

In spite of the defections, many of the original leaders have continued to form branches of the G12 movement, following in Castellanos's footsteps. Currently, the MCI in Bogotá claims to have established 55,000 cell groups with about 550,000 members worldwide.

Clifton L. Holland

See also: Charismatic Movement; Pentecostalism, Yoido Full Gospel Church.

References

Castellanos, César. *Developing a Supernatural Leadership*. Bogotá, Colombia: G12 Editors, 2003.

Castellanos, César. *The Revelation of the Cross*. Bogotá, Colombia: G12 Editors, 2003.

Castellanos, César. *Win through the G12 Vision*. Bogotá, Colombia: G12 Editors, 2006.

■ Gabon

Gabon, a country on the Atlantic coast of Africa between the Republic of the Congo (Brazzaville) and Equatorial Guinea, is home to some 1,486,000 people (2008), most members of one of the country's large Bantu people groups. The equator passes through the center of its 99,500 square miles of territory.

Gabon has been an inhabited area for several thousand years, but in the 16th century it was invaded by the Myene and in the next century by the Fang peoples. Amid the various Bantu groups in the area, the Fang emerged as the dominating force. Europeans had begun to visit the area in 1472 (the Portuguese), and sailors from various nations continued to land on the coast to collect slaves and ivory. The Myene and Fang cooperated with the Europeans in these endeavors. In the middle of the 19th century, as the slave trade was winding down, Libreville, now the country's capital, was founded as a city for freed slaves.

The French, who controlled Gabon for many years, had little interest in exploiting its resources and used it primarily as a conduit to more interesting parts of Africa. Only in the late 20th century did Western interests begin to focus upon the valuable uranium and oil deposits. The country made a rather peaceful transition to independence in 1960.

The many different peoples had a variety of traditional religions, most of which have been replaced by Christianity. The veneration of ancestors was a common theme among them. There were also various secret societies, the most important being the Bwiti, a male group dedicated to the remembrance of the great ancestors. It developed quite strongly among the Fang and more recently began to admit females to initiation. Members consume the eboga root, which possesses psychedelic properties and is used in initiation ceremonies in place of water baptism. Bwiti emerged in the late 19th century. Suppressed during the colonial era, it developed a branch that incorporated Christian elements and was then legalized in 1970. The Bwiti is now the third largest religious group in Gabon.

Christianity was introduced to Gabon by Capuchin missionaries who arrived from Italy in the 1600s. However, they were expelled by the Portuguese in 1777. In the 19th century the Congregation of the Sacred Heart of Mary and the Holy Ghost Fathers be-

Gabon

Religion	Followers in 1970	Followers in 2010	% of Population	Annual % growth 2000–2010	Followers in 2025	Followers in 2050
Christians	508,000	1,258,000	90.5	1.76	1,536,000	1,887,000
Roman Catholics	321,000	799,000	57.5	3.05	945,000	1,145,000
Independents	62,500	246,000	17.7	1.35	307,000	380,000
Protestants	92,000	172,000	12.4	0.84	230,000	310,000
Muslims	4,000	64,500	4.6	1.77	80,000	100,000
Ethnoreligionists	17,000	43,000	3.1	1.77	45,000	45,000
Agnostics	0	12,500	0.9	2.54	20,000	26,000
New religionists	300	10,500	0.8	1.78	15,000	20,000
Baha'is	200	600	0.0	1.77	1,000	1,800
Atheists	0	400	0.0	0.70	800	1,500
Total population	**529,000**	**1,390,000**	**100.0**	**1.77**	**1,698,000**	**2,081,000**

GABON

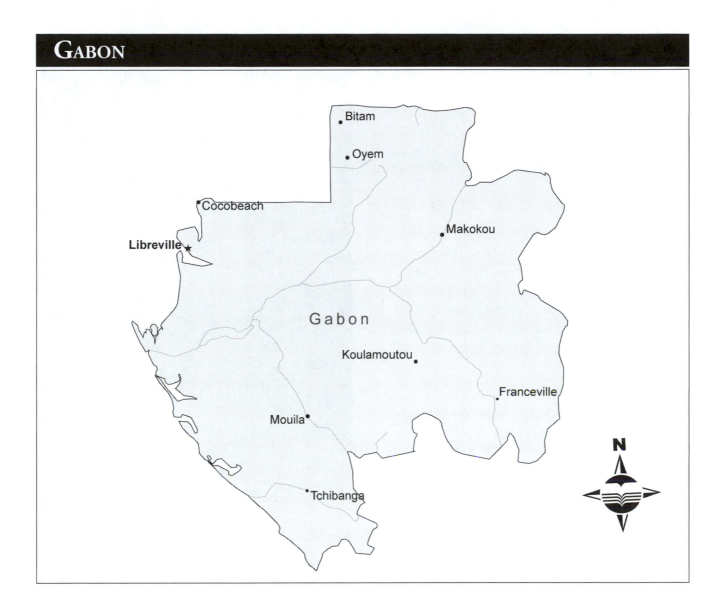

came the backbone of the Roman Catholic Church presence in the region. Libreville became the center of church activity in the 1850s, and the Vicariate Apostolic of Senegambia and the Two Guineas established, with the vicar residing in Gabon. In 1863 the area was divided into several vicariates and the Vicariate of Libreville created. In 1958, Libreville was elevated to archdiocesan status and a new Diocese of Mouila created. A third diocese was set apart in 1969.

The Evangelical Church of Gabon had its beginnings when missionaries from the American Board of Commissioners for Foreign Missions arrive in 1842. They turned their work over to American Presbyterians in 1870, who in turn gave way to the Paris Mission

(Reformed Church of France) in 1892. The Gabon mission became independent in 1961. In 1934, the Paris Mission encouraged the Christian and Missionary Alliance to begin work in the southern half of the country, their mission maturing as the Evangelical Church of South Gabon.

The Roman Catholic Church remains the largest church in the country, claiming upwards of 60 percent of the population. Besides the two larger Protestant churches, there are a few smaller groups, including the Jehovah's Witnesses; the Kimbanguist Church (Église de Jésus Christ sur la terre par le prophète Simon Kimbangu), which arrived from the Congo in the 1950s; and the indigenous Evangelical Church of Pentecost.

There is a small Muslim community, most of whom follow the Sunni Malikite School. The community received a boost in 1973, when Albert Bongo, who had become president of Gabon in 1967, announced that he had converted to Islam. The Baha'i Faith entered the country in the years after World War II. As is common in most former French colonies, there are several lodges of the Ancient and Mystical Order Rosae Crucis.

J. Gordon Melton

See also: American Board of Commissioners for Foreign Missions; Ancient and Mystical Order Rosae Crucis; Baha'i Faith; Capuchins; Christian and Missionary Alliance; Evangelical Church of Gabon; Holy Ghost Fathers; Jehovah's Witnesses; Kimbanguist Church; Malikite School of Islam; Paris Mission; Reformed Church of France; Roman Catholic Church.

References

Gardinier, David E. *Historical Dictionary of Gabon*. Metuchen, NJ: Scarecrow Press, 2006.

Hamilton, B. A. "The Environment, Establishment, and Development of Protestant Missions in French Equatorial Africa." Ph.D. diss., Grace Theological Seminary, 1959.

Kasule, O. H. "Muslims in Gabon, West Africa." *Journal of the Institute of Muslim Minority Affairs* 6, no. 1 (1985): 192–206.

Klein, C. M. *We Went to Gabon*. Harrisburg, PA: Christian Publications, 1974.

Stoecklin, P., et al. *L'Église Evangélique du Gabon, 1842–1961*. Alençon, France: Imprimerie Corbière et Jagain, 1962.

■ Gambia

Gambia is a small African nation that exists along the Gambia River, which flows into the center of Senegal. Gambia is completely surrounded on three sides by Senegal, the Atlantic Ocean forming its western border. Its 2,861 square miles are home to 1,735,464 people, most of whom are members of various African peoples. Almost half of Gambia's citizens are from the Mandingo people (42 percent), who moved into

Woman observes Friday prayers near the central mosque in the Gambian capital, Banjul. (AP/Wide World Photos)

the area in the 15th century. They shared power along the river with the kingdom of Mali. The Portuguese arrived in 1455, and their presence caused a significant amount of the economic life to shift toward the ocean.

In 1618 the British purchased Gambia from Portugal and thus established Great Britain's initial foothold in western Africa. The British worked the river and developed a system of gathering slaves for transport to its colonies in North America and the Caribbean. The British saw the area primarily as a source for slaves, and neither the government nor the British churches saw it as an area for missionary work. Meanwhile, beginning in the early 19th century, Islam became the dominant religion in the country.

After the end of the slave trade, Gambia lost its economic importance to Great Britain and was transformed primarily into an irritant for France, which

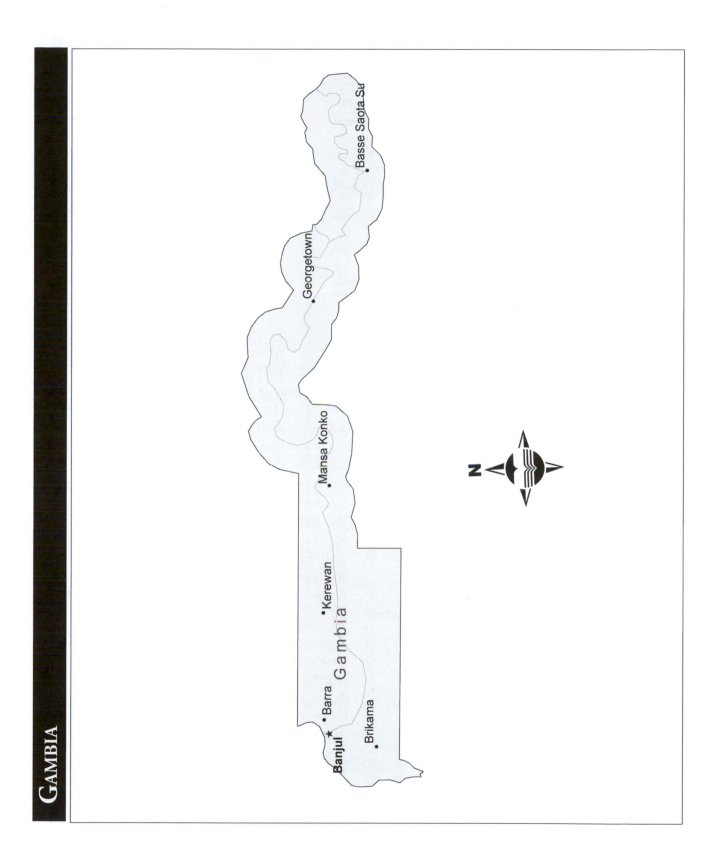

Gambia

Religion	Followers in 1970	Followers in 2010	% of Population	Annual % growth 2000–2010	Followers in 2025	Followers in 2050
Muslims	408,000	1,598,000	86.6	3.07	2,220,000	3,215,000
Ethnoreligionists	55,600	138,000	7.5	3.16	140,000	150,000
Christians	14,500	81,400	4.4	5.10	129,000	210,000
Roman Catholics	9,300	48,500	2.6	6.71	80,000	140,000
Independents	800	17,200	0.9	3.74	25,000	35,000
Protestants	1,600	8,600	0.5	4.24	14,000	24,000
Baha'is	4,100	16,000	0.9	3.16	27,000	42,000
Agnostics	0	11,300	0.6	3.16	17,400	30,000
Hindus	100	300	0.0	3.18	400	800
Atheists	0	80	0.0	3.32	150	300
Total population	**482,000**	**1,845,000**	**100.0**	**3.16**	**2,534,000**	**3,649,000**

controlled Senegal. In 1889, the French and British reached an agreement that set the present border between Gambia and Senegal. Gambia became autonomous in 1963 and in 1965 became an independent nation in the British Commonwealth.

Although some traditional religion remains in Gambia, the great majority of the people became Muslim (Sunni Malikite School of Islam) in the 19th century. Both the Tijaniyya and the Muridiyya Sufi Brotherhoods are also present, having come into the country from Senegal. In 1960, the Ahmadiyya Muslim movement also established a small presence. The Baha'i Faith began a growth phase in the 1960s.

It was not until 1816 that an Anglican chaplain made his way to Gambia. Later missionaries from the Society for the Propagation of the Gospel in Foreign Parts established a small mission. The Church of England's work was incorporated into the Diocese of Gambia, which in 1951 became part of the Church of the Province of West Africa. Representatives of the Methodist Church came in 1821, and Gambia became a launching pad for Methodism's expansion throughout West Africa. The first permanent mission of the Roman Catholic Church was established in 1849. There is now a Catholic diocese, established in 1957, whose bishop resides at Banjul. Many of the priests are Holy Ghost Fathers from Ireland.

These three churches dominated the Christian community through the mid-1950s. Together they consti-

tuted the Christian Council of Gabon, which in turn is affiliated with the World Council of Churches. However, beginning with the World Evangelical Crusade (now WEC International), which entered the country in 1957, several evangelical organizations have begun a new missionary effort. The primary effort has come from the Association of Baptists for World Evangelism, an American-based evangelical missionary sending organization that began sending missionaries in 1979. The first missionary couple, Mel and Ruby Pittman, was the vanguard heralding the arrival of what had become by the end of the 20th century a team of 17. The Southern Baptist Convention opened a mission in 1982.

J. Gordon Melton

See also: Ahmadiyya Movement in Islam; Baha'i Faith; Church of England; Church of the Province of West Africa; Holy Ghost Fathers; Methodist Church; Muridîyya; Roman Catholic Church; Society for the Propagation of the Gospel in Foreign Parts; Southern Baptist Convention; Tijaniyya Sufi Order; World Council of Churches.

References

Babou, Cheikh Anta. *Fighting the Greater Jihad: Amadu Bamba and the Founding of the Muridiyya of Senegal, 1853–1913*. Athens: Ohio State University Press, 2007.

Behrman, Lucy C. *Muslim Brotherhoods and Politics in Senegal*. Lincoln, NE: iUniverse, 1999.

Laughton, J. R. C. *Gambia: Country, People and Church in the Diocese of Gambia and the Rio Pongas.* London: SPG, 1938.

Maranz, D. E. *Peace Is Everything: World View of Muslims in Senegambia.* Dallas: Summer Institute of Linguistics, 1993.

Quinn, C. A. "Mandingo Kingdoms of the Senegambia: Traditionalism, Islam, and European Expansion." Ph.D. diss., Northwestern University, 1972.

Wilks, Ivor. *Wa and the Wala: Islam and Polity in Northwestern Ghana.* Cambridge: Cambridge University Press, 2002.

Ganesh Chaturthi

Ganesh Chaturthi is a Hindu holiday that celebrates the birthday, actually the creation, of the deity Ganesh. There are a variety of tales related to Ganesh's birth; possibly the best known begins at a time when the god Siva, who commonly dwelt on Mount Kailas, left his abode. While he was away, his wife Parvati desired an attendant who could protect her privacy while bathing and prevent incursions by unwanted personages who might appear at her front door. She decided to create a son who could perform such a task and named him Vinayak. When Siva returned, he did not recognize the new person in front of his home and Vinayak did not recognize Siva. Vinayak refused him entrance, and Siva beheaded Vinayak with his trident.

Later, when he discovered what he had done, he sent some of his attendants into the nearby forest with instructions to bring him the head of the first living creature they encountered. That creature turned out to be an elephant. When they returned, he placed the elephant's head on the headless body of Vinayak and breathed life into him. Vinayak sprang to life and emerged as Ganesh, now recognized as the son of Parvati and Siva.

Siva then said that when people begin their worship, they should first worship Ganesh and dedicate to him all their future efforts. Such worship would ensure success and prevent failure. Thus Ganesh emerged as the god of prosperity and good fortune, and the remover of obstacles.

Statue of the Hindu elephant-headed deity Ganesh, Gayatri Pariwar Center, Chicago. (J. Gordon Melton)

Another tale of Ganesha's birth begins with Siva slaying Aditya, the son of a sage. Siva restored the boy's life, but failed to calm his enraged father, Kashyapa, who cursed Siva. He doomed Siva's son to the loss of his head. The curse happened as Kashyapa had spoken. Siva retrieved the head from an elephant owned by the god Indra to replace it.

A third tale has Parvati throwing her used bathwater into the Ganges River only to have it drunk by the elephant-headed goddess Malini. Malini subsequently became the mother of a baby that had four arms and five heads—all shaped like an elephant. The baby was claimed as her own by the river goddess Ganga, while Siva asserted the claim of Parvati. He also removed four of the heads and then placed him on a throne as the "Controller of Obstacles."

The multiplication of stories about Ganesh indicates the prominent place he began to assume in Hindu rituals, often being the first deity mentioned, and the place he came to have in most Hindu temples. An increasing number of temples were dedicated to him as the primary deity. Interestingly, in spite of the prominent place Ganesh had, public festivities were not a part of Hindu culture until the 19th century. There was an annual Ganesh festival, but it was usually held in homes or the several Ganesh temples.

Lokmanya Tilak (1856–1920), an ardent Indian nationalist and the first popular leader of the Indian Independence movement that sought to overthrow British colonial rule, struggled with various obstacles to his goal, one being the social chasm that existed between India's ruling Brahmin caste and the masses of people in the various lower castes. Through the 1890s he began to suggest that the Ganesha Chaturthi celebration should be transformed into a National Festival and become a tool facilitating a grassroots unity between Indian peoples. He saw Ganesh as a god for every man. He had observed the Ganesha Chaturthi celebrations in Maharashtra and its capital Bombay (now Mumbai), where it had emerged as an important local festival. It would become an important festival across India through the first half of the 20th century.

Tilak was the first to promote large public images of Ganesha in outdoor tents, and he added the practice of creating many images of Ganesh, all of which were immersed on the 10th day of the festival. He viewed the festival as facilitating community participation and involvement in the 10 to 12 days of spiritual talks, dance, dramas, music, debates, and general festivities. The activities occasioned the coming together of people of all castes, at a time when large social and political gatherings were forbidden by the British.

Ganesha Chaturthi is celebrated during the month of Bhaadrapada on the Hindu lunar calendar, starting on the fourth day of the waxing moon. The day usually falls in August or September on the Common Era calendar.

During the 10 days (12 days in Maharashtra) of activities, *aarthi* (worship centered on the offering of light from wicks soaked in ghee or camphor to a deity) is performed daily. Kumkum, turmeric, and saffron powder, used for social and religious markings, is thrown over the idol. Food is offered before the statues.

A main activity of the celebration is the creation of numerous statues of Ganesh, which become the focus of prayers for good fortunes and success in the coming year. The festival climaxes with the procession of the many images of Ganesh great and small to the local shoreline where all the statues will be immersed in the water, with prayers that he will return to the place the next year. It is considered unholy to keep the image of Ganesh after this day.

In recent years, as the festival has grown in popularity, and as commercial interests have entered the statue-making market, a problem of pollution has arisen. The clay Ganesh statues used for many years were replaced with a variety of statues from non-biodegradable materials and their sheer quantity was a problem. Various cities have taken steps to promote an eco-friendly celebration relative to the immersion rituals and the materials being used in them.

Constance A. Jones

See also: Calendars, Religious; Common Era Calendar; Devotion/Devotional Traditions; Kailas, Mount/Lake Manasarovar.

References

Bhagwat, A. K., and G. P. Pradham. *Lokmanya Tilak: A Biography*. Mumbai; Jaico Publishing House, 2008.

Brown, Robert A. *Ganesh: Studies of an Asian God*. Albany: State University of New York Press, 1991.

Mukuncharandas, Sadhu. *Hindu Festivals (Origin Sentiments & Rituals)*. Amdavad, India: Swaminarayan Aksharpith, 2005.

Raina, Anita Raina. *Understanding Gaṇapati: Insights into the Dynamics of a Cult*. New Delhi: Manohar Publishers, 1997.

Gardnerian Wicca

In its narrower sense, "Gardnerian Wicca" refers to one initiatory lineage within contemporary Pagan Witchcraft whose members can trace a line of their initiators back to Gerald Brosseau Gardner (1884–1964). In a wider sense, the term is sometimes used to character-

Gerald Brosseau Gardner, founder of the Gardnerian Wicca tradition. (Raymond Buckland/Fortean Picture Library)

ize many forms of the new religion of Wicca (the only modern religion born in Britain) that share elements of the strictly defined "Gardnerian tradition." ("Tradition" in Wicca can be loosely compared to "denomination" in Protestant Christianity.)

Gardner was born in a suburb of Liverpool, where his father was a partner in a prosperous firm of timber importers. He had little formal education; due to acute asthma, he was often sent on sea voyages to warmer Mediterranean climates with his nurse-governess. When he was 16, his governess married a tea plantation owner in Ceylon (Sri Lanka, at that time a British colony). He worked two years for the couple and then took a managerial job on another plantation. During his early adult years he became a Freemason. He later managed rubber plantations in Borneo and Malaysia and, after contracting malaria, took employment with the colonial government inspecting rubber plantations and overseeing the legal opium trade. He retired in 1936, and

returned with his English wife, Donna, to live on the south coast of England at Highcliffe near Bournemouth. During his years of contact with South Asian cultures he had become intensely interested in such ideas as reincarnation, shamanism, and magic.

Gardner claimed to have met a handful of surviving British witches, to have been initiated, and to have been given permission to write about the Craft, first as fiction (*High Magic's Aid*) and then as nonfiction (*Witchcraft Today*). Some historians of the Pagan revival, such as Aidan Kelly and Ronald Hutton, question whether any such coven actually existed or whether Gardner and some friends themselves created it. Philip Heselton, on the other hand, argues that the coven did exist in his book *Wiccan Roots* and suggests who its members were. Thus far, no independent source as to a pre–World War II Pagan Witchcraft has been found, whereas its existence is well documented after 1950. Thanks partly to Gardener's openness to the British news media, Gardnerian Wicca enjoyed steady growth throughout the 1950s and 1960s, aided by books and interviews that caused interested people to seek out him and his later coveners.

Gardnerian Wicca spread to North America first through Gardener's books and later in the persons of Raymond and Rosemary Buckland, an English couple who came to Long Island in the early 1960s. By then the American science-fiction writer Margaret St. Clair had already absorbed Gardner's *Witchcraft Today* and included many of its elements in her 1963 novel *Sign of the Labrys.* Most American and Canadian Gardnerian witches (in the stricter sense) trace their lineage to the Bucklands, although Raymond Buckland, a frequent writer on Wicca, would in the 1970s downplay the importance of such lineage, going so far as to start his own from-scratch tradition, "Seax Wicca" (Saxon Witchcraft).

Gardnerian Wiccans regard Wicca as an initiatory mystery religion, not a mass movement. There are three degrees of initiation, with the first making one a priest or priestess and the second conferring the right to teach the Craft. The third qualifies one to form one's own coven, although sometimes second-degree witches may also do so. Ideally, a coven would have a high priestess (Witch Queen) and a high priest (Magus), both of the third degree, and no more than 13 members.

Gardnerian covens tend to be hierarchical, with leaders ritually addressed as "Lady" or "Lord." Third-degree initiates gain greater prestige based on the number of covens which have "hived off" from theirs. Each coven is autonomous, although persons judged to have broken their initiatory oaths may be shunned.

The ritual year is based upon a series of eight Sabbats at the solstices, equinoxes, and in-between cross-quarter days, plus Esbats, or magic-working and coven-business sessions, which may be held at the full moon.

All Gardnerian Wiccans are expected to copy their teachers' "Book of Shadows," a collection of core ritual scripts, chants, and other material, to which the student may later add. The eight seasonal rituals are not changed, however, as part of a deliberate effort to continue a shared current of energy that each generation adds to, a form of "group soul." Followers believe that they will reincarnate in circumstances permitting them to rejoin their coveners in their next lives.

Gardnerian covens emphasize the "drawing down" or "carrying" of their deities, a form of trance-possession similar to that found in Vodou and Candomblé. Among contemporary Wiccans, they have made this a hallmark of their practice.

Initiates themselves estimate that there are approximately 220 to 230 covens with a total of about 3,600 initiated Gardnerian-lineage witches in North America.

In another sense—that popularized by historian of religion Aidan Kelly—most Wicca is "Gardnerian," if it includes these elements that do not seem to have been part of English witchcraft before Gerald Gardner's writings were published: an asexual Godhead manifesting as a God and Goddess; ritual leadership primarily or ideally female; seasonal and lunar rituals performed within a magic circle, with elemental guardians invoked at each cardinal direction; a belief in reincarnation; the idea that Wicca is a revived ancient religion with its own theology, not merely a loose collection of magical practices.

None of these characteristics are unique to contemporary Wicca, but collectively they go a long way toward defining it. The widespread influence of Gardner's and his followers' writings (notably Doreen Valiente [1922–1999], who served as his high priestess in the 1950s and authored several books of her own) have exercised a magnetic influence on other forms of witchcraft and caused them to align with this broadly "Gardnerian" model.

Covens in the Gardnerian tradition operate as autonomous bodies tied together fraternally by their shared lineage and practice. Gardnerians may be contacted through the Gardnerian Tradition Web Ring on the Internet in which a number of Gardnerian covens participate.

Chas S. Clifton

See also: Goddess Spirituality; Reincarnation; Spring Equinox; Summer Solstice; Winter Solstice.

References

Clifton, Chas S. *Her Hidden Children: The Rise of Wicca and Paganism in America.* Lanham, MD: AltaMira Press, 2006.

Gardner, Gerald B. *High Magic's Aid.* London: Michael Houghton, 1949.

Gardner, Gerald B. *The Meaning of Witchcraft.* Wellingborough, UK: Aquarian. 1959.

Gardner, Gerald B. *Witchcraft Today.* London: Rider, 1954.

Heselton, Philip. *Gerald Gardner and the Cauldron of Inspiration.* Milverton, UK: Capall Bann, 2003.

Heselton, Philip. *Wiccan Roots: Gerald Gardner and the Modern Witchcraft Revival.* Freshfields, UK: Capall Bann Publishing, 2000.

Hutton, Ronald. *The Triumph of the Moon: A History of Modern Pagan Witchcraft.* Oxford: Oxford University Press, 1999.

Kelly, Aidan. *Crafting the Art of Magic.* St. Paul, MN: Llewellyn, 1991.

St. Clair, Margaret. *Sign of the Labrys.* New York: Bantam Books, 1963.

Valiente, Doreen. *The Rebirth of Witchcraft.* London: Robert Hale, 1989.

Garifuna Religion

The ethnic group known as the Garifuna, or Black Carib, exists today in Central America, the Caribbean, and various cities in the United States, Canada, and

A Garifuna dancer performs on Corn Island, Nicaragua. (AP Photo/Esteban Felix)

England (a total population of about 100,000 to 150,000) and can be distinguished by their unique cultural patterns: language, religion, crafts, music, dance, and lifestyle. Garinagu is the plural form of the singular word Garifuna and is the collective name preferred by the representatives of this population in Belize today.

The history of the Garifuna ("cassava-eating people") begins on the Island of St. Vincent in the eastern Caribbean, which was originally inhabited by a mixture of Caribe and Arawak tribes (linguistically Maipuran and Arawakan, or Island Carib) from mainland South America prior to the period of Spanish colonization that began in 1492. Soon after their initial contact with Europeans, the Island Carib began to absorb individual Europeans (from Spain, France, and England) and West Africans (mainly from shipwrecked Spanish slave ships) by means of capture or rescue. By 1700, a new ethnic group emerged on St. Vincent that

was racially and culturally distinct from that of the Island Caribs: the Garifuna.

In terms of their language and cultural patterns, the Garifuna are an Afro-Amerindian people (called *zambos* by the Spanish) who have blended various traits of their ancestors to create a unique social system with a strong emphasis on music, dance, and storytelling and with its unique brand of religion that consists of a mixture of Indian, African, and Roman Catholic beliefs. Another distinction is that the Garifuna are matrifocal, which means that the women are the center of the household and that descendants trace their bloodline (consanguineal) through their mother's family.

In November 1997, the Garifuna celebrated the 200th anniversary of their arrival on the shores of Central America, after being forcibly removed by the British from the Island of St. Vincent in 1797. After conquering many of the Spanish-held islands in the Caribbean, the British decided to take control of the

French-held island of St. Vincent during the 1770s. By 1783 the British had dominated the French inhabitants and their slaves, and had attempted to subjugate about 7,000 to 8,000 Garifuna. Many Garifuna were killed in battles with the British or died from European diseases during this period. During 1795–1797, the British hunted down, killed, or captured the remaining Garifuna population, destroyed their homes, and deported on 8 or 9 ships about 2,250 survivors to the Island of Roatan in the Bay Islands, off the coast of Honduras.

However, the Garifuna leaders considered Roatan to be unsuitable for such a large population and requested help from the Spanish authorities at Trujillo, on the mainland of Honduras. By the end of September 1797, about 1,700 Garifuna had been resettled near Trujillo by the Spanish, who hoped that the Garifuna would provide them with needed manpower for the development of farming communities on the north coast of Honduras.

By 1900, the Garifuna had established their own settlements along the Caribbean coast of Central America, predominantly in Honduras, Guatemala, and Belize (known at that time as British Honduras), but also at Sandy Bay in Nicaragua. The principal settlements were at Stann Creek and Punta Gorda in Belize; Livingston, near Puerto Barrios, in Guatemala; and at scores of locations along the northern coast of Honduras, near the major cities of Puerto Cortés, Tela, La Ceiba, and Trujillo. In 1974, it was estimated that the Garifuna population in Honduras was about 60,900, with about 10,600 in Belize, 5,500 in Guatemala, and 800 in Nicaragua. With few exceptions, most of these settlements were located within 200 yards of the sea, at river mouths, freshwater lagoons, and protected bays. Also, during the 1970s, thousands of Garifuna were reported to have migrated to U.S. cities (New York, Boston, New Orleans, and Los Angeles), where the men typically served in the U.S. merchant fleet. More recently, Garifuna families have been reported in port cities of Canada and Great Britain.

Soon after their arrival in Central America in 1797, the Garifuna were considered by the Spanish and British settlers to be "devil-worshippers, polygamists, and speakers of a secret language," which strengthened the Garifuna's resolve to live apart in their own settlements, maintain their independence, and conserve their culture. The Garifuna songs and dance styles display a wide range of subjects, such as work songs, social dances, and ancestral traditions; one of the most popular dances is called "La Punta," which is performed at wakes, holidays, parties, and other social events. Some of these traditional dances and ceremonies have to do with the Garifuna's respect for the dead: the Amuyadahani ("bathing the spirit of the dead"), the Chuga ("feeding the dead"), and the Dugu ("the feasting of the dead").

The Garifuna perform these religious rites and ceremonies because, like many Amerindian and African societies, they believe that the spirits of their dead ancestors, which are both good and evil and have a direct impact on the lives of people in the living world, must be respected, worshipped, and appeased. This religious tradition is known as Animism, or Spiritism.

Although some Garifuna adopted Catholicism on the Island of St. Vincent during the French occupation or after arriving on the Spanish-controlled mainland of Central America, this was more a "political decision" rather than an authentic conversion to Christianity. After migrating to the south coast of Belize in 1833 and establishing permanent settlements, some Garifuna accepted the presence of Anglican, Methodist, and Baptist missionaries in their villages and eventually the establishment of English-speaking Protestant churches and schools. Later, the Seventh-day Adventists and the Church of the Nazarene developed churches and schools in Garifuna villages in Belize. In Honduras, there are a few Baptist churches among the Garifuna, near Tela.

The core of Garifuna culture is their traditional Afro-Amerindian rites and rituals that are practiced in every Garifuna settlement, and the *buwiye*, or shaman (male or female), is the direct psychological link between the ancestors and the souls of the living. An important part of their religious ceremonies involves the use of songs, drinking, and dance, accompanied by drums and other musical instruments, which sometimes induces a trance-like state of consciousness (called "spirit-possession") during which time a person may enter the spirit-world and communicate with the ancestors, according to practitioners.

These ceremonies—which are similar in some respects to Vodou, Santeria, and Myalism-Obeah (Myalism is an African adaptation of Christianity, and Obeah is the related witchcraft element of that religious system) practices in Haiti, Cuba, Puerto Rico, and Jamaica, respectively—are used to mourn the dead, heal the sick, protect family members from harm, do harm to one's enemies, discern the future, assure good fishing and harvests, find a mate, help the dead achieve peace and happiness in the next world, and appease alienated spirits. Rum is often administered ritually to begin a ceremony or induce a trance; it is thrown out of the doors and windows to attract the spirits; it is sprinkled upon the dancers, drummers, and the possessed to cool and sooth; it is used to cure those seeking relief from physical and psychological ills; and it is used to anoint the sacred table at the end of the ceremony. Food, flowers, and candles are normally used in these ceremonies as well, but there is no mention of animal sacrifices being used as in Vodou, Santeria, and Myalism-Obeah rituals.

Although many Garifuna today speak Creole English and/or Spanish, most continue to use their traditional language that is a unique blend of Arawak, Caribe, French, Yuroba, Banti, and Swahili.

Clifton L. Holland

See also: Ancestors; Church of the Nazarene; Death; Roman Catholic Church; Santeria; Seventh-day Adventist Church; Spirit Possession; Vodou; Witchcraft.

References

Davidson, William V. "Black Carib (Garifuna) Habitats in Central America." In *Frontier Adaptations in Lower Central America*, edited by Mary W. Helms and Franklin O. Loveland. Philadelphia: Institute for the Study of Human Issues, 1976.

Gonzalez, Nancie L. *Sojourners of the Caribbean: Ethnogenesis and Ethnohistory of the Garifuna.* Urbana: University of Illinois Press, 1988.

Olmos, Margarite Fernández, and Lizabeth Paravisini-Gebert, eds. *Sacred Possessions: Vodou, Santería, Obeah and the Caribbean.* New Brunswick, NJ: Rutgers University Press, 1997.

www.centrelink.org/belize.html.

Gaudiya Math

The Gaudiya Math family of institutions represents the most visible form of Vaishnavism, the worship of Vishnu, in the world outside India and, increasingly, within India itself. It traces its origins to the life of Chaitanya Mahaprabhu (1486–1533), the great saint and ecstatic of Bengal, whom Gaudiya Math followers hold to be an incarnation of Krishna (Vishnu's avatar) himself.

Like many modern Indian religious movements, the Gaudiya Math had its birth in the reforming period of the 19th century, when its spiritual father, Kedarnath Datta Bhaktivinoda (1838–1914), commonly known as Bhaktivinoda Thakur, undertook to reveal the theological depth of the form of Vaishnavism taught by Chaitanya. Bhaktivinoda's son, Bhaktisiddhanta Saraswati (1869–1936), was the actual founder of the Gaudiya Math in 1918, creating a modern institution to promote Vaishnavism. In so doing, he made a number of radical changes in the external forms of the religion, which can be summarized as (1) a new attitude to social organization, known as *daiva Varnashram*, which rejects all hereditary spiritual rights; (2) a more intellectually based religious life, rejecting the quietist and mystical approaches that predominated in traditional Vaishnava circles; and (3) a strict moralism, fundamentally rejecting abuses that had grown out of antinomian elements in the tradition.

The evangelical fervor that Siddhanta Saraswati brought to his preaching resulted in the establishment of 64 branches of his *math* (monastery) before he died in 1936. His conviction of the depth of the Vaishnava tradition inspired him to send disciples to England and Germany to spread the teachings, though with limited results. He left behind him a large number of highly committed and learned disciples, many of them *sannyasi* (in the renounced order of life). His succession was troubled, however, and a first schism took place in 1943, when Bhakti Vilasa Tirtha rejected the leadership of Bhakti Prasad Puri and became *acharya* (teacher) of the Chaitanya Math. Puri Maharaj's organization is now officially known as the Gaudiya Mission. Other disciples of Siddhanta Saraswati became disillusioned with the leadership of both these acharyas and left to form their own independent institutions in the 1940s and 1950s. Most prominent among these sannyasis were Bhakti Rakshak Sridhar, Bhakti Dayita Madhava, Bhakti Prajnan Keshava, Bhakti Hridoy Bon, Bhakti Saranga Goswami, and Bhakti Kusum Madhusudan. Most of these acharyas established separate branches in Calcutta and Nabadwip-Mayapur (the birthplace of Chaitanya Mahaprabhu) and generally had a stronghold in some regions of West Bengal, Assam, or Orissa. Some of them also established branches in other parts of India, such as Delhi, Bombay, and Chandigarh, where they often served a predominantly Bengali clientele. A. C. Bhaktivedanta Swami (1896–1977), who started the International Society for Krishna Consciousness (ISKCON), was a relative latecomer and founded his society in 1967 in the United States (after an earlier, failed attempt to form another institution, the League of Devotees, in Jhansi in 1953).

Although these various Gaudiya maths had differing degrees of success in India prior to the spreading of the Hare Krishna movement internationally, ISKCON's unprecedented accomplishments around the world had undeniable repercussions on its relatives. In the early stages, the relationship of ISKCON to the Gaudiya Maths was problematic, due to Bhaktivedanta Swami's having been something of an outsider in his spiritual master's original movement. However, Bhaktivedanta Swami had strong friendships with two prominent sannyasi godbrothers, Bhakti Rakshak Sridhar (1895–1983), founder of the Chaitanya Saraswata Math, and Bhakti Prajnan Keshava (1898–1968), founder of the Gaudiya Vedanta Samiti. These relations were renewed following his return to India with his disciples from the Americas and Europe, and after his death in 1977, many of those disciples went to seek instruction in the Gaudiya Vaishnava religious tradition from Sridhar and Bhaktivedanta Narayan, one of Keshava's most prominent disciples. Another senior disciple of Siddhanta Saraswati, Bhakti Promode Puri (1899–2000), became a source of attraction to Westerners interested in the more authentic Gaudiya Math culture. Puri Maharaj became the first president of the World Vaishnava Association in 1994.

Sridhar's successor, Bhakti Sundar Govinda (b. 1929) (a Bengali), continues to travel all over the world and make disciples. Some of Sridhar's Western disciples have also enjoyed considerable success, particu-

larly Bhakti Aloka Paramadvaiti (b. 1953), a Swiss national and disciple of Bhaktivedanta Swami, who founded his own organization, VRINDA, which now has more than 100 centers, most prominently in South America. Paramadvaiti has also been the driving force in reviving the World Vaishnava Association (Visva Vaishnava Raja Sabha), an attempt to coordinate the activities of the disparate Gaudiya maths. This project has met with limited success, and there are few joint projects by the various institutions, though, with the significant exception of ISKCON, most are members.

Another prominent Western disciple of Bhaktivedanta Swami who accepted Sridhar as *siksha guru* (teacher) and formed an independent society is Swami Bhaktivedanta Tripurari. The Gaudiya Vaishnava Society's northern California monastery, Audarya, is its only math. Swami Tripurari has concentrated on making a literary contribution, rather than on establishing maths and making disciples. His writing focuses on presenting esoteric Gaudiya Vaishnava doctrines in contemporary language. He has also successfully established an Internet congregation that transcends sectarian boundaries and serves the entire international Gaudiya Vaishnava community.

The above-mentioned Bhaktivedanta Narayan (Gaudiya Vedanta Samiti), who performed the funeral rites (*samadhi*) for Bhaktivedanta Swami, is the most charismatic force in the Gaudiya Vaishnava world today and has attracted the largest number of disciples outside of India, with followers on every continent and a strong publishing program in several languages. Narayan has his principal center in Mathura, India.

Bhakti Ballabh Tirtha, the current acharya of the Chaitanya Gaudiya Math, has also been particularly active worldwide and has disciples in the United States, England, and Russia, but this math's principal strength is in Assam. Bhakti Promode Puri (Gopinath Gaudiya Math) also has a following in Russia.

Doctrinally, there is not much to distinguish the Gaudiya Math from ISKCON. The principal differences are in form—the Gaudiya Math has not been overly influenced by Western elements. ISKCON has generally been suspicious of the Gaudiya Math's learning and charisma.

The Gaudiya Math has generally taken a more traditional form in India, with a single acharya generally inheriting the institution from his predecessor. The ritual of the Gaudiya Math is fairly standard throughout all the institutions, with few of the individual leaders leaving much of an individual mark. They pride themselves on fidelity to the traditions established by Siddhanta Saraswati. Though different Gaudiya Math institutions have branches throughout India, the Bengali language predominates as the language of hymns (*kirtan*), which are, as in traditional Bengali Vaishnavism, an important means of communicating doctrine. This is in contrast with ISKCON, which concentrates on chanting the Hare Krishna mantra rather than using the Bengali-language hymnal of Bhaktivinoda Thakur. No hymn tradition has been established in any other languages than Bengali, Sanskrit, and to a much lesser extent, Hindi. Liturgically, the Gaudiya Math tends to admit of little influence from India's different vernacular Vaishnava traditions.

Also worth mentioning here is "Jagat Guru" Siddha Svarupananda, the somewhat idiosyncratic founder of the Chaitanya Mission based in Hawaii. A disciple of A. C. Bhaktivedanta Swami, he is perhaps the most Westernized of all representatives of this tradition, with a less intensely scholastic approach to spiritual life. He has opened centers in Poland and other Eastern European countries, as well as in the Philippines, Australia, and New Zealand, and is a founding member of the World Vaishnava Association.

Jan Brzezinski

See also: Chaitanya, Shri Krishna; Devotion/Devotional Traditions; International Society for Krishna Consciousness; Vaishnavism; World Vaisnava Association; Yoga.

References

De, S. K. *Early History of Vaisnava Faith and Movement in Bengal*. Calcutta: K. L. Mukhopadhyay, 1961.
Gelberg, Steven, ed. *Hare Krishna, Hare Krishna*. New York: Grove Press, 1983.
Paramadvaiti, Swami B. A. "Our Family the Gaudiya Math: A Study of the Expansion of Gaudiya Vaisnavism and the Many Branches Developing around the Gaudiya Math." http://www.vrindavan.org/English/Books/GMconded.html. Accessed September 15, 2001.
Sridhara, Deva Goswami Bhakti Raksaka. *Sri Guru and His Grace*. San Jose, CA: Guardian of Devotion Press, 1983.
Thakura, Bhakivinoda. *The Bhagavat: Its Philosophy, Its Ethics, and Its Theology*. San Jose, CA: Guardian of Devotion Press, 1985.
World Vaisnava Association. http://www.wva-vvrs.org. Accessed April 24, 2009.

Gedatsu Kai

A Japanese new religion founded by Okano Seiken (1881–1949) in Tokyo in 1929. After founding Gedatsu Kai, Okano was ordained at Daigoji (Shingon Buddhism) in 1931. For a time Gedatsu Kai received legal recognition as a subsidiary organization of Shingon Buddhism, and it was then called Shugendô Gedatsu Kyôkai, but with the end of World War II, it withdrew from the Shingon organization.

According to Gedatsu Kai, humans desire wealth, fame, sex, food, and other necessities, but they run into trouble whenever the search for these five (necessary for survival) becomes redirected to mere satisfaction for the individual. They then fall into life's tragedies—ignorance of karmic law, hereditary problems, and selfish thoughts. The object of religion is to move from the problems and resultant suffering to a state of enlightenment that will include calm resignation and complete peace of mind. Gedatsu Kai offers a method of attaining enlightenment (*gedatsu*) through developing wisdom, purifying the emotions, and improving will power.

Gedatsu Kai, literally the association of deliverance, reveres the Kami Tenjinchigi (the source of all being) and the Buddha Gochi Nyorai (a name borrowed from esoteric Buddhism). Hannya Shingyô is the most recited sutra in Gedatsu Kai. Ongohô Shugyô, which has to do with possession and mediation, is one of its main exercises. When performing Ongohô Shugyô, members kneel before a *kami*, or Buddha altar, holding a special spiritual card between their hands, and meditate. Spirits light on the card and present requests for purifying ritual and give warnings. The messages are interpreted, not by the person engaged in Ongohô Shugyô, but by a mediator posted alongside.

Another ceremony of importance in Gedatsu Kai is the Amacha Kuyô ritual, in which members pour sweet tea on cards inscribed with the name of ancestral or other spirits, in the belief that the ceremony purifies suffering spirits. Amacha Kuyô is performed morning and evening before the home altar.

The current leader of Gedatsu Kai is Okano Seihô. In 2000, it reported 193,856 members. Most reside in Japan, but centers are now scattered around the Pacific Basin and in Europe, carried by members who have participated in the Japanese global diaspora. The headquarters is in Tokyo, but there is a "holy land" in the city of Kitamoto, Saitama Prefecture. In the United States, there are three centers, called churches, in Los Angeles, Sacramento, and Honolulu.

Gedatsu Kai
4 Araki-cho
Shinjuku-ku, Tokyo 160-0007
Japan
http://www.gedatsu-usa.org/

Keishin Inaba

See also: Devotion/Devotional Traditions; Meditation; Shingon Buddhism.

References

Earhart, Byron. *Gedatsu-kai and Religion in Contemporary Japan: Returning to the Center*. Bloomington: Indiana University Press, 1989.

Gedatsu Church of America. *Gedatsu Ajikan Kongozen Meditation*. San Francisco: Gedatsu Church of America, 1974.

Gedatsu Church of America. *Manual for Implementation of Gedatsu Practice*. San Francisco: Gedatsu Church of America, 1965.

Ichiro, Hori, et al., eds. *Japanese Religion: A Survey by the Agency for Cultural Affairs*. Tokyo: Kodansha International, 1972.

Geiger, Abraham

1810–1874

Rabbi and biblical scholar Abraham Geiger was one of the founders of Reform Judaism, a 19th-century attempt to create a form of Jewish belief and practice that responded to the new intellectual demands of the age. He was an early student of the historical critical study of the Bible, which within the Jewish community came to be known as *Wissenschaft des judentums* (the science of Judaism).

Geiger was born May 24, 1810, in Frankfurt, Germany, the son of a rabbi. He showed marked intellectual abilities as a youth and became an accomplished student of the Torah and Talmud; he also learned the classical languages, Latin and Greek. By the age of 19, he was at the University of Heidelberg (and later at Bonn) studying Syriac and Arabic, the additional languages he needed to study traditional Jewish texts. In 1832 he became the rabbi at Wiesbaden. While there, he completed his Ph.D. at Marburg (1834).

During his teen years, Geiger developed a liberal bent, which was manifest even as early as his bar mitzvah, when he chose to teach from the Torah in both Hebrew and German. His study of the different languages and the secular environment of the universities pushed him even further in a liberalizing direction. By the time he was at Marburg, he was demanding new freedoms to approach the Jewish texts using the new historical critical tools. Relative to the biblical books of Genesis and Exodus especially, the new critical approach offered a radically different view of the compilation of the text and of the history of the Jewish people.

Once in his rabbinical position, Geiger began to introduce reforms that tended to give the Sabbath service the appearance of a Protestant church. He also ran into opposition from an emerging Orthodox movement led by his old classmate, Samson Raphael Hirsh (1808–1888). In 1838 he was forced out at Wiesbaden and moved to Breslau, where the congregation was more accepting of the reforms he introduced (including a new prayer book) and the local government supported him. Like the Orthodox, he was concerned by the number of Jews who were simply assimilating into German society, but responded by articulating the position that Jews could assert their German identity in addition to their Jewish identity. Judaism could be a modern 19th-century religion that appealed to the contemporary culture.

Geiger suggested that Judaism could do without those elements of the traditional faith that separated Jews from their non-Jewish neighbors. He saw no need, for example, for traditional ritual and the Hebrew language. The Sabbath service could be largely in German, especially the traditional prayers and the sermon. He introduced an organ into the synagogue. He also abandoned the following of traditional kosher dietary laws and the wearing of peculiar apparel such as the head covering (*kippah*) and prayer shawl (*tallit*). His congregation went along with his changes in the Sabbath service, including the removal of references to a return to Zion, the Messiah, and the restoration of temple sacrifices. They balked at the complete abandonment of Hebrew and dropping the practice of circumcision.

Geiger worked for the spread of the Reform movement, and to that end founded a school to train Reform rabbis. Geiger died on October 23, 1874, in Berlin.

J. Gordon Melton

See also: Orthodox Judaism; Reform Judaism.

References

Geiger, Abraham, and Max Wiener. *Abraham Geiger and the Liberal Judaism: The Challenge of the Nineteenth Century*. Cincinnati, OH: Hebrew Union College Press, 1981.

Koltun-Fromm, Ken. *Abraham Geiger's Liberal Judaism: Personal Meaning and Religious Authority*. Bloomington: Indiana University Press, 2006.

Meyer, Michael A. *Response to Modernity: The History of the Reform Movement in Judaism*. New York: Oxford University Press, 1988.

Plaut, W. Gunther. *The Rise of Reform Judaism*. New York: World Union for Progressive Judaism, 1963.

Gelugpa

The Gelugpa (sometimes spelled Gelukpa) order of Tibetan Buddhism is the largest of its four major traditions. Prior to the Chinese invasion of Tibet in 1950, it maintained the three largest monasteries in the country —Ganden, Drebung, and Sera—all of which have been rebuilt in Tibetan communities in India. The tradition is particularly associated with scholasticism and oral philosophical debate and has produced many renowned meditation masters.

Gelugpa traces its origins back to Tsong Khapa Losang Drakpa (1357–1419), a noted scholar and meditator, as well as one of the greatest debaters of his time. He traveled all over Tibet and studied with masters from various traditions in an attempt to determine what teachings and practices should be considered normative. The Gelugpa order—whose name means "System of Virtue"—was founded as a reformist tradition, the explicit aim of which was to emphasize the centrality of scholarship and monasticism.

Tsong Khapa considered his tradition to be the successor to the Kadampa order founded by Atiśa (982–1054) and his disciple Dromdön (1004–1064). For the first few centuries after its establishment, the Gelugpa order mostly avoided political entanglements, but in the 17th century it rose to supremacy in Tibet, when the fifth Dalai Lama, Ngawang Losang Gyatso (1617–1682), became the temporal ruler of Tibet with the help of Mongol troops. From this time until 1959, successive Dalai Lamas ruled the country. Following the Chinese invasion and annexation of Tibet, the 14th Dalai Lama, Tenzin Gyatso (b. 1935), fled to India in 1959 and established a government in exile in Dharamsala.

During the Cultural Revolution (1965–1975), Chinese Red Guards destroyed most of Tibet's monasteries, including the major Gelugpa institutions. Gelugpas who followed the Dalai Lama into exile re-established the three major Gelugpa monasteries in south India, along with a number of smaller institutions, including two devoted to the study and practice of Tantric Buddhism. Today they continue to teach the traditional monastic curriculum, which is based on memorization of textbooks (*yikcha*) and oral debate (*tsöba*). In Tibet, meanwhile, the Gelugpa monasteries have been severely reduced in numbers by Chinese authorities. Prior to the Chinese invasion, the three main monasteries housed tens of thousands of monks, but today they are only allowed several hundred each.

The central meditation practice of the Gelugpa order is the "stages of the path" (*lamrim*) system, which is outlined in Tsong Khapa's magnum opus, *The Great Exposition of the Stages of the Path* (*Lamrim Chenmo*). The text begins with an analysis of the sufferings of ordinary beings and the ignorance that is their root cause, followed by descriptions of the proper mindset of a religious practitioner. After generating a sincere

Gelugpa Buddhist monks beat ceremonial cymbals at a morning prayer session marking the beginning of the Tibetan New Year, Dharmsala, India. (AP Photo/Ashwini Bhatia)

desire to escape from cyclic existence, a practitioner should develop the "mind of awakening," pursue the path of a bodhisattva (a being who wishes to become a buddha for the benefit of other sentient beings), and cultivate the "six perfections" (generosity, ethics, patience, effort, concentration, and wisdom), which together constitute the core of a buddha's awakened mind. The path is conceived hierarchically, and along with the traditional practices of Mahayana Buddhism, Tsong Khapa discusses how the techniques of Tantra should be integrated into the training program. The core Gelugpa text for the Tantric path is Tsong Khapa's *Great Exposition of Secret Mantra* (*Ngakrim Chenmo*).

Today the Gelugpa order remains the largest in Tibetan Buddhism, and its main reincarnate lama (*tulku*), the Dalai Lama, is generally considered to be the preeminent religious leader by all orders. He is not, however, the head of the Gelugpa order; this position is held by the Throne Holder of Ganden Monastery (Gan-

den Triba), who is appointed in recognition of his scholarship and moral authority. The headquarters of the order is at the Tibetan Colony in North Kanars, Karnataka. Since 1959, Gelugpa leaders have spread across Australia, Europe, and North America. Apart from the main body, several autonomous Gelugpa groups have emerged, including the New Kadampa Tradition, a Gelugpa group that has challenged the Dalai Lama's authority.

The Gelugpa tradition is also represented by a variety of independent organizations such as the Foundation for the Preservation of the Mahayana Tradition and the Buddhist International Alliance. Although the present Dalai Lama holds no official position in the Tibetan exile government (at his own insistence), he is the most prominent figure in Tibetan Buddhism and has been involved in negotiations with the Chinese government aimed at encouraging China to respect international human rights conventions and give Tibetans greater autonomy in internal affairs. The address of the Office of His Holiness the Dalai Lama is Thekchen Choeling, PO Mcleod Ganj, Dharamsala 176215, India. A directory of the related offices of the Central Tibetan Administration of the government-in-exile established by the Dalai Lama in 1959 may be found at http://www.lungta.cz/biblio/tibadr2.htm.

Gelukga
Tibetan Colony
Lama Camp No. 1
Mundgod
North Kanars, Karnataka 581411
India

John Powers

See also: Atisha; Dalai Lama III, Sonam Gyatso; Foundation for the Preservation of the Mahayana Tradition; Mahayana Buddhism; New Kadampa Tradition–International Kadampa Buddhist Union; Tantrism; Tibetan Buddhism; Tsong Khapa.

References

Gyatso, Tenzin (Dalai Lama XIV). *Path to Bliss: A Practical Guide to the Stages of Meditation.* Ithaca, NY: Snow Lion, 1991.

Gyatso, Tenzin (Dalai Lama XIV). *The World of Tibetan Buddhism.* London: Wisdom, 1995.

Hopkins, Jeffrey. *Meditation on Emptiness.* London: Wisdom, 1983.

Powers, John. *Introduction to Tibetan Buddhism.* 2nd ed. Ithaca, NY: Snow Lion, 2007.

Tsong Khapa. *Ocean of Reasoning: A Great Commentary on Nagarjuna's Mulamadhyamaka-karika.* Trans. by Jay Garfield and Ngawang Samten. New York: Oxford University Press, 2006.

General Baptist Evangelical Convention of Egypt

One of several bodies constituting the small evangelical Christian community in predominantly Muslim Egypt, the General Baptist Evangelical Convention originated in 1931 around the preaching of Seddik W. Girgis (d. 1980). Girgis had been raised in the Coptic Orthodox Church. However, in the 1920s, while working with the YWCA in Jerusalem, he came into contact with Baptists and adopted an evangelical faith. His Baptist friends arranged for him to go to the United States, where he attended Texas Christian University. After completing his B.A., he attended the Southwestern Baptist Theological Seminary (affiliated with the Southern Baptist Convention). He also joined a Baptist church and was ordained as a minister.

In 1931 he returned to his hometown, Fayyoum, some 65 miles south of Cairo, and started preaching to his neighbors and family. Over the next 30 years he established 6 churches and converted some 250 individuals. The General Baptist Evangelical Convention emerged in the late 1960s, and Girgis served as its president until his death in 1980. He began a magazine, *The Baptist Evangel,* in 1971. The church building in Fayyoum was closed for a time because the church members had been unable to obtain a building permit prior to erecting it.

Once his work was off the ground, Girgis began petitioning the Foreign Mission Board of the Southern Baptist Convention (SBC) for support, but it was not until 1956 that he got a positive response. They began to send financial support and occasional visitors to check on the work. Only in 1981 were they able to send a resident missionary to pick up the work left by the recently deceased founder. The SBC continues to support the work.

In Egypt, it is illegal to proselytize Muslims, and many of the converts to the church come from a nominal Christian background. There is also a constituency who maintain formal ties to Islam. In 2006, the church reported 1,300 members in 13 congregations. The church is a member of the World Baptist Alliance. It was a member of the World Council of Churches, but has withdrawn.

General Baptist Evangelical Convention of Egypt
PO Box 1248
Cairo
Egypt

J. Gordon Melton

See also: Coptic Orthodox Church; Southern Baptist Convention; World Council of Churches.

Reference

Wardin, Albert W., ed. *Baptists Around the World.* Nashville: Holman Publishers, 1995.

General Church of the New Jerusalem, The

The General Church of the New Jerusalem, one of several churches formed by followers of the teachings of Emanuel Swedenborg (1688–1772), the 18th-century Swedish visionary and theologian, was formally established in 1897 by 347 men and women. The individuals involved in the founding of the General Church for the most part had been associated with what was termed the Academy movement, which at first was a body within the General Convention of the New Jerusalem (now generally known as the Swedenborgian Church). The Academy was founded in response to differences of opinion with the General Convention regarding the authority of the religious writings of Swedenborg, organizational structure, and procedural matters. The Academy position was based on the following three principles: first, Swedenborg's writings were the Divine Word of God, equivalent in authority to the Old and New Testaments; second, the writings clearly ordained a hierarchical, or episcopal, form of church government; and third, regional associations of the General Convention had the right to develop their own governmental structure. The Academy movement immediately established its own theological school, and in quick succession it also founded a college and separate high schools for boys and girls. The Academy was formally founded in 1876, when it received its charter from the State of Pennsylvania.

In 1890, differences between the two groups within the General Convention came to a head, when Bishop William H. Benade (1816–1905) ordained another minister of the Pennsylvania Association into the third or episcopal degree of the priesthood. His action was censured by the General Convention. At that point, members associated with the Academy movement withdrew from the Convention and established their own church, called the General Church of the Advent of the Lord. For eight years this church of the Academy movement functioned as both a church and a school, with Bishop Benade presiding over both. Benade's autocratic style of leadership increasingly caused problems and, with a sense of necessity and much sadness, the membership of the Academy withdrew their support from Benade. In 1897, the General Church of the New Jerusalem was founded, as a religious body separate from but affiliated with the Academy of the New Church.

At the time of its founding, the membership of the General Church came largely from those who previously had chosen to disaffiliate themselves from the General Convention of the New Jerusalem. However, it also attracted members from many General Conference societies in Canada, England, and other parts of the British Empire. Thus from its beginning it was an international church. Baptism does not confer membership and confirmation must be freely chosen as an adult. Church growth is thus dependent on the successful recruitment of each new generation, as well as on individuals who discover the works of Emanuel Swedenborg and are motivated to seek out an organized church.

The executive bishop of the General Church is the chief governor and pastor of the church. He is selected by the Council of the Clergy, and his name is then referred to the Board of Directors of the church for counsel and response. The priesthood of the General Church is open only to men, while both men and women may serve on the Board of Directors. The Joint Council of the Clergy and the Board of Directors decide when and where the name of the proposed executive bishop will be placed before the General Assembly of the membership of the church for confirmation. The bishop serves in the office until he resigns, dies in office, or is separated from the office by the same procedure used in the selection process. The executive bishop governs the church with the assistance of counsel from both clergy and laity and the assembly of all church members.

The bishop receives counsel from the Council of the Clergy, which is convened on a yearly basis, either in a council of the whole body of the clergy or in regional councils around the world, all of which the bishop attends. In addition, he receives regular counsel from a consistory composed of priests that he selects. The composition of the consistory changes from time to time, and it dissolves when there is a change in

Bryn Athyn Cathedral in Montgomery County, Pennsylvania. Bryn Athyn is the headquarters of the General Church of the New Jerusalem. (Jeff Krushinski/Dreamstime.com)

the holder of the episcopal office. He also appoints lay members to serve on the Bishop's Council for a term of three years. Both men and women, particularly married couples, serve on that council.

A General Assembly of the members of the General Church is held at the call of the bishop every three or four years. The General Assembly, while it is composed only of those in attendance, represents the whole church. The Joint Council acts for and represents the Assembly in the interim between assemblies. The last General Assembly was in 2005, when the Reverend Thomas L. Kline was elected bishop of the General Church. In 2008 he issued a call to have "meaningful contact with at least one million people" during the next 30 years. This challenge will be met by planting new churches, developing the international church, sponsoring spiritual journey campaigns at existing churches, creating a robust Internet presence, and creating an online church.

The General Church data center reports that as of June 2009, there were 5,075 members, with a total international church population of 16,845. This latter figure represents a 15 percent increase from 2001. It includes children and youths up to the age of 19, who are baptized but not yet confirmed in the church, and adults who are affiliated with the church but not members. The General Church has members in more than 70 societies, circles, or groups in 50 countries around the world. The largest concentrations of members and affiliates are in the United States, Canada, South Africa, and Ghana.

Growth and development has been particularly strong in Africa. The General Church now has members in 11 African countries. In West Africa the size of the clergy has doubled since 2000, due in part to the establishment of two theological schools there: one in Ghana and the other in the Ivory Coast. Eleven men were ordained in 2008 and each of these schools currently has six men enrolled. Three elementary schools have been founded in Africa in the last 10 years. Two schools in Ghana now serve almost 600 students, and one in Kenya is educating approximately 150 students through the 10th grade.

Nine North American societies of the General Church have elementary schools with a total of 595 students. Another long-established school is located in Durban, South Africa, serving 59 students. Additionally, a number of the church societies sponsor nursery education programs. Education of the young is considered an important function of the General Church. Although members of the General Church do not always live in special New Church communities, and in fact most members probably live outside of them, they have built several residential communities, which are centered around a church and an adjacent General Church elementary school, in various parts of North America.

The emphasis on education in the General Church is not limited to elementary education. Soon after the founding of the Academy in 1876, for the purpose of training men in theology, a college and a high school were also established. In 2008 there were 230 students in the boarding high school that draws students from the Philadelphia area and more broadly from states and provinces in North America. During the 2008–2009 academic year Bryn Athyn College had an international student body of 150 from 14 different countries. A substantially larger number of students enrolled in the college in the fall of 2009 due to a decision to increase the size of the college and its role within the General Church. An extensive building initiative is underway and by the end of the year there will be a new science center and classroom building, and a new student life center to complement the four residential cottages completed by the fall of 2008. A recruitment drive promises to increase the student body by at least 30 students or 20 percent. Previously led by a priest president who oversaw the whole Academy, a layman was named president of the college in the spring of 2009 to oversee the result of these initiatives and to look to program development.

In recent years a controversy has developed within the General Church membership over the issue of the ordination of women. At the beginning of the 21st century, women cannot be trained for or ordained into the priesthood of the General Church. Currently there are 128 priests on the roll; 85 of them are actively serving the church in some capacity. The others are either unassigned or retired. Women are welcome to enroll in the master's program in Religious Studies that was inaugurated under the leadership of the Theological School in Bryn Athyn in 1996. Since then 11 men and 20 women have graduated from that program, with an average of 3 graduates per year. An associate dean of graduate studies was appointed in the spring of 2009 in order to further develop and promote the program.

Bryn Athyn, Montgomery County, Pennsylvania, has been the headquarters and episcopal center of this church since its founding. The Swedenborgian community of Bryn Athyn was created when the Academy moved the location of its schools from the center of the city of Philadelphia to the country, in Lower Moreland Township. The relocation of the schools outside the city had been deemed by church members to be culturally desirable and also beneficial to the physical health of the members. In 1916 Bryn Athyn was incorporated into a borough with its own mayor and Borough Council.

Currently, the offices of the General Church of the New Jerusalem are located in a building called Cairncrest, which was built by Harold Pitcairn (1897–1960), a member of the General Church and an aviator who developed the Auto Giro used in helicopter guidance systems. There are three other notable buildings in Bryn Athyn. One is Glencairn, designed by Raymond Pitcairn (1885–1966) as the home for his family, which has its own unique arts and crafts style. Today it is a museum that houses his medieval art and a growing collection of New Church art. The second is the Bryn Athyn Cathedral, which was built using a modern version of the guild system. In the cathedral, every detail is uniquely crafted so that no two objects in the building are the same. It, too, has a unique arts and crafts style. The third is Cairnwood, built by Carrère and Hastings in 1895 to be the family home of the Pitcairn family patriarch, John, his wife, Gertrude, and their children. In April 2009, these buildings and grounds were designated a National Historic Landmark District, one of only 119 in Pennsylvania and 2,500 in the United States. According to the Annual Report of Borough Council for the year 2007, the community of Bryn Athyn has a resident population of 1,318 individuals.

The General Church of the New Jerusalem
PO Box 743
Bryn Athyn, PA 19009
http://www.newchurch.org
http://www.newchurch.org/materials/publications/around/

Jane Williams-Hogan

See also: Swedenborg, Emanuel; Swedenborgian Church of North America; Swedenborgian Movement; Women, Status and Role of.

References
Block, Marguerite Beck. *The New Church in the New World*. New York: Octagon Books, Inc., 1968.
Swedenborg, Emanuel. *True Christian Religion*. West Chester, PA: The Swedenborg Foundation, 1996.
Williams-Hogan, Jane. "Institutional and Communal Response to the Writings of Emanuel Swedenborg in Britain and the United States." In *Scribe of Heaven: Swedenborg's Life, Work, and Impact*, edited by Stuart Shotwell and Jonathan S. Rose. West Chester, PA: The Swedenborg Foundation, 2001.
http://www.brynathyncollege.edu.

■ Georgia

Georgia is a country in the mountainous region of the Caucasus in Eurasia. Until 1991, Georgia was one of 15 republics comprising the former Soviet Union. It is bordered on the west by the Black Sea, on the north by Russia, on the south by Turkey and Armenia, and on the east by Azerbaijan. The territory of Georgia is 26,900 square miles. The population of 4.4 million is overwhelmingly (84 percent) ethnic Georgians with lesser numbers of Azerbaijanians, Armenians, and Russians and with a small number of a few ethnic minorities (such as Ossetians, Greeks, Curds, etc.). The city of Tbilisi is the capital of Georgia. Georgia is a unitary semi-presidential republic.

The territory of today's Georgia was inhabited in the third millennium BCE. As early as the sixth century BCE, the kingdom of Kolkhida in western Georgia had arisen. In the fourth century BCE, a second kingdom, Iberia (or Kartli), emerged in eastern Georgia. Both kingdoms were incorporated into the Roman Empire in the first century BCE.

The territory of Iberia and Kolkhida fell under a succession of foreign rulers, including the Eastern Roman (Byzantine) Empire and Muslim Arabs; several feudal states were created in the 8th to the 10th centuries. In 1008, Georgia was unified into one single independent kingdom. The period from the 11th to the 13th centuries is seen by many as a "golden époque" in the life of Georgia. It came to an end after devastating invasions of Gengis Khan in the 13th century and Tamerlane in the 15th century. The country was split again into many feudal princedoms. During 1500–1800, various parts of Georgia were fought over by neighboring Turks and Iranians. In 1783, eastern Georgia became a protectorate of the Russian Empire. It was finally annexed in 1801. By 1880, as a result of several wars with Turkey, Russia absorbed the rest of Georgia. In 1914, at the beginning of World War I, the territory of present-day Georgia was divided into four administrative units of the Russian Empire: the Tbilisi and Kutaisi *gubernias* and the Batumi and Sukhumi *oblasts.*

According to the 1897 census, of the total population in the territory of contemporary Georgia, 70 percent were Orthodox Christians, 15 percent Muslims, 11 percent followers of the Armenian Apostolic Church, 1 percent Jews, 0.8 percent Orthodox Old Believers, 0.7 percent Roman Catholics, and 0.5 percent various Protestants.

After the Russian Revolution of 1917, Georgia gained its independence in May 1918 and it was recognized by the Soviet government. However, Britain, Germany, and Turkey all sent troops to bring down what had become a Socialist government of the newly independent Georgia. In February 1921, the Soviets responded by sending troops into the country, and in 1922 Georgia became a part of the Soviet Union. Three autonomous territorial units were established within Soviet Georgia. Two of them—Abkhazia and South Ossetia—were based on ethnicity, while the third—

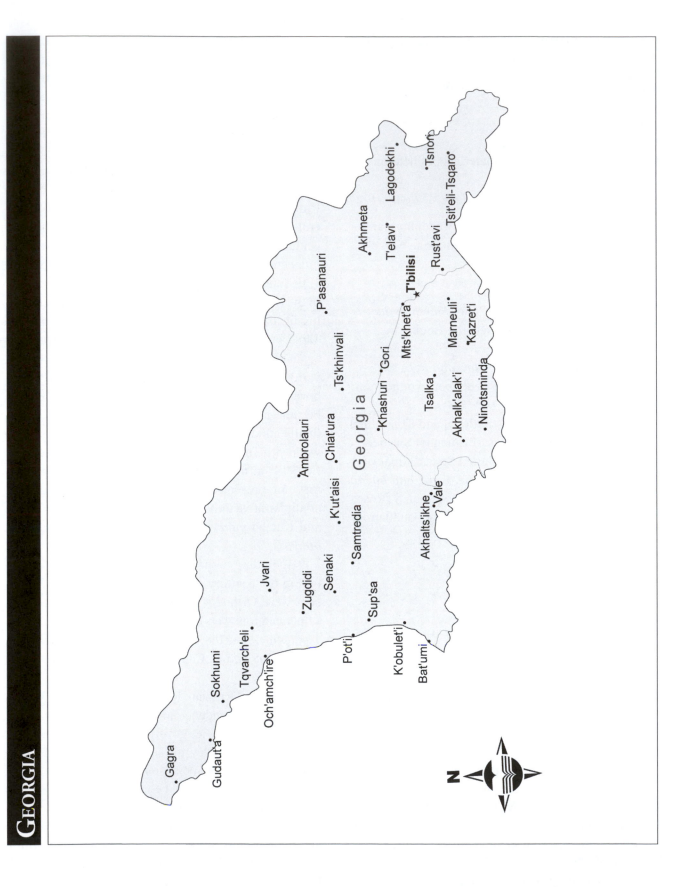

GEORGIA

Georgia

Religion	Followers in 1970	Followers in 2010	% of Population	Annual % growth 2000–2010	Followers in 2025	Followers in 2050
Christians	1,650,000	3,690,000	85.8	−0.80	3,437,000	2,769,000
Orthodox	1,608,000	3,565,000	82.9	−0.87	3,280,000	2,609,000
Roman Catholics	3,000	41,000	1.0	0.02	50,000	52,000
Marginals	100	33,000	0.8	2.24	40,000	40,000
Muslims	550,000	440,000	10.2	−1.97	386,000	295,000
Agnostics	1,706,000	140,000	3.3	−3.54	100,000	50,000
Atheists	776,000	17,000	0.4	−5.77	10,000	6,000
Jews	25,000	11,500	0.3	−2.61	9,000	8,000
Baha'is	500	1,800	0.0	−1.06	3,000	6,000
New religionists	300	300	0.0	−1.05	300	300
Total population	**4,707,000**	**4,301,000**	**100.0**	**−1.07**	**3,945,000**	**3,134,000**

Adjaria, which is populated by Georgian Muslims or Adjarians—was based on religion.

In 1988–1989, following the policy of democratization and liberalization introduced by the last Soviet leader, Mikhail Gorbachev (b. 1931), a strong nationalist movement developed in Georgia. Its goal was both to destroy the Communist system and to break away from the Soviet Union. In May 1991, the first Georgian president, Zviad Gamsakhurdia (b. 1939)—a representative of the nationalistic bloc Round Table–Free Georgia—was elected, and in December 1991 the breakup of the Soviet Union finalized the re-establishment of Georgia's independence. During 1991–1992, Georgia experienced civil war and unrest, combined with a growing separatist movement in its autonomous territorial units, South Ossetia, Adjaria, and Abkhazia. In March 1992, the military had ousted Gamsakhurdia, but obviously failed to control the situation in the country. The leadership was offered to Eduard Shevardnadze (b. 1928), who was a decades-long Communist leader in Soviet Georgia and who resided in Moscow at that time. In 1995, he was elected president of Georgia under the new Constitution that had just been adopted.

Meanwhile, the strong local separatist movements being supported by Russia achieved the de facto independence of Abkhazia and South Ossetia from Georgia. In 2003, Shevardnadze was deposed by the so-called Rose Revolution, accused by Georgian opposition and international observers of the falsification of the November 2 parliamentary elections. One of the leaders of the Rose Revolution, the U.S.-educated Mikheil Saakashvili (b. 1967), was elected president of Georgia in 2004. The reforms initiated by President Saakashvili aimed at enhancing the economy and military strength of the country. Politically, a high priority has been given to building close relationships with the United States and the North Atlantic Treaty Organization (NATO) (while distancing from Russia) and to gaining back control over secessionist regions of Ajaria, Abkhazia, and South Ossetia. In August 2008, the increasing tensions between Georgian armed forces and South Ossetian separatists resulted in an open military conflict. On August 7, after bombing the South Ossetian capital, Tskhinvali, the Georgian army entered into South Ossetia. On August 8, under the pretext of the killing by Georgians of several Russian peace-keepers and hundreds of South Ossetian civilians, the Russian army intervened into the conflict, ousting Georgian troops out of South Ossetia and advancing quickly into Georgia proper. During intense fighting there were many contradictory reports on the number of casualties on both sides and among both civilians and military personnel. Both Georgia and Russia claimed unnecessary violence on the part of the other side. On August 11, Russian peace-keeping troops stationed in the breakaway region of Abkhazia entered western Georgia. The full-scale war between Georgia and Russia (with the clear superiority of the latter) ended only after negotiations mediated by the president of the European Union, Nicolas Sarkozy. The so-called six point plan was signed by the Georgian President Saakashvili, by the president of Russia, Dmitri Medvedev, and by the separatist leaders Eduard Kokoity of South Ossetia and Sergei Bagapsh of Abkhazia. On August 25, 2008, Russia unilaterally recognized Abkhazia and South Ossetia as independent states and announced that Russian troops would be stationed there according to the agreements between Russian and the local governments and, therefore, the status of these troops was not regulated by the six-point peace plan.

The 2002 census provided data on the religious composition of the population of Georgia. According to this census, 84 percent are Orthodox Christians (mainly members of the Georgian Orthodox Church), 10 percent are Muslims, 4 percent are Gregorian Armenians (members of the Armenian Apostolic Church), and 0.8 percent are Catholics (both Latin-rite Roman Catholics and Byzantine-rite Catholics); 1.2 percent of the population is scattered among a variety of other Christian and religious minorities. It should be pointed out that Georgia has a long history of the peaceful coexistence of the various religious groups. Religious discrimination has been virtually unknown in Georgia.

The initial Christianization of Georgia has been traced to the first century CE. According to legend, lots were cast among Jesus' apostles to determine to which country each of them was to go with a mission, and the Holy Mother, the Blessed Virgin Mary, was assigned Georgia. Therefore Georgians consider their home country as "allotted to the Mother of God." Since the Mother of God stayed in Jerusalem, the Apostle Andrew went to Georgia. Western Georgia also received the Apostle Simon Canaanite (aka Simeon the Zealot), whose reputed grave is near the city of Sukhumi in the village of Komani.

The arrival of Christian clergy from the Byzantine Empire, the construction of Twelve Apostles Cathedral in Mtskheta, the ancient capital of the kingdom of Kartli (Iberia), and the baptism of the nation are all dated to 326 CE, just a short time after the legalization of Christianity and the first Council at Nicaea. The church in Kartli was initially under the jurisdiction of the Patriarchate of Antioch, but the Georgian Orthodox Church was granted independence from Jerusalem in 467. Consequently, the bishop of Mtskheta was elevated to the rank of catholicos. West Georgia, which was then a part of the Eastern Roman (Byzantine) Empire, gradually became Christian by the fifth century, and it came under the rule of the patriarch of Constantinople. Originally, the church in Georgia had joined with the Armenian Apostolic Church in the rejection of the decisions of the Council of Chalcedon in 451. However, it reversed its position in 697 and came again into full communion with other Eastern Orthodox churches.

As various conquerors (most of whom were Muslims) moved through Georgia, the struggle for independence became largely identified as a struggle for the defense of Orthodoxy, since many clerical and laypersons died as martyrs for their Orthodox faith.

In 1811, a decade after the Russian annexation of eastern Georgia, the head of the Georgian Church—the catholicos-patriarch—died. The independence of the Georgian Orthodox Church was abolished and it was incorporated into the Russian Orthodox Church (Moscow Patriarchate) as an Exarchate. The number of dioceses in the territory of Georgia was reduced from 13 to 4. The Georgian language in the church was largely replaced by the Church Slavonic liturgy, and forcible Russification of the church in Georgia began. After 1817, only Russian bishops were named as exarchs—the heads of the Exarchate of Georgia.

An independent Georgian Orthodox Church was re-established in 1917, but it was not until 1943 that it was formally recognized by the Patriarchate of Moscow.

After the break-up of the Soviet Union in 1991, the new important social role of the Georgian Orthodox Church in the independent post-Soviet Georgia was symbolized by the public baptism of Georgian President Eduard Shevardnadze in 1992. According to surveys, in 1993, 66 percent of the population in Georgia had declared that they considered themselves believers in a religion, and of those, 83 percent reported that they belonged to the Georgian Orthodox Church. At the same time, roughly the same proportion of respondents (80 to 82 percent) among those who called themselves nonbelievers and those who responded "don't know," also associated with the Georgian Orthodox Church. Thus, the overwhelming majority of the population sees the Georgian Orthodox Church as a national church and a symbol of Georgian statehood.

According to the Georgian Orthodox Church's decree (issued in 1991), priests and bishops are not allowed to be members of political parties or to participate in political activities, but indirectly various factions within the Georgian Orthodox Church have been involved in Georgia's politics. For instance, in the mid-1990s, the moderate head of the Georgian Orthodox Church, Patriarch Ilia II (born Irakli Ghudushauri-Shiolashvili, 1933), had forged an alliance with President Shevardnadze, while a conservative and anti-ecumenical group of Georgian Orthodox clergy has been linked to Georgian radical nationalists associated with ousted president Zviad Gamsakhurdia.

The ninth article of the Georgian Constitution declares full freedom of religion and the separation of the church and state, but it also acknowledges the "special role of the Georgian Orthodox Church in the history of Georgia." In the attempt to define this special role, some politicians have called for Orthodoxy to be declared the state religion. In several ways, the church operates already as an official body, and it has signed agreements about cooperation with the Georgian Ministry of Defense (1999) and the Ministry of Interior. In the 1990s, the Georgian state supported the Georgian Orthodox Church in opposing the spread of the so-called nontraditional and new religious movements into the country.

On March 31, 2001, the 188 members of the Parliament of Georgia passed a unanimous decision declaring the necessity of a Concordat (constitutional agreement) between the Georgian Orthodox Church and the state. The Concordat was signed on October 14, 2002. It stipulates, for example, that Orthodox clergy cannot be drafted into the army; the state recognizes marriages registered by the church; the property and lands owned by the church are tax-exempt; the state is obligated to implement joint educational programs and to support educational institutions of the Orthodox Church; and the 12 major Orthodox festivals are recognized as national public holidays.

Islam was first introduced to Georgia by the Arabs in the eighth century. However, it was not until the period when the Ottoman Empire and Persians (16th–19th centuries) had hegemony that a permanent Muslim community arose in the country. Although not a large number of Georgians were attracted to Islam, it has persisted through the centuries. A number of ethnically distinct Muslim communities exist today throughout Georgia. About 115,000 Muslims who live in Adjaria (West Georgia) are ethnic Georgians who adopted Islam during the reign of the Turks. The Islamic population of Georgia includes also ethnic Azerbaijanis living in southeast Georgia (about 290,000) as well as Chechens and Ingushs (12,000) in the villages of northeast Georgia, in the district of Akhmety. The Adjarian Muslims are Sunnis of the Hanafite rite, but there are both Shiites and Sunnis among Azerbaijanis. The religious practice of Chechens is largely of the various traditions of Sufism, of which there are more than 25, most important, the Qadiriyya and the Muridiyya brotherhoods. In terms of religiosity, the Adjarians are more superficial followers of Islam than Azerbaijanis and, especially, Chechens. Two major Islamic theological schools—madrasahs—function in the country and are situated in the capital, Tbilisi, and in the city of Marneuli.

Archaeological evidence confirms the presence of Jews in Mtskheta, the capital of the ancient eastern Georgian state of Kartli, in the first centuries CE. In western Georgia, Jews appear to have arrived in the sixth century, most likely from the Byzantine Empire. In the ninth century Georgia was the site of the birth of a new Jewish group that denied some Jewish laws concerning marriage and food. The group's founder, Abu-Imran Musa (Moshe) al-Za'farani, had moved to Tbilisi (then called Tiflis) from Babylonia. He was later known as Abu-Imran al-Tiflisi, and the group the Tiflis Sect. The group lasted some three or four centuries.

Today, Jewish religion in Georgia is represented by Orthodox Judaism. The Jewish community is subdivided in two groups: Georgian-speaking Sephardics and Russian-speaking Ashkenazi. While Sephardics can be considered as an indigenous population of Georgia, the origin of the community of Ashkenazi traces back only to the 19th century. At that time a number of retired soldiers of the Russian army who were Jews settled in Georgia. Consequently, until the 20th century, the Sephardics in Georgia lived almost exclusively in the countryside, while Ashkenazi were initially urban dwellers.

The number of Jews in Georgia peaked at around 61,000 in 1970, including 43,000 Sephardics and

18,000 Ashkenazi. It had decreased to fewer than 25,000 in 1989 (including 14,000 Georgian-speaking and 10,500 Russian-speaking) due to mass immigration to Israel and to the United States. The short period of Gamsakhurdia's radical nationalistic regime urged forward this process. The Jewish community continued to decrease in numbers through the 1990s. According to the 2002 census, only 3,541 Jews remain in Georgia. The vast majority of Georgian Jews live today in the capital Tbilisi (where they are served by two synagogues) and in the city of Kutaisi.

Most of the 33,000 Kurds who migrated to independent Georgia in 1918 did so because of the religious and political persecution conducted by the government of Turkey. They are Yezidis by religion. This Pagan religious teaching is based on Zoroastrianism, but it also has elements of Islam, Judaism, and Christianity. Kurds in Georgia are strict followers of religious traditions and prescriptions. According to the 2002 census, about 18,300 Yezidis are living today in Georgia.

The second-largest Christian group in Georgia are Gregorian Armenians (about 250,000 as of the census of 2002). Most of them (about 171,000) belong to the Monophysite Armenian Apostolic Church. Seven permanently functioning churches (two in Tbilisi and one each in Batumi, Nino Tsminda, Shaumjany, Akhalkalaki, and Akhalzikhi) along with many chapels in villages form the Georgian diocese of the Armenian Apostolic Church. Almost half of Georgia's Armenians live in southern Georgia, in the Province of Samtskhe-Javakheti. About one-third of the Armenian community resides in the capital Tbilisi.

The Roman Catholic Church was introduced to South Georgia at the time of the Ottoman Empire's rule. The Islamic conquerors were much more tolerant of Catholicism than of Orthodoxy, and many Orthodox Georgians preferred to convert to Catholicism rather than adopt Islam. Today Georgian Catholics (about 35,000 total) live mainly in the cities of Tbilisi and Kutaisi, and in South Georgia. The Catholic parishes in Georgia are part of the Apostolic Administration of Transcaucasia, which was established in 1994 and includes Georgia, Armenia, and Azerbaijan.

Protestantism came to Georgia initially through the spread of the Molokan movement. In the 1840s, members of this group who ran into trouble with the authorities in the Russian Empire were banished to Transcaucasia and established several villages in Djavakhetia, the mountainous area in South Georgia. In 1862, a German Baptist, Martin Kalweit (1833–1918), settled in Tbilisi. He began to hold worship services, primarily within the German-speaking community in the city. In 1867, he baptized the first Russian, Nikita Voronin. From that time the Baptist congregation grew, with services in both Russian and German languages. The Baptist movement in Georgia spread primarily among the Russians living there. One of them was Vasilii G. Pavlov (1854–1924), who studied in Germany and returned to become the leading force in spreading the Baptist faith in Transcaucasia. In 1912 the first Georgian-speaking members were baptized. After 1919, Baptist services were celebrated in the Georgian language on a regular basis.

In 1919, a Trans-Caucasian Union of Baptists was formed. In 1921, Georgian Baptists merged with the Russian Baptist Federation. The Baptist churches were closed during the period of harshest Communist religious repression (1937–1944), but in 1944 the first Baptist church was reopened under an umbrella organization of various Protestant groups, the so-called All-Union Council of Evangelical Churches–Baptists. Following the collapse of the Soviet Union, the Union of Evangelical and Baptist Churches of Georgia was formed. It is a member of the Baptist World Alliance. The Baptists in Georgia number about 18,000 faithful and have about 60 local churches (including 5,000 members and 8 churches in Tbilisi) and a theological seminary in Tbilisi. The Baptist congregations are divided along ethnic-linguistic lines: Georgian, Ossetian, Armenian, and Russian.

Aside from the Baptists, the Protestant denominations in Georgia are represented by Pentecostals (5,000 to 6,000 members in 70 local communities), Lutherans (about 1,000 persons living mainly in Tbilisi), Jehovah's Witnesses (the estimates vary greatly between 15,000 and 30,000), as well as by small groups of the New Apostolic Church and the Salvation Army.

A unique community of the Russian sect of Doukhobors in mountainous South Georgia numbered almost 7,000 in 1988, but it is almost extinct now, due to a mass migration to Russia. The remaining Doukhobors live today mainly in the village of Gorelovka in the Nino-Tsminda District.

Among religious groups that are relatively new to the country, the Baha'i community should be mentioned. The first Baha'i Local Spiritual Assembly in Georgia was formed in 1991. The first National Spiritual Assembly was elected by Georgian Baha'is in 1995.

Alexei D. Krindatch

See also: Armenian Apostolic Church (Holy See of Echmiadzin); Baha'i Faith; Baptist World Alliance; Doukhobors; Ecumenical Patriarchate/Patriarchate of Constantinople; Georgian Orthodox Church; Greek Orthodox Patriarchate of Antioch and All the East; Hanafite School of Islam; Jehovah's Witnesses; Mary, Blessed Virgin; Molokons; Muridîyya; New Apostolic Church; Orthodox Judaism; Pentecostalism; Qadiriyya Sufi Order; Roman Catholic Church; Russian Orthodox Church (Moscow Patriarchate); Salvation Army; Yezidis; Zoroastrianism.

References

Baltaden, S. K. *Seeking God: The Recovery of Religious Identity in Orthodox Russia, Ukraine, and Georgia.* De Kalb: Northern Illinois University Press, 1993.

Dowling, Theodore. *Sketches of Georgian Church History.* Ellibron Classics Series. Boston: Adamant Media Corporation, 2005.

Georgia Statistics. 2002 Population Census of Georgia. Population by Religious Beliefs. http://www.statistics.ge/_files/english/census/2002/Religious%20beliefs.pdf. Accessed July 15, 2009.

Malan, S. C., ed. *A Short History of the Georgian Church.* Trans. by P. Ioseliani. London: Saunders, Otley, 1866.

Roberson, R. *The Eastern Christian Churches: A Brief Survey.* 7th ed. Rome, Italy: Edizioni Orientalia Christiana, 2006. http://www.cnewa.org/generalpg-verus.aspx?pageID=182. Accessed July 15, 2009.

Skurat, K. *Istorija Pomestnykh Pravoslavnykh Cerkvej.* Moscow: Russkie ogni, 1994.

Spilling, Michael, and Winnie Wong. *Georgia (Cultures of the World).* Singapore: Marshall Cavendish, 2008.

Georgian Orthodox Church

The Georgian Orthodox Church (GOC) is the Eastern Orthodox Christian body that serves as the national church of the Caucasian country of Georgia. The great majority of Georgians are members of the church.

Archaeological findings testify to the existence of Christian communities in Georgia as early as the second and third centuries CE. At that time Georgia consisted of two states: the Kingdom of Kartli (or "Iberia" in Greek) in eastern Georgia and the Kingdom of Egrisi (or "Kolkhida" in Greek) in western Georgia. In Kartli, Christianity had become the state religion due to the missionary activity of "Equal to Apostles" Saint Nino, a woman from Cappadocia who came to Kartli from Jerusalem around 325. According to legend, Saint Nino was a close relative of Saint George, commonly recognized as a protector of Georgia. Under her ministry, Georgian Queen Nana (d. 363) and King Mirian III (r. 284–361) converted to Christianity, and then they requested the Byzantine emperor, Constantine (r. 306–337), to send clergy to Kartli in order to baptize the royal family. The construction of Twelve Apostles Cathedral in Mtskheta, an ancient capital of Kartli, and the baptism of the nation are dated to 326. Western Georgia, then a part of the Eastern Roman Empire, gradually became Christian by the fifth century, and it came under the jurisdiction of the patriarch of Constantinople. The Church of Kartli was initially under the Patriarchate of Antioch, but in 467 it was granted full independence (the so-called autocephaly) at the request of King Vakhtang Gorgaslan. The bishop of Mtskheta was elevated to the rank of catholicos. Consequently, the relations with the Holy Land, in particular with Jerusalem, have always had a special meaning for Georgia and for the GOC. Like other early Christian churches, the Georgian Church was involved in the disputes surrounding decisions of the Council of Chalcedon (451) regarding Christological definition. It was not until the end of the sixth century that Georgians finally joined with the Church of Constantinople and supported the decrees of the Chalcedon while splitting with the Armenian Apostolic Church (who rejected the decrees of Chalcedon).

Monasticism has flourished in Georgia since the sixth century and it peaked during the 10th to 12th

Jvari church above the city of Mtskheta, Georgia. This Georgian Orthodox church was built between 586 and 605 on the site where, according to legend, Saint Nino converted the pagan population to Christianity. (Shutterstock)

centuries. Georgian monasteries maintained regular contacts with monasteries in Jerusalem and Mount Sinai. Further, in the late 10th century, the Iviron Monastery was founded by Georgians on Mount Athos in Greece. The monks of the Iviron Monastery translated many religious books from Greek into Georgian. Georgians also built other churches and monasteries outside of Georgia in Palestine, Greece, Bulgaria, Syria, and Cyprus. Today, monasticism remains a significant feature of the contemporary GOC.

Initially in Kartli the Jerusalem liturgy of Saint James was celebrated, while the Byzantine liturgy was used in Kolkhida, in western Georgia. After East and West Georgia were united into one kingdom in 1008, the Byzantine liturgy celebrated in the Georgian language was adopted in the whole country. Also since that time the head of the GOC has been known by the title of catholicos-patriarch.

The period from the 11th to the 13th centuries is seen by many as a "golden époque" in the life of Georgia and GOC. It came to an end after the devastating invasions of Genghis Khan in the 13th century and Tamerlane in the 15th century.

During the period from 1500 to 1800, Georgia began to develop new contacts with the West and Russia. Further, looking for protection from Islamic invaders, Georgia has repeatedly requested assistance from Orthodox Russia. In 1783, Georgia became a protectorate of the Russian Empire. In 1801, upon the request of the last Georgian kings, George XII (1746–1800) and Solomon II of Imereti (1772–1815) (the country having split again in two parts in the 14th century), Georgia was declared a part of Russia by Emperor Alexander I (r. 1801–1825). In 1811, when the catholicos-patriarch of the Georgian Church died, the Catholicossate of Georgia was forcibly abolished, and the Georgian Church became a part of the Russian Orthodox Church (Moscow Patriarchate) with the status of exarchate. GOC lost its independence ("autocephaly"). The 13 dioceses of the church were reduced to 4, and the Georgian language was largely replaced by Russian and Slavonic in both the seminaries and the liturgy. Beginning in 1817, all exarchs of Georgia were ethnically Russians.

According to the 1897 census, of the total population in the territory of contemporary Georgia, 70 percent were Orthodox (members of the Russian Orthodox Church), 15 percent Muslims, 11 percent followers of the Armenian Apostolic Church, and 1 percent Jews. There were lesser numbers of Orthodox Old Believers, Roman Catholics, and Protestants.

In March 1917, after the abdication of the Russian Emperor Nicholas II, the autocephaly of the GOC was reestablished at a meeting of ethnically Georgian bishops, clergy, and laity. A new catholicos-patriarch of the GOC was elected in September 1917. After the Bolshevik Revolution in Russia (October 1917), Georgia existed as an independent country, but it was annexed by the Soviet Union in February 1921. The GOC, however, managed to retain its de facto independence from the Russian Orthodox Church, although this independent status was not recognized by the Moscow Patriarchate. The relations between the Russian and Georgian churches were broken, and the situation was aggravated by the fact that many Orthodox parishes in Georgia were predominantly Russian and had Russian priests. These parishes tended to remain loyal to the Moscow Patriarchate.

In 1943, the Moscow Patriarchate finally granted autocephaly to GOC, but this status continued to be questioned by the Ecumenical Patriarchate in Istanbul, which generally did not recognized Moscow's authority to grant autocephaly. The autocephaly of the GOC and its patriarchal rank were finally confirmed by the Ecumenical Patriarchate in 1990.

The situation of the GOC under the Soviet regime was similar to that of the Russian Orthodox Church. At the beginning of the 20th century, the GOC had nearly 2,400 parishes and 26 monasteries and 5 convents. Some 590 public schools were also run by the church. The Orthodox clergy numbered almost 2,000. In 1985, only 54 Orthodox churches remained open in the Soviet Republic of Georgia, along with 4 monasteries and 1 theological seminary in the capital city of Tbilisi.

In the late 1980s, the democratic reforms and the policy of political liberalization introduced by Mikhail Gorbachev in the Soviet Union triggered quick revival of the GOC. By 1990, the church had 200 parishes (divided into 15 dioceses) and 15 Orthodox monasteries. In addition to the seminary, a theological academy was open in Tbilisi in 1988. By 1999, GOC had 400 parishes, 30 monasteries, and 30 convents. The number of dioceses has increased to 27, served by 600 priests. In 2009, the Georgian Orthodox Church had 35 dioceses served by more than 1,000 parish clergy. There are now 2 theological academies (in Tbilisi and Gelati) and 6 seminaries around the country. According to the 2002 census, of a total Georgia's population of 4,380,000, 82 percent identified themselves as Georgian Orthodox. After the declaration of Georgia's independence (1991), the revival of the GOC has been further intensified by the growth of the church's political and social influence. The baptism of the Georgian president, Eduard Shevardnadze, in 1992 has been seen as a symbol of the important role that GOC plays in the newly independent Georgia. The 1994 agreement between the Georgian government and GOC introduced the teaching of religion in public schools under the program designed in cooperation with the GOC. Article 9 of Georgia's Constitution (adopted in 1995) declares full freedom of religion and the separation of the church and state, but, at the same time, acknowledges the "special role of the Georgian Orthodox Church in the history of Georgia." In the attempt to define that special role, some politicians have called for Orthodoxy to be declared the state religion.

On March 31, 2001, the 188 members of the Parliament of Georgia passed a unanimous decision declaring the necessity of a Concordat (constitutional agreement) between the GOC and the state. The Concordat was signed on October 14, 2002. It stipulates, for example, that Orthodox clergy cannot be drafted into the army; the state recognizes marriages registered by the church; the property and lands owned by the church are tax-exempt; the state is obligated to implement joint educational programs and to support educational institutions of the Orthodox Church; the

12 major Orthodox festivals are recognized as national public holidays.

The dynamic development of the GOC during 1990s was, however, accompanied by serious internal problems and tensions. Strong conservative and anti-ecumenical sentiments were growing within the GOC, specifically among the clergy in Georgian Orthodox monasteries. In an open letter published on May 17, 1997, the abbots of five monasteries threatened to break communion with the head of the GOC, Catholicos-Patriarch Ilia II, because of his ecumenical involvement (from 1979 to 1983, he served as president of the World Council of Churches). On May 20, 1997, in order to avoid a possible schism within the church, the Synod of Bishops voted to withdraw from both the World Council of Churches and the European Council of Churches. The leaders of the conservative opposition (who are in close contact with Old Calendarist groups from Greece), however, were not fully satisfied with this action and called to break communion with those national Orthodox churches that continue to participate in ecumenical organizations. These divisions within the GOC were to a significant extent associated with support for the various political factions. The moderate head of the GOC, Patriarch Ilia II (b. 1933), has forged an alliance with President Shevardnadze, while a conservative and anti-ecumenical group of Georgian Orthodox clergy has been linked to the Georgian nationalists related to the ousted president Zviad Gamsakhurdia.

In 2003, the so-called Rose Revolution deposed President Shevardnadze, who was accused by Georgian opposition and international observers of the falsification of the November 2 parliamentary elections. One of the leaders of the Rose Revolution, the U.S.-educated Mikheil Saakashvili, was elected president of Georgia in 2004. During the nonviolent Rose Revolution and transitional process of establishment of the new more pro-Western government, Patriarch Ilia II, made a strong appeal on behalf of the church against the use of arms and violence.

The administration of the Patriarchate of Georgia consists of 10 departments (External Affairs, Mission and Evangelization, Relations with Army and Law Enforcing Bodies, Relations with Prisoners, Search and Protection of Ecclesiastical Sanctities, Study of Non-Orthodox Denominations, Education, Publication, Folk Handicraft, Study of Ancient Georgian Sacred Songs). GOC supports a nationwide radio show, *Iveria*.

Since 1977, the GOC has been headed by His Holiness and Beatitude Ilia II, who has the title of "the Catholicos-Patriarch of All Georgia and Archbishop of Mtskheta and Tbilisi."

Alexei D. Krindatch

See also: Armenian Apostolic Church (Holy See of Echmiadzin); Ecumenical Patriarchate/Patriarchate of Constantinople; Greek Orthodox Patriarchate of Antioch and All the East; Mary, Blessed Virgin; Roman Catholic Church; Russian Orthodox Church (Moscow Patriarchate); World Council of Churches.

References

Baltaden, S. K. *Seeking God: The Recovery of Religious Identity in Orthodox Russia, Ukraine, and Georgia*. De Kalb: Northern Illinois University Press, 1993.

Dowling, Theodore. *Sketches of Georgian Church History*. Ellibron Classics Series. Boston: Adamant Media Corporation, 2005.

Georgia Statistics. 2002 Population Census of Georgia. Population by Religious Beliefs. http://www.statistics.ge/_files/english/census/2002/Religious%20beliefs.pdf. Accessed July 15, 2009.

Malan, S. C., ed. *A Short History of the Georgian Church*. Trans. by P. Ioseliani. London: Saunders, Otley, 1866.

Official website of the Georgian Orthodox Church (English version): http://www.patriarchate.ge/_en/?action=home. Accessed July 15, 2009.

Roberson, R. *The Eastern Christian Churches: A Brief Survey*. 7th ed. Rome, Italy: Edizioni Orientalia Christiana, 2006. http://www.cnewa.org/generalpg-verus.aspx?pageID=182. Accessed July 15, 2009.

Schmemann, Alexander. *The Historical Road of Eastern Orthodoxy*. Crestwood, NY: St. Vladimir's Seminary Press, 1977.

Skurat, K. *Istorija Pomestnykh Pravoslavnykh Cerkvej*. Moscow: Russkie ogni, 1994.

Gerizim, Mount

Mount Gerizim is the holy mountain of the Samaritans. The Samaritans have a version of the Old Testament that includes references to the mountain that do not appear in the Jewish Bible. Mount Gerizim was the location of their competing temple and the central location of their religion; it continues to be the central focus of their religious activities today.

Mount Gerizim is in the southern side of the valley in which the city of Nablus, or Shechem, sits, the northern side being Mount Ebal. It is about 2,900 feet above sea level, slightly shorter than Mount Ebal. It is the center of worship for the Samaritan community, most of whom live in the vicinity. They regard Mount Gerizim as the site of Abraham's attempted sacrifice of Isaac and of the Temple, both of which are positioned on Mount Moriah and in Jerusalem for Jews.

The mountain became a religious center designed to rival Jerusalem in the mid-fifth century BCE. The Samaritans established their own temple on Mount Gerizim and in the time of Alexander the Great, according to Josephus, it increased in size and magnificence. This seems to have aroused considerable antipathy with the Jews in Jerusalem, and both communities sought the support of the rulers of Palestine for the benefit of their own community. The Jews managed to destroy the temple on the mountain. Later on when Christianity became the state religion of the Roman Empire and a church was built on the mountain, this led to a violent Samaritan response, which briefly resulted in the sixth century CE in the recapture of the mountain and the destruction of churches in Samaria. This was put down quite quickly, though, and brought about the dispersal of the Samaritan population. Some must have remained, though, since a church was built on the summit of the mountain, which is rather flat, and was protected by a castle. The site remains today the place where Samaritans live, carry out their rituals, and await the coming of the Messiah.

Members of the ancient Samaritan community pray during the pilgrimage for the holy day of the Tabernacles, or Sukkot, at the religion's holiest site on the top of Mount Gerizim near Nablus, Palestine, October 25, 2007. (AP Photo/Kevin Frayer)

Mount Gerizim plays an enormous role in Samaritan life, and in their version of the Bible the place is mentioned in places where other mountains are mentioned in the Masoretic (Jewish) text. The many centuries of conflict and rivalry between the Jews and the Samaritans are symbolized by the differences in choice of holy mountains. In order for a Samaritan to be recognized as a Jew, he had to renounce any belief in the holiness of Mount Gerizim. There are various interesting remains on the mountain, including some stones that the Samaritans regard as sacred, together with parts of the church of the Virgin Mary and the wall built by Justinian. In the present day the Samaritan community lives on the slopes between the 10th of Nissan and the end of the Passover, using for their offerings not the summit of the mountain, even though this was the site of their original temple. They use a lower slope, perhaps because of the presence on the summit of a Muslim cemetery, which defiled the original site.

Oliver Leaman

See also: Abraham/Abram; Jerusalem; Mary, Blessed Virgin.

References

Kalimi, Isaac. "Zion or Gerizim? The Association of Abraham and the *Aqeda* with Zion/Gerizim in Jewish and Samaritan Sources." In *Boundaries of the Ancient Near Eastern World: A Tribute to Cyrus H. Gordon*, 442–457. JSOT Sup 273. Sheffield, UK: Sheffield Academic Press, 1998.

Magen, Yitzhak. "Mount Gerizim and the Samaritans." In *Early Christianity in Context*, edited by F. Manns and E. Alliata, 91–118. Studium Biblicum Franciscanum Collectio Maior 38. Jerusalem: Franciscan Printing,1993.

Stern, Ephraim, and Yitzhak Magen. "Mount Gerizim—A Temple City: Summary of Eighteen Years of Excavations." *Qadmoniot* 33 (2000): 74–118.

German Buddhist Union

The German Buddhist Union (GBU; Deutsche Buddhistische Union) is the umbrella organization of Buddhist groups, societies, and institutions in Germany. Since the organization is not aligned with any specific tradition, member societies are from the Theravada, Mahayana, Tibetan Buddhist, and Western Buddhist traditions. The Union is the only nationwide umbrella organization and widely recognized as the representative of Buddhism in Germany.

The GBU started as the German Buddhist Society in 1955, offering membership to both individuals and organizations. In 1958, the organizational structure was changed to an umbrella organization of Buddhist groups and societies only. The name adopted was German Buddhist Union, and it specified three aims: (1) to promote mutual understanding and cooperation between the different schools and traditions present in Germany, (2) to serve as a Buddhist representative for administrative bodies and other public institutions, and (3) to be a partner in interreligious dialogue.

During the first 25 years of its existence, the GBU remained small, with 7 to 8 member organizations only. As Buddhism generated increasing interest in Germany from the 1970s on, numerous new Buddhist groups and associations were founded. In the early 1980s, the GBU experienced a sharp increase, with new groups and organizations becoming members. This growth, accompanied by the wish to gain an officially established place in society and to firmly dissociate itself from new religious groups (such as the Bhagwan Shree Rajneesh movement), led to application for public recognition of Buddhism as an incorporated body in 1985. Although the GBU managed to meet legal prerequisites, especially those of a specific organizational structure and the provision of a commonly accepted doctrinal platform, the privileged status was not granted. The main reasons for the rejection were a lack of financial resources and the fact that too small a number of Buddhists were represented by the Union. Since 2008, the GBU has aimed to apply for recognition as an incorporated body.

The GBU is proud to present a Buddhist Confession (*Buddhistisches Bekenntnis;* a self-designation) that has been accepted by a wide range of traditions and schools. The friendly cooperation between the various Buddhist schools and groups in the GBU has been termed a "Buddhist ecumenism" (also a self-designation). The sharp increase in membership continued during the 1990s, doubling the members from 27 in 1994 to 59 in 2009. Many of the GBU members consist of numerous local meditation groups or centers; the organization thus comprises an estimated four-fifths of the more than 500 Buddhist groups, societies, centers, and organizations existent in Germany in the beginning of the 21st century. According to the GBU, the affiliated members attempt to realize an "authentic Buddhism" and all acknowledge the Buddhist Confession.

Legally, the GBU is a registered society with public benefit status. The Union is headed by a board of 11 persons, with a speaker coordinating the activities. Individual Buddhists can join the GBU via a membership in the Buddhist Community, which itself is a member of the GBU. Once a year, the GBU organizes a public conference, presenting varying topics. Since 1987, it has published the quarterly *Lotusblätter*, renamed and upgraded in 2004 as *Buddhismus aktuell*. The headquarters was established in Munich in 1986. The GBU is a member of the European Buddhist Union and the World Fellowship of Buddhists.

Deutsche Buddhistische Union
Amalienstr. 71
80799 Munich
Germany
http://www.dharma.de/dbu (in German and English)
Martin Baumann

See also: European Buddhist Union; World Fellowship of Buddhists.

References
Baumann, Martin. *Deutsche Buddhisten: Geschichte und Gemeinschaften.* 2nd ed. Marburg, Germany: Diagonal 1995.
Baumann, Martin. "The Transplantation of Buddhism to Germany—Processive Modes and Strategies of Adaptation." *Method and Theory in the Study of Religion* 6, no. 1 (1994): 35–61.
Deutsche Buddhistische Union. *Die Deutsche Buddhistische Union (DBU) und ihre Mitglieder in Selbstdarstellungen.* Munich: Deutsche Buddhistische Union, 1991.

■ Germany

Germany as a united nation-state in the modern sense came into being after the Franco-German War of 1871. Before, there was a millennium-long story of rivalry between numerous small and big German states, between principalities, kingdoms (for example, Bavaria, Prussia), and the Holy Roman Empire, a shifting loose confederation of mostly German-speaking states, generally with a German emperor, of which it has been said that it was neither holy nor Roman nor an empire. The different peoples were loosely connected by the

Refurbished Berlin Synagogue and its glittering new dome shine in a sea of houses in former East Berlin. The Byzantine-style structure was severely damaged during World War II. (Merlindo/Dreamstime.com)

Germany

Religion	Followers in 1970	Followers in 2010	% of Population	Annual % growth 2000–2010	Followers in 2025	Followers in 2050
Christians	70,124,000	58,123,000	70.6	–0.48	53,556,000	46,687,000
Protestants	34,467,000	25,800,000	31.3	–0.92	24,000,000	20,800,000
Roman Catholics	27,957,000	25,600,000	31.1	–0.70	23,800,000	20,500,000
Orthodox	610,000	1,100,000	1.3	1.10	1,150,000	1,150,000
Agnostics	5,552,000	18,055,000	21.9	2.03	18,850,000	18,500,000
Muslims	450,000	3,700,000	4.5	0.11	5,150,000	6,000,000
Atheists	1,928,000	2,000,000	2.4	1.28	2,174,000	2,150,000
Jews	32,900	230,000	0.3	0.08	250,000	250,000
Buddhists	5,000	88,000	0.1	0.08	130,000	180,000
Hindus	0	62,000	0.1	0.08	85,000	124,000
New religionists	66,000	58,000	0.1	0.08	80,000	95,000
Sikhs	2,000	25,000	0.0	0.08	30,000	36,000
Baha'is	9,400	13,000	0.0	0.08	20,000	40,000
Chinese folk	0	5,500	0.0	0.08	8,000	12,000
Ethnoreligionists	0	3,200	0.0	0.08	4,500	6,400
Confucianists	0	2,100	0.0	0.09	4,000	7,200
Total population	**78,169,000**	**82,365,000**	**100.0**	**0.08**	**80,341,000**	**74,088,000**

varying dialects of the German language (first referred to in Latin as *theodisca lingua*, from which the German expression *diutisc* was derived, first attested in the 10th century). From diutisc has come the modern *Deutsch*. People believed in the existence of local powers and deities (deities in trees, in rivers, on hills) that needed to be respected and approached in awe. In the course of the 5th to 10th centuries CE, Roman Catholic monks and nuns, supported by the ruling powers, led the peoples of the various central Western European territories to Christianity. During the Middle Ages (the 11th to the 15th centuries), the pope and the German emperor alternately struggled as rivals and cooperated.

In the early 16th century, the initial historic split between the Roman Catholic Church and reformist Protestantism took place, Martin Luther (1483–1546) providing the theological inspiration. Following Luther's translation of the New Testament into German (from the Greek and Latin versions) in 1521 and his public criticism of the pope and the practice of selling indulgences, an increasing number of German principalities and kingdoms dissociated from Rome and introduced the Protestant Reformation. The peace treaties of 1555 and 1648 politically sanctioned the split of the church. By those treaties, the principle was established

that the ruler of a region could determine its religion (in Latin, *cuius regio, eius religio*), and so parts of Germany became Protestant (following the Evangelical Church, as the church established by Luther was called), and other parts remained in the Roman Catholic Church. The subjects had to follow the principal's decision.

Within Protestantism, already in the 16th century the first splits occurred, and Pietistic denominations (emphasizing personal spirituality) came into being. Many principalities were in fact more or less mono-religious, but in the larger kingdoms people of both confessions (that is, of both the Evangelical and the Roman Catholic Church) resided, as well as marginalized Jews. Alongside this predominantly bidenominational set-up a small number of Free churches (for example, Baptists and Methodists), occult Esoteric groups, and metaphysical movements came into existence beginning in the 17th century.

Bi-confessionalism had also come about as a result of the legal secularization of 1803 and the territorial rearrangement of the German principalities following the Napoleonic wars (1806–1814). Along with the disappearance of states in which only one religion was recognized, a progressive dissolution of former state churches began, culminating in the legal separation of

GERMANY

church and state (in a now united Germany) of the Weimar Republic Constitution in 1918. In 1949, after the Nazi regime and World War II, the law of the Federal Republic of Germany (FRG) incorporated the relevant articles of the Weimar Constitution. Article 137 states that there is no state church, that the various "religious societies" have the right to organize themselves in an autonomous way, and that each may collect church taxes if it is recognized as a public body. More basically, article 4 guarantees the freedom of faith and religious confession. As for East Germany, the German Democratic Republic (GDR), its Constitution of 1949 adopted the same articles of the Weimar Constitution. Nevertheless, this did not prevent the state and the Communist Party of the GDR from imposing Marxist-Leninist ideology, nor did it prevent strong criticism of the Christian churches (mainly Protestant), and indeed of every faith. As a result, after 40 years of the GDR, the percentage of people not affiliated to a church or faith was the highest in Europe (70 percent non-affiliated). With the GDR joining the FRG and thus the formal ending of the GDR in 1990, the percentage of religiously non-affiliated people in the now united Germany became 26 percent of the whole population.

Around the beginning of the 20th century, new, non-Christian faiths and traditions had already emerged in or trickled into Germany. A few individual Baha'i, Buddhists, Theosophists, freethinkers, Anthroposophists, and others met in private circles, founded societies, and propagated their conviction in journals and public meetings. A different way of contributing to the enlarging religious pluralism of Germany came about during the 1960s, with the arrival of so-called guest workers (*Gastarbeiter*) from Turkey. Most of these workers and their families were Muslims (in the Sunni Hanafite tradition). After years of work in Germany, many opted to stay in the country where their children had grown up by now. A multitude of small, hidden mosques were built, a process that during the 1990s changed to a more visible appearance of Islam in Germany. In 2000, Islam, with some 3 million people, had become the third largest religious faith in Germany. Furthermore, the migration of people and flight of refugees from Near Eastern, African, and Asian countries had brought additional faiths and traditions, including other Islamic traditions, African Initiated Churches, Yezidis, Hindu, Sikh, and Buddhist followers.

Additionally, during the 1970s and 1980s, new religious movements such as the Hare Krishnas (International Society for Krishna Consciousness), Transcendental Meditation, the Neo-Sannyas movement of Bhagwan Shree Rajneesh (Osho Commune International), and the Church of Scientology had succeeded in finding a footing in Germany. A fierce public debate has ensued about whether these organizations are dangerous. Christian pastors and so-called sect specialists have been at the forefront of this polemical discussion, using their traditional societal power to define what is right and wrong.

Despite the fundamental enlargement of religious options and traditions, Christian churches have retained their dominant position within the religious pluralism in Germany. In 2009, of Germany's 83 million inhabitants, 24.8 million people were members of the Evangelical Church in Germany, and almost the same number of people were affiliated with Roman Catholicism (25.5 million). Free churches (1 million) and Orthodox churches (2.3 million) stay well behind the total of 4 million Muslims. Judaism has re-established itself in Germany after the persecution and Holocaust during Nazi rule, with 107,000 Jews affiliated with Jewish synagogues and 90,000 without such affiliation (often emigrants from Eastern European states). There are some 100,000 Hindus from India and Sri Lanka (Tamils), Tamil Hindus having been active in organizing and opening some 25 temples since the 1990s. The number of Buddhists can be estimated at some 150,000 people, two-thirds of whom are refugees and migrants from Asia. Other religious communities and new religious movements comprise a minority of some 120,000 to 140,000 followers altogether. In total, non-Christian faiths with about 10 million people constitute a growing minority of 12 percent. In contrast, the number of people not officially affiliated with a church or religious tradition is about 25 million, comprising more than a fourth of the population in Germany, with differences in East and West Germany.

Martin Baumann

See also: African Initiated (Independent) Churches; Church of Scientology; Evangelical Church in

Germany; International Society for Krishna Consciousness; Luther, Martin; Osho and the International Osho Movement; Roman Catholic Church; Yezidis.

References

Daiber, Karl-Fritz. *Religion unter den Bedingungen der Moderne.* Marburg, Germany: Diagonal, 1995.

Deutscher Bundestag, ed. *Abschlussbericht der Enquete-Kommission "Sogenannte Sekten und Psychogruppen": Neue religiöse und ideologische Gemeinschaften und Psychogruppen in der Bundesrepublik Deutschland.* Bonn: Referat Öffentlichkeitsarbeit, 1998.

Evans, Richard J. "Religion and Society." In *Rethinking German History: Nineteenth-Century Germany and the Origin of the Third Reich.* London: Allen and Unwin, 1987.

Hero, Markus, Volkhard Krech, and Helmut Zander, eds. *Religiöse Vielfalt in Nordrhein-Westfalen. Empirische Befunde und Perspektiven der Globalisierung vor Ort.* Schöningh Verlag, Germany: Paderborn, 2007.

Moltmann, Jürgen. "Religion and State in Germany: West and East." *Annals of the American Academy of Political Science* 483, no. 1 (1986): 110–117.

Religious Studies Media and Information Service (REMID), Marburg, Germany, 2009. *Religionsgemeinschaften in Deutschland: Mitgliederzahlen.* http://www.remid.de/remid_info_zahlen.htm. Accessed July 21, 2009.

Tworuschka, Udo, and Michael Klöcker, eds. *Handbuch der Religionen. Kirchen und andere Gluabensgemeinschaften in Deutschland.* Landsberg am Lech, Germany: Olzog, 1997. With updates and sections twice annually.

Germany, Hinduism in

Interest in Hindu concepts and ideas in Germany can be traced to 18th- and 19th-century philosophers and writers. Despite this early encounter, a lasting presence of Hindu people began no earlier than the second half of the 20th century, with immigrants and refugees coming from South Asia. Johann Gottfried Herder (1744–1803) and Romantic thinkers and poets such as Joseph Görres (1776–1848) and Novalis (1772–1801) idealized India as being synonymous with original religiosity and unity, virtues supposed to have been lost in Europe with the 18th-century Age of Enlightenment. This kind of idealization has continued to this day among some artists; it has also shaped the image of India and Hinduism held by many Western converts. In 2009, the number of Hindus living in Germany was estimated at about 100,000 people. Far from forming a homogeneous faith minority, Hindus fall into subminorities from India, Afghanistan, and Sri Lanka, as well as belonging to organizations formed by Western converts.

Indian Hindus, many of them businessmen, doctors, and engineers from Kerala, Bengal, or Gujarat, have come since the 1950s. The number was estimated at some 35,000 people in 2001. These individual professionals have become well established as professors, senior physicians, and businessmen. A fair number have married German partners and taken German citizenship. Despite their number, no permanent places of worship have been founded. Occasionally Indian Hindus meet in rented halls to celebrate the main Indian annual festivals, such as Durga-puja or Divali. Wealthy families invite a swami (teacher) to provide lectures or to perform specific life rituals.

Afghan Hindus came to Germany fleeing the civil war during the 1980s. Of some 66,000 Afghans in Germany, a minority of approximately 5,000 are Hindus. In 2009, they maintained a variety of well-organized and richly decorated temples, such those in Hamburg, Cologne, and Frankfurt am Main. These sites are often visited by Sikhs and Indian Hindus too.

Western Hindus come together in organizations such as the Ananda Marga Yoga Society (with some 200 members), Sahaja Yoga (200), Brahma Kumaris (300), the International Society for Krishna Consciousness (whose members are called Hare Krishnas, 350), Divine Light Mission (now known as Elan Vital, 1.500), Krishna Community (400), Transcendental Meditation Organization, now organized as the Global Country of World Peace (1,000, plus 5,000–10,000 "practitioners"), and Osho and the International Osho Movement (5,000). All together they number less than 10,000 people. In numerous local groups, they pursue devotional acts, read basic Hindu texts, and practice yoga and meditation. They provoked public debates during the 1970s and

1980s, when they were stigmatized as belonging to "cults" and "sects," but the controversy has calmed down since the mid-1990s. A less polemic and more factually oriented approach has emerged, which perceives these Hindu-faith-based groups as belonging to the category of new religions.

Tamil people from Sri Lanka have come to Germany as asylum seekers since the early 1980s. Among the 60,000 Tamil refugees and citizens in 2009, some 75 percent, or 45,000, were Hindus, the rest Catholic and Protestant. Despite the imposed geographic distribution of Tamils to all federal states of Germany, a clear concentration has evolved in North Rhine-Westphalia (NRW). In this region, 45 percent of all Tamil people live. They have established shops and social and political societies, and founded numerous temples. Of the 25 permanent temples (additionally there are temporary places of worship) in 2009, 15 were situated in NRW. The size of the temples varies, from little basement rooms to shrine rooms set up on the ground floor of a residential house to temples in spacious halls of converted industrial buildings. Hamm (in NRW), with its three separate temples for Vinayagar (Ganesha), Kamadchi (a goddess), and Murugan, has become the center of Hindu Tamil life in Germany. The Sri Kamadchi temple stages an annual procession attended by some 10,000 participants and visitors (Hindu Shankarar Sri Kamadchi Ampal Temple, Siegenbeckstr. 4, 59071 Hamm-Uentrop; http://www.kamadchi-ampal.de). Also, this temple is the only purposely built temple, constructed in South Indian style with a large *gōpuram* (tower) and seven separate shrines in the huge temple hall.

In general, until the mid-1990s migrant Hindus displayed a rather low public profile, despite their numbers. In contrast, media interests focused on convert Hindus and their religious practices. With the emergence of public processions and the founding of recognizable temples, there has been a shift to more public visibility of the immigrant Hindu minorities.

Martin Baumann

See also: Ananda Marga Yoga Society; Brahma Kumaris; Elan Vital/Divine Light Mission; Global Country of World Peace; International Society for Krishna Consciousness; Osho and the International Osho Movement; Sahaja Yoga.

References

Baumann, Martin. *Migration, Religion, Integration: Vietnamesische Buddhisten und tamilische Hindus in Deutschland.* Marburg, Germany: Diagonal-Verlag 2000.

Baumann, Martin. "Sustaining 'Little Indias': The Hindu Diasporas in Europe." In *Strangers and Sojourners: Religious Communities in the Diaspora,* edited by Gerrie ter Haar. Leuven, Belgium: Uitgeverij Peeters, 1998.

Baumann, Martin, and Kurt Salentin. "Migrant Religiousness and Social Incorporation: Tamil Hindus in Germany." *Journal of Contemporary Religion* 21, no. 3 (2006): 297–323.

Baumann, Martin, Brigitte Luchesi, and Annette Wilke, eds. *Tempel und Tamilen in zweiter Heimat: Hindus aus Sri Lanka im deutschsprachigen und skandinavischen Raum.* Würzburg, Germany: Ergon, 2003.

Religious Studies Media and Information Service (REMID), Marburg, Germany, 2009. *Religionsgemeinschaften in Deutschland: Mitgliederzahlen.* http://www.remid.de/remid_info_zahlen.htm. Accessed July 21, 2009.

Süss, Joachim. *Bhagwans Erbe. Die Osho-Bewegung heute.* Munich: Claudius, 1996.

Germany, Islam in

In 2009, 3.8 to 4.3 million people of the Muslim faith resided in Germany (up to 5.2 percent of the population). Some 63 percent, or 2.5 to 2.7 million, of these were Turkish Muslims, most of them in the Sunni Hanafi tradition, and 14 percent, or half a million, Muslims from Southeast Europe. Along with the dominant Sunni community (74 percent), there are also Turkish Muslims of the Alewite tradition (13 percent), and smaller groups of Shia Muslims (of Turkish, Iranian, and other descent, 7 percent), Sufis, Ismailis, and members of the Ahmadiyya movement in Islam (6 percent). Finally, there are also some 10,000 German Muslim converts.

The minaret of the local mosque in Gelsenkirchen, western Germany, is flanked by a German (left) and a Turkish flag. (AP Photo/Martin Meissner)

The current presence of Islam is based on the enlistment of Turkish men (very few women) for semi-skilled work in Germany during the 1960s. However, the history of Islam in Germany dates back to the mid-18th century, when in 1739 the Prussian king, Frederick William I, ordered the construction of a mosque in Potsdam (near Berlin) so that the Turkish soldiers serving in the Prussian army could faithfully practice their religious duties. In 1798, a first Muslim cemetery, owned by the Ottoman Empire, was authorized in Berlin. In the 1920s, due to Muslim diplomats, traders, and refugees living in Berlin (about 1,000 people), an initial Muslim community, consisting of Muslims from 41 nations, was established (1922).

A sharp increase of Muslim people resulted from a labor force shortage and the resultant signing of an employment agreement between West Germany and Turkey in 1961. Similar agreements were concluded with Morocco in 1969, and subsequently with Tunisia. The agreements foresaw a temporary influx of workers. A system of rotation was built into the program, and the so-called *Gastarbeiter* (guest workers) were intended to stay for one to three years only. Within 10 years, half a million Turkish workers came to Germany. In 1973, due to the oil recession, recruitment was stopped. The phase of family reunion commenced in the following year, and the guest workers moved from temporary housing to more permanent houses. A proliferation of Turkish social and cultural infrastructures, including small halls for prayer, developed during the 1970s and 1980s.

During the 1990s the children of the guest workers came of age, and they have occasioned a move of Islam into the public arena. Representative mosques, each with its minaret, quite different from the hitherto unnoticed, hidden prayer halls, have been built in various cities. Most often, the building of these publicly visible signs of Islamic presence were accompanied by emotionally laden controversies, as German-born residents complained about such overtly Islamic buildings. Still, the vast majority of places for prayer remain in converted halls or houses (some 2,300), as opposed to some 75 proper mosques. Mosques and prayer halls have assumed many functions, serving religious, cultural, and social needs. Some offer special programs for youth, women, or elderly people.

The primary Muslim organizations are the Turkish Islamic Union of the Authority of Religion (DITIB), a direct representative of the Turkish Ministry of Religion, and the Islamic Community Milli Görüs (IGMG; Islamische Gemeinschaft Milli Görüs). Influential are also the Sufi-oriented Association of Islamic Cultural Centers (VIKZ) and the Islamic Community Jama'at un-Nur (all four with headquarters in Cologne). In addition to these organizations, with which about half of the local mosques or prayer halls are associated, national umbrella organizations such as the Central Council of Muslims (ZMD; Zentralrat der Muslime in Deutschland) and the Islamic Council strive to function as general representatives of Muslims in Germany. However, so far factionalism and internal quarrels have prevented the formation of a unified body. The import of Turkish home policy, the alignment to specific Islamic schools and traditions, and the emphasis on the cultural-linguistic origin of immigrant Muslims strongly influence the heterogeneity of Islam in Germany. Despite this organizational disunity, the second generation's increasing share in the leadership has brought about a shift in orientation toward ambitions to establish Islam in Germany firmly and to foster processes of both public representation and acculturation. In political terms, in 2006 the Ministry of Inner Affairs established the "German Islam Conference," a meeting of Muslim representatives, politicians, and community workers. As the former migrants and guest workers have become German citizens and "German Muslims" (45 percent have acquired German nationality in 2009), the political meetings should foster an acknowledgment and understanding of the Muslim minority in Germany.

The various organizations, which, however, represent only some 40 to 50 percent of Muslims in Germany, can be contacted through the following: Zentralrat der Muslime in Deutschland (ZMD), Steinfelder Gasse 32, 50670 Köln, http://zentralrat.de and http://www.islam.de/ (in German); Islamrat für die Bundesrepublik Deutschland, Osterather Str. 7, 50739 Köln, http://www.islamrat.de/ (in German); DITIB, Türkisch-Islamische Union der Anstalt für Religion, Subbelrather Str. 17, 50823 Köln; IGMG, Islamische Gemeinschaft Milli Görüs, Boschstraße 61-65, 50171 Kerpen, http://www.igmg.de/; Islamische Gemeinschaft Jama'at un-Nur, Neustr. 11, 51063 Köln; and the Verband der Islamischen Kulturzentren (VIKZ), Vogelsanger Strasse 290, 50825 Köln, http://www.vikz.de/.

Martin Baumann

See also: Ahmadiyya Movement in Islam; Alevism; Hanafite School of Islam; Ismaili Islam; Sufism.

References

Al-Hamarneh, Ala, and Jörn Thielmann, eds. *Islam and Muslims in Germany*. Leiden: Brill, 2008.

Bielefeld, Heiner. *Muslime im säkularen Rechtsstaat. Integrationschancen durch Religionsfreiheit.* Bielefeld. Transcript, 2003.

Deutsche Islamkonferenz. *Muslimisches Leben in Deutschland.* Berlin: Bundesamt für Migration und Flüchtlinge, 2009.

Karakasoglu, Yasemin, and Gerd Nonnemann. "Muslims in Germany, with Special Reference to the Turkish-Islamic Community." In *Muslim Communities in the New Europe,* edited by Gerd Nonnemann, Tim Niblock, and Bogdan Szajkowski. Reading, UK: Ithaca Press, 1996.

Nöckel, Sigrid. *Die Töchter der Gastarbeiter und der Islam. Zur Soziologie alltagsweltlicher Anerkennungspolitiken.* Bielefeld. Transcript, 2002.

Schiffauer, Werner. "Islamic Vision and Social Reality: The Political Culture of Sunni Muslims in Germany." In *Islam in Europe: The Politics of Religion and Community,* edited by Steven Vertovec and Ceri Peach. Basingstoke, UK: Macmillan 1997.

Schiffauer, Werner. "Suspect Subjects: Muslim Migrants and the Security Agencies in Germany." In *The Social Life of Anti-Terrorist Laws: The War on Terror and the Classification of the 'Dangerous Other,'* edited by J. M. Eckert. Bielefeld. Transcript, 2008.

Yalcin-Heckmann, Lale. "Growing Up as a Muslim in Germany: Religious Socialization Among Turkish Migrant Families." In *Muslim European Youth: Reproducing Ethnicity, Religion, Culture,* edited by Steven Vertovec and Alisdair Rogers. Aldershot, UK: Ashgate 1998.

■ Ghana

Ghana, formerly the British colony known as the Gold Coast, is located on the Gulf of Guinea between Cote d'Ivoire and Togo. Much of its 89,000 square miles of territory is located along the Volta River. Today it is home to 23 million people, almost half of which are from the several groups of the Ashanti (or Akan) people.

The modern nation of Ghana began to take shape in the 14th century CE with the movement of the Ashanti people into the area, where they became rivals of the Denkyita state that controlled the coast. They

Ghana

Religion	Followers in 1970	Followers in 2010	% of Population	Annual % growth 2000–2010	Followers in 2025	Followers in 2050
Christians	4,806,000	15,309,000	61.5	2.80	20,475,000	27,828,000
Protestants	944,000	6,300,000	25.3	3.72	8,500,000	11,500,000
Independents	1,248,000	4,100,000	16.5	2.05	5,400,000	7,400,000
Roman Catholics	1,167,000	3,000,000	12.1	3.42	4,200,000	5,600,000
Ethnoreligionists	3,035,000	4,653,000	18.7	0.47	4,300,000	4,200,000
Muslims	1,200,000	4,800,000	19.3	2.52	7,000,000	9,500,000
Agnostics	9,000	75,900	0.3	2.27	150,000	250,000
New religionists	1,200	26,800	0.1	2.27	35,000	45,000
Baha'is	6,600	14,100	0.1	2.27	18,000	30,000
Hindus	1,000	4,900	0.0	2.26	7,000	14,000
Atheists	0	5,100	0.0	2.26	6,000	10,000
Chinese folk	0	750	0.0	2.29	1,200	1,500
Buddhists	300	500	0.0	2.28	1,000	2,000
Total population	**9,059,000**	**24,890,000**	**100.0**	**2.27**	**31,993,000**	**41,881,000**

emerged as a trading people who gathered the goods of the region and exchanged them for goods from the far north. This arrangement worked for several centuries, but in the 17th century, the Ashanti responded to the collapse of trade with North Africa by uniting and capturing several coastal cities. They then came into contact with Europeans and became partners in the slave trade.

The British attempts to stop the slave trade led to three different wars with the Ashanti (1806–1816, 1825–1828, and 1874). In 1875, the British established a protectorate over the coastal region, and 20 years later added the area in the north, where a new national political movement centered in Guinea threatened to spread. The Ashanti nation still controlled the central region. It was absorbed into the British colony, known as the Gold Coast, in 1902.

Pressure for independence grew after World War II, and in 1949 the Convention People's Party was founded by Kwame N'Krumah (1909–1972). He became the prime minister in 1952, and five years later the head of the first African colony to become independent. His attempts to reform the nation and his increasingly autocratic regime, however, met strong opposition, and in 1966 he was overthrown. A representative government was created in 1969. However, the next decades were marked by economic instability and frequent change of governments. Some stability has been offered by

Jerry John Rawlings (b. 1947), who came to prominence in 1979 and became president in 1982. He has survived several changes in the government and remained the country's president as the new century began. He was succeeded by John Kufour, whose second term concluded at the end of 2008.

The Ashanti (who dominate the central part of the country) and the Fanti (along the southern coast) make up 45 percent of the citizenry. Other important groups include the Ewe, Ga-Adanbe, Mole-Dagbane, Guan, and Gurma peoples. Approximately 25 percent of the people retain their traditional beliefs and practices.

Islam entered Ghana as early as the 1390s, in part due to the trade fostered by the Ashanti. Conversions to Islam were few until the 20th century, but Muslims (of the Sunni Shafiite, and Malikite schools) are now found across the nation. Muslims are strongest in the north, where such groups as the Wala and Dagoma are more than 50 percent Muslim. In 1969, some 200,000 Muslim immigrants in Ghana were expelled from the country, and many Muslim schools were closed. However, by that time the native Muslim community had become well entrenched. At the beginning of the new century, some 20 percent of the population of 20 million are Muslims.

Prior to 1969, the Muslim community had been dominated by the Ghana Muslim Community, headed by non-Ghanaians. After 1969, the Ghana Muslim

A Catholic church in Navrongo, northern Ghana. It is claimed by locals to be the largest mud church in the world. (iStockPhoto.com)

Mission (organized in 1957) and the Ahmadiyya Muslim movement (formed in Accra, the capital, in 1924) rose to prominence. Both formed modern Muslim schools and assumed a role in the post-independence culture. Most recently, missionaries sent by Al-Azhar University (Hanafite School) in Cairo, Egypt, have begun to proselytize in Ghana.

At the beginning of the 1990s, with the approval of the government, American Muslim leader Louis Farrakhan, head of the Nation of Islam, launched a mission in Ghana. In October 1994, he brought some 2,000 members from America to hold a five-day celebration of the work of Elijah Muhammad (founder of the Nation of Islam), the International Savior's Day, at which the Ghanaian president, Jerry Rawlings, spoke.

Christianity entered Ghana with initial missionary efforts of the Moravians, but no permanent work was established until 1828, when representatives of the Basel Mission settled in Christiansborg. The shaky work, headed by Europeans unused to the climate, was

rescued in 1843 by Jamaican Moravians, who finally built a stable congregation. The Basel missionaries built villages of Christian converts and created a school system. This work was transferred to the United Free Church of Scotland (now an integral part of the Church of Scotland) after World War I and eventually matured into the Presbyterian Church of Ghana.

British Methodists launched work in 1832 under the leadership of Thomas Birch Freeman (1809–1890), whose African heritage (by way of Jamaica) allowed him some comfort in his homeland. In 1838 he began the work among the Ashanti and emphasized education and indigenous leadership. The Methodist Church, Ghana became the leading church in the land and developed an education system capped by Bible schools and colleges.

As the British gained hegemony over the region, Anglicans moved in, headed by workers associated with the Church Missionary Society and the United Society for the Propagation of the Gospel (though Anglican services had been held in several locations along the coast since 1752). That work has now been incorporated into the Church of the Province of West Africa. The Salvation Army came in 1922. Nigerian (Yoruban) Baptists established the first Baptist congregations in 1918. Americans with the Assemblies of God brought Pentecostalism in 1931. In subsequent decades a spectrum of American and British groups staked out mission territories. The Southern Baptist Convention began an extensive mission in 1947.

Like the Muslims, the Christian community suffered in 1969, when all aliens without valid passports and work permits were expelled. Most Western missionaries and numerous Christians from neighboring countries were among the millions of people forced to leave Ghana.

The Roman Catholic Church first reached Ghana when the Portuguese explored the coast in the 15th century, but did not build an effective presence until the 1880s, when systematic work began. Following World War I, the White Fathers took the lead in building the church. The first Ghanaian bishop was consecrated in 1957. The church has been helped in the last generation by the spread of the Catholic Pentecostal movement.

African Initiated Churches began to arise early in the 20th century, and several, such as the Musama

GHANA

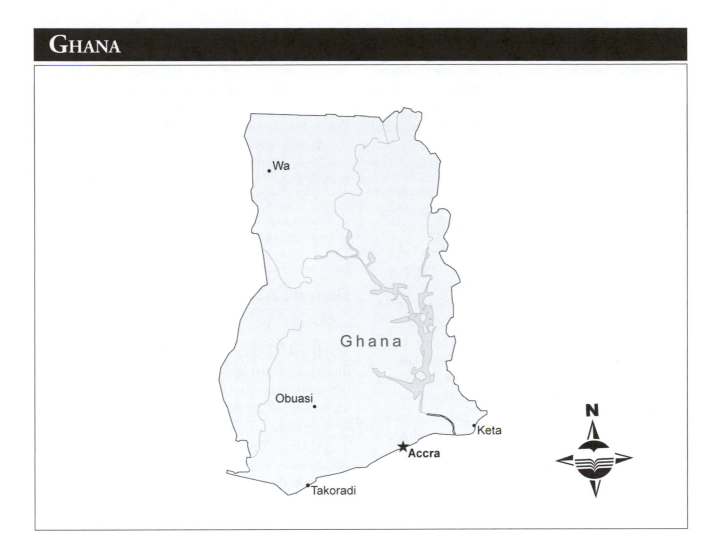

Disco Christo Church (also known as the Army of the Cross of Christ Church), have gone on to become international bodies. The Divine Healers Church now rivals the Methodist Church in size. Other churches, such as the Cherubim and Seraphim and the Harrist Church, have come to Ghana from neighboring lands. The very first Ghanaian independent church, the Church of the Twelve Apostles, was founded by a former member of the Harrist Church in 1914. Literally hundreds of different independent churches now operate in Ghana.

Many of the older missionary churches organized the Christian Council of the Gold Coast in 1924. That council evolved into the Christian Council of Ghana, now affiliated with the World Council of Churches. More recently, conservative evangelical churches have organized the National Association of Evangelicals of

Ghana, which is affiliated with the World Evangelical Alliance.

The Jehovah's Witnesses began work in 1924, and though banned in 1989, the organization now has more than 100,000 members. The Church of Jesus Christ of Latter-day Saints, also banned in 1989, now has 15,000 members and has erected a temple in Accra. The work in Ghana expanded for the first time in the years after the admission of people of African descent to the priesthood in 1978. The ban on the church was lifted in 1990.

Some Hindu traders from India had come to Ghana through the 20th century, but in 1977, a missionary (called the Black Monk of Africa) set up a Hindu monastery in Accra. It had a Ghanaian as its head and some two dozen African residents, who accepted the vows of renunciation as *sannyasi*. The monastery has developed a presence in various parts of the country through its establishment of clinics and social welfare structures. The Ananda Marga Yoga Society also has work in Ghana.

Additional small movements in Ghana include the Baha'i Faith, the Church Universal and Triumphant (from the United States), Soka Gakkai International (from Japan), and Chinese Buddhists.

J. Gordon Melton

See also: African Initiated (Independent) Churches; Ahmadiyya Movement in Islam; Ananda Marga Yoga Society; Assemblies of God; Baha'i Faith; Basel Mission; Cherubim and Seraphim/Eternal Sacred Order of the Cherubim and Seraphim; Church Missionary Society; Church of Jesus Christ of Latter-day Saints; Church of Scotland; Church of the Province of West Africa; Church Universal and Triumphant; Hanafite School of Islam; Harrist Church; Jehovah's Witnesses; Malikite School of Islam; Methodist Church, Ghana; Musama Disco Christo Church; Nation of Islam; Presbyterian Church of Ghana; Roman Catholic Church; Salvation Army; Shafiite School of Islam; Soka Gakkai International; Southern Baptist Convention; World Council of Churches; World Evangelical Alliance.

References

Asamoah-Gyadu, J. Kwabena. *African Charismatics: Current Developments within Independent Indigenous Pentecostalism in Ghana*. Leiden: Brill Academic Publishers, 2004.

Barker, P., ed. *Five Hundred Churches: A Brief Survey of Christianity in Ghana*. Accra: Christian Council of Ghana, 1978.

Debrunner, H. W. *A History of Christianity in Ghana*. Accra: Waterville Publishing House, 1967.

Fisher, Robert B. *West African Religious Traditions: Focus on the Akan of Ghana*. Maryknoll, NY: Orbis Books, 1998.

Greene, Sandra E. *Sacred Sites and the Colonial Encounter: A History of Meaning and Memory in Ghana*. Bloomington: Indiana University Press, 2002.

The Rise of Independent Churches in Ghana. Accra: Asempa Publishers, 1990.

Silverman, R. A., and D. Owusu-Ansah. "The Presence of Islam among the Akan of Ghana: A Bibliographical Essay." *History of Africa* 16 (1989): 325–337.

Soothill, Jane E. *Gender, Social Change and Spiritual Power: Charismatic Christianity in Ghana*. Leiden: Brill Academic Publishers, 2007.

Wilks, Ivor. *Wa and the Wala: Islam and Polity in Northwestern Ghana*. Cambridge: Cambridge University Press, 2002.

Wyllie, Robert W. *The Spirit-Seekers: New Religious Movements in Southern Ghana*. American Academy of Religion, Studies in Religion No. 21. Missoula, MT: Scholars Press, 1980.

Ghazali, Abu Hamid al-

1058–1111

Abu Hamid al-Ghazali is one of the most famous Muslim intellectuals, known especially for his promotion of Sufism as integral to true Islam. He was born in the early years of the Bagdad-based sultans of the Seljuk dynasty that ruled from Jerusalem to Bukhara.

Al-Ghazali was born in 1058 in Tus, in the eastern part of what is now Iran. In his late teen years he spent time under the guidance of Sufi shaykh Yusuf al-Nassaj. He then became a student of al-Juwayni (d. 1085), one of the famous imams of the time. Recognized for his brilliance, al-Ghazali was invited to teach in the court of Nizam al-Mulk, the vizier of the Seljuq leaders, and he became a professor at the Nizamiyah College in Baghdad in 1091.

In 1095 al-Ghazali left his teaching position and adopted the life of a Sufi mystic. After travels to Damascus, Jerusalem, and Mecca he moved to Tus, his birthplace. He had a band of disciples who joined his monastic path. In 1106, near the start of a new century, he began teaching again, this time at Nishapur. He died in his hometown in 1111.

Though more than 400 works bear his name, many are falsely attributed to him and others are questionable. He is most famous for *Ihyā ulūm ad-dīn* (*Revival of the Religious Sciences*) and its promotion of a mystical understanding of Islam. Critics have accused him of killing Muslim philosophy, while defenders assert he released Islam from the grip of Aristotle. His epistemic struggles seem genuine in his autobiographical account *Munqidh min al-Dalal* (*Deliverance from Error*) though they were dismissed by some as a ruse to pass himself off as a genuine searcher. Historians of philosophy have noted the significant parallels between al-Ghazali and Descartes.

His appreciation of Sufism is sometimes overstated. He valued the Sufi path but not without caution. For example, he warned about false imitation of mystical encounters as a hypocritical substitute for genuine ecstasy. He damned those who pretend a state of intimacy with God as rationale for disobeying God's law. He also said that overzealous Sufi mystics could get lost in fancy if there is no grounding in reason. There is also some evidence that al-Ghazali had personal experience of the depression that can accompany the ecstatic path.

His appreciation of Sufism was held in balance with his commitment to reason and, more important, to the Koran and Sunna of the Prophet. Here are his words: "the one who calls for pure uncritical acceptance in complete isolation from reason is ignorant; just as the one who is satisfied with nothing but reason, independent of the lights of the Koran and the Sunna, is deceived." He also wrote of change that does "not come about through constructing a proof or putting together an argument, but by a light that God Most High cast into my breast. And that light is the key to the greater part of knowledge. And whoever thinks that the unveiling of things divine depends upon strict proofs has in his thought narrowed down the wideness of God's mercy."

Al-Ghazali wrote works of jurisprudence and tomes that sought to combat alleged heresies within Islam. He was one of the major critics of Ismaili doctrine and practice though his perspective was tainted by longstanding bigotry toward Ismaili Islam in the Seljuq and Sunni establishments of his day.

James A. Beverley

See also: Bukhara; Damascus; Ismaili Islam; Jerusalem; Mecca; Sufism.

References

Griffel, Frank. *Al-Ghazali's Philosophical Theology.* New York: Oxford, 2009.

McCarthy, R. J. *Freedom and Fulfillment.* Boston: Twayne, 1980.

Watt, William Montgomery. *The Faith and Practice of al-Ghazali.* London: Allen and Unwin, 1953.

Ghost Dance

The term "Ghost Dance" refers to several Pan-Indian religious movements that spread among Native American people in the late 19th century in response to the European-American encroachment in the American West. The first of these movements began in the later 1860s when Wodziwob (ca.1844–ca.1873), of the Northern Paiute people, visited the spirit world while in a trance state, following which he conveyed prophecies of a restoration of conditions prior to contact with Europeans. During the years leading up to Wodziwob's pronunciations, the Paiute had experienced much suffering directly related to their being pushed off their traditional lands—disease, hunger, and a drought.

Wodziwob started the movement using the traditional Round Dance of the Paiutes, to which he added rites aimed at increase and healing. The movement brought no noticeable change to the Paiute and died out within a few years. By that time, however, it had spread to the West Coast. In California and Oregon, Noreliputus, a chief of the Yana-Wintu people, was inspired to found the Earth Lodge Religion, which added an element to the original movement, namely, the idea that believers would be protected from imminent apocalyptic changes by going underground into subterranean earth lodges, especially constructed for that purpose. As the movement spread northward toward Mount Shasta, dreams and dance were emphasized.

In north-central California, among the Hall Parwin people, a prophet named Lame Bill introduced what became the Bole-Maru Religion. This took the elements of the Paiute Ghost Dance in a somewhat different direction. While emphasizing dance and ceremony it replaced many of the predictions of apocalyptic events with an emphasis on belief in God, an afterlife, and moral reform, especially related to the abandonment of major personal vices. The movement produced a spectrum of innovative dances, including some for women. The movement has survived to the present.

The Bole-Maru Religion inspired the Big Head Religion, so named for the elaborate head piece worn

American artist Frederic Remington's interpretation of the Oglala Sioux Ghost Dance at Pine Ridge Indian Reservation, South Dakota, as it appeared in *Harper's Weekly* magazine in 1890. The Ghost Dance was a messianic movement that preached the promise of Indian freedom from the white man. (Library of Congress)

by the lead dancers. It also spread among northern California groups. Its dances were characterized by the presence of a foot drum and several kinds of rattles. The unique aspect of the movement was its traveling with the ritual instruments. A group would attain the ritual materials, perform the dances, and then pass the items to the next group, and the cycle would be repeated. The movement was present within any given group only when they owned the ritual instruments to carry out the dances.

In the late 1880s, a new Ghost Dance movement began among the Northern Paiute under the leadership of Wovoka (ca. 1856–1932). Wovoka emerged as a prophet in the mode of previous Paiute prophets. On January 1, 1889, during an eclipse of the Sun, he entered a trance state and visited the spirit world where he received teaching to be shared with his people. He offered a broad set of promises—the resurrection of those who had died, an end of the misery and death they had been experiencing, and the renewal of the land.

He preached a way of moral regeneration that included the abandonment of lying, stealing, and cheating; living in harmony with one's neighbor; and making peace with the white people. He proposed dancing, done in five-day increments, as the means of bring about the prophesied changes.

Wovoka was soon adorned with messianic expectations and news of his prophecies and pronouncements from the spirit world spread across the American West. His teachings and the dance he proposed spread to Native people from the Mississippi River to the Pacific Ocean. As it spread, numerous local variations developed in both belief and practice. Many hoped that white people would simply disappear and the buffalo would be restored. Many dancers reported a variety of visionary experiences and personal spirit contacts while dancing.

The rapid spread of the dancing movement alarmed the white people then in the midst of a major migration that saw hundreds of thousands moving from east of the Mississippi River to populate the emerging western states. Their fear that the dance heralded a massive Native American uprising led to a variety of repressive measures beginning with its being generally outlawed.

The most notable adaptation occurred among the Arapaho and Lakota peoples where a "shirt" said to be bulletproof was worn by the dancers. They saw the dances as bringing an imminent change, while many whites saw it as simply another war dance. That belief partially undergirded the military being called in to suppress the dance. The combination of the faith in the shirt and the fear of the dance among the white people culminated in the massacre of dancers and their families at Wounded Knee Creek in South Dakota.

On December 28, 1890, just two weeks after the unfortunate shooting death of Lakota Chief Sitting Bull and the officer attempting to arrest him, a group of 350 Lakota under Chief Big Foot encountered a force from the U.S. Army's 7th Cavalry along Wounded Knee Creek. The next morning, the troop commander ordered the Lakota to surrender their weapons immediately. Yellow Bird, the group's medicine man, started dancing and urged everyone to put on their sacred shirts in defiance of the troops. Amid the excited verbal exchanges that began, a shot was fired and the troops opened fire. When the firing finally stopped, some 150 Lakota had died. It appears that most of the troops that died or were wounded met their fate from unregulated friendly fire.

The Ghost Dance largely disappeared after Wounded Knee, and most certainly any belief in the powers of the sacred shirt. However, the movement survived in pockets for several decades. Among the Kiowa, for example, it had inspired a variant dance practice called the Feather Dance, so named for the eagle feather given to practitioners to be worn during the dance. The Kiowa had settled in eastern Oklahoma in the 1860s. They continued to practice the Feather Dance until threats of withholding government support money forced its discontinuance in 1916.

J. Gordon Melton

See also: Lakota, The; Native American Church.

References

Hirschfelder, Arlene, and Paulette Molin. *Encyclopedia of Native American Religions*. New York: Facts on File, 2000.

Kehoe, Alice. *The Ghost Dance: Ethnohistory and Revitalization*. Detroit, MI: Thompson Publishing, 1989.

Mooney, James. *The Ghost Dance Religion and Wounded Knee*. New York: Dover Publications Inc., 1896.

■ Gibraltar

Gibraltar, a peninsula located off the coast of southern Spain, is a United Nations territory administered by the United Kingdom. Though a mere 2.5 square miles of land mass, it is strategically placed immediately north of the Straits of Gibraltar and a mere 20 miles from Morocco. It is home to approximately 28,000 people, an eclectic mixture from a variety of European and North African backgrounds. Though the largest segment of the population is of Spanish heritage, the residents of Gibraltar have persistently rejected Spanish hegemony over their home.

The island was occupied by England in 1704. Spain formally ceded hegemony to England with the Treaty of Utrecht a decade later. Since the 1960s, Spain has actively worked to regain control, an effort blocked by a plebiscite in 1967. Following England and Spain working out an agreement for joint sovereignty, in 2002 the citizenry voted to reject the agreement. In 2007, a new Constitution, which assigned local autonomy and rejected any notion of the peninsula being a colony, granted the United Kingdom responsibility for defense, foreign relations, internal security, and financial stability.

The Roman Catholic Church had begun work on Gibraltar in 1492, but once the British assumed control, the church was suppressed. However, the church survived and remains by far the largest religious body on the island. In 1910 the work was organized into a diocese, whose bishop was immediately subject to Rome through the Office for the Propagation of the Faith.

The Anglican Church was introduced by the British in 1704 and has primarily served residents of British extraction. A Diocese of Gibraltar was organized in 1842, which included Anglican parishes across southern Europe around the Mediterranean rim all the way

GIBRALTAR

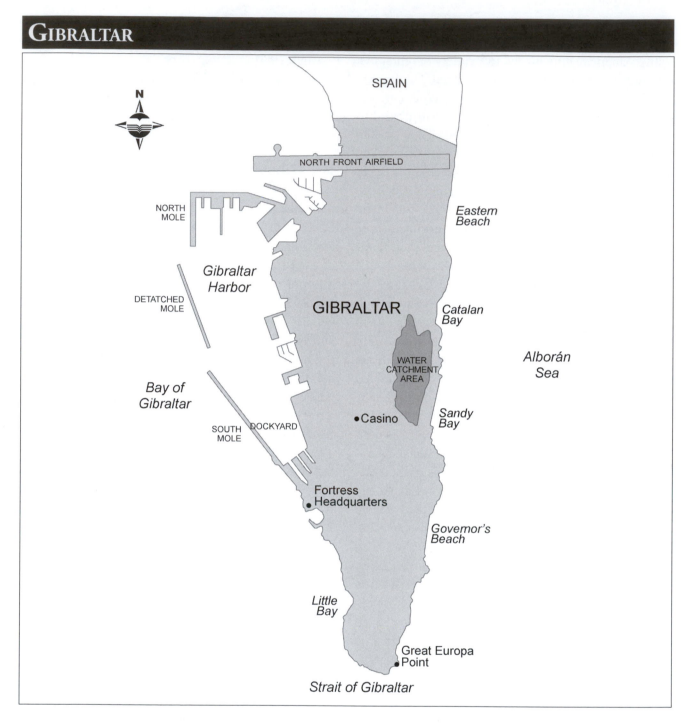

to Turkey. More recently, the Anglican work in Europe outside of the British Isles has been reorganized into the comprehensive Church of England's Diocese of Europe, which includes English-speaking parishes in some 45 countries. The work in Gibraltar has been reorganized into an archdeaconry.

Also following the British arrival, Methodists (associated with the Methodist Church [United Kingdom]

and Presbyterians (related to the Church of Scotland) established work. The Seventh-day Adventist Church arrived early in the century. Gibraltar is part of the Spanish Union of Churches. The Jehovah's Witnesses established their presence around 1955.

In 1492, at a time that Spain was considering what to do with the Jews in its midst, the government heard proposals that Gibraltar would be a site to exile some

Gibraltar

Religion	Followers in 1970	Followers in 2010	% of Population	Annual % growth 2000–2010	Followers in 2025	Followers in 2050
Christians	21,700	25,700	88.1	1.21	25,700	23,600
Roman Catholics	19,100	22,600	77.6	1.19	22,700	20,600
Anglicans	1,900	1,900	6.5	0.00	1,900	1,700
Protestants	360	420	1.4	3.88	420	460
Muslims	2,000	1,400	4.9	1.23	1,500	1,500
Agnostics	30	770	2.6	1.54	900	1,000
Jews	590	570	2.0	1.25	600	600
Hindus	260	530	1.8	1.23	350	400
Baha'is	30	100	0.3	2.18	120	150
Atheists	0	80	0.3	1.12	120	120
Total population	**24,600**	**29,200**	**100.0**	**1.23**	**29,300**	**27,400**

of them, especially the Marranos, or hidden Jews. No one acted upon the suggestion. Thus it was not until the British occupation that Jews from North Africa began to arrive. By 1749, when they received legal status, there were some 600, and 2 synagogues had been erected. The Jewish community has risen and fallen over the years. It peaked at around 2,000 in the middle of the 19th century, but had dropped back to approximately 600 by the end of the 20th century.

Beginning in 1961, Moroccans began to arrive in Gibraltar. They brought their Sunni Islam (of the Malikite School) with them. Several thousand now reside on the island. There are also a minuscule number of Hindus and Baha'is.

J. Gordon Melton

See also: Baha'i Faith; Church of England; Church of Scotland; Jehovah's Witnesses; Malikite School of Islam; Methodist Church; Roman Catholic Church; Seventh-day Adventist Church.

References

Jackson, William Godfrey Fothergill. *The Rock of the Gibraltarians: A History of Gibraltar*. New York: Hyperion Books, 1991.

Kadesh, Sharman. *Jewish Heritage in Gibraltar: An Architectural Guide*. Reading, UK: Spire, 2008.

Knight, H. J. C. *The Diocese of Gibraltar: A Sketch of Its History, Work and Tasks*. London: SPCK, 1917.

Leckey, Colin. *Dots on the Map*. London: Grosvenor House Publishing, 2006.

Upon This Rock, 1769–1969: A Short History of Methodism in Gibraltar. Gibraltar: n.p., 1969.

Glastonbury

Glastonbury, a town in Somerset, southwest England, is identified in local pre-Christian lore as the mythical Isle of Avalon, a word derived from the Celtic deity Avalloc (or Avallach), who ruled the underworld. Glastonbury Tor, a teardrop-shaped hill, dominates the landscape around the town, and the surrounding plain, the Summerland Meadows. Now surrounded on three sides by the River Brue, in times past, at least part of the year, it was an island. A prominent landmark through much of Britain's prehistoric eras, it became a focus of popular religion and legend. Modern Esoteric practitioners have added significantly to its spiritual lore.

Inhabited as early as 300 BCE, residents found it to be an easily defended position with a natural moat. Called "Ynis Witrin" or Isle of Glass, the Tor was connected to the surrounding territory by a narrow strip of land, above water only at low tide. The Romans, for whom the nearby city of Bath was a favorite, used Glastonbury, where several trade routes converged, for the movement of goods. In the seventh century, a Celtic Christian monastic community settled on top of the Tor. The tower attached to their center is the only remaining structure on the Tor proper. Some sources say the monastery was founded by the Welsh Saint David late in the sixth century. It was afterward relocated to

View of Glastonbury Tor and St. Michael's Tower in Glastonbury, England. St. Michael's Tower is all that remains of the church constructed there in about the 15th century. (iStockPhoto.com)

the foot of the hill and in the 10th century became the home of the future saint, Dunstan (d. 988). Dunstan was one of the leaders of the monastic revival in England of the late 10th century, and he launched the history of Glastonbury as a center of British monastic life.

Over the next 500 years, Glastonbury grew to become one of the largest and wealthiest abbeys in the land, and its abbot's influence reached across the country to the highest levels of the royal court in London. The object of King Henry VIII's (r. 1509–1547) attack in the 16th century, the monastery and church fell into ruins.

Prior to the rise of the church in the area, however, there are layers of myths and legends to be encountered. In the not too distant past, the high ground on which the church sits was surrounded by water. The high ground is believed by many to have been a center for the development of human settlement, culture, and worship in the region. In the Middle Ages, stories identifying Glastonbury with Avalon linked the region with King Arthur and his knights of the Roundtable. Avalon was reputedly the final resting place of the good king.

Placing King Arthur at Glastonbury/Avalon also leads to another popular legend, that during the early years of Jesus' life not covered in the Bible, he accompanied Joseph of Arimathea, supposedly his great uncle, to Glastonbury. Then, after Jesus' crucifixion, Joseph of Arimathea came into possession of the cup used at the Last Supper. He used the cup to catch some of the blood that flowed from Jesus' body as he was crucified. He returned to Glastonbury bringing the cup with him. He buried the cup (which came to be known as the Holy Grail) just below Glastonbury Tor. Shortly thereafter, a spring, now called Chalice Well, began to flow. Its water was a source of health and youthfulness. If one accepts the story of Joseph and the cup, the real purpose behind the Knights of the Roundtable becomes the discovery of the Holy Grail. On a more practical level, the story of Joseph served to bolster later British claims to have a Christian history that stood independently of Rome.

The legends that had grown up around Glastonbury were inexorably linked to the history of the old Celtic church/monastery in 1190, when the monks residing in Glastonbury Abbey claimed to have found the tomb of Arthur in the graveyard of the abbey south of the Lady Chapel. In the tomb was a lead cross about a foot long, with a Latin inscription: *Hic iacet sepultus inclitus rex arturius in insula avalonia*" ("Here lies buried the renowned King Arthur in the Isle of Avalon"). The artifact is now generally believed to be a hoax perpetrated by the monks designed to link Avalon and Arthur to the town and abbey. It worked, and Glastonbury became a popular pilgrimage site.

The bones in the tomb (reputedly of Arthur and Genevieve) were placed in caskets. King Edward I (r. 1270–1307) visited the abbey in 1278, at which time the remains were put in a black marble tomb that was placed before the high altar in the abbey church. Unfortunately, Glastonbury did not stand in the face of King Henry VIII's dissolution of the monasteries in 1536. Subsequently, the abbey was vandalized and Arthur's remains disappeared.

After the destruction of the abbey, Glastonbury's prominence faded considerably, but in the 20th century was revived as part of the growing popular and academic study of the Arthurian legends (that has included the identification of nearby Cadbury Hill with Camelot) and of the ancient monolithic structures in neighboring Wiltshire (especially Stonehenge). Then late in the century, Esoteric metaphysical believers and Christian mystics took up residence in and near Glastonbury to revel in older legends.

Glastonbury's profile was initially heightened in the 1920s by Katharine Maltwood. An amateur student of the Arthurian legends, she began to study large-scale maps of the countryside surrounding Glastonbury Tor. She noticed in the patterns of the earthworks, field tracks, river banks, and other artifacts of the landscape, what appeared to be a gigantic star map. As shown in the illustrations of her 1929 book, *A Guide to Glastonbury's Temple of the Stars*, the land features picture what could be seen as the 12 signs of the zodiac in a giant circle with Glastonbury Tor in the center.

The form of this terrestrial zodiac, as Maltwood (and countless later researchers) have designated it, is circular with a circumference of 30 miles. Some of the zodiacal figures are two to three miles in length. They could be seen only from some miles in the air. If one accepted the idea of the Glastonbury zodiac, then one would also have to suggest that many centuries before the megalith builders, there was a community at Glastonbury that was able to shape the terrain so to form the mystical and astrological patterns.

Contemporaneously with Maltwood, Frederick Bligh Bond (1864–1945), a local historian interested in Spiritualism, began to direct excavation of the abbey that proved remarkable for the number of discoveries he made over a relatively short period. In the wake of the discoveries, Bond disclosed that he had directed the work from the guidance he received from the spirit of a former monk who claimed to have lived at the abbey in its heyday.

In the decades since World War II, Glastonbury has come to life as one of Britain's foremost Esoteric/New Age centers. All of the sites associated with the old legends have been well marked, and the town now rivals Stonehenge as a magnet for tourists to Western England. A variety of New Age and alternative groups have opened centers in Glastonbury, and a number of alternative religious events now occur there weekly. All of this activity has led to a veritable library of material about Glastonbury ranging from tracks by true believers to the very skeptical volume by Robert Dunning, *Christianity in Somerset* (1970). Dunning claims that all of the stories about the region originated in the 12th century as part of a deliberate attempt of the monks to raise money by promoting pilgrimage to the abbey.

J. Gordon Melton

See also: Astrology; New Age Movement; Stonehenge; Western Esoteric Trdition.

References

Fortune, Dion. *Avalon of the Heart*. London: Aquarian Press, 1971.

Greed, John A. *Glastonbury Tales*. Bristol, UK: St. Trillo Publications, 1975.

Lewis, Lionel Smithett. *St. Joseph of Arimathea at Glastonbury*. London: James Clarke, 1976.

Maltwood, Katharine. *A Guide to Glastonbury's Temple of the Stars.* London: James Clarke, 1964.

Roberts, Anthony. *Atlantean Traditions in Ancient Britain.* London: Rider and Company, 1977.

Wilcock, John. *A Guide to Occult Britain.* London: Sidgwick & Jackson, 1976.

Williams, Mary, ed. *Glastonbury: A Study in Patterns.* Hammersmith, UK: RILKO, 1969.

Global Church of God

See Living Church of God.

Global Country of World Peace

The Global Country of World Peace is the major organization currently behind the worldwide spread of the practice of Transcendental Meditation (TM). Since 2000, it has superseded the World Plan Executive Council.

The practice of TM is generally ascribed to Guru Dev, the teacher of Maharishi Mahesh Yogi (1917–2008). Guru Dev is a title of respect and endearment given to Swami Brahmananda Saraswati (1870–1953), Shankaracharya (spiritual and ecclesiastical leader) of Jyotir Math, one of the oldest and most prominent centers of Hinduism in India. Maharishi emerged in 1957 with the mission of telling the world about the benefits of engaging in meditation. Maharishi had spent 13 years with Guru Dev prior to his public career.

In 1958–1959, Maharishi made his first world tour, during which he introduced TM to the West. That year he founded the Spiritual Regeneration movement, which became the first organization for the spread of TM in the West. In 1965, it was joined by the Students International Meditation Society. He had spectacular success, in part due to the endorsement by several celebrities, most notably the Beatles.

In 1972, he announced the World Plan, the overall strategy for spreading TM and its theoretical base, the Science of Creative Intelligence. Maharishi argued that TM was not a religious practice and that the Science of Creative Intelligence is an ancient science, not a reli-

Maharishi Mahesh Yogi, founder of the Transcendental Meditation movement and the Global Country for World Peace, pictured in 1967. (AP Photo)

gious philosophy. Based upon that understanding, the practice of TM has been introduced into many countries with the backing and assistance of secular governments from Zimbabwe to Romania. However, in other places, most notably the United States, it has been seen as a religious activity and government support has been denied.

TM is based on the effortless repetition of *bija* mantras, individual syllables drawn from the Tantric traditions of India. Mediation consists of the repeated silent mental repetition of a sound. The sound, called a mantra, is given to the person at the time of initiation into the practice. The particular sound is determined by the age of the initiate.

According to the Science of Creative Intelligence, the universe is underlain by an absolute field of pure being—unmanifest and transcendental. The Science of Creative Intelligence teaches how to contact this underlying reality, pure being, via meditation. The ultimate goal is God-realization. This Science of Creative Intelligence is seen as the summation of the wisdom of

India. A significant amount of research now supports the value of meditation and its healthful effects on the body.

The most controversial practice espoused by the TM movement is the TM-Sidhi Program, which claims to teach people to levitate, a practice called yogic flying. The skepticism about such claims, including the accusations of people who took the program and refuted its effectiveness, has undermined the movement's credibility in many quarters.

The World Executive Council was structured in a number of divisions. The International Meditation Society introduced the general public to meditation. The Students International Meditation Society focused on young adults, while the Spiritual Regeneration movement focused on older adults. The Foundation for Creative Intelligence worked with the business community. Maharishi International University in Fairfield, Iowa, offered a four-year college curriculum with instruction integrated with the practice of TM. The Natural Law Party functioned as a new political party that ran candidates for office in those countries where it was allowed to operate. The Maharishi Vedic Approach to Health has introduced a version of the Indian ayurvedic system of medical treatment to the West.

In 2000, Maharishi announced the formation of the Global Country of World Peace, a nation without borders, which would approach the concerns of world peace by focusing upon the divisive influence of nationalism and national borders on human society. The Global Country has largely superseded the World Plan Executive Council and is now the major structure organizing and directing the TM movement. Organized as a nation without borders, the Global Country has 40 ministries developed from the 40 branches of Vedic literature. It issues its own money, though the places that the currency can be used are quite limited. His Majesty Raja Nader Raam was named the first sovereign of the Global Country. According to the movement, "The sovereignty of the Global Country of World Peace is in the domain of consciousness and its authority is in the invincible power of Natural Law, which brings fulfillment to and upholds and nourishes every country's constitution."

The Global Country of World Peace launched a plan to establish at least two Peace Palaces, one for each gender, in the major urban centers of the world, including 240 of the largest cities in the United States. Each Peace Palace, drawing on the belief that the practice of TM by groups of people promotes world peace, is seen as a center that radiates peace to the surrounding community. Each Peace Palace is to be made ideally from marble and designed following Vedic architecture. While they are under construction, a number of Maharishi Enlightenment Centers still exist to provide instruction in TM.

In the new Global Country, Maharishi International University in Fairfield, Iowa, has become Maharishi University of Management (the name change actually occurred in 1995). The community that has grown up around the university has been named the Maharishi Vedic City. All the buildings have been either built or revised according to Vedic architecture, the most noticeable feature being that all entrances now face east. In addition, each building now has a designated silent space in its center called a *Brahmasthan* and a roof ornament painted gold called a *kalash*.

The TM movement has also envisioned the opening of a new Central University, being formed in Kansas —the geographic center of the United States. The university will be home to some 10,000 students, all practicing TM together at the same time. The university will be the Western parallel of the World Capital of Peace, in India, the seat of power of Raja Nader Raam and the home of the different rajas (administrators) and ministers of the Global Country, as well as 6,000 Vedic pandits (meditators, learned custodians of the ancient wisdom of TM).

In 2004, the national offices of the Natural Law Party in the United States was closed and the party's former presidential candidate John Hagelin organized the U.S. Peace Government, dedicated to creating permanent peace in the United States and the world. The U.S. Peace Government will be organized on a model of the government in the United States (a president, vice president, state governors, city mayors, etc.) and will ensure that "proven peace-creating programs," that is, the TM programs, are established across the country.

The TM movement claims that more than five million people practice TM and many more have been initiated. By 2003, there were more than 40,000 teachers of TM. At this point, all of the teachers were asked to become recertified. An unknown minority of them went through the process, though enough to maintain the teaching centers throughout the world. The Global Country of World Peace continually develops programs to facilitate the permeation of all realms of society with the practice of TM and has developed an extensive Internet presence (http://www.globalgoodnews .com/; http://www.globalcountry.net/; http://global countryofworldpeace.net/; http://www.maharishipeace palace.org/; http://www.tm.org; http://www.alltm.org/).

The TM movement builds much of its program around the 600 studies that have been conducted on TM and its practitioners. It is their belief that these studies have validated the benefits of TM on both the individuals who practice and every area of society where a critical mass of meditators exist. The movement urges every nation to establish Peace Palaces in order to safeguard its independence and sovereignty, and promises that Peace Palaces will make the nations invincible. It is also the claim that when individuals practice TM and the advanced TM-Sidhi program together in groups, there will be a measurable reduction in societal stress, crime, violence, and conflict and a parallel increase in coherence, positivity, and peace throughout the society.

The following addresses are all old. In the last years of Maharishi's life, the movement was centered in Vlodrop, Holland. Now the main centers of power appear to be in India, though this is in flux. One thing that is clear is that none of the Western heavy hitters (Hagelin, Bevan Morris, Tony Nader, etc.) are in Fairfield. They barely visit. Caution needs to be exercised in relation to addresses for the "center" of the Movement. Websites and the U.S. site are the safest at present.

Maharishi Shiksha Sansthan
Maharishi Nagar
Noida-Dadri Road
Gautam Buddha Nagar, UP 201 304
India

Maharishi Invincibility Center
11501 Huff Ct
Kensington, MD

J. Gordon Melton

See also: Hinduism; Meditation; Yoga.

References

Gilpin, Geoff. *The Maharishi Effect: A Personal Journey Through the Movement That Transformed American Spirituality*. New York: Tarcher-Penguin, 2006.

Maharishi Mahesh Yogi. *The Science of Being and the Art of Living*. London: International SRM, 1966.

Mason, Paul. *The Maharishi: The Biography of the Man Who Gave Transcendental Meditation to the West*. Shaftesbury, Dorset, UK: Element, 1994.

Orme-Johnson, David W., and John T. Farrows, eds. *Scientific Research on the Transcendental Meditation Program: Collected Papers I*. Seelisburg, Switzerland: Maharishi European Research University Press, 1977.

White, John. *Everything You Want to Know about TM, Including How to Do It*. New York: Pocket Books, 1976.

Globalization, Religion and

Religion has always been on the move. Some argue that religion was the first globalizing force in the world. Even before nation-states were formed, Christian, Muslim, and Buddhist missionaries, conquerors, traders, and travelers carried beliefs, rituals, and sacred objects and texts with them. However, in the past three decades, cheaper and better means of communication and transport has meant that this process of contact, exchange, and negotiation has taken an enormous leap. When scholars started writing about globalization in the early 1990s, they were mostly analyzing the economic aspects of this process. Globalization was then associated with a triumphant narrative of global capitalism due to the fall of Communism in the late 1980s and early 1990s. In this light, globalization would be a process by which the entire world would come to modernity, leading to cultural homogenization (or "MacDonaldization," since it was associated with U.S. imperialism).

In the past 15 years, much has changed in our understanding of globalization. The narrative of globalization as homogenization has been replaced by one in which homogenization and heterogenization are driving forces. Key concepts of hybridity (Garcia Canclini 1995; Werbner and Modood 1997) and Creolization (Hannerz 1997; Rocha 2006a) came into vogue to explain how the encounter between the global and the local takes place and the new forms it engenders. Robertson (1995) has coined the trope of "glocalization" to make it explicit that the global and the local are two facets of the same process. Furthermore, empirical studies have shown that global flows do not radiate only between central metropolitan powers and peripheries, in a North-South direction. Global flows radiate from a multiplicity of centers, and they have diverse itineraries and directions.

If globalization was first seen as an economic process, the increasingly prominent political and cultural roles religion plays in the world, and the intensification of flows of migration, commodities, ideas, and beliefs, have forced scholars to include religion as an important site of investigation. For instance, Turner (2001) argues that the globalization of the Western model of private religious faith and practice has elicited fundamentalism. Fundamentalism, he writes, "attempts to ensure the dominance of religion in the public spheres of law, economy and government" (2001, 133). Moreover, we have seen in the past decade that the tensions between (Christian and Muslim) fundamentalism on the one hand, and hybridity engendered by globalization on the other, take place in the everyday practices of actors involved. Many scholars have called for an anchored or grounded study of globalization (Levitt 2003, 2006, 2007; Vásquez and Marquardt 2003) to understand how religious practices, discourses, and norms are actually lived and transformed.

Indeed, global flows of religion are driven not only by religious institutions themselves, but also by migrants, refugees, tourists, pilgrims, and the Internet. By allowing transnational membership, religion presents itself as a map through which individuals, particularly transnational migrants, and organizations attempt to locate themselves amid fragmentation and dislocation generated by globalization (Vásquez and Marquardt 2003, 53). Indeed, religion is an important aspect in the insertion of migrants in the country of settlement as well in transnational processes (Levitt 2001, 2007;

Tweed 2002). That is, migrants' religious practices and beliefs have an influence on the host society by exposing it to religious diversity, and because migration continues to impact on the life of the homeland, these new forms are then carried back to the homeland and are re-created there, a phenomenon that Levitt (1999) calls "social remittance."

Furthermore, religion plays an important role for migrant communities. It usually is the first port of call when migrants arrive in the new country. For instance, religious institutions work as a support network to help Brazilians cope with the pressures and anxieties of migration to Australia (Rocha 2006b). Because they are not part of the government apparatus of the host country, diasporic religious institutions support undocumented and documented migrants in finding employment and housing, understanding the rules and laws of the new country, and counsellng them in spiritual and psychological matters.

In addition, religious institutions may also assist in reinforcing identity and sense of belonging by offering migrants a vicarious home away from home. Migrants can meet fellow migrants, worship in their own language, eat their own food, and celebrate holidays together. In this context, for many they play more a social than a religious function. Because of this heightened social function, many migrants who were not religious in the homeland may start frequenting religious institutions in the host country. By contrast, religious belonging may supersede national belonging even before some communities leave the homeland, as in the case of the Muslim and Hindu diasporas. As a result, conflicts from the homeland may be played out in the host countries (for instance, when transnational communities of local religious minorities seek political autonomy like the Sikh militancy in Britain). Diasporic communities may also influence politics in the homeland (for example, support to the Hindu nationalist BJ party by constituents of the Hindu diaspora).

Religious institutions are also part of this process of religious globalization. They may provide for a single ethnic community, with missionaries sent from the homeland with the mission of keeping migrants in the fold. They may also cater for a multicultural congregation, uniting locals and migrants or different migrant communities in the same place of worship.

Multicultural congregations, in particular, help migrants integrate since they meet locals who can assist them in practical terms while locals see migrants as brothers and sisters in their faith. Levitt (2001) has observed three types of transnational religious organization: extended, negotiated, and re-created. "Extended" refers to churches in the sending and receiving countries "which are connected and directed by a single authority, but enjoy autonomy at the local level" (2001, 12) like the Catholic Church. "Negotiated" refers to transnational religious organizations that are "much less hierarchical and centralized" and whose ties are "not subject to a set of pre-established rules that must constantly be worked out," such as Protestant churches (2001, 15). Finally, "re-created" transnational religious organizations are established when there is no religious infrastructure in the host country so migrants ask for "guidance and resources from the sending country" (2001, 18). To the latter, I would add that not only does the sending country contribute resources, but migrants receive guidance from their diasporic communities in other countries. A good example would be Brazilian Spiritists in Sydney contacting and receiving resources from the Brazilian Spiritist center in New York (Rocha 2006b). Furthermore, this third category can be used to analyze the role of non-migrants in importing religious practices and beliefs that carry kudos in their country. A case in point would be Buddhism in Western countries.

Moreover, tourists, as modern pilgrims, are also agents of change in the receiving community and in their homeland. In late modernity, sacred and secular pilgrimages intersect, and new sites are added to traditional pilgrimage sites such as Lourdes, Santiago de Compostela, Jerusalem, and Mecca. Globalization has made it cheaper and easier for pilgrims/tourists to reach and create new sacred pilgrimage sites such as Graceland, the local of the fatal car crash where Princess Diana died, Ground Zero, and most recently Michael Jackson's Neverland ranch in California. Many scholars have studied the impact of spiritual tourism/pilgrimage on individuals and communities (Badone and Roseman 2004; Coleman and Eade 2004).

Finally, the Internet has made religions more accessible and participatory. While religious institutions use the Internet to disseminate their beliefs, the increasing number of religious virtual communities and websites run by individuals exemplify how religion is meaningful in the contemporary world. Indeed, the Internet has expanded and strengthened the attributes of religious modernity (privatization of religion, religious pluralism, and the constitution of a market place) as well as the reinforcement of fundamentalist identities.

Cristina Rocha

See also: Fundamentalism; Modernity; Pilgrimage; Roman Catholic Church; Spiritism.

References

Badone, Ellen, and Sharon Roseman, eds. *Intersecting Journeys: The Anthropology of Pilgrimage and Tourism*. Urbana and Chicago: University of Illinois Press, 2004.

Coleman, Simon, and John Eade, eds. *Reframing Pilgrimage: Cultures in Motion*. London and New York: Routledge, 2004.

García Canclini, Néstor. *Hybrid Cultures: Strategies for Entering and Leaving Modernity*. Minneapolis and London: University of Minnesota Press, 1995.

Hannerz, Ulf. "The World in Creolisation." *Africa* 57, no. 4 (1997): 546–559.

Levitt, Peggy. "Social Remittance: A Local-Level, Migration-Driven Form of Cultural Diffusion." *International Migration Review* 32, no. 4 (1999): 926–949.

Levitt, Peggy. "Between God, Ethnicity, and Country: An Approach to the Study of Transnational Religion." In *Transnational Migration: Comparative Perspectives*. Princeton, NJ: Princeton University Press, 2001.

Levitt, Peggy. "'You Know, Abraham Was Really the First Immigrant': Religion and Transnational Migration." *The International Migration Review* 37, no. 3 (2003): 847.

Levitt, Peggy. "God Needs No Passport: Trying to Define the New Boundaries of Belonging." *Harvard Divinity Bulletin* 34, no. 3 (2006). http://www.hds.harvard.edu/news/bulletin_mag/articles/34-3_levitt.html. Accessed July 19, 2009.

Levitt, Peggy. *God Needs No Passport: Immigrants and the Changing American Religious Landscape*. New York: The New Press, 2007.

Robertson, Roland. "Glocalization: Time-Space and Homogeneity-Heterogeneity." In *Global Modernities,* edited by S. L. M. Featherstone and Roland Robertson. London: Sage, 1995.

Rocha, Cristina. *Zen in Brazil: The Quest for Cosmopolitan Modernity.* Honolulu: University of Hawaii Press, 2006a.

Rocha, Cristina. "Two Faces of God: Religion and Social Class in the Brazilian Diaspora in Sydney." In *Religious Pluralism in the Diaspora,* edited by P. Patrap Kumar, 147–160. Leiden: Brill, 2006b.

Turner, Bryan. "Cosmopolitan Virtue: On Religion in a Global Age." *European Journal of Social Theory* 4, no. 2 (2001): 131–152.

Tweed, Thomas. *Our Lady of the Exile: Diasporic Religion at a Cuban Catholic Shrine in Miami.* Oxford: Oxford University Press, 2002.

Vásquez, Manuel, and Marie Friedmann Marquardt. *Globalizing the Sacred: Religion Across the Americas.* New Brunswick, NJ, and London: Rutgers University Press, 2003.

Werbner, Pnina, and Tariq Modood, eds. *Debating Cultural Hybridity: Multicultural Identities and the Politics of Anti-Racism.* London: Zed Books, 1997.

Gnostic Catholic Church

The Gnostic Catholic Church, a contemporary occult church, exists as an integral part of the thelemic (from the Greek, *thelema,* or will) magical order Ordo Templi Orientis (OTO). It is actually one faction of the Nouvelle Église Gnostique Universelle, which in 1890 was initiated as a new Gnostic tradition by Jules-Benoît Doinel du Val-Michel (1842–1903). In 1867, the year before his marriage, Doinel claimed that as part of an apparition of the Virgin Mary, Jesus had also appeared and consecrated him as a bishop. Through the next years, he focused his reading on occult literature, and then around 1890, during a Spiritualist séance, he accepted a second consecration that led directly to his founding of the Nouvelle Église Gnostique Universelle. Through the church, Doinel hoped to revive the mystical doctrines attributed to the second-century theologian Origen, most important, the idea of the pre-existence of soul and the related belief in metempsychosis, or reincarnation. Assuming the position as patriarch of the new church, Doinel proceeded to consecrate four bishops, each of whom went on to establish separate lineages from which several dozen distinctive Gnostic jurisdictions have emerged.

In 1892, Doinel consecrated Gerard Encausse (1865–1916), the author of several occult texts under the pen name Papus. Papus took Doinel's Gnosticism into the milieu of the German and British occult orders. Papus remained loyal to the Église Gnostique Universelle, a faction of the church that emerged in 1908. However, as a bishop he possessed authority to consecrate others without reference to his superior, and it is claimed by some that he in fact consecrated both Theodor Reuss (1855–1923) and Aleister Crowley (1875–1947), who as leaders in the Ordo Templi Orientis brought the Gnostic Catholic Church into the OTO orb. Evidence of these consecrations is somewhat weak.

Early in his work for the OTO, Crowley wrote a Gnostic Mass that integrated thelemic themes in a liturgy that followed the form of the Roman Catholic Mass, though no Christian teachings remained. In 1917 Reuss translated Crowley's Mass into German and began designating himself as the leader of the Gnostic neo-Christians and the Swiss legate of the Église Gnostique Universelle, then headed by Jean Baptiste Bricaud (1881–1934), reportedly consecrated by Papus in 1911. Reuss later accepted several additional consecrations, while Bricaud (albeit unsuccessfully) advocated the use of Crowley's Mass in Freemason circles.

During the years under Karl Johannes Germer (1885–1962), the Ordo Templi Orientis almost ceased to exist, and the performance of the Gnostic Mass was put aside. Then in 1957 in Switzerland, Hermann Joseph Metzaer (1919–1990), a leader in the OTO, accepted consecration as a bishop of the Gnostic Catholic Church from Herbert Fritsche (1911–1960), and then succeeded Fritsche as patriarch in 1960. Following Germer's death, in 1963, he called together German OTO leaders and was selected by them as the new international outer head of the Order of the OTO. He then revived the OTO, along with the Gnostic Catholic Church.

In America in the 1970s, Grady McMurtry (1918–1985) revived the OTO by assuming the role of caliph of the order and argued that he was therefore patriarch of the Gnostic Catholic Church. McMurtry claimed authority to lead the OTO from some emergency documents he had been given by Crowley in the mid-1940s. He argued that the same documents gave him an implied consecration as a bishop. McMurtry's role as head of the church was questioned, given the lack of documentation of Crowley's consecration by Papus and the lack of an act of consecration of McMurtry.

McMurtry's successor, William Breeze, put the controversy over the church to rest when he was consecrated anew by Jack Hogg, a bishop of the Gnostic Church of Thelema. Hogg's lineage could be traced directly to Doinel and has been supplemented by the lineage of Orthodox bishop Joseph René Vilatte (1855–1929), through the small theosophically oriented American Catholic Church. All ninth-degree members of the American OTO are now consecrated as Gnostic bishops. The outer head of the OTO is also considered the patriarch of the Gnostic Catholic Church.

The American branch of the Gnostic Catholic Church may be contacted at JAF 7666, New York, NY 10116. Gnostic church services are held across North America and in 18 countries where the OTO has affiliated lodges and groups.

J. Gordon Melton

See also: Crowley, Aleister; Gnostic Churches; Gnosticism; Ordo Templi Orientis; Thelema.

References

Anson, Peter. *Bishops at Large*. London: Faber and Faber, 1964.

Koenig, Peter R. "Herman Joseph Metzger—OHO of the O.T.O. and Patriarch of the Gnostic Catholic Church." http://www.cyberlink.ch/~koenig/bishops.htm. Accessed April 24, 2009.

Koenig, Peter R. "Stranded Bishops." http://www.cyberlink.ch/~koenig/bishops.htm. Accessed April 24, 2009.

Ward, Gary L., Bertil Persson, and Alan Bain, eds. *Independent Bishops: An International Directory*. Detroit, MI: Apogee Press, 1990.

Gnostic Churches

The Gnostic Churches comprise a number of new religious movements, most of which originated from the spiritual experience of Jules-Benoît Doinel (1842–1903). Doinel was born in Moulins (France), in 1842, into a pious Catholic family, sharing a special devotion to the 16th-century Jesuit saint Stanislas Kostka (1550–1568), who appeared to Doinel in mystical visions when he was a teenager. These visions eventually got young Doinel in trouble with his teachers at the Jesuit Seminary of Montciel, which he entered in 1859 and from which he was expelled in 1861. He decided then to become a lay archivist and historian rather than a Jesuit priest, and graduated from the famous École des Chartes in 1866. His first appointment as an archivist was in Aurillac. By that time, Doinel had abandoned Roman Catholicism altogether and was active as a spiritualist medium. In 1868, however, he married actress Stéphanie-Françoise Le Clerc (1835–1873), a pious Catholic who brought him back into the Roman fold. In 1869, he was appointed archivist of the city of Niort and, while still claiming to be a good Catholic, resumed his practice as a spiritualist medium. After Stéphanie's death in 1873, he remarried in 1874, this time to a lady with strong family ties to (rather anti-Catholic) French Freemasonry, which he ultimately joined in 1884.

By that time, he had held the post of archivist in Orléans (a very important position) since 1875 and had again abandoned the Roman Catholic Church. French Freemasonry was in need of a competent archivist, and Doinel was called to Paris to take on the directorship of the Masonic Museum. In 1882, he joined Monodism, a short-lived religious movement led by Guillaume Monod (1800–1896), the son of the famous Swiss Reformed scholar Jean Monod (1765–1836); Guillaume claimed to be the new Messiah and to represent the Second Coming of Jesus Christ. In 1890, Doinel met Papus (Gérard Encausse, 1865–1916), who was then the leader of the Martinist Order and other occult organizations, which the archivist quickly joined. Doinel was a true collector of occult society memberships, and he also joined the Theosophical Society. His studies led him toward a particular interest in ancient Gnosticism and Catharism. He shared these interests in Paris with Countess Maria Mariátegui (1830–1895), who later became the duchess of Pomar by marriage, and was a friend of Madame Helena P. Blavatsky (1831–1891), as well as other Theosophical luminaries.

How Doinel came to found the Gnostic Church is a tale that he himself told in different ways during his later years. According to one version, in June 1890 during a Spiritualist séance at the home of the duchess of Pomar, the spirits of 41 Cathar bishops appeared and consecrated Doinel as patriarch of a newly established Gnostic Church. True or not, by late 1890 Doinel was actively consecrating Gnostic bishops, including Papus and another well-known French esoteric author, Paul Sédir (pseudonym of Yvon Le Loup, 1871–1926). By 1892, there were enough Gnostic bishops to convene a synod, which confirmed Doinel as patriarch with the name of Valentinus II. The same synod consecrated yet another French esoteric author, Léonce Fabre des Essarts (1848–1917), as bishop under the name of Synésius. Between 1890 and 1894 Doinel, using a mix of Gnosticism and Catharism, published both a catechism and a ritual for the Gnostic Church. In December 1894, however, Doinel repudiated both Freemasonry and the Gnostic Church, and in 1895 publicly announced his return to the Catholic fold. In May 1895, using the pseudonym of Jean Kostka (the latter being the surname of the Jesuit saint to whom he was so devoted in his youth), he published a book under the title of *Lucifer démasqué* (*Lucifer Unmasked*), in which he claimed that the devil himself was behind Freemasonry, the Theosophical Society, and the Gnostic Church.

Never one to remain in the same church for long, however, Doinel wrote to Fabre des Essarts (who, in the meantime, had been elected the new patriarch of the Gnostic Church) on December 31, 1899, claiming that he had never really abandoned Gnosticism and was returning to the Gnostic Church, not as patriarch, but as one of its bishops. In 1902, on the other hand, he published a rather pious book of Catholic poetry. Doinel died on March 16, 1902, with both Roman Catholics and Gnostics claiming that he had died while still embracing the tenets of their respective faiths.

Unlike Doinel, Fabre des Essarts remained a Gnostic bishop and patriarch throughout his whole life, and

presided over the expansion of the Gnostic Church from France into Belgium, Germany, Russia, Italy, and the United States. During this period, René Guénon (1886–1951), the famous French esoteric author, was also consecrated as a Gnostic bishop (in 1909) under the name of Palingénius, but remained a member of the Gnostic Church for only a short time. Another well-known French esoteric author (and Martinist leader), Jean Bricaud (1881–1934), was consecrated a Gnostic bishop in 1901, but went on in 1907 to head a schism that established what was initially known as the Catholic Gnostic Church, but which from 1908 on became known as the Universal Gnostic Church. Bricaud's branch eventually attracted most members of the original Gnostic Church led by Fabre des Essarts (who died in 1917) and his successors, Léon Champrenaud (1870–1925) and Patrice Genty (1883–1964).

The two branches (the Gnostic Church and the Universal Gnostic Church) merged in 1960 under the leadership of Robert Ambelain (1907–1997), who, as leader of the Universal Gnostic Church, had succeeded Constant Chevillon (1880–1944), who had been assassinated by Nazi collaborators, and Henry-Charles Dupont (1877–1960). Ambelain, a successful writer of popular esoteric books, had established yet another independent branch in 1958: it was known as the Apostolic Gnostic Church, and it too was part of the 1960 merger. In 1967, Ambelain left his position as patriarch to pursue other interests, and in 1983 the Apostolic Gnostic Church (which was the name it maintained from the 1960 merger) ceased to exist as an international body. A dozen small Gnostic churches, however, continue to this day to survive on a national basis, particularly in France and Belgium (Rosicrucian Apostolic Church, Gnostic Apostolic Church), Italy (Italian Gnostic Church: Via San Zanobi 89, 50129 Florence, Italy, although the activity appears to be somewhat reduced after the death of its longtime leader Bishop Loris Carlesi, 1915–2006), the United States, and Barbados (Apostolic Gnostic Church), and they have kept alive Doinel's ideas and rituals right up to the present time.

The different branches of the Gnostic Church established by Doinel in 1890 should not be confused, however, with other new religious movements, also known as Gnostic churches; some are completely independent of the Doinel tradition described above (such as several independent Gnostic churches active in California or throughout the United States); others derive from branches of the Ordo Templi Orientis. The latter include the Gnostic Catholic churches, which operate within several branches of the OTO loyal to the tradition of Aleister Crowley (1875–1947), although Crowley claimed episcopal orders from Doinel, and the Gnostic churches operating within the Gnostic Movement, founded by Samael Aun Weor (1917–1977).

Cristina Rocha

See also: Crowley, Aleister; Gnostic Catholic Church; Gnostic Movement; Ordo Templi Orientis; Roman Catholic Church; Theosophical Society (America); Western Esotericism.

References

Introvigne, Massimo. *Il ritorno dello gnosticismo.* Carnago, Varese, Italy: SugarCo, 1993.

Kostka, Jean (Jules Doinel). *Lucifer démasqué.* 1895; rpt., Geneva-Paris: Slatkine, 1983.

Le Forestier, René. *L'Occultisme en France aux XIXème et XXème siècles. L'Église Gnostique.* Milan: Archè, 1999.

Gnostic Movement

More than 100 independent organizations, known as Gnostic movements or Gnostic churches, claim as their founder Victor Manuel Gómez Rodriguez (1917–1977), an esoteric master born in Bogota (Colombia) and known under the pen name of Samael Aun Weor. Raised as a Roman Catholic, Weor later became a spiritualist, a Theosophist, and a member of the Fraternitas Rosicruciana Antiqua (Ancient Rosicrucian Brotherhood) founded by Arnoldo Krumm-Heller (1876–1949). Krumm-Heller was a friend of the British magus Aleister Crowley (1875–1947), and also operated a Catholic Gnostic Church, in which he probably consecrated Weor a bishop. Weor published his first popular esoteric book, *The Perfect Matrimony*, in 1950, and about the same time in Mexico City established a Universal Christian Gnostic Church. Weor's death in 1977 generated an endless sequel of schisms. They all differ on matters relating to leadership, doctrine, and ritual, but all venerate Weor as a superhuman master, and as the Messiah of the Aquarian Age. Some of the branches have several thousand members, particularly throughout Latin America, and also in Latin Europe and Quebec, with others in the United States, Australia, New Zealand, Asia, and Africa.

Weor's thought is syncretic and includes themes drawn from Theosophy, Krumm-Heller, Aleister Crowley, George Ivanovich Gurdjieff (ca. 1866–1949), and other masters. The three keys to Weor's system (or the "three factors of the consciousness revolution") are death, rebirth, and sacrifice. Death here means the destruction of all the negative psychological factors that prevent human awakening. Rebirth involves the birth of a higher alchemical body, achieved through sexual magic in the shape of the "AZF Arcane," a form of *karezza*, which is the technique aimed at halting a sexual experience just before orgasm. Sacrifice means spreading to humanity in its entirety the wisdom the initiate has acquired. In order to achieve the three stages of Weor's consciousness revolution, secret rituals (in seven degrees), study, astral projection, and astral travels have to be undertaken. The initiate's itinerary is divided into three stages, known as exoteric, mesoteric, and esoteric (a terminology also used by Gurdjieff). Weor's main sexual practice, the above-mentioned form of karezza, also known by the tantric name *Sahaja Maithuna*, is regarded as the only permissible sexual magic. All other forms (including those prevailing in the Ordo Templi Orientis groups inspired by the teaching of Aleister Crowley) are regarded as illicit, and ultimately controlled by a "Black Lodge" for its own satanic ends.

Drawing a map of the Weor groups is a difficult task, with new schisms occurring frequently. The largest group is the Gnostic Institute of Anthropology Samael and Litelantes (IGASL), which until her death in 1998 was led by Weor's widow, Arnolda Garro Gómez (known as Maestra Litelantes; 1920–1998). It has currently some 18,000 members and was established in 1989, when Arnolda left the original Gnostic Association of Anthropological and Cultural Studies over a dispute about the copyright on Weor's writings. The American branch of Arnolda's Institute is the American Institute of Gnostic Anthropology, which has several dozen centers throughout the United States listed in the website for the organization at http://www.gnosisusa.org.

The Gnostic Association of Anthropological and Cultural Studies (Internet site at http://www.ageacac.org) still exists under the joint leadership of Hypatia Gómez, Weor's daughter, and Victor Manuel Chavez, while Osiris Gómez, Weor's son, took over the leadership of the Gnostic Institute of Anthropology, together with Roberto Tejada, after his mother's death. Tejada, however, later left Osiris and established his own organization under the name Círculo de Investigación de la Antropología Gnóstica (CIAG).

Among other branches, a few are worthy of mention: (1) the Gnostic Association of Anthropological, Cultural and Scientific Studies, established in Spain in 1992 by Oscar Uzcátegui Quintero, one of Weor's closest associates (headquarters: Avenida de América 26/10F, 18006 Granada, Spain; website: http://www.ageac.org); several of Uzcátegui's disciples in turn have established their own independent branches; (2) the Center for Gnostic Studies (Centro de Estudios Gnósticos, CEG), perhaps the fastest-growing branch, a splinter from Arnolda's branch, guided by Ernesto Barón in 2001; Cloris Rojo Barón, Ernesto's wife, separated from her husband and created a separate branch that appears, however, to be moribund; (3) the Gnostic Christian Universal Church, founded by Colombian master Teofilo Bustos (1936–2005), known as the Venerable Master Lakshmi and currently headquartered in Uruguay (http://www.gnostico.com and http://www.gnosis2000.com); (4) the Gnostic Christian Universal Movement in the New Order, established in Colombia in 1960 by Joaquín Enrique Amortegui Valbuena (1926–2000), known as the Venerable Master Rabolú, a group that enjoyed a certain notoriety in the media thanks to its apocalyptic features and the idea that a planet named Hercólubus may soon collide with Planet Earth, thus destroying humanity forever. Many "Weorite" groups are quite secretive, and some have decided to close their websites, which were active in the 1990s.

Massimo Introvigne and PierLuigi Zoccatelli

See also: Crowley, Aleister; Gnostic Catholic Church; Gurdjieff, George Ivanovitch; Ordo Templi Orientis; Roman Catholic Church; Tantrism; Theosophical Society (America); Western Esoteric Tradition.

References

Weor, Samael Aun Weor. *Manual of Revolutionary Psychology*. Los Angeles: Gnostic Association, 1987.

Weor, Samael Aun Weor. *The Perfect Matrimony*. New York: Adonai Editorial, 1980.

Zoccatelli, PierLuigi. "Il paradigma esoterico e un modello di applicazione. Note sul movimento gnostico di Samael Aun Weor." *La Critica Sociologica* 135 (Fall 2000): 33–49.

Gnosticism

The term *Gnostic* was originally applied to a spectrum of groups that emerged to prominence in the second century CE as competitors to the Christian church. Questions about the origin of the groups remain a source of intense scholarly discussion, and estimates for the date of their origin range from the first century CE to the first century BCE. Until the 20th century, the Gnostics were known primarily from the writings of Christian heresiologists such as Saint Irenaeus (ca. 125–202), whose famous text *Against Heresies* included excerpts of the writings of various Gnostics such as Valentinus and Carpocrates, both of whom lived in the second century CE.

The study of Gnosticism was elevated from its status as a subtopic under Christian heresies in 1945, with the discovery of an ancient Gnostic library in the Egyptian desert at Nag Hammadi. The fourth-century site yielded complete copies of books such as the Gospel of Truth (initially recognized from the several quotes in Irenaeus's writings) and the Gospel of Thomas, a heretofore unknown collection of sayings attributed to Jesus. These books, along with the *Pistis Sophia*, a Gnostic collection published in 1900, have provided a whole new perspective on the Gnostic groups and have led some to question the conventional view of Gnosticism as a singular movement. The renewed interest in Gnosticism has also focused attention on the Mandeans, possibly the only Gnostic group that has survived from the ancient Mediterranean. The Mandean community is centered in southeastern Iraq.

Gnosticism was described by Irenaeus and other Christian writers as a heretical form of Christian teaching. However, in light of the new findings, the Gnostic tradition has come to be seen as a religious community in its own right that began to interact with the Christian movement already in the first century and incorporated Christian elements into its own teachings. Christian Gnostics believed that they possessed the clearest understanding of the message of Christ, the knowledge (Greek: *gnosis*) that allowed them to encounter spiritual reality and attain salvation.

To the Gnostics, God was a remote reality, utterly unknowable and transcendent. They described the world as the product of a series of emanations that originated in God—those closest to God being purely spiritual, and those closest to Earth being characterized by the gross materiality of earthly life. The material world was inherently bad, and only in escaping from it could one obtain salvation. Human beings were seen as sparks of divinity who had been trapped in this lower world. The gnosis allowed them to escape their fate and return to their spiritual home. In some groups, the God of the Hebrew Bible was pictured as a lesser deity, the demiurge, characterized by human passions. In contrast, Christ was seen as a totally spiritual being who appeared in human form (only seeming to have a material existence) to show the way back to the spiritual realm.

Gnosticism, apart from the Mandeans, appears to have died out by the fifth century, but the impulse it represented continued to reappear at various times and places throughout Europe, most prominently among the Bogomils toward the end of the first millennium CE in Bulgaria and the Cathars (or Albigensians) in southern France. Gnosticism had a great affinity to the kabbalistic teachings of mystical Judaism, which found expression in the Christian Kabbalah movement that emerged in the 16th century. A new burst of Gnosticism began with the Kabbalah movement and with the 17th-century movement called Rosicrucianism. This reborn Gnosticism is discussed elsewhere in this encyclopedia as the Western Esoteric tradition, which includes Rosicrucianism, Freemasonry (18th century), Theosophy (19th century), and a host of occult and metaphysical groups spawned in the 20th century, culminating in the New Age movement.

Whereas Christian leaders and scholars have tended to see Gnosticism as the oldest and most persistent Christian heresy, Western Esoteric leaders in the 20th century took the opportunity provided by the free religious environment to reclaim Gnosticism as a contemporary living tradition. Gnostic Christian groups have appeared on the fringe of the Christian community, incorporating the Gospel of Thomas into their canon of Scripture. Other Esoteric groups have claimed the Gnostic heritage by incorporating the term into their name, though without any significant reference to the ancient Gnostic texts; these include the Gnostic Catholic Church and the Gnostic movement.

A very few groups have attempted to base their religion directly on the ancient Gnostic writings. The most prominent representatives of this latter type include the Gnostic Society, based in southern California and headed by Gnostic Bishop Stephan A. Hoeller, and the Gnostic Society in the Kingdom of Norway, founded by Terje Dahl Bergersen.

Gnostic Society
4516 Hollywood Blvd.
Los Angeles, CA 90029
http://www.gnosis.org/~gnosis/gnostsoc.htm

Gnostic Society in the Kingdom of Norway
Bruchion-Center for Gnosis and Art
c/o Capella Santa Sophia
Jan Valentin Saether
Brugt. 3
0157 Oslo
Norway
http://terje.bergersen.net/gsn/

J. Gordon Melton

See also: Freemasonry; Gnostic Catholic Church; New Age Movement; Western Esoteric Tradition.

References

Couliano, Ioan P. *The Tree of Gnosis: Gnostic Mythology from Early Christianity to Modern Nihilism.* New York: HarperCollins, 1992.

Filoramo, Giovanni. *A History of Gnosticism.* Oxford: Basil Blackwell, 1990.

King, Karen L. *What Is Gnosticism?* Cambridge, MA: Belknap Press of Harvard University Press, 2005.

Logan, Alastair H. B. *Gnostic Truth and Christian Heresy: A Study in the History of Gnosticism.* Edinburgh: T. & T. Clark, 1996.

Pearson, Birger A. *Ancient Gnosticism: Traditions and Literature.* Minneapolis, MN: Fortress Press, 2007.

Robinson, James M. *The Nag Hammadi Library in English.* San Francisco: HarperSanFrancisco, 1990.

Rudolph, Kurt. *Gnosis: The Nature and History of Gnosticism.* New York: HarperCollins, 1987.

Smoley, Richard. *Forbidden Faith: The Secret History of Gnosticism.* New York: HarperOne, 2007.

Williams, Michael Allen. *Rethinking "Gnosticism": An Argument for Dismantling a Dubious Category.* Princeton, NJ: Princeton University Press, 1996.

God, Existence of

Debate about the existence of God has preoccupied many of the leading thinkers of Judaism, Christianity, and Islam, the Western religious traditions of humanity. For such thinkers, as for critics of each religion, it is not enough to simply accept the purported divine revelation behind one or more of these faiths. For these thinkers, both skeptic and believer, the existence of God is a proper subject of philosophical and theological debate. Even those who decry the need for religions to take philosophy seriously have to do so in order to state their case against its value or relevance.

There were two early signals that Judaism and Christianity would both be facing the topic of God in relation to the concerns of philosophy. The first had to do with the impact of Greek thought on Philo of Alexandria (ca. 20 BCE–40 CE), the father of Jewish philosophy. Though Philo's philosophy impacted the early Christian movement more than the Jewish world of his day, he was the earliest important Jewish thinker to wrestle with the relationship of Moses to Plato.

The second signal that Judeo-Christian thought about God would be seen through or in relation to the lens of philosophy was how quickly Christian leaders became preoccupied with Plato, Aristotle, and other

Greek philosopher Aristotle, whose philosophical writings had a significant impact on the development of Western intellectual history. (Jupiterimages)

philosophers. Paul's trip to Athens is mentioned briefly in the Acts of the Apostles and he gives a warning about philosophy in his epistle to the Colossians. For the most part, however, first-century Christians were not overly concerned with philosophy. Their emphasis was on the proclamation of the revelation from God through Jesus.

While proclamation continued in the second century, an apologetic emphasis was beginning. Its first focus was on proving the superiority of the Christian revelation to that of Moses. This was a significant motif in Ignatius, Barnabas, and Justin Martyr (100–165 CE), the earliest of the church fathers. However, even in Justin Martyr's *Dialogue with Trypho* we have clear proof of the significance of Greek philosophy for Christian thinkers. Justin claims that at a time in his life "contemplation of ideas furnished my mind with wings so that in a little while I supposed that I had become wise." He goes on to contrast this "stupidity" with the prophetic message about Jesus that he learned from an old man. Justin's critique of philosophy must not be overstated since he used Plato as an ally on various topics.

The apologetic against Greek thought continued in Tatian (110–180 CE), Theophilus of Antioch, Athenagoras (fl. 170), and Clement of Alexandria (155–215). With Tertullian (ca.160–ca. 220), however, the apologetic took a decisively negative turn. Tertullian speaks of the Apostle Paul's recognition that philosophy corrupts truth with its "mutually repugnant sects." He then goes on with his famous rhetorical questions: "What indeed has Athens to do with Jerusalem? What concord is there between the Academy and the Church? What between heretics and Christians?" Thus, he commands: "Away with all attempts to produce a mottled Christianity of Stoic, Platonic, and dialectic composition! We want no curious disputation after possessing Christ Jesus, no inquisition after enjoying the gospel!" (*Against Heretics*, VII).

Tertullian's radical demarcation between Christianity and philosophy was largely neglected until post-Reformation times. Origen (185–254) gave philosophical argument an important place, as did Gregory of Nyssa (fl. 370) and other theologians, including Augustine (354–430). Etienne Gilson even points out how Augustine foreshadowed Descartes in using similar tactics to set aside skepticism, as in this line from *City of God*: "Even in error, I should have to exist in order to be in error." Augustine is confident in God's existence as provable, though some make themselves blind to the obvious.

Augustine, like Tertullian, put reason at the bidding of theology, but Augustine showed far more comfort in combining faith and reason. This comfortable union of faith and reason continued, with little interruption, for 1,000 years, whether in Orthodox or Catholic circles. Belief in God was held with increasing certainty, even as Christian apologetic adapted, especially in Thomas Aquinas (1225–1274), to the discovery of the thought of Aristotle. There were a few

Christian thinkers wary of philosophy, notably Bernard of Clairvaux. Donald Wiebe notes the importance of Bernard in his work *The Irony of Theology and the Nature of Religious Thought*.

Aristotle had an earlier impact on Islamic thought. His writings were most influential on Al-Kindi (805–873), the father of Islamic philosophy, Al-Farabi (ca. 872–950/951), Avicenna (ca. 980–1037), and Averroes (1126–1198), known to Muslims as Ibn Rushd.

These thinkers used Aristotle to strengthen the case for Islamic orthodoxy, though al-Ghazali (1058–1111), like Bernard, had suspicions of the rationalist mindset. Al-Ghazali never tires of asking in his *Incoherence of the Philosophers* "Do you know this through the necessity of reason or through speculating with it?"

By the time of Aquinas the arguments for God were similar in Christian, Islamic, and Jewish circles. Anselm of Canterbury (1033–1109) had formulated the ontological argument. The cosmological argument was used in a restrained way by Moses Maimonides (1135–1204), the greatest of medieval Jewish thinkers, in his *Guide to the Perplexed*. Aquinas focused his attention on various facets of the cosmological argument in his *Summa contra Gentiles* and *Summa Theologica*.

The teleological argument was used by Averroes (following Aristotle) and also by Aquinas. The latter states: "We see that things which lack knowledge, such as natural bodies, act for an end, and this is evident from their acting always, or nearly always, in the same way, so as to obtain the best result. Hence it is plain that they achieve their end, not fortuitously, but designedly." This is the last of the five proofs to God from the *Summa Theologica*. Of course, Aquinas, the other Christian thinkers noted above, Muslim apologists, and Maimonides all noted the importance of moral argument in advancing the case for God. The first Christian apologists loved to point out the inferior morals of Pagans in contrast to the virtuous disciples of Christ.

The large unanimity and certainty about God in the Western religious tradition was diminished with the emergence of skepticism in the 16th century. At the same time that Martin Luther (1483–1546) and John Calvin (1509–1564) were questioning Catholic doctrine, the West was discovering the writings of Sextus Empiricus (d. 210), the Pyrrhonian writer. Thus, there was a double blow to the confident claims of Western religion.

This story has been documented most closely by Richard H. Popkin, the great historian of philosophy. His work *The History of Skepticism* shows how "the Reformation controversy had opened up Pandora's box in seeking the foundations of certain knowledge" and that this theological crisis was compounded by a larger epistemological skepticism. The latter was advanced most powerfully by Michel de Montaigne (1533–1592) and his *Apologie de Raymond Sebond*. Popkin notes that "Montaigne's genial Apology became the coup de grace to an entire intellectual world. It was also to be the womb of modern thought, in that it led to the attempt either to refute the new Pyrrhonism, or to find a way of living with it."

Many Catholic and Protestant thinkers turned to fideism, the belief that faith is independent of and superior to reason as a means of reaching truth about God, as an alternative to the earlier Christian rationalism and the new skepticism. It was not always easy to tell if the fideists were true believers working in apologetics or real skeptics hoping for the demise of Christian faith. A creative non-fideism apologetic came from René Descartes (1596–1650), who used a skeptical motif to re-establish the certainty of one thing ("I think, therefore, I am") from which he moved to solid proof for the existence of God. However, the foundations of knowledge had basically changed. Since Descartes all observations about the existence of God are made in the context of doubt and competing visions of reality, Christian and otherwise.

Christian and Jewish confidence about God was further impacted by the emergence of biblical criticism. The early proponents were Isaac La Peyrere (d. 1676), Baruch Spinoza (d. 1677), and Richard Simon (d. 1612), the French critic. Doubts increased dramatically with the confident Enlightenment theories of Immanuel Kant (1724–1804) and David Hume (1711–1776), especially in his famous essay against miracles. In a further blow, the next century provided Charles Darwin's argument for evolution and a subsequent withering of trust in the teleological argument for God. All of this formed the background to the Catholic affirmation of papal infallibility (1870) and the emergence of an anti-intellectual Protestant Fundamentalism in the early decades of the 20th century.

Both Judaism and Islam have faced modern crises as well, though not so much related to the vagaries of argument. Muslim scholars had to cope with the collapse of the Ottoman Empire and the triumph of Western powers. Jews have had their own doubts come to the fore in reaction to Adolf Hitler's Holocaust. This and other modern horrors have made it easy for critics to deny God on the basis of the problem of evil. This is one of the main arguments of the new militant atheists like Richard Dawkins and Christopher Hitchens. For them God is a delusion, and religious belief is a form of insanity.

In spite of five centuries of increasing agnosticism, belief in God continues. Western religious thinkers, residing in an increasingly globalized world, are more cognizant of other faiths. At the same time, the Western apologetic for God is now set increasingly in a postmodern context. Even Christian rationalists must acknowledge Jacques Derrida's impact. Karl Barth would have seen postmodern malaise as perfect proof of the value of fideism. Gilson wrote once that "all the Barthian Calvinist asks of philosophy is that it recognize itself as damned and remain in that condition."

Various Christian apologists have continued to opt for rational confidence about God. This includes the famed populist C. S. Lewis (1898–1963) and philosophers Alvin Plantinga (b. 1932) and Richard Swinburne (b. 1934). The case for God was strengthened with the 2004 announcement that Antony Flew (1923), the famous British philosopher, had abandoned atheism. He was impressed by a recent reformulation of Aristotle's proof for God, the evidence for big-bang cosmology, and the teleological arguments of the Intelligent Design movement. Proponents of the latter, including William Dembski, Michael Behe, Phillip E. Johnson, and Stephen Mayer, are often the objects of ridicule by Dawkins and other mainstream scientists.

Carl Becker points out that "whether arguments command assent or not depends less on the logic that conveys them then upon the climate of opinion in which they are sustained." This bears reflection given the changing opinions about the existence of God in Western thought. Becker describes the trajectory this way:

"It has taken eight centuries to replace the conception of existence as divinely composed and purposeful drama by the conception of existence as a blindly running flux of disintegrating energy." He quotes with approval the words of Aristophanes: "Whirl is king, having deposed Zeus." Of course, this verdict commands assent only in certain climates of opinion.

James A. Beverley

See also: Agnosticism; Atheism; Augustine of Hippo; Calvin, John; Globalization, Religion and; Luther, Martin; Thomas Aquinas.

References

Becker, Carl. *The Heavenly City of the Eighteenth-Century Philosophers.* New Haven, CT: Yale University Press, 1932.

Dawkins, Richard. *The God Delusion.* New York: Houghton Mifflin Harcourt, 2006.

Dembski, William, and Michael Ruse. *Debating Design.* New York: Cambridge, 2004.

Flew, Antony, and Roy Abraham Varghese. *There Is a God.* San Francisco: HarperOne, 2007.

Gardner, Martin. *The Whys of a Philosophical Scrivener.* New York: Quill, 1983.

Gay, Peter. *The Enlightenment.* New York: Knopf, 1966.

Gilson, Etienne. *The Christian Philosophy of St. Augustine.* New York: Random House, 1960.

Griffel, Frank. *Al-Ghazali's Philosophical Theology.* New York: Oxford University Press, 2009.

Inglis, John. *Medieval Philosophy and the Classical Tradition.* Richmond, UK: Curzon Press, 2002.

Küng, Hans. *Does God Exist?* New York: Doubleday, 1980.

Norris, Richard A. *God and World in Early Christian Theology.* London: Adam & Charles Black, 1966.

Plantinga, Alvin. *Warranted Christian Belief.* New York: Oxford University Press, 2000.

Popkin, Richard H. *The History of Scepticism.* Berkeley: University of California Press, 1979.

Stroud, Barry. *The Significance of Philosophical Skepticism.* Oxford: Clarendon Press, 1984.

Swinburne, Richard. *The Existence of God.* New York: Oxford University Press, 2004.

Wiebe, Donald. *The Irony of Theology and the Nature of Religious Thought.* Montréal: McGill-Queen's, 1991.

Goddess Spirituality

Goddess spirituality seeks to redress the imbalance it perceives in monotheistic traditions where the image of the Divine is overwhelmingly male and to envisage and celebrate the Divine as She as well as He. Goddess spirituality can be a radical challenge to the teaching of the world's monotheistic traditions, envisaging the Divine as immanent as well as transcendent and for many challenging also the accepted hierarchies and power relationships of Western society. There has been a strong identification, for example, with the environmental and climate change movements, which protest against capitalist and state exploitation of natural resources.

Some women have remained within Christian churches but have sought to adapt and enhance the liturgy and theology with enriched images and concepts of the Divine as Mother as well as Father. Some Jewish women have found in the Kabbalah and the matriarchs of the Bible images that can update Judaism to meet contemporary women's needs. Others have sought to find spiritual expression and fulfillment in other traditions, both West and East, and in indigenous spirituality.

The Goddess spirituality movement has been fostered by women's emancipation and growing social, political, and cultural participation from the 19th century on, but Goddess spirituality is not solely the preserve of women. Many men of deep spirituality have questioned the concept of a supreme male deity and contemporary Goddess spiritualities have been welcoming to men both heterosexual and gay. In the early 20th century, British colonial magistrate and Tantric scholar Sir John Woodroffe, writing as Arthur Avalon, advocated a return to a religion where Goddess and God were equal. All things were possible, wrote Sir John, when the supreme personifications of the Divine were God and Goddess who "give and receive mutually, the feminine side being of equal importance with the masculine." In the mid-20th century, writer Dion

Fortune wove Goddess spirituality into literature for public consumption in novels that described a religion of Goddess and Horned God, drawing on European mythologies with Kabbalistic overtones. In the late 1940s a retired British colonial administrator, Gerald Brousseau Gardner, had his own personal vision of the Goddess and created what was in effect a new religious synthesis by grafting ideas of Goddess worship, heavily seeped in the classics of his boyhood education, onto the remnants of the British witchcraft tradition.

Gardner's Wicca, as the synthesis came to be known, incorporated gender essentialism and a focus on heterosexuality that was unattractive in the latter half of the 20h century to many women attracted to Goddess worship as a manifestation of their feminism.

Newer feminist interpretations of Goddess-based witchcraft arose, particularly in the United States through the work of Starhawk. Wicca already venerated the natural world as a theaphony. Starhawk made more explicit the radical activism of many Goddess worshippers. From the 1980s on, Goddess spirituality, nature religion, and environmental activism have gone hand in hand. Goddess spirituality has had increasing inspiration from Buddhism, and many female bodhisattvas and Goddess figures are now revered in the West by women who think of themselves as Buddhists and by those who practice primarily a Goddess-based spirituality. Tara from Tibetan Buddhism and Chinese Buddhism's Guan-Yin (Kannon in Japan) are widely revered by Goddess-oriented women.

Goddess spirituality has been evolving rapidly as the first generations of Goddess-worshipping women have developed Goddess worship for family celebration and the religious education of children. This has led to the establishment of summer festivals and camps and family worship activities.

For Goddess-oriented women, there are numerous religious routes to ordination, including the Covenant of Unitarian Universalist Pagans (a branch of the Unitarian Church) and organizations such as the Fellowship of Isis and the Reformed Congregation of the Goddess.

Vivianne Crowley

See also: Fellowship of Isis; Gardnerian Wicca; Tibetan Buddhism; Wiccan Religion; Women, Status and Role of.

References

Avalon, Arthur [Sir John Woodroffe]. *Shakti and Shakta*. New York: Dover, 1918, 1978.

Billington, Sarah, and Miranda Green, eds. *The Concept of the Goddess*. London and New York: Routledge, 1996.

Crowley, Vivianne. *The Goddess Book of Days*. London: Vega, 2002.

Johnson, Cait, and Maura D. Shaw. *Celebrating the Great Mother*. Rochester, VT: Destiny Books, 1995.

Raphael, Melissa. *Thealogy: Discourse on the Goddess*. Sheffield, UK: Sheffield Academic Press, 1999.

Roberts, Wendy Hunter. *Celebrating Her: Feminist Ritualizing Comes of Age*. Cleveland, OH: The Pilgrim Press, 1998.

Starhawk [Miriam Simos]. *The Spiral Dance: A Rebirth of the Ancient Religion of the Great Goddess*. San Francisco: Harper and Row, 1979.

Golden Temple

The Golden Temple, located in the city of Amritsar, Punjab, India, has emerged as both the symbolic and administrative center of the Sikh religion. The temple, or more properly *gurdwara* or place of worship, is surrounded by a manmade lake (that is, fed by a spring) and the lake is surrounded by a complex of buildings that includes an information office, a museum, and shrines to notable Sikh leaders.

Until the early 16th century, only a small lake and associated forest existed where now a city is located, but Guru Nanak (1469–1539), the founder of the Sikh faith, came to this lake for meditation and eventually retired here. After Nanak's death, his followers made pilgrimages to the lake, which acquired an aura of sanctity, much derived from the stories of people being healed, even of leprosy, by the lake's water. The lake became known as Amritsar, or "pool of the nectar of immortality."

After Nanak's death, a set of successive gurus (teachers) led the small Sikh community. The third guru, Amar Das (1479–1574), left the task of building an appropriate place for worship to his successor, Ram

India's Golden Temple in the Punjabi city of Amritsar is Sikhism's holiest site. (iStockPhoto.com)

Das (1534–1581), who oversaw the enlargement of the lake and began the construction of the temple. The fifth guru, Arjan Dev (1563–1606), completed the initial work. Three years after the temple's completion in 1601, the Adi Granth, the collection of the writings of the gurus that constitute the Sikh scriptures, were formally installed inside the Har Mandir (Temple of God). As the temple became identified with the still relatively small Sikh community, its enemies occasionally focused on it. They destroyed it several time in the 18th century, the last time in 1767. On each occasion the Sikhs rebuilt it. Since the upper exterior of the temple was covered with gold in 1830, it has been commonly referred to as the Golden Temple. Close by the complex of temple buildings are dormitories and dining halls where all persons, irregardless of their religion, race, or gender, may find free room and board.

Pilgrims approach the Golden Temple along a causeway over the Pool of Nectar. At the beginning of the causeway is a small temple, the Akal Takht. As they pass over the causeway and circumambulate the temple, they find entrance doors on each of the four sides, a sign of the openness of the faith to all seekers coming from all directions. The Adi Granth's throne dominates the temple's main room of the temple. Within the temple, pilgrims find a tank filled with water from the spring that feeds the lake. Here they wash their soul and some pray for healing. As each day begins, a priest brings the Adi Granth from the Akal Takht to the Har Mandir, where it is placed on its symbolic throne. As the day progresses, he and others will read from it. At the end of the day, the Adi Granth is wrapped in ritual cloths and returned to the Akal Takht.

The world took notice of the Golden Temple in 1984 after a group seeking to create a separate Sikh nation (for which some Sikhs had argued through the 20th century) took residence within. Their cause was opposed by most Indians and then prime minister Indira Gandhi (1917–1984). In his search for independence, Sikh leader Jarnail Singh Bhindranwale (1947–1984) had made the Golden Temple his headquarters. In her efforts to suppress the independence movement, Gandhi vowed to capture Bhindranwale even at the cost of invading the temple's sacred space. When Bhindranwale refused to surrender, she ordered Indian army troops into the temple. In the process the Akal Takhl was largely destroyed, and many of the separatists, including Brandranwale, along with a number of unsuspecting pilgrims who had been trapped in the temple when the siege began, were killed.

For her invasion of the Golden Temple, Gandhi earned the enmity of the Sikh community, including the elite group of Sikhs who served as her personal bodyguards. Two of those bodyguards assassinated her in retaliation for the violation of the Golden Temple.

Guru Nanak had been opposed to the idea of making pilgrimages, thus Sikhs are reluctant to equate visits to Amritsar as making a pilgrimage. However, the temple and surrounding environment are the regular terminus of people visiting from far and near in search of spiritual and moral refreshment. Relatively close to Amritsar, visitors will also be able to find, including the gurdwara at Tarn Taran built in honor of Guru Arjun Dev, the gurudwara at Gobindwal built by Guru Amar Das and the memorial to Guru Angad Devji at Hazoor Sahib.

J. Gordon Melton

See also: Devotion/Devotional Traditions; Nanak, Guru; Pilgrimage; Sacred Texts.

References

Dogra, Ramesh Chander, and Gobind Singh Manusukhani. *Encyclopedia of Sikh Religion and Culture*. New Delhi: Vikas, 1995.

Duggard, K. S. *The Sikh People Yesterday and Today*. New Delhi: UBS Publishers' Distributoirs, 1993.

Parker, Victoria. *The Golden Temple*. Chicago: Raintree, 2003.

Singh, Jagit. *Temple of Spirituality or Golden Temple of Amritsar*. Columbia, MO: South Asia Books, 1998.

Tully, Mark. *Amritsar: Mrs. Gandhi's Last Battle*. Columbia, MO: South Asia Books, 1998.

Grace Communion International

See Worldwide Church of God.

Grail Movement, The

The Grail movement is an old and historically important international Esoteric organization, now divided among two main rival branches. The movement was founded by Oskar Ernst Bernhardt (1875–1941), a German Esoteric author known under the pen name of Abd-ru-shin (Parsi: Son of Light). He was born in Bischofswerda (Germany) in 1875, and from 1900 on traveled extensively in the Middle and Far East, the United States, and Europe; he also published several novels, short stories, and theatrical pieces. The outbreak of World War I found him, a German citizen, in an enemy country, the United Kingdom, and he was interned on the Isle of Man. In 1923, he circulated the first parts of *The Grail Message*, the publication of which continued through to 1937.

The Grail Message, a complicated Esoteric work, found interested readers, particularly in Germany, France, the former Czechoslovakia, and Austria. Bernhardt decided to settle in Austria, at the Vomperberg (Tyrol), together with a handful of followers of what later became known as the Grail movement. In 1938, Austria was occupied by Nazi Germany: *The Grail Message* was banned, the Vomperberg Center closed, and Abd-ru-shin arrested. Released from jail in September 1938, he was banished first to Schlauroth (near Görlitz, Saxony), and then to Kipsdorf, where he died in 1941. His wife, Maria Freyer (1887–1957), continued his spiritual mission within the framework of the Grail movement, which was directed for several years after her death by the children she had from a previous marriage, Irmgard (1908–1990), Alexander (1911–1968), and Elizabeth (1912–2002), who all legally changed their last name to Bernhardt. Their leadership was not recognized by the large Brazilian branch, directed by Roselis von Sass (1906–1997), who established a splinter group known as Ordem do Graal na Terra. Other schisms occurred in the present-day Czech Republic. The most important problems, however, were born from the will of Irmgard Bernhardt, who was the legal owner of both the Vomperberg Center and the copyright on Abd-ru-shin's books. Irmgard left the Vomperberg to her granddaughter Claudia-Maria (in turn, the natural daughter of a disciple she had adopted; 1948–1999) and to Claudia-Maria's husband, Siegfried (who also legally changed his last name to Bernhardt), and the copyrights to her brother-in-law Herbert Vollmann (1903–1999), the husband of her sister Elizabeth Bernhardt. Although Irmgard expressed in her will the hope that all her relatives might peacefully cooperate, this was not the case, particularly after Vollmann's death in 1999. The two branches of the movement—called in the United States the International Grail movement (led by Vollman's heirs, the owners of the copyrights) and the Grail movement of America (led by Siegfried Bernhardt, who controls the Vomperberg)—are now in fact completely separate.

The Grail Message includes 168 talks, explaining the structure of the whole universe and of the laws that govern it. The border between the divine and human realms is the Grail Castle, where the holy cup of the Grail represents God's direct irradiation. Creation is the spread of God's rays, with their consequent and gradual cooling beyond this border. This is how different planes of the universe were generated, a scheme very reminiscent of that found in the thought of Helena P. Blavatsky (1831–1891), one of the founders of the Theosophical Society. First came the original spiritual level, then the spiritual level and additional levels successively down to matter, all originating, it is believed, from the cooling and solidification of the divine rays. Crucial for this descent of the rays are two characters, known as Parsifal and the pristine Queen, or Mother. A force flows down from the Holy Grail and sustains the whole of creation. Planet Earth is part of the creation's denser and lower level. Human beings, however, keep within themselves a spiritual spark capable of reminding them of their divine origin. By cultivating this spark through successive reincarnations, humans can tran-scend the lower planes of matter, achieve a higher spiritual consciousness, and ultimately return to their heavenly home.

At the Vomperberg, and in other places, the Grail movement celebrates three spiritual feasts each year: the Feast of the Holy Ghost (Pentecost) on May 30, the Feast of the White Lily on September 7, and the Feast of the Radiant Star on December 29. The total membership of the main branch of the Grail movement (splinter groups not included) is currently 16,000. The international readership of *The Grail Message* is certainly much larger. The headquarters are located at the Vomperberg Center, although the international correspondence address is the movement's publishing house.

International Grail Movement (Vollmann branch)
Verlag der Stiftung Gralsbotschaft
Schukertstrasse 8
D-70192 Ditzingen
Germany
http://www.graal.org

Grail Administration (Siegfried Bernhardt branch: in
    the U.S.–Grail Movement of America)
Vomperberg, Grals-Siedlung
6134 Vomp/Tirol
 Austria
http://www.grailnet.org
    Massimo Introvigne and PierLuigi Zoccatelli

See also: Blavatsky, Helena P.; Theosophical Society (America); Western Esoteric Tradition.

References

Abd-ru-shin (Oskar Ernst Bernhardt). *In the Light of Truth. The Grail Message.* 3 vols. Vomperberg, Austria: Alexander Bernhardt, 1985.
Abd-ru-shin (Oskar Ernst Bernhardt). *The Ten Commandments of God. The Lord's Prayer.* Vomperberg, Austria: Alexander Bernhardt, 1982.

Granada, Spain

Located in southeastern Spain, the city of Granada (Arabic: Gharnata) was a medieval center of culture and learning located at the foot of the Sierra Nevada where the Darro and Genil rivers meet. Its strategic

The Alhambra, located in Granada, Spain, stands as a reminder of Spain's Moorish heritage. (Ralph Paprzycki/Dreamstime.com)

location had drawn settlers since prehistoric times. The city developed a large Jewish population after the Roman destruction of Jerusalem and its temple in 70 CE, but attained its heights under Muslim rule between the 8th and 15th centuries. It was incorporated into Christian Spain in 1492.

The Jewish community sided with the Muslim invaders in 711 and assisted in their bringing the city into the swiftly expanding Muslim Empire. Then, following the destruction of the Umayyad dynasty in Damascus, one of the heirs, Abd ar-Rahman (r. 756–788), made his way to Spain and re-established Umayyad rule with a base in Cordoba. He soon incorporated Granada into his new kingdom. It grew through the next century to become the capital of a province under the Cordoba caliphate declared by Abd ar-Rahman III (r. 912–961) in 929.

Unfortunately, the caliphate ran into serious succession problems early in the 11th century that would lead to its downfall in 1031. However, even as the caliphate's troubles began to manifest, Granada was attacked and largely destroyed in 1011. Out of the ruins the independent Taifa of Granada emerged in 1013. At this time, the Jewish and non-Jewish sections of the city were united and the present name, Granada (Spanish for pomegranate), was adopted. The new kingdom lasted until 1091. The Taifa was established by a Berber (North African) general named Ibn Ziri (r. 1013–1020), who founded the Zirid kingdom and made Granada its urban center.

Ibn Ziri saw to the building of the Great Mosque of Granada, whose beauty by all accounts rivaled those in Seville and Cordoba. He was also responsible for the construction of the Casbah (old section of the city), whose wall enclosed the royal palace and the commercial and residential quarters. Greater Granada was itself surrounded by lush orchards, most being of pomegranates.

While continuing under Muslim rule, Granada would successively fall under the authority of the Almoravid dynasty based in northwest Africa in 1091 and then the Almohad dynasty in 1166. Spanish Muslims led by Ibn al-Hud overthrew the Almohad forces in the 1230s only to have power wrested from him by Muhammad Ibn al-Ahmar, who established the Nasrid dynasty and proclaimed himself sultan of Granada in 1238.

In the meantime, the reconquest of Spain by Christian forces was well underway and Cordoba had already fallen to the Christian kingdom of Castille. The sultanate of Granada survived more than two and a half centuries as the last Spanish Muslim state by becoming a vassal state to Castille, to whom it paid tribute, and operating out of a balance of power policy between Christian rivals (Castille and Aragon) and Muslim forces sitting just across the Straits of Gibraltar in North Africa. Interestingly, the Nasrid sultanate brought Islamic culture in Spain to its zenith. The major symbol of Muslim rule was the Alhambra (the Red), a fortress resting on top of Sabika Hill, which served as the royal capital. Muhammad Ibn al-Ahmar began the construction of the Alhambra complex and his successors added to it decade by decade until it was pronounced completed during the reign of Muhammad V (r. 1354–1359, 1362–1391).

The Nasrid dynasty is remembered for its allegiance to the Malikite School of Islam (the dominant legal school across North Africa) and the associated strong support of Sufism (also the case in much of North Africa, especially Algeria and Morocco). Muhammad Ibn al-Ahmar used Sufi symbols to legitimate his authority. The dynasty identified itself as "those who make [Islam] victorious through God."

The educational life of Granada was focused in the Madrasah of Granada, started in 1349 by Sultan Yusuf I (r. 1318–1354). The school remained active until the suppression of the Muslim community in 1499. Subsequently, its building was confiscated and the library lost in a fire. It would be succeeded by what became the University of Granada, founded on a grant from King Charles V (r. 1516–1556) in 1526.

The fall of Muslim Granada was occasioned by the merging of Castille and Aragon through the marriage of King Ferdinand (1452–1516) of Castille and Queen Isabella (1451–1504) of Aragon. Granada was surrendered to Christian Spain in 1492, by which time Granada's population had become overwhelmingly Muslim. Large numbers of Granada's Christians and then the Jews had migrated to other parts of Christian Iberia through the 15th century. The initial capitulation agreement of 1492 provided Muslims the right to retain their customs and their religion.

The expected conversion of the majority of the population did not occur, and in 1499 Catholic leaders began a program of mass conversion and forced baptism—a clear violation of the surrender document. Some citizens revolted, which then became the occasion of the authorities to revoke the treaty altogether. The state now demanded the quick conversion or emigration of all of Spain's Muslims. The great majority converted, but many remained secret believers in their old faith. Evidence of the continued Islamic practices of the new Christian converts led King Philip III (r. 1598–1621) to decree their expulsion from Spain early in the 17th century.

Even before the Muslims were integrated into the Christian community, the same year that Granada fell, a decree demanding that Jews convert or leave Spain also destroyed the Granada Jewish community and the old Jewish neighborhood was demolished.

A new Christianized Granada emerged through the 16th century, and Spanish Catholics subsequently migrated to the city from across the country. The city's mosques were turned into churches or otherwise converted into Christian structures. Two of the structures begun early in the 16th century would join the list of architectural wonders in the city: the Granada Charterhouse, a Carthusian monastery, and the new Granada Cathedral. The cathedral was built over the site of the older Grand Mosque. It would take almost two centuries to construct (1523–1704). The monastery of the Carthusians, begun in 1615, would take three centuries to complete, but emerged as a magnificent example of Spanish baroque architecture. A number of other architecturally significant churches would also be built (or begun) during the 16th century.

J. Gordon Melton

See also: Cathedrals—Christian; Cordoba; Malekite School of Islam; Roman Catholic Church; Sufism.

References

Buluggin, Abd Allah b. *The Tibyan: Memoirs of Abd Allah b. Buluggin, the Last Zirid Emir of Granada.* Trans. and ed. by Amin T. Tibi. Leiden: Brill, 1986.

Coleman, David. *Creating Christian Granada: Society and Religious Culture in an Old-World Frontier City, 1492–1600.* Ithaca, NY: Cornell University Press, 2003.

Harris, A. Katie. *From Muslim to Christian Granada: Inventing a City's Past in Early Modern Spain.* Baltimore: Johns Hopkins University Press, 2007.

Harvey, L. P. *Islamic Spain, 1250 to 1500.* Chicago: University of Chicago Press, 1900, 1992.

Nash, Elizabeth. *Seville, Cordoba, and Granada: A Cultural History.* New York: Oxford University Press, 2005.

Reilly, Bernard F. *The Medieval Spains.* Cambridge: Cambridge University Press, 1993.

Grand Mosque, Damascus

Damascus is one of, if not, the oldest city in the world, and its Grand Mosque, though built in the eighth century CE, rests on a site that had successively been the home to various Pagan worship centers and a Christian church.

On the site now home to the Grand Mosque, the Aramean people built a temple around 1000 BCE. Rome conquered the city in 64 BCE, and later saw to the erection of a temple to Jupiter on the site. The Roman temple was constructed on an elevated rectangular platform. It measured some 1,163 by 1,001 feet. There was a square tower at each corner.

In the post-Constantinian world of the late fourth century, the Jupiter temple was superseded by a Christian church dedicated to John the Baptist. In a century in which reputed Christina relics came into their own, the church claimed to have among the most valuable: the head of John the Baptist (the biblical record noting that he died by beheading). The church became a popular pilgrimage site.

The Muslims conquered Damascus in 636 and initially shared the building with Christian worshippers. They built a prayer hall adjacent to the church. The Umayyad caliph al-Walid (r. 705–715) had the church demolished and a new large mosque, magnificent as befitting its role in the city that had become the center of Muslim power, put in its place. It included a large prayer hall (525 feet in length), an even larger courtyard, and many rooms for pilgrims. The Prophet's mosque in Medina was used as a basic model.

Al-Walid compensated his Christians subjects for the church and allowed them to rebuild elsewhere in the city. The relics of John the Baptist, who is also mentioned in the Koran, remained in the possession of the new mosque.

The builders took materials from a number of still-standing Pagan temples, and even columns from the Church of Mary in Antioch. The courtyard was faced with marble, glass, and gold. Included in the construction was what may be the largest golden mosaic in the world, covering some 43,000 square feet. This mosque is somewhat unique in having three minarets. The Minaret of the Bride dates to the 9th and 12th centuries; the Minaret of Jesus to the 13th century; and the Minaret of Qat Bey to the 15th century. Of the three, the Minaret of Jesus, is the tallest. Local tradition suggests that this will be the site of Christ's return to Earth on the Last Day.

The Umayyad mosque has suffered damage several times due to fires (1069, 1893), the Mongol conquest and destruction, and Tamerlane's overrunning the city in 1401.

In 1979, the mosque was included in the old city of Damascus, which was declared a World Heritage site by the United Nations Educational, Scientific and Cultural Organization (UNESCO). In 2001 Pope John Paul II (r. 1978–2005) visited the mosque to view the relics of John the Baptist. It was the first time a pope had made a visit to a mosque.

J. Gordon Melton

See also: Damascus; Medina; Mosques; Relics.

References

Bahnassi, Afif. *The Great Omayyad Mosque of Damascus: The First Masterpieces of Islamic Art.* Damascus: Tlass, 1989.

Burns, Ross. *Damascus: A History.* London: Routledge, 2007.

Great Disappointment

The Great Disappointment is the name given to the severe letdown felt by the followers of William Miller's Adventist teachings when Christ did not return in 1844. Miller, a Baptist preacher from New York, had suggested in the 1830s, based upon his study of the Bible, that Christ was to return around 1843.

The keystone to Miller's understanding of the immediate future was Daniel 8:13–14, "Then I heard one saint speaking, and another saint said unto that certain saint which spake, How long shall be the vision concerning the daily sacrifice, and the transgression of desolation, to give both the sanctuary and the host to be trodden under foot? And he said unto me, Unto two thousand and three hundred days; then shall the sanctuary be cleansed." This passage he coupled with Daniel 9:24, "Seventy weeks are determined upon thy people . . . to make an end to sins." He understood prophetic "days" as referring to mundane years, an idea based on biblical passages such as Ezekiel 4:6, "I have appointed thee each day for a year." Hence 70 weeks became 490 days/years.

Miller believed that the end of the 70 weeks was 33 CE, then the commonly accepted date of Christ's death and resurrection. If that was the case, the 70 weeks began in 457 BCE. Counting 2,300 years from that date brought him to 1843. With this essential chronology set, Miller was able to fill in the details of how Bible prophecy had predicted human history to that point. He began to share these findings with ministers in his community and as early as 1832 published a series of articles concerning his conclusions in a newspaper, the *Vermont Telegraph*, which led to a 64-page booklet the next year, *Evidences from Scripture and History of the Second Coming of Christ about the Year 1843*.

At the beginning of 1843, Miller stated that he believed that Christ would return between March 21, 1843, and March 21, 1844. When Christ failed to return in March 1844, Miller confessed his error and left his own movement. A minority also defected from the movement, but some followed Samuel Snow (1806–1870), who suggested October 22, 1844, was the more correct date. It is the despair that followed the failure of this second date that became known as the Great Disappointment. It resulted in a period of chaos and the division of the movement into several factions from which would eventually come the Seventh-day Adventist Church, the Jehovah's Witnesses, and the Worldwide Church of God.

J. Gordon Melton

See also: Adventism; Jehovah's Witnesses; Seventh-day Adventist Church; Worldwide Church of God.

References

Land, Gary. *Adventism in America*. Grand Rapids, MI: William B. Eerdmans Publishing Company, 1986.
Nichol, Francis D. *The Midnight Cry*. Takoma Park, MD: Review and Herald, 1944.

Great Mosque, Djenné, Mali

The Great Mosque of Djenné, constructed in 1907, is representative of the emergence of Islam as the dominant religion in much of West Africa, with much of that spread coming through the evangelical efforts of merchants and traders. Djenné was formally founded around 800 CE as a trading center connecting Timbuktu and the desert region to the north and east with Guinea and the rain forest region to the south and east.

According to tradition, a local ruler, Koi Kinboro, converted to Islam and in his enthusiasm for his new faith had his palace converted. Records are scarce concerning the size and appearance of the first mosque, but it was large enough that Sheikh Amadou Lobbo, who conquered Djenné during the Tukulor War, ordered the original mosque demolished in 1834, as he considered it to be too lavish for a mosque. The only portion of the original building that survived was an enclosure containing the graves of local leaders. In 1861 the city was conquered by the Tukulor emperor al-Hajj 'Umar and was then occupied by the French in 1893. The French oversaw a re-creation of the original building, which was completed in 1896. However, that building was demolished after the decision was made to build what is now the present mosque, designed by the architect Ismaila Traoré, then the head of Djenné's guild of masons.

The new mosque was constructed of sun-baked mud bricks and laid with a mud-based mortar, the whole structure being covered with a mud plaster. The materials have been developed locally over the centuries and function to insulate the building during the day and keep it relatively warm through the night. The building was constructed on a raised platform (surface area 62,500 square feet), which keeps it above the water line when the nearby river floods. The annual flooding of the Bani River transforms Djenné into an island.

A roof covers half of the mosque while the other half is an open air prayer hall or courtyard. The prayer wall faces toward Mecca (east) and also overlooks the city marketplace. Rising above the prayer wall are three large minarets, each containing a spiral staircase leading to the roof.

The Great Mosque, the largest building in the world made of mud, was included in that part of Djenné designated a World Heritage Site by the United Nations Educational, Scientific and Cultural Organization (UNESCO) in 1988. Once open to non-Muslims, it was closed following its use in a photo shoot that was deemed to be in violation of the building sanctity.

J. Gordon Melton

See also: Mosques.

References

Imperato, Pascal J., ed. *Historical Dictionary of Mali.* Lanham, MD: Scarecrow, 1996.

Jenkins, Mark. *To Timbuktu: A Journey Down the Niger.* New York: William Morrow, 1997.

Mans, Peter. "Djenne: Living Tradition." *Saudi ARAMCO World* (November–December 1990): 19–29. http://www.saudiaramcoworld.com/issue/199006/djenn.-living.tradition.htm.

Great White Brotherhood

The Great White Brotherhood (GWB) is perhaps the most publicized and controversial millenarian new religious movement that appeared in the former Soviet Union in the early 1990s. The founder of the GWB, an electronics engineer named Yuri Krivonogov, became interested in ways of "releasing the energetic potential of humankind" and "directing" human behavior during the 1980s. In 1990, he set up the Atma Medical Centre

Great White Brotherood religious sect leader Maria Tsvigun, who calls herself Maria Devi Christos, 1995. (AP PHOTO/Efrem Lukatsky)

(or Institute of Soul) in Kiev, the Ukrainian capital, which was intended to study and propagate esoteric methods of healing. He soon met Maria Tsvigun (b. 1960), a young Ukrainian journalist who had had a "special experience" during an abortion operation, and recognized her as the "living God." Following their marriage and "persecution" by Ukrainian legal authorities (a criminal investigation of financial irregularities), the Atma Medical Centre rapidly evolved into a religious community, and its leaders became the "divine duo" of Maria Devi Christos and Ioann Swami.

They announced a 1,260-day period of spreading the message of the living God, which Maria Devi Christos had already begun and which would culminate in her "sacrificial death," followed within three days by her resurrection on November 14, 1993, in the ancient Cathedral of St. Sophia in Kiev. On that day, at least 700 members of GWB arrived in Kiev, but were prevented by the Ukrainian police from joining Maria Devi and her closest adherents, who had managed to enter the cathedral. The leadership of the group were later arrested and sentenced to imprisonment for "causing damage to citizens' health under the guise of religious rituals and for seizure of state property." In prison, Maria Devi denounced her former husband as a "fallen Cain" and divorced him. She was released in 1997 under an amnesty and married Vitaliy Kovalchuk (High Priest John-Peter II in the former movement's hierarchy). The divorce caused a split among the remaining members, several dozens of whom continued to operate underground in both the Ukraine and Russia. After unsuccessfully attempting to register with authorities what they claimed to be a cleaned-up movement, the followers of Tsvigun and Krivonogov reverted to semi-underground operation.

The name of the movement alludes to an interest in, and the claim to have been initiated into, the ancient esoteric wisdom of "the White Brothers." This "Great Brotherhood" is thought to be a fraternity of enlightened spiritual beings, or the "sixth race," who after their ascendance from mortals to the higher realm remain responsible for the spiritual progress of human beings. This claim seems to indicate Krivonogov's and Tsvigun's familiarity with ideas of Helena. P. Blavatsky (1831–1891), co-founder of the Theosophical Society; with works of Helena Roerich (1879–1955) and Nicholas Roerich (1874–1947), founders of the Agni-Yoga Society, which was highly popular in the late Soviet Union (1970s–1980s); and with the legacy of Omram Mikhael Aivanhov (1900–1986), the Bulgarian mystic and founder of the Universal White Brotherhood, who became well known in Russia in the late 1980s. Krivonogov's early teachings were also influenced by various other alternative techniques and teachings that were available in the emerging Soviet New Age movement, and the more broad cultic milieu of the 1980s, such as bio-energetics, various forms of yoga and meditation, Neuro-Linguistic Programming, and the like. Reference to Eastern religious teachings is evident in the names adopted by the leaders (Swami and Devi). At the same time, in the early days the GWB emphasized the ability of the leaders to provide therapeutic remedies and to enhance the human potential of its followers. As the religious community developed, however,

millenarian features became increasingly prominent and were grafted onto the Christian apocalyptic motifs of Living God, God's Sacrifice, Resurrection, and Redemption. These millenarian features were embodied in the teaching of *Yusmalos.*

Yusmalos (a contraction of the two first names of the leaders and *logos*) depicted the current state of the world in dualistic terms as governed by a Satanic conspiracy on the one hand, but, on the other hand, blessed with the presence of the Living God, which gave prospects for salvation to "144,000 saints" (an apparent reference to the biblical book of Revelation). The early teachings of the GWB had strong political overtones, with both anti-Western and anti-Communist elements. The Satanic conspiracy was occasionally referred to as "American-Israeli" or "Jewish-Masonic," and only Slavs could be the elect few; God was said to be "Russian." At the same time, the post-Communist reality was seen as a hangover of Communist injustices, which could only be overcome by the establishment of a strong theocracy based on the "true religion." The "sacrifice" of Maria Devi Christos was seen as the beginning of the new era of "divine theocracy." It remains unclear, however, whether her "death" was expected to be a physical or purely symbolic act.

During the early 1990s, dozens of small "Usmalian" communities organized around these beliefs emerged in Russia and Ukraine, which had the recognizable features of world-rejecting millenarian groups anticipating the imminent end of the world. Their young members (some under 18) were expected to sever all ties with their biological parents, adopt an extremely ascetic lifestyle, and devote all their time to spreading the message. Indeed, in 1992–1993, all major Russian and Ukrainian cities were covered with leaflets featuring Maria Devi Christos and her stark message of the impending catastrophe and repentance.

After the failure of the end of the world to materialize and the split in the leadership, the millenarianism of GWB diminished considerably. Maria Devi Christos renounced its most controversial features and attributed their origins to the "evil" influence of her former husband. Since 1994, followers have tended to claim that the movement stemmed from the "respectable" traditions of Theosophy and Agni Yoga. Maria Devi Christos has published several books of poetry with the message of love and happy family life as ways to achieve eternal salvation, that is, to become members of the "sixth race" that will survive the Final Judgment and inherit the Earth (a clear reference to Helena Roerich's ideas from Agni-Yoga). Similar changes have occurred in the movement's practices, which have evolved from strong asceticism and hostility to the outside world to more moderate attitudes and even attempts to cooperate with public institutions. At the same time, the movement still sees the West, in particular the United States, as evil, believes in the "Judeo-Masonic" conspiracy, and claims the salvationist mission of the Slavic people. The continuing semi-underground existence of the GWB makes it difficult to know the extent to which these changes have affected different subgroups within the movement. This is compounded by continuing persecution of members of the GWB by police and local authorities in Russia and Ukraine.

The early activities of the GWB served as one of the triggers of the Russian and Ukrainian anti-cult movements. The anti-cultists exaggerated the GWB's controversial features and numerical significance to point to the general dangers from a spectrum of religious groups that emerged en masse in the former Soviet Union in the early 1990s. The very name of the group became synonymous with a dangerous destructive cult that capitalizes on vulnerabilities of hapless post-Soviet youth. The anti-cultists took the figure of 144,000 "destined to salvation" as representing its actual membership whereas in reality the movement is unlikely to have had more than 1,000 members at the peak of its activities.

Marat S. Shterin

See also: Aivanhov, Omraam Mikhael; Blavatsky, Helena P.; Energy; Theosophical Society (America); Universal Great Brotherhood.

References

Borenstein, E. "Articles of Faith: The Media Response to Maria Devi Christos." *Religion* 25, no. 3 (1995): 249–266.

Filatov, S. "Sects and New Religious Movements in Post-Soviet Russia." In *Proselytism and Orthodoxy in Russia*, edited by J. Witte Jr. and M. Bourdeaux. Maryknoll, NY: Orbis, 1999.

Shterin, Marat. "New Religions in the New Russia." *Nova Religio* 4, no. 2 (2001): 310–321.

Great Zimbabwe

In 1871, Europeans discovered Great Zimbabwe, the large medieval (abandoned) city located on the plains between the Limpopo and Zambezi rivers. It is the largest prehistoric stone structure in sub-Saharan Africa and it presented a problem as their understanding of the "primitive" state of the local inhabitants kept them from ascribing its construction to their ancestors. It was 60 years later before more thorough archaeological investigation proved that the Shona, the Bantu people whose presence in the area was dated back to fifth century CE, were responsible for the complex of buildings. The initial construction of the city, which encompassed some 1,800 acres, is now dated to around 1100 CE. Its growth and habitation continued through the mid-15th century.

Once its origin was understood, the story of Great Zimbabwe quickly unfolded. At its height, Great Zimbabwe would have been home to upwards of 20,000 people. Of these, the majority resided in those parts of the site now called the Hill Complex and the Valley Complex. Those of higher status, including the religious functionaries, lived on the higher land, while those of lower status (the workers and herdsmen) inhabited the valley.

Placement of the city was dictated on the one hand by the nearby substantial gold deposits and on the other by the nearby location of pre-existing trade routes. The main problem was water, a scarce resource, though grasslands for cattle and wildlife were abundant. Overcoming the water shortages, the city flourished for more than three centuries. Its far-reaching trade has been documented from as far away as China and Persia. It continued to produce a variety of goods from the iron forge it operated close by.

Much of the interest in Great Zimbabwe is directed toward a third component of the complex called the Great Enclosure. The 32-foot-high wall of the enclosure was constructed without mortar. Inside its circumference (800+ feet), there are brick altar-like structures, interior walls, pillars, and stone monoliths.

The Great Enclosure at Great Zimbabwe, most likely built by the Bantu-speaking Shona. Great Zimbabwe, which comprises 100 acres of stone buildings, was the center of a thriving trade region up until the 15th century. (Corel)

Research into the uses of the Great Enclosure (both religious and secular) has been hampered by modern alterations of various features, including the removal and relocation of some of the pillars. Enough remains, however, that scholars have discerned that the builders had some knowledge of astronomy. A pattern on the southeast corner of the outer wall, for example, appears to mark the Summer Solstice, and a large interior passageway appears to be positioned to align with the Milky Way during the Summer Solstice. This latter observation resonates with the worldview of the local residents in which the Milky Way plays a prominent role. Other markers in the Great Enclosure appear to indicate the arrival of the Spring and Fall equinoxes.

The residents abandoned Great Zimbabwe in the middle of the 15th century. The most likely explanation is that they exhausted the local grassland and used up the forest, though the lack of written records may mean that the real reasons are forever lost.

In 1986, the United Nations Educational, Scientific and Cultural Organization (UNESCO) designated Great Zimbabwe a World Heritage Site.

J. Gordon Melton

See also: African Traditional Religions.

References

Barnes-Svarney, Patricia. *Zimbabwe*. Philadelphia: Chelsea House Publishers, 1999.

Garlake, Peter S. *Kingdoms of Africa*. Oxford: Elsevier Publishing, 1978.

Vogel, Joseph O. *Great Zimbabwe: The Iron Age in South Central Africa*. New York: Garland Publishing, 1994.

■ Greece

The Greek peninsula and its associated islands, which constitute the modern nation of Greece, have been inhabited for some 5,000 years. The main body of the peninsula and its associated islands jut out into the Mediterranean Sea and its several adjacent local bodies of water—the Adriatic Sea, the Sea of Crete, and the Ionian Sea. Greece's northern border is shared with Albania, Macedonia, Bulgaria, and Turkey. It is home to 10.2 million people.

In the second millennium BCE the Achaean people emerged as the ruling elite of the region. They founded the Mycenaean Empire, covering present-day Greece and Crete. The Dorians swept through the area and rose to dominance as the first millennium BCE began. Over the next centuries a set of city-states arose in the area. In the eighth century the increase in population and lack of resources forced the Greeks to turn outward to the Mediterranean Sea. They became great traders, established colonies throughout the region, and made Greek the language of international commerce.

During the sixth century, Athens began its rise to prominence among the city-states, and during several centuries of prosperity great strides were made in the setting down of laws, scientific observations, literature, and philosophical thought, developments that have had implications for all humankind. The growing influence of Greece culminated in the rise of Philip of Macedonia, who subdued the peninsula. Philip's son, Alexander the Great (r. 336–323 BCE), built an empire that included North Africa, the Arabian Peninsula, Persia, and territory as far as India. The fracturing of Alexander's empire after his early death set the stage for the rise of Rome. Rome conquered Greece in 146 BCE.

Greece remained a part of the Roman Empire for many centuries. When in the fourth century CE the empire was divided, Greece was tied to the eastern part of the empire, known as the Byzantine Empire because its capital was Byzantium (later called Constantinople, and later still, Istanbul); as Christianity was established as the religion of the empire, Greece was brought under the hegemony of the Eastern Orthodox Church. Greece was under the direct authority of the patriarch in Constantinople.

Constantinople fell to the Turkish Muslims in 1456, and within a few years Greece also fell. The Turks remained in Greece as an occupation force for the next four centuries and in 1718 formally incorporated Greece into the Ottoman Empire. By the beginning of

Greek Orthodox church in Oia, on the island of Santorini. (Dareon/Dreamstime.com)

the 19th century, the Ottoman Empire was showing its weakness, and in 1830 the Greeks were able to force the creation of an independent Greek state, minus the area in the northeast around Thessalonica. The country was ruled by a king through the rest of the century, but in 1911 a Parliament was created. The country was overrun by the Nazis during World War II. Political instability has marked the postwar decades, the country reaching its lowest point during the harsh repressive military dictatorship that began in 1967. The dictatorship ended in 1974. Since 1975 the country has operated under its new democratic Constitution.

The introduction of Christianity to Greece is described in the New Testament as resulting from a dream experienced by the Apostle Paul during which he heard a call to come to Macedonia. He subsequently traveled through the land, stopping at Thessalonica, Berea, Philippi, Corinth, and Athens. He later wrote letters to believers in Thessalonica, Philippi, and Corinth that became part of the Christian scriptures.

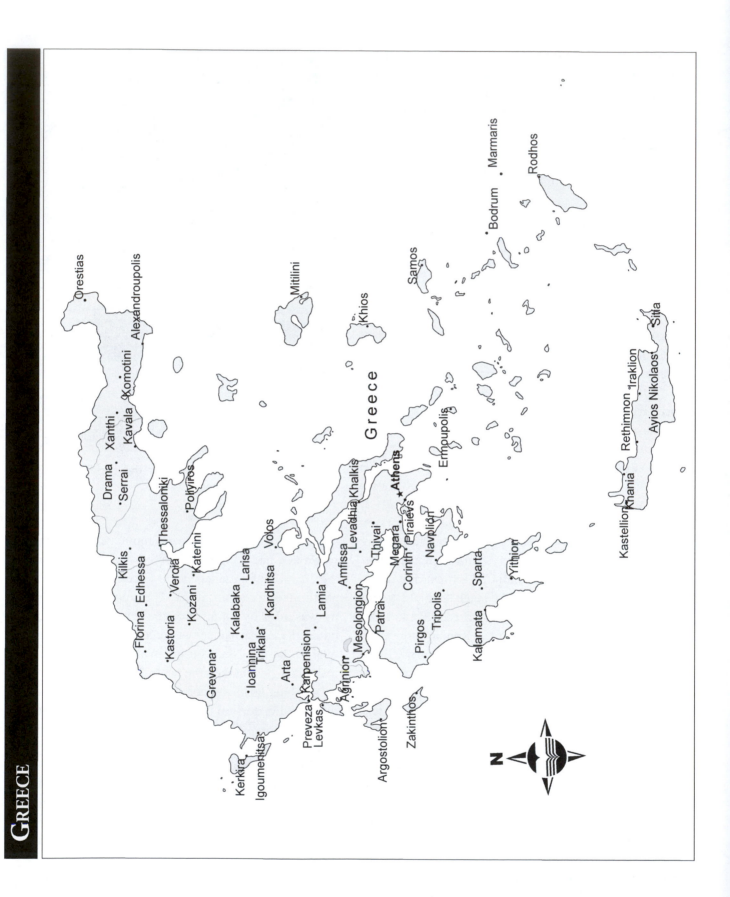

Greece

Religion	Followers in 1970	Followers in 2010	% of Population	Annual % growth 2000–2010	Followers in 2025	Followers in 2050
Christians	8,643,000	10,419,000	92.9	0.21	10,322,000	9,842,000
Orthodox	8,517,000	10,320,000	92.0	0.04	10,175,000	9,660,000
Marginals	50,200	58,000	0.5	0.52	55,000	60,000
Roman Catholics	45,700	140,000	1.2	18.47	175,000	185,000
Muslims	130,000	475,000	4.2	0.23	500,000	500,000
Agnostics	10,000	260,000	2.3	0.82	340,000	380,000
Atheists	5,000	31,000	0.3	0.23	40,000	50,000
Hindus	0	15,000	0.1	0.23	17,000	18,000
Jews	3,800	5,500	0.0	−0.17	5,500	5,000
Sikhs	0	5,700	0.1	0.23	6,000	6,000
New religionists	1,000	2,200	0.0	0.23	2,500	3,000
Spiritists	0	1,000	0.0	0.22	1,500	2,000
Buddhists	0	600	0.0	0.22	1,000	1,500
Baha'is	200	200	0.0	0.22	300	500
Total population	**8,793,000**	**11,215,000**	**100.0**	**0.23**	**11,236,000**	**10,808,000**

The rise of Christianity to a position of power in the Roman Empire led to its pushing aside the Pagan faith that had previously dominated in Greece and the other religions that had come to Greece along the trade routes established across the Mediterranean and through Alexander's kingdom. Christianity completely replaced what had come before though it was deeply influenced by the philosophy that had grown out of the encounter of Greek religion and the East, especially by the thought of Plato and the neo-Platonists, Judaism alone surviving. Over the next centuries the theology and liturgy of the Eastern Orthodox Church developed, and the Orthodox Church distinguished itself on various points from the Roman Catholic Church of the Latin-speaking part of the empire. Authority in the Eastern Greek-speaking church came to be shared by the patriarchs in Constantinople, Antioch, Jerusalem, and Alexandria.

The takeover of Greece by Turkey did not greatly change the church's position in Greek society, though the church became one symbol of the Greek people's survival during the long years of Turkish rule. However, after the coming of independence in 1830, a break with the Ecumenical Patriarchate followed. In 1833, the government issued the first formal statement declaring an independent national church free from the authority of the patriarch, who still resided in Turkish territory. It was not until 1850 that the independence of the church was recognized. Not included in the jurisdiction of the Orthodox Church of Greece are some of the Greek islands, still in the jurisdiction of the Ecumenical Patriarchate, and most important, the independent Monastic Republic of Mount Athos.

In 1924, the Church of Greece made what many considered a crucial change in adopting the Gregorian calendar, which replaced the traditional Julian calendar. This move was seen by many as a step away from the received tradition of the church and led to major schism by bishops, priests, and parishes who continued to adhere to the Julian calendar. Over the years, the True (Old Calendar) Orthodox Church of Greece has further divided over the issue of cooperation with the Church of Greece, which has participated in the larger ecumenical movement, even to the point of joining the World Council of Churches.

The Church of Greece remains the faith of the overwhelming majority of Greek citizens, but almost immediately after it came into being as an autonomous body, it had to make room for other Christian churches. Some posed little problem, such as churches like the Episcopal Church, the Armenian Apostolic Church (Holy See of Echmiadzin), or the Ancient Church of the East, which served small expatriate communities and offered no program for proselytization. However, in 1858, a Protestant movement, later known as the Greek Evangelical Church, was the first of a number of Protestant and Free church bodies that attempted to develop missions in Greece. At various times these churches have faced severe repression and in recent decades were the object of concern of the Greek police, who considered them subversive of national policy.

The most successful of non-Orthodox bodies have been the Jehovah's Witnesses, who began activity in Greece in 1900. They have also been the group that has received the most attention from both the Orthodox Church and the state in its attempt to protect the position of the church in Greek life. During the 1990s, the arrest of Jehovah's Witnesses led to the Greek government receiving two significant judgments from the World Court for violations of religious freedom documents to which it had agreed. These rulings have eased the situation in Greece somewhat.

During the 1960s, although not open to the new religions that were otherwise proselytizing throughout Europe, Greece became a setting for the development of the Western Esoteric tradition in the phase that came to be known as the New Age movement. Many New Age devotees described their work as nonreligious, though it was spiritual.

J. Gordon Melton

See also: Ancient Church of the East; Armenian Apostolic Church (Holy See of Echmiadzin); Ecumenical Patriarchate/Patriarchate of Constantinople; Episcopal Church; Free Churches; Greek Evangelical Church; Jehovah's Witnesses; New Age Movement; Orthodox Church of Greece; Roman Catholic Church; True (Old Calendar) Orthodox Church of Greece; World Council of Churches.

References

Burch, S. L. "The Beginning of the Protestant Mission to the Greek Orthodox in Asia Minor and Pontos." M.A. thesis, Fuller Theological Seminary, 1977.

Dietrich, B. C. *Tradition in Greek Religion.* Berlin: de Gruyter, 1986.

Frazee, C. A. "The Orthodox Church of Greece: The Last Fifteen Years." *Indiana Social Studies Quarterly* 32, no. 1 (1979): 89–110.

Hart, L. K. *Time, Religion and Social Experience in Rural Greece.* Lanham, MD: Rowman and Littlefield, 1992.

Hore, Alexander Hugh. *Eighteen Centuries of the Orthodox Greek Church.* Whitefish, MT: Kessinger Publishing, 2007.

Woodhouse, C. M. *Modern Greece: A Short History.* London: Faber and Faber, 2000.

Greek Catholic Church

In 1829, the sultan of the Ottoman Empire rescinded the law requiring Roman Catholics following an other-than-Latin liturgical order to be subject to the Orthodox Church. That law had meant that the small number of Greek Catholics in Greece and Turkey worshipped in churches under the jurisdiction of the Ecumenical Patriarchate, based in Istanbul. The small community of Greek Catholics, now allowed to have their own congregations, began to grow in the 1850s after missionary work was launched among the Greek Orthodox by a Roman Catholic priest. A modest number of parishes emerged through the remainder of the 19th century. In 1895, the Assumptionist Fathers settled in Constantinople, where they oversaw a Greek seminary and two parishes. In 1911, Pope Pius X organized the Greek Catholic parishes in Turkey into an exarchate and appointed Isaias Papadopoulos as the first bishop.

In the 1920s, almost all of the Greek Catholics moved to Athens, the result of an agreement between the two countries for a general relocation of expatriates to their homeland. The emergence of a body of believers in Greece affiliated with the Roman Catholic Church has caused considerable tension over the years in a land in which the Greek Orthodox Church is considered the national religious body. The Greek Orthodox Church has actively opposed both Protestant and Catholic presence in the country, but is especially opposed to the Greek Catholic Church, which it sees as easily confused with an Orthodox church. Catholics must conform to a set of special laws designed as obstacles to any movement of Orthodox believers into the Greek Catholic Church.

The several parishes of the Greek Catholic Church have a total membership of 2,325 (2009). There is still one parish in Istanbul. The church is led by Bishop Dimitrios Salachas (b. 1939), who took office in 2008.

Greek Catholic Church
Odos Homirou 9
106 72 Athens
Greece
http://www.elcathex.com/

J. Gordon Melton

See also: Ecumenical Patriarchate/Patriarchate of Constantinople; Roman Catholic Church.

References

Liesel, N. *The Eastern Catholic Liturgies: A Study in Words and Pictures.* Westminster, MD: Newman Press, 1960.

Roberson, Ronald G. *The Eastern Christian Churches—A Brief Survey.* 5th ed. Rome: Edizioni Orientalia Christiana, Pontificio Istituto Orientale, 1995.

Greek Evangelical Church

The roots of the Greek Evangelical Church can be traced to the work of Jonas King (1792–1869), a Congregationalist minister sent to Greece by the American Board of Commissioners for Foreign Missions following the Greek War for Independence that ended in 1828. He settled in Greece, met and married a Greek woman, started a school, engaged in welfare work, and preached as opportunity allowed. In 1848 the authorities arrested and deported King. Through the influence of the American government, he was eventually allowed to return.

It was not until 1866, just three years before King's death, that the first community of a future church was organized. King was by this time being aided by a young man, Michael Kalopothakis, who had been present at King's trial in 1848 and as a result had converted to Protestantism. He went to New York, studied at Union Theological Seminary, and then returned to his native land. He led in the erection of the first church building in 1871. By 1885 three congregations existed, and a synod was organized. In the meantime, evangelistic work had been conducted in the Greek commu-

nity in Turkey by the British Mediterranean Mission. This effort was to have a significant effect upon the work in Greece. As a result of the Greek-Turkish War of 1922, many Greek people left Turkey and returned to Greece. As a result of the sudden jump in membership that followed, the synod was reorganized as the Greek Evangelical Church.

The church is conservative in its theology and places great emphasis on the authority of the Bible. It has developed a strong Sunday school and youth program. The church is headed by a general assembly that meets semi-annually.

In the years since World War II, the church appears to have attained a stable position in Greek society, though many still consider it a foreign element in Greek culture. It continues to evangelize and has developed a broad social service program. In the 1990s it opened a mission in Albania.

In 2005 the church reported approximately 5,000 members. Affiliated churches can now be found in Cyprus, Germany, and the United States, where many members have immigrated. It is a member of both the World Alliance of Reformed Churches and the Reformed Ecumenical Council, as well as the World Council of Churches.

Greek Evangelical Church
24 Marku Botsari St.
GR-117 41 Athens
Greece

J. Gordon Melton

See also: Reformed Ecumenical Council; World Alliance of Reformed Churches; World Council of Churches.

References

Bauswein, Jean-Jacques, and Lukas Vischner, eds. *The Reformed Family Worldwide: A Survey of Reformed Churches, Theological Schools, and International Organizations.* Grand Rapids, MI: William B. Eerdmans Publishing Company, 1999.

Van Beek, Huibert. *A Handbook of the Churches and Councils: Profiles of Ecumenical Relationships.* Geneva: World Council of Churches, 2006.

Greek Orthodox Patriarchate of Alexandria and All Africa

This is the second-ranking autocephalous church in the Eastern Orthodox communion and includes all the Orthodox Christians on the continent of Africa.

The city of Alexandria was founded by Alexander the Great in 332 BCE, and it quickly become one of the great cultural and political centers of the ancient world. According to tradition, Saint Mark the Evangelist brought Christianity to the city in the first century CE, and the new religion began to spread in the sizable Jewish community that had long flourished there. By the end of the second century Christianity had been embraced by the majority of the city's Greeks and was growing in the local Egyptian population, and a renowned catechetical school had been established. The community was persecuted by the Roman emperors in the third century, but came into its own after Constantine's Edict of Milan granted religious freedom to Christians in 313.

The Church of Alexandria was soon torn by theological controversies and efforts to suppress various heresies that sprang up. The Byzantine emperors enforced the Christological teaching of the Council of Chalcedon (451), which had the support of local Greeks but was rejected by the great majority of the Egyptian Christian population. When the Arab armies took Alexandria in 642, the Egyptian Christians were free to organize themselves into what eventually became today's Coptic Orthodox Church. The Arabs singled out the Greek minority for special persecution because of their links to the former Byzantine rulers. The Turkish conquest of Egypt in 1517 brought an end to the persecutions but gave rise to a greater dependency on the Ecumenical Patriarchate of Constantinople. Some of the Greek patriarchs began to live in Constantinople, and at times the ecumenical patriarch appointed them to office. The Alexandrian Patriarchate sank deep into poverty and often had to turn to the Russian Orthodox Church (Moscow Patriarchate) for support. The church experienced a renaissance in the 19th century when the Egyptian rulers began to encourage Greeks to settle in Egypt. After 1846 the patriarchs resided permanently in Egypt once again, and the involvement of the Ecumenical Patriarchate in the administration of the Alexandrian Church ended in 1858.

Patriarch Meletios II (1926–1935) promulgated a new set of regulations for the Patriarchate and modified his title to include "of All Africa" in the place of the former "of All Egypt." His successor Christophoros recognized a spontaneous movement of indigenous Africans toward Orthodoxy that began in Uganda and spread to Kenya and Tanzania. By 1998 there were more than 100 African Orthodox priests in East Africa, presided over by the world's first black African Orthodox bishop. The growing membership among Africans compensated for the shrinking of the Greek community in Egypt.

The Patriarchate is governed by regulations that provide for a synodal system of administration and a process of patriarchal election that involves both clergy and laity. The Holy Synod, made up of at least 7 metropolitans (currently 24), must meet at least once a year but ordinarily gathers semiannually. Through the efforts of Archbishop Makarios III of Cyprus, an Orthodox Patriarchal School was opened in Nairobi in 1981. The membership of the Patriarchate today includes approximately 100,000 black Africans and 150,000 others, mostly ethnic Greeks scattered across the continent. It is an active member of the Middle East Council of Churches and the World Council of Churches.

Greek Orthodox Patriarchate of Alexandria and All
    Africa
His Beatitude Patriarch Theodoros II
PO Box 2006
Alexandria
Egypt
http://www.greekorthodox-alexandria.org/

Ronald Roberson

See also: Coptic Orthodox Church; Ecumenical Patriarchate/Patriarchate of Constantinople; Middle East Council of Churches; Russian Orthodox Church (Moscow Patriarchate); World Council of Churches.

References

Meinardus, O. F. A. *Christian Egypt: Ancient and Modern*. Cairo: American University/Cairo Press, 1970.

Orthodoxia. Regensburg, Germany: Ostkirchliches Institut, issued annually.

Roberson, Ronald G. *The Eastern Christian Churches—A Brief Survey.* 7th ed. Rome: Edizioni Orientalia Christiana, Pontificio Istituto Orientale, 2008.

Greek Orthodox Patriarchate of Antioch and All the East

This is the third-ranking autocephalous church in the Eastern Orthodox communion. It includes the Orthodox Christians in Syria, Lebanon, and other parts of the Middle East.

Founded in 300 BCE, the city of Antioch quickly became one of the most important urban centers of the eastern Mediterranean. The new religion arrived very early in the city; according to the New Testament book of Acts (11:26), it was there that the followers of Jesus were first called Christians. The single-bishop model of church government appears to have originated in Antioch, and most scholars agree that the Gospel of Matthew was composed there. The growing community was periodically persecuted in the third century CE, but flourished after Emperor Constantine's Edict of Milan (313) granted freedom of worship to Christians. The School of Antioch was renowned as a center of biblical studies advocating a literal interpretation of scripture and emphasis on both the humanity and divinity of Christ.

The Council of Chalcedon (451) established Antioch as a patriarchate but reduced its size by ceding much of its territory to Constantinople and the new Patriarchate of Jerusalem. Chalcedon also triggered a schism within the Church of Antioch, the larger portion rejecting the Christological teaching of the Council and eventually forming what is today the Syriac Orthodox Patriarchate of Antioch and All the East. After Antioch fell to the Arabs in 638, the Greeks who allied with Byzantium and who had accepted Chalcedon experienced many years of persecution. The Greek Patriarchate prospered again from 969, when the Byzantine Empire regained the city, until 1085, when it fell to the Seljuk Turks. During this period of Byzan-

tine rule the older West Syrian liturgy of Antioch was replaced by the Byzantine liturgy. In 1098 the Latin Crusaders took Antioch and established a kingdom that lasted nearly two centuries. A line of Latin patriarchs was set up, while a Greek succession continued in exile.

The Greek Patriarchate returned to Antioch after the city was taken by the Egyptian Mamelukes in 1268. By now Antioch had been reduced to a small town, and the Patriarchate moved permanently to Damascus in the 14th century. The area fell to the Ottoman Turks in 1516 and remained under their control until World War I. The Christians of the area had been reduced to a minority, and the church was further weakened by the activity of Western missionaries. A domestic quarrel among the Orthodox resulted in the election of two patriarchs in 1724, one Catholic and one Orthodox, and the church split into separate Greek Orthodox and Melkite Greek Catholic communities. Even though in recent centuries the faithful have been composed almost entirely of Arabs, the line of ethnic Greek patriarchs continued until 1898, when the last Greek patriarch was deposed. An ethnic Arab patriarch was elected the next year, and all subsequent patriarchs have been Arabs.

Today the Patriarchate's Holy Synod is composed of the patriarch and all the active metropolitans. Meeting at least annually, it has the purpose of electing the patriarch and other bishops, preserving the faith, and taking measures against violations of ecclesiastical order. There is also a General Community Council made up of the Holy Synod and lay representatives. Meeting twice a year, this body is responsible for financial, educational, juridical, and administrative matters. When a new patriarch needs to be chosen, the council selects three candidates, one of which is then elected by the Holy Synod. Patriarch Ignatius IV (elected 1979) has been very active in the ecumenical movement and has encouraged dialogue with the Syrian Orthodox Church and the Melkite Catholic Church in an effort to reunite the three main segments of the ancient Antiochian patriarchate. In 1970, the Patriarchate established St. John of Damascus Academy of Theology, located near Tripoli, Lebanon, which in 1988 was incorporated into Balamand University.

There has been extensive immigration from the homeland of this church in Syria and Lebanon to various parts of the world in recent decades, especially to North and South America. The Antiochian Orthodox Christian Archdiocese of North America also includes a number of Western-rite parishes, for the most part composed of former Episcopalians. The archdiocese maintains a website at http://www.antiochian.org. The total membership of the patriarchate today is about 750,000.

Greek Orthodox Patriarchate of Antioch and All the
    East
His Beatitude Patriarch Ignatius IV
PO Box 9
Damascus
Syria
http://www.antiochpat.org/

Ronald Roberson

See also: Melkite Catholic Church; Syriac Orthodox Patriarchate of Antioch and All the East.

References

Downey, G. *Ancient Antioch.* Princeton, NJ: Princeton University Press, 1963.

Dick, Ignace. *Les Melkites: Grecs-Orthodoxes et Grecs-Catholiques des Patriarcats d'Antioche, d'Alexandrie et de Jérusalem.* Turnhout, Belgium: Editions Brepols, 1994.

Korolevsky, Cyril. *Christian Antioch.* Trans. by John Collorafi. Fairfax, VA: Eastern Christian Publications, 2003.

Greek Orthodox Patriarchate of Jerusalem

This is the fourth-ranking autocephalous church in the Eastern Orthodox communion. It includes the Orthodox Christians living in Israel, Palestine, and Jordan.

The earliest Christian community in Jerusalem was decimated by the Roman destructions of the city in 70 and 135 CE. By the time the church in Palestine was organized in the late second century, the bishop of Jerusalem was subordinate to the metropolitan of Caesarea Maritima within the Patriarchate of Antioch. After peace was granted to Christians by Constantine in 313, Jerusalem became a great center of Christian life and pilgrimage, in part because of the Basilica of the Holy Sepulchre and other churches built by Constantine and his mother, Helen. Given its newfound importance, the Council of Chalcedon in 451 made Jerusalem a patriarchate ranking immediately after Antioch in status.

Christian Jerusalem suffered a terrible disaster in 614 when it was sacked by invading Persians, who destroyed most of its churches and monasteries. In 637 the city surrendered to the Arab armies that had besieged it for four months, and subsequently under Arab rule much of the population gradually converted to Islam.

In 1099, Jerusalem fell to the Crusaders, who established a Latin kingdom that endured for almost a century. Rome created a Latin Patriarchate of Jerusalem, but a line of Greek patriarchs continued in exile, usually residing in Constantinople. They began to live in or near Jerusalem again following the destruction of the Crusader kingdom by the Seljuk Turks in 1187. In 1247 the city was taken by the Egyptian Mamelukes, and in 1516 it fell to the Ottoman Turks, who ruled the city for 400 years.

Under Ottoman rule various Christian groups frequently struggled for control of the holy places in Jerusalem. In the mid-19th century the Turks confirmed Greek control over most of them. This arrangement remained in place under the British mandate beginning in 1917 and under subsequent Jordanian and Israeli administrations.

Even though most of the Patriarchate's faithful, including most of the married parish priests, have long been ethnic Arabs, since 1543 all the patriarchs of Jerusalem and most of the bishops have been ethnic Greeks drawn from the Brotherhood of the Holy Sepulchre, a monastic community headquartered in the Monastery of St. Constantine and St. Helena in Jerusalem. This has been a source of tension, which broke into the open several times in the 19th century and which continues today. The Holy Synod has vigorously resisted efforts to promote ethnic Arabs to the Episcopate and eventually the Patriarchate, and has continued to affirm its Greek character.

Under its current charter, the Patriarchate has both a synod and a mixed council. The patriarch presides

Greek Orthodox Patriarch of Jerusalem, Theofilos III (right), walks with bishops as he takes part in Easter mass at the Church of the Holy Sepulchre in Jerusalem's Old City, April 23, 2006. (AP Photo/Kevin Frayer)

over the Holy Synod, which can have no more than 18 members and is composed of metropolitans and provincial bishops as well as titular bishops and archimandrites appointed by the patriarch. Questions are decided by majority vote; ties are broken by the patriarch. The mixed council, composed of laity and clergy and over which the patriarch also presides, provides for lay input into the decision-making process.

The Patriarchate is a member of the World Council of Churches and the Middle East Council of Churches. At present it has jurisdiction over Jordan, Israel, and the areas under the control of the Palestinian Authority. Total membership is estimated at 200,000, with no more than 3,500 remaining in Jerusalem itself.

Greek Orthodox Patriarchate of Jerusalem
His Beatitude Patriarch Theophilos III
PO Box 19632-633
Jerusalem
Israel

Ronald Roberson

See also: Jerusalem; Middle East Council of Churches; World Council of Churches.

References

Pulcini, T. "Tensions between the Hierarchy and Laity of the Jerusalem Patriarchate: Historical Perspectives on the Present Situation." *St. Vladimir's Theological Quarterly* 36 (1992): 273–298.

Purvis, James D. *Jerusalem: The Holy City: A Bibliography.* 2 vols. Metuchen, NJ: Scarecrow, 1988.

"Règlement du patriarchat grec orthodoxe de Jérusalem." *Proche Orient Chrétien* 8 (1958): 227–242.

Vatikiotis, P. "The Greek Orthodox Patriarchate of Jerusalem between Hellenism and Arabism." *Middle Eastern Studies* 30 (1994): 619–629.

GREENLAND

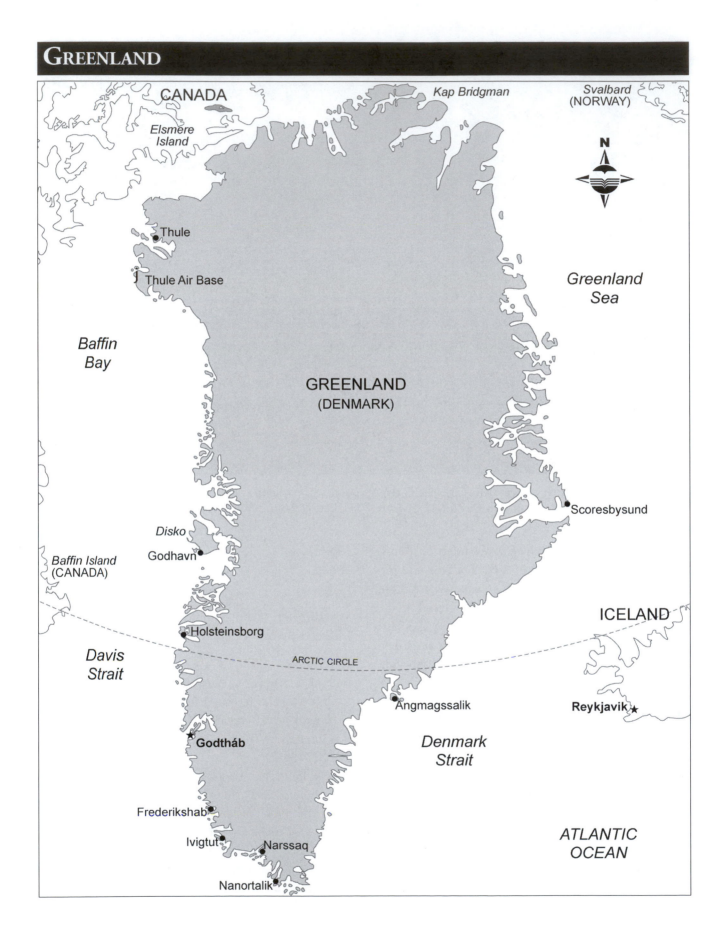

CANADA

Kap Bridgman

Svalbard
(NORWAY)

*Elsmere
Island*

N

Thule

Thule Air Base

*Greenland
Sea*

*Baffin
Bay*

**GREENLAND
(DENMARK)**

Scoresbysund

Disko

Baffin Island
(CANADA)

Godhavn

ICELAND

Holsteinsborg

*Davis
Strait*

ARCTIC CIRCLE

Angmagssalik

Reykjavik ★

Godtháb ★

*Denmark
Strait*

Frederikshab

*ATLANTIC
OCEAN*

Ivigtut

Narssaq

Nanortalik

■ Greenland

Greenland, the world's largest island, is located in the North Atlantic between Iceland and the more northerly islands of Canada. Most of Greenland's 836,330 square miles is covered in ice the year round and thus sparsely populated (57,600 in 2008). It was originally settled by Inuit people (Eskimos), and they remain the dominant element of the population. The majority of people live along the southwest coast, where the capital Nuuk (or Godthåb) is located.

Greenland played an important role in history as a staging area for the Viking exploration of America. Eric the Red established a colony in the 10th century that lasted until the 14th century. The land was rediscovered in the 16th century. In 1815 Denmark claimed it as a colony and established a new Danish settlement in 1894. It was made an integral part of Denmark in 1953, and Greenlanders elected two members to the Danish Parliament (the Folketing). Denmark granted local autonomy in 1979 but maintains hegemony over Greenland's foreign affairs.

Danish Lutherans established work in Greenland in 1721, and Lutheranism retains the allegiance of the majority of the population. The dean of the church, who lives in the capital, works under the bishop of the Lutheran Church in Denmark who resides in Copenhagen. The majority of the Inuit have been baptized, but there is evidence of some continued allegiance to their pre-Christian faith in the far north. The traditional religion was built around the veneration of a female deity, called variously Nerrivik or Sedna, the Old Woman of the Sea.

During the 20th century, a spectrum of churches, from the Roman Catholic Church to the Seventh-day Adventist Church and the Jehovah's Witnesses, developed congregations, but all have had relatively little success. Pentecostals from several Scandinavian countries arrived in the years after World War II, and the Christian Brethren, who had had great success in the Faeroe Islands, initiated work in 1970.

J. Gordon Melton

See also: Christian Brethren; Jehovah's Witnesses; Roman Catholic Church; Seventh-day Adventist Church.

References

Larsen, W. *Kirken under polarstjernen: Fra den grønlandske kirke.* Copenhagen: Lohse, 1972.

Minion, R. *Religions of the Circumpolar North.* Edmonton, Canada: University of Alberta/Boreal Institute for Northern Studies, 1985. BINS Bibliographical series.

Gregory VII Hildebrand

ca. 1021–1085; r. 1073–1085

Gregory VII stands out from his papal colleagues for the reforms he initiated during his decade as pope, though he is far more famous for the successful assertion of

Greenland

Religion	Followers in 1970	Followers in 2010	% of Population	Annual % growth 2000–2010	Followers in 2025	Followers in 2050
Christians	45,600	56,700	95.8	0.35	60,100	59,300
Protestants	35,000	39,900	67.4	0.20	41,600	40,000
Marginals	120	300	0.5	−4.86	500	800
Independents	0	340	0.6	6.96	600	900
Agnostics	100	1,500	2.5	4.33	2,500	3,500
Ethnoreligionists	500	450	0.8	0.45	400	200
Baha'is	200	380	0.6	0.45	550	800
Atheists	0	120	0.2	0.54	180	250
Muslims	0	20	0.0	0.00	30	50
Total population	**46,400**	**59,200**	**100.0**	**0.43**	**63,800**	**64,100**

Portrait of 11th-century pope Gregory VII. He was a vigorous proponent of ecclesiastical reform and an opponent of abuses such as clerical marriage and control of the Church by laity. (Library of Congress)

papal power in his clash with Henry IV (r. 1084–1105), the emperor of the Holy Roman Empire.

The future pope was born in poverty and obscurity around 1021 at Soana in Tuscany, Italy. The young Hildebrand was given a way up and out of his parents' life through his education in a monastery in Rome and the subsequent opportunity to attend the Lateran school. As a teenager, he joined the Benedictine Order, where he was recognized for his intellect and skills. He was invited to the Vatican and served a variety of diplomatic roles to several popes. The arbitrary nature of kingly rule manifested during the reign of Gregory VI (1046–1047), when he was exiled from Rome; however, Leo IX (r. 1049–1054) brought him back to Rome and actually paved the way for Hildebrand's own path to the papacy. Leo campaigned against simony (the purchasing of ecclesiastical office) though he is remembered as the pope at the time of the official break between Rome and the Eastern Orthodox Church. Hildebrand would live to see him under house arrest for a year after his army was defeated by a rising Norman kingdom in southern Italy.

Hildebrand would work for the election of the man who became Pope Alexander II (r. 1061–1073) and assist him in developing a program to further needed reforms. He also used his diplomatic skills to bring about a reconciliation with the Normans. Thus it was almost expected when in 1073, following the death of Alexander II, Hildebrand was elected pope.

As Gregory VII, the new pope moved quickly to continue the reforms he had helped institute during the previous two decades. He began with a decree against simony. He then forbade the practice of lay investiture. It was common in Germany, France, and England, for example, for the ruler to formally hand over the lands attached to the diocese along with the symbols of the bishop's office to each new bishop. Rulers opposed Gregory's measures and in places ignored him as they continued installing bishops with the insignia of their office.

Henry IV reacted to Gregory in 1073 by declaring him deposed. Hildebrand responded by both deposing and excommunicating the emperor. In 1074, with his throne at stake, the emperor backed away and submitted to the papal decisions. Gregory absolved him for his actions, but the conflict did not end. In 1080, Hildebrand again excommunicated Henry IV, but public opinion now seemed to be on Henry's side. Henry IV took advantage of the situation and of Gregory's reduced support by marching on Rome. When he finally seized Rome in 1084, Gregory fled to his hometown, where he died on May 25, 1085.

Under Gregory, Rome experienced its greatest power relative to the secular states of Europe, but the Holy Roman Emperor also demonstrated the limits of that power. Gregory made a variety of claims that few others recognized, over additional territories, and moved more successfully to expand papal influence by establishing diplomatic relations with all the nations of Europe Within the church, he moved on additional reforms, including the strengthening of the celibate clergy, and made an honest attempt to heal the rift with Constantinople.

Gregory was canonized in 1606 by Pope Paul V (r. 1605–1621), and his feast day was subsequently set for May 25.

J. Gordon Melton

See also: Roman Catholic Church.

References

Blumenthal, Uta-Renate. *Papal Reform and Canon Law in the 11th and 12th Centuries*. Brookfield, WI: Ashgate, 1998.

Cowdrey, H. E. J. *Pope Gregory VII, 1073–1085*. Oxford: Oxford University, 1998.

Cushing, Kathleen. *Papacy and Law in the Gregorian Revolution*. Oxford Historical Monographs. New York: Oxford University, 1998.

Macdonald, Allan John. *Hildebrand: A Life of Gregory VII*. London: Methuen, 1932.

Vincent, Marvin Richardson. *The Age of Hildebrand*. Edinburgh: T. &T. Clark, 1897.

■ Grenada

Grenada is an island off the Venezuelan coast, north of Trinidad and Tobago. To its west is the Caribbean Sea and to the east is the Atlantic Ocean. Its 133 square miles are home to 91,000 people (2009), over 90 percent of whom are of African descent. Two small islands to the north of Grenada, Carriacou and Petite Marti-nique, part of the Grenadine archipelago in the Windward Islands chain, are dependencies of Grenada. The remaining Grenadine islands are the nation of St. Vincent and the Grenadines.

When Christopher Columbus became the first European to discover Grenada in 1498, it was largely inhabited by the Carib people, who had previously displaced the Arawak people. The Spanish sailors who came to the island in the decades after Columbus overruled his name choice, and their name, Grenada, a reference to southern Spain, stuck. The Natives resisted any Spanish settlement and it was not until 1650 that the French fought a war with the inhabitants and conquered the island at the cost of all the Native population. The British almost immediately challenged the French, who began importing slaves from Africa to work the land. The British finally won control, under the Treaty of Versailles (1783), part of the complex settlement of the American Revolution. The British moved quickly to lay out sugar plantations and bring in large numbers of Africans to work them. Slavery was finally abolished in 1834.

Grenada remained under British control, first as a crown colony (1877), and then as an associate state within the British Commonwealth (1967), until becoming fully independent in 1974. In 1983, a Marxist military council took control of the island and attempted to establish a Socialist state. Six days later the island jumped on to the front page when it was invaded by

Grenada

Religion	Followers in 1970	Followers in 2010	% of Population	Annual % growth 2000–2010	Followers in 2025	Followers in 2050
Christians	93,500	101,000	96.6	0.89	103,000	90,100
Roman Catholics	60,000	55,300	52.7	0.40	53,500	45,100
Protestants	9,900	27,600	26.2	2.90	28,800	25,000
Anglicans	20,000	12,300	11.7	−1.96	12,000	11,000
Spiritists	400	1,400	1.3	0.94	1,400	1,200
Agnostics	100	1,000	1.0	7.34	1,400	1,600
Hindus	50	700	0.7	0.95	1,000	1,200
Muslims	220	340	0.3	0.95	500	700
Baha'is	120	140	0.1	0.97	160	200
New religionists	50	40	0.0	1.25	50	80
Atheists	0	20	0.0	1.49	20	30
Total population	**94,400**	**105,000**	**100.0**	**0.94**	**108,000**	**95,200**

GRENADA

The map shows Grenada with the following labeled locations: Petit Martinique, Hillsborough, Grand Bay, Carriacou, Ronde Island, Sauteurs, Victoria, Tivoli, Gouyave, Grenada, Grand Roy, Grenville, Marquis, St.George's, Saint Davids, Belmont, Calivigny.

forces from the United States and those of six other Caribbean nations. The Marxist leadership was ousted, and the following year, a general election re-established a democratic government, which has since remained in place.

The French brought the Roman Catholic Church to Granada and a slight majority of the residents belong to it. In 1956, the Diocese of St. George was created. It was a suffragan diocese to the archdiocese of Port-of-Spain (Trinidad) until 1974, when its became a suffragan to the archdiocese of Castries (St. Lucia). The Diocese oversees parishes across Granada and on Carriacou and Petite Martinique.

As British power was established on the island, both the Anglican and Methodist churches arrived in 1784 and 1789, respectively. The congregations are now part of the Church in the Province of the West Indies and Methodist Church in the Caribbean and the Americas. The other church with multiple parishes is the Seventh-day Adventist Church, which arrived in 1903. Now the third largest group on the island, its work is part of its South Caribbean conference. There are also congregations of Pentecostals, the largest following going to the Pentecostal Assemblies of the West Indies and the New Testament Church of God (related to the Church of God [Cleveland, Tennessee]).

J. Gordon Melton

See also: Church in the Province of the West Indies; Church of God (Cleveland, Tennessee); Methodist Church in the Caribbean and the Americas; Roman Catholic Church; Seventh-day Adventist Church.

References

Brizan, George I. *Grenada: Island of Conflict.* Oxford: MacMillan Caribbean, 1998.

Parker, J. A. *A Church in the Sun.* London: Cargate, 1959.

Schoenhals, Kai P. *Grenada.* Santa Barbara, CA: ABC-CLIO, 1990.

Steele, Beverly A. *Grenada: A History of Its People.* Oxford: MacMillan Caribbean, 2003.

Zwernerman, Andrew. *Bloody Terms: The Betrayal of the Church in Marxist Grenada.* South Bend, IN: Greenlawn Press, 1986.

■ Guadeloupe

Guadeloupe, an overseas department of France, includes several islands in the northeast edge of the Caribbean Sea, the main three islands being Basse-Terre, Grande-Terre, and Marie-Galante. Nine of the islands, with a land area of 1,706 square miles, are inhabited by some 445,000 people (as of 2004).

The islands were originally inhabited by the Arawaks, who were in turn overrun by the Caribs. The Spanish attempted to invade the islands in 1493, but were driven off by the Caribs. Finally, the Caribs were defeated by the French in the 1630s, and the latter began to develop the sugar industry. They imported a number of Africans to work the plantations. By the early 18th century, the Africans had completely replaced the Caribs.

In 1815, France renounced the slave trade and restructured its Caribbean possessions as colonies. Slavery was abolished, and to build the labor force indentured servants from India were brought to the Island. Following World War II, Guadeloupe was designated an overseas department, a status granting it much local autonomy.

In 1523, the first missionaries of the Roman Catholic Church on the islands were killed by the Caribs, but later missionaries from the various orders (Capuchins, Dominicans, Jesuits) had more success following the establishment of French authority. In 1816, a prefecture for Guadeloupe and Martinique was established, and in 1850 Guadeloupe was named a suffragan diocese and attached to the Diocese of Bordeaux, in France. The first priest of African descent was ordained in 1925, and the first bishop in 1970. Today, Guadeloupen priests and nuns serve throughout the French-speaking world. The church counts more than 90 percent of the population as Catholic.

Protestant missionary efforts began with the Moravians, who started work in the West Indies in the 1750s. They had only modest success, however. Missionaries from the Reformed Church of France established substantial work, now existing as the Église Evangélique de la Guadeloupe. It has been eclipsed, however, by the Seventh-day Adventist Church, which entered the field in 1965 and is the largest Protestant body in the country. The Adventist churches are part of the French Antilles-Guiana Union Mission. Some success has also been registered by the Jehovah's Witnesses, who came to the islands in the mid-1930s.

A variety of Holiness and Pentecostal groups, most from the United States, have established small works in Guadeloupe since World War II, but most have only one or two congregations.

Indian immigrants from Tamil arrived as workers in the middle of the 19th century. They have developed

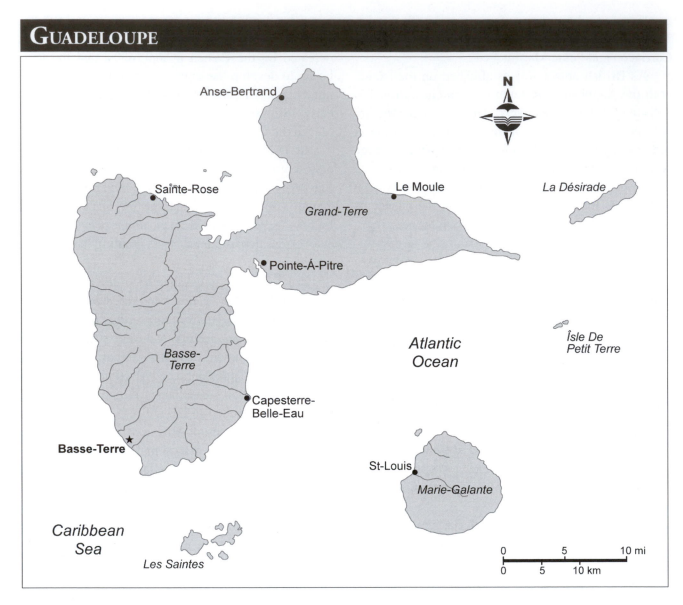

GUADELOUPE

Guadeloupe

Religion	Followers in 1970	Followers in 2010	% of Population	Annual % growth 2000–2010	Followers in 2025	Followers in 2050
Christians	312,000	435,000	95.8	0.80	455,000	434,000
Roman Catholics	307,000	405,000	89.3	0.36	421,000	395,000
Protestants	11,100	34,000	7.5	1.99	38,000	40,000
Marginals	5,000	16,500	3.6	0.07	25,000	30,000
Agnostics	2,900	8,600	1.9	0.79	12,500	18,000
Atheists	2,000	2,800	0.6	0.79	4,000	5,000
Hindus	0	2,300	0.5	0.79	3,000	4,000
Spiritists	0	1,700	0.4	0.80	1,700	1,700
Muslims	3,000	1,700	0.4	0.80	1,600	1,600
Baha'is	500	1,600	0.4	0.80	2,500	3,400
New religionists	100	200	0.0	0.85	350	500
Total population	**320,000**	**454,000**	**100.0**	**0.80**	**481,000**	**468,000**

Catholic church of Saint Peter and Saint Paul in Ponte a Pitre, Guadeloupe. (iStockPhoto.com)

a new religion that synthesizes elements of Catholicism and Hinduism. It is centered upon two female deities, Malieman, the Virgin Mary, and Mari-amma, the Tamil goddess of disease. Islam has been brought to the islands by immigrants from Syria, most of whom are Sunnis. There are also members of the ubiquitous Ancient and Mystical Order Rosae Crucis.

J. Gordon Melton

See also: Ancient and Mystical Order Rosae Crucis; Capuchins; Dominicans; Jehovah's Witnesses; Jesuits; Reformed Church of France; Roman Catholic Church; Seventh-day Adventist Church.

References

Brady, R. E. *Guadeloupe: Mission Field in the West Indies.* Brookhaven, MS: the author, 1966.

La Croix, O. "The French Presence and the Church in Martinique and Guadeloupe." In *New Mission for a New People: Voices from the Caribbean,* edited by D. I. Mitchell. New York: Friendship Press, 1977.

■ Guam

Guam is the southernmost island of the Mariana Islands, and it shares much of the history of the Marianas

GUAM

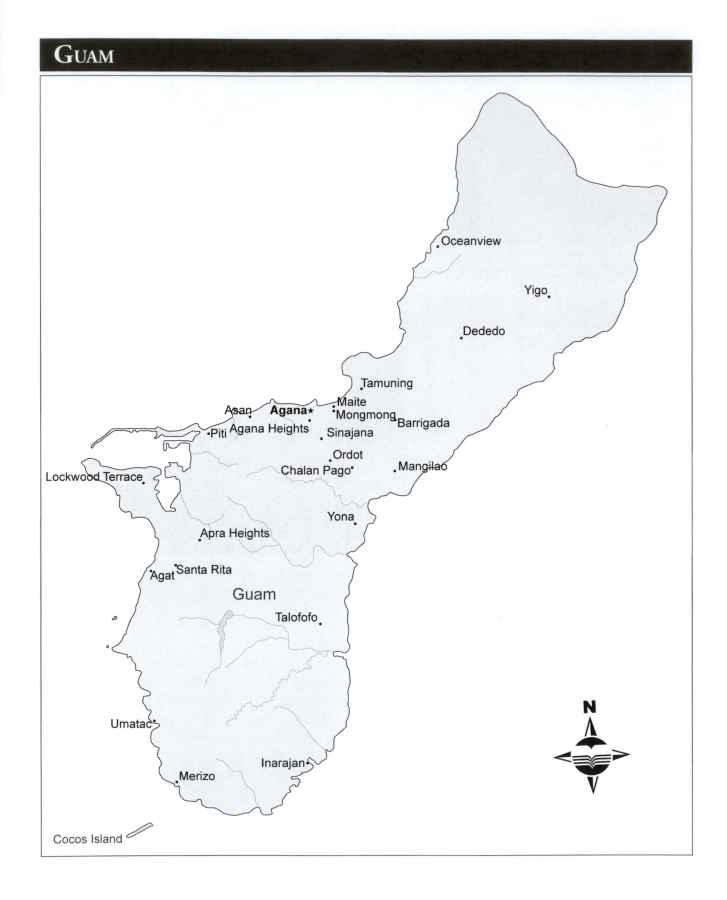

Guam

Religion	Followers in 1970	Followers in 2010	% of Population	Annual % growth 2000–2010	Followers in 2025	Followers in 2050
Christians	82,300	169,000	94.1	1.63	193,000	215,000
Roman Catholics	70,000	138,000	76.7	1.50	152,000	164,000
Protestants	13,100	26,000	14.4	2.48	32,000	38,000
Independents	1,000	4,400	2.4	4.41	6,000	8,000
Agnostics	700	3,100	1.7	4.55	7,000	11,000
Baha'is	500	2,100	1.2	1.67	3,500	5,500
Buddhists	200	1,900	1.1	1.67	3,000	5,000
Chinese folk	650	1,800	1.0	1.67	2,200	2,300
New religionists	0	750	0.4	1.69	1,100	1,500
Ethnoreligionists	1,000	630	0.4	1.68	700	700
Confucianists	150	180	0.1	1.64	300	400
Atheists	0	130	0.1	1.60	300	500
Muslims	0	60	0.0	1.65	200	300
Total population	**85,500**	**180,000**	**100.0**	**1.67**	**211,000**	**242,000**

and Micronesia in general. The lonely island, a mere 224 square miles, rests in the Pacific Ocean 1,000 miles east of the Philippine Islands. Some 176,000 people reside there.

The island was settled in prehistoric times by the Chamorro people, Micronesians. They first encountered Europeans when Ferdinand Magellan arrived in the area in 1521. The Spanish ruled the island and at various times in the last half of the 17th century attempted to exterminate the Native population. By the middle of the 18th century, fewer than 5,000 Chamorros were left alive. The present population is a product of intermarriage with the Spanish and with a number of Filipinos who migrated there along the Spanish trading route.

Guam came into U.S. hands in 1898 as a result of Spain's defeat in the Spanish-American War. After being reclaimed from Japanese control in 1944, it became a major U.S. military center. Guam was part of the trust assigned to the United States by the United Nations, which also began to urge the island's independence. Guam did not participate with the rest of the Marianas in the formation of the Federated States of Micronesia.

Guam remains an American territory. It has a semi-autonomous government that operates under the U.S. Department of the Interior. Residents are U.S. citizens, and the local political system is similar to the U.S. state governments. The island elects one representative (non-voting) to the U.S. House of Representatives. A third of the island is still controlled by the military.

During the Spanish era, the Roman Catholic Church became the dominant religion of the people, and with the intermarriage of the Chamorros with the Spanish and Filipinos, a unique form of Spanish Catholicism became institutionalized on the island. More than 90 percent of the population identify themselves as Roman Catholics.

The large number (more than 20,000) of U.S. military personnel on the island reflects the general spectrum of American religion. Military chaplains hold services for Catholic and Protestant and Free church believers. Jehovah's Witnesses are active on Guam, and there is one congregation of the Church of Christ, Scientist. Members of the Church of Jesus Christ of Latter-day Saints were among the service men and women stationed there during World War II, and following the war the church organized congregations that reached out to local residents. The work on Guam is now designated the Micronesia Guam Mission.

J. Gordon Melton

See also: Church of Christ, Scientist, Church of Jesus Christ of Latter-day Saints; Free Churches; Jehovah's Witnesses; Roman Catholic Church.

References

Mitchell, R. E. "Patron Saints and Pagan Ghosts: The Pairing of Opposites." *Asian Folklore Studies* 45, no. 1 (1986): 101–123.

Rogers, Robert F. *Destiny's Landfall: A History of Guam.* Honolulu: University of Hawaii Press, 1995.

Sullivan, J. *The Phoenix Rises: A Mission History of Guam.* New York: Seraphic Mass Association, 1957.

Guan Yin's Birthday

Guan Yin (aka Kwan Yin; Kannon [Japan] and Chenrezig [Tibet]) is one of the most ubiquitous presences in the world of Chinese religion and among Mahayana and Vajrayana Buddhists everywhere. Also known as Avalokitesvara (a male deity), Guan Yin is the goddess of compassion in Mahayana Buddhism. She also frequently graces the altar of Daoist temples throughout China, where she is frequently compared to the Virgin Mary in Roman Catholicism.

The veneration/worship of Avalokitesvara emerged in China in the third century CE, where it became especially identified with the Pure Land sect, which offered members the goal of rebirth in the heavenly Western Paradise. Three bodhisattvas—Amitabha Buddha, Mahasthamaprapta, and Avalokitesvara—are central to Pure Land practice. As the lord of compassion, Avalokitesvara is seen as an emanation of Amitabha or Amida Buddha (the leader of Pure Land) and as the guard of the world in the time between the departure of the historical Buddha and the future appearance of the coming Buddha, Maitreya.

Guan Yin was introduced in the Lotus Sutra, a Buddhist writing that appeared in 406 CE. Through the next centuries, Guan Yin would evolve as a female equated with Avalokitesvara. Vajrayana Buddhists (most identified with Tibet but also present in Mongolia and China) further popularized Guan Yin as a beautiful, white-robed goddess. She came to be known as the Perceiver of the World Sounds, that is, the cries of those who suffer. She works to relieve all suffering.

Several accounts are given of Guan Yin's origin, but the most popular relate to the story of Miao Shan,

Statue of Guan Yin, the Buddhist goddess of mercy. (J. Gordon Melton)

a seventh-century Chinese princess, who seems to be the source of the feminine representation of Guan Yin.

Miao Shan's parents did not appreciate their daughter, who at an early age expressed an overriding concern to help others. They berated her and forced her to do menial tasks. They finally allowed her to go to a convent, but asked the nuns to mistreat her. Given the barren land in which the monastery was located, they were amazed at her ability to gather wood and tend a flourishing garden.

When the king heard about these miracles, he decided that he was going to kill Miao Shan. After all, the nuns were supposed to have tormented her. But as his henchmen arrived at the monastery, a spirit came out of a fog of clouds and carried her away to safety on a remote island. She lived there on her own for many years, pursuing a life of religious dedication. She was later in a position to give of herself to save her father. Only after traveling to the island to meet the person who had saved his life, did he realize it was Miao Shan and repent of his bad treatment of her. At that moment, the 1,000 arms of 1,000 eyes of Avalokitesvara appeared and Miao Shan disappeared.

As early as the seventh century, Buddhist monks visited Putuo Shan, an island off the coast of Zhejiang, east of Ningpo and south of Shanghai. Later settling there, they built temples and identified this island as the place where Miao Shan had lived and devoted her life to healing and to saving sailors from shipwreck. They spearheaded both the identification of the island with Guan Yin and the veneration of her through northern China.

Guan Yin has numerous manifestations. She is depicted in various forms and her hand posed with appropriated mudras. She almost always is clothed in a long, flowing white robe or dress. She might be holding a rosary, a symbol of her devotion to Buddhism; the Lotus Sutra; a vase that pours compassion on to the world; or a willow branch. She is also seen as assisting barren women and is thus on occasion pictured, like the Virgin Mary, with a child in her arms.

Guan Yin's birthday is celebrated on the 19th day of the 2nd lunar month, usually in March on the Common Era calendar. It is a day for pilgrimages and events at the several temples and shrines in the island, but throughout the Mahayana and Vajrayana world it is acknowledged. In addition to her birthday, Guan Yin is saluted on two other days: her enlightenment day on the 19th day of the 6th lunar month (June) and her renunciation day—when she become a nun—on the 19th day of the 9th lunar month (September).

Guan Yin temples may now be found around the world. Prominent examples include the Kannon temples in northern Tokyo and in Kamakura, Japan; the temple on Waterloo Street in Singapore; Kek Lok Si Temple in Penang, Malaysia; and the Kuan Yin Temple in Honolulu, Hawaii, one of the oldest functioning Buddhist temples in the United States.

Through the centuries, Buddhist have also shown a particular penchant for erecting large statues of Buddha and the Buddhist bodhisattvas. Currently, the largest such statue is one of Guan Yin located at Sanya in Hainan Province of the People's Republic of China.

Completed in 2005, its stands 354 feet. (In contrast, the Statue of Liberty stands at a mere 151 feet.) The Guan Yin statue also eclipses the largest Buddha statue, located at Ushiku, Japan (328 feet), not to mention the well-known Buddha of Kamakura, a mere 36 feet.

J. Gordon Melton

See also: Bodhisattva; Mahayana Buddhism; Mudras; Putuo Shan; Statues—Buddhist; Tibetan Buddhism.

References

Blofeld, John. *Bodhissatva of Compassion: The Mystical Tradition of Kuan Yin*. Boulder, CO: Shambhala, 1978.

Karcher, Stephen. *Kuan Yin*. London: Time Warner, 2003.

Palmer, Ramsey, Kwok. *Kuan Yin: Myths and Prophecies of the Chinese Goddess of Compassion*. San Francisco: Thorsons, 1995.

Yu, Chun-Fang. *Kuan Yin*. New York: Colombia University Press, 2000.

■ Guatemala

The Republic of Guatemala is the most populous country in Central America, bordered by the Pacific Ocean to the west and the Caribbean Sea to the east, and adjacent to Mexico (west and north), Belize (northeast), Honduras (east), and El Salvador (southeast). The total population of Guatemala was 12,728,111, according to the July 2007 census. Most of Guatemala's population is rural, although urbanization is accelerating in the departmental capitals and in the national capital of Guatemala City (estimated population 2,156,348).

Guatemalan society is divided into two main ethnic categories: Amerindian and *ladino*. More than half of Guatemalans are descendants of indigenous Mayan peoples. Hispanicized Mayans and *mestizos* (mixed Spanish and Amerindian ancestry) are known as ladinos. However, the major factors for determining the size of the Amerindian population by the government have been language and dress, rather than race, which tends to underestimate the strength of the Amerindian population. According to Wycliffe Bible Translators' *Ethnologue* (2005), the population of Guatemala was

Guatemala

Religion	Followers in 1970	Followers in 2010	% of Population	Annual % growth 2000–2010	Followers in 2025	Followers in 2050
Christians	5,384,000	13,993,000	97.3	2.48	19,303,000	26,509,000
Roman Catholics	4,346,000	12,100,000	84.2	2.98	15,377,000	19,961,000
Protestants	269,000	2,400,000	16.7	4.24	3,500,000	5,200,000
Independents	104,000	1,800,000	12.5	4.37	2,700,000	3,800,000
Ethnoreligionists	5,000	120,000	0.8	2.51	140,000	160,000
Agnostics	9,000	140,000	1.0	5.11	280,000	480,000
Atheists	3,000	62,000	0.4	2.51	100,000	160,000
Spiritists	10,000	30,000	0.2	2.51	42,000	60,000
Baha'is	4,400	20,700	0.1	2.51	45,000	80,000
Chinese folk	1,000	4,400	0.0	2.51	5,800	9,000
New religionists	1,000	2,400	0.0	2.51	4,000	6,000
Buddhists	1,000	2,500	0.0	2.50	3,600	6,200
Jews	1,000	1,200	0.0	2.49	1,200	1,200
Muslims	0	1,100	0.0	2.52	1,500	1,800
Total population	**5,419,000**	**14,377,000**	**100.0**	**2.51**	**19,926,000**	**27,473,000**

55 percent Amerindian, 44 percent mestizo, and about 1 percent other races. Fifty-four living languages are spoken in Guatemala (not including those spoken by immigrant groups) among 23 ethnolinguistic groups, with Spanish being the dominant language (about 44 percent, followed by the principal Mayan languages of Quiché, Mam, Cakchiquel, and Kekchí).

The current president of Guatemala (r. 2008–2012), Alvaro Colom Caballeros of the Unidad Nacional de la Esperanza (UNE), is a center-left politician, industrial engineer, and Mayan priest who studied traditional Mayan cosmology under the guidance of the priest Cirilo Pérez Oxjal, a respected Quiché leader and former president of the Consejo Continental de Ancianos de América. Colom was elected president in November 2007 due to the strong support he received from the politically mobilized Amerindian population that had grown tired of being marginalized by ladinos within Guatemalan society and was resentful of ladino dominance in national politics.

Christianity remains a strong and vital force in Guatemalan society, but its composition has changed during generations of political and social unrest. Historically, the dominant religion has been Roman Catholicism. In 1980, 84.2 percent of the population was reported to be Roman Catholic; 13.8 percent was Protestant (most of whom identified as evangelicals); and

about 2 percent was identified with "other religious groups" (including traditional Mayan religions) or had "no religious affiliation." However, by 1990, the Catholic population had declined to 60.4 percent (a decline of 24 percentage points), while the Protestant population increased to 26.4 percent (an increase of 12.6 percentage points); 2.1 percent were adherents to "other religions"; and 11.1 percent had "no religious affiliation" (CID-Gallup Poll, June 1990).

Surprisingly, during the decade of the 1990s, a series of public opinion polls revealed little change in religious affiliation between 1990 and 2001. However, between 2001 and 2006, the size of the Protestant population increased from about 25 percent to almost 31 percent in 2006, while the Catholic population remained relatively constant at 55 to 57 percent. Those affiliated with other religions also remained steady at 2 to 3 percent, while those with no religious affiliation declined to about 10 percent.

A characteristic of most cities, towns, and villages in Guatemala is the presence of a Catholic church situated on the central square or plaza. The Metropolitan Cathedral (original construction 1782–1815) in Guatemala City is a visible sign of the historical presence of the Catholic Church in the life of the nation.

The mestizo population of Guatemala has strong ties to traditional Roman Catholicism brought to the

GUATEMALA

Americas by Spanish missionaries, who themselves carried the cultural baggage of their Iberian homeland with its pre-Christian Celtic spirituality and medieval Roman Catholicism. Consequently, the general religiosity of the ladinos of Guatemala contains elements of European as well as Amerindian "popular Catholicism" (syncretism).

The Roman Catholic Church   Conquistador Pedro de Alvarado y Contreras (1495–1541) and his army

San Andres Xecul Catholic church, Guatemala. (Maria T. Weinmann/Dreamstime.com)

invaded Guatemala during 1523–1527 and subjugated many of the Amerindian peoples to even more than the customary atrocities. The Amerindians rapidly declined under the imposed system of slavery and heavy tribute. Alvarado was subsequently appointed governor of Guatemala by Charles I of Spain (r. 1516–1556) and remained its governor until his death.

Even before the conquest was complete, the Dominican friars had taken up residence among the Quiché and had begun the difficult task of converting the Mayans to the Catholic faith. In 1530, Father Francisco Marroquín (1535–1563) arrived from Spain to organize the Catholic Church in Guatemala, and in 1533 he was confirmed as the country's first bishop. He gave special attention to the indigenous people and their languages, becoming particularly proficient in Quiché, into which language he translated the catechism.

Beginning in 1536–1537, Spanish friar Bartolomé de las Casas (1484–1566) established a Dominican convent at Santiago de Guatemala for the conversion of the natives, and applied methods of peaceful evangelization in the region of Vera Paz. Las Casas became well known for his advocacy of the rights of Amerindian peoples of the Americas, whose cultures he described with great care.

With the added assistance of the Franciscans, who entered the territory in 1541, the general "conversion of the Indians" was gradually accomplished, though the geography prevented extensive contact with remote Amerindian groups. In the early years of Spanish colonization, the Catholic clergy protected indigenous peoples who lived near the missions. Laws were passed in 1542 at the instigation of Catholic missionaries that attempted to eliminate some of the harsher practices of exploitation that had been imposed on Amerindians living in remote areas by Spanish authorities.

During the colonial period the Catholic Church was an agency of the Spanish Crown, although the friars' evangelization methods sometimes occasioned conflict with the civil authorities. Catholicism in Guatemala developed around the veneration of the saints; local lay religious associations, called *cofradías*, were charged with caring for the saint's images in local communities. Cofradías in Guatemala are a mix of Spanish and Amerindian practices.

Santiago de Guatemala was made a diocese by Pope Paul III on December 18, 1534. The Diocese of Guatemala was raised to a metropolitan see by Pope Benedict XIV on December 16, 1743, with the dioceses of Nicaragua and Comayagua (Honduras) being subordinate to it. By 1750, more than 424 Catholic churches and 23 missions had been established in the territory of Guatemala.

The Diocese of San Salvador, erected by Pope Gregory XVI (r. 1831–1846) in 1842, and the Diocese of San José de Costa Rica, erected in 1850, also became part of the Metropolitan Church of Santiago de Guatemala. Together with the Archdiocese of Guatemala, these four subordinate dioceses (Nicaragua, Honduras, El Salvador, and Costa Rica) constituted the ecclesiastical Province of Central America.

Historically, the Roman Catholic Church has had a strong popular base among ladinos and Europeans but has met with more resistance in predominantly Amerindian areas of the country where indigenous religious beliefs and practices are maintained. Spanish missionaries played a critical role by establishing new religious, social, and economic structures in the colony; building monasteries, churches, and schools with forced Indian labor; and helping to organize the Mayan labor force for the new cacao and indigo plantations.

Independence from Spain in the 1820s and the emergence of a new economic class of coffee growers in the later 19th century, which included many German immigrants, weakened the hegemony of the Catholic Church. Politically, Guatemala achieved its independence from Spain in 1821–1823, after nearly 300 years of Spanish colonial rule, when the Captaincy-General of Guatemala became the United Provinces of Central America. In 1838, the independent Republic of Guatemala was created under rebel leader Rafael Carrera (1814–1865). In 1852, Carrera's government signed a Concordat with the Vatican, repealed the anticlerical legislation established under the rule of Francisco Morazán (r. 1829–1838), reinstated the Catholic reli-

gious orders, and allowed the Catholic clergy to operate the nation's few schools.

Following the death of Carrera in 1865, the Liberal Justo Rufino Barrios came to power (r. 1873–1885) and the Catholic Church was again subjected to harsh legislation. The Jesuits were again expelled, the archbishop and bishops were exiled, tithes were eliminated, convents and monasteries were closed, church property was confiscated, priests were prohibited from wearing clerical garb and were barred from teaching, religious processions were proscribed, and civil marriage was declared obligatory. These anticlerical laws so crippled the Catholic Church in Guatemala that it has never recovered its former influence. In addition, Barrios also declared "religious freedom" and invited Protestant denominations to establish churches and schools in his country.

It was not until the 1930s that the Roman Catholic Church began to recover some of its former power and prestige in Guatemalan society. Under the dictatorship of General Jorge Ubico (r. 1931–1944), the Catholic Church was able to exercise more political influence, but when Ubico was overthrown in 1944 by a coalition of progressive army officers and civilians who were intent on modernizing Guatemala, the Catholic Church felt that its own social and political power was being attacked.

During the 1940s and 1950s, the Catholic hierarchy and its lay organizations—the Society for the Propagation of the Faith and Catholic Action—joined forces with the Anti-Communist Party (PUA) and other right-wing organizations to counteract the liberalizing trends of the nation's democratically elected, reformist civilian governments during the period 1944–1954. Around 1949, a new Catholic reform movement began in Guatemala, called Acción Católica (Catholic Action), a militant lay Catholic organization engaged in the "re-conversion of Guatemalan Indians," among other things. Their tactics caused deep resentment in the traditional Mayan communities. This reform movement also produced renewed attacks by Catholics on the Protestants and on Bible reading.

In 1950, Colonel Jacobo Arbenz Guzmán (r. 1950–1954) won the presidency. He accepted support from the clandestine Guatemalan Communist Party before and after the election and later promoted the legalization of the Communist Party. Conservatives and officials of the Catholic Church used anti-Communist rhetoric to attack the Arbenz administration, which led to the triumph of the CIA-engineered, right-wing military coup d'etat led by Colonel Carlos Castillo Armas.

Under President Castillo Armas's (r. 1955–1957) regime, thousands of people were killed in a purge of Communists and radical nationalists. At the same time, a new Guatemalan Christian Democratic Party was established in 1955 with strong support from the Catholic Church. The new government removed restrictions on the Catholic Church by allowing ownership of property, the entrance of foreign clergy and religious workers, Catholic religious instruction in the public schools, and wedding services officiated by priests. In turn, the Catholic hierarchy "blessed the military government" and supported its anti-Communist ideology and Cold War tactics.

One characteristic of this entire modern period, especially after the mid-1960s, was the frightful abuse of human rights by repressive, right-wing military dictatorships with the tacit support of the Conservative, anti-Communist elements within the Catholic hierarchy. Military and paramilitary counterinsurgency operations, mostly in the countryside against leftist guerrilla forces, led to the killing of tens of thousands of alleged "political dissidents and their supporters" between 1960 and 1996, many of whom were Mayans. Some exiled priests and nuns formed the "Guatemalan Church in Exile" and continued to try to draw international attention to the bloody civil conflict between repressive government armed forces and the "popular insurrection" led by leftist guerrilla rebels.

In response to the increasingly autocratic rule of General José Miguel Ramón Ydígoras Fuentes, who took power in 1958, a group of junior military officers from the military academy revolted (1960). When they failed, several went into hiding and became the nucleus of the 13th of November Revolutionary Movement (MR-13), which pursued armed insurrection against the government for the next 36 years (1960–1996). The civil war evolved into the brutal repression by military forces of all dissidents (including Catholic priests, nuns, and lay leaders), *campesinos* (rural peasants), and any indigenous communities suspected of collaborating with the insurgents.

The Guatemalan National Revolutionary Unity (URNG) was formed as a guerrilla umbrella organization in February 1982. Finally, in 1996, a peace accord signed by the Guatemalan government and the URNG ended the longest civil war in Latin American history. The URNG transformed into a legitimate political party.

During the 1950s, the Catholic Church was revitalized by the arrival of many new foreign priests, nuns, and other religious workers (mostly with a conservative political orientation), which provided needed resources for establishing new churches and schools and for expanding its social assistance efforts throughout the country. Some of the reforms introduced by the Second Vatican Council had a significant impact on the Mayans because the language of the liturgy was changed from Latin to vernacular languages; the change to Spanish was immediate, but increasingly the Mayan languages were used in indigenous areas.

In December 1973, the Catholic Charismatic Renewal (CCR) was established in Guatemala as a "laymen's apostolic organization" authorized by the hierarchy of the Roman Catholic Church. The CCR gained popularity among middle- and upper-class Guatemalans until certain restrictions were implemented by Catholic authorities beginning in June 1974 under the supervision of a Pastoral Service Team, led by Monseñor Ramiro Pellecer. As a result, many "Spirit-filled" Catholics chose to leave the Catholic Church and join evangelical churches, especially in Guatemala City. By September 1979, the CCR had grown strong enough to fill the National Stadium during a rally led by Father Francis McNutt, then a Dominican priest.

The Catholic voice in Guatemala is often discordant as Catholics respond to a variety of social concerns. Individual Catholics frequently hold opinions that diverge from the hierarchy, and the hierarchy itself is not always unified. Within the Catholic Church in Guatemala social stances on issues such as abortion, ordination of women, and divorce tend to mirror those of the Vatican. Abortion is illegal in the Guatemalan Penal Code, but family planning is available in much of the country.

The modernization of the Catholic Church that came with the Second Vatican Council (1962–1965) dovetailed with aspects of the older Catholic Action movement's agenda; there was a push for more direct pastoral involvement with social concerns. In Guatemala this resulted in a wave of cooperative and social organizing. Catholic Action's "Christian base communities" stressed education and consciousness-raising, and cooperated with one another throughout the highlands. They presented an alternative to both the guerrillas and the government, and, in many cases, peacefully supported the political goals of the guerrillas. This movement was attacked in the late 1960s and again in the late 1970s and early 1980s, when many priests and religious workers were killed or threatened.

During the 1970s, Catholic religious orders began an intensive missionary effort in isolated areas where indigenous groups practice Mayan spirituality. A school was established to train expatriate missionaries in the cultural practices of the indigenous groups, and in language acquisition, politics, and social concerns.

During the 20th century, the Catholic Church, as an institution, supported the status quo fostered by Conservative government policies that favored ladino society over Amerindian groups and that defended "national security" over human rights. However, a minority of Roman Catholic leaders (including bishops, priests, and nuns) dissented and opted to defend the interests of the poor and oppressed. Some of these priests and religious workers became martyrs for their faith during the Guatemalan civil war as well as in the aftermath.

The majority of the members of male Catholic religious orders in Guatemala have always been expatriates, primarily from Spain, Italy, and North America. Indigenous leaders were seldom trained. Native languages, values, and music were usually ignored and sometimes repudiated. In 1970, less than 15 percent of all Catholic clergy and religious workers were native Guatemalans.

In March 2009, the Guatemalan Catholic Church administered two archdioceses: the Archdiocese of Guatemala led by Archbishop Cardinal Rodolfo Quezada Toruño, appointed in June 2001, and the Archdiocese of Los Altos Quetzaltenango-Totonicapán (erected in 1996) led by Archbishop Oscar Julio Vian Morales, S.D.B., appointed in April 2007. In 2001, the 2 archdioceses reported a total of 14 dioceses and 428 parishes, which were served by 359 diocesan priests and 461 religious priests (for a total of 820), 6 permanent deacons, 769 male religious workers, and 2,059 female religious workers.

The Protestant Movement Pioneer efforts were made by English Baptist missionaries and laymen in the British colony of Belize to distribute the scriptures in the Spanish territory of Guatemala. The first known effort took place in 1824 when Joseph Bourne, an English Baptist missionary stationed in Belize Town, visited the ports of Ysabal in Guatemala and Omoa in Honduras.

Frederick Crowe (1819–1846), a young English seaman who had became a Baptist in Belize City in 1837, accepted an offer from the Eastern Coast of Central America Commercial and Agricultural Company in January 1841 to move to the new settlement of Abbottsville, where he worked as a school teacher and served as a voluntary chaplain. While residing in Abbottsville, Crowe made a difficult journey to Guatemala City as a missionary and Bible salesman (colporteur). Although Crowe was supported in his efforts by a few Liberal families, he was strongly opposed by the Catholic clergy and Conservative politicians, who forced his expulsion from Guatemala in April 1846.

Liberal President Justo Rufino Barrios (1873–1875) finally established freedom of speech and worship in Guatemala. Barrios also invited the Presbyterian Church of New York City (now an integral part of the Presbyterian Church [U.S.A.]) to send missionaries to Guatemala. Reverend John Clark Hill arrived in late 1882 to begin work in Guatemala City among 30 to 40 distinguished English-speaking foreigners who were already Protestants. The English worship services in Guatemala City, begun by Hill in 1882, were continued by James R. Hosmer and a succession of other pastors. Today, the nondenominational Union Church, located in Plazuela España, traces its founding to that date. This is the oldest Protestant church in Guatemala.

The third Protestant missionary organization to work in Guatemala was the Central American Mission (now known as CAM International, with headquarters in Dallas, Texas), which sent Mr. and Mrs. Edward Bishop to Guatemala City in 1899. The first CAM church established at a major intersection in the capital city became the "mother church" to hundreds of

CAM congregations throughout the country. The Central American Evangelical Church Association (CAM-related) became one of the largest Protestant denominations in Guatemala and assumed an important role in training pastors and lay leaders for the whole non-Pentecostal evangelical movement, originally through its Central American Bible Institute (founded in 1926), superseded in 1965 by the Central American Theological Seminary (known as SETECA).

By 1935, other Protestant mission agencies were working in Guatemala. The Church of the Nazarene traces its origins to work begun in 1901 by missionaries affiliated with The Pentecostal Mission (TPM), which merged into the Church of the Nazarene in 1915. In 1902, the California Friends Mission (Quakers) began its ministry in the southeastern part of the country, near the border with Honduras and El Salvador, with headquarters in the Department of Chiquimula. The Seventh-day Adventist Church arrived in 1908 and began work in Guatemala City and Quetzaltenango, the nation's second largest city. The Christian Brethren began work in Guatemala in 1924 through the ministry of Carlos Kramer in Quetzaltenango, a German-heritage Guatemalan and former Presbyterian.

The Pentecostal movement had its origin in Guatemala in the ministry of the Reverend and Mrs. Amos Bradley, who served in Guatemala affiliated with the Pentecostal Holiness Church (PHC, organized in 1911 in North Carolina). The Bradleys were that denomination's first missionaries in Central America during 1913–1918, while serving in Guatemala and El Salvador. Previously, the Bradleys had been independent Holiness missionaries in Guatemala between 1909 and 1912.

In 1916, Thomas Pullin and Charles Furman of the United and Free Gospel Missionary Society (Turtle Creek, Pennsylvania) arrived in Guatemala with their wives to begin an itinerant evangelistic ministry in El Quiché, Totonicapán. In 1920, both couples returned to the United States to strengthen their base of support. When Furman and his family returned to Guatemala in 1922, they were affiliated with the PHC. In 1934, while on furlough in the United States, Furman joined the Church of God (Cleveland, Tennessee) and returned to Guatemala to become that denomination's first missionary in the country. He proceeded to

visit PHC churches and encourage the leaders to join him in the ranks of the Church of God, which resulted in 14 PHC churches switching their affiliation to the Church of God. By 1980, this Pentecostal denomination had grown to 664 churches and 234 missions with 34,451 members.

Pastors and missionaries of the Assemblies of God in El Salvador began work in the Department of Jutiapa, Guatemala, in 1927; however, it was not until 1937–1938 that Ralph Williams and John Franklin were successful in organizing the first six churches in Guatemala. By 1940, 20 churches had been organized and work had begun in 36 additional towns. Following a healing campaign by T. L. Osborn in Guatemala City in 1953, the Assemblies of God work began to grow more rapidly. In 1990, there were 1,385 churches, 2,329 preaching points, 1,630 ordained pastors, 2,379 lay pastors, 8 Bible institutes, and 224,751 adherents. Total baptized membership was estimated to be about 127,500 in 1990.

The Prince of Peace Evangelical Church Association was formed in 1956 by José María Muñoz in Guatemala City among a group of believers that had left the Central Assembly of God. Many of the early members of this new denomination had been members of other evangelical churches, but were drawn to Muñoz's ministry because of his popular radio ministry and powerful Pentecostal preaching. From a group of 100 in 1956, membership grew to 4,500 in 1967 and to 29,130 in 1980 with 567 congregations.

The Elim Christian Mission began as a house church in 1962 in Guatemala City, led by a well-known medical doctor and radio personality, Dr. Otoniel Ríos, who became an evangelical during the Evangelism-in-Depth campaigns in 1961. In 1973, Ríos terminated his medical practice to devote himself to a full-time pastoral ministry and building up a large central church, which grew to 3,000 members in 1979 after the congregation moved into a new auditorium. By 1980, the ministry of Elim included 147 congregations (churches and missions) with a total membership of 15,290, with a growing association of sister churches in El Salvador.

The Charismatic Renewal movement began in Guatemala during 1969–1970 with small group meetings among both Catholics and Protestants, some of which were led by Tim Rovenstine of World MAP.

Rovenstine was instrumental in bringing Catholics and Protestants together in the beginnings of the movement in the early 1970s, aided by visiting members of the Full Gospel Business Men's Fellowship, members of the Word of God Community in Ann Arbor, Michigan, and Father Francis MacNutt and his team of Charismatic leaders that included Methodist pastors Joe Petree and Tommy Tyson.

One of the main ecumenical bridges between Catholics and Protestants during the 1970s and 1980s was the John 17:21 Fellowship, which was associated with David du Plessis in the United States and Europe. However, a Latin American branch of the John 17:21 Fellowship was established by U.S. Charismatic pastors Robert Thomas, Paul Northrup, and Bill Finke (all former missionaries in Latin America), together with local leaders, in Guatemala City after the destructive 1976 earthquake, which resulted in massive relief and development operations by local and international service organizations. The Latin American branch of the John 17:21 Fellowship was coordinated by Robert Thomas (a pastor in Los Altos, California), who worked closely with Friar Alfonzo Navarro and the Catholic Missionaries of the Holy Spirit in Mexico City.

Protestantism in Guatemala has become a very diverse phenomenon after a century of growth and development since the first missionaries arrived. A 1978–1981 national survey of the Protestant movement in Guatemala conducted by a PROCADES-SEPAL (Proyecto Centroamericano de Estudios Socio-Religiosos/Servir a Pastores e Lideres) research team revealed the presence of more than 200 denominations and independent church associations with 334,453 baptized church members (15 years or older) in 1980. Between 1960 and 1980, the national Protestant average annual growth rate was 11.8 percent. The total Protestant population of Guatemala was estimated by PROCADES to be 13.8 percent in 1980, up significantly from a mere 2.8 percent in 1950.

Despite differences of tradition, doctrine, and practice, many of the leaders of the respective Protestant denominations in Guatemala met together periodically, although informally, to discuss common problems and resolve conflicts during the period 1909–1935. However, a formal structure was organized in 1935 to facilitate interdenominational cooperation, the Synod of the Evangelical Church in Guatemala. In 1951, the Evangelical Synod was restructured and its name changed to the Evangelical Alliance of Guatemala (AEG).

On February 4, 1976, Guatemala City and a large part of the country (16 of 22 departments) were severely shaken by a major earthquake that registered 7.5 on the Richter scale, which caused massive destruction and loss of life. Out of a total population of approximately 5,500,000, more than 22,000 were killed, more than 77,000 injured, and more than 1,000,000 made homeless. This was called the most severe natural catastrophe in Central America during the 20th century.

The response of Protestant denominations and service agencies, both national and international, to the survivors in the aftermath of this earthquake was swift and significant, in terms of both emergency assistance and more long-term community development activities. This produced a favorable reaction among those who received immediate as well as long-term assistance from evangelical organizations, with a resulting burst of growth in attendance and membership of evangelical churches.

With growing social strength in Guatemalan society, the Protestant community in general has taken more interest in the humanitarian problems and needs of the larger society and a more active role in community affairs, but not necessarily in politics. Their theology tends to be pre-millennial and their hope is that God will "rapture" them out of this present evil world to escape the Great Tribulation.

During the period 1960–1980, Guatemala became a showcase for the growth of the Protestant movement in Latin America, but the enthusiasm of evangelical leaders regarding continued high rates of church growth in Guatemala often exceeded the reality. A series of public opinion polls taken between 1990 and 2001 in Guatemala helped to correct some of the erroneous growth projections made by evangelical leaders: the CID-Gallup company reported that the Protestant population was 26.4 percent in May 1990 and 25 percent in April 1996. Early in 2001, SEPAL conducted a public opinion poll in Guatemala that showed Protestants to be 25.3 percent of the national population. Therefore, it seems clear that the size of the Protestant population had not changed in Guatemala in more than a decade, although the number of Protestant congregations had continued to increase: from about 6,450 in 1980, to 9,298 in 1987, to about 18,000 in 2001. It seems logical to assume that if the number of Protestant congregations grew by 258 percent between 1980 and 2001 that the total membership probably increased by a similar rate of growth. So why did the size of the Protestant population remain stable at about 25 percent between 1990 and 2001?

One possible explanation is that there may have been "a great falling away" (desertion or exodus) of Protestant adherents in Guatemala during the 1980s–1990s due to discouragement about the performance of evangelical politicians, such as General Efraín Ríos Montt (military dictator during 1982–1983) and Jorge Serrano (president during 1990–1993). During the 1980s, evangelical public opinion was divided for and against support for General Ríos Montt, who offended many people—Catholics and Protestants alike—by his public radio messages that blended anti-Marxist rhetoric with evangelical sermons. The leadership of the Evangelical Alliance of Guatemala, which represents most evangelical organizations in the country, decided to back off from publicly supporting Ríos Montt and to distance themselves from his government to avoid a possible negative backlash and persecution of evangelicals should General Ríos Montt be overthrown. When this happened in 1983, the expected backlash did not take place.

In 2001, Southern Baptist missionary Roger Grossman reported the following statistics on adherents, based on his extensive national research project: Assemblies of God (600,540), Church of God (Cleveland, Tennessee) (487,984), Independent (188,421), Prince of Peace Church (179,038), Seventh-day Adventist Church (175,849), Association of Central American Churches (162,175), Pentecostal Church of God (136,743), Church of the Nazarene (102,345), Elim Christian Mission (105,435), all Baptists (75,648), all Presbyterians (65,800), Bethany Church (60,000), MIEL (43,929), New Church of God (28,129), Galilee Church of God–Anderson, Indiana (25,705), Friends/Quakers (23,347), Church of God of Prophecy (22,984), Evangelical Mission of the Holy Spirit (18,790),

Calvary Church (17,730), Verbo (14,649), Evangelical House of God (14,104), Living Water Church–Agua Viva (11,693), and Voice of God Church (11,047). All other Protestant groups had less than 10,000 adherents each.

In 2009, evangelical mega-churches (congregations with more than 2,000 members) in Guatemala City included the Christian Fraternity (Jorge H. López), the House of God Church (Carlos "Cash" Luna), El Shaddai Church (Harold Caballeros), Elim Central Church (founded by Dr. Othoniel Ríos Paredes, now called Iglesia de Jesucristo Palabra Mi–El Central), Showers of Grace Church (Dr. Ángel Edmundo Madrid Morales), and Ebenezer Ministries of Guatemala/Ebenezer Church of Christ (Sergio Enríquez).

Ecumenical relations in Guatemala are complex, with strong divisions between Pentecostal and non-Pentecostal leaders and their respective denominations. Nevertheless, many conservative evangelical leaders are represented by the Guatemalan Evangelical Alliance (Alianza Evangélica de Guatemala, AEG) at the national level, regardless of their denominational affiliation. However, a few of the most conservative denominations (called Fundamentalists) are not members of AEG and do not support its activities, such as the Trinitarian Bible Society (affiliated with the Independent Board of Presbyterian Foreign Missions), the Christian Brethren (Hermanos Libres), Baptist Bible Fellowship International, and the independent Christian Churches and Churches of Christ. Internationally, AEG is affiliated with the Latin American Confraternity of Evangelicals (CONELA), which is associated with the World Evangelical Alliance (WEF).

Also, the Latin American Council of Churches (CLAI), affiliated with the World Council of Churches (WCC), has a few members in Guatemala. CLAI membership is divided into two categories: the only full-member is the Episcopal Church of Guatemala; fraternal members include the Evangelical Center of Pastoral Studies in Central America (Centro Evangélico de Estudios Pastorales en Centroamérica), located in Zona 2, Ciudad de Guatemala, and the Guatemalan chapter of the Mesoamerican Christian Community (Comunidad Cristiana Mesoamericana), also located in Zona 2, Ciudad de Guatemala.

Other Religions Between 2001 and 2006, those affiliated with other religions remained steady at 2 to 3 percent, while those with "no religious affiliation" (this includes agnostics, atheists, no preference, and no response) were about 12.5 percent, according to two polls: CID-Gallup in November 2001 and Latinobarámetro in 2006.

Included in the "other religions" category were non-Protestant marginal Christian groups: the Church of Jesus Christ of Latter-Day Saints (see below), the Jehovah's Witnesses (364 congregations with about 24,000 members and 68,650 adherents in 2005), Philadelphia Church of God, Yahweh's House of God, Light of the World Church (Guadalajara, Mexico), Voice of the Cornerstone (Puerto Rico), Children of God (The Family International), United Church of Religious Science, Christadelphian Bible Mission, Growing in Grace Ministries International (Miami, Florida), and Mita Congregation and the People of Amos Church, both from Puerto Rico.

Mormon missionaries first arrived in Guatemala in 1947. The first official meeting was held in a rented building on August 22, 1948, with 66 people in attendance. Later that year, John F. O'Donnal baptized the first convert in Guatemala. By 1956, 3 small congregations with a membership of about 250 had been established. Membership grew to 10,000 by 1966, and 18 years later, when the Guatemala City Temple was dedicated in 1984, membership had risen to 40,000. By 1998, according to the church's official statistics, membership had quadrupled again to 164,000. In 2007, the Mormon Church reported 1 temple and 418 congregations with 215,186 members. If these last statistics are valid, then the Mormon Church was larger than most Protestant denominations in Guatemala at that time. (Note: Roger Grossman's 2001 study reported only 55,441 Mormon adherents nationally.)

There are three Eastern Orthodox denominations in Guatemala. (1) The Orthodox Catholic Church of North and South America (with headquarters in Akron, Ohio) ordained José Imre as bishop of Guatemala in 1990, with headquarters in Tiquisate, Department of Esquintla; this denomination operates a seminary in the municipality of Nueva Concepción, Esquintla. Prior to 1988, the Guatemala jurisdiction was known as the Catholic Orthodox Church of Guatemala and Latin America. (2) The Apostolic Orthodox Catholic Church of Guatemala was legally established in 1995 under the jurisdiction of Archbishop Antonio Chedraui, Metropolitan of Mexico, Central America, Venezuela, and the Caribbean, which is affiliated with the Holy Synod of the Patriarchy of Antioch (headquarters in Damascus, Syria). The Orthodox Parish of Guatemala is centered at the Orthodox Catholic Church of the Transfiguration (dedicated in 1997), which is located at the Rafael Ayau Orphanage in Zone 1 of Guatemala City and led by Hieromonje Padre Atanasio Alegría. Associated with this church body is the Orthodox Monastery of the Holy Trinity Lavra Mambré, which was founded in 1986 by Mother Inés Ayau García and Mother María A. Amistoso with the blessing of Metropolitan Damaskinos Papandreu. Although the monastery was originally located in Guatemala City, a new complex of buildings was constructed on the shores of Lake Amatitlán during the 1990s, under the leadership of Madre Inés. (3) The Orthodox Old Apostolic Catholic Church of Guatemala and Central America is led by Archbishop José Adán Morán Santos, with headquarters in Colonia Inde of Villa Nueva, a southern suburb of Guatemala City.

Guatemala is also now home to the spectrum of the world's religions including the following: Animism, Baha'i Faith, Islam, Judaism, Chinese religions, Japanese religions (Mahikari Divine True Light), Buddhism, and Hinduism.

Buddhist organizations include Antigua Sangha (Vietnamese Zen); Buddhist Center of Guatemala City (Tibetan, Karma Kagyu, Diamond Way lineages); Friends of the Dharma; Kagyu Dak Shang Choling; Buddhist Center of Huehuetenango; Buddhist Group of Guatemala (Tibetan); Casa Tibet Guatemala (Lhundrup Tongpa Ling); and Losang Chogyel Study Group (Vajrayana, Tibetan, Gelugpa lineages).

Hindu organizations in Guatemala include International Society for Krishna Consciousness (ISKON), International Sri Sathya Sai Baba Organizations, Transcendental Meditation (TM, now organized as the Global Country of World Peace), and Vaisnava Mission.

Western Esoteric groups include Grand Universal Fraternity, the Ancient and Mystical Order Rosae

Crucis (AMORC), Universal Gnostic Movement, New Acropolis Cultural Centers. Psychic-Spiritualist–New Age groups include the Spiritist Association, Guatemalan Heliosophical Network, Spiritual Magnetic School of the Universal Commune, Ishaya Techniques, Church of Scientology, the Unification Movement, Raelian Movement, and Silva Mind Control/Silvan Method.

Many of the Amerindian peoples practice religious syncretism, which combines their ancient animistic beliefs and practices with a Roman Catholicism imposed on them by civil and religious authorities during the Spanish colonial period (1521–1821). The result is a "popular Catholicism" that retains significant elements of Amerindian spirituality, which includes animistic beliefs and practices such as magic (white and black, good and evil), witchcraft (*bujería*), herbal healing (*curanderismo*), and shamanism (the shaman is an intermediary with the spirit world). Animistic beliefs are strongest among the Amerindians who are the least acculturated to ladino society, and who live in the central highlands or the rainforests of the lowlands in the Petén region of northern Guatemala. However, since the end of Guatemala's civil war (1960–1996), there has been a resurgence of Mayan Spirituality in the predominantly Mayan areas of the Central Highlands, among both Roman Catholics and Protestants.

Also, Garifuna Religion (among the Black Carib) and Creole religion (among English-speaking West Indians: Myalism and Obeah) is practiced on the Caribbean coast in Livingston, Puerto Barrios, and surrounding areas. In addition, there are numerous psychics, mediums, clairvoyants, and astrologers who announce their services in local newspapers.

Clifton L. Holland

See also: Ancient and Mystical Order Rosae Crucis; Assemblies of God; Baha'i Faith; Baptist Bible Fellowship International; Charismatic Movement; Christian Brethren; Christian Churches and Churches of Christ; Church of God (Cleveland, Tennessee); Church of God of Prophecy; Church of Jesus Christ of Latter-Day Saints; Church of Scientology; Church of the Nazarene; Dominicans; Family International, The; Franciscans; Garifuna Religion; Global Country of World Peace; International Society for Krishna Consciousness; Jehovah's Witnesses; Jesuits; Latin American Council of Churches; Light of the World Church; Mita Congregation; Presbyterian Church (U.S.A.); Raelian Movement International; Religious Science; Roman Catholic Church; Seventh-day Adventist Church; Spiritism; Unification Movement; Witchcraft; World Council of Churches; World Evangelical Alliance.

References

Barry, Tom. *Inside Guatemala.* Albuquerque, NM: The Inter-Hemispheric Education Resource Center, 1992.

Berberian, Martha. *Frederico Crowe: Una Biografía.* Guatemala City: Ediciones Sa-Ber, 1995.

Berberian, Samuel. *Dos Décadas de Renovación Carismática en América Latina: Un análisis histórico de la Renovación Carismática en América Latina (1960–1980).* 3rd ed. Guatemala City: Ediciones Sa-Ber, 2002.

Berryman, Phillip. *The Religious Roots of Rebellion: Christians in Central American Revolutions.* Maryknoll, NY: Orbis Books, 1984.

De las Casas, Bartrolomé. *Brevíssima relación de la destrucción de las Indias.* 1552; rpt. Madrid: Editorial EDAF, 2004.

Escobar, David. *Historia del Movimiento Evangélico en Guatemala.* Tomo I: 1524–1882. Guatemala City: Editorial Cristiana PUBLICAD, 2000.

Gordon, Raymond G., Jr., ed. *Ethnologue: Languages of the World.* 15th ed. Dallas, TX: SIL International. http://www.ethnologue.com/, 2005.

Grossman, Roger. "Interpreting the Development of the Evangelical Church in Guatemala, 2002." Ph.D. diss., Southeastern Baptist Theological Seminary, 2002.

Holland, Clifton L., ed. *World Christianity: Central America and the Caribbean.* Monrovia, CA: MARC-World Vision International, 1981.

INDEF-PROCADES & SEPAL. *Directorio de Iglesias, Organizaciones y Ministerios del Movimiento Protestante en Guatemala, 1981.* Guatemala City: INDEF-PROCADES & SEPAL, 1981.

Jeter de Walker, Luisa. *Siembra y Cosecha*. Tomo 1, *Las Asambleas de Dios de México y Centro-américa*. Deerfield, FL: Editorial Vida, 1990.

PROLADES. *A Chronology of Protestant Beginnings in Guatemala, 1824–1980*. http://www.prolades.com/cra/regions/cam/gte/chron-cam-guate.pdf (accessed March 15, 2010).

PROLADES. *Public Opinion Polls on Religious Affiliation in Guatemala: 1990–2008*. http://www.prolades.com/cra/regions/cam/gte/guat_polls_1990-2008.pdf (accessed March 15, 2010).

SEPAL. *Reporte Preliminar: El Estado de la Iglesia Evangélica en Guatemala, 2001*. Guatemala City: Servicio Evangelizadora para América Latina (SEPAL), 2001.

Woodward, Ralph Lee. *A Short History of Guatemala*. Guatemala City: Editorial Laura Lee, 2005.

Zapata, Virgilio A. *Historia de la Iglesia Evangélica en Guatemala*. Guatemala City: Génesis Publicidad, 1982.

■ Guinea

Guinea, a former French colony on the west coast of Africa, is situated between Sierra Leone and Guinea-Bissau. It also shares borders with Liberia, Cote d'Ivoire, Mali, and Senegal. Some 9.8 million people (2008) reside on its 95,000 square miles of territory. It is the home to no less than 16 different African peoples, among whom the Fulahs, Mandingos, Malinkes, and Susses form the largest blocs in the population.

Guinea was a rich land, with notable gold deposits in its northern highlands. At various times through the centuries, parts of Guinea were incorporated into empires ruled from neighboring power centers. They were, for example, on the edge and frequently part of the various Fulani states centered in Senegal and Mali. Then in 1870, a man named Samori (1840–1900) rose from humble beginnings to become the Almany (a title indicating his combined political and religious role) of a state that approximated the present country of Guinea (plus parts of Mali and the Cote d'Ivoire).

Portuguese had traveled the coast of Guinea for several centuries and established trading posts prior to Samori's emergence, but it was during his rule that the French began to move into the heart of the country from Senegal. He fought his first battle with French troops in 1886. He fought the French for the next 12 years but was finally defeated, taken prisoner, and exiled. The country remained a French colony until 1958, when, following a negative vote on President Charles de Gaulle's plan to transform Guinea from a colony to a member of the French Community, the local leadership proclaimed the country's independence.

The popular leader of the independence movement, Sékou Touré (1922–1984), died in 1984. Shortly thereafter a coup was led by Colonel Lansana Conté, who continues to head the government.

Guinea

Religion	Followers in 1970	Followers in 2010	% of Population	Annual % growth 2000–2010	Followers in 2025	Followers in 2050
Muslims	2,559,000	6,904,000	68.8	1.83	10,381,000	16,926,000
Ethnoreligionists	1,199,000	2,730,000	27.2	1.68	3,500,000	4,600,000
Christians	55,400	362,000	3.6	4.56	610,000	1,069,000
Roman Catholics	48,400	270,000	2.7	11.78	450,000	750,000
Protestants	3,100	93,000	0.9	1.44	150,000	280,000
Independents	1,300	30,000	0.3	1.47	50,000	90,000
Agnostics	4,000	18,000	0.2	1.88	35,000	80,000
Buddhists	0	9,000	0.1	1.88	13,000	20,000
Atheists	1,000	5,300	0.1	1.88	8,000	15,000
Baha'is	100	150	0.0	1.88	500	1,200
Total population	**3,819,000**	**10,028,000**	**100.0**	**1.88**	**14,547,000**	**22,711,000**

GUINEA

Traditional religions of the Guinea peoples have remained strong in this land, where Christianity and Islam have vied for the heart of the population. The Kissi, Loma, and Gbande peoples, who traditionally have occupied the forest lands in the southeast near the borders with Sierra Leone and Liberia, have been most resistant to conversion. Also many of the Malinke and Kpelle have retained their religion.

Islam (of the Sunni Malekite School) entered Guinea in the 18th century, the Fulani people being the primary instrument. The majority of Guineans are now Muslims. The strongest support has appeared among the Dialonke, Garakole, and Susu peoples. Many of the country's Muslims are members of the Tijaniyya Sufi Order, an order that was developing in North Africa at about the same time that Islam was moving into Guinea. In the 20th century, the community has further diversified with the introduction of the Ahmadiyya Muslim movement from Pakistan. Also, since World War II the Baha'i Faith has begun to spread.

Portuguese arrived along the coast of Guinea in 1462. Catholicism was introduced at the trading centers, but there was no effort to evangelize the interior. It was not until 1877 that Roman Catholic missionaries, in the form of the Holy Ghost Fathers, arrived, by which time Islam already had established its claim on much of the region. The first mission station was opened at Boffa. The White Fathers arrived in 1896, by which time the French had almost completed their conquest of the land.

The Roman Catholic Church grew steadily through the 20th century, growth marked by the ordination of the first Guinean priest in 1940, the establishment of the first archdiocese (Conakry) in 1955, and consecration of the first African archbishop in 1962. The Holy Ghost Fathers were in charge of the archdiocese, and the White Fathers worked in the neighboring diocese of N'Zékékoré. Then in 1967, as the country was struggling to become independent, all foreign priests and nuns were expelled. Only eight priests remained work eventually matured into the Evangelical Protestant Church.

By 1967, several other churches had also established missions, most prominently the Church of the Open Bible, an American Pentecostal group that entered in 1952. The Paris Mission and the Anglicans had both established work in the nation's capital city, Conakry. Each of these three efforts lost all their missionary leadership in 1967, and the churches have remained weak. Anglican churches are part of the Diocese of Guinea, which now includes both Guinea and Guinea-Bissau, part of the Church of the Province of West Africa.

The Christian community remains relatively small, 2 to 3 percent of the total population of approximately 10 million. Some 65 percent of the population profess Islam, and the remainder continue to follow their traditional religion. There are few signs of new religious impulses, though several evangelical groups (most notably the New Tribes Mission, SIM USA [formerly the Sudan Interior Mission] and the Southern Baptist Convention) opened work in the 1980. The Southern Baptists have a small work among the Susu people, and more recently the National Baptist Convention, U.S.A., has launched missionary activity.

J. Gordon Melton

See also: Ahmadiyya Movement in Islam; Baha'i Faith; Christian and Missionary Alliance; Church of the Province of West Africa; Holy Ghost Fathers; Malekite School of Islam; National Baptist Convention, U.S.A.; Paris Mission; Roman Catholic Church; Southern Baptist Convention; Tijaniyya Sufi Order.

References

"The Church in Guinea." *International Fides Service* (Rome) no. 2695 (January 7, 1976): 6–9.

Laughton, J. R. C. *Gambia: Country, People and Church in the Diocese of Gambia and the Rio Pongas*. London: SPG, 1938.

■ Guinea-Bissau

Guinea-Bissau, a small country sandwiched between Senegal and the Republic of Guinea, includes three major river valleys (the Geba, Cacheu, and Corubal)

People walk past a mosque in Conakry, Guinea. (AP Photo/Schalk van Zuydam)

to carry on the work. The church was forced to quickly recruit more priests and rebuild, which it has subsequently done.

Protestants did not enter the country until 1918, when the Christian and Missionary Alliance (CMA) began work in the Niger River Valley. It expanded primarily by working among groups that had to that point retained their traditional faith, rather than from the Muslim community. The CMA has taken the lead in producing Bibles and other literature in the various languages spoken in Guinea. Like the Catholics, CMA missionaries were expelled in 1967, but the CMA was able to negotiate an arrangement whereby 26 missionaries were allowed to remain, though their activity was for a period very restricted. Many of these were at the church's two schools at Telekoro and Mamou. Thus they were able to focus on leadership training and continue the process of translating the Bible. Their

Guinea-Bissau

Religion	Followers in 1970	Followers in 2010	% of Population	Annual % growth 2000–2010	Followers in 2025	Followers in 2050
Ethnoreligionists	333,000	809,000	43.6	3.11	1,100,000	1,500,000
Muslims	184,000	817,000	44.1	3.76	1,443,000	3,110,000
Christians	66,800	202,000	10.9	0.90	316,000	595,000
Roman Catholics	59,600	140,000	7.6	−0.75	200,000	350,000
Independents	0	40,000	2.2	3.13	70,000	150,000
Protestants	2,500	22,500	1.2	8.97	45,000	95,000
Agnostics	500	23,200	1.3	3.31	50,000	110,000
Atheists	0	1,700	0.1	3.10	3,500	8,000
Baha'is	50	350	0.0	3.05	600	1,000
Total population	**584,000**	**1,853,000**	**100.0**	**3.11**	**2,913,000**	**5,324,000**

and the Bijagos Archipelago, which includes a number of islands in the Atlantic Ocean immediately off the coast. A population of 1.5 million people resides on its 10,800 square miles of territory.

Early in the second millennium BCE, the area was incorporated into different kingdoms centered in Senegal and Mali, but the people eventually attained their independence, only to see the Portuguese begin to create settlements along the coast at the end of the 15th century. At this time the area was home to no less than 40 different peoples, the most numerous being the Fulani, Mandingos, Mandes, and Balantes.

The Portuguese gradually established a colony, which became the source of slave labor. The country itself was turned over to a private company, which forced many into the cultivation of crops designed for export, while the majority of the population were living at subsistence levels. The country was impoverished and left in ignorance. However, in this situation in the1950s a resistance movement began to develop, led by Amilcar Cabral (d. 1973). His goals were made plain in the name of the organization he founded, the African Party for the Liberation of Guinea and Cape Verde (the Portuguese island off the coast that had been a processing center for the slave trade). The movement turned into a war for liberation, which won the country's freedom in 1973. As he realized his life's work, Cabral was assassinated by Portuguese agents. The United Nations moved quickly to recognize the new nation, and its establishment played a major role in the coup that ended the harsh dictatorship in Portu-gal and led to the dismantling of the Portuguese colonial empire.

The new government was taken over in a coup in 1980, and a Marxist dictatorship took control. A multiparty democracy was put in place in 1991, but the poverty of the country has made it continually unstable. It was the scene of a civil war in 1998–1999 followed by an interim government, which fell following a coup in 2003. Former dictator Joao Bernardo "Nino" Viera was elected president in 2005.

The majority of the people of Guinea-Bissau retain allegiance to the traditional religions of the land, and are the overwhelming majority in the western half of the country farthest from the coast. The Banyum, Bayot, and Manjaco peoples have remained virtually untouched by either Islam or Christianity.

Christianity came to Guinea-Bissau with Franciscans who arrived in 1462 with the first wave of Portuguese traders. Their work came under the jurisdiction of the new Diocese of St. James of Cape Verde erected in 1532. They were later joined by Jesuit priests, but made only slow progress at wooing converts into the church. The low point of the church was in 1929, when only one priest remained in the entire country. In 1940 (as part of an agreement between Portugal and the Vatican), Guinea-Bissau became a mission independent of Cape Verde, and a new missionary effort began. The relative success in more recent decades was indicated by the mission's elevation to the status of a prefecture apostolic in 1955 and the establishment of the Diocese of Bissau in 1977.

GUINEA-BISSAU

The development of the Roman Catholic Church was overshadowed by the movement of Islam into the country, especially in the 18th century. Sunni Islam of the Malikite School came to dominate the Sominke, Fulakunda, and Susu peoples, mostly in the southern and eastern portions of the country, and the Diola in the west. However, even Islam has had only relative success, with only 40 percent of the population of 1.8 million people being attracted to it.

Protestantism did not manifest in Guinea-Bissau until the Worldwide Evangelization Crusade (WEC), headquartered in England, established work in Bissau. Its work spread along the coast and in the islands of the archipelago. Like the Roman Catholic Church, it has found progress difficult. In the 1990s the Evangelical Church of Guinea (Igreja Evangélica da Guine), founded by the WEC, still had only a few thousand members. It is the largest Protestant work in the country. There is also a small Anglican presence attached to the Diocese of Guinea of the Church of the Province of West Africa and the small Guinea-Bissau Mission of the Seventh-day Adventist Church, part of the larger Sahel Union Mission, which includes a number of countries in West Africa.

Of some interest, there is a small Druze community in Guinea-Bissau consisting of approximately 100 expatriates from Lebanon. The continued civil unrest has tended to discourage the founding of new religions.

J. Gordon Melton

See also: Church of the Province of West Africa; Druze; Malikite School of Islam; Roman Catholic Church; Seventh-day Adventist Church.

References

Callewaert, Inger. *The Birth of Religion Among the Balanta of Guinea-Bissau*. Stockholm: Almquist & Wiksell International, 2000.
Gonçalves, J. J. *O islamismo na Guiné Portuguesa*. Lisbon: Agência-Geral do Ultramar, 1961.
Laughton, J. R. C. *Gambia: Country, People and Church in the Diocese of Gambia and the Rio Pongas*. London: SPG, 1938.
Rema, H. P. *História das missões católicas da Guiné*. Braga, Portugal: Editorial Franciscana, 1982.
Willis, H. *The Light Shines in the Darkness: The Story of the Evangelical Church of Guinea-Bissau, 1940–1974*. Balstrade, UK: WED, 1996.

Gurdjieff Foundations

During his life, G. I. Gurdjieff (ca. 1866–1949) worked closely with a number of students in Europe and America in what remains essentially an oral teaching tradition that emphasizes the need to develop a new quality of participation in all aspects of life. Today, study of his ideas and practices exists in several locales. The primary locale represents direct descent from Gurdjieff and consists of a network of organizations operating largely under the titles Gurdjieff Foundation or Gurdjieff Society and other organizations founded by individuals who left Gurdjieff or his students to establish independent groups. As the most direct conduit from Gurdjieff himself, the Foundations are considered the organization that most completely represents his teaching.

Shortly before his death, Gurdjieff related to his chief student, Jeanne de Salzmann (1889–1990), that a nucleus of people should be prepared in order to respond to the demand that would arise. In the early 1950s, Madame de Salzmann began to coordinate groups dedicated to the Work (the body of ideas and practices that Gurdjieff introduced). Soon after, centers identified by the names Societe d'Etudes et de Recherches pour la Connaissance de l'Homme (SERCH, later named Institut Gurdjieff) in Paris, Gurdjieff Foundation in New York and Caracas, and Gurdjieff Society in London were established, with one or more direct students in charge of each center. From these major centers, a growing number of organizations have begun in Europe, North America, South America, Australia, South Africa, the Middle East, and the Far East. Local organizations offer various forms of the Work, and, collectively, they remain the repository of Gurdjieff's musical and dance creations and direct the publication of Gurdjieff's writings and music.

Most of Gurdjieff's direct students, as well as their own students, have been associated with the Foundation/ Society organization. The network remained under the leadership of Jeanne de Salzmann from Gurdjieff's death in 1949 until her death in 1990. She traveled widely and saw to the publication of Gurdjieff's *Life Is Real Only Then, When "I Am,"* and a volume of Gurdjieff's early talks, *Views from the Real World.* With director Peter Brook (b. 1925), she adapted *Meetings with Remarkable Men* into a film. She preserved and taught the "movements" or sacred dances taught by Gurdjieff and created several films that demonstrate some of the essential aspects of the Work through movements. Following her death, her son Michel de Salzmann (1923–2001) maintained a link among the Foundations until his death in 2001.

At the local level, work groups are selected, organized, and led by senior members, usually acting as a council. Councils coordinate across localities to sponsor events and create projects. The relation of the Foundations to each other is cooperative rather than based on a central authority. The Foundations collaborate in order to develop a sense of responsibility to the influence that Gurdjieff brought. The link among local organizations is the teaching itself, not a formal or hierarchical structure.

In 2003, the International Association of Gurdjieff Foundations (IAGF) was chartered in Switzerland by four founding members: the societies in Paris, London, New York, and Caracas. Meetings of the IAGF occur twice a year on a rotating basis in Europe, Britain, the United States, and South America, primarily to share the efforts and experience derived in the different member institutes.

As a path devoted to development of consciousness, the Work does not involve belief or formal rites, but calls for direct experience and understanding. Essential to Gurdjieff's teaching is the principle that the Work, begun as quiet, inner observation of oneself, must eventually emerge into everyday life. He provided many inner exercises and practices to make use of the events of ordinary life for growth of awareness and attention. In the Foundations, practical work takes place through small group meetings, movements, exercises, study, and a wide range of activities including music, art, crafts, and manual work, all of which are intended to make possible the use of each aspect of everyday life for the growth of awareness.

Two central activities constitute the pillars or primary activities of Work in the Foundations: group meetings and movements. Other activities derive from and facilitate these primary activities.

Small Group Meetings Group meetings have been an integral part of the Work since its inception. Small groups experiment with exercises of attention and discuss questions that arise from study of the teaching undertaken in the conditions of everyday life. Participation in a group allows a student to deepen personal inquiry by learning from others' experiences.

In spite of the confidentiality practiced in Work groups, accounts of small group exchanges, with both Gurdjieff himself and later group leaders, are published. Of particular interest is a collection of exchanges with Lord Pentland (1907–1984), born Henry John Sinclair, a student of Gurdjieff who served as president of the Gurdjieff Foundation of New York from its inception in 1953 until his death. Accounts of group meetings with Lord Pentland show how students pose inquiries and an accomplished teacher of Gurdjieff's ideas responds.

As support for small group work, members sit quietly in order to develop awareness of bodily sensation and to observe internal processes and tensions in the body. Gurdjieff taught that sitting quietly without tension and without identification with thoughts brings energy and can help in formulating and realizing an aim. These "sittings," observed in small groups and individually, provide a means for self-knowledge and inner verification of Gurdjieff's teaching about the human condition.

Movements and Dances   Gurdjieff included in his teaching rhythmic exercises, called movements, which he says parallel dances performed during temple rites in Asia and the Middle East. According to Gurdjieff, movements have two aims: self-knowledge and development of a new quality of attention that can include the whole person: body, mind, and feeling. Movements are said to express precise metaphysical laws and to allow a direct and personal experience of different qualities of energy. A student can experience intimations of another dimension of reality. In recognition of these transformative possibilities, Gurdjieff also referred to movements as "sacred dances" and "sacred gymnastics."

Each movement involves a sequence of positions and displacements of the body performed in changing patterns, usually accompanied by music. The challenge of movements is that they require instantaneous coordination of body and mind. Movements help a student develop awareness of the state of the body and its participation—as both ally and obstacle—in the search for consciousness. Because movements are taught in classes, each student can observe how a personal inner search is connected with that of others.

Other activities that derive from and support the two primary pillars of the Work, small group meetings and movements, include the following.

Music   Gurdjieff maintains that he composed music in order to transmit understanding of universal laws through direct perception of the effect of vibrations on the organism. He explains that "objective music" can convey a precise understanding of the laws of vibrations and can produce in all listeners a predictable and identical result, unlike "subjective music," which is produced and received differently by different people. With music, Gurdjieff invokes the teaching of correspondences; study of the microcosm of music is an inquiry into universal laws and processes that also operate at the macrocosmic level.

The corpus of 200 or so musical compositions written by Gurdjieff and Thomas de Hartmann ranges widely as to form and effect. Some pieces echo folk melodies and rhythms; others include chants and dances; still others are hymns and prayers.

Study of Ideas   According to Gurdjieff, ancient teachings brought an understanding of how a fine energy can enter human existence. Study of ideas can provide, he says, a way in which this energy from higher sources can enter the life of a person. In order to appreciate the universal source from which all great teachings derive, Work groups study ideas from ancient traditions, including Christianity, Islam, Buddhism, Hinduism, and nature religions, along with Gurdjieff's ideas. Study of ideas, alone and in groups, calls for an integration of the ideas of the teaching with personal experience. Gurdjieff stressed the need to study the ideas of his teaching at all levels, from personal to universal, and to spend time pondering the meaning of personal experience in relation to larger planetary forces.

Practical Work   Working with craft materials or tools with a directed attention can provide impressions of how awareness, emotional attachment, and physical activity are interrelated. Groups regularly assemble for a period (day, weekend, or longer) to work at preparation of meals, housekeeping, gardening, writing, building construction, and crafts, such as weaving, sewing, and pottery. Work periods usually begin by setting a common intention to experiment with some aspect of self-observation during practical activities. At common meals, members exchange their individual observations in a group setting.

Activities with Children and Young People Since Gurdjieff's teaching is a way in everyday life, the Foundations value and devote attention to the education of children. Following Gurdjieff's teaching about the cultural and educational forces that deny development of essence in formative years, members work with children to encourage growth of essence and to ameliorate habitual imitation of others.

Although these activities are carried out for members only, essential aspects of the teaching are periodically presented to the public through conferences, lectures, concerts, and the publication of relevant writings. The Foundations do not proselytize widely for new members, which may in part account for the charges of secrecy that have arisen from time to time. Today, approximately 2,500 to 3,000 people worldwide are involved in the Foundation network.

No notable controversies have occurred within the Foundations since their beginning in the early 1950s. However, some older students separated from the mainstream of the work and formed groups of their own. Numerous other organizations are led by individuals who claim no historical lineage with Gurdjieff or his direct students, yet use a term from Gurdjieff's teaching, particularly the term "Fourth Way," in definition of their respective missions. An even more subtle diffusion of his ideas and practices into the larger culture includes spiritual teachers and professionals who cite Gurdjieff or his teaching in the development of their own systems. In many instances, the interpretations of his teaching given within these forms of dissemination have little or no relation to the way these ideas are approached and experienced within the Foundations.

Links to all Foundations throughout the world can be obtained at www.IAGF.org.

The Gurdjieff Foundation of New York: http://www.gurdjieff.org/foundation.htm.

Constance A. Jones

See also: Gurdjieff, George Ivanovitch; Western Esoteric Tradition.

References
de Dampierre, Pauline. "The Role of Movements." In *Gurdjieff: Essays and Reflections on the Man and His Teaching*, edited by J. Needleman, G. Baker, and B. Panafieu, 290–295. New York: Continuum, 1996.

Gurdjieff International Review. http://www.gurdjieff.org/.

Jones, Constance A. *G. I. Gurdjieff e la sua eredita*. Turin, Italy: Elledici, 2005.

Meetings with Remarkable Men. Peter Brook, director, with the collaboration of Jeanne de Salzmann. New York: A Parabola Release, 1978.

Needleman, Jacob. "The Gurdjieff Tradition," In *Dictionary of Gnosis and Western Esotericism*, edited by W. J. Hanegraaff, in collaboration with Jean-Pierre Brach, Roelof van den Broek, and Antoine Faivre. Leiden: Brill, 2006.

Needleman, Jacob, George Baker, and Bruno de Panafieu, eds. *Gurdjieff: Essays and Reflections on the Man and His Teaching*. New York: Continuum, 1996.

Ouspensky, P. D. *A Further Record: Extracts from Meetings 1928–1945*. London: Arkana, 1986.

Ouspensky, P. D. *In Search of the Miraculous: Fragments of an Unknown Teaching*. New York: Harcourt Brace, 1949.

Patterson, William Patrick. *Ladies of the Rope: Gurdjieff's Special Left Bank Women's Group*. Fairfax, CA: Arete Communications, 1999.

Patterson, William Patrick. *Voices in the Dark*. Fairfax, CA: Arete Communications, 2000.

Pentland, John. *Exchanges Within: Questions from Everyday Life Selected from Gurdjieff Group Meetings with John Pentland in California 1955–1984*. New York: Continuum, 1997.

Rawlinson, Andrew. *The Book of Enlightened Masters*. LaSalle, IL: Open Court, 1997.

Rosenthal, Laurence. "Gurdjieff and Music." In *Gurdjieff: Essays and Reflections on the Man and His*

Teaching, edited by J. Needleman, G. Baker, and B. Panafieu, 301–310. New York: Continuum, 1996. "A Teacher of Dancing." Whole issue of *Gurdjieff International Review* 5, no.1 (Spring 2002).

Gurdjieff, George Ivanovitch

ca. 1866–1949

George Ivanovitch Gurdjieff was a spiritual teacher who brought a message of inner awakening and a method of self-development that is increasingly studied in the West today. The body of ideas and practices that he introduced, called the "Work," reflects the Western Esoteric (alchemical) tradition that integrates humanistic and scientific concerns and requires effort on the part of the aspirant to awaken to the process of inner transformation.

A defining feature of this work on oneself is that it is meant to take place in the cauldron of everyday life. Specific to Gurdjieff's method is his emphasis on the direct awareness of the triadic structure of humans, the three centers of body, mind, and feeling. The harmonious development of this triad, called by Gurdjieff the three "brains," brings balance to the whole being and allows access to a new dimension of consciousness.

Born in Alexandropol, in the southern Caucasus, at the crossroads of diverse cultures, traditions, and languages, Gurdjieff dedicated his early life to the search for meaning. He was convinced that an ancient knowledge exists that could illuminate the true place of human existence within the cosmic scheme. He relates how, as a boy, he wished to understand the meaning of human life and humanity's position in the universe. The force of these questions led him to investigate many sources, but in each he found contradictions, even among accomplished practitioners and scholars. In search of a non-contradictory understanding, he read widely in science and religion, and studied formally both medicine and Orthodox Christian theology. His writings portray early interest in a broad spectrum of philosophical and religious issues, as well as the history of science in the West and the technological advances of his day.

With the belief that understanding of his concerns could be found among ancient traditions in the Middle

Portrait of the Greco-Armenian mystic George Ivanovitch Gurdjieff, who founded the Institute for the Harmonious Development of Man in 1919. (Library of Congress/Janet Flanner-Solita Solano papers)

East and Asia, he decided to forgo further academic study and to search for surviving traces of these traditions. In his account, *Meetings with Remarkable Men*, he describes travels in the Middle East, Egypt, Ethiopia, Tibet, Central Asia, and the Hindu Kush. Sometimes on his own and sometimes with a group of associates who called themselves Seekers of Truth, he spent more than 20 years in what he describes as relentless inquiry—traveling, learning languages, surveying ancient documents and monuments, studying with spiritual teachers, and visiting religious centers and remote monasteries.

Meetings with Remarkable Men, an interweaving of travel, spiritual quest and allegorical teaching, relates that he studied many traditions, including Esoteric teachings in both East and West. Each adventure, he says, served his quest for an understanding of the sense and significance of life on earth, particularly human life. His later creations, including expositions of his ideas, music, dance, and psychological exercises, indicate a variety of influences, which he does not identify. Even with these influences unidentified, his writings refer often to world religions (including Christianity, Judaism, Islam, Buddhism, Hinduism, and Zoroastrianism) as well as ancient teachings from Greece, Babylon, Egypt, and the fabled Atlantis.

After more than 20 years of searching in remote schools and monasteries of the Middle East and Central Asia, he appeared in Moscow in 1912 with an all-encompassing teaching that wove cosmology, metaphysics, social critique, and spiritual practice into a design for personal evolution. This was the beginning of Gurdjieff's career as a teacher. His first students were drawn mainly from the Russian intelligentsia. Among these was Peter Demianovich Ouspensky (1878–1947), philosopher, mathematician, and journalist, who by this time had received recognition in intellectual circles through publication of *Tertium Organum*, a treatise on the nature of the universe, first published in Russia in 1911. Ouspensky relates that he immediately recognized that what he had published was conjecture and that Gurdjieff offered more—an understanding, beyond conjecture, about the universe and humanity's place in it. Ouspensky was an avid student in the Moscow days and documented this time in a monograph, *In Search of the Miraculous*, which remains a major exposition of the teaching.

A core of students began to collect in Russia, including Sophie Grigorievna (1874–1963), referred to consistently as Mme Ouspensky; Thomas de Hartmann (1885–1956), an accomplished musician and composer who later collaborated with Gurdjieff in creating a corpus of music that expresses elements of the teaching; and de Hartmann's wife, Olga (1885–1979), who later served as Gurdjieff's secretary and was a significant contributor to the development of Gurdjieff's mission in France, the United States, and Canada.

Leading his students out of the chaos of the Russian Revolution, in 1921 Gurdjieff settled in France, where he based his activity until his death in 1949. At first he lived with some of his students at the Prieuré des Basses Loges at Fontainebleau-Avon and later moved to an apartment in Paris. During this period he also set out his ideas in his major work, *Beelzebub's Tales to His Grandson*, as well as in *Meetings with Remarkable Men*, written in the form of a spiritual autobiography.

Between 1929 and 1948, Gurdjieff traveled to the United States nine times to meet with Work groups, oversee translation of his writing, and to attend to what he called the "material question," that is, finances. Over the years he supported a large extended family of émigrés, as well as the upkeep of the Prieuré. Throughout the 1930s, Gurdjieff diversified his activities. New groups were established in France, England, and the United States. During the German occupation of Paris, from 1940 to 1944, Gurdjieff conducted group meetings, under discreet and often stressful circumstances, in his apartment near the Place de l'Etoile. Groups continued to meet after the liberation. In 1947, after Ouspensky's death, Gurdjieff made his last trip to America and authorized Mme Ouspensky to publish her husband's account of his time with Gurdjieff. Gurdjieff died in Paris on October 29, 1949. He was memorialized with the rites of the Russian Orthodox faith at Alexandre Nevski Cathedral in Paris and buried at Avon near Paris.

Gurdjieff left a large corpus of sacred dances and exercises called "movements" and, in collaboration with Thomas de Hartmann, more than 200 musical compositions.

Constance A. Jones

See also: Gurdjieff Foundations; Western Esoteri Tradition.

References

Driscoll, J. Walter. *Gurdjieff: A Reading Guide*. Los Altos, CA: Gurdjieff Electronic Publishing, 1999.

Driscoll, J. Walter, and the Gurdjieff Foundation of California. *Gurdjieff: An Annotated Bibliography*. New York: Garland Publishing, 1985.

Gurdjieff, G. I. *Beelzebub's Tales to His Grandson: An Objectively Impartial Criticism of the Life of Man*. London and New York: Penguin Arkana, 1999.

Gurdjieff, G. I. *Life Is Real Only Then, When "I Am."* London and New York: Penguin Arkana, 1999.

Gurdjieff, G. I. *Meetings with Remarkable Men*. London and New York: Penguin Arkana, 1985.

Gurdjieff, G. I. *Views from the Real World: Early Talks in Moscow, Essentuki, Tiflis, Berlin, London, Paris, New York, Chicago, As Recollected by His Students*. Foreword by Jeanne de Salzmann. London and New York: Arkana, 1984.

Gurdjieff International Review. http://www.gurdjieff.org/.

de Hartmann, Thomas A., and Olga A. S. *Our Life with Mr. Gurdjieff*. Rev. by Thomas C. Daly. San Francisco: Harper and Row, 1983.

Meetings with Remarkable Men. Peter Brook, director, with the collaboration of Jeanne de Salzmann. New York: A Parabola Release, 1978.

Moore, James. *Gurdjieff: The Anatomy of a Myth, a Biography*. Shaftsbury, UK: Element, 1991.

Needleman, Jacob. "The Gurdjieff Tradition." In *Dictionary of Gnosis and Western Esotericism*, edited by W. J. Hanegraaff, in collaboration with Jean-Pierre Brach, Roelof van den Broek, and Antoine Faivre. Leiden: Brill, 2006.

Needleman, Jacob, George Baker, and Bruno de Panafieu, eds. *Gurdjieff: Essays and Reflections on the Man and His Teaching*. New York: Continuum, 1996.

Nott, C. S. *Teachings of Gurdjieff: The Journal of a Student*. London: Routledge & Kegan Paul, 1961.

Ouspensky, P. D. *In Search of the Miraculous: Fragments of an Unknown Teaching*. New York: Harcourt Brace, 1949.

Rawlinson, Andrew. *The Book of Enlightened Masters*. LaSalle, IL: Open Court, 1997.

de Salzmann, Michel. "Footnote to the Gurdjieff Literature." In *Gurdjieff: An Annotated Bibliography*, edited by J. Walter Driscoll and the Gurdjieff Foundation of California. New York: Garland, 1985.

Tchekhovitch, Tcheslaw. *Gurdjieff: A Master in Life*. Toronto: Dolmen Meadows, 2006.

Vaysse, Jean. *Toward Awakening: An Approach to the Teaching Left by Gurdjieff*. London: Routledge & Kegan Paul, 1980.

Walker, Kenneth. *A Study of Gurdjieff's Teaching*. London: Cape, 1957.

Walker, Kenneth. *Venture with Ideas*. London: Cape, 1951.

Webb, James. *The Harmonious Circle*. New York: Putnam, 1980.

www.gurdjieff.org.

www.IAGF.com.

Guru Gobind Singh's Birthday

Guru Gobind Singh was the 10th guru (teacher) acknowledged as the leader of the Sikh community, and the one who held up the Guru Granth Sahib, the Sikh scripture, as his successor guru. Thus Gobind Singh was the last living guru acknowledged by the Sikh community. The birthday celebration allows for special acknowledgment of his role in shaping the Sikh community. The most important Sikh holidays are *gurpurbs*, or festivals occasioned by birthday or martyrdom of one of the 10 gurus, and this is no exception.

Guru Gobind Singh was born the son of Guru Tegh Bahadur at Patna Sahib, in the state of Bihar, India, on December 22, 1666 (on the Gregorian calendar). He was raised at Annadpur, a Punjabi city founded by his father and now a Sikh holy site. He emerged to adulthood at a time of great stress within the Sikh community, which was suffering abuse by the Muslim ruler under which they lived. He articulated a principle later known as Kshatradharma, a form of spiritual practice that values the "protection of the seekers and destruction of the evildoers." This principle fit a militant response to discriminatory and persecutory actions. On several occasions Gobind Singh led forces and won battles in defense of the community.

The principle of Kshatradharma would lead him in 1699 to the organization of the Khalsa, the Order of the Pure, a military-religious fraternity originally consisting of those men who acknowledged their willingness to give their life for the guru. The khalsa later expanded to include all within the Sikh community, formally entered by baptism, the adoption of the name Singh (lion) (or in the case of women, the name Kuar [princess]). Sikh's give Guru Gobind Singh credit for turning the tide against Mughal oppression in India.

Along with his military and organizational accomplishments, Sikhs also point to his intellectual activity, which included authoring a number of treatises concerning what might be termed the Khalsa spirit. His writings would later be collected into a separate volume, the Dasam Granth, which is revered second only to the Guru Granth Sahib by Sikhs.

The guru's birthday is now celebrated on what is January 5 on the Common Era calendar, which is the 23rd day of the month of Poh on the new Sikh Nakanshahi Calendar. Members of the community celebrate by gathering at the *gurdwara* (a Sikh house of worship) for special programs remembering Gobind Sing's life.

J. Gordon Melton

See also: Calendars, Religious; Sikhism/Sant Mat.

References;

Kapoor, Sukhbor Sing. *Sikh Festivals*. Vero Beach, FL: Rourke Publishing Group, 1989.

Singh, Babir. *Message of Guru Govind Singh and Other Essays*. Amritsar: Punjab University, 1997.

Singh, Bhagat Lakeshman. *Short Sketch of the Life and Work of Guru Govind Singh, the Tenth and Last Guru*. Ottawa: Laurier Books, 1995.

Guru Purnima

Guru Purnuma is the annual day when Hindus show special veneration to their spiritual teacher, their guru. It is observed on the day of the full moon (*purnima*) in the Hindu lunar month of Ashadh (which occurs in June or July of the Common Era calendar). Primary honor on this date is given to an acknowledgment of the legendary Bhagwan Ved Vyasa, the first guru, who in Hindu lore is credited with compiling all the Vedic hymns available at the time, dividing them into four parts based on their ritual use. He is also credited with writing the 18 Puranas and the great epic of India, the

During Guru Purnima, an Indian Hindu devotee prostrates himself before the *mahant* (religious leader) Ravi Shankar, on the banks of the Ganges in Allahabad, India, July 2, 2004. (AP photo/Rajesh Kumar Singh)

Mahabharata. The Mahabharata dates to the third century BCE, with parts that may be as old as the ninth century. The Puranas date to the third to fifth centuries CE. Nevertheless, Vyasa supplies the original image of what a guru is and should be.

Besides the first gurus there have been many spiritual teachers throughout history and many exist today. Thus Guru Purnima becomes the occasion of especially honoring one personal guru in the present. Many Hindus believe that every spiritual aspirant needs a teacher who can dispel darkness and guide him or her to spiritual enlightenment. On this day, the aspirant should serve and worship the guru (*vyasa puja*), speaking of her or his life and teachings. One pattern for observing Guru Purnima is to meditate on the guru and chant his prayers; perform worship of the guru's feet; attend *satsang* (a gathering) in which discourses extol the glory of devotion to the guru; fasting; and prayer. The day ends as the devotee renews his or her resolve to make future spiritual progress.

It has become a common practice in some Hindu circles to have a special day of guru worship on the birthday (day of physical appearance) of the guru and to commemorate that day (Vaysa Puja) annually by issuing a book that will include pictures of the guru, excerpts of teachings, and accounts of his or her life.

Constance A. Jones

See also: Hinduism.

References

Harshananda, Swami. *Hindu Festivals and Sacred Days.* Bangalore: Ramakrishna Math, 1994.

Muktananda, Swami. *The Perfect Relationship: The Guru and the Disciple.* South Fallsburg, NY: Siddha Yoga Publications, 1999.

Mukuncharandas, Sadhu. *Hindu Festivals (Origin Sentiments & Rituals).* Amdavad, India: Swaminarayan Aksharpith, 2005.

Gush Emunim

Gush Emunim, the Bloc of the Faithful, is an Orthodox Jewish group founded in the wake of the Six-Day War of 1967, which pitted Israel against Syria, Jordan, and Egypt. As a result of the war Israel occupied new territory far beyond the borders fixed in 1949 by the armistice following its War of Independence, but part of historic Israel.

Immediately, a group led by Rabbi Tzvi Yehuda Kook, the son of the revered Rabbi Abraham Isaac Kook (1865–1935), former chief rabbi of Palestine, began planning to build Jewish settlements on this new land, even as the government of Israel considered returning it for peace with its Arab neighbors. The younger Kook believed Jews should possess all the territory included in the Israel of biblical times (including ancient Israel, Judea, and Samaria). He came to believe that possession of that land was a prerequisite for the coming of the promised Messiah.

Gush Emunim builds on the tradition of religious Zionism as expounded by such leaders as Rabbi Zvi Hirsch Kalischer (1795–1874), Rabbi Judah Alkalay (1798–1878), and Rabbi Samuel Mohilewer (1824–1898). As a minority movement among Zionists, the religious supporters organized the Mizrachi (Spiritual Center) movement in Vienna in 1901, at a conference called by Rabbi Isaac Jacob Reines (1839–1915), the organization's first president. Like all Orthodox Jews, they believed that a Messiah would come, and that he would reconstruct the temple and initiate a great Jewish empire that would be the instrument for establishing peace and prosperity for the world's people. They were also content, to some extent, to await the Messiah's coming. Rabbi's Kook's followers, the Gush Emunim, have given up waiting and operate on the idea that the Messiah wants or needs them to help prepare the way. According to the Gush Emunim, beyond the mere establishment of the state of Israel, the Temple Mount in Jerusalem needs to be cleared, the temple rebuilt, and all the biblical lands settled by Jews.

To carry out their program, once east Jerusalem was in Israeli hands, a member climbed to the top of the Wailing Wall and unfurled an Israeli flag. A short time later, Kook and some of his followers rented rooms at an Arab-run hotel in Hebron, the first step in a program to create a large number of settlements throughout the West Bank. Gush Emunim, though small, has additional support through their political party, the Tehiya Party, which, though also relatively small, has been able to block government attempts to return conquered land to Palestinian control. While unable to swing a large number of Israelis to its full program of religious messianism, in the 1970s they found the public supportive of the basic notion of Israel's territorial expansion.

The Gush Emunim have remained a small but important group in Israel. In 1980, some of the group were responsible for a failed attempt to blow up the Dome of the Rock, an important Muslim site in Jerusalem built in the seventh century. In the 1990s, rabbis sympathetic to the Gush Emunim position advocated disobedience to military orders to leave the occupied territories. At the same time, because of his activity in pursuing the peace process with the Palestinians, they called Prime Minister Yitzhak Rabin a traitor. In November 1995, Rabin was assassinated.

Gush Emunim, though small in membership, has sympathetic supporters throughout Israel for some of its primary affirmations, especially its desire to expand Israel's borders and provide no concessions to an independent Palestine. It remains somewhat secretive, especially as it has been supportive and knowledgeable about continuing violent incidents in Israel.

J. Gordon Melton

See also: Orthodox Judaism.

References

Gorenberg, Gershom. *The End of Days: Fundamentalism and the Struggle for the Temple Mount.* New York: Free Press, 2000.

Lustick, Ian. *For the Land and the Lord: Jewish Fundamentalism in Israel.* New York: Council on Foreign Relations, 1988.

Morrison, David. *The Gush: Center of Modern Religious Zionism.* Lynbrook, NY: Gefen Books, 2003.

Newman, David, ed. *The Impact of Gush Emunim: Politics and Settlement in the West Bank.* New York: St. Martin's Press, 1985.

Segal, Haggai. *Dear Brothers: The West Bank Jewish Underground.* Woodmere, NY: Beit Shamai Publications, 1988.

Sprinzak, Ehud. *Brother against Brother: Violence and Extremism in Israeli Politics from Altalena to the Rabin Assassination.* New York: Free Press, 1999.

Gutenberg, Johann

ca. 1398–1468

Though he lived and died a devout Roman Catholic, Johann Gutenberg is revered among Protestant Christians. His invention of moveable type is widely credited with both shaping Protestantism's orientation on the biblical Word and allowing the movement's relatively rapid spread through Europe in the mid-16th century.

Little is known of Gutenberg's early life. He was probably born in Mainz, Germany, around 1398, but only emerges out of obscurity around 1430, when his family moved to Strasbourg. By this time, he had gained some knowledge of metallurgy, which would serve him well in later life, and once in his new home he formed a partnership with Johann Fust, a well-to-do businessman.

Gutenberg actually had made several notable improvements of the printing press of his day, but they all take second place to his perfecting of a form of type based on individual letters that fit neatly on a single page and produced pages that were aesthetic to the reader. The use of individual letters allowed Gutenberg to quickly rearrange them to form new pages and thus greatly speed the process of producing books. The first book printed with the new press and technique was the Bible in Latin. This book, now known as the Gutenberg Bible, was published around 1455.

Shortly after demonstrating to the world the viability of their new techniques, Gutenberg and Fust had a falling out. Fust, having supplied the capital for the adventure, was impatient about recovering his investment. He sued Gutenberg and came into possession of the press, the type used for the Bible, as well as a whole new set of type that Gutenberg had prepared for a Psalter. Fust later published the Psalter.

Gutenberg had to locate a new patron, which he found in the person of Conrad Humery, the chancellor of the council in Mainz. With Humery's support, he produced the *Catholikon*, a grammar and alphabetic lexicon in 1460. The profit from the sales did not replace his losses to Fust and he lived the remaining years of his life in relative poverty. In 1565, Archbishop Adolf of Nassau began assisting Gutenberg, but

Portrait of Johann Gutenberg, German engraver who invented mechanical movable-type printing in Europe. (Library of Congress)

his support was little above bare subsistence. Few took notice when he died in Mainz, probably in 1468. His burial place is unknown.

Gutenberg emerged briefly into the public light, but faded back into obscurity before the impact of his accomplishments could be appreciated. His impact on Western history and religion, however, was immense. The new printing press he had produced aligned perfectly with the theology of the Word developed by Martin Luther. It allowed Protestants to identify the Word of God with the Bible and to incarnate their theology by printing the Bible in mass quantities in local languages and making it readily available to all. Equally important, in the early stages of the Reformation, Protestants proved more capable of quickly printing and distributing propaganda material that consolidated popular support against their Catholic opposition. The emphasis on the written Word, the authority of the Bible, and the study of the Bible by individual believers would become a defining characteristic of Protestantism that continues to the present day.

J. Gordon Melton

See also: Luther, Martin.

References

Davis, Martin. *The Gutenberg Bible.* London: British Library, 1996.

Ing, Janet. *Johann Gutenberg and His Bible.* New York: The Typophiles, 1988.

Kapr, Albert. *Johann Gutenberg: The Man and his Invention.* Trans. by Douglas Martin. London: Scolar Press, 1996.

Man, John. *Gutenberg: How One Man Remade the World with Words.* New York: Wiley, 2002.

Scholderer, Victor. *Johann Gutenberg: The Inventor of Printing.* 2nd ed. London: British Museum, 1970.

Thorpe, James Ernest. *The Gutenberg Bible: Landmark in Learning.* San Marino, CA: Huntington Library, 1975.

■ Guyana

Guyana, on South America's northern coast, is located between Venezuela and Surinam. Its southern border is shared with Brazil. The former Dutch colony has 76,000 square miles of land, much of it hot and humid and along the three main rivers—the Essequibo, the Demerara, and the Berbice. Most of the population of 771,000 reside on the northern coastal plain.

Human beings may have reached what is today the country of Guyana as early as 35,000 years ago. In modern times it came to be the home of two people, the Arawak people, who inhabited the coast, and the Caribs in the interior. Eventually, the more warlike Caribs displaced the Arawaks, a process repeated several times as both groups moved into the islands of the Caribbean. They bequeathed to the region, its name, Guyana, or "land of waters."

Christopher Columbus sailed along the coast of Guyana in 1498, but the first European settlers were from Holland. The Dutch constructed a fort in 1616,

Hindus offer morning prayers in a Vishnu temple in Georgetown, Guyana. Many Hindu families have been living in Guyana since the first Indian slaves arrived there in 1838. (Prakash Singh/AFP/Getty Images)

the first of several settlements to facilitate trade. The Dutch West India Company administered the colony into the 18th century. As agriculture increased in the mid-1600s, the Company began to import African slaves, and the shrinking Native population moved inland. In the 1770s, Guyana became contested territory, and after four decades during which it changed hands several times, it became a British possession in 1814, and was known as British Guyana. The British retained control until independence in 1966, when it assumed the name Guyana. Since 1968, the People's National Congress has been the leading political party.

The Guyanese Constitution guarantees religious freedom. During the early decades of independence, however, the Marxist-oriented governments promoted atheism, one symbol of which was the nationalization of all the schools operated by various religious groups. Religious groups and buildings are registered through the government's Ministry of Home Affairs. The presence of foreign religious personnel is strictly regulated.

Indigenous religions have survived in the interior of Guyana, especially among the Arekung, Macushi, and Warrau peoples. But Christianity is now followed by a slight majority of the people, and Guyana has possibly the highest percentage of adherents to Hinduism of any country in the Americas (32 percent).

Roman Catholicism was introduced in 1657 by brothers of the Capuchin Order, but their work did not survive. Missionaries from the Netherlands Reformed Church and the Moravian Brethren arrived later in the century. The first Reformed church was erected in 1720, and Dutch Lutherans built a church in 1743, both primarily serving the Dutch community. The Reformed Church had a policy of not allowing either Africans or Guyanese people to become members.

GUYANA

Guyana

Religion	Followers in 1970	Followers in 2010	% of Population	Annual % growth 2000–2010	Followers in 2025	Followers in 2050
Christians	383,000	370,000	50.6	0.10	337,000	228,000
Protestants	96,000	195,000	26.7	2.06	195,000	145,000
Roman Catholics	110,000	88,000	12.0	0.00	85,000	60,000
Anglicans	100,000	52,000	7.1	−4.71	50,000	45,000
Hindus	227,000	241,000	32.9	0.14	227,000	160,000
Muslims	63,800	61,300	8.4	0.14	58,000	40,000
Ethnoreligionists	20,000	17,400	2.4	0.14	15,000	10,000
Baha'is	1,700	13,000	1.8	0.14	13,500	11,000
Agnostics	3,000	11,000	1.5	1.37	12,000	10,000
Spiritists	7,000	9,600	1.3	0.14	9,000	8,000
Atheists	1,000	4,100	0.6	0.14	5,000	4,000
Chinese folk	1,000	2,100	0.3	0.14	2,600	2,000
Buddhists	2,000	1,800	0.2	0.14	4,000	4,000
Jews	50	60	0.0	0.00	100	100
Total population	**709,000**	**731,000**	**100.0**	**0.14**	**683,000**	**477,000**

A new era in Guyanese religion began with the establishment of British control. The London Missionary Society entered the country in 1807, and the Church of England was established as the favored religious community in 1810. State support was withdrawn from the Reformed Church, and it was gradually superseded by the Church of Scotland (Presbyterians), that church having been established in 1766 by several plantation owners. It began to receive state funds in 1837.

Methodism in the islands had a unique beginning. It was brought to Guyana by freed slaves from Nevis in 1802. The church was then supplemented by British immigrants. Rounding out the Guyanese scene were the Canadian Presbyterians (1885) and the Seventh-day Adventist Church (1887). During the 20th century, notable work was founded by the Ethiopian Orthodox Tewahedo Church, the Assemblies of God, and an independent evangelical sending agency, the Unevangelized Fields Mission, which now works in the country's interior. Among the more interesting indigenous churches are the Jordanites, an independent Pentecostal church, and the Hallelujah Church, which emerged in the interior in the 1870s under the leadership of a new prophet named Abel.

Protestant Christians associate with each other across denominational lines through the Guyana Council of Churches, an affiliate of the World Council of Churches. Conservative Protestants are associated in the Guyana Evangelical Fellowship, which is related to the World Evangelical Alliance.

The Roman Catholic Church was re-established in 1826 with the arrival of an initial priest. The effort proved quite successful, and a vicariate was erected a mere 11 years later. The Diocese of Georgetown was designated in 1956. Catholicism now has the largest following in Guyana, followed by the Anglicans, whose work is now a diocese of the Church of the Province of the West Indies, and the Assemblies of God.

Following the abolition of slavery in 1833, the British turned to India as a source of labor. Indians (most of whom were Hindus) were recruited for work on plantations and brought to Guyana as indentured servants. They were largely from rural India, predominantly male, with 10 percent children and 30 percent female. Those between the ages of 10 and 20 were counted as adults. Some 200,000 were transported to Guyana, and their descendants now constitute 53 percent of the population. Many left Hinduism for Christianity, as the British made it an official policy for Hindus to become Christians before they could be eligible for the better civilian jobs.

Traditional Hinduism underwent some development as people from different parts of India were thrown together on plantations with Africans and members of the Native peoples. Various forms of traditional Hinduism, both Vaishnava and Saivite, remain popular, most of the temples being associated with the Hindu Orthodox Guyana Sanathan Dharma Maha Sabha, the largest single religious group in the country. Hindu priests have organized the Guyana Pandits Society. Two popular Hindu holy days, Diwali and Holi (Phagwa), are celebrated as national holidays.

There are small groups associated with the International Society for Krishna Consciousness, the Sri Sathya Sai Baba Organization of Guyana, and the Arya Samaj. There is also a chapter of the Vishwa Hindu Parishad.

A percentage of the Indian immigrants to Guyana were Muslim, the great majority being Sunnis of the Hanafite and Shafiite schools. There are lesser numbers of Ismailis and Shias. The Shiites, who have no separate mosque, have felt some discrimination from the Sunni majority, especially with the growth of a vocal Wahhabi presence. Guyana's pluralistic culture has provided fertile ground for both branches of the Ahmadiyyas, the Ahmadiyya Movement in Islam and the Ahmadiyya Anjuman Ishaat Islam, Lahore, and for the Baha'i Faith.

Although most Africans brought to Guyana (who currently constitute approximate one-third of the population) have become Christians, some have also become Hindus and Muslims, while a noticeable minority have continued to practice a form of their traditional African faiths. These now find expression in Guyanese Vodou (with a base in Ashanti religion from West Africa) and Spiritism, their life being somewhat affected by the improved communications between Caribbean lands and by the injection of the Rastafarian movement from Jamaica. One African-derived religion, the Comfa religion, focuses on the ancestral spirits of the various ethnic groups that constitute Guyanese society.

In November 1987, Guyana became the scene of one of the more dramatic religious events of the 20th century. More than 900 members of the Peoples Temple who had established an agricultural colony in a rural part of the country were involved in a massive act of murder and suicide. Although this event occurred in isolation from the ongoing life of Guyanese religions as a whole, it affected the larger religious community worldwide.

J. Gordon Melton

See also: Ahmadiyya Anjuman Ishaat Islam, Lahore; Ahmadiyya Movement in Islam; Arya Samaj; Assemblies of God; Baha'i Faith; Church of England; Church of Scotland; Ethiopian Orthodox Tewahedo Church; Hanafite School of Islam; International Society for Krishna Consciousness; London Missionary Society; Netherlands Reformed Churches; Peoples Temple; Rastafarians; Roman Catholic Church; Seventh-day Adventist Church; Shafiite School of Islam; Spiritism; Vodou; Wahhabi Islam; World Council of Churches; World Evangelical Alliance.

References

Aksharananda, Swami. "Hinduism in Guyana: A Study in Traditions of Worship." Ph.D. diss., University of Wisconsin, 1993.

Gibson, Kean. *Comfa Religion and Creole Language in a Caribbean Community*. Albany: State University of New York Press, 2001.

Gibson, Kean. *Sacred Duty: Hinduism and Violence in Guyana*. Princeton, NJ: GroupFive, 2005.

Hoyte, Hugh Desmond. *Hinduism, Religious Diversity and Social Cohesion: The Guyana Experience*. N.p.: Guyana National Printers Limited, 1987.

Jayawardena, C. "Religious Belief and Social Change: Aspects of the Development of Hinduism in British Guiana." *Comparative Studies in Society and History: An International Quarterly* 8, no. 1 (1966): 211–240.

Premdas, R. R. "Religion and Reconciliation in the Multi-Ethnic States of the Third World." Ph.D. diss., McGill University, 1991.

H

Haein-sa Temple

Located in a valley at the foot of Gaya Mountain in the Hapcheon-gun region in South Gyeongsang Province, the Haein-sa Temple is one of the Three Jewels Temples of the Republic of (South) Korea. Each temple was designed to represent one of the Three Jewels of Buddhism—the Buddha, the Dharma, and the Sangha. Haein-sa Temple is focused upon the Dharma, Buddha's teachings. The name of the temple, Haein, is drawn from Korean phrases that refer to the enlightened world of Buddha and/or humankind's naturally unpolluted mind (Buddha nature).

The temple was initially built in 802, the story of its founding mixing history and legend. Its founding is tied to two Korean monks, Suneung and his disciple Ijeong, who had been away studying in China. On their return at the beginning of the ninth century, they discovered the wife of King Aejang (r. 800–809) ill with a tumor. The monks reputedly tied a piece of string to the tumor and ran it to a nearby tree. They subsequently began chanting and all were surprised to see the tumor shrink and the tree wither. King Aejang built Haein-sa out of gratitude for the healing of his wife. Another story has a more mundane account, namely, that the two monks secured the support of the dowager queen, who financed the monastic complex. As originally conceived, the temple was a base for Hwaom Buddhism and its propagation of the Avatamsaka or Flower Garland Sutra. Today it is a Son (Zen) Buddhist center.

Haein-sa is entered through three gates that lead to the courtyard. Straight ahead up a flight of stairs is the main hall. Constructed in 1818 on foundations laid in the ninth century, it is dominated by seven statues of Buddhas and bodhisattvas—the central statue being of a mega-statue of Vairocana. Of the rest, two—Avalokitesvara and Popgi, or Born of Truth Bodhisattva—are made of iron. The others—Manjushri, Ksitigarbha, Samantabhadra, and a second statue of Vairocana—are carved from wood. The wooden Vairocana, Manjusri, and Samantabhadra statues were all carved from a huge ginkgo tree during the rule of the Koryo dynasty (r. 918–1392). Additionally, the main hall is graced with a set of paintings of Buddha's life painted during the Choson (or Joseon) dynasty (1392–August 1910).

As worthy as is the main hall of attention, it pales beside what is to be found above and behind it—the Janggyeong Panjeon complex. The halls of the complex are the depositories for the 81,258 wooden printing blocks upon which are found the complete text of the Tripitaka Koreana. These blocks date to the time of King Gojong of Goryeo (r. 1213–1259), whose lengthy reign was marked by prolonged warfare with Manchuria. He turned to Buddhism to protect the nation, and in that effort he had the texts of Buddhist scriptures transferred to the printing blocks. The project took 16 years and was carried out on Kanghwado Island near Seoul. The project was completed in 1252. An earlier set, carved in the 11th century, was burned by Mongol invaders.

The Janggyeong Panjeon complex was built to hold the blocks. The four halls were expanded and renovated during the reign of King Sejo (r. 1455–1468) in 1457. These halls survived the various fires at the temple through the centuries and the devastation of the Korean War (1950–1953). A pilot sent to bomb the temple during the war found himself unable to release his bomb load. As a result he was initially court-martialed

Stupa in a courtyard at the ninth-century Haein-sa Temple complex, South Korea. (Carmen Redondo/Corbis)

and imprisoned but later released and honored for what was seen as brave act.

At present, the temple is a permanent home to about 220 monks (including novices) while the 15 hermitages just outside the temple complex house some 200 women. Also, around the temple, 500 mountain men reside.

J. Gordon Melton

See also: Korean Buddhism; Songgwangsa; T'onngdo-sa Temple.

References

Chung, Byung-jo. *History of Korean Buddhism.* Eddison, NJ: Jimoondang, 2007.

"Haein-sa: The Temples of the Learning." Buddhapia. http://eng.buddhapia.com/_Service/_ContentView/ETC_CONTENT_2.ASP?PK =0000766183&danrak_no=&clss_cd=&top _menu_cd=0000000808. Accessed May 15, 2009.

Hagia Sophia

The construction of Hagia Sophia, one of the great monuments of Byzantine Christianity, was completed in 538 CE in what was then Constantinople (now Istanbul, Turkey) after almost six years of building work under the mandate of the Emperor Justinian, following the destruction of the previous church on the site during a rebellion in 532. The elevated site had, it is believed, been a Pagan temple when Constantine I (272–337) came to power early in the fourth century and transformed Christianity from a persecuted religion into a state-supported church. The original church was erected between a smaller, hastily completed church, the original cathedral for the city, and the emperor's palace complex. It was constructed during the emperorship of Constantine's son, Constantius II (317–361), whose reign began in 337. It was dedicated near the end of his time in power in 360. The gold and silver items he donated to the church were lost when

Arian Christians vandalized the church in 381, an act occasioned by the church council meeting there. The Council of Constantinople had reaffirmed the Nicene Creed and offered further condemnation of the theological position of Arius (260–336).

In 404, John Chrysostom, the archbishop of Constantinople, was exiled by the Emperor Arcadius (377–408) because he had made critical remarks about his wife. Riots erupted during which the church was destroyed. It fell to the Emperor Theodosius II (401–450) to build a new church, which was completed in 415. That church would stand until the riots of 532. The so-called Nike riots began over disagreements relative to sports competition (which carried underlying political dimensions). They led to the destruction of a large portion of the city, including the cathedral church.

Emperor Justinian I (483–565) took the occasion of the rebuilding of the city to inaugurate construction of a church that would be the most magnificent in existence. In this effort, he recruited the two most renowned architects of the day: Anthemius of Tralles (Aydin) and Isidorus of Miletus. He also stayed involved in the building's development and brought in resources from different parts of the empire (including materials taken from older Pagan temples), as needed or desired. It was completed on December 27, 537. The finished cathedral was the largest in the world for a millennium, until supplanted by the Cathedral at Seville in 1520.

The building was erected on a square base over which was placed a large dome, approaching the size of that of the Pantheon in Rome. The central dome has a maximum diameter of 102 feet, 6 inches. It reaches 182 feet, 5 inches above the floor. The dome was all the more unique because of 40 windows that were placed around its base. It was the first pendentive dome in history, a pendentive being an innovative device that permits the placing of a circular dome over a square room by carrying the weight of the dome to the four corners of the building base.

Above and beyond the ravages of time, the church was subject to the periodic earthquakes that affect the area and to the actions of those who attacked the city through riots and war. Just 20 years after the church's completion, the city was hit by earthquakes in 553,

557, and 558, requiring significant repairs. Additional damage was incurred in 869 and 986.

In 1204, frustrated Crusaders, unable to accomplish their goals in the Holy Land, turned on Constantinople and amid the sacking of the city did not leave Hagia Sophia untouched. This action still affects the relationship between Eastern Orthodoxy and the Roman Catholic Church. Then in 1453, the Ottoman Turks captured Constantinople and soon afterward converted the church into a mosque. They added minarets, but preserved the interior frescoes and mosaics (though they later covered them with plaster). The interior worship structures were altered to fit requirements for a mosque, including the establishment of worship toward Mecca.

Istanbul had been the headquarters of the Ottoman Empire until its fall in the years after World I. In 1935, Kemal Ataturk (1881–1938), then the head of the new secularized Turkish government, ordered Hagia Sophia converted into a museum on February 1, 1935. Ataturk visited the museum a few days later, on February 6, 1935. It remains a museum to the present.

J. Gordon Melton

See also: Cathedrals—Christian; Istanbul; Mosques.

References

Balfour, John Patrick Douglas. *Hagia Sophia*. New York: W. W. Norton & Company, 1972.

Harris, Jonathan. *Constantinople: Capital of Byzantium*. New York: Hambledon/Continuum, 2007.

Mainstone, Rowland J. *Hagia Sophia: Architecture, Structure and Liturgy of Justinian's Great Church*. London: Thames & Hudson, 1988.

Swainson, Harold. *The Church of Sancta Sophia Constantinople: A Study of Byzantine Building*. Boston: Adamant Media Corporation, 2005.

■ Haiti

The Caribbean island nation of Haiti shares the island of Hispaniola with the Dominican Republic. Its 10,600 square miles of territory includes the western third of Hispaniola's land. Its 8.9 million citizens (2008) are almost totally of African descent.

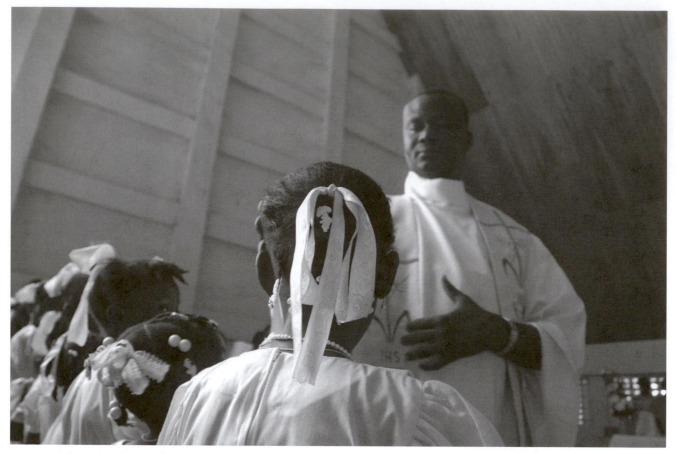

A young girl is confirmed at a Catholic ceremony in Gonaives, Haiti. (David Snyder/Dreamstime.com)

Estimates of the number of inhabitants on the island of Hispaniola at the time of Columbus's arrival in 1492 vary from 500,000 to 2 million. Within 50 years, they had been reduced to a few hundred, such that the Spanish were forced to turn to African slaves as a replacement labor force. Although the island's native religious cultures, those of the Taino and Carib, all but perished with their bearers, certain indigenous Caribbean influences are still notable in Haitian Vodou. Zaka, the Vodou spirit of agriculture, for instance, is perhaps a derivative of an indigenous corn spirit.

As early as 1502 the Spanish were shipping enslaved Africans to the island, empowered by the 1454 papal bull *Romanus pontifex*. Slaves were forcibly baptized Catholic, yet their conversion was usually cosmetic. African religious traditions, despite their prohibition, thus thrived in the colony, especially in maroon communities, absorbing Catholic elements and eventually becoming the religion known as Vodou.

In response to an increasingly uncontrollable French presence on the island's northwestern coast, the Spanish ceded the western third of the island to the French at the Treaty of Ryswick in 1697. Statistics reveal the explosion of the French plantation system that followed: when the treaty was signed, there were roughly 2,000 slaves in the nascent French colony of Saint-Domingue, whereas by 1789, more than 600,000 slaves labored for the colony, at one point producing one-third of all sugar consumed in Europe.

French Catholicism in Saint-Domingue was hampered by a weak and factional priesthood, whose conversion of enslaved Africans was largely a perfunctory gesture required by article 2 of the *Code Noir*, the royal decree governing the treatment of slaves in French colonies. The arrival of the Society of Jesus in 1704 marked a significant change in this regard. French Jesuits learned African languages and established a more genuine mission for more than half the colony's slaves.

HAITI

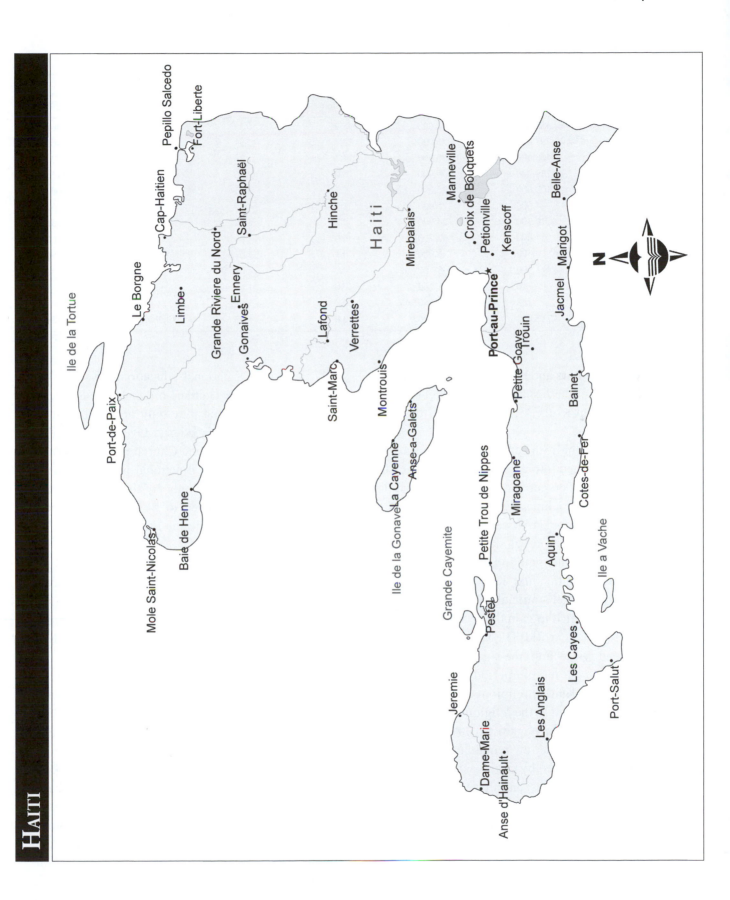

Haiti

Religion	Followers in 1970	Followers in 2010	% of Population	Annual % growth 2000–2010	Followers in 2025	Followers in 2050
Christians	4,555,000	9,574,000	95.2	1.53	11,617,000	14,340,000
Roman Catholics	3,797,000	7,285,000	72.4	1.51	8,500,000	10,000,000
Protestants	400,000	1,480,000	14.7	1.88	2,000,000	2,700,000
Independents	139,000	500,000	5.0	2.36	750,000	1,116,000
Spiritists	100,000	273,000	2.7	3.11	330,000	400,000
Agnostics	44,000	175,000	1.7	4.93	300,000	450,000
Baha'is	10,700	24,900	0.2	3.42	40,000	55,000
New religionists	1,000	3,700	0.0	1.64	4,500	6,000
Atheists	500	6,000	0.1	12.01	10,000	18,000
Muslims	1,500	2,400	0.0	1.64	2,700	4,500
Chinese folk	0	260	0.0	1.66	300	500
Jews	100	240	0.0	1.61	300	500
Total population	**4,713,000**	**10,060,000**	**100.0**	**1.63**	**12,305,000**	**15,275,000**

Colony administrators and plantation owners soon became suspicious of the Jesuits, however, accused them of insubordination to the Crown, and had them expelled in 1763.

By the end of the 18th century persistent slave resistance mushroomed into a national revolt following an August 1791 Vodou ceremony at Boïs Caiman led by a slave named Boukman Dutty. Over the next 13 years of revolt, the popular Africa-based religion served to unite and inspire the rebel slaves to defeat Napoleon's forces and finally gain independence in 1804.

Independent Haiti's first leaders (who declared Catholicism the nation's official religion, which it remains today) struggled to gain the recognition and respect of the rest of the world. The Vatican, for example, refused to send priests until the signing of a concordat in 1860. The 54-year interim period was one of especial importance in Haitian religious history, as Vodou was further crystallized as the religion of the peasantry (despite new prohibitions against it). As for the Haitian Catholic Church, the few remaining priests in the new republic were joined by clerics who had been expelled from other colonies, and these men provided a dubious and inadequate sacerdotal leadership for Haitian Catholics. In such a disorderly ecclesial climate, popular Catholicism developed more unrestrainedly in Haiti than anywhere else in the Americas.

Shortly after the signing of the concordat in 1860, French Catholic missionaries came to Haiti and aggressively developed a national educational system. Not until the 1950s were Haitians ordained in significant numbers, and even then they only accounted for 20 percent of the country's priests. Over the course of these 100 years the Catholic Church was transformed into the largest and most functional institution in the country, rivaled in power only by the Haitian armed forces, and was kowtowed to by all Haitian heads of state, save the recalcitrant François Duvalier (r. 1957–1971).

Besides educating and ministering to the better part of the population, the Catholic Church hierarchy in Haiti has until very recently sought to eradicate Vodou from Haitian society. Three formal "antisuperstition" campaigns were waged to this end, in 1896, 1913, and 1941–1942. The last of these saw the Haitian government put the military at the church's disposal, and the resultant repression of Vodou practitioners and destruction of a treasury of national art represents one of the great tragedies in Haitian religious history.

Tempered by the spirit of the Second Vatican Council (1962–1965) and inspired by the force of Liberation Theology, the popular Haitian Catholic Church has changed radically in recent decades, both becoming acculturated and taking sides with the poor. Vodou rhythms and drums are now common features in Catholic Masses, and Catholic base communities have emerged as a potent political force, known collectively as *tilegliz* (Haitian Creole: little church). Empowered by Pope John Paul II's March 1983 visit and forceful declaration that "Something must change here," the tilegliz movement served to rally the masses against the oppressive Duvalier regime, eventually leading to the dramatic departure of Jean-Claude Duvalier in 1984 and the election of populist priest Jean-Bertrand Aristide as president in 1990.

As in other Latin American nations, the Charismatic Renewal is recently having a strong impact on Haitian Catholicism. The direct emotional religious experiences normally associated with Protestant Pentecostal revivals now feature in many Haitian Catholic Masses, and the annual national Charismatic convention in Port-au-Prince draws tens of thousands and is marked by dramatic healings, speaking in tongues, and witnessing.

A recent survey of more than 1,000 households in rural Haiti shows that as many as 30 percent of Haitians today are Protestant. Though surprising, this figure is in reality a reflection of Haiti's participation in the hemisphere-wide turn of Third World Catholics to Protestant Pentecostalism. Protestantism in Haiti, moreover, has a long history, beginning with the 1817 establishment of the Methodist Wesleyan Mission. Other Protestant sects emerged in Haiti in ensuing decades, including the Baptist, Episcopalian, and Seventh-day Adventist churches. Today, most major Protestant sects count significant numbers of followers in Haiti; the largest is the Convention Baptiste de' Haite, which was founded in 1924 and by 1986 counted 120,000 members.

Religious freedom is enjoyed today by all of Haiti's nine million citizens. Vodou has gained greater respect and is widely appreciated as a source of Haitian pride and identity and a driving force behind Haiti's rich artistic culture. Although small numbers of Buddhists, Muslims, and members of the Baha'i Faith can be found in Port-au-Prince, by far the most influential religious movements besides Christianity in Haiti are Freemasonry and Rosicrucianism, both of which date to the colonial era. Although the esoteric nature of these movements precludes any estimation of their numbers, many Haitian heads of state have been Masons, and historically the Catholic Church hierarchy has been troubled by the attraction of its flock—and especially of upper-class Haitian Catholics—to Freemasonry and Rosicrucianism.

Terry Rey

See also: Convention Baptiste de' Haite; Freemasonry; Roman Catholic Church; Seventh-day Adventist Church; Vodou.

References

Bellegarde-Smith, Patrick. *Fragments of Bone: Neo-African Religions in a New World*. Urbana: University of Illinois Press, 2005.

Bellegarde-Smith, Patrick, and Claudine Michel, eds. *Haitian Vodou: Spirit, Myth, and Reality*. Bloomington: Indiana University Press, 2006.

Conway, F. J. "Pentecostalism in the Context of Haitian Religion and Health Practice." Ph.D. diss., American University, 1978.

Dayan, Colin. *Haiti, History, and the Gods*. Berkeley: University of California Press, 1998.

Desmangles, L. G. *The Faces of the Gods: Vodou and Roman Catholicism in Haiti*. Chapel Hill: University of North Carolina Press, 1992.

Greene, A. *The Catholic Church in Haiti: Political and Social Change*. East Lansing: Michigan State University Press, 1993.

McAlister, Elizabeth. *Rara! Vodou, Power, and Performance in Haiti and Its Diaspora*. Berkeley: University of California Press, 2002.

Michel, Claudine, and Patrick Bellegarde-Smith, eds. *Vodou in Haitian Life and Culture: Invisible Power*. New York: Palgrave Macmillan, 2006.

Rey, Terry. *Our Lady of Class Struggle: The Cult of the Virgin Mary in Haiti*. Trenton, NJ: Africa World Press, 1999.

Simpson, G. E. *Religious Cults of the Caribbean: Trinidad, Jamaica, and Haiti*. Rio Piedras: Institute of Caribbean Studies, University of Puerto Rico, 1980.

Hanafite School of Islam

The Hanafite School of Islam is one of four *madhhabs* (schools) of jurisprudence recognized as orthodox within the Sunni Muslim world. Islam is centered upon submission to God (Allah) and obedience to the

Sunni Muslim men pray at Abu Hanifa Mosque in central Baghdad, Iraq, as they mark the first day of Eid. Eid is a Muslim holiday that marks the end of the holy month of Ramadan. (AP Photo/Karim Kadim)

shariah, or law. As Islam developed, necessary decisions over acceptable and unacceptable behavior led to the elevation of jurisprudence within the Muslim community as a variety of interpretations of the Koran and the Sunnah, the collection of *hadith* (the sayings and action of the prophet Muhammad and his companions). Through the first centuries of Islam, different collections of hadith appeared and only slowly did a consensus emerge concerning what constituted the authentic hadith.

Abu Hanifah (699–767) was a merchant in Kufa, in Mesopotamia (modern-day Iraq). He used the lessons of his mercantile experience when he turned to legal studies. After being a student for many years, he became a teacher and instructed many in his system.

He left no writings behind and it was left to two students, Abu Yusuf (ca. 731–198) and Muhammad ibn al-Hasan al-Shaybani (749–ca. 804), and later scholars to develop the Hanafi perspective. A large body of legal commentaries produced by scholars over the centuries now forms the library of the Hanafi School. As Hanafi thought developed, it contended for acceptance with the Malikite and Shafiite schools. In the 9th and 10th centuries, the Abbasid Empire tended to favor the Shafiite School and the Hanafi approach went into eclipse. However, with the rise of the Ottoman Empire, the Hanafi School was revived and became the dominant school in those lands under its control. It has thus survived as the dominant school of Islam in Turkey and Egypt and the lands between (Syria, Lebanon, Jordan) and eastward into central Asia, Pakistan, India, and China (though challenged by Shia Islam in Iran and Iraq).

Muslim legal thought has four sources—the Koran, the Sunnah, the consensus of the *ulama* (community of those knowledgeable in Islamic law and theology), and reasoning by analogy, the latter principle allowing a general broadening of areas covered by the law. Like the other schools of jurisprudence, Hanafi legal scholars agree upon the importance of the Koran and the traditions passed through the Sunnah as important, and give due reverence to the consensus of the ulama. However, the Hanafi are distinguished by the relative importance they give to the use of analogy (*qiyas*) and tolerance of a resulting range of opinion (*ra'y*) on some issues. Hanafis use human reason to compare a current situation with one for which legislation already exists. Thus the Hanafi School has been seen as the most liberal of the four schools and the one that has been most open to issues of personal freedom.

The liberality of the Hanafis made them the object of attack by the Traditionalists, especially the Hanbalite School that rejected the use of analogy and placed its emphasis upon a conservative reading of the Koran and Sunnah. Those forces that opposed the Ottoman Empire, which had adopted the Hanafite system for its legal discourse, cited their opposition to the Hanafite School as part of their rationale for fighting the empire.

J. Gordon Melton

See also: Abu Hanifa; Hanbalite School of Islam; Malikite School of Islam; Shafiite School of Islam; Shia Islam.

References

Coulson, Noel J. *Conflicts and Tensions in Islamic Jurisprudence*. Chicago: University of Chicago Press, 1969.

Coulson, Noel J. *A History of Islamic Law*. Edinburgh: Edinburgh University Press, 1994.

Hallaq, Wael B. *A History of Islamic Legal Theories: An Introduction to Sunni Usul al-Fiqh*. New York: Cambridge University Press, 1997.

Horrie, Chris, and Peter Chippindale. *What Is Islam?* London: Virgin Publishing 1998.

Schacht, Joseph. *An Introduction to Islamic Law*. Oxford: Oxford University Press, 1964.

Watt, Montgomery. *The Majesty That Was Islam*. New York: Praeger Publishers, 1974.

Hanbalite School of Islam

The Hanbalite School of Islam is one of the four *madhhabs* (schools) of jurisprudence deemed orthodox within the world of Sunni Islam. The school traces its origin to Ahmad ibn Hanbal (780–855). Born in Baghdad, he would travel widely across the Arabian Peninsula and throughout the Muslim world. Though he never authored a single book on jurisprudence (*fiqh*), after his death, his students (including his son, Abd Allah (d. 903) gathered his writings, including a number of *fatwas* (legal pronouncements), which once assembled manifested the breadth of his work on the *shariah* (Islamic law).

Hanbal, though a student of Muhammad ibn Idris ibn al-Abbas ibn Uthman ibn Shafi (767–820), the founder of the Shafiite School of Islam, developed a more strict approach to legal interpretation that centered upon the Koran and the Sunnah, the collection of *hadith* (the sayings and action of the prophet Muhammad and his companions). He played down the role of the *ulama* (community of those knowledgeable in Islamic law and theology) and reasoning by analogy, which had become so established in the Hanafite School. The result was a more rigid approach to Islam

that among other opinions developed a significant dislike of Sufism as a departure from orthodox Islam.

The Hanbalite School grew strong during the 9th and 10th centuries, but in 945 the new Buwayhid dynasty (which favored the Shia Islam) turned against the Hanbalites. The school enjoyed a revival under subsequent dynasties in the 11th and 12th centuries. Though not the most favored at court, the Hanbalites remained active through 15th century during which time one of its most celebrated teachers, Ahmad ibn Taymiyya (d. 1328), appeared. The school further suffered in popularity with the rise of the Ottoman Empire, which favored the Hanafite School. The Hanbalite School survived mainly in pockets on the Arabian Peninsula.

The Hanbalite School experienced a revival in Arabia during the career of Muhammad ibn Abd-al-Wahhab (ca. 1703–1791). He founded a movement closely identified with the Hanbalite perspective (though many Hanbalite scholars have not supported it). The identification of the Saud family in Arabia with the Wahhabi movement provided an agenda for their moving against the Ottoman Empire and led in the 1930s to the establishment of the modern state of Saudi Arabia. Wahhabism is now the professed faith of the ruling elite in Saudi Arabia and Hanbalism the majority religious community in Saudi Arabia, which is home to a variety of Islamic schools, and the Hanbalite legal system forms the basis of state law. The Hanbalite School exists as a minority party in India, Egypt, and Syria.

J. Gordon Melton

See also: Hanafite School of Islam; Ibn Hanbal, Ahmad; Malikite School of Islam; Shafiite School of Islam; Wahhabi Islam.

References

Coulson, Noel J. *Conflicts and Tensions in Islamic Jurisprudence*. Chicago: University of Chicago Press, 1969.

Coulson, Noel J. *A History of Islamic Law*. Edinburgh: Edinburgh University Press, 1994.

Hallaq, Wael B. *A History of Islamic Legal Theories: An Introduction to Sunni Usul al-Fiqh*. New York: Cambridge University Press, 1997.

Horrie, Chris, and Peter Chippindale. *What Is Islam?* London: Virgin Publishing 1998.

Schacht, Joseph. *An Introduction to Islamic Law.* Oxford: Oxford University Press, 1964.

Watt, Montgomery. *The Majesty That Was Islam.* New York: Praeger Publishers, 1974.

Hanukkah

Hanukkah (or Chanukah), sometimes referred to as the Festival of Lights, is an eight-day holiday recalling the events of the Maccabean Revolt, the reclaiming of hegemony over the Temple at Jerusalem, and a reliving of the celebration that followed. These events occurred in the second century BCE, when Judea was part of the Seleucid Empire, one of several empires that arose following the death of Alexander the Great and the subsequent breakup of his great empire. During the second century, Antiochus IV Epiphanes (r. 175–164) emerged as the Seleucid ruler.

Much of the regime of Antiochus IV was taken up with efforts to assert control over Egypt, which were blocked by the Roman Empire in 168. Meanwhile, in Jerusalem the high priesthood had become embroiled in corruption, as Antiochus began appointing to the office those who bribed him. When a dispossessed Jewish high priest seized the moment, raised an army, and attacked the city of Jerusalem, Menelaus, the high priest Antiochus had chosen, fled the city. In return, Antiochus moved on Jerusalem and, in 167, restored Menelaus and then massacred many Jews. He then decided to go further and incorporate the Jews into the Hellenic world. He successively looted the Temple, outlawed the Jewish religion, and ordered the worship of Zeus as the supreme god. To enforce his orders, he had an altar to Zeus erected in the Temple upon which pigs were sacrificed. This desecration of the Temple was later termed the "abomination of desolation."

Antiochus's actions, especially relative to the Temple, galvanized many to fight against Seleucid rule and provoked a large-scale revolt originally led by Mattathias (d. ca. 166) and his five sons, the most famous among them being Judah the Hammer or Yehuda HaMakabi (Maccabee). In 164, the Maccabees succeeded in recapturing the Temple; they then purified it and rededicated it. The Maccabees called for an eight-day celebration to commemorate the re-consecration of the Temple. This story is retold in the apocryphal first book of Maccabees.

Missing from the oldest account of the story of the Temple restoration is any mention of a miraculous occurrence that reputedly accompanied this initial celebration. It seems that the olive oil needed to keep the lamp in the Temple lighted was lacking. Only enough for one day was available. In spite of the lack of oil, the lamp in the Temple was kept burning for eight days—equal to the time required for a fresh batch of olive oil to be prepared. At a later date, the leaders of the community instituted Hanukkah to commemorate the miracle that occurred during the original celebration of the rededication of the temple.

Several explanations of the events following the Maccabean Revolt have been offered. Some have suggested that the eight-day celebration was in fact the holding of the festivals of Sukkot (the Feast of Tabernacles) and Shemini Atzeret, for their proper celebrations had not been possible during the years of the revolt. These two holy days combined take eight days.

Modern scholarship on the Maccabean era has suggested that what propelled Antiochus to introduce the decrees outlawing Judaism was not Hellenistic zeal but rather a determination to quash an internal provincial civil war. These scholars focus on the fighting in Jerusalem among the followers of the various claimants to the high priesthood. Since the Temple and Judaism seemed to lie at the center of the civil war, Antiochus subsequently decided to extirpate Judaism and demand that the Jews adapt Greek culture and religion.

Modern Hanukkah is an eight-day celebration starting on the 25th day of the month of Kislev on the Hebrew calendar, which places it in late November or December on the Common Era calendar. There is a story told in the second book of Maccabees concerning the relighting of the altar fire by Nehemiah as the result of a miracle that had occurred on Kislev 25. This event from an earlier era appears to be the reason Judah Maccabees selected Kislev as the day for the rededication of the altar in 165 BCE.

Observance is carried out through a set of rituals performed each day of the eight days. Most are family-

An Ultra-Orthodox Jewish family lights candles on the fifth night of Hanukkah in the Mea Sharim neighborhood of Jerusalem. (AFP/Getty Images)

based and occur around the evening meal, the most important being the lighting of the candles soon after nightfall. On the first night a single light is lit, that number increasing by one each of the eight nights. The Hanukkah *menorah* has room for nine candles, the ninth, the *shamash* or guardian candle, should be higher than the others and is used to light the other candles. As the candles are lit, specific blessings over the lights and remembering God's miracles are said.

Other objects closely associated with Hanukkah are the *dreidel*, a four-sided spinning top that is used in a game that children play on the holiday. Also it is customary to eat foods fried in oil on the holiday. These include potato pancakes called *latkes* and jelly donuts.

In the modern West, Hanukkah has become a time of gift giving. The custom may be dated from 17th-century Poland when children were given money to pass on to their teachers. Eventually money was given to the children to keep for themselves. While most Hanukkah money was and remains in the form of small coins, Hanukkah in the modern world serves as the occasion for larger monetary gifts. Hanukkah also seems to have been the inspiration for chocolate companies to create coin-shaped chocolate covered in gold or silver foil.

In the late 20th century, Hanukkah was increasingly seen as one of a set of winter-season holidays that have absorbed elements of the secular side of Christmas, especially its gift giving. For some, it has become an occasion to give, especially to children, a gift on each night of the holiday. The eight days of Hanukkah are official holidays in Israel.

J. Gordon Melton

See also: Christmas; Judaism; Sukkot.

References

Bloch, Abraham P. *The Biblical and Historical Background of Jewish Customs and Ceremonies.* New York: KTAV Publishing House, Inc., 1980.

Eckstein, Yecheil. *What You Should Know About Jews and Judaism.* Waco, TX: Word Books, 1984.

Greenberg, Irving. *The Jewish Way: Living the Holidays.* New York: Jason Aronson, 1998.

Posner, Raphael, Uri Kaploun, and Sherman Cohen, eds. *Jewish Liturgy: Prayer and Synagogue Service through the Ages.* New York: Leon Amiel Publisher/Jerusalem: Keter Publishing House, 1975.

Schauss, Hayyim. *The Jewish Festivals: A Guide to Their History and Observance.* New York: Schocken, 1996.

Hanuman Jayanti

Hanuman Jayanti is a Hindu holiday that celebrates the birth of Hanuman, the popular deity who appears as a monkey. Actually, he is of the *vanara*, the race of ape-like humanoids who play a prominent role in the India epic Ramayana. The vanara were created by the gods to assist the deity Rama in his battle against the demon Ravana. They possess strength and a spectrum of godly traits. Hanuman led the vanara in the fight against Ravana.

Hanuman is said to have been born to Anjana, a vanara who prior to her birth on Earth was a celestial being. There are several places that lay claims to be the spot of Hanuman's birth. The several stories about Anjana and Kesari, her husband, describe them as devotees of Siva and Hanuman as a product of that devotion.

The fifth book in the Ramayana is primarily concerned with the many adventures of Hanuman. They tell of his strong devotion, especially to Rama and Sita, his strength, his magical powers, and his ability to subdue evil spirits. He is often pictured having ripped opened his chest to show a picture of Rama and Sita, the deities he carries in his heart.

Statue of the Hindu monkey-god, Hanuman, Sri Ranganathaswamy Temple, India. (Yuliya Kryzhevska/Dreamstime.com)

Hanuman temples are found in most towns of any size throughout India. Hanuman Jayanti is celebrated during the Hindu lunar month of Chaitra (March–April), the exact day varying in different areas. The most distinct celebrations occur in Tamil Nadu and Kerala, in southernmost India, where the Hanuman Jayanthi is celebrated in the lunar month of Margazhi (December–January). Wherever it is celebrated, however, on the selected day, spiritual talks will be given in Hindu temples (and not limited to those especially dedicated to the deity.) These talks will begin early in the morning. Hanuman was reputedly born at sunrise, and at this moment, the talks will be paused while sacred food (Prasad) will be distributed among those at the temple.

In one of the stories about Hanuman, he observed Sita applying *sindhur* (the unique mark found on the foreheads of most Indian women) to her head. Hanuman inquired into the rationale for it, and Sita indicated that it would ensure a long life for her husband (Rama). Hanuman then took the material and smeared it over his entire body, an act aimed at ensuring Rama's immortality. In remembrance of this account, devotees visit Hanuman temples and apply sindhur from the Hanuman statues to their foreheads. Devotees expect this act to bring them good fortune.

Constance A. Jones

See also: Hinduism.

References

Harshananda, Swami. *Hindu Festivals and Sacred Days.* Bangalore: Ramakrishna Math, 1994.

Mukuncharandas, Sadhu. *Hindu Festivals (Origin Sentiments & Rituals).* Amdavad, India: Swaminarayan Aksharpith, 2005.

Sharma, Nath. *Festivals of India.* New Delhi: Abhinav Publications, 1978.

Shekar, H. V. *Festivals of India: Significance of the Celebrations.* Louisville, KY: Insight Books, 2000.

Welbon, Guy, and Glenn Yocum, eds. *Religious Festivals in South India and Sri Lanka.* Delhi: Manohar, 1982.

Harer

Harer is a small city in eastern-central Ethiopia, almost due east of Addis Ababa in the Ahmer Mountains. In recent centuries it has emerged as the primary Islamic pilgrimage site on the continent of Africa. Harer appears to date to the seventh century CE. Islam entered the city under the aegis of Shaykh Abadir, who in the 10th century established Islam with the assistance of 44 saints. Then in 1520, the empire builder from Somali, Ahmad Gran (1506–1543), captured the city and transformed it into the center of a large Muslim state. The Ethiopians who recaptured the city a half century later were from the Ethiopian Oromo people who also happened to be Muslims. The Muslim rulers relied on the large city walls, erected by the widow of Ahmad

Gran, to assist them in maintaining a degree of independence, which lasted until Egyptian forces invaded the region in 1875 and occupied Harer. Two years later Menelik II (1844–1913) incorporated it into Ethiopia proper. He replaced the main mosque of the time with what is now the Medhane Alem Cathedral, a church of the Ethiopian Orthodox Tewahedo Church.

During the years of Muslim rule, Harer was essentially closed to non-Muslims. The first European to see Harar was Sir Richard Burton, who made his way there in 1854. Today, the city remains home to some 82 mosques and more than 100 Muslim shrines. Three of the mosques date to the 10th century, while the largest, al-Jami, was erected in the 11th century. Among the most visited sites is that of the tomb of the city's founder, Abadir, which several times weekly is the scene of Sufi ceremonies.

In 2006, Harar was added to the list of World Heritage Sites designated by the United Nations.

J. Gordon Melton

See also: Ethiopian Orthodox Tewahedo Church; Mosques; Pilgrimage; Sufism.

References

Munro-Hay, Stuart. *Historical Ethiopia: A Book of Sources and a Guide to Historical Sites.* Trenton, NJ: Red Sea Press, 2000.

Trimingham, John Spencer. *Islam in Ethiopia.* London: Oxford University Press, 1952.

Harrist Church

William Wade Harris (1865–1929) received a call in 1910, while in a Liberian prison for treason, to be a prophet to take God's word to those who had never heard it. The Spirit came on him, and after his release, he began to preach from the Bible about the one true God, healing from disease, and the rejection of practices associated with traditional religions. In 1913 and 1914, he began preaching in Cote d'Ivoire and the Gold Coast (Ghana). Rejecting Western clothing and walking barefoot, Harris wore a long white calico robe, a turban, and black bands crossed around his chest. He carried a Bible, a gourd rattle, a bowl, and a staff in the shape of a cross.

The whole population of the regions through which he passed accepted him as the messenger of God. People traveled from distant places to hear Harris and be baptized, and as a result his message penetrated deep into the interior. He sent out disciples to carry his message and methods far and wide. On the Ghanaian coast, Harris confronted traditional priests, many of whom were converted. Opposition from Catholic missionaries caused him to return to Cote d'Ivoire, where he was accused of intimidation and fraud, arrested, and beaten; he was deported from Cote d'Ivoire toward the end of 1914. Over the next 10 years, Harrist believers were systematically suppressed and village prayer houses destroyed. Harris returned to Liberia and lived in relative obscurity until his death in 1929.

Harris never intended to form a separate church, and he directed people to existing (especially Catholic and Methodist) churches, but he also encouraged converts to build their own prayer houses where there were no churches; in those houses they were to worship, led by a minister and 12 apostles chosen by the village community. Tens of thousands of his followers formed these village churches in Cote d'Ivoire and the Gold Coast. Thousands of Harris's followers soon found themselves at odds with Methodist financial policy, their prohibition of polygyny, and the Methodist liturgy, so different from the African hymn-singing and dancing practiced by Harris. These followers organized themselves into the Harrist Church (Église Harriste), apparently after receiving the prophet's approval to do so just before Harris died in 1929. As symbols of his prophetic authority, Harris gave John Ahui a cane cross and a Bible, and Ahui was thereafter designated Harris's successor.

The Harrist movement was severely persecuted by the French administration, and for many years its adherents had to meet secretly. Many coastal Ivorians, however, increasingly identified it with the nationalist struggle, and it began to grow rapidly. Sometime after 1931, Ahui began preaching as Harris had done and organizing churches, but he was still severely restricted. After about 1945, people who had been baptized by Harris began leaving mission churches to join or to establish Harrist churches. The Harrist Church in Cote d'Ivoire was officially constituted in 1955, and Ahui became its preacher bishop, and later pope. In 1964, the church was officially recognized as one of four national religions, the others being Islam, Roman Catholicism, and Protestantism. Since 1972, the church has tried to modernize and has a renewed emphasis on healing and the eradication of witchcraft.

In 1990, the church had an estimated 176,000 members, one of the four largest churches in the Ivory Coast. Ahui died in 1992 and was succeeded by Supreme Preacher Cessi Koutouan Jacob as spiritual head of the church.

Église Harriste
BP 337
Bingerville
Cote d'Ivoire
http://www.egliseharriste-ongapa.ci (in French)

Allan H. Anderson

See also: African Initiated (Independent) Churches; Methodist Church.

References

Haliburton, Gordon M. *The Prophet Harris: A Study of an African Prophet and his Mass Movement in the Ivory Coast and the Gold Coast, 1913–1915.* London: Longman, 1971.

Hastings, Adrian. *The Church in Africa, 1450–1930.* Oxford: Clarendon, 1994.

Walker, Sheila S. *The Religious Revolution in the Ivory Coast: The Prophet Harris and the Harrist Church.* Chapel Hill: University of North Carolina Press, 1983.

Hasidism

Hasidism is a form of Orthodox Judaism that emphasizes mystical experience, the direct encounter with the divine. Although it draws upon various Jewish mystical texts from centuries past, Hasidism began with the career of Israel Baal Shem Tov (born Israel ben Eliezer, referred to by the acronym the Besht; 1698–1760). A Baal Shem is one who possesses the secret mystical knowledge of the names of God and who works miracles out of that knowledge. It is reported that as a young man the Besht studied with a mystical

Ultra-Orthodox Hasidic Jews, members of a devout sect, celebrate Purim at a synagogue in the Mea Shearim neighborhood in Jerusalem, March 27, 2005. (Gil Cohen Magen/Corbis)

teacher, or *tzaddik*, from a secret order called the Tzadikim Nistarim, in which he became a leader. He also became familiar with the Kabbalah, one of the older Jewish mystical teachings, and in 1724 began a 10-year period of withdrawal to study the Bible and the Kabbalah. He also claimed to have been in regular contact with Ahiya of Shilo, a prophet who lived during the reign of the ancient King David. His retreat was climaxed in 1736, when he received a revelation concerning his future career.

Israel Baal Shem Tov settled in Mezshbozsh, Poland, and began to teach Hasidism. He taught that each individual could have a living experience of faith, and he encouraged people to cleave to God in their daily life. The sense of oneness with God would lead to joy, which would in turn be expressed in ecstatic dance and prayer. An approach to Judaism that emphasized devotion and piety over law and learning had an im-

mediate appeal to many in the impoverished communities of Polish Jewry, and the movement spread to Jewish communities throughout the Slavic countries.

The Hasidic movement was organized around a set of teachers (called *rebbes* or tzaddiks) who were known for their mystical, psychic, miracle-working powers as much as their learning. Tzaddiks became associated with a particular Jewish community, and their followers flocked to these centers to be with the tzaddik on special occasions and for extended periods of study and prayer. Tzaddiks emerged throughout Poland, Hungary, Lithuania, Ukraine, Russia, Belarus, and other nearby countries.

Leadership within the movement was generally passed from father to son or nephew, and different Hasidic groups came to be known both by the town in which the tzaddik lived and by his family name. Two Hasidic groups stand out for their distinctiveness.

Bratslav Hasidism developed around Nachman of Bratslav (1772–1810). At the time of his untimely death, he was heard to have said, "My light will glow till the days of the Messiah." His followers interpreted the remark to mean that he would have no successor, and the community he called together has continued without a rebbe to lead them. The Lubavitcher rebbe survived the Holocaust and moved to the United States, where he and his successors have spearheaded the growth of a global new Hasidism. Lubavitch Hasidim has also become known for the millennial expectations that have grown up around their recently deceased rebbe, Menachem Mendel Schneerson (1902–1994).

Hasidism was almost destroyed by the Holocaust. Nazi forces overran much of the Hasidim's homeland in Eastern Europe, and only a small percentage survived. The rebbes that escaped migrated primarily to the United States and Palestine. Among the survivors was Yoel Teitelbaum (1887–1979), the rebbe for Satmar Hasidism, a group well known for their opposition to Zionism and the establishment of the state of Israel. Today, most Hasidic groups have their headquarters in the United States (many in Brooklyn, New York) and Israel.

In the 1960s, a new generation of teachers from the Hasidic tradition appeared as leaders of a variety of neo-Hasidic groups. The movement was partially inspired by the writings of theologian Martin Buber (1878–1965). Rabbi and musician Shlomo Carlebach (1926–1994) was a popular figure of this new generation of mystically oriented Jews. The most successful of the new Hasidic groups, however, appears to be the Kabbalah Learning Centre, founded in 1922 by Rabbi Yehuda Ashlag (1886–1955), but now headed by Rabbi Philip S. Berg, the author of many books on the Kabbalah and Jewish mysticism.

J. Gordon Melton

See also: Kabbalah Learning Centre; Lubavitch Hasidism; Orthodox Judaism; Satmar Hasidism.

References

Bokser, Ben Zion. *The Jewish Mystical Tradition.* New York: Pilgrim Press, 1981.

Buber, Martin. *The Origin and Meaning of Hasidism.* New York: Horizon Press, 1960.

Fishkoff, Sue. *The Rebbe's Army: Inside the World of Chabad-Lubavitch.* New York: Schocken, 2005.

Idel, Moshe. *Hasidism.* Albany: State University of New York Press, 2007.

Rabinowicz, Tzvi. *The Encyclopedia of Hasidism.* Northvale, NJ: Jason Aronson, 1996.

Rabinowitz, H. A. *A Guide to Hasidism.* New York: Thomas Yoseloff, 1960.

Healing Tao

The Healing Tao is among the best known popular Daoist groups in the West. It teaches a regulated system of inner alchemy and is famous for popularizing ritual sexual practices. It was founded by Mantak Chia (b. 1944), a Thai-born Chinese, who was trained in Hong Kong and has a background in both Eastern and Western medicine, as well as traditional Daoist practices. He claims his teachings are a body of esoteric knowledge, previously hidden from the world but now being made available and accessible to the general public.

Chia is said to have begun self-cultivation at the very young age of six with Buddhist meditation training, martial arts, tai chi, and kundalini yoga. Of his many teachers, the most influential was from the Lungmen sect of Quanzhen Daoism. This teacher, called One Cloud, gave him transmission and a mandate to teach and heal.

Chia systematized his knowledge, and in 1974 he established the first of his schools in Thailand (called the Natural Healing Center). In 1979, he moved to New York and opened the Taoist Esoteric Yoga Center. This center, which became the Healing Tao Center, attracted Euro-American students who helped him organize a national seminar circuit. In 1994, Mantak and his wife, Maneween (whom he subsequently divorced), moved back to Thailand to establish an international Healing Tao Center in Chiang Mai, which caters to wealthy Europeans and Americans.

Meanwhile, Chia's principal student, Michael Winn, runs a Healing Tao University each summer in upstate New York that bills itself as the "largest summer 'Chi' retreat program in the world." This program is no longer officially affiliated with Mantak Chia, and Winn has added several new techniques, but Chia is a guest teacher every year. There are currently some 1,000 certified Healing Tao instructors globally.

The Healing Tao program consists of 15 courses, the first 9 being introductory, the next 3 intermediate, and the final 3 advanced, which can only be reached after many years of practice. The first 9 include connecting the microcosmic orbit, developing the Inner Smile, and practicing the Six Healing Sounds. The personal goals of those who practice Chia's form of Daoism include the expansion of consciousness and improvement of their health, guided by the master through the workshops he has structured.

Healing Tao has its international headquarters at the Universal Tao Center in Thailand, where Mantak Chia now resides. Michael Winn now heads Healing Tao USA, which may be reached at PO Box 20028, New York, NY 10014. Healing Tao USA has a website at http://www.healingtaousa.com.

Universal Tao Center
274 Moo 7, Laung Nua
Doi Saket, Chiang Mai 50220
Thailand
http://www.universal-tao.com

Elijah Siegler

See also: Quanzhen Daoism.

References

Chia, Matak. *Awaken Healing Energy through the Tao*. New York: Aurora Press, 1983.

Chia, Matak. *Taoist Ways to Transform Stress into Vitality: The Inner Smile/Six Healing Sounds*. New York: Aurora Press, 1985.

Chia, Matak, with Michael Winn. *Taoist Secrets of Love: Cultivating Male Sexual Energy*. New York: Aurora Press, 1984.

Helena, Flavia Iulia

ca. 248–328

Flavia Iulia Helena, mother of Constantine the Great, Roman empress, and alleged discover of the True Cross,

Saint Helena and the emperor Heraclius at the Gate of Jerusalem, altarpiece of Santa Cruz de Bleza, late 15th century. (The Art Archive/Corbis)

was probably born in Drepanum in Bithynia (later renamed Helenopolis in her honor) around 248 in humble circumstances. She was of low social origin and was working as a maid in an inn when she met Constantius (ca. 250–306), who would rise to be emperor of the Western Roman Empire. Out of their concubinage the later emperor Constantine the Great (r. 306–337) was born in Naissus (modern Niš) ca. 272/273.

Constantius left her when he became a member of the tetrarchy in 293.

Constantine's rise to power in 306 brought Helena to the imperial court, where she gradually gained a prominent position. Coins and inscriptions mention her as Nobilissima Femina and from 324 until her death she held the title of Augusta, indicating that she was considered an important member of the imperial family. She may have lived at Constantine's court in Trier until 312. After Constantine had defeated Maxentius at the Milvian Bridge (October 28, 312), Helena probably came to live in Rome. The fundus Laurentus in the southeast corner of Rome, which included the Palatium Sessorianum, a circus, and public baths (later called Thermae Helenae), came into her possession. Several inscriptions (*CIL*, 6.1134, 1135, 1136) found in the area are evidence for a close connection between Helena and the fundus Laurentus. So is her interest in the newly found basilica Ss. Marcellino e Pietro, which was built in the area that belonged to the estate (*Lib. Pont.* I, 183); she was buried in a mausoleum attached to this basilica. Part of the Palatium Sessorianum was possibly shortly after her death transformed into a chapel, now known as the church of S. Croce in Gerusalemme.

Although it has been suggested that she was sympathetic toward the Christian faith from her childhood on, Helena most probably converted to Christianity following Constantine, who after 312 began to protect and favor the Christian church.

At the end of her life she journeyed through the eastern provinces of the Roman Empire. This journey, which took place ca. 326–327, is elaborately described by the church father Eusebius in his *Life of Constantine* (*VC* 3.41–47). Because of Eusebius's description—he is mainly concerned with her visit to Palestine, and he describes her religious enthusiasm, her desire to pray at places where Christ had been, and her care for the poor and needy—her journey is generally considered a pilgrimage. However, it is more likely that she traveled through the East for political purposes having to do with problems within the Constantinian family. Eusebius ascribes the foundation of the Constantinian churches in Bethlehem and on the Mount of Olives to her. He also connects her with the construction of the Church of Holy Sepulchre in Jerusalem.

Helena acquired her greatest fame by her alleged discovery of the True Cross. Her presence in Jerusalem and the description Eusebius presented of her stay in Palestine led ultimately to connecting Helena with the discovery of the Cross. The connection between the Cross, relics of which were present and venerated in the Church of the Holy Sepulchre since at least the 340s, is only first attested in the sources at the end of the fourth century. The legend of Helena's discovery of the Cross most probably originated in Jerusalem in the last quarter of the fourth century and rapidly spread over the whole Roman Empire. The story is told by prominent late antique Christian authors such as Ambrose, Paulinus of Nola, and the church historians Socrates, Sozomen, and Theodoret. The legend is known in various versions of which the best known is the Judas Kyriakos legend. According to this version Helena found the Cross with the help of the Jew Judas, who afterward converted to Christianity and became bishop of Jerusalem. This version, known in particular from Jacobus de Voragine's *Legenda Aurea* (13th century), was widespread in the Middle Ages; it was translated into vernacular languages and a favorite subject for iconographic representation, of which Piero della Francesca's frescoes in Arezzo are the most famous.

Shortly after her visit to the East Helena died at the age of about 80 in the presence of her son (Eus. *VC* 3.46) either late in 328 or the beginning of 329. Her porphyry sarcophagus is now in the Vatican Museums.

Apart from Rome, Trier and Hautvillers, which claim to possess her remains, have a lively Helena folklore. So does Britain: according to a medieval tradition Helena was a native of England; it gave rise to various British Helena legends. She is often venerated together with her son, Constantine, in particular in the Eastern Church. Her feast day in the Eastern Church is May 21 and in the Roman Catholic Church August 18.

Jan Willem Drijvers

See also: Constantine the Great; Jerusalem; Relics.

References

Baert, Barbara. *A Heritage of Holy Wood: The Legend of the True Cross in Text and Image.* Leiden: Brill, 2004.

Borgehammer, Stephan. *How the Holy Cross Was Found: From Event to Medieval Legend.* Stockholm: Almqvist & Wiksell International, 1991.

Drijvers, Han J. W., and Jan Willem Drijvers. *The Finding of the True Cross: The Judas Kyriakos Legend in Syriac.* Introduction Text and Translation, CSCO 565, Subs. 93. Louvain, Belgium: Peeters, 1997.

Drijvers, Jan Willem. *Helena Augusta: The Mother of Constantine the Great and Her Finding of the True Cross.* Leiden: Brill, 1992.

Pohlsander, Hans A. *Helena: Empress and Saint.* Chicago: Area, 1996.

Heng Shan

Heng Shan is the name of two of the five sacred mountains of China. The one designated the Daoist mountain of the north is located in Shanxi Province. The Daoist mountain of the south is located in Hunan Province. It is easy to confuse them as they bear the same name and are both within this very select group of sacred sites.

Heng Shan (Shanxi) rose to prominence during the Zhou dynasty (1045–256 BCE) and veneration of the mountain melded with the new concept of the worship of Tian (heaven). The Zhou sought to legitimize their authority by reference to the Mandate of Heaven, a Chinese idea similar to the Western notion of the divine right of kings. The ruler, as the "Son of Tian," governed by divine right. It was noted that the ruler's losing his throne meant that he had lost the mandate. It was also the case that repeated natural disasters and rebellions were evidence that the present ruling family had lost the mandate.

The mountain is the reputed home of the mountain god whose worship is focused at the Shrine of the Northern Peak, originally built during the Han dynasty (202 BCE–220 CE). This mountain, due to its location, frequently changed hands with the ups and downs of the Chinese empire, and this shrine was on several occasions destroyed and rebuilt. Today, no Daoists reside there.

Over the years, Heng Shan has become known for its hanging temples and monasteries that cling to the steep mountainsides in seeming defiance of gravity.

One of the hanging temples of Heng Shan, China. (Iralis/Dreamstime.com)

These are Buddhist centers, the most famous being the Buddhist Hanging Monastery, a wooden temple and monastic complex of some 40 halls that is supported by a relatively small number of wooden posts. It was originally built in 491 CE, and is one of the oldest Buddhist temples in the whole region. The current existing monastery was largely rebuilt in the Ming dynasty (1368–1644) and maintained through the Qing dynasty (1644–1911), with a major restoration effort in 1900.

Heng Shan (Shanxi) rises 7,087 feet and is one of the highest mountains in China. Heng Shan (Hunan), the 4,232-foot Daoist sacred mountain of the south, is noted for its beauty and the large forests on its slopes. It became the site of numerous Daoist and then Buddhist temples. With the decline of Daoism generally in China, many of the Daoist sites were abandoned, and their preservation has become a matter of grave concern.

Heng Shan is also the source of Mist Tea, one of the more cherished teas of a land that values its teas.

The origin of the tea is tied to Tanyue Buddhist Temple, the largest temple complex in southern China, located near the foot of the mountain. Destroyed and rebuilt on several occasions, the present temple was reconstructed during the Qing dynasty with plans inspired by the Imperial Palace in Beijing. The main halls of the complex rest on 72 stone pillars symbolizing the 72 peaks of the mountain. According to the stories, the tea was developed during the Tian Bao period (742–756 CE) when a monk attached to the Nanyue Temple observed a white snake burying tea seeds in the ground near the temple. From tea plants grown on that spot, Master Ching Yan, the monk, used water from a spring in a nearby cave in which to boil his tea. That spring later became famous as Hu Pao, or Running Tiger Spring.

Near Tanyue is Zhusheng Si, the Imperial Blessings Monastery, built shortly after Nanyue, but reconstructed and renamed in 1705 for an anticipated visit of Emperor Kangxi (r. 1661–1722), who never arrived. From Tanyue and Zgusheng Si, a path up the mountain passes many temples, both Buddhist and Daoist, and culminates at the top of the mountain, where the Daoist temple (Zhurong Gong [Wishing for Harmony Palace]) is located.

J. Gordon Melton

See also: Daoism; Hua Shan; Song Shan; Tai Shan; Temples—Buddhist.

References

Einarsen, John, ed. *The Sacred Mountains of Asia.* Boston: Shambhala, 1995.

Geil, William Edgar. *The Sacred 5 of China.* London: John Nurray, 1926.

Hahn, Thomas H. "Daoist Sacred Sites." In *Daoism Handbook*, edited by Livia Kohn, 683–708. Leiden: Brill, 2004.

"Sacred Mountains of China." Places of Peace and Power. http://www.sacredsites.com/asia/china/sacred_mountains.html. Accessed May 15, 2009.

Hermetic Order of the Golden Dawn

Established in England in 1888, the Hermetic Order of the Golden Dawn has strongly influenced contem-

MacGregor Mathers performs his rites of Isis. Mathers is primarily known as one of the founders of the Hermetic Order of the Golden Dawn. (TopFoto/Fortean/The Image Works)

porary Western magical beliefs and practices ever since. The Golden Dawn drew on a range of ancient and medieval cosmologies and incorporated them into a body of ceremonial practices and ritual grades centered on the Kabbalistic Tree of Life, an important symbol within the Jewish mystical tradition representing the sacred emanations of the Godhead. In addition to the Kabbalah, the Golden Dawn also drew on the Hermetic tradition, which had its roots in neo-Platonism and underwent a revival during the Renaissance. Roscrucianism, Freemasonry, and the medieval Tarot were also significant elements.

The Hermetic Order of the Golden Dawn was formally established in London on February 12, 1888, when its three founding figures, Samuel Liddell MacGregor Mathers (1854–1918), Dr. William Wynn Westcott (1848–1925), and Dr. William Robert Woodman (1828–1891), signed a document headed "Order of the

G.D." All three were members of the Societas Rosicruciana in Anglia (SRIA) and it was through this esoteric Masonic organization that they had met each other. Westcott had acquired a manuscript in cipher form that had been discovered among the papers of a deceased member of the SRIA, and he claimed to have found among the leaves of the cipher manuscript the name and address of a certain Fraulein Anna Sprengel, said to be an eminent Rosicrucian adept. On her authority, and following a lengthy correspondence, Westcott announced in Masonic and Theosophical circles that he had been instructed to found an English branch of her German occult group, calling it the Hermetic Order of the Golden Dawn.

Westcott invited his colleague from the SRIA, Samuel Liddell Mathers, to expand the cipher material so that it could form the basis of a "complete scheme of initiation." Mathers developed the five Masonic grades into a workable system suitable for the practice of ceremonial magic and as a result the Isis-Urania Temple of the Golden Dawn was established in London on March 1, 1888, with Mathers, Westcott, and Woodman confirmed as leaders of the Order. In a relatively short time it would be followed by other branches: the Osiris Temple in Weston-super-Mare, the Horus Temple in Bradford, the Amen-Ra Temple in Edinburgh, and the Ahathoor Temple in Paris.

In due course the Hermetic Order of the Golden Dawn attracted a distinguished membership, including such figures as the distinguished homeopath Dr. Edward Berridge; the Scottish Astronomer Royal William Peck; Arthur Edward Waite, an authority on the Kabbalah, Rosicrucianism, and the Holy Grail legends; the distinguished poet William Butler Yeats, who would later win the Nobel Prize; well-known physician and pioneer of tropical medicine Dr. R. W. Felkin; lawyer John W. Brodie-Innes; the well-known fantasy novelists Arthur Machen and Algernon Blackwood; and the controversial ritual magician and adventurer Aleister Crowley. The Order also included within its membership several notable women, among them Annie Horniman, later a leading patron of Irish theater; artist Moina Bergson, sister of the influential French philosopher Henri Bergson and future wife of Samuel Mathers; Celtic revivalist Maude Gonne; actress Florence Farr; and in later years the Christian Kab-

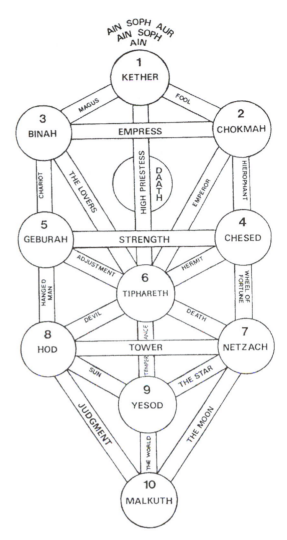

The Golden Dawn Tree of Life

balist Violet Firth, better known as the magical novelist Dion Fortune.

As Freemasons, Westcott and Mathers were strongly attracted to the concept of ritual degrees, and the grades of the Hermetic Order of the Golden Dawn were formulated in a manner that would align them symbolically with the *sephiroth*, or levels of mystical consciousness, upon the Kabbalistic Tree of Life. Four of the five ritual grades had Latin names: Zelator (corresponding to the sephirah Malkuth on the Tree), Theoricus (corresponding to Yesod), Practicus (corresponding to Hod), and Philosophus (corresponding to Netzach). There was also a Neophyte grade which, in a symbolic sense, was located below the Kabbalistic Tree of Life because at this stage the candidate who had just entered the Golden Dawn had not yet embarked on the magical exploration of the higher spheres on the Tree.

In addition, there were ritual grades associated with the Inner, or Second, Order of the Golden Dawn known as the Red Rose and the Cross of Gold: Rosae Rubae et Aurea Crucis. These grades were Adeptus Minor (corresponding to Tiphareth), Adeptus Major (corresponding to Geburah), and Adeptus Exemptus (corresponding to Chesed). By passing through the ritual grade of Adeptus Minor the ceremonial magician entered what Mac-Gregor Mathers referred to as the Vault of the Adepts. The candidate was bound symbolically on the Cross of Suffering while also witnessing "the resurrection of the Chief Adept, who represented Christian Rosencreutz, from a tomb within an elaborately painted, seven-sided vault." No ritual grades were assigned to the three remaining sephiroth on the Kabbalistic Tree of Life. Sometimes referred to as the Third Order, the spheres of Kether, Chokmah, and Binah were said to be the domain of Secret Chiefs—inspirational spiritual masters who were believed to guide the Order from the inner planes.

The Hermetic Order of the Golden Dawn began to fragment into various splinter groups during the period between 1900 and the end of World War I, and the practice of ceremonial magic in the West then became increasingly dominated by Aleister Crowley's doctrine of thelema (Greek: will). Wicca—contemporary Pagan witchcraft—would not emerge as a major Esoteric movement until the 1950s and 1960s, following the repeal in 1951 of the British Witchcraft Act forbidding the practice of witchcraft. Nevertheless, the historical influence of the Hermetic Order of the Golden Dawn has been considerable. All modern occult perspectives—including Wicca, Goddess spirituality, and the Thelemic magick of Aleister Crowley—owe a debt to the Golden Dawn for integrating the principal sources of the Western Esoteric tradition in the late 19th century and initiating a transformative process that continues more than 100 years later.

Neville Drury

See also: Ancient and Mystical Order Rosae Crucis; Crowley, Aleister; Freemasonry; Mathers, Samuel Liddell MacGregor; Thelema; Wiccan Religion; Witchcraft.

References

Gilbert, Robert A. *Revelations of the Golden Dawn: The Rise and Fall of a Magical Order.* Slough, UK: Quantum/Foulsham, 1997.

Howe, Ellic. *The Magicians of the Golden Dawn.* London: Routledge & Kegan Paul, 1972.

King, Francis. *Astral Projection, Magic and Alchemy.* London: Spearman, 1971.

King, Francis. *Ritual Magic in England.* London: Spearman, 1970.

Regardie, I., ed. *The Golden Dawn.* Vols 1–4. Chicago: Aries Press, 1937–1940.

Hiei, Mount

Mount Hiei, located a short distance northeast of Kyoto, Japan, has been a major disseminating point of Japanese Buddhism. Unlike other mountains, Mount Fuji, for example, Mount Hiei has not been thought of as a "sacred" mountain in and of itself. Rather, it has been the home to sacred centers and the site of a number of important historical events.

Mount Hiei's association to Buddhism began following the return of the monk Saicho (767–822 CE) from China. He settled on Mount Hiei in 785 and three years later built a small temple, Hieisan-ji, which was renamed Enryaku-ji in 823 by the emperor after Saicho's death. His choice of a location like Mount Hiei was most likely influenced by his time in China, where he was studying T'ian-tai Buddhism (known in Japan as Tendai Buddhism) and spent considerable time at Mount T'ian-Tai.

At the time the center at Mount Hiei was established, Theravada Buddhism dominated life at Nara, the major center of Buddhism in Japan; all ordinations of monks followed the Theravada format, and all occurred at Nara. Saicho used his considerable influence at court in Kyoto to gain permission to hold the first Mahayana ordinations in Japan at Mount Hiei. In succeeding centuries, a number of important leaders of Japanese Buddhism would study at Mount Hiei, including Honen (1133–1212), founder of the Pure Land Jodo-shu; Shinran (1173–1262), founder of Pure Land Jodo Shinshu Buddhism; Nichiren (1212–1282), founder of the Nichirenshu; Eisei (1141–1215), the founder of Japanese Rinzai Zen Buddhism; and Dogen (1200–1253), founder of Soto Zen Buddhism.

J. Gordon Melton

See also: Dogen; Jodo-shinshu; Jodo-shu; Nara; Nichiren; Nichirenshu; Saicho; Tian Tai/Tendai Buddhism; Zen Buddhism.

References

Groner, Paul. *Saicho: The Establishment of the Japanese Tendai School.* Honolulu: University of Hawaii Press, 2000.

Kasahara, Kazou, ed. *A History of Japanese Religion.* Tokyo: Kosei Publishing, 2001.

High Holy Days

See Days of Awe.

Hildegard of Bingen

1098–1179

Hildegard of Bingen was a unique and influential woman in the Roman Catholic Church of Germany. A mystic, she rose to be an advisor to some of the most powerful men of her day.

Born to a noble family, at a young age Hildegard began to experience visions. At the age of eight she was placed in the care of a woman named Jutta, a young woman from a wealthy and prominent family. Jutta had thought of entering a convent, but chose instead to become an anchoress. As such she would lead an ascetic life dictated by being enclosed inside a small room with only a small window through which food would be passed in and refuse passed out.

An anchoress would spend the day in sessions of prayer and contemplation broken by work such as sewing. Before entering the room, with the understanding that she was becoming dead to the world, the future anchoress would receive last rites accompanied with a funeral ceremony. Hildegard and Jutta began their life together as anchoresses in 1112 at Disibodenberg in

Illumination of Hildegard of Bingen, a 12th-century visionary abbess and an established theologian, from the Abbey of St. Hildegard, Hesse, Germany. (INSADCO Photography/StockphotoPro)

the Palatinate Forest. As Jutta also had visions, many people came to visit the two women.

Jutta died in 1136, at which time the community of nuns at Disibodenberg bestowed the title of "magistra" (master) on Hildegard and the abbot asked her to become the prioress. Hildegard asked Archbishop Henry I of Mainz, who finally agreed. Hildegard and about 20 nuns moved to St. Rupertsberg in 1150. In 1165 she formed a second convent at Eibingen. Hildegard had been hesitant to share her visions until 1141, when at the age of 42, she received instruction in a vision to write down all she saw and heard.

In 1147, Saint Bernard of Clairvaux (1090–1123) persuaded Pope Eugenius III (r. 1145–1153) to create a commission to investigate the nature of Hildegard's visionary life. The pope asked Hildegard to finish her writings, so with papal approval, Hildegard was able to complete her first major work, *Scivias* (*Know the Ways of the Lord*), which recounts 26 visions about the Christian doctrine of salvation. The commission later determined that she was a true mystic. As her fame spread through Germany and beyond she wrote additional works, including plays, a medical encyclopedia and handbook, and several well-known hymns. She also traveled around Germany to give public speeches at monasteries and cathedrals. In her mature years, she became one of the most influential women of her time. Through her many letters she advised popes, statesmen, emperors, and heads of different monasteries.

Hildegard died September 17, 1179. There have been four attempts to have Hildegard named as a saint, but all have fallen short with naming her beatified. In spite of the failure to complete the formal process of canonization, her name was added to the *Roman Martyology*, a list of saints, and many have considered her as such. Her feast day is September 17. Hildegard also appears in the calendar of saints of both the Church of England and its American sister church, the Episcopal Church.

Hildegard left vivid descriptions of the physical sensations that accompanied her visions. These records have been examined by modern physicians and psychologists. They have suggested that she was describing what today is known as scintillating scotoma, a common visual effect that precedes migraine headaches.

J. Gordon Melton

See also: Church of England; Episcopal Church; Roman Catholic Church; Saints.

References

Flanagan, Sabina. *Hildegard of Bingen, 1098–1179: A Visionary Life.* London: Routledge, 1990.

Hildegard von Bingen. *Hildegard von Bingen's Mystical Visions: Translated from Hildegard's Scivias.* Trans. by Bruce Hozeski. Santa Fe, NM: Bear & Company, 1995.

King-Lenzmeier, Anne H. *Hildegard of Bingen: An Integrated Vision.* Collegeville, MN: Liturgical Press, 2001.

Palmquist, Mary, ed. *The Life of the Holy Hildegard.* Collegeville, MN: Liturgical Press, 1995.

◆ Hinduism

Hinduism became a global religion in the 20th century. For millennia restricted to the Indian subcontinent, Hindus currently reside in some 150 countries. The universal outreach has not been only geographical. Rather, the modern reinterpretation of Hindu ideas and practices has paved the way to attracting converts and sympathizers beyond the Indian people. As during the classical epoch of Hinduism, the modern epoch continues to be prosperous and dynamic in bringing forth new forms, ideas, and practices of Hindu ideas and devotion.

"Hinduism," a Problematic Term   The term "Hinduism" is a Western construction invented in the early 19th century by British colonial administrators and Orientalists. The construction and usage of the notion is built on a differentiation, current in the subcontinent, previously altering its meaning according to European understanding. Persian conquerors of the late sixth century BCE used the word *Hindu*, a Persian variant of Sanskrit *sindhu*, to denote both the region and the people living nearby and beyond the Indus River (the region of today's Pakistan). Muslim rulers, who invaded North India beginning in the eighth century, took over the term and used it to demarcate Muslims from their non-Muslim Indian subjects. The Muslims' exclusive term "Hindu" was then adopted by 18th-century European Orientalists and administrators in an altered mode. Since all people of the subcontinent were conceived of as followers of the one so-called heathen religion, the term "Hindoo" subsequently replaced the previous notion of "Gentoo" (heathens, from Latin *gentiles*, Portuguese *gentio*). Thus, all different Indian religious traditions—except Islam—prevalent in the 19th-century British Raj came under the heading of "Hindoo." From this the abstraction "Hinduism" was derived, first used in English in 1829.

Since then, the notion of "Hinduism" suggests a coherent religion to be found all over India. The construction fails to convey, however, the apparent diversity and heterogeneity that it both subsumes and ignores. Related to the empirical situation in the subcontinent (and now also overseas), it would be more appropriate to speak of a number of distinct but related religious traditions or religions existing side by side within so-called Hinduism. The encompassing of diverse regional religious traditions under the one heading of Hinduism has stirred up both academic and practical problems of communal and national representation. The same terminological problematic applies to the designation "Hindu," as a person is not a "Hindu in general" but rather a "Hindu in particular"—for example, a Gujarati Vaishnava or Tamil Shaivaite, placing emphasis on specific deities, sacred texts, ways of worship (*puja*), religious teachers, and so on.

Hindus seldom employ the notion "Hinduism" as a self-description, using as an alternative a term of their own—*sanatana dharma* (perennial or eternal faith). This term remains elitist, in particular as it is applied more to philosophical interpretations of the diverse Hindu traditions than to the multifarious local manifestations of practice and faith.

Main Historical Epochs   This article subdivides the approximately 3,000-year-long history of Veda-based traditions, or Hinduism, into five broad epochs, highlighting the main developments and changes. (The references section directs the reader to topics and voices that deserve a fuller treatment than is possible here, in particular with regard to women, Dalits [so-called untouchables], the veneration of goddesses, worship, and the performing arts.)

The Harappa Culture   Early 20th-century archaeological excavations made known the existence of large towns, such as Mohenjo Daro and Harappa, with some 40,000 inhabitants each, on the banks of the Indus River. It is assumed that these towns already existed in the first half of the third millennium BCE. This Indus Valley civilization, also designated as Harappa culture, knew the art of writing, evidenced in carved seals. The people built impressive houses of brick supplemented by a drainage system. The script has still not been deciphered, and thus the many archaeological findings are subject to contrasting interpretations and speculation. Speculations also abound in the religious sphere. Evidence suggests cults of fire and fertility, but it is not yet clear whether the many female figures excavated relate to the veneration of a mother goddess or are mainly paraphernalia for fertility rites. Seals seem to have been used like protective amulets.

Epoch of the Veda or Brahmanism   According to established theory (though challenged recently), Indo-European people known as the Aryans (Sanskrit: *arya*, noble, honorable) invaded the northwestern plains of the Indian subcontinent during the first half of the second millennium BCE. It is not yet known for certain whether this incursion of the Aryans destroyed the Harrapa culture or whether the civilization had already come to an end because of ecological catastrophes (droughts). The Indo-European immigrants settled down near the River Sindhu (Indus) and subsequently went on to reach the Ganges River regions. Their language was an Indo-European tongue that developed into Vedic Sanskrit and later into classical Sanskrit. From those early days, Sanskrit has been the exclusive, sacred language of Vedic Brahmanism and Hinduism. Sanskrit texts, some of them more than 3,000 years old, provide ample evidence of the religious ideas, rituals, and culture of the Aryan people. The texts form a huge corpus of scripts that developed over a period of several centuries. These hymns and manuals on ritual and philosophy had previously been passed down from generation to generation by word of mouth and were written down between 1200 and 500 BCE. The collection of texts is called Veda from the Sanskrit root *vid* (knowledge). The Veda is spiritually audible, meaning that ancient seers (*rishi*) saw or "heard" the knowledge thanks to their superior intuition. Collectively, the four text groups of the Veda are called *shruti* (that which was heard). This knowledge is timeless, not subject to change. It is of nonhuman origin; it was not invented or composed by the seers.

The Veda consists of four collections, each divided into four sections. The collections are the Rig, Sama, Yajur, and Atharva; the sections in each of these collections are Samhita (hymnic compositions), Brahmana (ritual treatises), Aranyaka (forest books), and

Upanishad (sitting near [the teacher], philosophical treatises). The stated sequence is roughly in chronological order, the Rig Veda Samhita being the earliest text (written down around 1200 BCE) and the Upanishads being the latest (composed from 800 to 500 BCE). The Veda is primarily a liturgical text, being used in the ritual honoring of the deities. The central religious practice was the sacrifice (Sanskrit: *homa, yajna*), in which the ritual specialist, the *brahmana* (also known as *brahmin* and *brahman*) propitiated the gods. Sacrificial ingredients were milk; ghee or purified butter; curds; various grains; and the *soma* plant. Also, domestic animals such as sheep, goats, cattle, or horses were offered by way of ritual slaughter. The substances offered would be given into the fire and through this transported to the deities (the *deva* invoked). Most important was the correct recitation of the hymns and *mantras* (sounds, verbal formulas); only the priest was eligible to perform these rituals. The Aryans primarily worshipped Agni, the fire god; Soma, a hallucinogenic plant; Varuna, the custodian of the "law" or cosmic order (*rita*); and Indra, the warrior god. According to the texts and the brahmans, these rituals were essential and indispensable to sustain the cosmic homology— that is, the correlation of the cosmos and man's position in it.

In the course of time, the priestly brahmans came to dominate the religious practice and to establish their ritual monopoly. The kings also were especially in need of rites to legitimize and stabilize their power. The dominant position of the brahmans, undisputed until the middle of the first millennium BCE, provides valid ground to call this Vedic epoch the time of the brahmans, or Brahmanism. The early texts also outlined the fourfold classification of Vedic society along general social strata into which a person was born (Sanskrit: *varna*). According to Rig Veda 10.90, 12, the four varnas are the brahmana or priest; the *kshatriya*, or warrior and ruler; the *vaishya*, or farmer, trader, and commoner; and the *shudra*, or serf. The classification was straightforward and exclusive, based on ritual purity. A change of one's varna and thus one's social status was not possible. The first three classes were called the twice-born, due to a special ritual ceremony. The male members of those varnas underwent the initiation ceremony called *upanayana*, receiving the sacred

thread. The girl's equivalent to the upanayana ceremony was a rite during her first menstruation, performed especially for brahman daughters. During the epic epoch and subsequent centuries, this rough classification along varnas subdifferentiated along manyfold *jatis*—that is, specific occupational and residential so-called castes into which a person was born.

The youngest group of texts, the Upanishads, comprise the "end of the Veda" (*vedanta*). In these texts the change from a sacrificial worldview to a more person-centered search for liberation (*moksha*) became manifest. The knowledge of the correct performance of the ritual shifted to a knowledge based on insight and realization of inner wisdom. It was in the Upanishads that the central terms and concepts of classical "Hinduism" (that is, Veda-based traditions) were formulated and expounded. Both with regard to the Vedic and epic epoch, it is paramount to bear in mind that not a single, systematized Veda-based religion dominated the Indian subcontinent. Rather, a parallelism of various religious traditions and strands, at times markedly influenced by local cults, existed.

Epoch of the Epics or Classical Hinduism   The time of so-called classical Hinduism can roughly be set from the late 6th century BCE to the 11th century CE. The shift from the Vedic to the epic epoch is based on both socioeconomic and religious changes. These took place in the seventh and sixth centuries BCE. During that time span, northern India witnessed an increase in urbanization and occupational differentiation. A self-content trading strata emerged, and the numerous smaller kingdoms were replaced by larger ones. In religious terms, during these centuries a variety of renouncer traditions emerged. Among the many *shramana*, or ascetic movements, prevalent in those days were the Buddhist and the Jain traditions. Like the many other renouncer traditions, they questioned the ritualistic predominance and the religious monopoly of the brahmans. The many shramana movements and orders of *sadhus* (good men, renouncers) and *sadhvis* (good women) accepted the authority of the Veda. In contrast, the Buddhists and Jains questioned the attributed sacred status of the texts. The two later came to be labeled as heterodox or heretic, and in the course of succeeding centuries various means were taken either

Bronze figure of the dancing Hindu god Shiva (Siva). One of the three principal gods in Hinduism, Shiva is associated with death and regeneration. (Corel)

to destroy their centers of learning or to conceptually absorb the teachings and religious practices. At times, powerful rulers such as the famous kings Ashoka (268–233 BCE) and Kanishka (first century CE) supported the Buddhist *sangha* (order); at other times dynasties such as the Guptas (320–600 CE) were less favorable and more in support of the brahmanical sacrificial traditions. In particular, from the Guptas on, the brahmanical traditions regained their central socio-political status in the Indian subcontinent, as these were concerned with the ritually legitimized status of the king, the maintenance of boundaries between the social strata, and the regulation of a person's behavior according to the general principle of *dharma* (order, obligation). Nevertheless, since the middle of the first millennium BCE and parallel to the established brahmanical traditions, groups of ascetics and renouncers came into existence. These advocated a homeless life, depended for food on alms, and minimized, in varying

degrees, personal ownership of possessions. These ascetics, by virtue of their austere life and yogic exercises, became religious authorities in their own right. To them lay devotees came for spiritual advice and instruction as well as to have *darshan* (sight, seeing the divine) and to receive *prasad* (food from the gods). In this way, apart from the heterodox traditions, the strand of brahmanical sacrificial tradition(s) was faced with a strand of nonestablished, and often nonresident, authority of sacred knowledge and practice, based on the Veda.

During the epic epoch, both the central religious ideas of "mainstream" Hinduism crystallized and the leading gods and deities stepped forth. The separate section below will explain the main sociopolitical and doctrinal ideas, and thus we now turn to the emergence of the devotional veneration of one god (*ishtadeva*, deity of choice). The strengthening of the devotional, or *bhakti*, movement, in the southern subcontinent in particular, the expanding popularity of the epics and the Puranas among the general population, as well as the absorption of pre-Vedic and non-Aryan religious forms had their impact on this long-term development. In this way, during the second half of the first millennium CE, the main Hindu traditions, with their focus on Shiva, Vishnu, and Devi (goddess), took shape. Although the latter often is subsumed under the former—that is, the goddess being the wife or consort to Shiva and thus forming a part of the Shaivite tradition—it rightfully can be argued to speak of a line or strand of its own. The god Shiva in one of his many manifestations is known as a Himalayan ascetic, residing on the sacred mountain Kailas. Often he is venerated in the form of a *linga*, a smooth, cylindrical stone. He is also associated with a divine family, his wife Parvati personifying Shiva's female energy, *shakti*, together with the sons Ganesha and Skanda (or Murukan). Shiva is an ambivalent god, being both destructive and benevolent.

Like Shiva, Vishnu is described iconographically in many stories and myths in the Puranas. The followers of Vishnu, called Vaishnavas, venerate him in one of his 10 *avataras* (incarnations). Most important among these are the figures of Rama and Krishna; they form central figures in the great epic stories. The goddess tradition is associated with powerful female deities such as Kali, Durga, and many local goddesses. The character of the goddesses is often ambivalent; they can give life and fertility, but can also generate destruction and death. Their followers are called Shaktas; the devotional and ritual strand refers back to both tantric texts and non-Aryan practices. At various times—and a process going on these days also—formerly local goddesses may be identified with the pan-Indian Devi, providing additional legitimation for their veneration and their inclusion in brahmanical worship.

These deities were honored both at home and in temples. Brahmans performed a manifold complex of rituals, in particular in the temples. From the sixth century CE on, important temple cities evolved. These cities were not only centers of commerce and administration but also ritual centers, with the temple at the hub of the town and the streets radiating outward. The city formed the capital of the regional kingdom, and brahmanical ritual and the temple supported the power and sovereignty of the dynasty. Outstanding examples of such royal-religious cities were Madurai, Citamparam, and Kanchipuram in Tamil Nadu (South India), or Puri in Orissa (East India) with the Jagannatha temple.

Finally, notable during the first millennium CE, Hindu (and Buddhist) practices and concepts spread to Southeast Asia by way of Indians in search of economic wealth. Records provide evidence that brahmans, kshatriyas, vaishyas, as well as renouncers crossed the sea to find a living and wealth in foreign lands. This process, stretching from the 1st to the 13th centuries, has become known as the Indianization of mainland Southeast Asia and the archipelago. The local courts employed Indian warriors and priests to settle their power and to legitimize their reign ritually. Hindu and Buddhist elements were not so much superimposed on as creatively absorbed by the local nobility and elite. Localized versions of the Ramayana and other important doctrinal sources evolved, incorporating indigenous legends and myths. With the advance of Islam and the supremacy of Theravada Buddhism in Siam (Thailand) and Laos, the Sanskritic culture in Southeast Asia came to its end. In Bali, however, the particular version of Indo-Javanese culture and religion has survived to this day.

Epoch of Postclassical Hinduism and Islamic Rule
Spanning the time from about 1100 to 1800, this epoch witnessed less innovative religious impulses than the preceding epoch of classical Hinduism or the succeeding one of neo-Hinduism. Of paramount political importance was the gradual conquering of India by Muslim rulers, beginning with the raids of Mahmud of Ghazni in northwest India (977–1030). Later, the Delhi Sultanate (1206–1526) was followed by the Mughal Empire (1526–1757). Although neither the Mughals nor—gradually from 1757 on—the British actually imposed their religion on the Indians, both esteemed their religion as superior. They looked down upon Hindu beliefs and practices. In the 15th century, Muslim-Hindu syncretistic interpretations evolved. Most prominent among these new understandings were the concepts and practices proposed by bhakti poet Kabir (1440–1518) and Nanak (1469–1539). Nanak founded the Sikh tradition and was the first of a line of 10 gurus, based in the Punjab. Also notable was the religiously

tolerant rule of the great Mughal emperor Akbar (r. 1555–1605). The Hindu traditions, differentiated along regional and devotional lines, also had some outstanding interpreters such as the *dvaita* renouncer Madhva (13th century). In line with his view, the Bengali saint Chaitanya (1486–1533) founded the Gaudiya Vaishnava *sampradaya*, or subtradition. His ecstatic dancing and singing enabled him to experience the love of Radha and Krishna. In the 20th century, the Bengali Vaishnava Prabhupada felt inspired by Chaitanya and Madhva, founding the International Society for Krishna Consciousness in New York in 1966. Other important theologians and poets of the 16th and 17th centuries, spreading their devotional form of religiosity in vernacular rather than Sanskrit verses, were Vallabha (1479–1531), Tulsidas (ca. 1532–1632), and Dadu (1544–1660), as well as Tukaram (1608–1649) and Ramdas (1608–1681). The latter two praised Hinduness and glorified past "golden ages."

Epoch of Neo-Hinduism, British Rule, and Independence From the 16th century on, the Portuguese started to establish trading posts on the Indian coast. They were followed by Dutch, French, and British companies, all striving to gain a share in the lucrative trade in spices. The British strengthened their commercial and administrative position gradually. In 1757, the British East India Company secured Bengal by military force. Over the course of the next 100 years, the company was able to spread its commercial and military influence all over India. The Indian economy was changed to mainly the exporting of goods, which consequently ruined local trade and business. English became the official language of the administration and the law courts. In 1858 the British Crown officially adopted India as its colony, establishing a centralized administration for the whole country.

The industrialization of the Indian economy was accompanied by the establishment of the British educational system as well as the arrival of Christian missionaries. Earlier on, British administrators and scholars had started to study and collect the numerous sacred texts. Charles Wilkins translated the Bhagavad Gita into English in 1785, followed by William Jones's translation of the Manusmriti in 1789. Christian missionaries aimed to convert members of the high castes,

though with little success. They strongly criticized Indian customs such as child-marriage and the self-immolation of widows (*sati*). Such criticism was also voiced by Indian social reformers, most notably the Bengali Ram Mohan Roy (1772–1833). Influenced by Muslim and Christian ideas, in particular by the Unitarians, Roy formed the Brahmo Samaj in 1828. He intended to spread a rational, ethical monotheism, which according to him had its roots in the Upanishads and Brahma Sutra. The society was modeled on Christian reform movements and met regularly for religious services during which passages from the Upanishads were read, hymns sung, and sermons delivered. Some 50 years later, Dayananda Saraswati (1824–1883) founded the Arya Samaj in 1875. He emphasized a return to the Veda and denied the authenticity of Puranic Hinduism. The Arya Samaj criticized brahman-based ritual worship of images or "idols," worked for the uplift of women, and glorified an assumed "golden Vedic age."

The Brahmo Samaj and Arya Samaj organizationally and conceptually pioneered what came to be known as neo-Hinduism or Hindu Renaissance. They were followed by other influential reformers and their organizations, most notably Vivekananda (1863–1902, disciple of Ramakrishna), Shri Aurobindo (1872–1950), and Mohandas K. Gandhi (1869–1948). These and other spokesmen were strongly influenced by Western ideas and Christian values, making use of these in order to bring about a revival of Hinduism and an independent India. Religious reforms and a burgeoning Indian nationalism went hand in hand, reclaiming an "unpolluted," sovereign Aryan past. These Western-educated reformers used the English language to spread their ideas, circulated texts and pamphlets, stressed social services, and criticized what they saw as degenerated Hindu customs and practices. They constructed a Hinduism based on reason and ethical spirituality, equal or superior to Christianity and Islam. Although this reformist Hinduism has acquired the image of representing "typical Hinduism" in the West, especially championed by Vivekananda and the Vedanta Society (founded 1894), in India itself the various reform movements have attracted only small followings. Their religious impact has remained confined to the educated, urban strata of Indian society, not reaching the mass of the Hindu people.

The movement for Indian self-rule (*svaraj*) grew stronger in the 1920s and 1930s, headed by Gandhi and his campaign based on the principle of *satyagraha* (holding fast to the truth). India gained independence in 1947, Nehru becoming its first prime minister. Based on democratic ideals and a secular Constitution, Hindu political nationalists questioned the latter in particular during the last two decades of the 20th century. The nationalists used the religious argument to a large extent for the achievement of political and ideological aims. A climax was reached with the destruction in 1992 of the Babri mosque (built in 1528) in Ayodhya. Communalism and the right-wing *Hindutva* policy (making India Hindu) have since undermined the country's self-claimed prestige as the most numerous secular democracy of the world.

The late-19th-century reinterpretation of Hinduism along Western organizational models and ideas was vital to paving the way for a trans-Indian outreach of Hinduism. Vivekananda's famous speech at the 1893 World Parliament of Religions in Chicago and his two-year stay in the United States made him the first effective proponent of Hinduism as a universal religion. An idealized image of India as the land of spiritually superior gurus (grave persons) and of Hinduism as a religion of tolerance and deep devotion reinforced previously held Western glorifications (prevalent since the late 18th century). This positive perception was strengthened as Hindu teachers, swamis, and gurus started to visit the West from the 1950s onward. A variety of groups and organizations were founded, and they won followers among the hippies and the counterculture. Most prominent have become the Transcendental Meditation (now organized as the Global Country of World Peace) of Maharishi Mahesh Yogi; Swami Pabhupadas's International Society for Krishna Consciousness; Shree Hans Ji Maharaj's Divine Light Mission (superseded by Elan Vital); the Ananda Marga Yoga Society, founded by Shree Shree Amandamurti; the neo-Sannyas movement (Osho Commune International), centered on the teachings of Bhagwan Shree Rajneesh (Osho); the Brahma Kumaris; and Sahaja Yoga.

Hindu practices, customs, and ideas had left India prior to this export of spiritual practices, however. Between 1838 and 1917, Britain's colonial authorities recruited workers from India for labor in the mines and sugar fields in South Africa, the Caribbean, and the Malayan-Pacific region. Also, laborers left India to build the railway in East Africa and to earn a living as traders there. The overall number of these indentured workers is estimated to have been in excess of 1.5 million. Communities of Hindu and, to a lesser degree, Muslim Indians were formed in the faraway colonies. The religious heritage was not abandoned, despite attempts to convert the Indians to Christianity. Rather, the religious belonging and rituals were maintained and handed down the generations. As a result, sizable Hindu communities have existed from the time of indentureship in such scattered locations as Trinidad, Guyana, Surinam, East and South Africa (Natal), Mauritius, Malaysia, and the Fiji Islands.

A very different trajectory has brought hundreds of thousands of Indians to the West since the 1960s. Because of changes in foreign policy (especially that of the United States), shifts in immigration policies, and the need for increased work forces abroad, Indians were allowed to immigrate to Canada, the United States, and Australia. Furthermore, Indians had begun a significant move to Great Britain following Indian independence, and beginning in the 1950s settled in other European countries as well. Finally, because of the oil boom, workers were needed to build new houses and cities in the Near East, and many Indians lived there temporarily. A widespread network of communications has been set up by Hindus in the different places, using the airplane, telephone, Internet, and e-mail to maintain contact with fellow Hindus abroad and in India. Also, as is the case with the converted "Western" Hindus, the Indian Hindu communities and their newly erected and consecrated temples are often visited by gurus and swamis from India. Confined for three millennia to the Indian subcontinent (with the exception of Indianized Southeast Asia), during the 20th century Hinduism became a globally distributed religion.

Principal Concepts and Practice At the close of the Vedic and the shift to the epic epochs, the texts of the Aranyakas and Upanishads expounded on the principal concepts of classical Hinduism. The notion of *dharma* started to become a leading religious concept: dharma, though untranslatable in any Western language, as it has no direct semantic equivalents, conveys the meaning of duty, norm, obligation, and cosmic law or order. A Hindu person is said to act according to the dharma of his or her *varna* and *jati*—that is, to stick to the obligations and restrictions imposed by one's birth. Birth and rebirth in specific jatis is dependent on the person's *karma* (action). All living beings are thought to be reborn repeatedly in the cycle of death and rebirth (*samsara*), this according to the cause and effect of the actions and deeds a person had performed in life. There are different "disciplines" (*yoga*, from the Sanskrit root *yuj*, to control) or "paths" (*marga*) to gain *moksha*, or liberation, from this beginningless cycle: the path of action (*karma marga*) entails the path of unselfish action—that is, of fulfilling one's duty (dharma) without expecting praise or blame. The path of knowledge (*jnana marga*) is constituted by attaining scriptural knowledge and by this "true insight" into the real nature of the universe. The path of devotion (*bhakti marga*), most emphasized throughout the great epic Bhagavad Gita, outlines as means for final liberation the surrender to and wholehearted trust in the god venerated. Basic to these different paths is the fundamental correspondence of the all-pervading ultimate reality or truth (brahman) and the human soul (atman). To reach liberation is to understand this basic unity of brahman and atman. The Chandogya Upanishad explains this nonseparatedness in the famous conversation between Uddalaka Aruni and his son Shvetaku: the father asks the son to dissolve salt in water and says that brahman and atman are united in a similar manner. The father ends the teaching in explaining: "The finest essence here—that constitutes the self of this world; that is the truth; that is the self (atman); and that is how you are (*tat tvam asi*)" (6.13).

The two great epics, the Ramayana and the Mahabharata (including the Bhagavad Gita), in particular, expound on and make known the central Hindu concepts and the different paths to liberation. These epics, composed from 200 BCE to 300 CE and followed by other texts, such as the Manusmriti (codes of law), the Puranas (old stories), *sutras*, and *shastras* (normative and scientific texts), all belong to the category of *smriti* (remembered, handed down). Smriti texts are of human authorship; they explain, comment on, and prescribe ideas and life-styles touched on in the Vedas. Although theoretically this literature is of lesser authority than the Vedas, it has played a far more important role in the lives and religiosity of Hindus for the last 2,000 years. In particular, the sutras and shastras provide a normative structuring of a person's obligation (dharma), both with regard to one's position in society (that is, duties according to one's varna) and with regard to one's stage of life (*ashrama*). These two concerns together became known as *varnashrama*-dharma. Its fulfillment was a sign of brahmanical orthopraxy, and in many Hindu traditions this model codified the ideal of a "true Hindu life." *Smarta* brahmans are especially proud and eager to follow the teachings and prescriptions of the smriti texts. The four different stages that a male "twice-born" (*dvija*) is expected to take are: *brahmacarya*, the stage of boy student, learning the Veda; *grihastha*, the stage of householder, raising a family; *vanaprastha*, the stage of hermit or forest-dweller, retiring from the householder's duties; and *samnyasa*, the final stage of renouncer, concentrating on final liberation. The obligations of married women are generally referred to as *stri*-dharma, the duties of the wife. According to the Manusmriti, women are to be subject to male control and authority throughout their lives; they have to be docile and virtuous.

As mentioned, of paramount importance to teaching basic Hindu ideas, norms, and practices to the common Hindu were the two great epics, the Ramayana and Mahabharata. Some two and a half millennia later, these mythological dramas continue to attract an unsurpassed interest. The stories and their morale are told by parents to their children, set on stage by village theater groups, and broadcast in phenomenally successful television productions in the 1980s. The Ramayana, or story of King Rama, exists in a multitude of versions, the most widely known being the one attributed to Valmiki. The main plot of the story is the abduction of Princess Sita, wife of Rama, by the demon Ravana and the freeing of Sita and her return to Ayodhya with the help of the monkey general Hanuman. The story's moral centers on the fulfillment of one's dharma—that is, on loyal obedience to one's social role and obligations. In the same way, the Mahabharata highlights the virtues of devoted service to and dutiful observance of one's dharma. The main part of the story circles around struggles for throne succession among cousins, culminating in a battle between the Pandavas and the Kauravas. The eve of the battle sets the scene for the Bhagavad Gita (Song of the Lord), the well-known dialogue between Krishna and Arjuna. Doubtful Arjuna, who is hesitant to fight his relatives, is convinced by his charioteer Krishna that it is his social and religious obligation, or dharma, to go into the war. As a member of the warrior class, he has to fulfill his duty. Krishna, though disguised as charioteer, is really the supreme Lord, and he offers Arjuna guidance in the same way a teacher (guru) instructs his pupil. In the 18 chapters of the Gita, the 3 principal disciplines or paths to attain liberation from the cycle of death and rebirth are also explained prominently, among many further themes.

The shaping and codifying of basic Hindu concepts and norms from the middle of the first millennium BCE on was accompanied by the development of different philosophical systems and the growth of so-called sectarian or tradition-wise worship of particular deities from the middle of the first millennium CE. From around the third to the sixth centuries CE, theologians and philosophers worked out six so-called orthodox perspectives or systems (darshana) commonly identified in Hindu thought. Each system is based on a specific text and commentaries, containing logic, analysis, and scriptural exegesis. The samkhya darshana advocates a dualistic and atheistic differentiation of self or spirit (purusha) and matter (prakriti). The yoga darshana, based on the Yoga Sutra of Patanjali (fifth century), builds on the dualism of samkhya. It focuses, however, on the spiritual discipline required for the self to attain moksha, or liberation. The mimamsa darshana places its emphasis on right action (dharma), whereas the nyaya darshana elaborates on a system of logic, leading to liberation. The vaisheshika darshana constitutes a system of atomistic analysis of the categories of dharma and their constituent elements. Finally, the vedanta darshana, like the mimamsa darshana a system of Vedic exegesis, concentrates on the Upanishadic teaching on ultimate reality (brahman). In the following centuries, the vedanta system was differently interpreted by philosophers and renouncers. Most prominent among the many have become Shankara (ca. 788–820), Ramanuja (1017–1137), and Madhva (1238–1317). Shankara favored the nondualist, or advaita, vedanta and established that viewpoint as the touchstone of a revived smarta orthodoxy. He was

founder of 10 orders of samnyasis (renouncers) and set up 4 (or 5) principal monasteries (mathas) or seats of learning (vidyapithas). The leading men of these seats are renowned spiritual and normative leaders known as Shankaracharyas (masters [in the tradition] of Shankara), playing an important role through the centuries and up to the present. Ramanuja taught a qualified nondualist, or vishishtadvaita, Vedanta different from Shankara's theology. He disagreed with Shankara on the nature of brahman, the individual selves, and the world. Ramanuja was the leader of a Shri Vaishnava Order (followers of Vishnu), arguing that Vishnu-Narayana is the ultimate brahman, his relation to the world and souls being "qualified" as substance to attribute. In contrast to Shankara's and Ramanuja's understandings, Madhva exposed a dualist, or dvaita, vedanta. He stressed the absolute sovereignty of God and differentiated the fivefold set of absolute distinctions between (1) God and souls, (2) God and the world, (3) souls and souls, (4) souls and the world, and (5) matter in its different aspects. These theological conceptualizations cannot be differentiated from philosophical systematizations; a sharp distinction is hardly possible.

Worship and the veneration of the chosen deity take many different forms in the Hindu traditions and sampradayas. To the vast majority of people, the above sketched philosophical investigations are rather less known. The bulk of devotees engage in the recitation of the name of the deity, in praying to the various gods and goddesses and receiving darshan, in joint singing at a meeting (samkirtana, bhajana singing), in night vigils of prayer and song, and in attending fire sacrifices in the temple or at home. Individual prayer is more prevalent than congregational forms of worship. A devotee may concentrate on a mental image of a god or pray in front of an image that expresses a divine spirit (murti). The honoring and worship can be daily, or it can be performed occasionally before the home shrine and without a foot ever set in a temple. Also, some may go on a pilgrimage (tirthayatra) to the holy spots in India, while many will attend the various specific festival days (utsava, yatra), celebrated throughout the year. One of the most popular forms of worship is the puja, the ritual offering of hospitality to a god or goddess as a most welcome and honored guest. The brahman offers flowers, camphor, water, light, fruits, and food, as well as mantras to venerate the deity. At specific days and occasions, a ritual bathing (*abhishekam*) will take place, the brahman offering a number of precious ingredients to the deity. As an expression of one's faith and devotion, a devotee may give gifts (*dana*) and undertake fasts and vows (*vrata*). In life-cycle ceremonies, memorial rites, and rites of expiation, the favor of the deity is sought through prayer and invocations. Of particular practical importance for many Hindus is the knowledge of auspicious times according to astrological constellations. In ancient times these were used to determine the appropriate times for Vedic sacrifices, and it has become a common belief that terrestrial events correspond to celestial phenomena. The constellations are held to have a direct effect on important life events. Hindus consult an astrologer or a brahman to have a horoscope cast, providing information about beneficial and unfavorable times. According to the days and hours specified, children's ritual names are selected, marriages arranged and performed, debts paid, businesses started, travels undertaken, and much more. In contrast to Western astrologies, the Hindu system considers the Moon rather than the Sun to be of fundamental importance.

Martin Baumann

See also: Ananda Marga Yoga Society; Arya Samaj; Asceticism; Brahma Kumaris; Brahmo Samaj; Chaitanya, Shri Krishna; Elan Vital/Divine Light Mission; Global Country of World Peace; India, Hinduism in: Ancient Vedic Expressions; India, Hinduism in: Medieval, Classical, and Modern Periods; International Society for Krishna Consciousness; Kailas, Mount/Lake Manasarovar; Nanak, Guru; Osho and the International Osho Movement; Patanjali; Sahaja Yoga; Shaivism; Shaktism; Vaishnavism; Vedanta Societies; Yoga.

References

General

Brockington, J. L. *The Sacred Thread: A Short History of Hinduism*. Delhi: Oxford University Press, 1981, 1992.

Cush, Denise, Catherine Robinson, and Michael York, eds. *Encyclopedia of Hinduism*. London and New York: Routledge, 2008.

Dubois, Abbe J. A. *Hindu Manners, Customs and Ceremonies*. Trans. by Henry K. Beauchamp. Calcutta: Rupa and Co., 1993.

Flood, Gavin, ed. *The Blackwell Companion to Hinduism*. London: Wiley-Blackwell, 2003.

Flood, Gavin. *An Introduction to Hinduism*. Cambridge: Cambridge University Press, 1996.

Jones, Kenneth W. *Socio-religious Movements in British India*. Cambridge: Cambridge University Press, 1989.

Knott, Kim. *Hinduism: A Very Short Introduction*. Oxford: Oxford University Press, 1999.

Michaels, Axel. *Der Hinduismus: Geschichte und Gegenwart*. Munich: Beck, 1998.

Conceptual Considerations

Dalmia, Vasudha, and Heinrich von Stietencron, eds. *Representing Hinduism: The Construction of Religious Traditions and National Identity*. New Delhi: Sage, 1995.

International Journal of Hindu Studies, Springer, 3 vols. published annually, since 1997.

King, Richard. *Orientalism and Religion: Postcolonial Theory, India and "The Mystic East."* London: Routledge, 1999.

Sontheimer, Günther D., and Hermann Kulke, eds. *Hinduism Reconsidered*. New Delhi: Manohar, 1989.

Sweetman, Will. *Mapping Hinduism: Hinduism and the Study of Indian Religions, 1600–1776*. Halle and Saale, Germany: Verlag der Franckeschen Stiftungen, 2006.

Main Historical Epochs and Modernity

Baird, Robert D., ed. *Religion in Modern India*. Delhi: Manohar, 1995.

Coedès, Georges. *The Indianized States of Southeast Asia*. Trans. by Susan Brown Cowing. Ed. by Walter F. Vella. Honolulu: East-West Center Press, 1968.

Copley, Antony, ed. *Gurus and Their Followers: New Religious Reform Movements in Colonial India*. Oxford: Oxford University Press, 2000.

Dumont, Louis. *Homo Hierarchicus: The Caste System and Its Implications*. Trans. by Mark Sainsbury. Chicago: University of Chicago Press, 1970.

Hartsuiker, Dolf. *Sadhus: Holy Men of India.* Singapore: Thames and Hudson, 1993.

Hatcher, Brian A. *Eclecticism and Modern Hindu Discourse.* Oxford: Oxford University Press, 1999.

Hawley, John Stratton, and Donna Marie Wulff, eds. *Devi: Goddesses of India.* Berkeley: University of California Press, 1996.

Kumar, Radha. *The History of Doing: An Illustrated Account of Movements for Women's Rights and Feminism in India, 1800–1990.* New Delhi: Kali for Women, 1993.

Larson, Gerald James. *India's Agony over Religion.* New York: State University Press of New York, 1995.

Luden, David, ed. *Making India Hindu: Religion, Community, and the Politics of Democracy in India.* Delhi: Oxford University Press, 1996.

Marriott, McKim. *India through Hindu Categories.* New Delhi: Sage, 1990.

Nilakanta Sastri, K. A. *Development of Religion in South India.* New Delhi: Munshiram Manoharlal, 1978.

Pechilis, Karen. *The Graceful Guru: Hindu Female Gurus in India and the United States.* Oxford: Oxford University Press, 2004.

Richards, Glyn. *A Sourcebook of Modern Hinduism.* London: Curzon, 1985.

Sharma, Arvind. *Classical Hindu Thought: An Introduction.* Oxford: Oxford University Press, 2000.

Singer, M. B. *When a Great Tradition Modernizes: An Anthropological Approach to Indian Civilization.* New York: Praeger 1972.

Stutley, Margaret, and James Stutley. *A Dictionary of Hinduism: Its Mythology, Folklore and Development 1500 B.C.–A.D. 1500.* London: Routledge and Kegan Paul, 1977.

Thapar, Romila. *Interpreting Early India.* Oxford: Oxford University Press, 1992.

Tharu, Susie, and K. Lalita, eds. *Women Writing in India, 600 B.C. to the Early Twentieth Century.* London: Pandora Press, 1991.

van der Veer, Peter. *Religious Nationalism: Hindus and Muslims in India.* Berkeley: University of California Press, 1994.

Williams, Raymond Brady, ed. *A Sacred Thread: Modern Transmission of Hindu Traditions in India and Abroad.* Chambersburg, PA: Anima Publ., 1992.

Hindu Traditions Overseas and in Diaspora

Baumann, Martin, Brigitte Luchesi, and Annette Wilke, eds. *Tempel und Tamilen in zweiter Heimat: Hindus aus Sri Lanka im deutschsprachigen und skandinavischen Raum.* Würzburg, Germany: Ergon, 2003.

Bromley, David G., and Larry D. Shinn, eds. *Krishna Consciousness in the West.* Lewisburg, PA: Bucknall University Press, 1989.

Coward, Harold, John Hinnells, and Raymond Brady Williams, eds. *The South Asian Religious Diaspora in Britain, Canada, and the United States.* New York: State University of New York Press, 2000.

Dabydeen, David, and Brinsley Samaroo, eds. *Across the Dark Waters: Ethnicity and Indian Identity in the Caribbean.* London: Macmillan, 1996.

Forsthoefel, Thomas A., and Cynthia Ann Humes, eds. *Gurus in America.* New York. State University of New York Press, 2005.

Jacobsen, Knut A., ed. *South Asian Religions on Display: Religious Processions in South Asia and in the Diaspora.* London: Routledge, 2008.

Jacobsen, Knut A., and Pratap Kumar, eds. *South Asians in the Diaspora. Histories and Religious Traditions.* Leiden: Brill, 2004.

Knott, Kim. *My Sweet Lord: The Hare Krishna Movement.* Wellingsborough, Northamptonshire, UK: Aquarian Press, 1986.

Punzo Waghorne, Joanne. *Diasporas of the Gods: Modern Hindu Temples in an Urban Middle-Class World.* Oxford: Oxford University Press, 2004.

Rukmani, T. S., ed. *Hindu Diaspora: Global Perspectives.* Montreal: Concordia University, 1999.

Vertovec, Steven. *The Hindu Diaspora: Comparative Patterns.* London: Routledge, 2000.

Principal Concepts and Practices

Bahadur, Om Lata. *The Book of Hindu Festivals and Ceremonies.* New Delhi: UBS, 1995.

Bhardwaj, S. M. *Hindu Places of Pilgrimage in India*. Berkeley: University of California Press, 1973.

Eck, Diana L. *Darshan: Seeing the Divine Image in India*. New York: Columbia University Press, 1981, 1998.

Fuller, Christopher J. *The Camphor Flame: Popular Hinduism and Society in India*. Princeton, NJ: Viking, 1992.

Huyler, Stephen P. *Meeting God: Elements of Hindu Devotion*. New Haven, CT: Yale University Press, 1999.

Kinsley, David. *Hindu Goddesses: Visions of the Divine Feminine in the Hindu Religious Tradition*. Berkeley: University of California Press, 1986.

Kumar, P. Pratap. *The Goddess Laksmi: The Divine Consort in South Indian Vaisnava Tradition*. Oxford: Oxford University Press, 1997.

McGilvray, Dennis B. *Symbolic Heat: Gender, Health and Worship among Tamils of South India and Sri Lanka*. Middletown, NJ: Grantha, 1998.

Hirsch, Samson Raphael

1808–1888

Samson Raphael Hirsh, a rabbi for more than 35 years in Frankfurt, Germany, is today counted one of the major voices in the founding of the modern Orthodox movement in Judaism. During his Hamburg years, he wrote a number of books, edited a magazine, and headed a school that integrated Jewish and secular studies, and through which he propagated his basic idea of Torah im Derech Eretz (Torah with the way of the land).

Hirsh was born June 20, 1808, in Hamburg, Germany, where he also spent his early years. While he was attending public schools, his parents saw to his Jewish education in the home. His grandfather, Mendel Frankfurter, had founded the Talmud Torah, a Jewish religious school in Hamburg, and his father was an active observant Jew.

By the time Hirsch began his training for the rabbinate, he had come to the idea of synthesizing tradi-

tional Jewish teachings with Western culture. After his ordination as a rabbi, he pursued further studies in classical languages, history, and philosophy at the University of Bonn, where he would meet Abraham Geiger (1810–1874), later a founding leader of Reform Judaism. Hirsch assume his first rabbinical position at Oldenburg, Saxony, and then in 1846 was named the district rabbi of Moravia (in what is now the Czech Republic).

While in Moravia in 1851, he developed a concern over the assimilation of the Jewish community into the larger culture, and immediately after he assumed his long-term post at Frankfurt, he launched an initiative to create Jewish schools, ritual baths (*mikvas*), and slaughter houses (*kashruit*) that would provide kosher food. On the Sabbath, he assumed some of the outward form of the popular Jewish Reformers. He wore a robe similar to the Protestant Christian clergy, delivered his sermons in the vernacular, and shaved off his beard. The synagogue had a male choir and emphasized the study of the Tanakh (Jewish Bible) over the study of the Talmud.

At the same time, Hirsh emerged as a defender of traditional Judaism. While at Oldenburg, he had published the *Nineteen Letters of ben Uziel* (1836), an articulate and even unique defense of "orthodoxy" that recognized the existence of and responded to the developing Reform movement in a way traditionalists had previously felt unnecessary. Two years later he released *Choreb*, a rationalist explanation and defense of the mitzvah, the traditional 613 commandments that Jews find in the Torah, which he followed with a commentary on the Torah (Jewish Bible).

Hirsch planted one foot in the modern world, while arguing that Jews could adhere to Jewish law and participate in modern society. This position became known as neo-Orthodoxy and the resultant neo-Orthodox movement emerged as the first effort among traditionalists to counter the rise of Reform. Hirsh rejected any attempt to abrogate Jewish ritual law (*halakhah*) and the subtle undermining of tradition he perceived in the historical approach to Judaism asserted by theologian Zechariah Frankel (1801–1875). He affirmed that God was the author of the Torah and that God had dictated Jewish law via oral tradition. Thus he concluded that Jews could embrace all of Western culture in so far as it did not conflict with or distract from the observance of Jewish law.

In Frankfurt, Hirsch emerged as a capable opponent of Reform Judaism and led in the formation of the modern Orthodox movement, whose members observed traditional Jewish practice while as far as possible fully interacting with Western society. After guiding the Frankfurt community for more than three decades, Hirsh passed away December 31, 1888, in Frankfurt, where he was also buried. Hirsch is credited with assisting traditional Judaism's successful countering of the new threat of cultural assimilation and in the process with creating the Orthodox movement

J. Gordon Melton

See also: Geiger, Abraham; Orthodox Judaism; Reform Judaism.

References

Hirsh, Samson Raphael. *Collected Writings of Rabbi Samson Raphael Hirsch.* 8 vols. New York: Philip Feldheim, 1996.

Liberles, Robert. *Religious Conflict in Social Context: The Resurgence of Orthodox Judaism in Frankfurt Am Main, 1838–1877.* Westport, CT: Greenwood Press, 1985.

Meyer, Michael A. *Response to Modernity: A History of the Reform Movement in Judaism.* New York: Oxford University Press, 1988.

Rosenbloom, Noah H. *Tradition in an Age of Reform: The Religious Philosophy of Samson Raphael Hirsch.* Philadelphia: Jewish Publication Society, 1976.

Aga Khan I, spiritual leader of the Nizari Ismailis, a Shiite Islamic sect that returned to prominence in British India during the early 20th century. (Dumasia, Naoroji M, *The Aga Khan and His Ancestors: A Biographical and Historical Sketch,* 1936)

His Highness Prince Aga Khan Shia Imami Ismaili Council

The His Highness Prince Aga Khan Shia Imami Ismaili Council is the administrative authority, operating under the leadership of the Aga Khan, for the contemporary Nizari Ismaili Muslim community. The Nizari Ismailis, as a separate branch of Ismaili Islam, originated during the years of the Fatimid dynasty in Egypt. In 1094 CE, Abu Mansur Nizar (1045–1095) succeeded his father Abu Tamim Ma'add al-Mustansir bi'llah (d. 1094) as caliph of Egypt and imam for the Ismaili

community. However, some part of the population favored his younger brother, Abu'l-Qasim Ahmad (1074–1101). A civil war resulted, and Nizar was defeated and subsequently executed. His death appeared to end his cause, but Ismailis in Persia and Iraq continued to recognize his lineage. After the fall of the Fatimid dynasty and the suppression of Ismaili belief in Egypt, the Persians became the center of the surviving community.

For several centuries, Ismaili life was centered upon the famous mountain fortress at Alamut in northern Persia (and similar mountain fortresses in Syria and Lebanon). During this era, the Ismailis became known as the Assassins, a name derived from their use of hashish, but later applied to their practice of sending out trained killers to assassinate their enemies. Their life at Alamut was brought to an end by the Mongols in 1256, and the last of the mountain outposts were finally overrun by the Ottomans in the 16th century. They were left as a minority Muslim community, but they still possessed a leadership in the lineage of Nizar, whom they believed to be in a direct familial lineage with Muhammad through his daughter and his son-in-law Ali. In the 1830s, the leader was given the honorific title, Aga Khan, by which he and his successors have since been known.

During the Alamut years the Ismaili community expanded to India when a number of missionaries began to build what became a growing following in Gujarat and the Sind (now part of Pakistan). By the beginning of the 19th century, the largest groups of Ismailis resided in India. Thus when the Aga Khan was forced out of Persia in 1840, it was only natural that he would assume a new residence among his followers in India. Locally, his followers became known as Khojas. Here they developed a distinctive literature focused in *ginans*, a variety of hymnlike poems utilizing local languages that embody Ismaili theological and speculative beliefs.

The contemporary Nazari Ismaili community is under the absolute spiritual guidance of the Aga Khan, a belief that was spelled out in the 1986 constitution granted to the community. The administration of the community is placed in the hands of the His Highness Prince Aga Khan Shia Imami Ismaili Council, which takes on life through a number of national and local councils that are found wherever the Nizari Ismailis have spread. During the 19th century, many Ismailis began to move to East Africa and in the 20th century to Europe and North America. It is estimated that there are some 30 million Nazari Ismailis worldwide.

During the first half of the 20th century, the Aga Khan authorized the formation of a spectrum of institutions for social and economic development on the Indian subcontinent and in East Africa. These have now been grouped in the Aga Khan Development Network, which includes the Aga Khan Foundation, the Aga Khan Educational Services, the Aga Khan Fund for Economic Development, Aga Khan Health Services, Aga Khan Planning and Business Services, the Aga Khan Trust for Culture, Aga Khan University (Pakistan), and the University of Central Asia (with projected campuses in Tajikistan, Kyrgyzstan, and Kazakhstan). The network may be contacted through its Internet site, http://www.akdn.org, or at its international offices at 1-3 Avenue de la Paix, PO Box 2369, CH-1211 Geneva 2, Switzerland. Several of the national councils have websites.

J. Gordon Melton

See also: Ismaili Islam; Shia Islam.

References

Daftary, Farhad. *A Short History of the Ismailis.* Princeton, NJ: Marcus Wiener Publishers, 1998.

Dadtary, Farhad, and Zulfikar Hirji. *The Ismailis: An Illustrated History.* London: Azimuth Edition/ Institute of Ismaili Studies, 2008.

Frischauer, Willi. *The Aga Khans.* New York: Hawthorn Publishers, 1971.

Jackson, Stanley. *The Aga Khan.* London: Odhams Press, 1952.

Nanjio, A. *The Nizari Isma'ili Tradition in the Indo-Pakistani Subcontinent.* Delmar, NY: Caravan Books, 1978.

Hoa Hao Buddhism

Hoa Hao Buddhism (Phat Giao Hoa Hao, or PGHH) is a Vietnamese reformist Buddhist movement combining Buddhism and the cults of ancestors. Hoa Hao is considered by its followers to be a reform branch of Buddhism. It does not have an institutionalized priesthood and rejects many of the ritual aspects of orthodox Mahayana Buddhism. For instance, even the most dedicated followers of Hoa Hao, who would in more orthodox traditions be monks, are allowed to live with their families and are not required to shave their heads. Hoa Hao followers worship Buddha at least twice a day. Hoa Hao altars display no Buddha statues but a piece of brown cloth. Their flag is rectangular and brown, bearing no symbols.

Hoa Hao followers believe that their movement is an extension of the Buu Son Ky Huong (literally, "Strange Fragrance of Precious Mountains") sect, which was established in Vietnam in 1849. Hoa Hao Buddhism was launched in 1939 by charismatic 20-year-old visionary Huynh Phu So. His teaching

Members of the Hoa Hao Buddhist sect participate in an interdenominational prayer for peace, April 22, 1975, at Saigon Cathedral. The banner above them reads "Pray for peace." (AP Photo)

highlighted basic Buddhist doctrines and the concept of "Four Debts," namely, duties to ancestors and parents, to the Fatherland, to one's compatriots, and to Buddhist values. The new Buddhist movement was named after Huynh Phu So's birthplace—Hoa Hao village in Tan Chau District, Chau Doc Province, which is in the Mekong Delta near the Cambodian border.

Within a few months, Huynh Phu So gained the adherence of half a million followers. Also, in 1939 the young leader had composed four volumes of traditional Vietnamese verses, which aimed at propagating the basics of Hoa Hao doctrine. These works, composed in the language of ordinary speech, totaled about 150,000 words, and more than 800,000 copies were distributed.

During World War II, the Hoa Hao started a military build-up. When Vietnam declared its independence in 1945, Huynh Phu So allied with the Viet Minh to resist the French troops. On September 21, 1946, Huynh Phu So established the Social Democrat Party of Vietnam (Viet Nam Dan Chu Xa Hoi Dang, also known as Dan Xa). But the alliance between the Hoa Hao and the Viet Minh did not last. In 1947 Huynh Phu So was invited for talks by the Communists and executed. Beliefs that Huynh Phu So's avatar will soon descend to Earth still persist among the Hoa Hao, constituting a potentially explosive amalgamation of millenarian themes and motives of personal allegiance.

In the wake of the 1954 Geneva Agreements, the Hoa Hao community suffered persecution under the regime of Ngo Dinh Diem. Only after the overthrow of Diem in November 1963 did the Hoa Hao Buddhists reorganize themselves and elect a new administrative body. Since the end of the Vietnam War in April 1975, Communist authorities have confiscated thousands of Hoa Hao properties, abolished its management structure, and banned its major celebrations. Also prohibited is the dissemination of Hoa Hao sacred scriptures.

The Vietnamese government officially recognized the Hoa Hao community only in May 1999, when a group of 160 Hoa Hao delegates convened a congress in An Giang Province with government approval. However, many domestic Hoa Hao followers, as well as expatriate Hoa Hao activists, do not recognize the validity of this congress, since they see it as subject to government control.

Hoa Hao followers are concentrated in the Mekong Delta, particularly in provinces such as An Giang and Chau Doc. According to the Vietnamese government officials, there are 1.3 million Hoa Hao believers. Church-affiliated expatriate groups suggest that there are more than 2 million.

The international authority of the movement has moved to the United States and may now be contacted at the first address given below, or at the mailing address that follows.

Hoa Hao Buddhist Church
c/o Central Council of Administrators
2114 W. McFadden Ave.
Santa Ana, CA 92704
PO Box 3048
Santa Fe Springs, CA 90670
http://www.hoahao.org (English and Vietnamese)
Sergei Blagov

See also: Buddhism; Devotion/Devotional Traditions.

References

Biography and Teachings of Prophet Huynh Phu So. Santa Fe Springs, CA: Hoa Hao Buddhist Overseas Office, 1983.

Hue Tam Ho Tai. *Millenarism and Peasant Politics in Vietnam.* Cambridge: Harvard University Press, 1983.

Holi

Holi is a Hindu festival that takes place on the day of the full moon in the Indian lunar month of Phalguna (generally in February or March of the Common Era calendar). While celebrated by Hindus around the world, observation is most intense in places identified with the deity Krishna, an incarnation of the deity Vishnu, such as the Braj region in the state of Uttar Pradesh, India. Within Braj, the land of Krishna, one finds Mathura, the traditional birth place of Krishna, and Vrindavan, the town now located where Lord Krishna spent his childhood days. Here the celebration may be stretched into two weeks or more.

In India three stories are told as to why this day is celebrated. Devotees of Vishnu, called *vaishnavas*, tell of Hiranyakashipu, the king of demons, who had been granted a boon by Brahma, making it almost impossible for him to be killed. As a result he grew arrogant and went on a destructive rampage. He also attempted to stop the worship of the gods, placing himself in their stead.

Hiranyakashipu's son, Prahlada, was a devotee of Lord Vishnu. He refused to stop his worship of Lord Vishnu, even at his father's command. In spite of several threats from Hiranyakashipu, Prahlada continued offering prayers to Lord Vishnu. Hiranyakashipu attempted to kill him. When his attempts failed, he commanded his son to place himself on the lap of his sister, Holika, on top of a fire. Holika was immune to fire as she wore a protective shawl. Prahlada followed his father's command while also praying to Vishnu to keep him safe. As the fire roared into flame, the shawl flew from Holika and encased Prahlada who survived unharmed. Holika was consumed. Holi remembers the burning of Holika. (Later Lord Vishnu killed Hiranyakashipu.)

A second tale concerns an ogress called Dhundhi, a female monster who specially troubled small children who became fed up with her. She had received a boon from the deity Siva that made her difficult to kill. Siva, however, left her vulnerable at one point: she could be endangered by boys going about acting crazily.

The king of the region affected by the ogress asked the local priest what to do. The answer was that on the 15th day of the month of Phalguna, he should have the village collect wood and grass and set them on fire with mantras. As the fire burned, they should clap their hands, circle the fire three times, and make noise with laughter and song. The noise and the fire would get rid of the monster. The legend states that on the day of

People smear colored powder on each other during Holi festivities in Mumbai, India. The Holi festival, also called the Festival of Color, celebrates the start of spring and is associated with the Hindu god Krishna. (AP Photo/Rafiq Maqbool)

Holi, the boys united and chased Dhundhi away by their shouts, abuses, and pranks. Today on Holi young boys are permitted to use rude language without their elders taking offense, while children enjoy burning Holika again.

A third story concerns the deity Siva's third eye, pictured in most representations resting in the middle of his forehead. The story is told that his wife Umā came up behind him and covered his eyes with her hands. As a result, the world sunk into darkness. Again to save the world, Siva developed a third eye on his forehead. When he opened that eye, the light returned to the world. Holi is a celebration of the day that Siva initially opened his third eye, one consequence being that Kamadeva, the god of love, was reduced to ashes.

Holi is an ancient festival, very likely one that began before the Common Era. In one early form married women celebrated the happiness and well-being of their families, but in a way that left in place a vari-

ety of sexual and erotic elements suggesting that the Holi may have derived from spring fertility rites. In some places in India, for example, sexually explicit songs may be sung and men might carry penis-shaped objects to brandish. One of the names for the festival is Kamamahotsava, or the celebration for the God of Love.

Today, Holi is the festival of color, and the most popular festival activity is the throwing or shooting of colored water on everyone. In recent years water balloons have become popular. People will commonly wear white clothes so that all the varied colors are visible on each participant. It was also not uncommon in years passed for men to drink generously of *bhang*, a potent marijuana concoction, during the celebrations.

Holi is a public holiday in most states in India.

Constance A. Jones

See also: Janmashtami; VRINDA/The Vrindavan Institute for Vaisnava Culture and Studies.

References

Harshananda, Swami. *Hindu Festivals and Sacred Days.* Bangalore: Ramakrishna Math, 1994.

Mukuncharandas, Sadhu. *Hindu Festivals (Origin Sentiments & Rituals).* Amdavad, India: Swaminarayan Aksharpith, 2005.

Sharma, Nath. *Festivals of India.* New Delhi: Abhinav Publications, 1978.

Shekar, H. V. *Festivals of India: Significance of the Celebrations.* Louisville, KY: Insight Books, 2000.

Welbon, Guy, and Glenn Yocum, eds. *Religious Festivals in South India and Sri Lanka.* Delhi: Manohar, 1982.

Holiness Movement

The Holiness movement developed in the 19th century as a revival of interest in the teachings of John Wesley (1703–1791), the founder of Methodism. Wesley had pictured the life of the Christian as one of growing in grace, culminating in the attainment of a level of perfection that he termed "sanctification." Although Wesley saw the Christian life as one of striving, the attainment of this new grace of sanctification was, like the beginning of the Christian life, seen as a result of God's gracious action, not human striving.

Among Methodists in America, the preaching of sanctification as a second act of grace immediately available to the serious Christian gave a slightly different slant on Wesleyan teachings. Within the camp meeting setting, the emphasis upon a life of growth in grace prior to sanctification was de-emphasized in favor of a focus upon the individual believer's prayer for the immediate attainment of perfection by God's action. The result was a fellowship in which the sanctified life became the norm of Christian church life.

This new emphasis on sanctification gained favor throughout the several Methodist denominations (including the Wesleyan Methodist Church and the Free Methodist Church) in the decades immediately after the American Civil War, but began to lose favor with the bishops and church intellectuals in larger branches in the 1880s. The result was that during the next generation many Holiness advocates left the Methodists to form or join independent Holiness churches, while at the same time creating independent Bible colleges and seminaries for the training of ministers. In the early 20th century these churches began to coalesce into the major Holiness denominations, such as the Church of the Nazarene and the Pilgrim Holiness Church (now a constituent part of the Church of God [Anderson, Indiana]). In the meantime, several of the old Methodist denominational bodies, especially the Wesleyan Methodists (now a constituent part of the Wesleyan Church) and the Free Methodist Church of North America, continued their identification with the Holiness movement, while the several larger churches (later to become part of the United Methodist Church) steadily backed away from it.

Through the 20th century, the Holiness churches became worldwide bodies through an extensive missionary program. The larger Holiness churches now have affiliate congregations in most of the countries of the world, and several now report a majority of their membership residing outside North America. In North America, Holiness churches have fellowship through the Christian Holiness Partnership. Also, in the early 20th century, the Holiness movement became the birthplace of a new movement, Pentecostalism, which continued to share its emphasis on Holiness.

J. Gordon Melton

See also: Christian Holiness Partnership; Church of God (Anderson, Indiana); Church of the Nazarene; Free Methodist Church of North America; Methodism; Pentecostalism; Wesley, John; Wesleyan Church.

References

Bassett, Paul M. *Holiness Teaching—New Testament Times to John Wesley.* Kansas City, MO: Beacon Hill Press, 1997.

Dieter, Melvin Easterday. *The Holiness Revival in the Nineteenth Century.* 2nd ed. Metuchen, NJ: Scarecrow Press, 1996.

Jones, Charles Edwin. *The Wesleyan Holiness Movement: A Comprehensive Guide.* Metuchen, NJ: Scarecrow Press, 2005.

Kostlevy, William. *Historical Dictionary of the Holiness Movement.* Metuchen, NJ: Scarecrow Press, 2001.

Lindstrom, Harold. *Wesley and Sanctification*. New York: Abingdon Press, 1946.

Peterson, David. *Possessed by God: A New Testament Theology of Sanctification and Holiness*. Downers Grove, IL: IVP Academic, 2001.

Holy Catholic Church in Japan

See Anglican Church in Japan.

Holy Ghost Fathers

The Holy Ghost Fathers, officially the Congregation of the Holy Ghost under the Protection of the Immaculate Heart of Mary, is a religious order of the Roman Catholic Church composed of both priests and lay brothers. The Order, commonly referred to as the Spiritans, was founded in Paris, France, in 1703 by Claude Francis Poullart des Places (1679–1709). The original intent was the supplying of the French church with trained priests, and the first project was a seminary. The founder died in 1709 and the Order's first two members a year later; it survived, but did not receive official approval until 1734. The Order began to take an interest in missionary work during the 18th century. Their first missionary was sent to Canada in 1732. During the 19th century, several missionaries were sent to West Africa.

The Order was almost destroyed in the aftermath of the antireligious sentiments generated by the French Revolution. Disbanded, it was restored in 1804, but did not truly revive until the 1850s, under its new superior general, Francis Libermann (1804–1852), a converted Jew. In 1841, Libermann had founded the Congregation of the Holy Heart of Mary and sent priests to Guinea in West Africa. Out of contacts between Libermann's order and the Holy Ghost Fathers in Africa, the two orders decided to merge in 1848. Libermann became the head of the merged group.

Under Libermann's guidance the Order spread across Europe and North America, where a number of schools, including seminaries for the training of priests, were established. Here men were recruited for work in the rest of the world—South America, the West Indies, Africa, and the islands of the Indian Ocean. By the middle of the 20th century, the Holy Ghost Fathers had sent more missionary personnel (more than 1,700) to Africa than any other single religious order. Several, including Archbishops Prosper Augouard (1852–1890) (Congo) and Alexandre Le Roy (1854–1938) (Gabon), became honored church leaders of note.

The Spiritans entered the United States as early as 1794, and eventually centered their work in Pittsburgh, where Duquesne University was opened in 1878. In 1889, they founded an initial mission to African Americans in Pittsburgh. They subsequently joined forces with Saint Katherine Drexel and the Sisters of the Blessed Sacrament to build a broad mission with African American communities throughout the United States.

The Congregation has its headquarters in Rome. There are numerous Internet sites for the Spiritans reflective of its various provinces.

Congregation of the Holy Ghost
Clivo de Cinna 195
I-00136 Rome
Italy
http://members.attcanada.ca/~spilav/TheSpiritans
.html

J. Gordon Melton

See also: Monasticism; Roman Catholic Church.

Reference
Koren, H. J. *The Spiritans: A History of the Congregation of the Holy Ghost*. Pittsburgh: Duquesne Studies, Spiritan Series I, 1958. Rev. ed. *To the Ends of the Earth*. Pittsburgh: Duquesne University Press, 1983.

Holy Orthodox Church in Japan

Eastern Orthodoxy spread to Japan in 1861 when Nikolai Kassathin (1836–1912), a priest, arrived as a representative of the Russian Orthodox Church. He began work on the island of Hokkaido, and within several decades had converted some 20,000 people and opened churches across the country. He had the vision of an indigenous church, and rather than ask for fur-

Holy Resurrection Cathedral in Tokyo, center for the Holy Orthodox Church in Japan. (Joe Jones)

ther priests from Russia, he began to recruit priests from among the converts. He was able to create a missionary society to expand the work and was rewarded for his efforts by being made bishop and then archbishop of the growing mission. Toward the end of the century, the spread of the church was hindered, first by the policies of the government, and then especially by the strong anti-Russian sentiment that developed as a result of the Russo-Japanese War (1904–1905).

In 1919, following the Russian Revolution and the establishment of the Soviet Union, the church in Japan, under Metropolitan Sergei Tikhomiroff, established itself as an independent body. It took the name Nippon Harisutosu Kyokai (Japan Orthodox Church). Archbishop Nikolai's policy of quickly building an indigenous church allowed the church to survive the period of most intense nationalism during the last years of the

Meiji regime and World War II. It remained a separate body and was not forced into the Protestant-based United Church of Christ in Japan. After the war, the church developed strong relationships with the independent Russian Orthodox community in the United States (now the Orthodox Church in America) and accepted episcopal oversight from them until 1965, when relations were normalized with the parent body in Moscow.

The Holy Orthodox Church became autonomous in 1970 under its own episcopal leadership. The first Japanese archbishop, Metropolitan Theodosius (1935–1999), assumed leadership of the new church. He was succeeded by the current primate, His Eminence Daniel (Nushiro, b. 1938), archbishop of Tokyo and metropolitan of all Japan. The archbishop resides in Tokyo, where the Cathedral of the Holy Resurrection has become a popular site for visitors. The church is organized around its three dioceses. It remains at one in doctrine and practice with Orthodoxy worldwide.

The Holy Orthodox Church has more than 25,000 members and sponsors a seminary in Tokyo. It joined the World Council of Churches in 1973.

Holy Orthodox Church in Japan
Nicholai do, 1-4 chome
Surugadai Kanda
Chiyoda-Ku, Tokyo 101
Japan
http://plaza15.mbn.or.jp/~fnagaya/ (Japanese and
    Russian)

J. Gordon Melton

See also: Eastern Orthodoxy; United Church of Christ in Japan; World Council of Churches.

References

Van Beek, Huibert. *A Handbook of the Churches and Councils: Profiles of Ecumenical Relationships.* Geneva: World Council of Churches, 2006.
Van der Bent, Ans J., ed. *Handbook/Member Churches/World Council of Churches.* Geneva: World Council of Churches, 1985.

Holy Spirit Association for the Unification of World Christianity

See Unification Movement.

Holy Week

Holy Week commemorates the last week of the earthly life of Jesus Christ. It covers the events of his triumphal entry into Jerusalem, the Last Supper, the arrest, and his death by crucifixion. Beginning with the sixth Sunday of Lent, Holy Week includes Palm Sunday, Maundy Thursday, and Good Friday. Two lesser observed days of this week are Spy Wednesday and Holy Saturday.

The earliest reference to Holy Week observances appears in the writings of the *Pilgrimage of Ætheria* in fourth-century Jerusalem. From this time forward, we have records of Christians from all over the world taking pilgrimages to Jerusalem to participate in rites and re-enact the final events of Christ's life. Eventually, distinct practices for each special day of Holy Week spread throughout the wider Christian world.

Palm Sunday   The first of Holy Week celebrations, Palm Sunday focuses on Jesus' triumphal entry into Jerusalem when he was heralded as Messianic King. Worship services include the blessing of the palms outside the church and a procession into the church with participants waving palm branches and singing songs of celebration.

Holy Thursday (Maundy Thursday)   Holy Thursday revolves around the last supper Jesus shared with his disciples and consequently commemorates the institution of the Eucharist (Communion). As well, according to John 13, Jesus washed the disciples' feet during the meal. He then commanded them to wash one another's feet. Consequently, Maundy Thursday incorporates the rite of foot washing in many denominations. The term "maundy" comes from the Latin *mandatum* (cf. the English "mandate") in John 13:34, referring to the new commandment Jesus gives his disciples to love one another as he has loved them.

After Maundy Thursday services, it is customary in some church traditions to remove all of the altar coverings and decorations. Crosses are also removed or veiled until Easter Sunday morning. As well, Maundy Thursday begins what is known as the Easter Triduum, a three-day period devoted to special prayer and observance that runs through Good Friday to Easter Sunday.

Good Friday   On this day, the church commemorates Jesus' arrest, trial, crucifixion and suffering, death, and burial. It is traditionally a day of fasting and the Eucharist is not celebrated. Liturgies will often focus on the "Seven Last Words of Christ" and follow the "Stations of the Cross." Crosses remain veiled and the altar remains completely bare, without decorations, texts, candlesticks, or altar cloths.

Another common service for Good Friday is Tenebrae (Latin for "shadows" or "darkness"). Sometimes this term is applied generally to all evening church services on the last three days of Holy Week. More specifically, however, it is used for the "Service of Darkness" or "Service of Shadows" held in the evening of Good Friday.

Holy Week, and thus Lent, ends on the evening of Holy Saturday. Easter Sunday morning thus marks the beginning of a new period in the liturgical calendar.

In Roman Catholic and Eastern Orthodox churches, Holy Week is marked with church services almost every day from Palm Sunday to Easter. Protestant Churches vary widely, with some, like the Anglicans, approaching the Catholic and Orthodox churches in their frequency and intensity, while others recognize only Good Friday and/or Maundy Thursday; still others, especially the Free churches, have abandoned special services during Holy Week.

Kevin Quast

See also: Easter; Eastern Orthodoxy; Jerusalem; Lent; Liturgical Year; Pilgrimage; Roman Catholic Church.

References

deChant, Dell. *The Sacred Santa: Religious Dimensions of Consumer Culture.* Cleveland, OH: Pilgrim Press, 2002.

Nocent, Adrian. *The Liturgical Year.* Vol. 3: *The Paschal Triduum, The Easter Season.* Collegeville, MN: Liturgical Press. 1977.

Ramshaw, Gail. *The Three Day Feast: Maundy Thursday, Good Friday, Easter.* Minneapolis, MN: Augsburg Fortress, 2004.

Senn, Frank. *Christian Liturgy: Catholic and Evangelical.* Minneapolis, MN: Augsburg Fortress, 1997.

Stevenson, Kenneth. *Jerusalem Revisited: The Liturgical Meaning of Holy Week.* Washington, DC: Pastoral Press, 1988.

Thurston, Herbert. "Holy Week." In *The Catholic Encyclopedia.* Vol. 7. New York: Robert Appleton Company, 1910.

Homosexuality

The world religions seem to agree widely that homosexuality is deviant and its rejection is deeply rooted in the context-sensitive concepts of sexuality and gender relations. It is important to keep in mind that homosexuality is a modern category of sexuality referring to a certain sexual orientation that is generally understood as the attraction to and preference of the same sex that goes beyond mere homosexual acts. Owing to its age the traditional literature of world religions doesn't apply to this concept with its contemporary connotations but only corresponds to homosexual practices. Nevertheless, in the discussion about the acceptance of homosexuality, religious authorities refer to their normative scriptures to define their position. Thus it is important to outline the main arguments made in the traditional literature that are applied by the authorities and still bias the present attitudes toward homosexuality. Due to their common background the Abrahamic monotheistic religions of Judaism, Christianity, and Islam have very similar concepts of sexuality and gender roles. Their concepts of normative heterosexuality are derived from the belief that man and woman were created by God to complement each other. While the Islamic tradition teaches that they were created from the same sort of clay, the image of splitting the primordial Adam in two persons (Judaism) or creating Eve from Adam's rib (Christianity) leads to the belief that Adam and Eve—originally one—have to regain this genuine unity, which in this world is attained by marriage. This is reinforced by the fact that only the sexual intercourse between a man and a woman results in procreation, which again is the foremost legitimacy for sexual intercourse (this has been very strict in Christian perception, while Judaism and Islam agree on the understanding of sexual intercourse as a sacred act that can be enjoyed within a marriage while it doesn't have to lead to the requested procreation at any rate). This perception of legitimate sexuality implies the prohibition of same-sex relations, as they are neither fit to regain the unity of man and woman nor are they focused on procreation. For the Abrahamic religions, the center of reference to prohibit homosexual relations is the story about Lot and the people of Sodom, who tried to mass rape Lot's angelic guests represented as males, even though he offered to them his daughters instead. As a divine punishment for this sin Sodom is destroyed and all its inhabitants killed (Old Testament: Genesis 19:1–11; Koran: Sura 7:80–84,

26:165–166). Generally applied passages of the New Testament don't refer to Sodom (Romans 1:26–27; 1 Timothy 1:10) and besides the story of Lot there are commandments in the Holiness Code of the Old Testament (Leviticus 18:22; 20:13) prohibiting same-sex relations; there are several *hadith* where Muhammad condemns homosexual acts (in his Farewell Sermon). Nowadays concerned Jews, Christians, or Muslims make an effort to change attitudes toward homosexuality, for example, by reinterpreting the sin of the Sodomites as a transgression of hospitality laws rather than a sexual sin. Homosexual Muslims who have a specifically bad standing in Islamic societies allude to the homoerotic poetry of Sufism and stories about catamites. Another argument for the acceptance of homosexuals is the importance of love in a relationship, which can't be denied to same-sex couples that should be accepted as equal to heterosexual couples and thus granted the right to legally marry.

As a conglomeration of several different traditions the attitude of Hinduism toward homosexuality can hardly be generalized. The Hindu literature widely ignores it, except for a few remarks in the epics and the Puranas that include same-sex relations while condemning promiscuity in general (the Mahabharata declares it as a reason for impotence; XIII.145.52). Furthermore some passages about homosexual practices are enclosed in the Kamasutra (KS II.9) as well as several sections in both the canonical and the secular law that provide specific but minor punishments (Manu XI.68, XI.175). In total there are few explicit prohibitions of homosexual relations in the traditional literature and the religious Hindu attitude may be relatively tolerant, but as a culture it isn't. Hinduism is very permissive about conjugal sex foremost with the intention of procreation, but sexual relations are not discussed in public and homosexual acts are seen as a transgression of the natural order. Neo-Hinduism is very hostile toward homosexuals; gays and lesbians have to suffer from serious discrimination and violent abuses. NGOs and LBTG-activists are fighting for equality—for example, the Naz Foundation India Trust accomplished the decriminalization of homosexual relationships between consenting adults in a legal battle in 2009.

Similar to Hinduism the diversity of Buddhist tradition has led to divergent perceptions that depend on the historical period and the geographical location. There is a general neutrality regarding homosexuality in so far as the Pali canon, the normative scripture for the Buddhist Sangha, prohibits any kind of sexual intercourse or stimulation; within this homosexuality is just one of many prohibited practices (Vinayapitaka, Parajika I). From a Buddhist point of view any form of desire is harmful on the way to salvation; sexual intercourse is especially negative in its effects because, resulting in procreation, it reconstitutes the humans' bondage to *samsara*. This rule for the Buddhist monks and nuns, however, does not apply to the laity. In the lay Buddhist context homosexuality is rarely mentioned as a transgression although extramarital relations are generally perceived as illicit. Homosexuality is often understood as a result of negative karmic consequences or as a flaw that will lead to a bad reincarnation. In some times and places, however, especially members of higher social strata had same-sex relations, like the emperors of China during Han times, who as a matter of course had male lovers, or even monks, for example, in 14th-century Japan, where older monks took young novices (*chigos*) as lovers. The legitimacy of the latter might be explained by the fact that homosexual relations can't result in procreation and therefore are less harmful on the spiritual way. Nowadays Buddhist attitudes toward homosexuality are as diverse as they have always been. Religious authorities that commented on the matter so far, for example, the Dalai Lama, were not entirely positive, but homosexual Buddhists are usually not restrained by religious beliefs but social condemnation. On a religious level there are means of identification with the stories about the close and devotional relationships between a bodhisattva or Gautama Buddha and a close male companion like Ananda in the Jatakas, which are perceived as homoerotic.

In the Abrahamic traditional literature female homosexuality, or lesbianism, is widely ignored; some religious authorities expand the prohibition of male homosexuality to lesbianism, but most of them don't regard same-sex relations between women as intercourse because there is no penile penetration; thus they classify it solely as immoral and prosecute it with lesser penalties. In contrast to that Hindu law books mention sexual relations between women and these are punished much more severely than those between men because female virtue and chastity were a greater concern than the right sexual role of the man. On the other hand homosexual practices between women are depicted in the Kamasutra (KS V.6) without apparent judging. The Buddhist Bhikkhunivibhanga of the Pali canon refers to sexual acts between nuns that are prohibited but solely entail repentance (Pacittiya III, IV).

Today attitudes may differ from the traditional perceptions of homosexuality but its acceptance still depends on the respective cultural and socio-political circumstances. While some religious authorities and especially individual believers open up to homosexuals or encourage their acceptance by introducing new interpretations of the traditional literature, others are insisting on prohibitions. In consequence of the process of globalization and secularization many cultures presently fear the decline of their traditional values and moral standards due to a compelling impact of the West. In this regard homosexuality as a sexual orientation is often depicted as an "invention" or a characteristic of the immoral Western societies. This perception of homosexuality as a characteristic trait of the enemy or the foreigner is characteristic throughout history —there are many examples of cultures that began prohibiting homosexual acts along with adultery to distinguish themselves from the other (Jews in Hellenistic times; the Christians in contrast to some pagan cults, etc.).

Today homosexuals in most cultural and regional contexts are actively trying to improve their standing in society and their situation within their religious system. However, if homosexuality is socially condemned or illegal, lesbians and gays don't have much of a chance to fight for their rights, because of serious social consequences or legal penalties for solely coming out of the closet.

Céline Grünhagen

See also: Buddha, Gautama; Hinduism; Islam; Judaism.

References

Comstock, Gary David, and Susan E. Henking, eds. *Que(e)rying Religion: A Critical Anthology.* New York: Continuum Publishing Company, 1997.

Swidler, Arlene, ed. *Homosexuality in World Religions.* Valley Forge, PA: Trinity Press International, 1993.

http://www.bigeye.com/sexeducation/religion.html.

■ Honduras

The Republic of Honduras, formerly known as Spanish Honduras to differentiate it from British Honduras (now Belize), is about the size of Ohio—just over 43,278 square miles. The country is bordered on the west by Guatemala, on the southwest by El Salvador, on the southeast by Nicaragua, on the south by the Pacific Ocean at the Gulf of Fonseca, and on the north by the Gulf of Honduras, which is part of the Caribbean Sea. It has an estimated population of almost 7.5 million (2007).

Today, Honduras is the second poorest country in Central America and has an extraordinarily unequal distribution of income and a high unemployment rate. The economy relies heavily on a narrow range of exports, notably bananas and coffee, making it vulnerable to natural disasters and shifts in commodity prices.

In mid-2000, the national literacy rate was 80 percent and the total population was very homogeneous. Approximately 5,517,000, or 90 percent, of its population was *mestizo* (mixed Spanish and Indian blood), about 7 percent Amerindian (Lenca, Chorti, Chorotega, Pipil, Miskito, Pech, Sumo, and Tol), about 2 percent Afro-Caribbean (Garifunas and Creoles), and about 1 percent Caucasian. Honduras has the distinction of having the largest Garifuna (Afro-Amerindian origins, also known as Black Caribs) population in Central America.

The Constitution provides for freedom of religion and the government generally respects this right in practice. Although there is no state religion, the Honduran Armed Forces has an official Catholic patron saint. Government officials consult with Catholic Church officials and occasionally appoint Catholic clergy to quasi-official commissions on key subjects of mutual concern. Prominent Catholic and Protestant clergymen have been represented on more than a dozen governmental commissions, including the National Anticorruption Council.

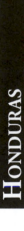

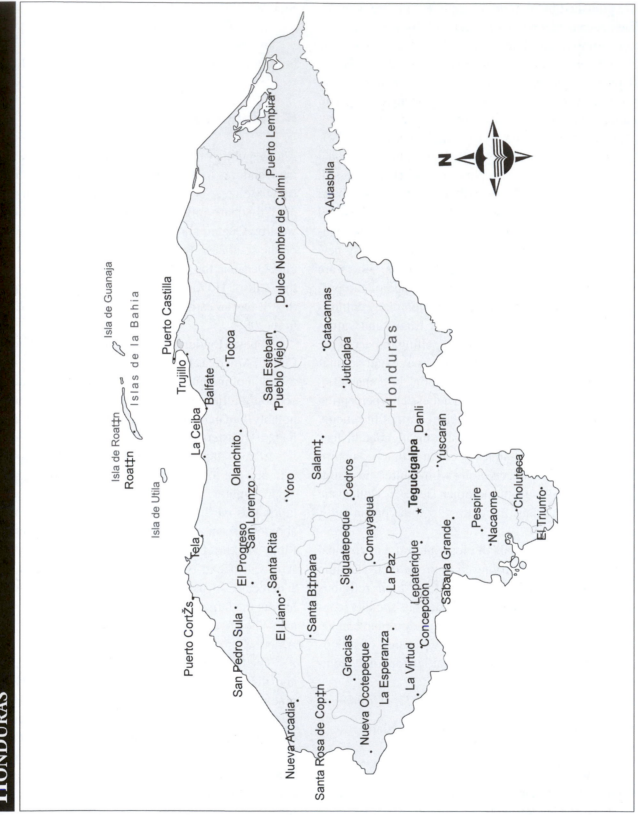

HONDURAS

Isla de Guanaja
Isla de Roat‡n
Roat‡n
Islas de la Bahia
Isla de Utila

Puerto Castilla
Puerto Lempira
Dulce Nombre de Culmi
Auasbila

Trujillo
Balfate
Tocoa
San Esteban
Pueblo Viejo
Catacamas

La Ceiba
Olanchito
Juticalpa
Honduras

Tela
San Lorenzo
Yoro
Salam‡
Cedros
Tegucigalpa
Danli
Yuscaran

El Progreso
Santa Rita
Siguatepeque
Comayagua
Pespire
Nacaome
Choluteca

Puerto Cort Žs
El Llano
Santa B‡rbara
La Paz
Lepaterique
Sabana Grande
El Triunfo

San Pedro Sula
Concepcion

Gracias
La Virtud

Nueva Arcadia
La Esperanza

Santa Rosa de Cop‡n
Nueva Ocotepeque

N

In May 2007, a national public opinion poll conducted by CID-Gallup that measured religious affiliation reported the following: Roman Catholics, 57 percent; Protestants, 36 percent; and "other religions" and those claiming "no religion" (or providing "no answer"), 17 percent. Previous polls reported that about 4 percent of the population was affiliated with "other religions" and about 12 percent claimed "no religion" (or "no answer").

The Roman Catholic Church has been the most affected by competition with other religious movements and by the process of secularization within Honduran society since 1950. Despite the historical ties of Hondurans to the Catholic Church, national public opinion polls taken by CID-Gallup between 1997 and 2007 in Honduras revealed a steady decline in the number of Catholic adherents and a significant increase in Protestant adherents, while those affiliated with "other religions" and those claiming "no religion" remained proportionally about the same. On the one hand, Catholic adherents declined from about 95 percent in 1950 to 63 percent in 1997, and to 47 percent in 2007, or less than half of the total population. On the other hand, Protestant adherents increased from less than 5 percent in 1950 to 21 percent in July 1997, and to 36 percent in May 2007. According to many observers, this represents the most significant increase in Protestant adherents in Central America during the past several decades.

Prior to Spanish colonization, the Caribbean coast was populated by the Miskito, Sumo, and Rama peoples of Macro-Chibchan origin (the predominant group in Colombia) who lived in scattered fishing villages on the coast and along the inland waterways, whereas the Pacific coast was largely home to ethnolinguistic groups that migrated south along the Pacific coast from present-day Mexico as early as 1000 BCE, including the Lenca, Chorti (Mayan), Chorotega, Pipil, Pech, and Tol. The Mayan civilization in Central America stretched from southern Mexico into Guatemala, El Salvador, and Honduras. The ethnic Maya of western Honduras have managed to maintain substantial remnants of their ancient cultural heritage. The Chorti (also known as Ch'orti') language is spoken today by approximately 15,000 people, but many are bilingual in Spanish also.

Spanish Admiral Christopher Columbus explored the northern coast of Honduras and landed on the mainland, near modern Trujillo (Colón Department), in 1502. The country was named Honduras ("depths") for the deep waters off its coast, known today as the Bay of Honduras. In 1532, the Province of Honduras consisted of one Spanish settlement on the Caribbean coast at the port of Trujillo, which was founded in May 1525 by Juan de Medina.

After Pedro de Alvarado defeated the Amerindian resistance headed by chief Çiçumba in 1536, the Spaniards began to dominate the entire country. Alvarado imposed the *repartimiento de labor*, a colonial labor system whereby the natives were forced into low-paid or unpaid labor for a portion of each year. When the Spanish authorities began mining both gold and silver in the 16th century, they further enslaved the Native peoples (Amerindians) and imported Africans to work in the mines.

Beginning in the mid-1600s, the British claimed a Protectorate over the Mosquito Coast, which today forms part of the Republics of Honduras and Nicaragua. Trading settlements were subsequently established by the British, who armed the residents. The Miskito Kingdom successfully resisted Spanish conquests and allied itself with the British for self-protection and trade benefits.

Honduras gained its independence from Spain in 1821 but was briefly annexed to the independent Mexican Empire. In 1823, Honduras joined the newly formed United Provinces of Central America. Soon, social and economic differences between Honduras and its regional neighbors created harsh partisan strife among regional leaders, which brought about the federation's collapse in 1838–1839. Restoring Central American unity was the officially stated chief aim of Honduran foreign policy until after World War I.

All democratic elections in Honduras have been dominated by two major political parties, the Honduran Liberal Party (PLH, center-left) and the Honduran National Party (PNH, center-right). The PNH dominated the country between 1933 and 1957. In 1963, a military junta overthrew the democratically elected government of President Ramón Villeda Morales (r. 1957–1963) and established an authoritarian regime that held power until 1982, when Roberto Suazo Córdova (PLH) became president.

The administration of General Policarpo Paz García (b. 1932; r. 1978–1982) was noted for its corruption and military repression, including the activities attributed to the infamous Battalion 3-16, a secret right-wing paramilitary death squad trained by the CIA that kidnapped, tortured, and assassinated many political dissidents of the military dictatorship. In 1980, the military junta headed by General Paz García decided to restore the nation to civil rule under a new Constitution, and subsequently Roberto Suazo Córdova (b. 1927; r. 1982–1986) was elected president.

Carlos Roberto Reina Idiáquez (1926–2003; r. 1994–1999) inherited a relatively difficult economic situation from the previous administration. He was able, however, to launch a "moral revolution" to defeat corruption and mismanagement, and most of his reforms were realized by the end of his first year in office. Then in 1998, Hurricane Mitch caused such massive and widespread loss that Reina's successor, Carlos Roberto Flores Facussé (b. 1950; r. 1998–2002), observed that 50 years of progress in the country had been reversed. The powerful hurricane obliterated about 70 percent of the crops and an estimated 70 to 80 percent of the transportation infrastructure. Across the country, some 5,600 people were killed, and the economy lost some $3 billion. Estimated recovery would take nearly two decades.

The Roman Catholic Church   Roman Catholicism arrived in Honduras with the early Spanish explorers and settlers, and it dominated the religious life of the country until the 1950s, when Protestant groups began to multiply rapidly throughout the country. The first Franciscans arrived in 1521, followed by Mercedarian missionaries in 1548, to begin the task of evangelizing and baptizing the Amerindians, and subsequently forcing them to build churches and convents in the settled communities across the land. The Franciscans were given the difficult and risky task of evangelizing Amerindians in unconquered lands, whereas the Mercedarians worked mainly among subjugated Amerindians in the *reducciones* (organized communities) near the mission stations, where they were given religious instruction and used as laborers by the missionaries; other

captives were distributed among the Spanish colonists as slave labor. Convents were established by the Mercedarians in Comayagua, Tegucigalpa (Francisco Morazán Department), Gracias (Lempira Department), Tencoa (Santa Barbara Department), and Choluteca.

The first Catholic bishop of Honduras was friar Cristóbal de Pedraza (1485–1553), who arrived in 1539 and settled in the town of Trujillo (founded in 1525), which is located on a bluff overlooking the Bay of Trujillo; this area has a very hot and humid climate, which created unhealthy living conditions. In addition, the British, Dutch, and French pirates took their toll of destruction on Trujillo during the 16th to 18th centuries. Bishop Pedraza was succeeded in 1555 by Gerónimo de Corella, who chose the town of Nueva Valladolid (now Comayagua) as his seat, due to its central geographical location in the interior, its relative safety from pirate attacks, and its more favorable climate. The Diocese of Comayagua was established in 1561 from the Diocese of Santiago de Guatemala, under Bishop Corella. In 1601, Catholic missions among the "savage Indians" on the north coast were attacked by English pirates, and the Spanish colonists and missionaries were scattered. Consequently, most Amerindians in that region "relapsed into their original savagery."

The revolution of independence from Spain in 1821 did great damage to the Catholic Church. Before that time there were more than 300 Catholic churches and missions (called "ecclesiastical foundations") and public worship was conducted nearly everywhere with some dignity. All foreign priests were expelled in 1821. The revolutionary government, by 1842, had confiscated most of the property owned by the church. Since then the parishes depended on precarious voluntary offerings to support public worship, and the number of clergy diminished in number by 1902. The episcopal city of Comayagua suffered greatly from the civil wars during the period of the Federation (1823–1839), and by 1902 had not regained its former size or prosperity.

Between 1878 and 1880, the new president of Honduras, imposed by the Liberal government of Guatemala, confiscated some of the church's resources and abolished the payment of tithes by the state to the church. These oppressive acts greatly hampered the

Hondurans pray during a mass celebrating the Feast of Virgin Suyapa at a Roman Catholic church near the capital Tegucigalpa, February 3, 1998. Thousands of piligrims gathered from all over the country to worship the Virgin Suyapa, the patron saint of Honduras. (AP Photo/Eugene Hoshiko)

proper formation of the clergy, public worship, and the administration of the dioceses. By 1902, the Catholic seminary had been reopened, but it was subject to many governmental restrictions.

In 1908, Bishop Joseph María Martínez Cabanas (1841–1921, bishop of Comayagua, 1902–1921) was assisted by five parish priests in the Department of Comayagua. Nationally, there were 70 secular priests but no foreign religious priests, because the government had not allowed them to return since their expulsion in 1821.

At that time, the wealthier classes of the Diocese of Comayagua, with very few exceptions, were indifferent to religion. There were no parochial schools, because the people of the pueblos were unable to support them after paying taxes for the public schools. Moreover, the clergy were unable to conduct parochial

schools because of their obligation at all times to move about from one small town to another among the widely scattered villages in mountainous terrain.

In 1902, the Diocese of Comayagua, which included the entire Republic of Honduras, had a population (exclusive of "uncivilized Indians") of 684,400 inhabitants, mostly baptized Catholics, except on the northern coast and in the Bay Islands, among the Creoles, Garifunas, and Miskitos. In 1916, the Diocese of Comayagua was relocated and renamed the Diocese of Tegucigalpa, and it was elevated to an archdiocese under Archbishop Santiago María Martínez y Cabanas (1842–1921).

The current archbishop of Tegucigalpa (appointed in 1993) is Cardinal Oscar Andrés Rodríguez Maradiaga, S.D.B. (b. 1942, became a bishop in 1978 and a cardinal in 2001); he was ordained a priest of the

Salesians of Saint John Bosco in 1970. Archbishop Rodríguez is cardinal titular of the Church of Santa Maria della Speranza in Tegucigalpa. Today, the Honduran Catholic Church is divided administratively into eight dioceses (the percentages are the proportion of Catholics in relationship to the total population in each diocese): Tegucigalpa (75 percent), Comayagua (92.2 percent), Choluteca (87.4 percent), Juticalpa (90.9 percent), San Pedro Sula (66.7 percent), Santa Rosa de Copán (90 percent), Trujillo (67.1 percent), and Yoro (82 percent). This reveals that the dioceses of San Pedro Sula, Trujillo, and Tegucigalpa have the lowest proportion of Catholic adherents in the country, in that order. It is assumed that the proportion of Protestant adherents is higher in those three dioceses than in the others.

During past centuries, the Roman Catholic Church in Honduras failed to develop into a strong national institution. In 1970, 86.3 percent of the religious priests in Honduras were expatriates (mainly from Spain), 9 percent were from other Latin American countries, and only 5 percent were Hondurans. As late as 1990, the Honduran Catholic Church was one of the most dependent national churches in Latin America, with a large number of expatriate priests, lay brothers, and nuns. In fact, Honduras still has a very high proportion of expatriate religious priests. In 2002, the Archdiocese of Tegucigalpa reported 168 diocesan priests and 214 religious priests (a total of 382), 255 non-ordained male religious, and 561 female religious (nuns), distributed among 168 parishes in 7 dioceses in the whole country.

Diverse tensions arose within the Honduran Catholic Church during the 1960s and following years, which resulted from challenges posed by the Second Vatican Council (1962–1965), the Conference of Latin American Bishops held in Medellín (Colombia) in 1968, Latin American Liberation Theology, and the Catholic Charismatic Renewal movement. These powerful new currents polarized Catholic bishops, priests (diocesan and religious), lay brothers and sisters (members of religious orders), and the laity in general into various factions. *Traditionalists* wanted the church to remain as it was prior to the reforms approved by the Second Vatican Council (mid-1960s), with an emphasis on apostolic authority, orthodox theology, the sacraments, and personal piety. *Reformers* generally supported the church's post–Second Vatican Council stance of modernization and toleration of diversity based on its official social doctrine. *Progressives*, inspired by reforms approved at the Second Vatican and Medellín conferences, sought to implement the new vision for "a preferential option for the poor" through social and political action aimed at transforming Honduran society and establishing greater social justice through peaceful democratic means. *Radicals* adopted the Marxist-inspired Liberation Theology and advocated violent revolution by the people as a means of overthrowing the military dictatorship and creating a Socialist state that would serve the poor marginalized masses. *Charismatic agents* sought to transform the spiritual and communal life of Catholics by means of the power and gifts of the Holy Spirit (including the "baptism of the Holy Spirit" and "speaking in tongues"), rather than by political and social activism.

Since 1925, the patron saint of Honduras has been the Immaculate Virgin of Suyapa. Her statue (only 2.3 inches tall), which allegedly was discovered in 1747 and was credited with her first miracle in 1768, normally resides in the small Iglesia de Suyapa. However, during the week of her feast day on February 2, the statue is moved to the much larger Basilica de Suyapa to accommodate the crowds of pilgrims who travel from all over Central America to pray and ask her for a miracle. Each town and city has annual celebrations (*fiestas patronales*) for its patron saints, and special religious celebrations are held all over the country during Holy Week, which ends on Easter Sunday.

The Protestant Movement   Between 1768 and 1950, Protestantism in Honduras experienced slow but steady grow. The first Anglican missionary, Christian Frederick Post (1768–1785) from Philadelphia, was sent out by the Society for the Propagation of the Gospel in Foreign Parts (SPGFP). Post arrived at the Black River settlement in 1768, and additional Anglican chaplains followed. In spite of their troubles with the climate, Anglican schools and chapels were established among the Amerindians and Africans, but few converts were made among the whites.

Anglican chaplains and missionaries continued to serve on the Miskito Coast until the mid-20th century. Anglican work in Honduras was transferred to U.S.

jurisdiction in 1947, eventually becoming a missionary district of the Episcopal Church with headquarters in the Panama Canal Zone. In 2000, there were 41 Episcopal congregations (churches and missions) in Honduras, with about 2,900 members.

Protestant missionary activity increased during the 19th century with the arrival of British Wesleyan missionaries in the Bay Islands, where the first Methodist society was formed during 1844–1845. Between 1887 and 1892, missionaries of the Belize District of the Wesleyan Methodist Church formally entered the mainland of Honduras, where English-speaking congregations were established among Belizean and West Indian (Creole) migrants. During the 1930s, these congregations were taken over by a new mission agency from the United States, the African Methodist Episcopal Church. In 1949, the United Brethren in Christ Mission (UBCM) arrived on the Caribbean coast of Honduras, and soon absorbed the remaining English-speaking Methodist congregations. In 1952, the UBCM began work among the Spanish-speaking population in central Honduras, and by 1986 the work had grown to 34 churches, 8 missions, and 1,677 members. In 2005, this denomination had an estimated 67 churches and 2,880 members.

Another Methodist missionary society entered Honduras in 1957, the Wesleyan Methodist Church (now the Wesleyan Church), which also began work among the English-speaking population on the Caribbean coast. By 1978, 6 churches had been established, with about 260 members. In 1986, most of the English-speaking Methodists in the country were affiliated with the Conference of the Methodist Church on the Caribbean and the Americas. In 2005, there were an estimated 12 Methodist churches and 750 members in Honduras.

The Baptists in British Honduras (now called Belize) responded to invitations from West Indian Baptists in the Bay Islands to come and help them, and the first Baptist missionaries were sent from Belize to the Bay Islands in 1846. Although in 1978 there were only 7 churches and 110 members in the Baptist Association of the Bay Islands, by 2005 the work had grown to an estimated 82 churches and 4,550 members.

Baptist work on the mainland, begun by the Conservative Baptist Home Missionary Society in 1951,

grew to 66 churches and 1,470 members along the Caribbean coast by 1978. In 1960, the Conservative Baptists established Radio Station HRVC in the capital, initially broadcasting on short-wave, but adding medium-wave in 1965. In 1978, this was the only evangelical radio station in Honduras and was listened to throughout the country. In 1986, there were 119 congregations with 2,269 baptized members affiliated with the Conservative Baptist Association (now CBAmerica) in Honduras, mainly resulting from the efforts of U.S. missionary George Patterson in the port city of La Ceiba. By 2005, there were an estimated 190 churches and 3,960 members in this Baptist Association.

Three other Protestant groups entered Honduras during the latter part of the 19th century, the Seventh-day Adventist Church (1887), the Central American Mission (1896), and the Christian Brethren (1898). Initially, the Adventists concentrated their efforts on the English-speaking population of the Bay Islands and on the coastal mainland. By 1978, Adventist work in Honduras was equally divided among Spanish-speakers in the interior and English-speakers on the north coast and the Bay Islands. At that time, the Adventist Mission included 55 churches, 97 mission stations, and about 18,400 baptized members. In 2000, Adventist work had grown to an estimated 100 churches and 22,200 members, which made this denomination one of the largest Protestant groups in the country. Also present in Honduras are the Church of God (Seventh-day) and the Seventh-day Adventist Church Reform movement.

Missionaries of the Central American Mission (now called CAM International) entered Honduras in 1896 with the express purpose of evangelizing the Spanish-speaking population, mainly in the nation's interior regions. Five CAM missionaries launched a pioneer effort in the mountain villages, while others concentrated their efforts on regional market centers. By 1985, CAM reported 154 churches and 21 mission stations with about 7,600 baptized members. In 2000, CAM work had grown to 270 churches and missions with 8,130 members, affiliated with the Association of Central American Churches of Honduras.

The Christian Brethren (the Open Brethren branch of the Plymouth Brethren movement from England) began work in the San Pedro Sula area in 1898 led by

Christopher Knapp and, after 1911, by Alfred Hockins, an agent for the British and Foreign Bible Society. Hockins later became a missionary affiliated with Christian Missions in Many Lands (1919) and remained in active ministry with the Christian Brethren in Honduras until his death in 1978. By 1936, 12 small congregations, called Gospel Halls, had been established in the San Pedro Sula and Trujillo regions on the north coast. About 1950, missionary efforts were started in the interior of the country, and the Christian Brethren almost doubled their membership during the next decade. From 164 congregations and about 15,000 members in 1985, the Association of Gospel Halls grew to 250 congregations and an estimated 23,000 members in 2000.

During the 20th century, Protestant mission efforts in Honduras increased significantly with the arrival of dozens of new mission agencies and hundreds of new missionaries, mainly from the United States following World War II. The California Yearly Meeting of Friends (Religious Society of Friends, or Quakers) established mission work in Guatemala in 1902, and by 1912 their activity had spread across the border into northwestern Honduras, based in San Marcos de Ocotepeque. Soon Quaker missionaries and national workers were active throughout the departments of Copán, Gracias, and Ocotepeque. However, due to the war between Honduras and El Salvador in 1969, the work of the Friends Mission in northwestern Honduras was severely affected, because many of the church members were Salvadorans who were forced to return to their own country during the conflict, while other members fled to Guatemala and to the interior of Honduras. In 1985, the Friends Church Association reported 61 congregations with only 1,185 members, but by 2000 the total membership had increased to 2,240.

Although, in 1914, the Quakers also began work in Tegucigalpa, located in the south-central mountain region, this field of service was administered separately and included mission stations in La Esperanza, Marcal, La Paz, and Juticalpa. However, in 1944 the Tegucigalpa Friends Mission was transferred to the supervision of the National Holiness Missionary Society (now called the World Gospel Mission [WGM]), due to serious financial and personnel shortages during World War II. At the time of the transfer, there were

5 Quaker churches, but by 1985 the Honduras Holiness Church reported about 2,400 members in 98 congregations. In 2005, this denomination had grown to an estimated 3,490 members in 130 congregations.

Other non-Pentecostal churches established in Honduras included the Evangelical and Reformed Church (now an integral part of the United Church of Christ) in 1935, with headquarters in San Pedro Sula. The Moravian Church began work in 1930 in the Mosquitia region among the Miskito Indians, as an extension of their older work in Nicaragua (begun in 1847). Missionaries of the Southern Baptist Convention first arrived in 1946 in Tegucigalpa, and in 1958 the National Convention of Baptist Churches of Honduras was organized with four churches and 22 missions. The Eastern Mennonite Board of Missions and Charities began work in 1950 on the Caribbean coast and later in Tegucigalpa.

Several other Baptist missions entered Honduras during the 1950s and 1960s: Baptist International Mission, Baptist Bible Fellowship International, Grace Baptist Churches, Baptist Mid-Missions, the Good Samaritan Baptist Mission, and a dozen independent Baptist groups. Also present in Honduras are the Church of the Nazarene, the Lutheran Church–Missouri Synod, the independent Churches of Christ, and several other small denominations.

The first known Pentecostal missionaries in Honduras visited the Bay Islands in the early 1900s, but it was not until 1931 that Frederick Mebius, an independent Pentecostal missionary working in El Salvador (he arrived there in 1904), crossed the border and helped established the first Pentecostal churches in western Honduras. The leaders of these new Pentecostal churches in Honduras requested help from the Assemblies of God in El Salvador during the mid-1930s. Several national workers soon arrived from El Salvador, but the first Assemblies of God missionaries did not enter Honduras until late 1940. From the very beginning, the work in Honduras was indigenous and self-supporting, although the Assemblies of God Board of Missions has aided the work by sending missionaries and funds for special projects. By 1985, the Assemblies of God of Honduras had 392 churches with 10,156 members. In December 2000, when the Assemblies of God of Honduras celebrated their 60th anniversary in the country, the number of churches had grown to more than 700, in addition to more than 320 preaching points; there were a total of 1,050 national pastors and 90,285 adherents (about 30,000 baptized members). There is an Assemblies of God mega-church in Tegucigalpa with more than 10,000 members. Also, this denomination operates three Bible institutes in Honduras.

The Church of God (Cleveland, Tennessee) arrived in the Bay Islands in 1944, when Fred and Lucille Litton went to Roatán and Utila to hold revival meetings among the English-speaking West Indian (Creole) population. Spanish-speaking work was begun in the 1950s in the interior of the country through the efforts of Mexican evangelist Josué Rubio, who established the first church in Tegucigalpa in 1951 with 53 members. By 1985, there were 371 churches with about 14,000 members; and in 2005 there were an estimated 690 churches with 21,200 Full Gospel Church of God members in Honduras.

The International Church of the Foursquare Gospel began work in Honduras in 1952 with the arrival of missionaries Edwin and Vonitta Gurney. Evangelistic efforts were launched in the capital city and in the departments of Cortés, La Paz, Santa Barbara, and Valle, in addition to other parts of the Department of Francisco Morazán, where Tegucigalpa is located. This denomination had numerous divisions and little church growth until the mid-1980s. Since then, several Foursquare evangelists have held citywide crusades in stadiums around the country, with attendance numbering 10,000 to 50,000 for each event and with thousands of reported conversions. La Cosecha (Harvest) Foursquare Church in San Pedro Sula is acclaimed as the "largest evangelical church in Honduras," with 20,000 attending weekly. In 2006, this denomination recorded 20,000 "decisions for Christ" and 13,000 water baptisms, and planted 17 new churches. There were a total of 250 Foursquare churches with 57,000 members in 2006.

The Prince of Peace Pentecostal Church, founded in Guatemala City by José María Muñoz in 1956, began its ministry in Honduras during the 1960s, mainly as a result of the influence of Muñoz's extensive radio ministry and the reputation of the large mother church in Guatemala. In Honduras, Prince of Peace experienced rapid growth in the mid-1970s, increasing from about 50 churches in 1974 to 125 in 1979. In the early 1980s, it declined due to dissension from within and the formation of splinter groups. However, in 1985, this denomination reported 143 churches and about 2,000 members. In 2005, there were an estimated 210 churches and 15,200 members in the Prince of Peace Church Association.

Other Pentecostal denominations in Honduras include (2005 estimates by Brierly): the United Pentecostal Church International (220 churches and 13,400 members), Philadelphia Church from Sweden (130 churches and 7,090 members), the Church of God of Prophecy (230 churches and 6,410 members), Center for Christian Formation (18 churches and 6,470 members), the Great Commission Churches (110 churches and 5,500 members), Elim Christian Mission (59 churches and 4,460 members), the Pentecostal Church of God from Puerto Rico (170 churches and 4,200 members), the independent Living Love Church (29 churches and 4,350 members), the Congregational Holiness Church (200 churches and 3,680 members), Gospel Crusade of Honduras (about 200 churches), and several dozen smaller groups with fewer than 3,000 members each in 2005.

During the early 1970s, when the Catholic Charismatic Renewal movement (its first retreat was held in 1973) began to grow among the upper classes in Tegucigalpa, several new ecumenical groups (fellowship groups of Catholics and Protestants combined) were formed, and some evangelical groups began to take on a Charismatic flavor. Some of these groups experienced significant growth, especially among young people and families involved in the business community. The Christian Love Brigade Association, led by Cuban pastor Mario Fumero, had 4 churches, 4 missions, and about 500 members in 1978. The Cenáculo Christian Center of Charismatic Renewal, pastored by Fernando Nieto, had 2 centers and 410 members in 1978; this group is affiliated with the Assemblies of God. Living Love Groups (Grupos de Amor Viviente), led by missionary Edward King, are affiliated with the Eastern Mennonite Board of Missions and Charities; this organization reported 13 Bible study and fellowship groups that ministered to about 700 people in 1978. Some Mennonite groups in San Pedro Sula and La Ceiba also had a Charismatic emphasis. Abundant

Honduras

Religion	Followers in 1970	Followers in 2010	% of Population	Annual % growth 2000–2010	Followers in 2025	Followers in 2050
Christians	2,638,000	7,277,000	96.6	1.96	9,290,000	11,498,000
Roman Catholics	2,413,000	6,025,000	80.0	1.74	7,350,000	8,800,000
Protestants	61,900	970,000	12.9	5.04	1,450,000	1,950,000
Independents	28,500	390,000	5.2	3.52	650,000	900,000
Spiritists	12,000	67,000	0.9	1.98	86,000	108,000
Agnostics	2,500	75,000	1.0	3.88	150,000	250,000
Ethnoreligionists	25,000	40,000	0.5	1.98	42,000	40,000
Baha'is	8,000	38,000	0.5	1.98	56,000	90,000
Atheists	1,000	16,800	0.2	1.98	25,000	40,000
Muslims	1,600	11,400	0.2	1.98	20,000	30,000
Buddhists	1,000	4,500	0.1	1.98	7,000	14,000
New religionists	1,000	2,400	0.0	1.98	5,000	7,500
Chinese folk	500	500	0.0	1.98	700	1,000
Jews	150	400	0.0	2.02	400	400
Total population	**2,691,000**	**7,533,000**	**100.0**	**1.98**	**9,682,000**	**12,079,000**

Life Christian Church (Iglesia Cristiana Vida Abundante) was founded in 1972 in Tegucigalpa by several families who had been active members of the Friends Church (Quakers). Sometime in 1979 during special meetings held with fasting and prayer (extended prayer meetings, called *vigilias*), some members of the group began "speaking in tongues." These Charismatic experiences transformed their worship and prayer services into something quite different from the traditional Quaker meetings, which created problems for them with the Friends denomination in western Honduras. In 1980, the Friends group in Tegucigalpa decided to become independent of the Friends denomination, under the leadership of pastor Evelio Reyes. The new Charismatic church grew from about 30 people in 1977 to several hundred by 1980—in 1991, Mario René López reported an attendance of about 3,400 in the main worship services.

Overall, according to a socio-religious study of Honduras conducted by World Vision International in 1986, the Protestant movement in Honduras included an estimated 2,644 churches and 645 missions, for a total of 3,289 congregations. The total membership was reported to be 149,313, with a Protestant community estimated at 450,000, or about 11.7 percent, of the national population of 3,838,031 (1985 estimate). Al-

though no national church growth studies have been conducted in Honduras since 1986, it is estimated that Protestant adherents increased from about 12 percent of the total population in 1985 to 21 percent in July 1997 (CID-Gallup poll), and to 36 percent in May 2007 (CID-Gallup poll).

The Evangelical Committee for Relief and National Emergency (CEDEN) was organized in 1974, following the disaster caused by Hurricane Fife, which hit the northern coast and caused widespread destruction and left 12,000 dead and an estimated 150,000 homeless. In 1985, CEDEN had the support of about 30 denominations and evangelical service agencies in Honduras. Temporary relief committees were formed by evangelicals to aid refugees during the war with El Salvador in 1969, to assist in earthquake relief in Managua in 1972, and to care for survivors of Hurricane Fife on the northern coast of Honduras in 1974. In response to these emergencies, as well as to growing social concerns among evangelicals, CEDEN was organized on a permanent basis. In 1985, its programs included agriculture and community development, well digging, public health, leadership training, communications, and audiovisual production. The organization of regional committees and offices gave CEDEN strong grassroots support among evangelicals in San Pedro Sula,

La Ceiba, Choluteca, and San Marcos de Ocotepeque, in addition to the Tegucigalpa-Comayagüela area.

The Evangelical Alliance of Honduras has existed since 1958, but was strongest in the early 1960s during the years of Evangelism-in-Depth. The Alliance has always been a fairly weak organization, mainly dedicated to representing the evangelical community before the Honduran government in matters relating to religious education, taxes, customs duties, and the like. Prior to 1958, an inter-mission committee served a similar function.

In 2008, the Latin American Confraternity of Evangelicals (CONELA)–related groups in Honduras were associated together in the Evangelical Confraternity of Honduras (CEH), which reported 212 member organizations, whereas the only Latin American Council of Churches (CLAI)–related groups in Honduras were the Evangelical and Reformed Church, the Episcopal Church, the Evangelical Mennonite Church, and the Evangelical Lutheran Church.

Other Religions   In May 2007, a national public opinion poll conducted by CID-Gallup measured religious affiliation and found that those claiming adherence to "other religions" and those claiming "no religion" (or providing "no answer") was 17 percent of the national population, but there was no breakdown of the percentages for these two categories. According to a previous CID-Gallup national public opinion poll conducted in July 1997, those claiming affiliation with "other religions" were 4 percent of the total population, and those claiming "no religious affiliation" (or "no answer") were 12 percent.

Included in the "other religions" category are non-Protestant marginal Christian groups, which include the Jehovah's Witnesses (231 congregations and 15,716 adherents in 2005); the Philadelphia Church of God; 2 Mormon denominations—the Church of Jesus Christ of Latter-day Saints (Utah Mormons: 220 congregations and 125,606 adherents in 2007) and the Reorganized Church of Jesus Christ of Latter Day Saints (now the Community of Christ); Light of the World Church (Guadalajara, Mexico); Philadelphia Church of God; God is Love Pentecostal Church and Universal Church of the Kingdom of God (both from Brazil); Mita Con-

gregation, the People of Amos Church, and the Voice of the Cornerstone Church (all from Puerto Rico); and Growing in Grace International Ministries (from Miami, Florida).

Also present in Honduras is St. John the Baptist Antiochian Orthodox Church (an autocephalous Eastern Orthodox Church with headquarters in Damascus, Syria), founded in San Pedro Sula in 1963 and composed of Palestinian Arabs (mainly from Bethlehem) who first arrived in Honduras in 1890s; the community totaled 592 in 1934, 812 in 1937, and 1,149 in 1986. A minority of the Palestinian immigrants is Muslim, and there is a Mosque in San Pedro Sula. A small Jewish community was established after World War II; today, there are two synagogues, in San Pedro Sula and Tegucigalpa.

Other world religions in Honduras include Baha'i Faith, Buddhism (largely among an estimated 7,500 Chinese immigrants and their descendants), Hinduism (International Society for Krishna Consciousness, International Sri Sathya Sai Baba Organization, and the Transcendental Meditation movement, aka Global Country of World Peace). The Western Esoteric tradition is represented by the Ancient and Mystical Order Rosae Crucis (AMORC), the Grand Universal Fraternity, and the Universal Gnostic Christian Church. Spiritualist-Psychic–New–Age groups include the Church of Scientology and the Unification Movement (Reverend Sun Myung Moon).

Native American religious traditions (animist) have survived from the pre-Columbian era and have been joined by the Garifuna religion among the Black Carib, who dwell in at least 50 communities on the Caribbean coast, and by Myalism (an African adaptation of Christianity) and Obeah (witchcraft) among the Creoles (West Indians), who are also concentrated on the northern coast. "Popular religiosity" (syncretistic) is practiced by a majority of the Hispanic Catholic population. Among practitioners of Amerindian, Black Carib, and West Indian religions and Hispanic Popular Catholicism, there are "specialists" who practice magic, witchcraft (*brujería*), shamanism (*chamanismo*), and folk healing (*curanderismo*). In addition, there are numerous psychics, mediums, clairvoyants, and astrologers who announce their services in local newspapers.

Satanic groups have been reported to exist in Tegucigalpa and San Pedro Sula.

Clifton L. Holland

See also: African Methodist Episcopal Church; Ancient and Mystical Order Rosae Crucis; Assemblies of God; Baptist Bible Fellowship International; Baptists; CBAmerica; Christian Brethren; Church of God (Cleveland, Tennessee); Church of God of Prophecy; Church of Jesus Christ of Latter-day Saints; Church of Scientology; Community of Christ; Episcopal Church; Franciscans: Friends/ Quakers; Garifuna Religion; Global Country of World Peace; International Church of the Foursquare Gospel; International Society for Krishna Consciousness; Jehovah's Witnesses; Light of the World Church; Methodist Church in the Caribbean and the Americas; Mita Congregation; Pentecostalism; Roman Catholic Church; Seventh Day Adventist Reform Movements; Seventh-day Adventist Church; Society for the Propagation of the Gospel in Foreign Parts; Southern Baptist Convention; Spiritualism; Unification Movement; United Church of Christ; United Pentecostal Church International; Wesleyan Church.

References

Brierly, Peter, ed. *World Churches Handbook.* London: Christian Research, 1977.

Catholic Statistics by Diocese for Honduras (2002). http://www.catholic-hierarchy.org/country/schn1.html. Accessed June 15, 2009.

Dussell, Enrique, et al. *Historia General de la Iglesia en América Latina.* Vol. 6, *América Central.* Salamanca, Spain: Ediciones Sígueme, 1985.

Grubb, Kenneth G. *Religion in Central America.* London: World Dominion Press, 1937.

Herrera, Feliciano. "Comayagua." In *The Catholic Encyclopedia.* Vol. 4. New York: Robert Appleton Company, 1908. http://www.newadvent.org/cathen/04151c.htm. Accessed June 15, 2009.

Holland, Clifton L., ed. *World Christianity: Central America and the Caribbean.* Monrovia, CA: MARC-World Vision, 1981.

Holland, Clifton L., ed. *Directorio de Iglesias, Organizaciones y Ministerios del Movimiento Protestante: Honduras.* San José, Costa Rica: PROCADES-CEDEN, 1979, 1982.

Iglesia Cristiana Luterana. *¿Los Nuevos Movimientos Religiosos en Honduras al Servicio de Quién? 1980–1989.* Tegucigalpa, Honduras: Iglesia Cristiana Luterana de Honduras, 1993.

López, Marlo René. "Historia y Misión del Protestantismo Hondureño." Tesis de Licenciatura en Teología, Seminario Internacional Teológico Bautista, 1992.

PROLADES y Visión Mundial Internacional de Honduras. *Estudio Socio-Religioso de Honduras.* Tegucigalpa, Honduras: Visión Mundial Internacional-Honduras, 1986.

PROLADES-RITA Database. "Ethnic and Religious Diversity in Honduras." http://www.prolades/cra/regions/cam/hon/hon-docs.htm. Accessed June 15, 2009.

U.S. Department of State. *International Religious Freedom Report 2007: Honduras.* http://www.state.gov/g/drl/rls/irf/2007/90258.htm. Accessed June 15, 2009.

Honen

1133–1212

Honen is a Japanese Tendai monk who broke with the Tendai tradition then prevalent and started his own school, Jodo (Pure Land) Buddhism. He is one of the greatest founders of religion in Japanese history.

Born into a prominent family in Mimasaka Province, he studied at the Tendai center on Mount Hiei, near Kyoto. During his time there he encountered the writings of Genshin (942–1017), a prominent Tendai scholar active at the beginning of the 11th century. Genshin advocated for devotion to Amitabha (known in Japan as Amida) Buddha. He believed that faith in Amida was the only possible route for Japan, which he believed had entered a degenerate age. Honen increasingly focused on the figure of Amitabha, the Buddha of the West, who had vowed to save all creatures and lead those with faith to the Pure Land, the western paradise. Whereas Genshin had focused upon visual meditation practices, Honen emphasized the verbal recitation of the *nembutsu*, a mantra that called upon Amida Buddha.

Starting in 1175 Honen began to preach this faith openly. He initially worked within the larger Tendai community, but the publication of his major work, *Collection of Passages*, in 1198, led to a break with Tendai. Then eight years later, the reigning emperor exiled Honen due to a scandal among his followers. He finally returned to Kyoto in 1211 but did not live beyond 1212. His six major followers then continued his work, with varying emphases and different outcomes. At least two major contemporary schools of Buddhist thought and practice (Jodo-shu and Honpa Hongwanji, plus the related Higashi Hongwanji) can be traced to Honen's influence.

Edward A. Irons

See also: Hiei, Mount; Jodo-shinshu; Jodo-shu; Pure Land Buddhism; Tian Tai/Tendai Buddhism.

References

Joji, Atone, and Hayashi Yoko. *An Anthology of the Teachings of Honen Shonin.* Los Angeles: Bukkyo University–Los Angeles Extension, 1998.

Soho Machida. *Renegade Monk: Honen and Japanese Pure Land Buddhism.* Trans. and ed. by Ioannis Mentzas. Berkeley: University of California Press, 1999.

Unno, Taitetsu. *River of Fire, River of Water: An Introduction to the Pure Land Tradition of Shin Buddhism.* New York: Doubleday, 1998.

Hong Kong Council of the Church of Christ in China

The Church of Christ in China can be traced to 1918, when a group of Protestant Christian leaders in China thought it necessary for the several mission-based churches to become united and form an indigenous church organization. They also realized that if they wanted to preach the gospel more effectively, they should conform to the three principles of self-support, self-governance, and self-propagation (hence its popular designation as the Three-Self movement). Those denominations that supported such a movement included the Presbyterian Church, the London Missionary Society, the Congregational Church, the Church of the United Brethren, the Methodist Evangelical Missionary, and the Swedish Missionary Society. By 1948 there were 24 synods, 110 associations, 2,767 local churches, 496 ordained ministers, 1,448 male and female preachers, and some 172,000 communicants. The church organization consisted of a national assembly, synods, district associations, and local churches.

The Hong Kong Council was formerly incorporated within the jurisdiction of the Sixth District Association of the Guangdong Synod of the Church of Christ in China. It was renamed the Hong Kong Council of the Church of Christ in China in 1953 and incorporated by legislation passed by the Legislative Council of Hong Kong in 1958 (Chapter 1095). Members of the Council basically included those churches, institutions, and schools that were originally members of the Sixth District Association, located in Hong Kong Island, Kowloon, the New Territories, Offshore Islands, and Macao. The Council became a self-supporting organization in 1974 and proclaimed as a Three-Self church in 1980. The Council emphasizes the universality and unity of the church, and focuses on sharing, witnessing, and service.

The Hong Kong Council of the Church of Christ in China is a uniting church organization and a member of the World Council of Churches. Its member churches come from different denominational backgrounds and church polities, but they share much: faith in Jesus Christ as Redeemer and Lord on whom the Christian church is founded; an earnest desire for the establishment of Christ's kingdom throughout the whole Earth; belief in holy scripture, made up of the Old and New Testaments, as the divinely inspired Word of God, and its supreme authority in matters of faith and life; and acknowledgment of the Apostles' Creed as the expression of the fundamental doctrines of a common evangelical faith.

Other than sharing these common beliefs, churches wishing to join the Council as members must also be willing to abide by several underlying principles. They must support the unity movement, emphasize democratic participation, and advocate the three-self principle. They must advocate equal rights for both sexes.

And they must practice a spirit of mutual respect, trust, and sharing.

By the end of 2008, the Council had 65 churches and preaching points in Hong Kong and Macao. These churches offer Sunday services in Cantonese, Mandarin, Fukienese, Hainan, and Swatow dialects. There are 68 ordained ministers and 124 preachers, and a congregation of 30,000 persons. Also, the Council sponsors 26 secondary schools, 2 evening secondary schools, 25 primary schools, 6 kindergartens, 1 special child care center, a family support center, and a campsite. Additionally, 24 primary schools and kindergartens are also operated by member churches. There are approximately 2,800 teachers and 58,000 students.

Hong Kong Council of the Church of Christ in
    China
Morrison Memorial Centre
191 Prince Edward Road West
Kowloon
Hong Kong
http://www.hkcccc.org

Kim-Kwong Chan

See also: London Missionary Society; World Council of Churches.

References

The Church of Christ in China: Church Unity in China and Church and Mission Co-operation. Shanghai: Willow Pattern Press, 1938.

Merwin, Wallace C. *Adventure in Unity: The Church of Christ in China.* Grand Rapids, MI: William B. Eerdmans Publishing Company, 1974.

Wong, Peter. *Words of the General Secretary.* Hong Kong: Hong Kong Council of the Church of Christ in China, 1983.

Honmichi

Honmichi (Original Way) honors both the founder of Tenrikyo, Nakayama Miki (1798–1887), and its own founder, Onishi Aijiro (1881–1958). The latter, a former member of Tenrikyo and one of its church leaders in Yamaguchi Prefecture, believed that the role of Nakayama Miki as mediator of divine truth to the Tenrikyo movement came to an end in August 1913 when the *kami* of truth, Kanrodai-Sama, decided to choose him as the *tenkeisha* (revealed one) and appointed him in Nakayama Miki's place as the mediator of divine revelation.

Tenrikyo finally expelled Onishi Aijiro in 1924, and in 1925 he established the Tenri Association for the Study of Heavenly Truth (Tenri Kenkyukai). In 1926 he and some 100 of his followers were imprisoned on the charge of *lese majesty*, a charge that was made against and led to the imprisonment of several other leaders, including Nakayama Miki, Deguchi Nao (of Omoto), and Deguchi Onisaburo (of Omoto). In the case of Onishi Aijiro, his crime consisted of expressing in a pamphlet, *Kenkyu Shiryo* (*Research Materials*), that the kami (gods) ruled Japan before Emperor Jimmu, the legendary first emperor of the nation, that the emperor himself was not of divine status, and that the then emperor was unfit to lead the nation. Released in 1935, he regrouped, but he was again imprisoned in 1938 for a breach of the Peace Preservation Law, and in 1939 his movement was disbanded.

On being released for a second time in March 1946, Onishi restarted his movement, giving it the new name of Tenri Honmichi (Original Way of Heavenly Truth). Later the Tenri part of the name was dropped, and the movement is now known simply as Honmichi.

Many of Honmichi's beliefs are derived from the Tenrikyo scriptures—the *Ofudesaki* (*Tip of Divine Writing Brush*) and the *Migakura-uta*—revealed by Tenri-O-no-Mikami (the creator god of both the universe and of humankind) to Nakayama Miki, the woman who founded Tenrikyo. At the center of Honmichi worship is the veneration of a group of 10 kami (the principal one of which is Tenri-O-no-Mikoto, God of Heavenly Reason), who are believed to be the core of the universe.

Hinokishin, or voluntary activity of a mental and physical kind, a pivotal idea in Tenrikyo, is also central to the teaching of Honmichi, where it often means the practice of the movement's teachings combined with selfless service to others.

Honmichi, and numerous other Japanese new and new, new religions (*shin shukyo* and *shin shin shukyo*, respectively), is persuaded that the solution to all ills lies in mind. Right mindfulness is the key to health, happiness, and peace, and thus great emphasis is placed on attaining, with the help of Kanrodai-Sama, the proper state of mind, and on using the mind in accordance with the will of God. Failure in these areas leads to misfortune, sickness, and unhappiness, all evil forces that obstruct God's efforts to assist humankind. The principal goal of human beings is to build paradise on Earth so that the human race can live united in peace and harmony.

Like so many other Japanese new and new, new religions, Honmichi is strongly millenarian. It is also apocalyptic, in that it preaches that world war and catastrophe will afflict the human race before the advent of paradise on Earth.

The current membership of Honmichi in Japan is estimated to stand at 316,000. There is only one overseas branch, and that is in the United States in Los Angeles.

Honmichi (Original Way)
4431 Wilshire Blvd.
Los Angeles, CA 90010

Peter B. Clarke

See also: Omoto; Tenrikyo.

References

Clarke, Peter B., ed. *A Bibliography of Japanese New Religions*. Eastbourne, UK: Japan Library, 1998.
Shimazono, Susumu. "The Development of Millennialistic Thought in Japan's New Religions: From Tenrikyo to Honmichi." In *New Religious Movements and Rapid Social Change*, edited by James Beckford. London: Sage, 1986.

Hossoshu

Hossoshu (Sect of Dharma Characteristics) draws doctrinal inspiration from the *vijnanavada* (consciousness-only) thought of Yogacara Buddhism, as propagated by Indian Buddhist philosopher-monk Asanga (fourth century CE) and Vasubandhu (fourth century CE). As a Buddhist school, Hossoshu has strong doctrinal links with Indian Buddhism. It intends to examine "the essential nature and phenomenal manifestations of all

existents." It asserts consciousness as the basis for the appearance of the phenomenal world.

Hossoshu is the Japanese equivalent of the Chinese Fa-hsiang-tsung, one of the 13 traditional Chinese Buddhist sects. The doctrines of Hossoshu, together with an idealistic analysis of phenomena, were transmitted into Japan four times: first, the Japanese monk Dosho (629–700), who studied the doctrine of *vijnaptimatrata* under Hsuan-tsang (602–664), upon returning from China in 660 founded Hossoshu in Japan; second, in 658 Chitsu and Chitatsu brought the doctrines of the Kusha School; third, in 706 the Korean monk Chiho brought the teaching; and fourth, in 735 Genbo (d. 746) brought to Japan the first complete Chinese Buddhist canon.

Hossoshu played an important role in the early stages of Buddhism in Japan. In the early phase of Japanese Buddhism, influential and famous monks such as Gyogi (668–749), Gomyo (750–834), and Jokei (1155–1213) belonged to Hossoshu. Jokei, in particular, revived Hosso doctrines with an intense critique of Honen's exclusive *nenbutsu* movement. Hossoshu was one of the six Nara sects of scholastic Buddhism introduced to Japan during the Nara period (710–794), which became the foundation for doctrinal innovations in the Kamakura period (1185–1336). During the medieval period (13th–16th centuries), three important monastic establishments—Horyuji (fl. 607), Yakushiji (fl. 680), and Kofukuji (fl. 710)—propagated its ideas and practices; in 1892 these three headquarters came under the rule of one single abbot. Though Horyuji seceded from Hossoshu in 1950, both Yakushiji and Kofukuji in Nara each have about 20 affiliated temples.

In Japan, though the word *shu* (sect) is quite often used to identify Buddhist denominations, in the Nara period it did not denote the doctrinal differences associated with the English term "sect." In particular, in the Nara period it referred to "a group of scholars who gathered together to study one tradition," but their examination was not by any means restricted to one tradition alone. In fact, initially all six Nara schools gathered and pursued their studies at Todaiji Temple in Nara.

Although the major role of the Nara schools such as Hossoshu was the introduction of the academic study of Buddhism, as propagators of Buddhism among the masses they were not successful. Their vast depth of knowledge in Buddhist doctrinal and philosophical issues did not reach the general populace in Japan. Although two Nara schools—Kusha and Jojitsu—had no adherents, the other four Nara schools, including Hossoshu, attracted members of the aristocracy. However, even they made very little effort to spread their teachings among the masses, since they were still preoccupied with performing rites and rituals for the protection of the nation, the royal family, and the aristocracy and with the promotion of culture and education. Only a few individuals, such as Gyogi of the Hossoshu, believed that as Buddhists they were expected to teach Buddhism and help the masses create a better life for themselves. Nevertheless, the doctrinal contributions of Hossoshu and other schools still continue to shape the curriculum of higher learning in Japanese Buddhist institutions.

Hossoshu
457 Nishinokyo-machi
Nara-shi 630
Japan

Mahinda Deegalle

See also: Mahayana Buddhism; Nara.

References

Ford, James L. *Jokei and Buddhist Devotion in Early Medieval Japan.* Oxford: Oxford University Press, 2006.

Hori, Ichiro, et al., eds. *Japanese Religion: A Survey by the Agency for Cultural Affairs.* Tokyo: Kodansha International, 1981.

Kashiwahara, Yusen, and Koyu Sonoda. *Shapers of Japanese Buddhism.* Tokyo: Kosei Publishing Co, 1994.

Matsunaga, Daigan, and Alicia Matsunaga. *Foundation of Japanese Buddhism.* 2 vols. Los Angeles: Buddhist Books International, 1987.

Hua Shan

Hua Shan, the Daoist sacred mountain of the West, is located in China's Shaanxi Province, some 75 miles east of the old capital at Xi'an. The tallest of the five major peaks rises some 6,550 feet. Legend places Daoist founder Laozi on Hua Shan, where he was said to have prepared the Elixir of Immortality. In later centuries, the mountain gained a reputation as a site where immortality drugs could be found.

The mountain became the home of the Quanzhen Daoists, whose community is presently centered on the imperial temple, Xi Yue Miao. Viewed from the temple, the five major peaks of the mountain resemble a lotus flower and as a result the mountain came to be known as the Lotus Mountain. Today the mountain is home to many Daoist poems and quotations that have been carved into its rock formation over the centuries.

Access to these carvings and other Daoist sites begins at Yu Quan Gong, the entrance temple, and follows a system of paths and steps cut from the rock and leading to each of the five peaks. These pathways are identified with the Dao, the Way, a basic concept in Daoist theology. The pathways were in place by the 16th century, by which time some 150 temples had been constructed at Hua Shan.

Among the important surviving temples at Hua Shan are the Shrine of the Western Peak (second century BCE), known as a site where mediums could contact the god of the underworld, and the Cloister of the Jade Spring, dedicated to one of the legendary founders of Daoism, Chen Tuan.

In 1998, the Quanzhen Daoists placed the mountain's temples under the hegemony of the China Daoist Association.

Edward A. Irons

See also: China Daoist Association; Daoism; Heng Shan; Laozi; Quanzhen Daoism; Song Shan; Tai Shan; Temples—Buddhist.

References

"The ARC China Sacred Mountains Project: 1995 to Date." Alliance of Religions and Conservation. 2008. http://www.arcworld.org/downloads/ Sacred%20Mountain2%20July%202008.pdf. Accessed May 15, 2009.

Einarsen, John, ed. *The Sacred Mountains of Asia.* Boston: Shambhala, 1995.

Geil, William Edgar. *The Sacred 5 of China.* London: John Nurray, 1926.

Hua Shan, the Daoist sacred mountain of the West, in China's Shaanxi Province. Legend places Daoist founder Laozi on Hua Shan, where he was said to have prepared the Elixer of Immortality. (Tersina/Dreamstime.com)

Hahn, Thomas H. "Daoist Sacred Sites." In *Daoism Handbook*, edited by Livia Kohn, 683–708. Leiden: Brill, 2004.

"Sacred Mountains of China." Places of Peace and Power. http://www.sacredsites.com/asia/china/sacred_mountains.html. Accessed May 15, 2009.

Hubbard, L. Ron

1911–1986

L. Ron Hubbard is the founder of the Church of Scientology, one of the most successful, if controversial, of the new religious movements founded in the 20th century. Hubbard, a former naval officer and a well-known writer of fiction and nonfiction, authorized the formation of the church in 1954, and over the years authored the material that embodied the church's developing beliefs and practices. These writings are now considered Scientology scriptures.

Lafayette Ronald Hubbard was born in Tilden, Nebraska, on March 19, 1911. His father was in the navy, and he traveled widely in his youth. He was an explorer, both during and after studying two years at George Washington University, though he made his living by writing. He served as an officer in the navy during World War II and returned to his writing career in the late 1940s.

Even before the war, Hubbard had developed a fascination with the human unconscious, and his hospital stay during the last years of the war further stimulated speculation about the nature of the mind and its role in illness and health. His initial writings on the question culminated in the publication of *Dianetics: The Modern Science of Mental Health* in 1950. The book became a nonfiction best-seller.

Hubbard gained both fame and notoriety for his new theories on the mind espoused through his books and lectures. He had a growing following for Dianetics, even as he redirected his attention from the mind to the human spirit. This change of focus led him to accept the idea of past lives (commonly called reincarnation) and the crucial role of the soul, which he termed the Thetan. The new approach resulted in his moving beyond Dianetics to Scientology.

As Dianetics and Scientology grew in popularity, medical authorities viewed it in the context of pseudoscience and illicit medical practice. The medical community's opposition led to the U.S. Food and Drug Administration raiding the Washington, D.C., church in 1963. At the same time, the Internal Revenue Service began to question the church's tax status. Legal problems spread to other countries. The growing militancy against Hubbard and the church led him in 1966 to create a separate structure, the Guardian's Office (GO), to respond to attacks upon the church. About the same time, he resigned all his administrative offices in the church and retired from public life to engage in the advanced research that would complete his understanding of Scientology. He continued to direct the church from behind the scenes. Among his more important actions was the founding of the Sea Organization (Sea Org), a fraternity of highly committed members, to whom were assigned the duty of delivering the most advanced teachings of the church to its members.

Increasingly frustrated by its inability to track the source of its problem with different government agencies, in the mid-1970s, the GO infiltrated a spectrum of agencies looking for its files. The discovery of this activity prompted an FBI raid in 1977 and two years later a trial at which several church leaders, including Hubbard's wife, were convicted. Following the convictions, he authorized what became the complete reorganization of the church including the disbanding of the GO and the emergence of the Religious Technology Center and the Church of Scientology International, through which the movement is now governed.

Hubbard continued to live quietly out of sight through this period, only emerging periodically to prove that he was still alive. He died January 24, 1986, in San Luis Obispo, California. There is no authorized biography of Hubbard, though the church he founded has published a series of booklets, the Ron Series, which explore various aspects of his life.

Hubbard taught that humans are spiritual beings (Thetans), immortal creatures who live thousands of embodied lives. Similar to other Western Esoteric groups, he believed that the Thetan had, through time, lost its way and forgot who it was. He proposed a complex of methods to realize individual identity as a Thetan and help people achieve a state beyond matter, energy, space, and time. This path is known in Scientology as the "bridge to total freedom." Hubbard designed Scientology classes and a counseling process called auditing (therapy) to help humans reach the state of "clear" and move beyond clear to become an Operating Thetan, or OT. Hubbard also claimed that the human dimension involves dealing with eight powerful drives or dynamics, including self-survival, group identity, and the spiritual dynamic.

Hubbard's navy career impacted his vision and plans for Scientology as an organization. He employed ships as instructional centers in the 1960s and while residing on a ship, created the Sea Org. Its members dressed in uniforms and adopted a military style and drive for efficiency in the implementation of its goals and practices.

James A. Beverley

See also: Church of Scientology; Western Esoteric Trdition.

References

Hubbard, L. Ron. *Dianetics: The Modern Science of Mental Health*. New York: Hermitage House, 1950.

Hubbard, L. Ron. *Scientology: A New Slant on Life*. Los Angeles: Bridge Publications, 2007.

Lamont, Stewart. *Religions Inc.* London: Harrap, 1986.

Lewis, James, ed. *Scientology*. New York: Oxford University Press, 2009.

Melton, J. Gordon. *The Church of Scientology*. Salt Lake City, UT: Signature Books, 2000.

Miller, Russell Miller. *Bare-faced Messiah*. New York: Henry Holt, 1987.

Hui Neng

638–713

Hui Neng is widely known in Mahayana Buddhism as the sixth patriarch of the southern line of the Chan

(Zen) School. He is a pivotal figure in Chinese Buddhist history, since he served to articulate rationalist concepts received from Indian Buddhism into irrational expression through Chinese Chan (later Korean Son and Japanese Zen).

Hui Neng's biography is found in the Platform Sutra of the Sixth Patriarch, an important indigenous Chinese text still widely distributed today. He was born in the heyday of the Tang dynasty (618–907). He did not desire to become a monk until he heard a sutra preached when he was 24. He then went to study with Hong Ren (602–675), today known as the fifth Chan patriarch. During his tutelage under Hong Ren, Hui Neng bested the rival priest Shen Xiu (ca. 605–706) in a poetry contest that has become legendary. Shen Xiu wrote:

> The body is like the Bodhi tree,
> The mind is like a clear mirror.
> At all times we must strive to polish it,
> And do not let any dust land on it.

To which Hui Neng replied:

> Originally there is no tree of Awakening
> Nor is there a stand for the clear mirror.
> From the very beginning, not one thing;
> Where could the dust land?

Due to the deep perception obvious in this poem, Hong Ren is said to have named Hui Neng his successor on the spot. Hui Neng was also given the bowl and robe that had belonged to Bodhidharma, the founder of the Chan lineage.

Hui Neng spent the rest of his life in southern China, at what is today the Nan Hua Temple. He trained 10 major disciples, including Shen Hui. Shen Hui went on to promote Hui Neng as patriarch of southern Buddhism. Although much of the story of Hui Neng is legendary, a reflection of the Platform Sutra, the individual no doubt lived and was a patriarch in the Chan lineage. All current active lines of Chan/Zen trace their lineages back to Hui Neng.

Edward A. Irons

See also: Bodhidharma; Mahayana Buddhism; Zen Buddhism.

References

Claery, Thomas. *The Sutra of Hui Neng: Grand Master of Zen with Hui Neng's Commentary on the Diamond Sutra.* Boston: Shambhala, 1998.

Dumoulin, Heinrich. *Zen Buddhism, a History: India and China.* New York: Macmillan, 1988.

Yampolsky, Philip B. *The Platform Sutra of the Sixth Patriarch.* New York: Columbia University Press, 1967.

Hui Si

515–577

A Chinese monk in the early period of Buddhism's development in China, Hui Si was well known in his day as a specialist in meditation. He was born in northern China, then under the rule of the northern Qi (550–577), a foreign dynasty. He later moved to Nanyue, in present-day Hunan, southern China. On nearby Heng Shan, one of China's sacred mountains, he built the Fu Yan Temple and the Can Jin Hill, both of which are still intact.

He was also the teacher of Zhi Yi, who later went on to found the Tiantai School of Chinese Buddhism. Hui Si emphasized the role of the intellect in Buddhism, which later manifested in Zhi Yi's teaching that both faith and intellectual activity were important in Buddhism. Zhi Yi compared them to a bird's two wings, noting that with one wing only, the bird cannot fly. Thus a Buddhist who abandons either faith or the intellect would be diverted from the path of liberation. Hui Si is also frequently mentioned as the transmitter of many of Zhi Yi's meditation techniques.

Edward A. Irons

See also: Heng Shan; Meditation; Tian Tan/Tendai Buddhism.

References

Chappel, David W., ed. *T'ien-t'ai Buddhism.* Tokyo: Daiichi-Shobo, 1983.

Chen, Kenneth K. S. *Buddhism in China: A Historical Survey.* Vol. 1, *Studies in History of Religion.* Princeton, NJ: Princeton University Press, 1964.

Hui Yuan

334–416

Hui Yuan was a student of Dao An (312–385), an early translator of Buddhist scriptures, based in the northern city of Chang An. In his early life he had been a student of the Chinese classical literature (Confucius, Laozi), but was converted to Buddhism after hearing Dao An's sermons.

In 402, Hui Yuan founded a religious community on Mount Lu called the White Lotus Society (*bailianshe*), not to be confused with the later revolutionary societies using that same name. The purpose of Hui Yan's society was to focus on Amitabha, the Buddha of the West, through meditation and chanting, in order to gain entry into Amitabha's western paradise. Hui Yuan's group became the fountainhead of Pure Land Buddhism, a movement that spread throughout East Asia and that remains active today.

Edward A. Irons

See also: Meditation; Pure Land Buddhism.

References

Blum, Mark L. *The Origins and Development of Pure Land Buddhism: A Study and Translation of Gyonen's Jodo Homon Genrusho.* Oxford: Oxford University Press, 2002.

Tanaka, Kenneth K. *The Dawn of Chinese Pure Land Buddhist Doctrine: Ching-ying Hui-yuan's Commentary on the Visualization Sutra.* Albany: State University of New York Press, 1990.

Zenryo, Tsukamoto. *History of Early Chinese Buddhism: From Its Introduction to the Death of Hui-Yuan.* Trans. by Leon Hurvitz. New York: Kodansha America, 1985.

Human-Etisk Forbund i Norge

Human-Etisk Forbund i Norge (Norwegian Humanist Association) was formed in 1956 by a group of parents in Oslo who had begun by seeking an alternative to the coming-of-age ceremony through which most Norwegian youth go in their 15th year. The ceremony confirms them as adult members of the Church of Norway (Lutheran), the state church of the land. Not wishing their offspring to participate in a ceremony related to a faith they rejected, the parents proposed an alternative civil ceremony, similar to one that had been in use in Denmark. They organized the first ceremony in 1951, and 34 youths participated.

In 1956 members of the informal Association for Civil Confirmation, as the parents called themselves, broadened their program to unite a variety of individuals who were interested in nonreligious approaches to ethical questions. Those who attended an initial gathering founded the Human-Etisk Forbund i Norge. The first leader was Kristian Horn, a professor of botany, who was able to enlist a number of colleagues from the academic and political world as supporters. They represented a spectrum of nontheistic perspectives.

The association has served over the years as a forum for discussions and the development of a community of shared values and ideas. Though realizing its shortcomings, they supported the program of "life and education" that schools began to offer in the 1970s. The program presented different religious perspectives in a somewhat objective manner, as opposed to the Christian teachings that had previously dominated the curriculum. That program was ended in 1996 by a new law that re-established Christian dominance in the state schools. By this time, however, the association had grown into the second largest religious/philosophical organization in the country.

In 2000, some 8,000 youth, about 15 percent of all Norwegian youth of the appropriate age, participated in the civil confirmation ceremony. The association has also prepared secular alternatives to other rites of passage for births (naming ceremonies), weddings, and funerals.

Norwegian Humanists also voiced their concerns over a law passed in 1997 making Christian education part of the school curriculum in the country. In 2004, the Human Rights Commission of the United Nations ruled that the new law violated the human rights of Humanist Norwegians and by implication others who are not members of the Church of Norway.

As the new century began, the association reported 64,000 members. Religious freedom became a reality constitutionally in Norway in 1979. Citizens pay religious taxes, and the Human-Etisk Forbund i Norge receives the religious tax money collected from its members. The association is a member of the International Humanist and Ethical Union.

Human-Etisk Forbund i Norge
Postboks 7644
St. Olavs Pl.
N-0130 Oslo
Norway
http://www.human.no (in Norwegian)

J. Gordon Melton

See also: Church of Norway; International Humanist and Ethical Union.

References

Cherry, Matt. "UN backs Norwegian humanists, overturns compulsory Christian education." http://www.humaniststudies.org/enews/index.php?id=167&article=2. Accessed April 24, 2009.

Stein, Gordon. *The Encyclopedia of Unbelief.* 2 vols. Buffalo, NY: Prometheus Books, 1985.

Humanism

Humanism is one form of nontheistic thinking that emerged in the 20th century in the context of liberalizing trends in American religion that sought to reconstruct religion around human aspirations, values, and moral needs rather than speculations about supernaturalism and divinity, especially those built upon reputed revelations of divine truth. Self-identified Humanists appeared at the beginning of the 20th century among members of the American Unitarian Association (now an integral part of the Unitarian Universalist Association), the Free Religious Association, and the American Ethical Union. Leading spokespersons included John H. Dietrich (1878–1957), Curtis W. Reese (1887–1961), Charles Francis Potter (1885–1962), and Theodore Abell (1891–1932). Potter was among the Humanists who in 1933 issued an early definitive statement of the Humanist perspective, the *Humanist Manifesto.* Other signers included philosopher John Dewey (1859–1952) and philosopher-historian John Herman Randall (1899–1980). The Manifesto suggested that the universe was self-existing and not (as Christianity proposed) created. It also rejected supernaturalism and

theism. The goal of life is the realization of human personality, and social ethics is a major tool in reaching that goal. New Manifestos issued in 1973 and 2003 have attempted to expand upon and update the original with a strong affirmation that human beings have a responsibility toward the whole of the human race.

Among the first organizations to form specifically around the Humanist perspective was the American Humanist Association. Over the next generation, the movement spread globally and was embodied by such organizations as the Human-Etisk Forbund i Norge (1951), the Sydney (Australia) Humanist Association (1960), the Indian Humanist Union (1960), the Humanist Society of New Zealand (1963), the British Humanist Association (1963), the Humanist Association of Canada (1967), and the Humanist Association of South Africa (1979). Many of these groups have come together in the International Humanist and Ethical Union, founded in 1952.

Among the most successful Humanist groups is Human-Etisk Forbund i Norge (Norwegian Humanist Association), which has more than 60,000 members and has become the second largest philosophical/religious association in the country. It began as a group of parents who wished to organize an alternative to the confirmation ceremony through which most Norwegian youth pass during their 15th year. The first 34 youth used the new civil ceremony in 1951. In the year 2000, some 8,000 (about 15 percent of the youth that age) selected the civil ceremony rather than that of the Church of Norway.

At the end of the 1970s, philosopher Paul Kurtz (b. 1925), a prominent Humanist and head of Prometheus Books, left the American Humanist Association and began to argue for what he termed Secular Humanism. In 1980 he organized the Council for Secular Humanism, which stood for not only a nontheistic Humanism, but a nonreligious Humanism. He saw Secular Humanism as an alternative, not just to traditional religion but to all religion, and circulated "A Secular Humanist Declaration," which outlined that perspective. More recently, Kurtz issued his commentary on the 1973 *Humanist Manifesto, Humanist Manifesto 2000: A Call for New Planetary Humanism.*

The Council and its sister organizations have taken a more aggressive anti-religious stance; they propose

Temple for Humanistic Judaism, in a Detroit suburb. (J. Gordon Melton)

scientific inquiry as the best method of reaching an adequate worldview and moral code. Like the religious Humanists, the Council is a member of the International Humanist and Ethical Union.

J. Gordon Melton

See also: Church of Norway; Council for Secular Humanism; Human-Etisk Forbund i Norge; International Humanist and Ethical Union; Unitarian Universalist Association.

References

Firth, Raymond. *Religion: A Humanist Interpretation*. Boston: Routledge, 1996.

Flew, Anthony. *Atheist Humanism*. Buffalo, NY: Prometheus Books, 1983.

Flynn, Tom, ed. *The New Encyclopedia of Unbelief*. Amherst, NY: Prometheus Books, 2007.

Herrick, Jim. *Humanism: An Introduction*. Amherst, NY: Prometheus Books, 2005.

Kurtz, Paul. *In Defense of Secular Humanism*. Buffalo, NY: Prometheus Books, 1983.

Lamont, Corliss. *The Philosophy of Humanism*. 7th ed. New York: F. Ungar, 1990.

Murry, William R. *Reason and Reverence: Religious Humanism for the 21st Century*. Boston: Skinner House Books, 2006.

Hungarian Reformed Church in America

The Hungarian Reformed Church in America, a representative of the Reformed Presbyterian tradition of the 16th century, has its origins in the spread of the

Protestant Reformation to Hungary and the subsequent migration of Hungarians to the United States where Hungarian Reformed congregations were established in the late 19th century. In 1904 an American Hungarian Reformed Church was formed under the care of the Reformed Church in Hungary. Following World War I, a series of negotiations with the Reformed Church in the United States let to the declaration in 1921 of the Tiffin Agreement, which mandated that the Hungarian Reformed Church in America would merge into the Reformed Church in the United States (now an integral part of the United Church of Christ).

Three congregations of the Hungarian Reformed Church did not accept the Tiffin Agreement. These congregations and four additional congregations formed after the issuing of the Tiffin Agreement subsequently came together as the Free Magyar Reformed Church in America, which in 1958 adopted its present name. That same year it joined the World Council of Churches.

The church adheres to Reformed theology as expressed in the Second Helvetic Confession and the Heidelberg Catechism. Its organization is a mixture of the presbyterian and episcopal systems, with a synod headed by a bishop and a lay curator. There are three classes: the New York, Eastern, and Western, each headed by a dean and lay curator. The synod, the highest legislative body, meets quadrennially.

In 2001, the church reported 6,000 members in the United States and Canada. It is ecumenically active, holding membership in the World Alliance of Reformed Churches.

Hungarian Reformed Church in America
c/o Andrew Harsanyi
220 4th St.
Passaic, NJ 07055
www.hrca.us

J. Gordon Melton

See also: Reformed Church of Hungary; United Church of Christ; World Alliance of Reformed Churches; World Council of Churches.

Reference

Van Beek, Huibert. *A Handbook of the Churches and Councils: Profiles of Ecumenical Relationships.* Geneva: World Council of Churches, 2006.

■ Hungary

The Carpathian Basin, where Hungary is located, is a relatively closed geographic unit in central-eastern Europe. The flat and open center of the surrounded area, called Plainland (Alföld), is broken only by a few rivers, of which the Danube (Duna) and Theiss (Tisza) are the most important. Once a Hungarian territory, the Highlands (Felvidék), located north of the Plainland, correspond to contemporary Slovakia and Carpato-Ukraine. Also a Hungarian territory until 1920, Transylvania (Erdély), east of the Plainland in today's Romania, is a high plateau. The rolling hills of the Transdanubian region (Dunántúl) stretch from the Danube to the foothills of the Austrian Alps. Crossing the river Drava, we enter the historical region of Southland (Délvidék), today's Croatia and Slavonia. The dominant language in Hungary is the *magyar* (Hungarian). Of the different national and ethnic minorities living in Hungary, the 600,000 Romas represent the largest group, but the German and Slovakian minorities are also significant. Hungarian minorities experience ethnic discrimination in most of the surrounding countries, especially in Slovakia, Serbia, and Romania.

In the capital city, Budapest, lives about 20 percent of the country's 10,030,000 inhabitants. The latest census in 2001 concluded that apart from the Catholics (55 percent), adherents of the Reformed Church of Hungary (16 percent), and those of the Lutheran Church in Hungary (3 percent), the membership of all other religious entities amounted only to 1.2 percent. About 15 percent were not affiliated, and 10 percent refused to answer the question probing religious affiliation. The larger liberal Protestant churches have associated together in the Ecumenical Council of Churches in Hungary, which is affiliated with the World Council of Churches. Some of the smaller, more conservative evangelical Christian congregations are now served by the Magyar Evangeliumi Aliansz, which is in turn associated with the World Evangelical Alliance.

The most important developments in the country's recent history include the regained freedom after the fall of the Soviet Union in 1990 and Hungary's joining the European Union in 2004. While open religious oppression—as practiced by the Communists— disappeared, tensions in church-state relationships are

HUNGARY

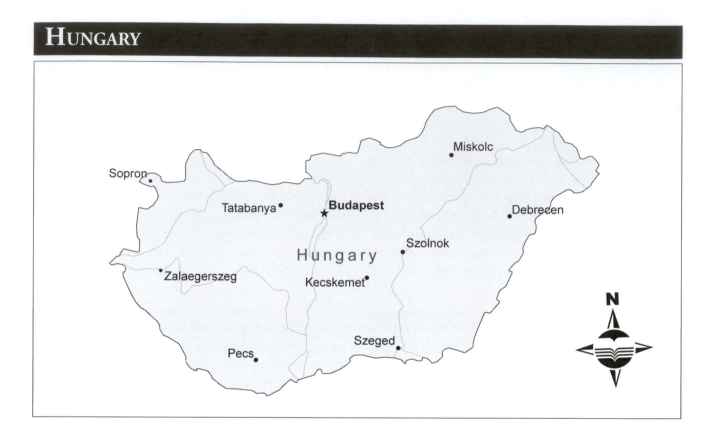

not uncommon. While the so-called national-Christian political forces protect and support the large Christian churches, the Liberal-Socialist parties guard the freedom of the smaller religious entities, especially that of the new religious movements in order to weaken the Catholic, Reformed, and Lutheran churches. The roots of these tensions along with the Hungarians' generally tolerant attitude toward religion go back at least to the late medieval history of the country.

The Hungarians, or Magyars, entered the Carpathian Basin toward the end of the ninth century after a long journey. In 1235, a Hungarian Dominican friar, Julianus, set out to find Magna Hungaria, the great land of the ancestors, and actually found a people whose language he could clearly understand beyond the Volga, in the territory of today's Bashkiria, a republic within Russia. Like the belief system of the other peoples of the Steppes, the Hungarians' faith consisted of animism, the veneration of totem animals, and, most of all, shamanism. According to this belief, the spirits know everything because being bodiless they can go anywhere. However, only the *táltos*, the Hungarian shaman, has the unique capability of communicating with the spirits of living and deceased creatures and with objects. The information gained in a voluntary ecstasy—what the Hungarians call *rejtôzés*, meaning to conceal oneself—enabled the táltos to be the Hungarians' clairvoyant, healer of humans and animals, advisor, and *regôs*, who preserved the Hungarians' cultural heritage. Even today, a few táltos can be found among Hungarians.

By the end of the ninth century, Hungarians moved into, and practically conquered, the Carpathian Basin. From there they launched their stormy, marauding raids on wealthy European cities for roughly a century. Various European rulers and aspiring rulers also hired them as mercenaries against their rivals. That was the time when the prayer "From the arrows of the Hungarians, save us, Lord" was introduced to the litany of the Catholic Church. From the middle of the 10th century, however, the European rulers recognized that by constantly ravaging each other's domains through the use of Hungarian mercenaries, they were all harming themselves. From their several defeats, the Hungarian leaders also realized that continuing raids would lead to self-destruction. Hence, it was in the interest of both the European and the Hungarian leaders to tame the restless and nomadic Hungarians by having them settle down in a defined territory and by incorporating them in Christendom.

The missionaries—most important, Bishop Pilgrim of Passau, and after him, Saint Adalbert of Prague—were able to turn to local traditions for support, because in the fourth century Christianity had had episcopal seats in the Roman province of Pannonia, a territory that later became Western Hungary. In addition, after the fall of the Avar Empire (796), Charlemagne, the Holy Roman Emperor, promoted the Christianization of Eastern Europe. Instead of Constantinople, the Hungarian leaders turned to Rome, partly because of Hungary's relatively favorable bargaining position in relation to the papacy, which was feuding with the German emperors. For Stephen, Hungary's first king, a crown from the pope not only meant the acknowledgment of Stephen's rule but also signaled his independence from both Byzantium and the German emperor.

Religious intolerance was not characteristic of Hungarians. King Ladislaus (1077–1095), instead of persecuting Paganism, started what has been called a campaign of canonization in 1083. It raised, among others, Stephen, his son, Emeric, and Bishop Gerard, the martyr tutor of Emeric, into sainthood. The canonizations served a twofold purpose. Apart from issuing mild warning to the remnants of Paganism, they also certified the presence of the nation and its rulers, the dynasty of Árpád, in Christian Europe. A large Ishmaelite population in the 12th century provides further evidence of the Hungarians' religious tolerance. They were able to practice their faith and were obliged to serve the king only in case of war, and even then only against non-Muslims. Similarly, the Jews had privileges even under King Béla IV (1235–1270); and only the Anjou period (1301–1395) introduced to Hungary the medieval version of anti-Semitism and persecution. Finally, Coloman (1095–1116), nicknamed the Book Lover (Beauclerc), issued a decree in which he stated, contrary to the views of contemporary European rulers, that witches who could assume different shapes and forms did not exist. However, while different religions existed peacefully in the Carpathian Basin under the reign of the House of Árpád, the primacy and dominance of Roman Catholicism was unquestionable.

Hungarian kings were involved in the wars against the Turks from the time of Sigismund of Luxemburg (1387–1437). After the Hungarian defeat at Mohács (1526), the country was divided into three parts, with decisive consequences, especially with respect to religion. The western and northern regions became a part of the Hapsburg Empire, and thus remained Catholic. The middle part, a triangle-shaped territory, whose peak extended far beyond the capital city and included the Alföld (Great Plain), the eastern half of Transdanubia, and the lower tip of Transylvania, was absorbed by the Ottoman Empire. The remaining part of Transylvania emerged as an independent principality, protecting and nurturing future Hungarian national aspirations. Meanwhile, the 16th-century religious Reformation begun by Luther also affected the religious life of Hungarians. Due partly to the influence of Johann Honter (1498–1549), the founder of the Lutheran national church of the German Saxons, the Transylvanian territory soon developed an overwhelmingly Protestant character. By the middle of the 16th century, Protestantism had become well established in the whole country. Although Hungary was not saved from denominational enmities, in comparison to Europe, it preserved its religious tolerance. In 1557, the Edict of Torda, which takes its name from what is now the Romanian city of Turda, was the first European declaration of the equality of religions and of guaranteed free religious practice.

The victory of the Holy League at the Battle at Zenta in 1697 meant the end of the Turkish occupation of Hungary, but at the same time, Hungary became, for all practical purposes, a colony of the Hapsburg Empire. The Catholic Hapsburgs launched an anti-Protestant campaign. Their intention was probably the weakening of the Hungarian nobility, the mere existence of which represented a threat to their plan of colonizing Hungary. The fact that the Hungarian nobility survived was partly due to the Protestant Transylvanian princes who generously donated noble titles, although mostly without land. A consequence of the Hapsburg policy was that Hungarian national feelings became closely linked to Protestantism, because the adherents of this faith offered greater resistance to the Hapsburgs and consequently suffered more than the Catholics.

Despite the restrictive measures of the Hapsburgs against the Protestants, Hungarian Catholics fared little better in the latter half of the 18th century than the Protestants. The explanation for the relative weakness of the Catholic Church contains at least three components: what was called Febronianism, a new theory of church-state relations implicitly suggesting that the territorial churches were subject to their local governments; Maria Theresa's decrees regulating the life of Hungarian Catholicism; and finally the actions of her son, Joseph II. During his 10-year rule (1780–1790), Emperor Joseph issued 6,206 decrees concerning religious life in his empire. Some of his orders were ignored, especially in the remote areas of his empire, and others created such upheaval that he soon withdrew them. Nonetheless many traditional religious customs disappeared under his reign. His more important religio-political decisions included the dissolution of the contemplative religious orders and some of the teaching orders. Toward the end of his life he realized that, despite his good intentions, his painstakingly meticulous regulations had made the lives of his subjects miserable. On his deathbed, he withdrew all of his orders, with the exception of three laws, including his famous decree of religious tolerance issued in 1781. The *edictum tolerantiale* guaranteed the free practice of the Protestant faith in any settlement where at least 100 families were of that faith.

Various Protestant or Free churches entered Hungary during the 19th century. The Baptist movement was brought to Hungary by Hungarian workers who went to Hamburg, Germany, in the mid-1840s to help rebuild the city. There they encountered the great German Baptist leader Johann Gerhard Oncken (1800–1884), who in 1846 sent three Hungarians back to their homeland to plant a church. That initial effort led eventually to the founding of the Baptist Union of Hungary in 1920.

Methodism in Hungary began at the start of the 10th century through the spread of literature among German-speaking residents of the country. Ministers from Vienna began to visit Batchka, in what is now Serbia, from which work spread to other German-speaking communities. The first Hungarian services were held in 1904, and initial organization in Budapest occurred the next year. In 1907, the work was made part of the Northern Germany Conference of the Methodist Episcopal Church (now an integral part of the United Methodist Church). The work was organized separately following World War I, but all the Hungarian work was, with the exception of the Budapest centers, in the new Yugoslavian state, or Austria. The work in contemporary Hungary originated from the Budapest work. It developed into an independent church following World War II.

Hungary's revolution in 1848–1849 brought about serious consequences for church-state relations. The new government issued the so-called Religion Bill of 1848, in which they disestablished Roman Catholicism as the state religion by proclaiming the full equality of all the "lawfully received" denominations. This term originates in Transylvanian terminology, where during the 16th century the Catholics, Lutherans, Calvinists, and Unitarians were admitted and legally "received" by the prince and the estates. It reappears also in article 43 of 1895, which mentions a "form of legal classification of religions." The first category consisted of the legally "received churches": the Catholic, Lutheran, and Reformed churches, the Jewish communities, the Eastern Orthodox Church, and the Unitarians. The second or so-called recognized churches contained most of the smaller denominations, including, starting in 1905, the Baptists and, starting in 1916, the Muslims. The religions in the tolerated category included the Adventists, the Methodists, the Millennialists, the Mormons, and the Nazarenes. Finally, a fourth group consisted of those religions that were banned, namely the Jehovah's Witnesses, the different Pentecostal movements, and, after 1939, the Church of the Nazarene. This categorization remained in force until the end of World War II.

Between the two World Wars, Hungary allied itself with Germany, expecting the abolition of the humiliating Trianon Treaty (1920), which reduced Hungary to a third of both its territory and its population. This alliance sealed not only the fate of 600,000 deported Hungarian Jews but also that of the whole country through the following Soviet occupation since it was used to justify the Soviet occupation of Hungary after World War II. The Communist era, for all practical purposes, meant the persecution of any organized religious life. The resistance of Cardinal Mindszenty

Interior of Doheny Synagogue in Budapest, Hungary. (iStockPhoto.com)

(1892–1975) and other ecclesiastical leaders resulted in their imprisonment, the banning of religious orders, the dissolution of religious organizations, and harassment of both ecclesiastics and lay persons. A certain change of attitude toward religion was experienced starting in the mid-1960s, resulting in greater tolerance, but religious people were considered second-class citizens throughout the whole Communist period.

There has been a Jewish community in Hungary since Roman times. It reached a height of 450,000 (within the boundaries set in 1920) in the 1930s in spite of varying levels of anti-Semitism. Some 250,000 Jews could be found in Budapest. Many restrictions on Jews were removed by the Emancipation Act in 1867, and Jews played an important role in the country's economic, intellectual, and cultural life for the next 60 years. The community, however, bore much of the brunt of the Holocaust, more than three-fourths of it perishing.

Fewer than 100,000 Jews currently reside in Hungary, the great majority in Budapest. The Federation of the Jewish Communities in Hungary provides some overall focus. There is a large synagogue in Budapest that serves as a unifying point of the religious community, and nearby a rabbinical seminary. The chief rabbi heads the Central Rabbinate. Hungarian Jewry is largely Reform in orientation, but there is an Orthodox synagogue in Budapest. The strong Hasidic life that had been present in Hungary was wiped out during the Holocaust, though a remnant survived in Israel and the United States.

The fall of Communism brought along the rehabilitation of religion, in the form of an open expression of appreciation, financial support, and the return of some of the ecclesiastical buildings nationalized under Communism. While the population is dominantly Christian—at least nominally—fewer than 20 percent of Hungarians consider themselves religious according

Hungary

Religion	Followers in 1970	Followers in 2010	% of Population	Annual % growth 2000–2010	Followers in 2025	Followers in 2050
Christians	8,784,000	8,687,000	87.4	−0.25	8,590,000	7,913,000
Roman Catholics	6,125,000	6,000,000	60.4	−0.76	5,700,000	5,100,000
Protestants	2,486,000	2,450,000	24.6	0.45	2,500,000	2,400,000
Orthodox	66,100	155,000	1.6	0.16	160,000	180,000
Agnostics	891,000	700,000	7.0	−0.44	500,000	300,000
Atheists	570,000	420,000	4.2	−0.29	220,000	100,000
Jews	90,000	98,000	1.0	1.29	90,000	90,000
Muslims	2,000	25,400	0.3	−0.25	35,000	40,000
Chinese folk	0	5,100	0.1	−0.25	6,000	7,000
Buddhists	300	4,400	0.0	4.32	6,000	8,000
Baha'is	100	300	0.0	−0.27	500	1,000
Total population	**10,337,000**	**9,940,000**	**100.0**	**−0.25**	**9,448,000**	**8,459,000**

to the teaching of their denominations. One of the consequences is that, although a sizable number of Hungarians favor the presence of religion in public life, another significant—and more energetic—segment of the population considers the public role of churches particularly undesirable. Another source of tension is the increasing number of new religious movements, even though their membership is negligible. Due to the sensation-mongering media and the anti-cult campaign launched by a former Protestant minister in 1993, the Parliament suspended the financial support of four so-called destructive sects: the Jehovah's Witnesses, the Church of Scientology, the International Society for Krishna Consciousness, and the Unification movement. As a consequence of international pressure, the suspension was revoked the next year. Organizations concerned with religious freedom paid closer attention to Hungary again in 2001, when a bill was proposed, unsuccessfully, to make the requirements of establishing a new church more demanding. On the whole, however, Hungary has at the beginning of the third millennium a more tolerant attitude toward religion than most formerly Communist countries.

Péter Török

See also: Baptist Union of Hungary; Church of Scientology; Church of the Nazarene; International Society for Krishna Consciousness; Jehovah's Witnesses; Lutheran Church in Hungary; Reformed Church of Hungary; Unification Movement; United Methodist Church; World Council of Churches; World Evangelical Alliance.

References

Hertsel, M. Y. *Christianity and the Holocaust of Hungarian Jewry*. New York: New York University Press, 1993.

Központi Statisztikai Hivatal (Central Statistical Office). *Népszámlálás 2001. 6. Területi Adatok* (Census 2001. 6. Regional Data). CD, 2003.

Lázár, István. *Hungary: A Brief History*. http://historicaltextarchive.com/books.php?op=viewbook&bookid=6 . Accessed October 1, 2008.

Tomka, M. *Church, State and Society in Eastern Europe*. Washington, DC: The Council for Research in Values and Philosophy, 2005.

Török, P. "Unity in Future? The Role of New Religious Movements in Post-Communist Hungarian Church-State Relationships." In *Moderné Nábozenstvo: Modern Religion*, edited by Zostavila Silvia Jozefciaková, 295–311. Bratislava: Slovakian Institute for Church and State.

Husayn ibn Ali ibn Abi Talib Al-

626–680

Al-Husayn ibn Ali is the grandson of the Prophet Muhammad and a martyr hero to the Shia branch of Islam.

Ali ibn Abi Talib, fourth caliph of Islam, cousin and brother-in-law of Muhammad, holds the body of the killed Imam, Safavid fresco, 17th century. (SEF/Art Resource, NY)

According to Muslim tradition, he was born in 626 CE, the son of Ali ibn Abi Talib (the fourth caliph) and Fatima, Muhammad's daughter. His death on October 10, 680, in Karbala, Iraq, represents one of the major turning points in Islamic history and marks the decisive break between Sunni and Shia Muslims.

The death of Muhammad in 632 CE created a crisis over leadership and proper succession to the prophet. Muslims who believe that Ali, Husayn's father, is the proper successor to Muhammad are known as Shia (a shortened form of Arabic words for faction or house of Ali). Ali, a cousin of the prophet and husband to Fatima, was chosen leader in 656 CE after the killing of Uthman, the third caliph after Muhammad. The previous caliphs were Abu Bakr (632–634) and Umar (634–644).

After Ali was assassinated in 661, Husayn and his older brother Hasan grudgingly recognized the rule of Mu'awiya, the first of the Umayyad caliphates.

Mu'awiya died in 680 and the caliphate passed to his son Yazid I. Husayn resisted Yazid's rule, and Yazid sent an army to arrest Husayn, who was traveling to Kofa to meet supporters. Negotiations failed and Husayn was killed during the Battle of Karbala in October 680. His head was sent to Yazid in Damascus. Yazid tried to shift blame for Husayn's death on others but to no avail. The Umayyad caliphate was henceforth burdened with opposition from Ali's house.

Shia Muslims observe Husayn's death every year. The lamentation is known as the Day of Ashura and takes place during Muharram, the first month of the Islamic calendar. Rites of mourning involve fasting, recitation of stories of Husayn's death, and flagellation. Some Shia view Husayn's death as atonement for sin. Sunni Muslims hold a Day of Ashura as well but they usually observe it as a celebration to honor the rescue of Jews from Egyptian bondage.

Husayn is regarded by Shiites not only as one of the true caliphs but also as an imam. In Shia Islam the title imam is reserved for those leaders descended from Muhammad who provide infallible leadership to the Muslim community (*umma*). Shiites are divided over the correct number of imams. Most Shia Muslims claim 12 (hence known as Twelvers) while the Ismaili count 7. Besides being the third imam, Husayn is also credited as one of the Fourteen Infallibles of Shia Islam.

There are accounts in Shia hadith (traditions) about the Prophet Muhammad foreseeing the death of his grandson. There are also miracles related to Husayn's martyrdom. The main focus of the traditions, however, is to invoke Husayn's purity and sacrifice and his willingness to travel the martyr's path.

James A. Beverley

See also: Ali ibn Abi Talib; Ashura; Damascus; Ismaili Islam; Karbala; Muhammad; Shia Islam.

References

Hourani, Albert. *A History of the Arab Peoples.* Cambridge, MA: Harvard University Press, 1991.

Nigosian, S. A. *Islam: Its History, Teaching and Practices.* Bloomington: Indiana University Press, 2004.

Shirazi, Imam Muhammad. *Husayn: The Sacrifice for Mankind.* London: Fountain Books, 2003.

Hutterites

The Hutterites originated in the early days of the Anabaptist uprising within the Protestant Reformation of the 16th century and are thus spiritual cousins of the other Anabaptists, the Mennonites and the Amish. Among the distinctive Anabaptist teachings, still adhered to today, were adult baptism, separation of church and state, and pacifism.

Many Anabaptists, fleeing persecution in Switzerland and other nearby areas, settled in Moravia. There, in 1528, one group pooled their property, including money, in keeping with their interpretation of Acts 2:44–45 and other biblical passages. In 1533 Jacob Hutter joined the group and soon emerged as its leader. He shaped it into a disciplined communal organization,

and the believers have been known by his name ever since. Persecution of the group continued, however, and Hutter was executed by the order of King Ferdinand I of Austria in 1536.

Although the Hutterites did have some good and prosperous times in Moravia after 1550, persecution continued to erupt periodically. In 1770, promised freedom from military service, among other things, they migrated to Russia. A century later, however, their exemption from military conscription was rescinded and they moved again. Beginning in 1874 they migrated to the United States, settling in South Dakota. There they founded three colonies, reflecting the organizational pattern that had prevailed lately in Russia. Each of those colonies became the founding locus of one of three Hutterite subgroups, or *leuts*, known after their

Hutterite girls at their home in the northwest United States, 1974. (AP Photo/Arts Club of Washington)

founding elders as the Schmiedeleut, the Dariusleut, and the Lehrerleut. The leuts, harboring some distinctions in theology and lifestyle, have operated largely separately ever since. The Schmiedeleut, in a disagreement over leadership, divided into two subgroups in the 1990s.

The Hutterites grew in obscurity for many years, founding new colonies as their population expanded. In 1917, however, the U.S. government imposed military conscription without provision for conscientious objection. Young Hutterite men were incarcerated for refusing military duty and two died of maltreatment in a military prison. Meanwhile, harassment and even mob violence were directed against the colonies. Assured of exemption from military service in Canada, the Hutterites sold all but one of their American colonies and moved to Alberta and Manitoba. The majority have lived there ever since, although as social conditions changed new colonies were founded in the United States as well. Today the Hutterites have more than 40,000 members in more than 400 colonies in four Canadian provinces and six American states.

Unlike the Amish, the Hutterites accept modern agricultural technology. They maintain full community of property and live in colonies averaging about 100 in population. Each colony is led by a minister and a farm superintendent, both always male. Families live in apartments and eat at a common dining hall in the center of the colony. Each colony maintains two schools, a German-language school for instruction in religion and traditional values and an English school with a curriculum much like those of schools elsewhere. Children usually go to school until about age 15, when they begin working in the colony full-time.

Young adults are usually baptized when they are in their early 20s and only thereafter marry. The Hutterites have proven to be one of the most fertile populations in the world, with an average, at some points in their history, of more than 10 children per family. Thus a colony can double in size and give birth to an offspring colony in 10 to 20 years. That rapid growth has led to the chief recent controversy surrounding Hutterism, over repeated purchases of large tracts of land for new colonies, which, other farmers contend, drives up the price of land and takes it away from non-Hutterite farmers. In recent years, however, Hutterite family size has begun to decline.

Hutterite colonies are largely independent. An elder is designated for each of the leuts, and the nominal headquarters of each leut is located at that elder's colony. Contact is best made through the website maintained by Schmiedeleut Hutterites at http://www.hutterites.org. It gives the name of the designated elder for the three leuts, and for the committee of elders that head the Committee Schmiedeleut, one of the groups formed in 1990s when that leut divided.

Timothy Miller

See also: Amish; Anabaptism; Communalism; Mennonites.

References

Hostetler, John A. *Hutterite Society*. Baltimore: Johns Hopkins University Press, 1974.

Huntington, Gertrude E. "Living in the Ark: Four Centuries of Hutterite Faith and Community." In *America's Communal Utopias*, edited by Donald E. Pitzer. Chapel Hill: University of North Carolina Press, 1997.

Riedemann (Rideman), Peter. *Account of Our Religion, Doctrine and Faith, Given by Peter Rideman of the Brothers Whom Men Call Hutterians.* Trans. by Kathleen E. Hasenberg. London: Hodder and Stoughton, with Plough Publishing House, 1950.

Index

Judaism (*continued*)
and the development of the modern
Jewish community, 1600
during the diaspora, 1598–1600
during the Greek and Roman eras,
1596–1598
in India, 1405–1406
martyrdom and, 1815–1816
Messianic Judaism, 1862–1863
origins of, 1593–1596
re-establishment of in Germany,
1204
sacred texts of, 1597–1598
in Suriname, 2760–2761
women's role in, 3117–3118
See also Hanukkah; Hasidism;
Orthodox Judaism; Passover;
Reconstructionist Judaism;
Reform Judaism; Synagogues;
Temples, Jewish
Judge, William Quan, 342, 356, 2846,
2848–2849
Judson, Adoniram, 92, 2001–2002
Julius Caesar, 2733, 2753
Justin Martyr, 1231

Kabbalah, 443
Kabbalah Learning Center, **1605–1606**
Kabila, Laurent, 775
Kabir, 1326, 1397
Kadampa School of Tibetan
Buddhism, 236
Kagyupa Tibetan Buddhism,
1606–1607
Kahihia, Benjamin, 30
Kailas, Mount/Lake Manasarovar,
1607–1608, 1607 (image),
1608 (image)
Kak, Subash, 226
Kali, 2601, 2601 (image), 2602
Kamakura, **1609–1610**
Great Buddha of, 100 (image)
Kamal-ud-Din, Khwaja, 56
Kamm, William, 2565
Kanada, Tokumitsu, 2232–2233
Kanaky (New Caledonia), **1610–1612,**
1611 (map), 1611 (table)
Kannon Jikeikai (Association for the
Worship of the Bodhisattva
Kannon), 51
Kaplan, Mordecai Menahem,
1612–1614, 1613 (image),
2369–2370, 2370 (image)

Karaites, **1614–1615**
Karbala, **1615–1617,** 1616 (image)
Kardec, Allan, 2693
Karma-Kagyupa Tibetan Buddhism,
1617–1618
Karo Batak Protestant Church,
1618–1619
Kashmir Saivism (Tantric Saivism),
1619–1620
Kassam, Abd al Karem, 1498
Kazakhstan, **1620–1624,**
1620 (image), 1621 (table),
1622 (map), 1623 (image)
Baptists in, 1623
Christianity in, 1623
Islam in, 1621
Russian expansion into,
1620–1621
Kedarnath, **1624**
Kedrovsky, John, 2152
Keech, William, 283
Keller, Otto, 36
Kellner, Carl, 2149
Kellogg, John Harvey, 2588
Kellogg, Will Keith, 2588
Kelly, William, 609
Kemal, Mustafa, 2903–2904
Kenya, 33, **1624–1629,** 1625 (image),
1626 (table), 1627 (map)
Buddhism in, 1629
Christianity in, 1626
Eastern religions in, 1628–1629
ecumenism in, 1628
historical mixture of Bantu and
Muslims in, 1624–1625
Islam in, 1626
Masai hegemony in, 1625
Mau Mau terrorist organization in,
1625
Roman Catholicism in, 1628
traditional religions in, 1626
Kenya Evangelical Lutheran Church,
1629–1630
Kenyatta, Jomo, 29, 1625–1626
Khama, Seretse, 380
Khan, Hazrat Inayat, 2739, 2740
Khan, Pir Vilayat, 2739–2740
Khan, Pir Zia, 2740
Khilafat movement, **1630–1631**
Khyentse Foundation, The,
1631–1633, 1632 (image)
Kikuyu Independent Schools Asso-
ciation (KISA), 29–30

Kikuyu Karing's Educational Asso-
ciation (KKEA), 29, 30
Kilham, Alexander, 987
Kim, Simon K., 127
Kim Il Sung, 1642
Kimball, Spencer, 688
Kimbangu, Simon, 31, 778, 1633,
1634, 2083
Kimbanguist Church, 31, **1633–1634**
King, Jonas, 1251
King, Martin Luther, Jr., 2311
King, Samuel, 840
Kiribati, **1634–1637,** 1635 (map),
1636 (table), 1636 (image)
Kiribati Protestant Church, **1637**
Kirpalani, Lekhraj Khubchand, 383
Kisaburo, Ueda. *See* Onissaburo,
Deguchi
Kitamura, Sayo, 2833
Kivuli, Daudi Zakayo, 36
Kivuli, John Mweresa, II, 37
Knapp, Martin Wells, 3097
Kneeland, Abner, 1148
Knight, Charles F., 433
Knight-Bruce, George W. H.,
719–720
Knox, John, 703, 2285
Ko Bong Soen Sa Nim, 1670
Ko Thy Byu, 2002
Köbner, Julius, 290
Kôdô Kyôdan, **1637–1638**
Kofuku no Kagaku, 1568–1569,
1638–1639
Kokuchu-Kai, **1639–1640**
Kolingba, André, 531
Kongtrul, Jamgon, 2124
Konkokyo, **1640–1641**
Kony, Joseph, 2922
Koran, the, 405
Allah in, 1515–1516
biblical material in, 1516
description of true believers in,
1517
eschatology of, 1517
Jesus in, 1516
major themes of, 1515–1516
Muhammad in, 1516
origin of, 1515
Korea, Democratic People's Republic
of (North Korea), **1641–1645,**
1642 (image), 1643 (map),
1644 (table)
missions in, 1642